Wyszków Memorial Book
(Wyszków, Poland)

Translation of *Sefer Wyszków*

Original Yizkor Book edited by: D. Shtokfish
Published in Tel Aviv in 1964
By the Wyszków Association of Former Residents in Israel and
Abroad
(Hebrew and Yiddish, 351 pages).

Published by JewishGen

**An Affiliate of the Museum of Jewish Heritage—A Living Memorial to the Holocaust
New York**

Wyszków Memorial Book
Translation of *Sefer Wyszków*

Copyright © 2020 by JewishGen, Inc.
All rights reserved.
First Printing: February 2020, Shevat 5780

Project Coordinator: Howard B. Orenstein
Photo Processing: Larry Gaum
Cover Design: Nina Schwartz, Impulse Graphics LLC
Indexing: Debbie Terman

Published by JewishGen, Inc.
An Affiliate of the Museum of Jewish Heritage
A Living Memorial to the Holocaust
36 Battery Place, New York, NY 10280

Printed in the United States of America by Lightning Source, Inc.
Library of Congress Control Number (LCCN): 2019948430
ISBN 978-1-939561-83-1 (hard cover: 784 pages, alk. Paper)

Cover credits:
Front cover: Center of the city, 1920s. Photo by Zaklad Chrzesc, Foto Znicz.
Courtesy of Howard Orenstein, McDaniel College, Westminster, MD.
Back cover: Tombstone fragments from "Lapidary" memorial, Wyszków.
 Courtesy of POLIN Museum of the History of Polish Jews, Warsaw, Poland.

JewishGen and the Yizkor Books in Print Project

This book has been published by the **Yizkor Books in Print Project**, as part of the **Yizkor Book Project** of JewishGen, Inc.

JewishGen, Inc. is a non-profit organization founded in 1987 as a resource for Jewish genealogy. Its website [www.jewishgen.org] serves as an international clearinghouse and resource center to assist individuals who are researching the history of their Jewish families and the places where they lived. JewishGen provides databases, facilitates discussion groups, and coordinates projects relating to Jewish genealogy and the history of the Jewish people. In 2003, JewishGen became an affiliate of the **Museum of Jewish Heritage—A Living Memorial to the Holocaust** in New York.

The **JewishGen Yizkor Book Project** was organized to make more widely known the existence of Yizkor (Memorial) Books written by survivors and former residents of various Jewish communities throughout the world. Later, volunteers connected to the different destroyed communities began cooperating to have these books translated from the original language—usually Hebrew or Yiddish—into English, thus enabling a wider audience to have access to the valuable information contained within them. As each chapter of these books was translated, it was posted on the JewishGen website and made available to the general public.

The **Yizkor Books in Print Project** began in 2011 as an initiative to print and publish Yizkor Books that had been fully translated, so that hard copies would be available for purchase by the descendants of these communities and also by scholars, universities, synagogues, libraries, and museums.

These Yizkor books have been produced almost entirely through the volunteer effort of researchers from around the world, assisted by donations from private individuals. The books are printed and sold at near cost, so as to make them as affordable as possible. Our goal is to make this important genre of Jewish literature and history available in English in book form, so that people can have the personal histories of their ancestral towns on their bookshelves for themselves and for their children and grandchildren.

A list of all published translated Yizkor Books in the project with prices and ordering information can be found at:
http://www.jewishgen.org/Yizkor/ybip.html

Binny Lewis, Yizkor Book Project Manager
Joel Alpert, Yizkor-Book-in-Print Project Coordinator

JewishGen
Yizkor Book Project

This book is presented by the
Yizkor Books in Print Project
Project Coordinator: Joel Alpert

Part of the
Yizkor Books Project of JewishGen, Inc.
Project Manager: Lance Ackerfeld

These books have been produced solely through volunteer effort
of individuals from around the world. The books are printed and
sold at near cost, so as to make them as affordable as possible.

Our goal is to make this history and important genre of Jewish
literature available in English in book form so that people can have
the near-personal histories of their ancestral towns on their bookshelves for themselves and for their children and grandchildren.

Any donations to the Yizkor Books Project are appreciated.

Please send donations to:
Yizkor Book Project
JewishGen
36 Battery Place
New York, NY 10280

JewishGen, Inc. is an affiliate of the
Museum of Jewish Heritage
A Living Memorial to the Holocaust

Acknowledgements

When my father, Jack (Yankel) Orenstein, died in 1996, I wanted to memorialize his life in some way. Born in Wyszkow, he lived and studied at the Yeshiva there (and several others in Warsaw) until arriving, as a teenager, in the US at the end of 1929.

In pursuit of my family's genealogy, I contacted the Executive Director of Jewish Records Indexing-Poland, Stanley Diamond. One of the first things he sent me was a photocopy of Sefer Wyszków (The Book of Wyszków), which consisted of chapters written by Holocaust survivors from the world-over who had lived in Wyszków before, during and briefly after World War II. There was only one problem: most of the chapters were written in Yiddish, although some in Hebrew. My meager facility with Yiddish and Hebrew made it next to impossible for me and most other English monolingual readers to fully appreciate the original collection of memoirs.

Fortunately, I discovered that JewishGen had begun a Yizkor Book Translation Project. Sefer Wyszków was among those listed, but my excitement was short-lived as only a few chapters were translated. I realized then that completing the translation of Sefer Wyszków allowed me a way to honor my father's passing. In short order, I was contacted by Frida Grapa Markuschamer de Cielak (of Mexico), whose family were also from Wyszków. She, along with noted Mexican historian, Enrique Krauze, also with roots in Wyszków, collaborated on a research project dealing with Jews from Wyszków, and they provided translations for several chapters from the Yizkor Book.

But, interest and funding for translations waned for a bit until a few individuals with keen interest in Wyszków offered their support, financial and otherwise, to help me complete the project. So, I must give major thanks to Alan Grosbard (California) and Mark Oland (Connecticut).

The vast majority of the Yiddish translations were expertly handled by Pamela Russ, a wonderful and generous person with exceptional skills who lives in Montreal, Canada. Likewise, the Hebrew translations primarily were handled by Chava Eisenstein of Jerusalem.

My thanks go to all those who voluntarily contributed translations along the way. Last, but definitely not least, I would like to thank two dedicated people associated with JewishGen: Lance Ackerfeld, the JewishGen Yizkor Book coordinator, and his able staff for fine tuning the presentation of all the translations online; and Joel Alpert, the coordinator for JewishGen's Yizkor-Books-in-Print project, without whom you would not be holding the book in front of you.

Special thanks to the National Yiddish Book Center in Amherst, Massachusetts and the New York Public Library for supplying the high resolution images used in this book.

Our sincere appreciation to Mr. Israel Pshetitsky, of the Wyszków Association in Israel, for permission to JewishGen, Inc. to use this material.

Howard Orenstein
Sefer Wyszków Translation Coordinator

History of Wyszków

The town of Wyszków, about 35 miles northeast of Warsaw, lies along the Bug River. Jewish people started to inhabit the town in the late 1700s and were engaged as merchants and craftsmen. In the 19th and 20th centuries, they began to engage with small trade. Before World War I, Jews owned various businesses such soda water factories, ice cream parlors, and a railway carriage production factory. Also, they were involved in processing forest products and established wood tar factories.

In the 19th century, the Hassidim began to play a greater role in the community and dominated it in the second half of the 19th century. The establishment of Yeshiva "Beis Yosef" in 1908 was an example of the influences of orthodox society.

After the town was invaded and occupied by the Germans in September 1939, the town commandant evicted all the Jews. Nearly 80 Jews and eight Poles were forced into a barn which was then set on fire. Everyone perished. During the first days of the occupation, the Germans rounded-up and killed approximately 1,000 Jews. As the war ensued, others were sent to death camps. Some Jewish residents of Wyszków managed to escape. Some reached Polish territory which had been occupied by the Russians. Those who managed to survive relocated to many countries around the globe, mostly the United States of America and the State of Israel.

This Yizkor Book serves as a memorial to all the victims of the Shoah from Wyszków and nearby towns.

Notes to the Reader:

We apologize ahead of time for the poor quality of images in the book. Often these images had been scanned from the original Yizkor books which were of poor quality to begin with, being copies of old photographs. Each transfer results in loss of quality. We have done the best we could, given the original material and the resources and technology at hand. Even though images often appear of higher quality on computer screens, that does not transfer to high quality images in print. A reader can view the original scans on the web sites listed below.

Within the text the reader will note "{34}" standing ahead of a paragraph. This indicates that the material translated below was on page 34 of the original book. However, when a paragraph was split between two pages in the original book, the marker is placed in this book after the end of the paragraph for ease of reading.

Also please note that all references within the text of the book to page numbers, refer to the page numbers of the original Yizkor Book.

The original book can be seen online at the New York Public Library site:
https://digitalcollections.nypl.org/items/0a63c1e0-28ae-0133-93de-58d385a7b928

or at the Yiddish Book Center web site:
https://www.yiddishbookcenter.org/collections/yizkor-books/yzk-nybc314240/sztokfisz-david-sefer-vishkov

In order to obtain a list of all Shoah victims from the town, the reader should access the Yad Vashem web site listed below; one can also search for specific family names using family name option. These lists are continually updated by Yad Vashem, so it is worthwhile to periodically search these lists.

There is much valuable information available on this web site, including the Pages of Testimony, etc.
http://yvng.yadvashem.org

A list of this book and all books available in the Yizkor-Book-In-Print Project along with prices is available at:
http://www.jewishgen.org/Yizkor/ybip.html

Geopolitical Information:

Located at 52°36' North Latitude and 21°28' East Longitude

Situated 31 miles NE of Warsaw, 17 miles ESE of Pułtusk.

Alternate names for the town are: Wyszków [Polish], Vishkov [Yiddish], Vyshkov [Russian], Vishkeve, Viszkuv

Period	Town	District	Province	Country
Before WWI (c. 1900):	Wyszków	Pułtusk	Warszawa	Russian Empire
Between the wars (c. 1930):	Wyszków	Pułtusk	Warszawa	Poland
After WWII (c. 1950):	Wyszków			
Today (c. 2000):	Wyszków			

Notes: Russian: Вышков / Вышкув. Yiddish: ווישקעוו. Hebrew: וישקוב

Jewish Population 3,207 (in 1897), 4,412 (in 1921)

Nearby Jewish Communities:
Kamieńczyk 3 miles E
Brańszczyk 6 miles ENE
Poręba Średnia 11 miles ENE
Poręba-Kocęby 11 miles NE
Jadów 12 miles SE
Łopianka 12 miles ESE
Tłuszcz 13 miles S
Długosiodło 13 miles NNE

Baczki 14 miles ESE
Pułtusk 17 miles WNW
Radzymin 17 miles SW
Brok 17 miles ENE
Serock 18 miles WSW
Stoczek 19 miles E
Wołomin 20 miles SSW
Różan 20 miles N

BALTIC SEA

LITHUANIA

RUSSIA

Vilnius ●

POLAND

BELARUS

GERMANY

Wyszków
●

● Poznan

Warsaw ●

● Lodz

● Prague

● Krakow

UKRAINE

CZECH REPUBLIC

SLOVAKIA

250 miles

0

0   250 Km   500 Km

POLAND - **Current Borders**

Hebrew Title Page of Original Yizkor Book

ספר וישקוב

הוצא ע"י אירגוני יוצאי וישקוב בישראל ובחוץ־לארץ

ארויסגעגעבן דורך די וישקאווער לאנדסמאנשאפטן אין ישראל און אין אויסלאנד

Translation of the Title Page of Original Yiddish Book

Wyszków Book

Published by the Wyszków Association of Former Residents in Israel and Abroad

Table of Contents

Introduction

A. The History of the Town, General Memoirs, and Descriptions

The Ancestry of Wishkov/Wyszków	D. Shtokfish	4
My Memories of Wyszkow	Menachem Kaspi (Srebrenik)	14
The town in the years 1891-1913	Max Chekhanov	35
30 years of community life	Yitzkhok Baharov/Barab	43
The yeshiva, synagogues, study places, and prayer quorums		53
The last rabbis of Vishkov		58
Bloody Polish "Games" of 1920	Mordkhe V. Bernshteyn	58
Polish-Bolshevik Terror in 1920	Y. Mitlsbakh	68
A Memoir of "That Year"	Liber Vigoda	71
Wishkov Remembrances	Yisroel Granat	73
Wishkov (Wyszków) During Bad and Good Times	M. Rabin	78
Pictures of the town	Baranek	89
Romantically, Socially, Idealistically	Yekhiel Bzhoza/Bzoza	94
A bundle of memories from days past	Haim Levin	97
Memories of the old town	Moyshe Stolik	100
A Wishkever Melody	Aron Pakht	104
The Wishkover Band; Dalekes	Itzkhok Marcuschamer	109
A day in town	Moishe Farbshteyn	115
Memories of our Young Years	Shmuel Niestenpover	120
Our train station, the Poremba settlement	Yankev/Yakov Palukh	124
The Poremba Settlement	Yankev/Yakov Palukh	129
From Wyszkow To Kibbutz Dafna	Yehuda Ilan	133

B. Political Parties, Societies, Organizations, and Institutions

Establishment Of The Zionist Association In Wyszkow	Mordechai Kronenberg	142
The First Pioneers in Town	Yisroel Kaluski	144
The Left Poalei Zion ["Workers of Zion"] and Its Youth	Yankev Shtelung	152
Along The Lines At The Shomer Hatzair In Wyszkow[1]	Leah Goldstein	163
In the Youth Movement Hashomer Hatzair	Bina Jakubowycz–Tabak	169
At The Religious "Ha'Shomer Ha'Dati" Youth Movement	Menakhem Nagel	173
On the Eve of the Jewish Community Elections in the Year 1931		177
The Wyszkower Loan Fund in the Year 1935	Paul. A. Kramer	178
Interest–Free Loan Fund for the Socialist Handworkers' Un-	Y.M. Czembal	180

ion

Sports Clubs and self-defense	Borukh Yismakh/Ismaj	186
The Sport Club "Maccabi"	Sh. Sh.	192
The Worker's Sports Club "Skala"	Mayer Leyb Holczman	197

C. Religious Life

Religious institutions and "Shtiblakh"[2]	Motl Venger	200
Wyszkow - A religious town	Velvl Olenberg	209
My Children Are Not Agnostics	Freyda Kaplovitch	214
The First Kheyder Metukan [Proper School][3]	F. M. R.	216
Student at "Darkhey Noam" Yeshiva Recalls[4]	Khaim Umyal	218
The Yeshiva "Beis Yosef"	Paul A. Kramer	220
Jewish Chains (A gratitude poem)	Rabbi Shimon Arie Kheyfetz	221
My Memories of the Yeshive	Shimon Zakharia Malowanczyk	223
The Keepers of the Sabbath in Town	Arie Shtelung Sokol	228
The Excommunication (der kheyrem)	Borukh Yismakh/Ismaj	231
Buried behind the Fence …	Y. M. Tzembal/Cembal	234
Cantorial Singing and Choirs in Wyszkow	Eliyahu Y. Brukhanski	239
The Guardians of the Sabbath Were Not Successful	Yosel Popowski	244

D. Personalities, Businessmen, Figures, and Types

Mordekhai Anielewicz, Commander of the Ghetto Uprising in Warsaw – Born in Wyszkow (in Hebrew & Yiddish)	Yisroel Gutman	249
	Jeheskel Rotenberg,	
Admo"r Rabbi Jacob Aryeh of Wyszkow–Radzymin	Moshe Scheinfield	255
Reb Khaim Henekh (Shtelung), Baal Tefilah [Prayer Leader]	Menakhem Shtelung	258
Reb Khaim Malkhiel (Brukhanski), the Khazzan [Cantor]	Y. Brukhanski	265
Yisroel Asman	Yosef Zajdenstat	267
Yisroel Asman's Folk Legends and Folklore	Sh. Ernst	268
Yisroel Asman in Los Angeles	Yekhiel Bzhoza	273
Community Activists (Wyszkower Personalities)	Yitzkhok Baharav	275
Henekh Kaluski	Avigdor Mondry	277
Dr. Laykher	Shimon Malovantczyk	278
Reb Motl Broder	Shimon Malovantchik	280
Reb Yakov Dovid Pszetitski	Shimon Malovantchik	281
Mordkhe Tchekhanov	Tch. (Khane) Appleboim	282
R. Simon son of Yehezkel Serbernik	Yerakhmiel Wilenski	284
Motl and Sore Baharov	Yitszkhok Baharav/Barab	289
A Very Ramified (Well–Branched) Family	Yitszkhok Baharav/Barab	290

R. Hanok (Heinoch) Kornet	Moshe Kornet	291
Grandpa, R. Israel-Isaac and Grandma, Freida-Perla	Isaac Weisman	292
To the Memory of my Father, Simkha Mushkat	H. Mushkat	294
Zvika Musberg	Penina Musberg	296
Zeev Holland		304
Abraham Tenenbaum	Hana and Borukh-David Tenenbaum	305
Isaac Zamir		306
Their Memories Must be Forever		308
Their memories must be forever: Henda the lady-butcher[Katzfke]	Yitzkhok Markuschamer	312
Noyke (Noakh'ke)	Yitzkhak Markuschamer	316
Hershele the Water Carrier	Yisroel Osman	320
Hershele Kurlap	Yisroel Asman	325
My Teachers	Motl Wenger	331
The Blind Rabbi	H.Mushkat	337
Ayzikl, the Teacher	M. Rabin	339
Itche–Metch der Klezmer (the Musician)	Yankl Mitlsbakh	343
Reyzele – Di Zogerin	Yakov Mitlsbakh	346
Hershl Melamed	Yankl (Yakov) Mitlsbakh	349
Mates–Faivl der Kremer (the Storekeeper)	Yankl Mitlsbakh	353
Hersh–Leyb, Shingle–Maker	Yankl Mitlsbakh	354
The Fishermen	Yankl Mitlsbakh	359
"Der Sfas–Emes"	M. Rabin	362
The Two Mutes	Yekhiel Bzhoza (Brzoza)	367
The rural doctor Malowanczyk	Yosl Popowski	371
Reb Sholom Refoelkes (Mikhalkes)	M. Federgreen	373

The Second Part – The Destruction of Wishkov

In the Wyszkow Forest (a poem)	Binem Heler	378
To Remember and Commemorate	Menachem Kaspi (Serbernik)	380
The first air-raid of Wishkov	Yoysef Gurni	384
In the first days of the destruction	Moyshe Venger	386
Opening of Fire, September 1939	Naphtali Kretsmer	390
The "Black Friday"	Leibel Popowski	393
The Nazi Murderers in Town	Kh. A. (YIVO-Wyszkow#1140)	397
Wyszkow in Flames	Tzvi Yakov Gemora	398
Struggling with Death	Lemel Rubin	400
In the Years of Misfortune and Anguish	Khane Srebro (nee Vengel)	415
Hitler's Murder of Children	Leah Direktor (Lerman)	432
My Experiences during the Occupation	Fanya Hertz	439
In the Forest with the Partisans	Fayvl Fular	445

The last request of a martyr   Abraham, Ben Soreh-Rifkeh   449

The Polacks Helped Kill the Jews of Wyszkow   Hebrew Newspaper   451

We Succeeded to Escape   Velvel Elenberg   452

Partisans and Ghetto–Fighters in the Forest of Wyszkow   453

With My Wandering Stick in Hand   Yitzchok Baharav/Barab   457

Dead Shadows Walk in the Marketplace …   Dr. Khaim Shoshkes   467

Rabbi (Tzvi) Borenstajn Visits Wyszkow in 1961   469

Part Three – Wishkevers in Israel and in the World

The Beginnings in Israel   Moishe Farbsztejn   472

Fifteen Years of the Irgun Yotzei Wyszkow b'Yisroel   Rabbi Yerakhmiel Wilenski – Grapa   476

The Wyszkower society in New York   Yekhiel Burstyn   496

Wyszkower in New York[5]   507

The Los Angeles Wyszkower Society   Avrohom–Dovid Taff   509

Wyszkower in Los Angeles   H. Muszkat   511

Various Activities   Beltche Taff (Yelin)   514

The Union of Wyszkow and Surrounding Areas in Argentina   Aryeh Shtelung   515

About Two Activists in the Wyszkower Society in Argentina   Y. Leiles   529

Yakov Shtelung (50 years of a social activist)   Y. M. Czembal   531

Wyszkower in Uruguay   Sh. Grapa & Kh. Wenger, Montevideo   534

Wyszkower in Cuba   Cz. Apelboim   536

The Wyszkower in Germany Ask for Help   Y.M. Kurt Kepel   537

Part Four – Yizkor

Remember   Dr. M. Dvorszki, S. Shalom   539

Kaddish   Yerakhmiel Wilenski   540

List of Wishkever Jews who died   542

The Rabbis of Wyszkow   Zev Radziminsky   583

Founders and management of Bank Lodovi   Stanislaw Wolski   605

Righteous Gentiles   606

Obituaries   607

Part Five – Additions

Index of Geographical Names   720

Index of Geographic Names   728

Index   737

Introduction

Translated by Pamela Russ

"*Sefer Wyszkow*" [Wyszkow Book] – the timely production of an eight-year writing and editing project, of communal efforts, and financial toil – is now being given over to the people of Wyszkow. The 356 double-sided pages recount in words and in pictures the history, development, and destruction of a Jewish community in Poland.

We, the survivors of the Holocaust from the Jewish town on the Bug [River], cannot think of this book simply as a memorial book – but we see it as the one and only permanent tombstone on the unknown graves of our dear, very familiar Wyszkower Jews who died as martyrs for the Name of God.

Externally, Wyszkow was not different from other similar settlements in pre-war Poland. But we, born and raised in the town, know that Wyszkow had in it something unique and specific not only in its landscape, appearance, and size, but mainly it was that its Jews were outstanding – the Shabbath ones and the weekday ones, the religious and the secular ones, those who believed in Zionism and those who were anti-Zionists. In particular, our Wyszkower Jewish youth was baked into our hearts, we who wanted to free the entire world and envisioned our own nation, as well as [in the hearts of] those who strove for the Ultimate Redemption, and thought that through that merit other nations would be redeemed as well....

The main intention of the *Sefer Wyszkow* is: to give life to the dead and all their shining faces, show them in their pains and joy, describe their efforts and struggles for their own existence and for national existence, tell how they formed the social, religious, and political life in Wyszkow and passed on to generations their tragic deaths in the ghettos, bunkers, forests, and wagons, sharing the fate of European Jewry, upon whom the Nazi murderers had put a death sentence.

The reader will judge whether these intentions were met. Unfortunately, some writings are missing about the activities of certain parties, friends of the organizations, and also a list of social activists who should certainly be perpetuated in our book-monument. The editor is not at fault here, but those *landsleit* who did not find it necessary to describe their activities and friends. We also ask for your understanding and forgiveness for any printing errors, mistakes in names and events – something that is impossible to prevent in a book of this sort.

Sefer Wyszkow is divided as follows:

a. history of the town, general memories and descriptions

b. parties, societies, organizations, and institutions

c. religious life

d. personalities, businessmen, figures, and types

e. destruction of Wyszkow

f. Wyszkower in Israel and around the world

g. Yizkor section

h. addenda

As much as the available material permitted, the chronology and a certain order were maintained. However, it was impossible to avoid the "sneaking in" of the "outside" material into individual sections. Thus, the reader will find much information about the parties, religious life, and personalities – in the general descriptions and remembrances. We are certain that the larger and smaller works will give a full, but not complete picture of the town.

In reference to the destruction of Wyszkow, there are no extensive descriptions in this book of the death of the town, because it was in the first few days of the war that the town was bombed and burned down, the residents fled, and only a few survivors held it in their holy obligation to describe the road of hell they experienced in strange places, in other ghettos, in the death camps, or in partisan units.

Another problem that there was for us was the so-called "language question." Our *landsleit* from abroad requested more Yiddish, and the Wyszkower in Israel were in favor that Hebrew be dominant in the book. The compromise that resulted: The works that were written in Hebrew – were included in the book in the original. Also, some important works were translated into Hebrew.

*

To conclude, our brotherly, warm thanks to the Wyszkower *landsmanschaften*–organizations and individuals in New York, Los Angeles, Argentina, Uruguay, France, and last but not least – in Israel (with the secretary of the *Irgun*, Mr. Yerakhmiel Wilenski at the head), for their true great, moral and material assistance in publishing our book.

A special thank you goes to our esteemed book editor, Mr. Dovid Shtokfish, for his boundless work in collecting, gathering, and editing the material, and also in putting it all together – literarily and graphically – the *Sefer Wyszkow*. Also noteworthy is the work of "the typesetter" [graphic designer], Mr. Yisroel Freedman, who poured a piece of his heart and soul into the pencilled lines so that our book should be better and more and more beautiful. The printing team, and the directing team of "*Defus Hakhodesh*" [Print (sheet) of the Month], deserves a thank you for their assistance. The merit for all those who helped with all their means to publish the *Sefer Wyszkow*, must be made known, that thanks to their strength, a small, but important town in Poland has been eternalized.

Menakhem Shtelung
Chairman of the *Irgun Yotzei Wyszkow be'Yisrael* [Society of Those from Wyszkow in Israel]
Tel Aviv, January 1964

[Page 11]

The Ancestry of Wishkov / Wyszków[1]
(To the history of the Shtetl)[2]
by D. Shtokfish (Ramat–Gan in 1946)

Translated in 2009 by Sylvia Schildt z"l[3]

Reviewed by Frida Grapa Markuschamer de Cielak (Mexico City)

and thanks to Pamela Russ (Montreal, Canada)

Translation donated by the Historian Enrique Krauze (Mexico City)

How long has Wyszków existed? How did the history of the shtetl take shape?

Not hard to answer both questions. Polish historic literature, also encyclopedias and lexicons of great European nations, have dedicated much space to this little town on the Bug River (Widłach Bugu in Polish[4]), along with researches and greater studies. The existing materials in the National Library in Warsaw specifically detail the history of Wyszków. However not much space is devoted to the history of the Jews in that shtetl. And also from the scant reports there is not much to glean, of how long Jews lived here, just as in other towns and little town, rooted in centuries but, not so much that one cannot dredge up the various tribulations, persecutions and pogroms[5]. The Jews of Poland did not have the power to withstand these on Polish soil, and Wyszków was no exception.

The First Mention of Wyszków

Wyszków is mentioned for the first time in Conrad's Document from the year 1302. Among the reckoned possessions of the Bishops[6] he mentions: Tuchlin/Tuczyn[7], Gura, Belina and Turina/Toruń and there, one that can be found is – Wyszków. (Info from "The Town of Wyszków," Geographic Dictionary of Crown–Poland. 14th Volume, Warsaw, 1895,Pages 147–148 by Bronislav Chlebowski)

Therein, it is related:

Wyszków, a municipal entity, earlier – a small village on the right bank of the River Bug, in the Pultusk Powiat (District, county or prefecture), away to the northeast 27 kilometers[8] from Serotzk/Serock and 45 kms[9] from Jablone/Jablon. Several kilometers below Kamientchik / /Kamieńczyk[10] the train station on the left bank of the Bug. It has a property (or a holding??) of a gated cloister[11] belonging to the parish[12]; an elementary school; a community office and a post office. It has over 150 houses and more than 3000 inhabitants, the majority – Jews. In the year 1827 there were 102 houses and 1283 inhabitants. In 1864 – 108 houses, among them – a gated one; 2354 inhabitants – among them – 543 Jews; It sits along the highway that leads from Warsaw to Bialystok; A railroad iron–line is being built that will connect Warsaw with Ostrolenka and will pass through the Wyszków station; Over the Bug, an iron bridge will be build.

Wyszków is an old–fashioned region and has always belonged to the Plotzker Church (Evangelical Church in Plotzk).

The Maczowsher Duke/Duke of Masovia, Treydom/Trojden[13] captured Wyszków with the cloister on the Bug River, and from Kamion on the Waisl/Vistula River/Wisła in Polish), as well as Targovna/Targowa (near Kamion which is located behind Warsaw).

[Page 12]

The sons of Treydom/Trojden: – Zhemovit//Siemowit and Kazhimiesz/Casimir I, returned all these properties to the Bishops.

This is why the latter returned the town of Wyszków to the Duke for 8 years (according to the act of the year 1347. Composed in Czerwinsk) and committed them to return the town after that time back to the Church (Locatat et Informatam), according to the Maczow Codex 58 and 59.

The Bishops from Plotzk/Płock had long since built their palace here and often had a good time there.

In the year 1502 the Bishop Wincenty Przerębski ceded the area with municipal rights that freed the inhabitants of any conscription (A.G. Chelminske).

King Zygmunt [14] the First allowed the Wyzskovers/citizens of Wyszków to build a bridge over the Bug and collect a toll for passing over the bridge. Zygmunt the Third/Sigismund III in the year 1599 gave rights to the local guilds (unions).

(Then), the son of that king, Karl Ferdinand (who was the Plotzker Bishop) built a comfortable palace here and settled in permanently. He died in the year 1655.

In the year 1657 the Swedes destroyed the shtetl. The flood that broke out completed the destruction.

Stanislaw August [15] complied with the request of Plotzker Bishop Michal Poniatowski, and severed the dependence of Wyzków on the bishops and in the year 1781 created markets and fairs. The Mieshtanes/Miesztanes (mixed unions), defending their recently acquired privileges, no longer wanted to overthrow the bishops. At the frequent disputes that broke out between the bishops and the Miesztanes commissars determined by the king, arbitrated them.

The "Tigodnik Ilustrowani" (Illustrated Week) of the year 1876 relates that Wyszków with community and parish comprised a space of 16.628 morgs [16] and 7,693 inhabitants, among them 6 prawoslavni (probably refers to orthodox worshipers), 21 protestants and 2,682 Jews, mainly in the town itself.

The area of Wyszków, which belongs to the government, comprised a distance of 1,280 morgs: forest – 20.654 mórg.

Gmina Wyszkow borders with the gmines/gmina (communes or municipalities or administrative districts) of [17] and Grembkow/Grebkow, Usawna(probably Olszanka), Boczeh (probably Gmina Brańszczyk or the shtetl Brzoza) and Rzasnik/Rząśnik. Surrounding (the gminas), this are the other components (other villages and settlements) in the area: Dombrowe(Yiddish)/Dabrowa(Polish); Grodzisk/Grodzisko; Mrotszk/Mrozyvc; Ozstczecze/Oszczerze; Pyeczkali/Pierzchaly; Falkow/Polkow; Fruszhew/Proszew; Pruczewska–Wiulka/Przetycz Wloscianska; Sukhodoly/Suchodoly; Wytanki(Y&P); Vishkow/Wyszkow; Zaleczhe/Zalecze and Zhomaki/Ziemaki.

A Memorial Whose Meaning Nobody Knows

In the year 1886 the same "Tigodnik Ilustrowani" (Illustrated Week) relates (Volume 13, page 232) about a obelisk with the insignia of the Vazas[18] in Wyszków.

Karl Ferdinand [19]), the 4th son of King Zygmunt/Sigismund the III (Vaza/Waza), Bishop of Plock, was on his later years a melancholic. (Julian Bartashevitch –Princes–Bishops, Warsaw, 1851). Traveling around his holdings he was pleased by the forested region along the River Bug, the shtetl Wyszków situated not far from Warsaw. There he built and settled into a very comfortable residence. There he died in the year 1655. His dead body was first transferred to Warsaw and then – to Cracow/Kraków, to the royal graves along the Wawel[20].

When the Swedish King Gustav Adolf occupied Poland, Wyszków was completely burned to the ground, despite the fact that it had a defense gate and guard towers.

Not far from the shtetl near the former tract that led from Warsaw to Lithuania, on a sufficiently formed foundation, stands a not–large obelisk of grey local marble. There is no inscription on it except the royal Vasa's/Wasa's insignia: a bundle of wheat on all four sides of the memorial. Cut out with a crude chisel, a second similar obelisk, also with the Vasa's insignia, stood on the opposite side of Wyszków. The stonecutter, carved on it the Vasa's insignia, unified wheat in a strange fashion, perhaps inadvertently, so that it looks more like a pitcher with two ears, than a bundle of wheat[21].

About 40 years ago (at abt. 1906), the inspector placed on the pedestal just a pyramidal tip and in the middle placed a compass with the royal insignia.

Along with the shtetl they, (the Swedish army of King Gustav Adolph), also burned all the Acts and the written reports in memory of the memorials that were set up.

The obelisks and inscriptions are silent and say nothing. Only from the insignias can one ascertain that the Princely Bishop of the Vasa/Wasa family put them up. A local legend relates that this is a remembrance of the coming together of two brothers, royal sons, one from Warsaw and the other from Lithuania of that period. They know to tell also about fantastic treasures that are entombed in the obelisks and are guarded by evil spirits. This was also the cause of dismantling one of the memorials. But they did not find – any treasures or documents. It seems that the great wealth that the Kingly Bishop possessed and held in one place until the end of his life, played to the fantasy of buried treasures.

Severin's[22] writing of Wyszków about this, in his historic sketches of the town Wyszków, (published through Hyppolyte Tchimbarovitch in the year 1841, pages 13–6, 32–35, 50–52) thusly assessed the meaning of both obelisks in the shtetl:

"A bit behind the town, near the former Warsaw tract, stands a memorial in the form of an obelisk, 18 meters tall, of grey marble, without any inscriptions, only with the insignia of the Vasa's. The upper part is destroyed by time. A second memorial with another insignia of the Vasa's, stood on the other side of town. But it was destroyed in barbaric fashion by an unknown hand and its fragments lie around still in the cloister cemetery. By whom and when these memorials were installed – no one knows. No Acts in the Cloister and Municipal Entities – have ever been found.

[Page 13]

But the legend relates that these memorials were put up after the two big epidemics, and this seems to be highly possible because of the double crosses found on their tops".

"Constant Influx of the Population"

The above-mentioned Severin, begins his historic overview of Wyszków with a citation from a poem:

"Under my feet, with silvered pearl/ swims the old Bug,/

around and around, with smiling greens/

have overgrown the bridge. ("Pshetland Warsaw", 10th band, 1890)

And further:

" In the Pultusk Circle, on Lithuanian soil, on a height, at whose feet wraps his currents the Old Bug – the Ganges of the Ancient Slavs, lies the shtetl Wyszków, which with one arm reaches the actual river"...

(Bishop) Wincenty Przerębski[23] with the insignia "Novene", the Crown–Chancellor and Bishop of Plotzk/Płock, on a Friday in the week of "Judica" in the year 1502, raised the village Wyszków, which had belonged to the Bishops, to the status of a town and granted it the following privileges:

1. The town's name should be no other than Wyszków.

2. Liberate the minorities from all the forced labor and obligations. They only have to pay taxes.

3. The council gave the magistrate the right to control the public size and weight with the possibility of punishment for counterfeiting, by the Chelmno (Kulm) Law – and the income from them appointed for some needs.

4. A free access to the burghers in Bishop's forests; to get timber for their urban needs.

5. Assignment of the state lawns.

6. From the income of the bath; of clothing–businesses around or in the hall; from sharp drinks or goods (merchindice); every 3rd penny must be appointed for the State.

7. Allow the urban population to start with small nets to fish in the Bug River.

8. He compensated the State of Wyszkow with the rights of the city of Pultusk, iliving up the right to determine alone the mayor and the council–men.

The original acts of the privileges were burned up, but the copies were found at the Bishops Archives.

The privileges of King Zygmunt the First[24] were given to the town of Wyszków at the Piatrokow Council in 1533, as equally endowed with all other start–up towns, was formally recognized on the 6th of January 1557 in Warsaw by King Zygmunt August[25].

In the year 1528, in the time of the Piatrkow Council, the town of Wyszków received from King Zygmunt the First permission to build a bridge across the Bug with the right to collect a toll for the benefit of the Plotzker Bishops.

The extent of the earlier Wyszków including its boundaries, are not known.

First the decree from a "committee for good order" in the year 1775 permanently reserved 3 plow fields measuring 12 wlach according to Chelminska measurement, as well as 73 places to 73 morg.(See again[16]).

The size of Wyszków it seems was rather spacious, because among the surrounding fields you can even today come upon foundations of gates and defense–towers. Legend says that Wyszków had reached as far as the village of Rybienko[26].

In the year 1841– Wyszków was a little town of 95 wooden and 8–gated houses in which there lived 1149 "heads" – more than half Jews. The insignia was in the form of a village rake.

Once the town possessed a council house built of wood, which was taken down in the year 1806 in order to place there a bridge for military use over the Bug. But then the bridge was burned down.

The shtetl has no factories of any kind (in 1946). A highway cuts through the middle of Wyszków that leads from Warsaw to Bialystok. The whole town is cobbled, but this does not prevent mud. At night it is lit with several lanterns.

A little river, which has two bridges, divides Wyszków from the village of Nadgozhe/ Nadgorze. Right after the bridge, just where the river flows into the Bug River, stands on a mountain, one of the oldest cloisters in all Poland, from the time of Boleslav Chrobry[27], or his follower, and has already been restored twice. The current, gated cloister was begun in the year 1790 and finished in 1793, with money from Krzysztof Hilary Szembek, the Plotzker Bishop[28].

The Cholera (epidemic of infectious gastroenteritis), which emptied the Polish provinces in the years 1581, 1634, 1708 and 1710, did not omit Wyszków. The last epidemic in the time of Ludwik Zaluski, the Plotzker Bishop (1722) entirely eliminated the population of people and animals.

And here the historian, allows himself an ugly anti–Semitic outburst, blaming the Jews for the plague, which has broken out:

[Page 14]

"The cholera of the year 1831" – writes Severin about Wyszków – "was a very mild one – but in the year 1837, a panic happened, especially in a town full of Jews, who were not noted for their cleanliness. When the last of them were driven into the forests, the plague ceased".

The main sustenance of the inhabitants was agriculture, which existed on a very low niveau. Next to the River Bug, which was arable, sizable income was derived from lumber from the surrounding forests – all the way to Dantzik (Danzig[29]). But even this was not able to lift their impoverished lifestyle.

There was nothing special to distinguish the character of the inhabitants, because of the constant influx of population, which consisted of various armies. The frequent change of government in the past and current centuries left no remarkable impressions on the town.

Below Folwark[30], there is a big salt–mine, built during the Prussian government, full of brlne (salt) carriages that haul (transport) salt from (the salt mines) from Wyelitczke(Wieliczkaand Czestochowa/Częstochowa, which is now such an important product for everybody.

In the spring, the river looks very welcoming with thousands of little boats swimming through filled with golden wheat from Wolin[31] and barges with wood rushing to the Baltic Sea ...

Wyszków in other sources

Thus is portrayed the history of the shtetl in Polish historic literature. But also serious scientific publications in various lands have not overlooked Wyszków and revealed an array of statistical publications in various times. In Meyer's Lexicon, which appeared in the year 1930 in Leipzig (12th volume, p. 1631), it is stated: Wyszków, a town in the Polish province of Warsaw, Pultusk Circle, in the year, 1921 – 9,084 inhabitants, half of them – Jews. Located on the Bug (River)and train line Tlushtesh/Tlutszcz– Ostrolenka, glass industry.

In the Parisian "Larousse" (1939, volume 6, page 1631) the number of inhabitants is given as 10,050 with factories and agricultural implements and machines. In Ritter's Geographic–Statistical Lexicon published in Leipzig a hundred years ago, (page 883, 5th edition), Wyszków still belonged to Russia, situated in the Plotzker Gubernye (political subdivision in Plock). The number of inhabitants – 1,290, and in the same lexicon, but published in the year 1910, (ninth edition, band 2, page 865, St. Petersburg), Wyszków belonged to the Lomzher Gubernye/Łomża gubernia.

More information about Jews is given in the Jewish Encyclopedia (5th volume, page 865, St. Petersburg): Wyszków – a settlement in the Pultusker gubernye/Pułtusk gubernia. Jews experienced no difficulties settling here. In the year 1856: – 1,023 Jews, 512 Christians. In the year 1897: – 5,038 inhabitants, of them, 3,207 Jews.

Our Memorial

A so–so lineage–letter (yikhes–briv) for the ancestry of a shtetl. But unfortunately the history of Jewish Wyszków was brutally and gruesomely chopped away in September 1939, with the outbreak of the 2nd World War. Since that date, it is no longer for Jews the history of a settlement, but lamentation for the murder of an entire Jewish community. The historic memorial of Wyszków is no longer like the obelisks on both sides of town, for which they do not in whose memory they were erected. Now in the year 1964, in the biggest city of the Jewish land, in Tel–Aviv – we have erected another "obelisk": – **Sefer Wyszków** – in memory of an active creative Jewish community, that distinguished itself with both Hassidism and worldliness; with Zionism and Socialism; with folkloric and communal activities.

Let this Book–Gravestone (Sefer Wyszków), serve as remembrance for the Survivors, calling up in them memories and feelings, with mourning and a hidden tear over the fate of a Jewish settlement that is no longer here......

Footnotes

1. Wyszków = neither Wishkov nor Vishkov, the correct Polish spelling is Wyszków.

2. shtetl = A shtetl(inYiddish) refers a small town with a large Jewish population in Central and Eastern Europe, before the Pogroms and the Holocaust.

3. The translator, Sylvia Schildt(z"l 2010) aided some time ago, by Frida Grapa–Cielak, Wyszków researcher for Dr. Enrique Krauze's Wyszków Project, tried as much as possible, to translate from the Yiddish text the correct spelling of the Polish and the non–Yiddish words with the best intention to have them correctly written, which in some cases was more than an impossible task. (But, Frida CIELAK, reviewed and added the names in their original Polish spelling.

4. Bug River = In Polish the correct name is Widłach Bugu

5. pogroms (pogrom in sing.) = A pogrom is a violent massacre or persecution of an ethnic or religious group, particularly one aimed at Jews.

6. Bishops = (Bishop in sing.) is the title of an ecclesiastical dignitary or clergyman who possesses the fullness of the priesthood to rule a diocese as its chief–pastor, primacy of the pope in due submission of the pope.

7. Tuchlin/Tuczyn = This presentation of 2 names with a diagonal line in between them, denotes that the first word is in the way it was pronounced and written in the original Yiddish texts, while the 2nd word after the diagonal, is the correct Polish spelling (alike to the following presentations: Turina/Toruń; Serotzk/Serock; Jablone/; Kamientchik/Kamienczyk; etc). Be aware that this similar presentation is to be found in most of the translated texts).

8. 27 kilometers (kms) = are abt. 16 miles.

9. 45 kms = are abt. 27 miles.

10. Kamientchik/Kamienczyk = Was a train–station 5 km east of Wyszków (3.18 mi).

11. cloister = A place, especially a monastery or convent, devoted to religious seclusion.

12. parish = A church territorial–unit under the pastoral care and clerical jurisdiction of a parish priest.

13. Treydom/Trojden, The Duke of Masovia = He was better known under his Belarusian name Trojden, but also as: Traidenis in Polish and in Yiddish he was called: Treydom! Trojden, the Grand Duke of Lithuania in the 13th century was the one who inherited parts of Warsaw and Liw, captured Wyszków with the cloister on the Bug River, from Kamion on to the Waisl (probably Vistula River (Polish=Wisła;), as well as Targovna (near Kamion which is located behind Warsaw).

14. Zygmunt the First = Zygmunt, in Polish; Sigismund I in English: (1467–1548, King of Poland.

15. Stanislaw August = He was Stanisław August Poniatowski, the last king of Poland.

16. mórg. = (mórgs, in plural) A unit of Polish land–measurement;(per Gerald Ortell's book on Polish parish records).

17. and *Not all the gmina names and the names of the surrounding villages, cities or settlements could be found in the correct Polish spelling, but for each found, the distance between it and Wyszkow was determined in order to have a better idea of what the author wanted to transmit.

He wrote: ...... Gmina Wyszków borders the gmines/gminas (communes or municipalities or administrative districts) of: Grembkow(Yiddish)/Gmina Grębków(Polish) and the village Grebkow is 8.78 kms/5.46 miles from Wyszkow; ; Uzawna(Y)&(no gmina starts in Polish with a U, so it could probably be Olszanka); **Boszeh** (Y)& (in Polish the gmina found is Gmina Brańszczyk and as a village or shtetl: Brzoza) and finally, the gmina mentioned as Ruczna(Y)/gmina Rząśnik (in Polish) The villages and settlements of the gminas in the area, (close to Wyszkow) are: Dombrowe(Yiddish)/Dabrowa(Polish) **or** Dabrowa Chotomowska 79 kms/49 miles); Grodzisk(Y)/Grodzisko(P) (3.4kms=2.11 miles from Wyszkow); Mrotszky(Y)/Mrozyvc(22.3 kms=13.84 mil.); Ozstczecze(Y)/Oszczerze(P)(2.2kms=1.36 miles); Pyeczkali(Y)/Pierzchaly(P) (1.13 kms=0.7 miles); Falkow(Y)/Polkow(P) (3.7 kms=2.5 mi); Fruszhew(Y)/Proszew(P)(5.7 kms=3.6 miles); Pruczewska–Wiulka(Y)/Przetycz Wloscianska(P)/Przetycz(57.6 km=35.8 miles).; Sukhodoly(Y)/Suchodoly(P) (5.7 kms=abt. 3 miles); Wytanki(Y&P)(4 kms=/abt. 3 miles); Vishkow/Wyszkow(0.0); Zaleczhe(Y)/Zalecze(P)/Zalesie Miasto(74.5 kms=46 miles) and Zhomaki(Y)/Ziemaki(P)(12.2 kms=7.6 miles).

18. Vazas or Wasas(plural) = It refers to the the Vaza/Wasa family of Polish Bishops.

19. Karl Ferdinand Vasa (in Polish: Karol Ferdynand Waza) = known also as Charles Ferdinand Vasa, was the Prince–Bishop, born October 13, 1613 in Warsaw, the 4th son of Zygmunt/Sigismund Vasa the III and Habsburżanki Constance, brother to John Casimir, half–brother of Wladyslaw Vasa the IV. Bishop of Wroclaw–1625, Bishop of Plock–1640 who died May 9, 1655 in his palace in Wyszkow, and for whom, a marble obelisk was build up in Wyszkow in his memory in 1655.

20. Wawel = is a fortified architectural complex erected over many centuries atop a limestone outcrop on the left bank of the Vistula River in Kraków/Craców, Poland.

21. Vasa's or Wasa's Royal insignia = A bundle of wheat, the Royal Wasa Insignia was on all four sides of the memorial. (This shield picture was not included in the original version in "Sefer Wyszkow", it was added here, for explanatory purposes only.

22. Severin = Timothy "Tim" Severin (born 1940) is a British explorer, historian and writer noted for his work in retracing the legendary journeys of historical figures.

23. Wincenty Przerębski = Vincent Przerębski, Bishop of Plock, obtained in March of 1502 the consent of the King John I Albert (in Polish: Jan I Olbracht) to broadcast the municipal rights in Wyszków, privileges established by the "Sejm" (the Prussian state parliament) The Bishop of Plóck was the representative of Polish Kings in the Prussian state parliament called "Sejm".

24. King Zygmunt the First. (1467–1548); He was also known as King Zygmunt I the Old King of Poland (Sigismund in English).

25. Zygmunt August II = was the Grand Duke of Lithuania from 1522; and the nominally King of Poland from 1529; in fact King of Poland from 1548 as King Sigismund II Augustus (1520 – 1572).

26. Rybienko Nowe (today) = A village in the administrative district of Gmina Wyszków, within Wyszków County, (in a distance of almost 2 km, 1.30 miles).

27. Boleslav Chrobry = He was nicknamed: "the Brave" or "Valiant," ruled as Duke of Poland from 992-1025 as the first King of Poland in 1025.

28. Krzysztof Hilary Szembek = (in English: Christopher), was Bishop of Plóck (born 1722 in White, Poland– died Sept. 5th, 1797 in Kraków) Was for 12 years, Bishop of Plóck (1785. 1797) was immersed in a disciple of the Jesuits in the years (1783–1784) served as a proxy functions Nuncio in Poland, and was the doctor's crown in the general confederation Targowica.

29. Dantzik/Dantzig = An older Dutch and German spelling variant of Danzig is Gdańsk.

30. Folwark mines = The mines produce iron; amber, and, mined at one time Folwark, near Rogoźno had salt deposits and springs medical baths.

31. Wolin, Poland = This name is shared by 2: An island in the Baltic Sea, located just of the Polish coast and a Polish town located on the southern tip on that island.

[Page 14]

My Memories of Wyszkow
by Menachem Kaspi (Srebrenik), Kfar Auno
Translated by Chava Eisenstein

My hometown Wyszkow was not an exceptional town. She didn't stand out with her history, and no remarkable individuals originated from her. She was always engrossed in problems that arise in a provincial town's life. The central pivot in the town's life was the Rabbi, the Shokhet (Kosher slaughterer), or their "Rivalry in the name of Holiness." The Rosh HaKahal, the dominant leader of the congregation, and the youth, who began awakening to the fact that they are missing something to hold onto and are hanging on to thin string.

When I sink into thought and bring up her figure from the bottom of the past, I try to remember and bring everything back to life, slowly the fog fades off, the town itself begins to appear as it was, with all its alleys, people, their problems, their difficult battles and struggles for life. Here is so–and–so; all week long he does not try to voice any opinion when ordinary Jews are schmoozing about current affairs or busy making jokes. He only bends down his head and nods with his beard to show he agrees to everything. Nevertheless, on Market Day, his eyes spurt sparks of fire and he is all tangled up, his feet are in constant heavy motion with his hands clapping in the effort of convincing one or another, like a gallant battling a heavy war.

With Sunrise

I awake early on a spring morning. The trees are at the peak of blossom, the whole town is enveloped in silence, except for the occasional passing wagons with their noisy iron wheels bumping their way over the stony pavement.

[Page 15]

I am pacing the street inhaling the pure and fresh air, the apple garden is so appealing. I jump over to a line of half cut–down trees. The planks of the fence around the apple garden are fastened one to another. I am searching for a breach so I can enjoy the smell and the sights, until I get to a stand where the fruit is for sale and I enjoy peeking on them. Behind is one of the "Fishers" who bought this garden, his lengthy beard twisting down to his clothes, with his fleshy nose he approaches me, he grabs my ears with the tips of his fingers.

"Yingel," what are you trying to smell around here. Go learn your Gemara. Moshe the blacksmith is banging with a sledgehammer, the sparks are reaching far and together with the ricochets – his cunning gaze. His face covered with soot and in his eyelashes are beginning to show a mysterious gloss, as though a black oven was opened and a flame is coming out. Fast go to Kheyder! Otherwise, you will be like me, and he picks up the heavy mallet and hammers even stronger. I feel so lucky that I am learning and will not have to work that hard.

I pass swiftly the red brick house, where the Police and the Post office are. Whenever I pass this place, fear mixed with curiosity overcomes me. I want to peek into the arched gate, and see all the secrets that are hiding there. Only once did I make it to look inside, when they brought the dead body of a gentile that committed suicide. Many people gathered around and I too pushed my way into the crowd, but I was chased away immediately and now I am not curious anymore. To learn I want!

The wagons with the meat from the slaughterhouse just arrived, and the butchers open their shops causing great commotion. "Yossel Butcher" the tall guy, his thin pale face with red veins protruding from under his skin in a crisscross design, each time he passes with a chunk of meat he knocks into something. "Yuta Zivia's son" the athlete, as if his body operates by springs, his face half laughing half–mad, but his eyes know no rest, and he roars at him: Hello! Of course you don't have sense! Each time you bump into the doorframe you knock your head until it losses its sense...you are laughing! Today they wanted to slaughter in the abattoir. I bought a nice cow, a real "Golden Bargain." They wanted to announce her as non–kosher, they found something in the lung, they didn't agree to puff it up, only I, the Shokhtim and the Rabbi were shaking like by the long–prayer. If it would be non–kosher I would have slayed them myself. They barely made it Kosher. And they pointed to me with their finger: "My Yeshiva Bokhur." My precious jewel, you study from the huge Gemara. Say, what are they stupefying our brains "these lovely Yidden" those predicated faces, Kosher – Glatt Kosher. For heaven's sake, I can't figure them out, if it is Kosher – so it is kosher for all, and if it is non–kosher, so what? Am I a Goy? I barely slip away from them and rush to the "Rinek" (town's square). Only my side curls blow backwards.

The "Rinek" is swarming with people, wagons and merchandize, a mixture of everything. The horses, their heads in the wagons, are lashing their pony (tails?) and are not stopping to eat. The gentile coachmen, their whips in hand, are busy curling their mustaches and trying to smell around if they can make some good deal with the "z'hidek" (Jew). Chaya is clasping her hands. Her abrasive face full with all sorts of blots and spots is turning red.

The scarf on her head is moving independently as she watches her short, stout husband approach. His pale face glittering as his praying shawl is tucked under his arm. Couldn't you make today's prayer shorter and chat some less? You forgot it's market day today? Will you keep an eye at this "taker"? He utters not a single word and comes closer, he pushes his way into the crowd of clients while his mouth is muttering: "cheaper than dirt, finest quality, real bargains" – as though he is still praying.

The "Rinek"

I try to perceive with one glance the "Rinek" the town's square, it is a wide huge square, with paved stones only at its ledges and all around there are many, many stores. On a regular day it's a pleasure to walk around here, with one glance you can surround all the various types of stores and the people standing on their threshold, their wide open mouth ready to catch any event, every word, eager to begin a conversation, even Kupchick, the Goy, will offer you to sniff tobacco. Today's "market" – everything is in great upheaval. The square filled with stalls and tables, crates, hanging clothes. Shiny boots, weird hats, and every moment someone else emerges, almost collapses under the heavy freight on his shoulder, as he rushes by he almost sweeps you along. All you see is a scrunched face, blown up face–muscles, hands and feet in constant motion continuously ready to jump, distorted tongue and jabbered language. I hardly break my way through to the wooden bridge, to breathe fresh air, that's where I remain, leaning onto the banister bent towards the Bug River, which is flowing in an endless stream. A slight wind comes sneaking from behind, and smooth/s my burning face from the hot sunrays that burst through the heavy clouds and mingle with the silver glimmer of the water flow.

New water streams pass in a torrent only to return. The Bug's waters come from afar carrying a silent yearning of wishes. Arms are held high and are carried afar, ligaments are drawn as a polished mirror, and I, the bridge, and everything is swished away, swept and taken by the endless stream like my heart's yearnings. Suddenly a lash twists on my neck and leaves me with scorching pain accompanied by a screeching voice: "Hey, Z'hidek! You and your side locks, get away from here, go to your Palestine." Yes, I should go away from here to My Palestine, to the Beit Midrash, to learn. Yes, I erred.

Lag Baomer "Maccabi" and "Hashomer Hatzaeir" March – on the bridge over the Bug

[Page 16]

"Go, Go"

The small synagogue was already empty of people, the sun flooded the place, everything is seen in its bright light. The clock on the wall with its Hebrew letters on its face, the pride of the synagogue. The heavy long tables that are attached to the floor. The sunrays, like beams of fire, light up the white wall and like a torrent of light directed on the black letters on the white background – "Law of Israel Association." When night falls, this corner looks like the darkest part here. You can only see people bent over the huge volumes nodding their head in approval to each word that comes from the Rabbi's mouth with a pleasure and enthusiasm. The wall isn't seen, nor the house, only a knot of people gathered together, and the inspiring Rabbi. The words circle around into the space of this nook. The light walls integrate in the emptiness of the synagogue. The electric bulbs in the seven–branched chandelier that hangs over the prayer page appear as pale sticks. Even the death wagon and the cleansing board that stand behind the synagogue, they, that always throw one into fear, at night, together with its shadow, make it seem, as if the dead souls are still hanging on to the wagon, they are coming to catch the holy prayer "Kedusha" and the "Shema," for the benefit of their souls. By day – the light of the sun slides off the black walls of the square wagon with its big white lettering "Justice Walks before Him" and I look for the footsteps of the praying people. The small synagogue (the small "Beit Medrash"), its outside lines are simple straight and clear, engraved altogether in white. This was the synagogue of the craftsmen: tailors, blacksmiths, carpenters, the nearing footsteps of heavy boots that are on battle for sustainment are heard. They fight the day, the praying. They leave at sunrise, to a day of arduous labor. The place is shrouded in lonesome mystery, you look for the heavy footsteps of those who implanted sorrow and sadness with their silent prayers, but there are no impressions left.

The open Gemara winks me: "please, come cry out your heart": "Avayei says, Rava says." A yearning voice and a rumbly heart fill the whole atmosphere of the synagogue. The echoes swirl their way up. The evil inclination is prompting and instigating: The synagogue is right here before you, the tables, benches are available, you can leap and jump on them without being disturbed, you can jump and spin from one table to the other to no end. Here goes Zelig Fischer, he comes on Market Day – how is it? And he yells to me: it's my "Shmedresh" (prayer house), my table, my clock, my synagogue, the tables are mine, the clock, and you are here to destroy! Get out of here! Again, I have to leave, I am a failure and a sinner.

I sneak to the "Ger'r Shtiebel." It's only across the street, sort of a dead alley divides between the small synagogue and the Khassidic Ger'r Shtiebel. Peeling walls, pieces of plaster caught within the many cob webs and on the feeble steps, not sure whether they are steps or plain slabs of earth, and in the dark hall are by now heard clearly the voices coming from inside. The worshipers are pacing back and forth, from time to time they scream out words, and go figure out if they are ending or only beginning the prayers. The tumult here is great. All those who finished praying and those that are still in the midst, their yelps ring high in the air, even the stones on the walls are shouting, everything is voicing and expressing.

Everyday Talk

Mendel Zrumber is sitting, his face all wrinkled, his thin beard and his direct inspecting eyes tell, that he is clever and good–hearted. He is learning with his son Torah, but he knows that it is in vain. The little brain of the youth is not doing any intake. Shmuel the purger, forever restless, reels his hands to his back and gives them a sudden jerk in conjunction with his feet. He manages to visit every corner and finger each book. From the corner of his eye he is reading something, his hands are holding a "Tanya" (practical and mystical fundamentals of Khabad) that was standing at the end of the bookcase, he leafs through it and through the heavy "Sfas Emes" besides the Talmud volume and a booklet of tales, turning its pages from cover to cover not finding interest in anything. His face is narrow but full, nature was ungenerous with his beard, therefore it is hard to tell its direction or color, his eyes show cleverness and inattentiveness, energy but no ambition, he wishes to hold on to something but he has so much to say that he becomes mixed up. Somehow, he approaches the table of Reb. Mendel. Reb. Mendel lets out a relieved breath. Nu, so you are watching the Torah penetrating my jewel's little head, it is a bit hard he says, with his characteristic hoarse voice. The tale goes about a Jewish farmer that came across the verse "shemesh bayoim lo **yakekah**" he screamed – eek! Such a horrible word in prayer just cannot be: it must be "lo **yabebah**." Hearing this treasure of a word makes Shmuel the purger jump: I know "Hebrew masters" that instead of saying "Lamenatzeakh" they say "Latzmaneakh" and many more samples like these with endless stories. He stood there with his foot on bench and hand on knee, his fingertips engrossed in his straggly beard. The young lads were always exchanging secret language with the Tefillin tied around their arms. They derived special pleasure of schmoozing with one sleeve raised and half of their cloak sloped over a shoulder with the Tefillin sticking out from an arm, like great adventurers. What a variety of words, always ready for further inspiration. When Shmuel and Reb Mendel got together, it always called for attention from these lads who would gather about and the talk would begin to liven up. Shmuel, out of contentment, would muster up new energy. I, too, would push through to be present. Shmuel used his strong hands and granted me an appropriate pinch on my cheek, which was never hard to tell if it is from affection or hate.

The Ger Khassidic Shtiebel as center of focus in town

On the outside, the Khassidic shtiebel of Ger appeared to be rundown, two neglected rooms, the second room was almost dark in spite of its windows, the sun never really came in, in the center stood four bare wooden poles. Still it contained a distinct charm. Here, didn't stand out any distinct characters with strong influential or social charisma. The shtiebel had its cut of alert merchants with a vague Torah knowledge, but they were men of action, they always sensed the reality and were aware of all happenings in town. From them emerged the town leaders, and they made the essential decisions. The activity in the shtiebel served as a ray of light for the youth in town.

The Young Pioneer

[Page 17]

Agudat Yisrael

When I entered this always–dim hall, I was drawn to the acrobatic steps that lead to the upper room. The two low–ceilinged rooms were filled with rows of books, secular books. How curious I am and wish to know what is going on in the big world, beyond the one, which surrounds me. And there I can peek into it. So I climb the stairs, perhaps the door is open. A meeting is being held now. The chairman is reciting some foreign language paragraphs, young lads that crave for breaking barriers are talking about a new movement – Torah garbed in orderliness and organization, to cast the Torah in new utensils. With burning eyes fused with enthusiasm, they talk about it. The library is open, long lines of shiny books are facing me, I swallow Marcus Lehman's books, with the pure love, nature in itself, the green fields. There are Khassidic movements that are against the idea, its boundary breaching! The youth is going to be consumed in fire!

Conflict between Ger and Alexander Khassidim

The Alexander Khassidim are poor, their means are meager, but they are affluent in Torah. They weren't even able to afford a special room for praying, and they were forced to wander around from one place to another until they found a place near the Bug River. A small narrow room, but its pleasantness for the soul mingled with the idyll, a human friendship reigned there of people deprived physically but free in their spirit. This Khassidic Home was a haven to escape life's sufferings. Here, mental tranquility was found. The praying went on quietly, with a reserved and soft spirituality. The prayers hovered all over the "shtiebel," they caressed, soothed and blended harmoniously in all hearts. On Shabbat morning, the shtiebel was veiled by the pleasant spirit of Gemara learning before prayers, and especially the prayers from Berish Cohen, that was a special silent melody, not the skyrocketing type, nor sadness of the soul, only natural accords of the essence of life and spiritual pleasure. Berish Cohen was busy all week long with commerce, but it didn't leave any mark on him, like raised voices or hand motions, mild, pleasant, quite and natural speech. His appearance brought niceness, his facial wrinkles flowed together with his straight beard, where all the hair found places neatly without getting tangled one another. He would come every Shabbat morning prior to prayers and learn Gemara. His gentle melody mixing with the rumbling of the river that was seen through the window, and created a wonderful combination of man and universe. He was one of those, destined to stand against the opening breaches and reclaim the insult of the Torah, of which the youth is dismantling. Sin leads to more sins and the young lads will "peek and get damaged.". If there are no kid–goats there will be no goats, and we will remain without Torah and without etiquette. The more famous amongst them is Reb Shimon, since two in the morning, and father is exerting his mind in study, he paces back and forth, hands in his belt, his face looks tired but his lips are still mumbling phrases and parts of sayings of the sacred secret "Zohar." "vekholho almin hukhrevoo mai taama m'shum d'adam lo huskan" (man failed to amend himself in the form of the almighty's image.) And they are continuing to corrupt. Woe to that son that is placed at the doorstep of immorality. What can the son do and not sin?! That's how he decided to go and devote himself against this verdict. And dissension developed.

The youth breaks loose into the street

It is hard to determine what came first: the awakening prior to the fight or the fighting prior to the awakening. The broken rickety steps always trembled under the constant running feet of the boys from the "Ger'r shtiebel" upstairs to the "Agudas Yisroel" offices and back. There were gatherings, meetings, a secretary was elected, disputes on secretarial issues and "Melave Malka" (end of Shabbat) meals. The low–ceilinged pitiable rooms were booming with action and traffic, young energy and enthusiasm. All of a sudden, the noise ceased, the Ger'r Shtiebel, that housed usually many tattered books, was now empty. The youth went somewhere far. Where are they? The youth was drawn to the outer edge. On Friday nights the section from Koshzushko street till the bridge that leads to the boardwalk, stores, houses, cannot be seen, only boys and girls. The streetlights throw a dim light over their radiating faces. Every now and then outbursts of girlish laughter or loud talk is heard. There is a pause and then they continue strolling back and forth, endless. Where are they walking to? "Out on the street," they reach the bridge, and look down on the dark cleft and continue to roam.

On Shabbat, the bridge sways along with the steps of the youth like a baby cradle. Some hold on to the benches along the bridge and enjoy the river's splendor, but usually the bridge is passed quickly, the forests charms are more attractive. With my heart pounding my brother Yossel pulls at my sleeve, how much longer will you stare at the unending water that makes its way through the pillars of the bridge. Fast, we have to reach the other end because of the "Eiruv" (ritual enclosure) poles that we laid under the bridge prior to the Shabbat. We pause to rest a bit, rifts of clouds hang over us as they grow wider. The sunrays fall on a white sky and return back to us. Eyes open widely, one can't help gazing at the faraway continuous fields all along the river. The fields and the river blend into thousands of colors. The forest is intoxicating, it awakens suppressed desires. Here go a couple, embracing each other, I always saw them. She – daughter of the blacksmith, she once looked like a gypsy: he – short and fat. They would walk together in an indifferent silence, in the forest their faces come to life. Hugging and heading to the thickness of the forest. In all directions of the forest, gatherings are taking place...meetings...and I am laying on the loose earth under the Conifer trees. The erect trees rise even higher, their branches tangled one in another. A silent wind sweeps over them and they move, echoing till afar. A sunray slides through leaving over fragments of sunlight, and I, am craving to join society that is hiding within the shadowy trees. Soon they will all come out from hiding and will gather here, me too.

Sports indorse us

Sport groups get together, the children try to get pennies from their mothers, they want to join and buy a ball and they come home without shoes and patience. They can't wait for Shabbat afternoon when they will run straight to the football ground near the Polish school. We climbed over the fence regardless the danger. The Jews are playing against the Poles. "Laizer Mesing" the painter, all hunched over, is watching his son getting into trouble with "Karp" the gentile, he squints his lips and waves his hand as though he is still holding the paintbrush. Avrem'l the janitor, hands on hips, face uptight, all ready to pounce and catch the ball. Avrem'l the son of Yaakov the Shokhet, his father tried all the methods that Torah should enter his mind, but in vain. In no time, he became the town's idol: all black, his masculine face conveyed skillfulness. His eyes rolling fast after the ball, everyone is watching him, praying that the gentiles Will – G–d forbid – not win. He caught the ball, everyone is thanking him with admiring glances. I look into his eyes so he should look back at me, after all – a neighbor. He does not notice me, as though I am non–existent. I wish they would get a "Goal" into him and he will explode, than he will not be so arrogant. Again, the gentiles come storming in, expressing derision, they want to kick "Moshke," Avrem'l goes out of the gate, and I follow him fearful, praying. I forgive him. Nothing is wrong, he should only be successful...

[Page 18]

A Short Illusion

On the road leading to Srotzk, after the Polish school, near the train bridge, stood alone a house, the last house of the city. It was stuck between rows of bushy trees and apple gardens. That is where they gathered to get ready for the march on the road. The boys stood in a row absorbed in thought, all of a sudden they straightened up like poles, all ready for self–sacrifice, physical and mental alike. A blue and white flag appeared. The faces didn't show any personal signs but a strong unity. The flag enwrapped them and transferred them to concepts of different galaxies. They sang with passion "Hatikva" – for the Land of Israel. And in front of my eyes I discovered a different Land Of Israel, not one of the world to come, of Mashiakh, but one of hope and anticipation, the actual Land Of Israel. Apparently, they were preparing for the May 3 march, Poland's Constitution Day.

This day brought great commotion. Dr. Laykher donated 100 zloty for decorating the big synagogue and the community gave something too. The great synagogue was a spacious building that occupied the whole corner of the street. Three entrances it had. Inside, two artisan lions stood upwards, upon entering, one would think they are alive and can swallow everything. The windows were arched in Gothic style. The synagogue was pleasant and when you came in you felt at liberty. You would always find you have a quorum of ten with which to pray. It gave a homely feeling. The big synagogue served as the central artery of the city and was now decorated with paper flags in all colors, chains connected between the huge chandelier and its glass tassels hanging down. Greenery and papers decorated the stage pillars, interwoven with red and white flags. The main entrance, the one opposite the Police, was always closed, probably from fear of unfavorable eyes of the neighbors across. This time was decorated with leaves in a gate shape and on top was the Polish Eagle. Around it – a Magen David with multi–colored electric bulbs. It seems as the Jewish Teaching: "You shall be light as an Eagle" – is trying to compete with the rude and rapacious Polish Eagle. One eyeing the other with weird terrifying glances; slowly they accustom to each other and spread their wings creating a peaceful canopy, as if communal understanding was found between us and the gentiles.

The Celebration and its results

The main entrance to the synagogue was open, the street was crowded with people, and the schoolchildren of "Powoschechna School" were lined up to six in a row. Everyone was happy, the friendly May–sun infused in all, joy and liveliness. There never was such a deep longing to the big synagogue, and when entrance was denied, I pushed my way through the Polish school kids. Inside the synagogue there was great noise and commotion, Dr. Laykher spoke Polish, his fleshy hands were pressed to his body as if he was a soldier. His voice rang as if coming from a record, he was stocky, and around his eyes was swelling. His whole appearance spoke of arrogance. Our Rabbi also showed up, tall and straight, his beard going down to his chest, thus adding dignity to his appearance. With his wide and banal speech, not forgetting to add "not to be counted,", that Poland shall grow and expand to all dimensions, as if there were no pogroms. He surpassed from his speech topic, and the crowds didn't like his words, when he finished with "Yidden, Fieldmarshal Pilsudski shall live," the Polish anthem "Jeszcze Polska" ("Even Poland") burst out of the school children's mouths, and it united with the praise and prayers from the synagogue, creating a queer combination.

Outside the parade, the fire department musical band played military march melodies. At the head of the firemen stood Pavlowski the Burmistrz (Mayor), the priest, the Gymnasia and after them the "Sokol" with red shirts, a twisted cord going through one of the sleeves passing through the arm. Their gaze is one of Polish insolence and pride. We feel uneasy, where are the Jewish delegates? They were trailing at the end of the parade, the Shikses are laughing "Zhidek," look on! Our flag, blue and white didn't awake my enthusiasm, it was embarrassed, we need it held up high, with our own strength.

"Let's over–smart them"

Anti–Semitic and national slogans showed up like truffles and mushrooms on the fences and walls in big letters: "Przez Zhidami" – "Don't buy by Jews". The Polish children harass the Jewish children at school, they come back crying, a drunkard chases the youth off the bridge. We are anxious and wondering, why didn't they protest? We walk a little on the avenue, to savor the scent of the chestnuts that are spread on both sides of the boulevard, they sway softly in accordance with the wind which touches their tops, and scatters shadows between the lines of light that penetrate the twigs and create sort of a game of light n' shadow and sooth the yearning of their soul, the disagreement that's hidden within them. Suddenly – a gentile knocks with a stick on my brother Zadok's head, blood is gushing, gone is the taste for life, it hurts me and I am aggravated that I don't know the language of this gentile, I would turn to him with a question: why do you hit someone whom you don't know, and didn't do you any harm? At the sound of horse galloping and wheels rolling from afar we would push aside, to stay away from his reach, but the gentile stands there alert with his whip "Batam go" ("Beat him up"). At night, I dreamt a nightmare – many gentiles, each with whip in hand, I am in the center, and they are screaming: "Batam go, batam go, batam go."

The streets begin to empty, they're lurking for us in all ways, there are many gatherings at the "Rinek," whispers pass from mouth to ear, each has only half of a story, sort of an unfinished pain, that he had some dispute with a gentile, what the gentile told him and what the Jew answered and how he gave him a decent "Stab" of sharp words. The revenge of the persecuted from their pursuers. Their imagination is busy weaving the resistance. The income decreases. "Pickets" appear, they descend into our lives. A non–Jew that buys by a Jew is related as if he is doing a crime or – a favor. The Jews have the feeling that they are being ostracized and if they are treated differently, it is as if receiving a kindness. Stories about how the "Endeks" (fascist anti-Semitic National Democrats) came into Jewish stores from the back door, and they tell about it in great length with much satisfaction. The masses at the "Rinek" starts thinning, every time another one of the stands liquidates and turns into a real pauper. Reb Itsche, a tall and upright Jew, his lengthy straight beard looks as entwined with iron threads, he gathers all the merchandise in one rag, to transfer it to the stand for market day. He always was in need of help from his sons to take out the merchandise of the market, and he himself would sink under the heavy merchandise, but now there is no need for his shoulder. His shut fist keeps the bundle on the shoulder and his next hand is holding a hotplate of coal to warm up his hands. In any case, he does not have anything to do. As he is chewing a piece of bread his glance falls on the merchandise and his mouth turns tasteless, as though he is eating a piece of cloth and is consuming it. The goods are becoming less and soon finishing. The gymnast "Piketnik" shows up, his hat with its angles is pressed on his head but tilted sideways, hands in pockets, and coat huddled to his body – an act of courage and energy. "Look," he shows with his finger in coat pocket together with coat, this "Zhidek" is displaying a little goods to deceive us, so we will think of him as poor, and we will buy by him. All his merchandize is under the table, that is why they are filled with money, because they cheat our brothers, he's warming his hands and doing nothing. And our brothers have to labor in the fields and sweat for "These Zhideks." His sons, seeing the gathering want to pounce on him, but their father stops them. That sleek face of the "Endek" didn't show any human expression. His tiny gray eyes blinking to all directions like a wild animal. When his mouth opened – laughter came rolling out turning his face to red, his bright head–cap was sprinkled with white snowflakes and mixed with his reddish face resembling the white and red Polish flag, the symbol of freedom. "Not a sound," Itsche cautions his sons, they are liable to accuse us with insulting the Polish nation, so to speak. The people sit near the stalls, warming their hands in the embers of the coals and staring at the inanimate hangers of clothes, shoes, hats, awaiting someone to purchase them. The snow falls slowly and covers the market. The stands, the merchants the gentiles, the "Piketniks." The atmosphere is befouled, everything is holding its breath, and from time to time a crow passes with its prey. Lets out a shriek – kra kra kra, and casts a black shadow.

[Page 19]

Effervescence and Rebellion

The young generation is bitter and disappointed. Hollowness, no activity and zero hope for something beneficial. Some try to lay hope on a change of the regime and on Socialism, they go underground, new cells are created and members go over the villages making propaganda. Terror in the Jewish streets increases, every Jewish youth is considered a Communist, at night they are seized from their beds straight to "Kartuze Breze" (a Jewish Ghetto during the Holocaust located in Eastern Poland). When Yankel Burstyn was mistakenly taken to jail there was great stimulation. Yankel Burstyn, the cobbler's son, the pride of his family, was a Torah Director, was the "Torah Reader" at the "Khok" society, which was a division of the great synagogue. When they undressed him and saw his "Talis Katan" (tzitzit) they said that even a religious Jew with a Talis Katan can be a Communist! We helpless people found a broken stem of support in the Communists; we viewed them as people who are fighting for a better future.

A very anxious commotion occurred before May 1. Upon morning, one would ask the other: who was arrested? Fear was on everyone, and on May 1 the whole city turned into a battlefield. People with clenched fists, deprived of life, waves of people came spilling into the city and into the "Rinek," a box was put, shouts of "Niech Dzie" ("let it be"), and "Przez" ("thus") echoing over the whole city. Some eye–glassed man walked up to the podium and gave a speech and police from all angles (started) "taking" men to jail.

Smells of Pogrom in the air

Waves of hatred carried the Polish nation, destroying every bit of worthiness. The Jews of the town are surrounded with an ocean of blind hatred, they stand alone in their hopeless war, the ability of making a living has dwindled drastically. Their spirit is dry, gone was the fighting between the two dynasties Ger and Alexander, or the Shomrei Shabbat Society and the political parties. Everyone realized how close the danger has come to one and all, there are no exceptions. The memory day of the "Miracle on the Wisla," the triumph over the Bolsheviks near the Wisla River in 1920 when the full war was near the town, rumors spread that they are preparing something "Joyful" for the Jews, at the "Rinek" the gathering has to raise the suspense with a little Jewish blood. "Hurra na Zhidov"("hurray for the Jews") I came home from Warsaw and found everyone panicky in fear, like the bird that found herself in a narrow place with an eagle loitering above, about to leap on her, suck her blood, crack her bones, and the bird is fluttering her wings. Who are we, what can we do in this ocean of axes and scythes and a lust for blood and lots of loot. Bialik's song comes to my mind: "Heaven, plead mercy on me! If you have a G–d, and G–d has a path, I – my heart is dead and no more prayer on my lips." I see my father, all bent over and immersed in the Khabad (Lubavitch) books, his pale face, exhausted, his creased forehead is like a stormy ocean with waves coming one after the other. And yes, he is looking for the path to G–d.

Kuschtshuska (Kosciuszko) Street

Slight Comfort

Chaim Meir Lis the baker, makes a living doing manual labor, he is from the noblemen amongst the Khabad men (Lubavitch Khassidim), more than once he organized a "Tanya" (practical and mystical fundamentals of Khabad) class and each time it dispersed, but his influence didn't vanish and he gained adherents. Tall, a bit bent, his long hands embracing the universe and all its contents, an introspect; he speaks slowly, sort of a string sound that opens human hearts. His face is one of a philosopher, he doesn't preach, doesn't rebuke. He shares his ideas with you, brings up intellectual thoughts from his heart's depths. No wrath nor emotion, only an all–containing eloquence. His ideas are irrefutable no matter who tries. Encouraging infusions of both, body and spirit, that do their job unnoticed. With this gloominess we got near him and he inspired us with a fresh source of faith. On the Shabbat nights, we would gather by him, not for loud singing and not for blurring bitter reality, but we derived a sense of calm and satisfaction. On those nights, the big synagogue was full with people that drew to your heart and soothed their broken torn soul by saying the psalms of the Great Psalmist of Israel. Still a fearful feeling and uneasiness is there, kind of premonition of what is to come.

The Last Sukkah

After Rosh Hashanah and Yom Kippur the tension lessened. Heightened spirits and preparation for dealing with the Almighty, the thought of what lays ahead brings the shivers. Now, after the intensive effort of prayer and fast, the tension loosens, shuffling their way home trying to avoid one another after meeting so many times and exchanging greetings for the new year and for Yom Kippur. If their eyes do meet at the entrance to the house, they nod their heads in automatic fashion.

[Page 20]

The "Maccabi" Orchestra

Reb Yankel the Shokhet, stepping fast, focusing – as always – on the same span. As he reaches the house, he pushes through fast as if he doesn't notice what's going on around him. His face expresses segregation: Please, I won't interfere with you and you don't interfere with me. Now with Sukkos approaching there is an artificial smile on his face, as if saying: it is Sukkot on the world, but it says: "Seven days you shall sit in your Sukkos" in plural form. However, I won't refrain of contact and one must adjust to his fate. Therefore, a Sukkah has to be made but there aren't any boards, and there is no place, and time is short. But, he murmurs to himself, and when boards they will have, will they have sense to manage? Do they know where to begin? Every year they make a Sukkah, but every year the same problems; Running around, arguing. When one takes some boards or something alike, to construct, immediately everyone crowds together, one grabs away from the other and they begin to fight. And suddenly everyone leaves and nothing gets moving until I lend a hand. I made once an experiment and left them by themselves; let them break their heads alone. They are always grumpy about me having the best place in the Sukkah and they grouch: here goes the VIP that takes the preeminent place and has the key and doesn't allow free entrance, so that their children won't come in and break everything. And what? If my wife occasionally brings geese into the Sukkah prior the slaughter on one of the weekdays following Sukkot? And Reb Nata, despite the fact that he doesn't lift a finger when we finish putting up the skhakh, he jumps in displaying his brass candlesticks intentionally in front of me. They are all like that. After everything is done, they arise with great commotion, what do you people see – for heaven's sake – in this Sukkah? Look how they pasted the boards crookedly, good–for–nothings like these – I have never seen. One time I decided not to interfere; why argue with them, is it in my interest? What do I have with them? But that turned out to be a mess and we almost remained without a Sukkah. And when I didn't watch them, they banged on the wall of Yosske the gardener – the Milkman's house, and they knocked over all his ceramic pots which he hangs on the other side of the wall. And to whom did they come? To Reb Yankel the Shokhet, and demanded from me to cover the damage. I was forced to roll up my sleeves and start working. The newly wed yeshivah student, the son–in–law of the "Amerikanke" digging the holes for the boards and Reb Yisroel and Zundel helped along, and so, after much effort I got them in and we finally finished. Should we start? What do you say Reb Shimon? We will start processing with the Sukkah. Concerning the boards – you will obtain them from our wealthy Reb Dovid Gurni, he prays at your "Shtiebel." And place for the Sukkah? Again arguments, a little effort with Reb Moshe Zuzel the smith, so he should allow the place for the Sukkah.

The house we lived in belonged to Yitzkhak Epstein, and is made out of layers of wood, it stands at the length of the narrow lot, like a salami. This was a courtyard – passage from one street to another, full of activity also of the children that attended the school, which was within the building. When Yankel Shokhet's daughters take out an easy–chair, and begin to laugh high and lively, showing a yearning and craving for something, their hinting damp eye glances – fill the whole yard with life and motion. In the past, a huge ground was here, and the children had space for play, until one bright day, when a fence was put up and started to move; going forward with the pushing of Reb Yitzkhak Epstein, and back from the pushing of Reb Moshe Zuzel, until the landlords came out – one pushed forward and the other pushed backwards and then the landlords came out, pushing one another, until fire sparks began to fly in the air, like the sparks that flickered from the smith's workshop. And since then the fence was set to the ruling of Moshe Zuzel, and the Sukkah, however you might think – was to be a must only in his plot.

Every year they would elect representatives, dignified men that should convince Reb Moshe to let build the Sukkah in his territory. They had to muster lots of patience and negotiating skill, for Reb Moshe was blessed with a great ability to bargain – out of habit, of bargaining daily with the peasants over the price for the wagons and bicycles and the hand clapping – to sign the agreement. Also, the Sukkah dispute brought out the best of his argumentative skill. He was overflowing with legends and stories, tales from the Midrash and from Ein Yaakov (compilation of Jewish lore from non–legal part of Talmud), which he heard nightly at the small synagogue, and here was a wonderful opportunity to prove his knowledge of Talmudic phrases and dictums. Now was the time that Reb Moshe will teach them – and they will listen, those "Sheine Yidden." And he always won. The dispute never ended at once. They had to come and come again until he felt they were tired enough, or he finally became disgusted and the long awaited approval was given, at the last moment.

The last year was very different, there was an indifference. A wishful thought crossed each one's mind; we wish we would be able to postpone the Sukkah matter for an unlimited time. Where is the awakening? The will, the joy of the Mitzvah? But time was very pressing, and there was no time to think, the necessity overpowered, and a Sukkah must be in the courtyard no matter what. With Reb Shimon and with the boards we managed – Reb Yankel with his thin nice voice, added. All the thoughts about the Mitzvah of Sukkah and its particular details is not viable as long as the Sukkah is not standing yet, and time is running short. We still didn't talk to Reb Moshe Zuzel like every year, this time Reb Yankel Shochet forgoes one ounce of his pride, of which he is normally very strict about...Reb Yisroel will contribute a hand, he has boards in advance in the corner, and maybe Moshe will give the place, like those times when they were successful at the end. The boards are laying already by the wooden fence of Reb Moshe's plot. Reb Moshe passes by, ...with his hat tilted to the side hiding part of his face. His slanted look crosses eyes on the boards that are leaning on the fence, and makes himself as if he doesn't see and it isn't related to him.

[Page 21]

The tenant representatives are heading to Reb Moshe. Nu, Reb Moshe, in heaven, you will sit with the righteous people and great scholars, your plot is as holy as Jerusalem itself, absorbed with Torah and Mitzvos. Reb Moshe as if you didn't hear. Reb Moshe, the boards and everything are ready for putting up the Sukkah, just give us the place. What do you want from me? Do you pay me rent? Go to Reb Yitzkhak Epstein, he is your proprietor, he should supply you with a Sukkah, leave me alone! I didn't let all the years, and this year too, not. Nothing doing. As much as they tried to convince and reprimand him, it didn't help. The tenants came running, it is an emergency, what will we do without a Sukkah? They whispered and scurried around. The more pious ones suggested making it at the place of Reb Yankel the smith; he is plain and unassuming and won't get into trouble with Talmud students, at the best place on his lot, the Sukkah should be made, but that's not a solution, because there is no exit to the lot, but for exiting through the windows, and the food has to be brought with ropes like by Rahav, the whore. Reb Yitzkhak Epstein – the landlord – rubs his hands, measures each one sideways, his tenants are so lost and he is delighted, let them suffer a bit, these takers, let them feel what I felt sweating over this house.

He takes a minor glance at the house that is as long like the Jewish Exile, they keep sitting motionless. Until he will see money from them, one can pass out. You could have become a little rich. Bad luck. He talks to them about expenses and rent and they roll their eyes upwards, like begging for mercy. But what can be done? There are the tenant's protection rules, and I am yet "Prezes" ("chairman") of the "community."

Reb Yitzchak, tall, high, a wide big black beard, assertive and energetic is fast to settle affairs without being disturbed of what others will say. Thanks to these traits, he was elected chairman of the community. As a member, he would go in and out of the council. His tenants were mostly G–d fearing Jews and almost all of them were engaged in sacred Jewish matters. Their faces displayed emotion and suffering, but they knew to rise above and not to breakdown. He despised their unconcerned stance. The apartment he lived in was always further away from his tenants. Now he energetically turned to put up his small Sukkah that was permanently on the roof with only small changes. He put the boards in an outstanding form, so they should be noticeable, and he laughed to himself – let them remain without a Sukkah once. Slowly, the day was passing, darkness began to prevail, everyone stood there numb and openmouthed, not having a choice they tried everything to appease Reb Moshe, but to no avail. Many of them turned to the smith's workshop, darkness spread over the place, the people and the workshop. Only sparks flew in all directions and drew an illuminated line that came and went and appeared again.

Reb Shimon, deep in thought, his heart directed to heaven, scrutinizing his own actions – what made Reb Moshe's heart more hardened than any other year. He got closer to Reb Moshe when the latter raised a hammer, but it slipped out of his hands, he panicked from the glorious gaze of Rabbi Shimon, who called out. Reb Moshe, did you learn the Mishna? Yes, Reb Shimon, I know, the smith replied. Well, there is a Mishna in the tractate of Bikurim: Reb Shimon said, when a Jew brought First Fruits to the Temple, a heavenly voice declared that he will merit to do so next year too. The question arises, what happens when a Jew is to die? – An insane thought enters his mind that year, and tells him not to bring his First Fruit. Reb Moshe, every year you permitted us to put up the Sukkah and we declared that so you shall do, next year too. Now, who knows what will happen? Reb Moshe, shaking with fear, instantly stopped the work and called with all his might: "Jews, good neighbors! Come here! Let us put up the Sukkah. Do you need wood? Come! Together, let's put up the Sukkah!....

And that was the last Sukkah. Hitler and his troops destroyed, burned, murdered and annihilated.

Communal prayer in face of the Nazi horrors

It was Election Day for the German parliament, May 1933, right before Hitler arose to power. The Rabbinate dedicated the day for communal devoted prayer. The big Synagogue in Wyszkow was full to capacity, everyone let go of all their doings, the shops, the stores were shut, everyone shared the common feeling, that today is to be sealed not only the fate of Germany, but first and foremost, of all Jewish people.

The community looked for one, who should lead the prayers, one that should express all the heaviness that hung in the air. And all eyes were pointed to the left corner, near the holy ark, that's where Reb Shimon Serevnik sat and learned and prayed daily, from early in the morning on. Also the Shamash, who was standing on the podium, was searching: who should be honored and called to read in the Torah

His eyes never approached this corner, where my father prayed, for the man did not await any honor. He was a humble unyielding soul, and no real results of any aspect can possibly come out of him.

This time honor was not in anyone's mind, but for, who will shake up the whole crowd, and will arouse the human conscience and emotion to shout bitterly to high–heavens.

My father got up and stood facing the public, he looked around with sad, sad eyes, his soul outpouring, he made his way with small steps towards the prayer pillar, his pale hands clutching the pillar when a silent yell came spilling out of the depths of his heart: "O, why are the nations astir".

Hearts shook, walls wavered.

People were inspired.

They burst out in a bitter cry:

"O why, why, why are the nations arising?!...."

"Morgenstern" Sport–Club

[Page 22]

The town in the years 1891-1913
by Max Chekhanov, New York
Translated by Edward Jaffe
Donated by Rona G. Finkelstein

I left Vishkov in 1913 on the way to America. At that time statistics showed that the town's Jewish population consisted of about 1500 families. It was calculated as follows: the large synagogue had 800 worshipers and the new synagogue – about 200, the Gerer Hasidim prayer house – 200; Alexander Hasidim – 200; Amshenover Hasidim – 50. And the same number of worshipers were in the Otvosk and Radziminer prayer houses. In the Dan Synagogue (also called the "German Synagogue" because there were some who wore "short dresses") worshipped about 100 persons. At that time there were a few private worshipping groups consisting of a few rich people and other pious Jews. At that time that was the population composition in town. Let's assume out of respect of the martyred that their statistics were correct.

Jewish income

At the beginning of the 20th century the Vishkov Jewish population could be divided into two groups: Mitnagdim and Hasidim. Two third of the population were Mitnagdim and one third Hasidim. Both the Mitnagdim and the Hasidim were very pious Jews. It appears to me that the difference between the two Vishkov groups was that the former prayed in the Ashkinazi style, and the latter in the Sfardi style.

As far as I remember, according to their income Vishkov's Jews fell into the following categories: shop keepers, money lenders, small business people, quite a few wood merchants and their workers, butchers, fish sellers, deliverers by horse and buggy, carriers, tailors, shoemakers, smiths, leather makers, horseshoe makers, tinmen, glass installers, pot makers, bakers, carpenters, turners, embroiderers, watch repairmen, rope makers, coppersmiths, goldsmiths, painters, and others. Then come the rabbis, beadles, bible teachers, ritual slaughterers, matchmakers, minstrels and musicians. There was also one Jewish doctor, a Jewish pharmacist, a Jewish female dentist and two paramedics. We also had three carbonated drinks factories, three ice cream factories, a scale factory, and a wicker chairs workshop. To that must be added the poor beggars, and those seeking alms from house to house. I believe, I cited all income earners of Vishkov at that time. The general economic condition of Vishkov's Jewish population can be detailed in the following manner: 1% rich people, 9% well to do, 40% middle class that had plenty to eat, 40% lower middle class that had just enough to eat, and 10% poor and indigent.

When did Jews settle in Vishkov

For as long as I lived in Vishkov I posed this question many times to the older town's people, but never obtained a satisfactory answer. I am not delving into the non-Jewish sources about the history of our town. As I remember there was no written record about our community in years past. All I know about the age of the Jewish community in our town is summarized below. When I was 11 years old, my late father took me once to visit the family plot at the Vishkov cemetery. My father pointed out the graves of four generations of our ancestors: the grave of his father, the grave of his grandfather, the grave of his great grandfather, and the grave of his grandfather's grandfather. When I asked my father whether other earlier members of our family are buried here, he responded in the affirmative. But he did not know where-their graves are located.

Is there a trace left of you, dear holy graves?

Vishkov's Rabbis

During my childhood there was a rabbi and a spiritual teacher in Vishkov. I knew the rabbi well because he lived adjacent to the same yard (the synagogue yard). As a child I frequently visited the rabbi's house and played with his grandchildren. I remember that the rabbi was a real pleasant person. A real lover of the Jewish people and all living creatures. He always had a smile on his gentle face. If he had to call somebody from the synagogue he asked me to do it. Although I was a small child, he knew me well and used to ask me gently "be so good" or "excuse me", "don't be insulted, please call so and so from the synagogue". The spiritual teacher I knew only by his appearance. Beyond that I knew nothing of him. Once there was an argument between the rabbi and the spiritual teacher. The argument was so intense that it caused a fight between their respective followers. The town's youths resorted to strange name calling of the two sides. The rabbi's supporters were called "bombers" and the spiritual teachers were called "turtles.""

There were also those who were "neutral" and called "trulelus.""

I did not understand the meaning of these strange names.

[Page 23]

I also remember that the quarrel led the "neutral" group to steal a Torah on the Jewish holiday of Hoshana-Raba which they took to a known Jew in the nearby village by the name of Vigoda. There they celebrated Shmini-Etzeret and Simcha-Torah. In the morning of the same Shmini-Etzeret a high ranking official with police and artillery soldiers arrived in Vishkov from the provincial town of Pultusk, and chased all worshippers away from the large synagogue.

The end result of this quarrel led to the arrest of the spiritual teacher. The incident made a lasting impression, many of the older people remember it to this day. Whatever happened to the spiritual teacher I do not know. I only know that the Vishkov Jews quieted down after this incident.

Many years later when the rabbi died, Vishkov's Jews selected as a religious authority a prestigious person from a rabbinical family. With the new rabbi I had a difficult and unpleasant incident that I remember to this day.

At that time I already had a bookstore in Vishkov where I sold Warsaw Jewish newspapers. As soon as the new rabbi arrived in town, he sent for me to come and see him. My late father, whom I appreciated and loved dearly, insisted that I comply with the rabbi's request. I did it because of my father's request.

When I came to see the rabbi, I greeted him and wished him much luck. I asked him why he called me. He immediately began reproaching me and asking why I decided to make a living by selling books and newspapers. I in turn asked ther rabbi why his friend, a pious so and so, can sell books and I cannot? It was true that the pious Jew did not sell newspapers. Instead of an answer the rabbi began shouting at me and in an angry voice stated that "I would rather see you sell pork than books". I responded to the rabbi by telling him that this type of advice he ought give his friend that sells books, and I promptly left. My late father later approved of my response. He too was not particularly happy that I dealt in books and newspapers. Nevertheless, he told me that the rabbi had no right to tell me to deal in pork.

Years later, the rabbi and I reconciled our differences. After World War I when I moved to America, the rabbi forgave me. He sent me a heartfelt letter in which he also thanked me for my participation in the Vishkov aid society in New York. Regretfully the rabbi, who later became the chief rabbi, together with his whole family was murdered by the Nazis.

The rich of Vishkov

As far as I remember, in my time in Vishkov about 15 Jews were considered to be wealthy. It is no exaggeration to doubt that any one of them was worth more than 100,000 rubles. Nevertheless, they were considered to be rich.

The Vishkov Jews did not excel in their generosity, with the exception of one who could be considered a very charitable man. But at the same time he behaved like a real dictator. He was involved in an unpleasant incident, when in the year 1912 the well known writer and philosopher, the famous late Hilel Zeitlin, could not come to a literary evening arranged by the town's youths in Vishkov. The gathering took place without Zeitlin's participation, whereupon the late writer B. Yaushzon described the incident in a brochure under the title "The Rabbi was Dragged to a Concert." It was said about another of Vishkov's rich that his daughter sympathized with the town's workers and taught some of them how to read and write, In the period of 1905-6 when the revolution was being suppressed by Czar Nicholas the second. The word circulating in town was that she did it because her father became non-observant.

Vishkov's Elite

Besides the rich we also had in Vishkov an elite. There were Jews claiming various progenitors. Some of them claimed the Amshinover rabbi as a relative. Others were proud to be associated with the Yabloner rabbi, the first Hasidic leader who left Poland for the land of Israel. He personally participated in the building of the town of Bnei-Brak. There were also Jews who prided themselves as relatives of Moishe-Tuvie Stanislaver (the great personality described in the "Day-Morning Journal" by the well known writer I. I. Troonk).

Others were proud for entirely different reasons. There were some that always claimed that Nochum Sokolov belonged to their family. Others I knew claimed to be related to the Warsaw Jewish book publisher B. Simin. There were others, the type you could meet in any Jewish town, who could demonstrate in writing that they are descendants of King David or even Maimonidis. Who could disprove it? There were others who prided themselves with personal achievements. In short we had in Vishkov a varied elite.

[Page 24]

Vishkov's old

I don't remember whether in my time there were too many real old people. Nevertheless, a few of them are deeply imbedded in my memory. One of the old people was said to be about 90 years of age. Others thought he was over 100 years old. I was too young to estimate his age. An interesting thing happened to him at his advanced age: he became a widower and then married for the second time a young and beautiful girl. A rumor circulated in town that the old groom was carried to the wedding canopy.

A second old man, I recall, belonged to a Mishna study group and was a respected citizen. The study group held an annual feast. It so happened that two members of the group brought their disagreements for resolution at such a feast. The whole group selected the old man to adjudicate the disagreement. Even though he was not a great Torah scholar, all followed his reasoning and as soon as he rendered a verdict, it was accepted by all. The Mishna study group in our town was generally known for the respect they paid to the town's old-people.

Vishkov's heroes

Vishkov had its heroes who showed real courage when Jews had to be protected. From my earliest childhood, I recall how two Vishkov Jews dispersed a market full of farmers. The reason for this incident I do not remember. I only know that both were honest and pious Jews. Apparently, the was generating a potential danger to the town's Jews.

I also remember a Vishkov young Jewish man, who served in the Czar's guard, who upon returning home on leave settled a dispute with a policeman, actually a "senior police officer." On Sabbath at midday, an arrested Jew was brought to Vishkov's market place by horse and buggy while being guarded by an out of town policeman. Upon arrival he screamed asking to be rescued from desecration of the Sabbath. Soon a large number of people gathered, including the Vishkov rabbi. The arrested was then transferred to the charge of the 'senior police officer'. The rabbi asked the officer to transfer the arrested Jew to his care until the Sabbath passes. The officer turned down the rabbi's request. Then our guardsman became embroiled and offered to assume responsibility for the Jew, until after the candles are lit. The policeman refused. Our Viskov young man became very upset and both began quarreling. After exchanging some words, our guardsman picked up the "senior officer" by a leg, lifted him above his head and turned him around three times, as if he was performing the ritual of "kaporot." The gathered crowd liked what they saw and gave the Jewish hero a loud cheer. After this incident the "senior police officer" escaped from Vishkov and the town got rid of a Jew hater.

I also remember when one November evening, newly recruited soldiers arrived in town. They became inebriated and began to beat Jews. Panic set in. Jewish storekeepers closed their businesses. I myself locked up my father's store (I was then about 11 years old). Soon thereafter two Jewish young man came out into the street and started beating the drunken Poles. The hooligans beat a hasty retreat and escaped as far as they possibly could go.

Once in the year 1907, a rumor spread that at the upcoming market day that the Poles will start a pogrom against the Jews. That was during the time when a bloody wave of pogroms swept through the Jewish towns and villages. Our Vishkov had a strong Jewish youth who organized a self defense force. As the market day neared the tension grew. But the self defense group was ready for any eventuality. As soon as the drunken Poles raised havoc, a Jew, actually one from a different town, engaged the hooligans and handily dispersed them. The town was spared a pogrom. As a consequence, the organized Vishkov.defense group was left with little to do.

Vishkov's revolutionaries

In the stormy year of 1905, in Vishkov as well as in other towns and villages of erstwhile Russia, the spirit of revolution against the czar was rising. I remember a group of Jews together with Poles leading a demonstration with banners proclaiming the czar's misdeeds. Later, a few participants in the demonstration were arrested and expelled. Among Viskov's Polish revolutionaries were also anti-Semites. A few such young Poles who belonged to the intellectual class (at least that is what they pretended) and claimed to be "revolutionary patriots" one sunny Sabbath afternoon attacked a group of Jewish boys and girls who were peacefully walking across the wooden bridge over the river Bug. The Poles berated the Jewish boys and girls with expressions and words as well as deeds that cannot be repeated or discussed.

[Page 25]

The town also had revolutionary fools. A Jewish worker told a joke about current affairs to a group of other Jewish workers who did not like one of the expressions. Therefore the "proletariat " beat up the poor Jewish worker. He was lucky to escape alive.

Another difficult incident is engraved in my memory. There was a tailor of woman's clothing in town. A worker like any other of his kind. He did not excel at anything. This tailor was shot and the murderers were not caught. During my time it was the only murder in Vishkov. Word got around that he had something to do with the stormy incidents at that time.

Vishkov's guards

There were only a few guards in town but they gave us plenty of trouble. Mostly it had to do with the existing czar's regime. Our Vishkov guards were no exception.

Once on an ordinary winter evening in the year 1908, 1 was at the Vishkov railroad station awaiting the daily package of Jewish newspapers from Warsaw. Suddenly a "senior guard" approached me and asked that I follow him. He took me to an empty field. Looking around and seeing that nobody was there he told me the following: "I know that your bookstore is kosher, you had controllers and inspectors who convinced themselves that you sell only approved books. You should, however, know that there are pious Jews who asked me to make trouble for you. And you should also know that there are preparations afoot to raid your bookstore and destroy your books. Therefore, I ask you that every first day of the month, according to the Russian calendar, you meet me at this very place, and bring mc thrcc rublcs. In other words, I want from you three rubles a month in order to protect you. And I also want something else: your father deals in Jewish lottery tickets which are illegal. Therefore, I demand that you bring with you a lottery ticket for every drawing, and I will leave your father alone".

For a moment I thought about the possibility of a raid on the bookstore. But I decided that it is not worth doubting his word, and I accepted all his proposals. Thus, I paid the "senior guard" three rubles per month until I left Vishkov.

I had another incident in my bookstore. One evening a group of boys were learning Hebrew literature in the store. We used to spend time as a group twice a week. We were taught by an older well-read and able colleague. Suddenly, two guards came in with a pretext of having to make a search for people holding an allegedly secret meeting to "depose the czar". I began to explain what we were doing, and in the meantime my friends stepped outside. One of the guards pursued them. Outside the door my friends played a trick, causing one of the guards in his haste to fall into a pit full of whiting that was prepared for a new building. Ultimately the guard came to me and demanded two rubles in order to cleanse the whiting from his soiled clothing. He excused himself for having disturbed us in the innocent study of Hebrew literature and promised never to disturb us again. However, he demanded for himself and his friend, the second guard, six rubles for not disturbing us in the future nor report the owner of the building for leaving an open whiting pit. I handed them the demanded sum and both guards from that time on developed a friendly attitude toward me.

I also remember another incident. Once on a beautiful and warm day, I went for a walk with a girl (actually my current wife). We passed the bridge and went onto the Lahav road. We were young, our feet were strong and the natural surroundings were beautiful, it was a real pleasure. On one side of the road flowed the river Bug and on the other side the eye was delighted with the blossoming spring trees of the famous Skisiver forest in our area. We walked deeper into the forest. Suddenly, from a hiding place jumped out two strange, unknown to us guards, with whips in their hands. One of them hit me with his whip across my shoulder. Instead of escaping, I came closer to the guard and asked why they are doing it to me. We are only friendly wanderers. One of them said they will stop hitting me and added that he sees for the first time a whipped Jew that does not run away. The guards wanted us to give them some coins and cigarettes to smoke. I took out a pack of cigarettes and they lit up. I put two other cigarettes behind their ears for later use. I also gave them the coins they requested. They "thanked" us and told us to return to town because they are looking for somebody that may cause a shoot out, and therefore it is best for us to go forth.

[Page 26]

I remember other things

I remember other things about our town that no longer exists. I remember Vishkov's groups of time past. The Burial Society, Mishna Study Group, a Shas Group, an Eyen Yakov Group, a Human Life Group, a Tilim study Group, a Dowry Group, a Visiting the Sick Group, a Money Lending Group, the Righteous Group, and a Secret Help Group.

I remember when a train passed through Vishkov for the first time and my parents carried me to view the new wonder.

I remember when Vishkov's people ran after the first car that passed through town.

I remember when gas light lamps were installed in Vishkov to provide light in the streets.

I remember when the first telephone line connecting Vishkov with Warsaw was installed.

I remember when Vishkov's Jews won several times the great Rabbis Lottery (that of Gerer and Alexander).

I remember when we sold in Vishkov under my direction 75 copies of Jewish newspapers, 60 of the Warsaw "Moment" and 15 of the Warsaw "Day".

I also had in my bookstore about 120 readers of Jewish and Hebrew books. There were also in Vishkov two subscribers of the Hebrew publication "Hazman" ("The Time"), two for the "Hatzfirah" ("The Dawn"), and one for "Hatzofeh" ("The Scout").

All of them appear alive in my memory, the devoted readers of Jewish and Hebrew works, and the loyal friends of the great national Jewish and Hebrew Journals. I remember them and others from our town where I spent 22 years of my life from 1891 till 1913. Where I was known as Abraham Mordekhi Chechenoviecki (now somewhat shortened to Max Chekhanov).

My town Vishkov – an interrupted song of a vanished Jewish life.

30 Years of Community Life
by Yitskhok Beharov
Translated by Sheldon Clare

Zionist beginnings

The origin of concrete Zionist work in Vishkov occurred in the year 1916. Thanks to the campaign for the "Keren Kayemet" (Jewish National Fund) alms boxes that were found in every Jewish home. The local Zionist organization was also established in the same year. In the presidium, the following were elected: Avraham-Moshe Levin, Moshe Ayon, and Henekh Kaluski. In the managing committee: Itcheh Shkarlat, Rafael Shkarlat, Moshe-Leib Kahn, Itcheh Barev, and Yosef Landau.

The Zionist organization was the most dominant in Vishkov. Masses of youth flowed into it. Even then, we owned our own small Zionist synagogue, that our friend, the Zionist Elyahu-Meier Goldman, bequeathed it in the names of Henkh Kaluski, Khaim-Noson Vengrov, Shmaiya Rapoport, Itcheh Barev. Here, I will recall others of our contemporary (actionists). Very possibly, I have certainly omitted names-this is a story of more than 40 years ago-they should therefore not feel missed. It happened simply unintentionally. These are the kind and loyal Zionist leaders: Leibish Pshetitsky, Meier Ihrlikht, Moshe Novominski, Shlomo Rozenberg, Avraham Brodatch, Yekhezkal Yagoda, Yitzkhok Neiman, Yakov Neiman, Pinkhas Feintzeig, Dovid Chervonagura, Moshe Sokol, Meier Shchigel, and others.

We were represented in the community with a united (DOZORES) and had a large representation on the city council. As the largest party, we obtained the only Jewish (LAVNIK) in City Hall. Noson Vengrov, was an important defender for the interests of the Vishkover Jewish population.

In 1926, through the Zionists, there was created the first educational institution, where from childhood on, it attempted to educate about Zionism and "Eretz Yisroel"- this was the "Gan-Y'ladim" (Children's Garden), also were organized Hebrew lectures for the Zionist youth. The learned scholars were Yitzkhok Shkarlat, Shapira, Pitchnik, and Bookshtayn. The sale of Zionist membership certificates was very intensive. Incidentally, every year, the eastern leader came to us, the saintly Rabbi Yitzkhok Nissenboim, of blessed memory. Every year, he used to appear at a lecture in the big synagogue. Large and small, all of Vishkov used to come to hear this witty speaker. His call to support the Land of Israel. He did not look upon this as if we had a lot of Jews. Also, from "Agudah", there was opposition to the Zionist principles. Every year, we raised for the "Keren Hayesod" some $1000. The devotion was (without bounds?). I remind myself: That in 1929, I happened to be with Shmaia Rapoport to accompany Rabbi Nissenboim during his (Keren Hayesod) campaign in Vishkov. We first went to the devoted Zionist Leibish Pshetitzki, stirred to tears, he spoke (HAZORAIM BADME'A BRANA YIKTZORO – Hebrew) and he drew upon more than he knew. Every year, he used to raise his fee (donation). He was the example and the other contributors emulated him. I will mention here the Zionist committee of the last 10 years. They were: Henekh Kaluski, Rafael Shkarlat, Shmaia Rapoport, Itcheh B'herev, Avraham Bradatch, Khaim-Noson Vengrov.

[Page 27]

Nagduzheh Street

The Library

Also in 1909, a group of enlightened youth began to think of putting up a library. Seeing in this institution an important cultural center for the city. One began to raise money and at the same time, some books were brought from Warsaw. But immediately, a difficult question was put forth: Where do we find a location for the library? Just now came a good opportunity: Bercheh Segal traveled to America. He lived on "Pshedmieshceh" near the Christian Filipovski. Bercheh's wife Khaveh, who loved Yiddish books, had with the agreement of the Christian, a liberal person, agreed to give their apartment for the library. Not looking on the fact that the library was found "Behind" (I think it means just out of the city) the city, the youth streamed en masse, and "sneezed" at this institution. The books were exchanged (borrowed) twice a week. Quickly it was shown that the library could not accommodate the inquiries of the readers. The amount of books was small. They were soon all read and the public requested more books. But where does one get money? Someone came up with the idea to create a drama section and the income of this concept would go to buying books. Because of this, the library indeed became richer with the works of great writers.

Also, with great strength, a lively cultural-activity was carried out and one used to bring lecturers from Warsaw such as the writer, Kh. D. Naumberg, the historian, Dr. I. Shiffer, the leader and Zionist Yitzkhok Grinboim and other personalities. In 1916, Yitzkhok Epshtayn and his family traveled from Vishkov to Russia. Only his son Moshe and his sister Henyeh remained – members of the Zionist organization. They gave up their house on Stodolneh Street for the movement. First, the library began to develop. It was comfortable for bookcases and for a special reading hall where the youth had an opportunity to engross themselves in a newspaper and in a book. In that era had indeed blossomed cultural-activities. A special speakers-circle was carried out with (KESTL OVNTN) and prepared lectures of literary and Zionist themes: Yitzkhok Shkarlat, Ehrlikh (a student), Yungshtayn, Shafar, Shapira. The management committee consisted of: Rafael Shkarlat, Moshe-Leib Kahn, Yitzkhok Shkarlat, Ehrlikh, Yosef Landau, and others.

Parties, Societies, Institutions

I want to further tell about a series of other organizations and institutes, which were active in Vishkov.

[Page 28]

As early as 1916, there was in Vishkov a Jewish workers-movement under the direction of the "Bund" (Socialist Labor Party). During the first city council election, they obtained 356 votes and 3 councilmen. Most important in the movement stood a cultural-developing youth. I will here recall the names that I remember: Dubanik, Yisroel Goldvasser, Yekhiel Bzhozeh, Simkhe-Yakov Vengrov (a brother of our Zionist Leader), Motl Rinek, and Avrohom Yedvob. They led a cultural-activity among the workers, gave lectures, brought outside lecturers, and organized a professional union. They also had a cooperative.

In the later years, the management of the "Bund" were the councilmen Simkha-Yakov Vengrov, Avrohom Yedvob, and Avrohom Yagoda. We had a society "AKHIEZAR' that used to occupy its time giving help to poor ill people - with a doctor and also with prescriptions. The administers of "AKHIEZAR" were: Moshe-Dovid Yoskovitch, Moshe B'herev, Ziske-Moshe Shteinberg, and Moshe Pshshchelenitz. The majority of them are now martyrs. In the same year, a (Loan-office?) was established familiar to us with the name "Tavazhistva" directed by the said institution. Those who gave out loans for the "lower middle class": Khaim-Dovid Goldvasser, Kerner, Avrohom-Moshe Levin, Mendl Shkarlat, and Dovid Gurney. At the head was Moshe Ayon. From the aforesaid small "Tavazhistva", later grew out the large "Peoples Bank" which received help from "Joint", (which led the Peoples Bank?), with its loans supported hundreds of merchants and artisans. There stood the devoted leaders: The artisans Moshe-Dovid Yoskovitch, Yitzkhok Khzhan, Fishl Bronshtein, and Yakov Holtzman. The bookkeeper was Moshe Ayon and his helper, Yakov Pzhemirover.

In 1919, I became married to the daughter of the wood merchant and sawmill-owner Yehoshua Sokol (may he rest in peace). I then opened a small business in Rinek. In time, I became one of the wholesale merchants and was one of the few who had the franchise to sell tobacco and cigarettes. (The last time the Polish government restricted the number of franchises given to Jews to sell tobacco and cigarettes. Only three Jews in each town had the right for the franchises. I was one of the three.) In those days, the tax was rather high. The finance office (Oozhand Skarbovi) was in Poltusk, where the appraisal committee sat and set the businessman's taxes as they understood. On the part of the Jewish businessmen from Vishkov (who were by the way in the majority), none of them sat on the committee. Of course, the contemporary attitude of the Jews in Poland, the appraisal committee put enormous taxes on the Jewish businessmen. Every attempt was made to run to Poltusk to repeal this personal injustice.

Then, together with Yitzkhok Mondrey, Yosef Vengazh, Shmuel Elboim, Yekhiel-Meier Rubin, and Eliahu-Meier Goldman, I spoke with the secretary of our community, Moshe-Yosef Abramchik, and it was called a general assembly of all Jewish businessmen in Vishkov. At the assembly was indeed created the first businessmen's-union, where also there was an election of the management of additional businessmen: Itschi B'herev-chairman, Yosef Vengozh-vice chairman, Yitzkhok Mondrey – treasurer; in the management: Pinkhas Piyenik, Sholem Zissman, Yitzkhok-Ber Rozenberg, Yekhiek-Meier Rubin, Yakov-Arieh Rabinovich. The secretary was the community secretary Moshe-Yosef Abramchik. We quickly presented ourselves in the tax-office in Poltusk.

As for the legal case (affair) of the taxes for the Vishkover Jewish businessmen, they should call upon the businessmen's-union. We rented a hall on Strazhatzkeh Street. The merchants and artisans then had an address to call upon against injustice, against incorrect tax-measures, against those that the (SAKVESTATORN) used to for taxes, transferred (bequeathed) ownership of housewares or workers' tools. The businessmen's-union immediately delegated the secretary Avramchik to Poltusk to take care of tax-matters for many Jews. After it was established if it was to determine, the amount of tax, every line of business and vocation used to send a representative to the appraisal-committee. Avramchik always accompanied them. Also the secretary of the "Khila" (community) was seen there. He knew all the Jews and was also of the opinion that one could indeed count on him. With this aspect, much was accomplished. "Not one Jew was saved from [simple or plain ruin]" – (This sentence doesn't make sense. Perhaps, he meant that no Jew was totally ruined.)

For a period of 14 years, I was the chairman of the businessmen's-union. In time, we approached the dear Jew (subsequently, a martyr) Dr. B. Leykher, who was the legal consul of the union and displayed a lot of initiative by defending the interests of Jewish artisans and merchants in general and for every particular individual. One case I will mention. In many Polish towns, a campaign began on the part of the (SHONAI-YISRAEL) to make the towns nicer and cleaner "Covered under the cloak" (I think this means not telling the Jews.) The so-called "urbanization". This campaign actually happened to the Jews. (GRAD) did not care for the Jewish neighborhoods, the Jewish streets, the Jewish homes, which they decided to tear down. One of the campaigns was to transfer the commercial markets far out of town. This was for the Jews a true evil decree. Constantly, the markets used to be in the built up market areas where Jews used to live and had their businesses. Moving the markets and fairs out of town had significance as the Jews would have remained literally without bread. In the new areas one would want to erect the "fresh-baked" businesses subsidized because of the anti-Semitic organizations. Also, Vishkov had been surrounded by this evil decree. The (STARASTEH) soon gave out a deadline to move the markets far from the town. The (words are missing) intervened with the mayor Volski. A liberal (words are missing) convinced him that he should with a delegation of the businessmen's-union travel to Voiyevadeh in Warsaw, so that the evil decree will be cancelled. Also the city was against the decree of (STARASTEH). Leading this delegation indeed stood Dr. Leykher. It was because of him that the decree was called off. We appointed Dr. Leykher as a life-long honorary member of the businessmen's-union in Vishkov.

[Page 29]

"Tarbut" school

Here, I wish to mention a second event from this dark time. When in Poland, the anti-Semitic agitation spread out not to buy from Jews, the (SEYIM-TRIBUNEH, same person?) the interior minister Skladovski declared, that it is permitted to have an economic anti-Jewish boycott. His familiar saying to permit this anti-Jewish agitation was: "Avshem- by all means". With the assistance of the official Polish authorities, more businesses were established-Polish, which had never been involved in commercial trade. Their only purpose was to crush Jewish existence. To help these so-called "businessmen" came the "picketers" group. Led by student hooligans (ruffians), who demonstrated in the streets with anti-Jewish slogans, "Svoy do Svegah" (this means: Go to your own kind, not to strangers). The police did not disturb these demonstrations. These were called peaceful demonstrations that were carrying out the minister's slogan "AVSHEM." The police only looked out for demonstrations bringing about scandal.

At one of these anti-Semitic demonstrations, when the excited masses went through the town with their slogans, they prevented a meeting in the market, near the iron-works of Pinkhas Feintzeig. There, one of the masses provoked a shot from a revolver. They soon found witnesses, saying that they saw shooting from Pinkhas Feintzeig's balcony. This began to show the first signs of a pogrom. They began to loot the goods from the market-stalls. But the merchant's-union with the Zionist (LAVNIK) Khaim-Noson Vengrov stood guard. Quickly, in the street, the mayor together with the police and the out-of-town police from Poltusk had intervened. We then were able to save Vishkov from a certain pogrom.

The merchants-union had created a popular merchants-bank, under the name "Bank Kupyetski." The bank took care of all possible "law?" and merchant-organizations, and gave loans, borrowed on goods-cargo, and helped with taxes. The presidium (board) of "Bank Kupyetski" consisted of Dr. Leykher, Mordkhe-Mendl Lemberg, Itzshe B'herev, and the management: Yitzkhok-Ber Rozenberg, Yitzkhok Epshteyn, Shmuel Elboim, Yosef Vengozh; Treasurer: Yitzkhok Mondrey, Bookkeeper: Moshe-Yosef Avramchik; Assistant: Zundl Elboim. The bank ran its constructive activity until the outbreak of the Second World War.

In Vishkov, there was also a "non-interest loan office," leading the office was: Yisroel-Moshe Tzembal, Moshe Shtern, Yakov-Dovid Pzhetitski; Secretary: Sheikeh Postolski; and Bookkeeper: Yakov Yacobovitch. This organization rescued a lot of Jews. A lot of artisans or small merchants had the opportunity to obtain a 300 zlotys loan with the privilege to repay the loan at 15 zlotys per week. There was also an "Agudas Haortodoksim" (Orthodox Association). This means an organization of "Agudas Yisrael" (Israel Association). This brought together the whole pious-religious-traditional Jewry. They had their representative in the community and also in the city hall. They created a "Beis-Yacov" school for girls. They had teachers from the center. From local women's association leaders they helped Tzirl and Hadassah Rozenberg (today in Israel). The leaders of the "Aguda" were: Khaim-Binyomin Vernik, Mordkhe Vinter, Borukh Tzluyak, Yakov-Moshe Plontschak, Khaim-Meier Lis. Here, there was a "Revisionist-Organization" with a really substantial-effect. At the top stood the leaders of the revisionists in Vishkov: Lipeh Kerner, dentist (Today in Israel) and my cousin (SHTELUNG?) Moshe, may he rest in peace. There was a department of the Women's Zionist Organization "WIZO" that assisted all Zionist campaigns. The leaders were: Brokheh Kalusky (Dr. Leykher's wife), Rivke Shkarlat, Rokhl Yonish. There was a "Mizrakhi" organization. They even had their own Gerer study hall (SHTIBL). They participated in all Zionist activites. Their management was composed of Yakov Levin, Yitzkhok-Meier Visotzky, Moshe Ostry, Leml Rubin. There was an activity led by the "Rightist Poele-Tzion" (Workers of Zion). They created in Vishkov the "Hakhalutz" and directed the training of groups. They sent a lot of pioneers to Israel, sent others, and also went themselves.Their leaders: Yisroel Kalusky, Shmaia Gurney, Khaim-B'nyomin Bruk. (All now in Israel).

A Group of Hekhalutz Friends

[Page 30]

Macabee - Vishkov 1931

Our Vishkover "Hashomer Hatzair" (Guardian of Youth) owned a large meeting hall, their own library with many Hebrew books from which the youth learned Hebrew and prepared to travel to the Land of Israel.The leaders were: Khaim B'herev, Falek Gurney, Levin, Khanscheh Shapira. Many of them are actually in Israel now. The leftist "Poele-Tzion" owned (ran) a "Workers Evening Courses Organization." They brought teachers from Warsaw.Their leaders were: Yisroel-Moshe Tzembal, Yakov Shtelung, Yakov Volman. They had representatives in all organizations. Vishkov also had a sports-organization "Macabee", with their own orchestra. Sport-exercise was carried out by Dr. Leykher, dentist Leshchinski, dentist's wife Gutshtat.They are all martyrs.

In the town's "Talmud Torah" (Hebrew School), the children of the less well-to-do parents studied. They did not have any means to pay tuition for private tutors.The Talmud Torah took up three homes near the large synagogue.The budget was put together with the help of the whole Jewish population.Everyone paid a weekly allowance and the community gave appropriate subsidies.The leaders of the Talmud Torah were: Morkhe-Mendl Alenberg, Yitzkhok Epshteyn, Yitzkhok-Ber Rozenberg.

The Organized Community

The major institution of the Vishkover Jews was the Jewish organized community (K'hileh). Between the (DOZORES?) representative of all parties was chosen through official election. On the basis of a proportional system. The community conducted with all the religious (HAKHARKHOTON?) of the Jewish population: Rabbinate, ritual slaughter, mikva, Midrash study (B'tai Midrashim). In the community budget, there was also an appropriate place for social help for the poor.The budget was put together by the community tax and receipts from the ritual slaughter. This maintained all the community's institutions.The community also had a say with the burial society. In the last period, the head of the community was Yitzkhok Epshteyn. 1st Vice-President – Henekh Kalusky , 2nd Vice-President 6#150; Morkhe-Mendl Alenberg, Secretary – Moshe-Yosef Avramchik. The budget of the community had to be approved by the "STARASTEH" in Poltusk. It is interesting to add a small detail.We Zionists put into the budget to help four pioneers who were travelling to Israel. The entire budget was approved. The "STARASTEH" however barred the position of helping the pioneers. For him, Israel was an "unkosher" legal matter.

"Shibulim" group of "Hashomer Hatzair"

The Yeshiva, Synagogues, Study Places, and Prayer Quorums
Translated by Sheldon Clare

The Vishkov Yeshiva, "Beis-Yosef" had a good name throughout the town, and here is the proof: Of the 200 students that studied there,the Rabbi commuted from "outside of town". The Yeshiva was above the big synagogue and was led by the spirit of the traditions of the late Rabbi Yosef Salanter. Rabbi Shimon Khofetz, the Yeshiva head, required nothing. His total pusuit was to educate the students with Torah. They should constantly learn, day and inght. He told the young men how to live in the world so that they could enjoy (benefit) from the next world.

[Page 31]

The Rabbi of the Yeshiva was Rabbi Avrahom Tzitrin, who later became recognized as a rabbi in a larger city. Besides this, other Torah readers gave Torah lessons. The Yeshive committee consisted of: The Gerer Hasid Reb Avrohom Lerner, the Hasid Reb Yakov Shmilkis, Reb Eli Rozen, Reb Butcheh the baker. His son-in-law Alter and other dear Jews, who took upon themselves the concern for the young men to sccurc a night's lodging, food, clean laundry, and other needs. An ardent and energetic women's committee helped the Yeshiva and its students. While for the older boys, there existed a kitchen. They used to arrange for the younger ones with different hosts to have "eating days" (GEGES'N TEG) and where they were to sleep. Our pious mothers did everthing so that the students could quietly study Torah and not worry with the necessities. The members of the women's committee were called "The Lady Trustees of the Yeshiva". Some of them I will mention: Rivche Astroviak, Khaveh Markuskhamer, Libeh Rubin, Dvorah the knitter, Ruzhkeh Molotek, and others.

One time after Passover, Khaveh Markuskhamer and Rivche Astroviak came into my place of business and asked for places for Yeshiva students to sleep. I alone studied in the Makover Yeshiva for a period of two years of "eating days" and slept in someone else's bed. Knowing the feeling and taste of a Yeshiva student, I quickly consented to their message (request). As long as the Yeshiva existed in Vishkov, two Yeshiva students slept at my place. One of them ate with us every Saturday and another (not one who slept here) ate with us every day. Besides the women's committee, there were also 20 Jews who were involved in a special Yeshiva-committee. Voluntarily, they took on the burden of worrying about the Yeshiva's needs. Although alone, one they did not have much to eat... Both committees created "pocket money" for the Yeshiva students – and alone we were very far from and being able to eke out a living.

Vishkov had 9 houses of worship and two minyanim (prayer quorums). They were all (distributed ?) at the big synagogue on Warsaw Street. There was concentrated almost all of the religious life of the town: The community, the Talmud Torah, that occupied three large rooms, the Yeshiva above, the mikva in the courtyard, the (HAKHNASAT-ORKHIM or visitors place) where every stranger could sleep overnight.

In the synagogue, there were prayers 8 times in the morning. There were 14 Torah scrolls. All three tables from afternoon to evening services were occupied with learners. At the right table, Reb Khaim-Yehoshua Friedman taught with the "Ein Yakov" group. In this group were tailors, shoemakers, and other tradesmen. They put down their scissor and iron, their kaftan and awl, the saw and hammer and came to satisfy their spiritual requirements. Caretakers of the "Ein Yakov" group were: Nisen Bzhezhinski, Yehuda-Yosef Malchik, Hersh-Fivl Gershkovski, Yakov Holtzman. At the middle table sat the "M'silat Yishraim" (Circle of Honesty) group wherethe rebbe was Reb Shimon Trebernik, the trustees: Fishl Bronshteyn, Khaim Markhevke, Shmuel Brama. The left side was taken up by the "Mishnaes" group. Trustees in the synagogue were: Yekhiel-Meier Domb, Hershl Holtzman, and the synagogue committee: Yakov Eikenboim, Moshe B'herev, Shmuel-Leib Holland.

The synagogue had two sextons: One was called Shmuleh , with the nickname "Moov". He had a helper Hershl, known with the popular name Hershenkeh and his wife Hinkeleh. Shmuleh's nickname "Moov" came about in that he was always with the Rabbi. One time, officials came to ask the Rabbi something. The Rabbi did not know Polish. In Polish, he asked the sexton Shmuleh (Hershenkeh's salary came from [DOS RED]?? Doesn't make sense ???). Since then, "Moov" remained as his nickname. His work consisted of sweeping the synagogue, kindling the Sabbath candles, preparing the water for the priestly benediction, bringing the wedding canopy with the poles to a wedding (The wine glass with the bottle of wine was carried by the head-sexton Shmuel). Hershenkeh's salary – came about by going to Jewish homes every Thursday and Friday and getting 5-10 groshn. He existed on this for a whole week and also celebrated the Sabbath- and Hershenkeh used to really celebrate the Sabbath with fish and meat...

Hershenkeh also had an additional-mission. Every Friday evening at
4 o'clock, he used to every summer and winter, arise and even in the dreadful
cold, went through the Vishkov streets and monotonously, but with a
wonderfully sweet melody, called out: "Jews, Jews, arise for Community
services (L'VODAS HABOORA)! And the Jews obeyed. They indeed arose and
went to the synagogue and collectively read Psalms. That is how Hershenkeh
continuously awoke the Vishkover Jews for services for 25 years. Awoke, not
always full (foodwise) and without warm clothing. Until one time when he
caught a bad cold and Dr. Leykher told him to stay in bed and not to worry
about going to awaken for Psalms... For a time, Hershenkeh, did not go out to
awaken. A Jew from Vishkov came to him, a tailor, and gave him 150 zlotys to
cede the good deed to awaken the Jews Friday evening for Psalms.
Hershenkeh sold this good deed, but the whole town was convinced that this
was surely not Hershenkeh's " Jews, Jews..." At a later time, Hershenkeh
became better. He began to cash in his "pension" – the weekly pay of 5-10
groshn. However, he looked bad. When someone asked what was the matter,
he answered that every night, he heard a voice from Heaven: "Hershl, Hershl,
what have you done? What answer will you give the next world, when they will
ask you why did you sell such a "mitzvah" (gave away such a mitzvah) for
money?" Hershenkeh and Hinkeleh wept, screamed and the Vishkov Jews
returned the 150 zlotys to the tailor. Hershenkeh took back his right to wake
the Jews for services. But on Friday nights, Hershenkeh already did not go
alone. His Hinkeleh went with him; she was afraid to leave him alone. His
chanting became weaker and weaker. One Friday evening, Hershkeleh indeed
fell (on his position?) during the awakening for services. Singing his song:
"Jews, Jews, arise..." He fell alone, collapsed...

Zhetchpospolita

[Page 32]

Itsche Shkarlat – One of the first Zionists in town

The small synagogue on Starazhatzkeh Street was for the "Psalms Society". Owning 6 Torahs and besides praying several times a day, they also studied a lot. They were called the "Synagogue of the Burial Society". On Varshever Street, one found the A.G. Zionist Synagogue, that carried the name of its owner, the late Eli-Meier Goldman who wrote it over to (during his lifetime?) to the Zionist organization, under the names of Henekh Kaluski, Itche B'herev, Shmaia Rapoport.

From the study houses came unconditionally the seniority of the Gerer study-house (Shtibl) on Strazhatzkeh Street, it was built by the wealthy Hassid Reb Z'khariya Kopolovitch. There, praying and studying occurred during the whole day. Through the window, the beautiful voices of the young men carried out while they taught a page of Gemora with Tosefet. Every evening, about 60 Jews sat at a long table in the first room and studied the "Daf-Yomi- The daily page". In the second house, ordinary older Hassidim sat. Gossiped (talked) about Torah, told stories about rabbis. I remember some of their names: Brukh Zeitog, Itche-Meier Tziviak, Hehoshua Sokol (my father-in-law), Motl B'herev (my father, a ritual slaughterer), Yakov Shokhet Blumshtayn, Izik M'lamed, Yitzkhok Mondry, Khaim-Henekh Shtelung – the Bal-musaf of Rosh Hashana and Yom Kippur (I cannot until this day forget his sweet and exalted praying), Yitzkhok-Hirsh Bialistok, Berish Tchervonogureh,

Sholem Zissman, Khaim-Khaikl Hiller, Yitzkhok Epshteyn – the (President?) of the community.

In the second Gerer study home on Varshaver Street, prayed the supporters of "Mizrakhi" and many young people, who used to travel to the Gerer Rabbi. They then understood that they could travel to Ger and simultaneously love "Eretz Yisrael." The trustees of the "Shtibl" were: Reb Moshe Oster, Khaim Kremer, Yakov Levin, Yitzkhok-Meier Visotski, and Leml Rubin.

In the Atvatzker study home, prayed the Vorker Hasids, who used to take advantage of every free moment to study Gemora and Tosefos. Reb Borukh-Mendl Burshteyn used to sit there day and night and study, while his wife Kreyndl was the "bread winner". Borukh-Mendl for his whole life went only in one direction: From his home to the Atvatzker study home – and returned. He sneaked along the walls so that no one would look at him, or to touch him. He became a martyr as other worshippers of the Atvatzker study home: Reb Yitzkhok-Ber Rozenberg, Reb Pinieh Pienik, M'shhaleh Psheshchelinietz, Yakov-Yosef Plonchik, Yisroel-Yosef Krishtal, Yakov Markuskhamer, Morkhe-Mendl Halenberg, Khiel-Meier Rubin. and many others.

One should also recall the Alexander study home with the dear Hasids and wonderful Jews, where the Torah-expert and scholar Shimon Srebnik (Khatzkls). The wonderful (SHEYNEH-actually means beautiful) Jews and Hasids: Reb Yekhiel Shultz, Berish Volinski, Zishe Kaluski, Mordkheh Khanhas, Feivl Shron, who together with their families, became martyrs. Of the distinguished Hasids in Rodziminer study home, I remember: Simkhe Shnek, who every Saturday, used to walk on the bridge after eating and there, said 10 pages of Gemora by heart, Dovid-Leib Domb, B'nyomin Brodek, Yosef Vangazh, Shepsl Borenshteyn, and others. In the "Pshedmiehshcheh" was found the large minyan of Reb Yoske Lakher. There, the neighborhood Jews prayed. Also the Porendzher shoemakers had their minyan, where they prayed Minkhe-Meiriv and every morning. Besides this, the dear artisans studied Ein-Yakov. They had praying and studying on their minds, rather than earning a living...

I will end my survey of the worship houses in Vishkov with the Amshinover study home and its dear Hasids: G'dalyahu Shokhet Tentshe, Tzvi Rozenberg (now in Israel), Moshe-Yosef Avramchik, Avromcheh Holland (FAR-SHTAT?)

[Page 33]

The Last Rabbi's of Vishkov
Translated by Sheldon Clare

The last great scholars and Rabbis that Vishkov possessed before the Holocaust were: The old Rabbi Reb Ben-Tzion Rozenboim, his son-in-law the teacher-instructor, scholar and brilliant student Reb Mendele Bresler, the great scholar and brilliant student Reb Yakov-Arieh Morgenshtern, a grandchild of the Kotzker, the Lamazer Rabbi's son, the son-in-law of the Amshinover Rabbi. After the death of the Radzhiminer Rabbi Reb Mendele, he became the Radzhiminer until the day the war broke out. His son, the scholar and sage Reb Dovid-Shlomo became the Vishkover Rabbi.

I do not remember the name of the last teacher-instructor in Vishkov – but also he – as all the pure and martyrs in town – all perished. I have attempted to recall from my memory certain figures of our annihilated holy community of Vishkov. I know that this is only a part: These are only bits (crumbs) of what our town had and possessed. I recalled the familiar, those who I knew. Those who I came together with them on various occasions, to cooperate or to see their activities. I know that I have omitted many names – they should not have a grudge against me. The (SHOROT) of mine should be a modest mourner's prayer to remember all the martyrs and purified ones (T'horim), who, along with the sayer of the mourner's prayer "perished for the martyrdom of being a Jew".

Bloody Polish "Games" of 1920
by Mordekhe V. Bernshteyn, Buenos Aires
Translated by Edward Jaffe
Donated by Rona G. Finkelstein

In the description of the Nazi wrought destruction in Poland, the various recollections, witnesses testimony and other documents relate the behavior of the Polish population during the Nazi murders of the Jews. Not only did the Poles behave in a passive manner toward the Nazi atrocities, but they were often active participants in the awful acts perpetrated against the Jews. Not only did they often serve as denouncers in towns and villages, pointing out the Jews to the Germans, but frequently handed over Jews who were hidden and actually participated in robbing Jews during "actions" and "resettlements", and ultimately becoming inheritors of the robbed goods and possessions.

Those who remember or know what the Poles did during the "honey times" at the creation of the independent Poland, after World War I, will not be surprised by the behavior of the Polish population, at least by its majority. When the Polish country took its first steps at the birth of the new "Zhetchpospolita", the Jews experienced pain and paid in blood at the creation of the new country.

This is not the place to discuss the wave of pogroms that took place in the years 1918-1919. Specific details, materials and documents are recorded in several publications. The classic work by the known activist of Poali-Zion. Leon Khazanovich, describes the facts, the documents, the pogroms and the excesses in 105 towns and villages in Poland in November-December 1918. [L. Khazanovich: The Jewish pogroms in November and December 1918. Acts and Documents. Stockholm, 1918.]

Two particularly horrible massacres carried out by the Polish military, the extermination In Lemberg of that time, and the shootings in Pinsk in Nisan of 1919 are described in special publications. [Joseph Bendoov: "The Lemberg Jewish Pogrom" (November 1918 – January 1919), Vienna. About Pinsk: Abraham-Asher Feinstein - "Story of a Catastrophe", Tel-Aviv, 1929.] Here we are discussing a second wave of anti-Jewish actions which came at the time of the communist invasion. At that time an anti-Jewish conspiracy developed in Poland. Circles of official military leaders, starting with orders from the general staff and down to the Polish underworld propagated a libel that Jews collaborated with Bolshevik "Revcoms", and that Jews spied for the Red Army, and shot at Polish military units, etc.

At that time in Poland there was already some Jewish representation in the form of the Jewish National Board, whose members were elected representatives in the Polish Seim (parliament). The National Board began to collect facts about the horrible actions; send their representatives to a series of places where pogroms or other misdeeds against Jews took place; published a series of materials; and brought into the Seim various presentations, etc.

The materials about this bloody period was published by the Jewish parliament faction in a series of issues where authentic facts were presented about the executions of hundreds in little towns. [Two articles under the name "Invasion by the Bolsheviks and the Jews" issued by the National Club of

Jewish representatives in Parliament for the Temporary Jewish National Advisory Board. Both appeared in Warsaw in 1921.]

[Page 34]

In the first collection there was material about an urgent presentation, entered on September 1920 in the Polish parliament by Jewish deputies: Greenbaum, Farbstein, Hartglas and others about the politics of Jewish persecution led by the Polish government. The presentation tells about pogroms in tens of little towns and hundreds of robberies and destruction incidents that were carried out by the Polish military in cooperation with local Polish groups (official and civil).

Among the documents that were presented, two were from Vishkov. We present these documents here translated into Yiddish. Such publications are a rarity, therefore it is important that this chapter not be missed in the "Book of Vishkov". The first document describes the protocol delivered by Joseph Gravitzky who was sent by the Jewish deputies group in the Polish parliament to Vishkov, in order to establish exactly what happened. The second document is a declaration obtained from some of the arrested Jews.

Actually I bring here three declarations attached to the documents which I succeeded in obtaining from one of the three Jews that signed document number 2.

Senatorska Garden

Document number 1

To the Deputies' Club of the Temporary National Council in the City (Warsaw).

In accord with your proposal of 27th of this month (August) I visited Viskov, and have the honor to submit the report about the incidents in that town. The information is based on statements I received from the injured and facts that I observed myself.

On the 11th of this month, in the afternoon, the Bolshevik military came into Vishkov. The military behaved reasonably peacefully. The Bolshevik commissar created a group of police to keep order in town. The police consisted of Christians and Jews. On the evening of the 18th of this month the police left town as a result of the Polish counteroffensive. Before leaving town the Bolshevik soldiers, particularly the rear guard (the group withdrawing last), robbed the stores and houses, particularly those belonging to Jews.

The same evening when the Polish military moved in, there were already occasional cases of robbery. The following morning words spread among the military by the Polish population that shots were fired from Jewish homes at Polish military personnel. Based on these declarations all inhabitants of the Reichman house were taken out to be shot.

[Page 35]

Chaim-David Goldwasser, 60 years old, his wife and three children.

Leo Zrenchi, 32 years old.

Samual-Leo Holland, 26 years old, with his wife and children. Haikal Hiller, 40 years old, with his wife.

Abraham Reichman, 65 years old, with his wife.

Moishe Barak, 32 years old, with his wife.

Eisik-Meyer Krishtol, 50 years old, with his wife.

Ytzkhak-Hersh Bialistok (the blind), 60 years old, and his wife. And other inhabitants of the house.

All above-mentioned were lined up in the yard, and were told that they are to be shot. The entire house was searched and money, clothing, and other valuables were taken. Thanks to a declaration by Polish neighbors that the rumors about shots having been fired from windows of this house have not been confirmed, the people were released.

Before the Bolsheviks left the town of Vishkov, several hundred Jews who feared possible war action, left town on the 17th of the month for Ostrov. Two days after their arrival in Ostrov, Polish soldiers entered the town. The Vishkov Jews turned to the military commander of Ostrov and the local mayor with a request for travel documents to Vishkov. They also asked for a police escort. They were afraid to go by themselves because the roads were full of military convoys. The mayor assigned to them 4 policemen, for which they paid 7300 marks.

Tuesday, the 24th in the morning they arrived in Vishkov. In the village Komisarka (7 miles from Vishkov) the Vishkov police already waited for them and together with the Ostrov policemen accompanied them into town. The Jews were brought into the firemen's hall. Immediately, a civilian Pole by the name of Liskevich showed up and declared that they will be shot because they are Bolsheviks. One half hour later they were transferred from the firemen's hall to the so called "senators garden".

In the garden were already assembled several hundred Polish inhabitants of the town, actually the worst element, mostly young. About 200 Jews were lined up four in a row and terribly beaten in the process. The police requested that the youths find Bolsheviks among the Jews, and at the same time they called the town's Christian citizens to bring forth their grievances against the Jewish Bolsheviks, among whom there were also old people.

Those identified as Bolsheviks were taken out of formation and beaten with whips, sticks and wires to which they attached stones, as well as with rifle butts.

From the magistrate's office were brought tables. At one table sat down the secretary of the regional court, Voevudski and two senior military officers. From the point where the Jews were lined up to the tables were stationed two rows of civilian Poles and soldiers. Every Jew who passed through between the rows of men to the table was beaten harshly from both sides with sticks, wires, whips, rifle butts and even with bayonets. Anyone who approached a table was searched, undressed and left wearing a shirt only. During the searches everything was taken from the Jews and they were asked to get up on a table. While standing on a table they were asked to shout "long live Poland, and death to the rabbi". They also had to ask the crowd: "does anyone have a request? Have I ever done anyone an evil deed?".

Meanwhile they were beaten without interruption. Naturally, some people from the crowd would speak up and say that someone was a Bolshevik or that he harmed someone. Later the Jew was thrown off the table in such a way that the table landed on him, making it impossible to get up. When they ultimately got up, they had to return through the lineup and the beating was repeated once again. During the beatings some Jews lost their consciousness.

During my visit I personally saw Jews with bleeding wounds. I also saw wounded women who were beaten when they tried to approach their brothers or fathers.

The action lasted from 9 in the morning till 3-4 in the afternoon and caused great anxiety among the Jewish population and among some Poles, causing the soldiers and policemen to shoot several times in the air to scare and "pacify" the crowd. I was told that prior to the commencement of the action, soldiers and policemen visited houses and invited the Polish population to gather in the garden for a "game". During the "game" I determined that the following were present: the town's mayor – Stanislaw Pavlovski, the town's physician – Ribka, the military physician – Sharkevich, two priests and many of the local intellectuals.

[Page 36]

After the action was over, the wounded and bloody Jews were brought to the town's jail and on the way were beaten again. The same happened inside the jail.

Now the Jews are in jail. While I was in Vishkov a temporary investigation was started and a few Jews were set free. In the coming days a larger number will be freed.

The arrested Jews are taken to work every day near the bridge over the river Bug. At work they are still beaten. They started to feed them one day before my arrival – Friday the 27th of this month. The citizen militia, composed of Christians only (among them are those who were policemen at the time of the Bolshevik invasion) are guarding the arrested. I determined that they let into the jail any passing soldiers who beat the inmates and are allowed to enjoy themselves.

The current town's commander has forbidden such behavior, and in the last couple of days such incidents were not repeated.

The Jewish population in town live under very difficult conditions. The beating of Jews and cutting of their beards by passing soldiers is a very frequent occurrence.

Warsaw, the 29th August 1920. I. Gravitzky

Wyszków

Do

Klubu Poselskiego przy Tymcz. Żyd. Radzie Narod.

w Miejscu.

Zgodnie z poleceniem Sz. Panów zwiedziłem dn. 27-go b. m. miasto Wyszków i mam zaszczyt przy niniejszym złożyć sprawozdanie z wydarzeń w Wyszkowie.

Wiadomości moje czerpałem z informacji poszkodowanych i faktów, których byłem naocznym świadkiem.

Dnia 11 b. m. w południe wkroczyły do Wyszkowa wojska bolszewickie. Wojska te zachowywały się względnie spokojnie. Komisarz bolszewicki utworzył milicję w celu utrzymania porządku w mieście. Milicja ta składała się z chrześcijan i Żydów. Dn. 18 b. m. wieczorem opuścili bolszewicy miasto wskutek kontrofenzywy polskiej. Przed opuszczeniem miasta żołnierze bolszewiccy, szczególnie arjergarda, obrabowali sklepy i domy, przeważnie żydowskie. Tego samego wieczora, kiedy wkroczyły wojska polskie, były już pojedyńcze wypadki rabunku. Nazajutrz rano zaczęły pomiędzy żołnierzami krążyć pogłoski, rozpowszechniane przez ludność polską, że z domów żydowskich strzelano do wojska polskiego. Na skutek tych pogłosek miano rozstrzelać wszystkich mieszkańców domu REICHMANA (ulica Rynek): Chaima Dawida Goldwassera, lat 60, z żoną i 3 córkami, Lejba Zrecznego, lat 32, Szmula Lejba Hollanda, lat 36, z żoną i dziećmi, Chajkla Millera, lat 40, z żoną, Abrama Reichmana, lat 65, z żoną, Mojsze Baraka, lat 32, z żoną, Ajzyka Majera Krystała, lat 50, z żoną, Mojsze Mendla Grinberga, Icka Hersza Białystoka (ślepy), lat 60, z żoną i jeszcze kilku mieszkańców (Żydów) tego domu. Wszystkich wyżej wymienionych ustawiono na podwórzu, oświadczając, że będą rozstrzelani. W całym domu zarządzono rewizję, podczas której zabrano pieniądze, bieliznę, kosztowności i t. d.

Wskutek zaświadczenia sąsiadów polskich, iż pogłoski o

...ch dwóch dni wypadki te już się nie powtarzały.

Ludność żydowska w mieście żyje w warunkach bardzo ciężkich. Bicie i obcinanie bród Żydom przez przechodzących żołnierzy są to zjawiska, które można obserwować na każdym kroku.

(—) J. Grawicki.

Warszawa, dnia 29 sierpnia 1920.

My, niżej podpisani: Icek BARAB, lat 29, Szlojme ROZENBERG, lat 28 i Icek NEUMAN, lat 23, zam w Wyszkowie, zeznajemy, co następuje:

We wtorek, dn. 17 b. m., udaliśmy się do Ostrowia. Byliśmy tam dwa dni, po upływie których wkroczyły do Ostrowia wojska polskie. Udaliśmy się wraz ze wszystkimi uciekinierami z Wyszkowa do Komendanta Wojskowego w Ostrowiu, do burmistrza tegoż miasta i prosiliśmy, żeby nam dali policjanta, któryby nas odprowadził do Wyszkowa. Baliśmy się chodzić bez policjanta, gdyż drogi były przepełnione żołnierzami. Burmistrz zgodził się na naszą propozycję i dał nam 4 policjantów, zaco zapłaciliśmy mu 7.300 mk.

W poniedziałek, dn. 23 b. m., policjanci zaprowadzili nas do Wyszkowa.

We wtorek, dn. 24 b. m., zrana przyszliśmy do Wyszkowa. Jeszcze w Komisarce (wieś o 7 w. od Wyszkowa) oczekiwało nas 5 policjantów z Wyszkowa, którzy razem z policjantami z Ostrowia wprowadzili nas do miasta. Po drodze przez miasto nie pozwolono nikomu podchodzić do nas ani wyglądać z okien. Strzelano na postrach do tych, którzy usiłowali porozumieć się z nami. Wprowadzili nas do szopy Straży Ogniowej, do której wszedł cywilny Polak Liśkiewicz i oznajmił, że jesteśmy bolszewikami i jako tacy będziemy rozstrzelani. Po upływie pół godziny wprowadzili nas do „Ogrodu Senatorskiego".

W ogrodzie ustawili nas w czwórki, przytem bito nas bez litości. Było tam wielu żołnierzy i policjantów, jak również cywilnych mieszkańców miasta. Policja kazała chłopcom Polakom, którzy się zebrali w ogrodzie, rozpoznać między nami bolszewików, a ci rozkaz ten spełnili. Jednocześnie z miasta zawezwano

A copy of the report to members of the Jewish parliament in the Polish Sejm about the bloody events of 1920.

Document number 2

Declaration We the undersigned: Itzkhak Barab, 29 years old, Shloima Rosenberg, 28 years old, and ltzkhak Neuman, 23 years old, residing in Vishkov, declare as follows:

Tuesday the 17th of the month (August) we went to Ostrov. We were there 2 days, after that Polish soldiers came into Ostrov. Together with the other refugees from Vishkov, we went to the military commander of Ostrov, the mayor of this town and asked that he assign a policeman to take us to Vishkov. We were fearful to go without protection because the roads were teeming with soldiers. The mayor agreed to honor our request and assigned 4 policemen, for which we paid 7300 marks.

Monday the 23rd of the month, the policemen took us to Vishkov.

Tuesday the 24th of the month in the morning we arrived in Vishkov.

In the village of Komisarka (7 miles from Vishkov) 5 policemen from Vishkov waited for us. Together with Ostrov's policemen they brought us into town. While walking through the town nobody was allowed to come close to us, not even to look through a window at us. Shots were fired to scare those who attempted to contact us. We were brought to the firehouse where the civilian Pole Liskevich declared that we are Bolsheviks and therefore we will be shot. A half hour later we were taken to the "senator park". In the park we were aligned four in a row and were beaten without mercy. There were present many soldiers, policemen as well as civilian inhabitants of the town. The police asked the Polish youth to identify Bolsheviks among the detainees. The youths carried out the order. At the same time they called the town's Christians to voice their grievances against the Jews.

[Page 37]

Among us were also old people. Those pointed out by the youths (as being Bolsheviks) were taken out of the rows and beaten with sticks, whips, wires to which stones were attached and so forth. These people were positioned separately. Then a table was brought and the secretary of the regional court, Voevudski, and two senior military man sat down. From the point where the rows of Jews (the so called Bolsheviks) were lined up and up to the table were stationed rows of civilians and soldiers. Every one of us who came through between the rows was cruelly beaten with sticks, whips and wires. When we approached the table we were searched and undressed and left standing wearing a shirt only. We were robbed of all our possessions. Then they asked us to get up on the table, from where we had to shout: "long live Poland and death to the rabbi". Naturally, the crowd voiced demands from every one of us for the presumed misdeeds we inflicted upon them.

Later we were thrown off the table by turning it upside down and landing the table on us. We were not allowed to get up, and while laying on the ground we were again beaten with whips and sticks. When we ultimately got up and went back through the rows we were beaten once again.

After this action, we returned bloodied (many of us lost consciousness) to our rows and were beaten again.

This action continued from 9 in the morning till 3 in the afternoon. At 4 o'clock we were put under the town's arrest. In the jail yard we were told to sit down like "Turks" – that is bend our legs under our bodies. Those who could not do it were beaten with rifle butts. We set like that (like "Turks") until 7 o'clock. Then we were taken into the garden for the night.

During the action in the garden, there were shouts in town from mothers, sisters and others. To quiet the crowd rifle shots were fired to scare the people.

During the action the following were present: the town's mayor Stanislaw Povlovski, the town's physician Ribka, Dr. Sharkevich, a military physician, the priest,and the so called intellectuals. We were beaten by the town's police, headed by commissar Stazinski.

Now we are under arrest. We are 200 locked up Jews. Soldiers are constantly allowed to come in to beat and humiliate us.

Read: Itzik Barab, Shloima Rosenberg, Itzek Neuman.

Additional explanations

As fate would have it one of the three Jews who signed the mentioned affidavit about the "games" in Vishkov, Itzkhak Barab (or as he was known in Vishkov, Itche-Motel the ritual slaughterer's son) survived the war. Exactly this Itzkhak Barab I met on the meandering roads in Samarkand and later in Buenos Aires. Seeing his name on the document, I could establish that it was the same person. From him I learned additional details which complete the picture of the bloody, torturous days of the Vishkov Jews.

Firstly, there is a question as to how did hundreds of Vishkov's Jews come to Ostrov. After the Bolsheviks were expelled, not only Vishkov's, but youths from many Polish towns and villages, found themselves outside their own towns. This happened not because Jews were Bolsheviks and retreated together with the Red Army (there were some, but a small minority) but because they were scared due to warning from the Poles that when "our people" (meaning Poles) will come, we will get even with the Jews for their service to the Bolsheviks. Actually, during the Bolshevik reign the "Revcoms" (Revolutionary Committees), the police (or militia) as well as other positions were to a large extent occupied by Poles from the general population. Generally, against such Poles no repressive measures were taken.

Many Jews (Itzkhak Barab among them), were hidden during the Polish reign because they did not want to serve in the Polish Army. At that time "patriotism" vis a vis the army was non-existent because of its extreme animosity toward Jews. Some were hidden outside their villages. When the Polish reign stabilized, some began coming back to their villages. Actually, for those who were hidden an amnesty was proclaimed absolving them from being deserters, provided they would report to the military commission.

[Page 38]

Hundreds of Vishkov's Jews who were in Ostrov as refugees, were generally far from being politically active and particularly from being Bolshevik sympathizers. These were young and old from business backgrounds who suffered from "red" confiscation of their business goods (or where business goods were not confiscated, they were simply "bought" for worthless rubles). Many of them were known for their Zionist sympathies, among them were some real Zionist activists.

The group which appealed to the Ostrov mayor to provide an escort to Vishkov consisted of about 100 men. The local Zionist activist Shultz was helpful in obtaining the required permission. The 7300 marks that was paid to the mayor was collected from the refugees. The people who signed the affidavit from jail were also (besides Itzkhak Barab who was mentioned above) the following: Shloima Rosenberg, then a bachelor; his father Itzkhak-Ber Rosenberg was a clever Vorker Hasid who owned a yard goods store. Shloima himself was a Zionist who later married Malka, Shmuel Elbein's daughter and lived in Warsaw where he had a leather business. He was killed together with his family and all other Warsaw Jews.

Itzkhak Neuman, his father a Gerer Hasid, had a wholesale business of salt, herring and oil. He was then a bachelor. Later married the daughter of Mendel Shkariat; after the wedding had a flour wholesale business. During the Nazi offensive of 1939 escaped with many other Jews to Bialistok. Itzkhak Barab actually met him in Bialistok together with his wife and 2 children. Neuman evidently took a Soviet passport and stayed in the Soviet occupied parts of Poland, and was killed together with his family by the Germans.

And now a few words about the people mentioned in the report by Joseph Gravitzky.

Chaim-David Goldwasser, a Gerer Hasid, had the whiskey monopoly. Evidently died before the World War II.

Samuel-Leo Holland, was a horse trader. Killed with his family during the Nazi reign, apparently in Yadeve, whereto he escaped from Vishkov.

Haykal Hiller, representative of Warsaw Jewish newspapers. He and his wife were killed. Some of his children may be in Israel.

Abraham Reichman, a tailor by trade. He owned a house from where the people were taken. He was a short time in America, where he made "a few dollars" and then returned and bought the house.

Moishe Barak, it should be Barab, brother of Itzkhak Barab, son of Motel Shokhet. He was a watch repairman. Killed with his family in the Warsaw ghetto.

Eizik-Meyer Krishtol. Had a tobacco store. Perished.

Moishe-Mendel Greenberg had a hardware business. The last years lived in Ostrolenko.

Itzkhak-Hersh Bialistok, who was blind, was killed with his wife in Vishkov, before the start of the general murder campaign. It ought to be added that Vishkov's sacrifices included two additional Jewish youths who were shot under the pretense of being "deserters". Abraham-Itzkhak the tailor, Frieda's son. The name of the second youth will perhaps be recalled by other Vishkov residents. This became known about a week or two after the above described "games" took place. The town's commandant called upon the chief rabbi Mendel Bressler to administer the death prayer for the two who were sentenced to death. They were shot beyond the confines of the town. Actually, many Poles had committed the sin of "desertion" but were never convicted for these offenses.

As a conclusion, a few additional details about Joseph Gravitzky who wrote the report about the story of Vishkov, according to the "Lexicon of the New Jewish Literature", Volume 2, New York 1958.

Born in Warsaw on November 8, 1900, died in Israel in December 1955. Lately went by the name of Joseph Rogav. Received a Jewish and general upbringing.

Graduated from Krinski's gymnasium (high school) in Warsaw and studied government science in Vienna. Was a member of the Zionist movement from his early youth. Was the founder and general secretary of the Ze'iri-Zion in Poland. In the years 1921-1932 was a member of the central committee and general secretary of the Zionist organization in Poland. In those years was a delegate to all Zionist congresses. In the years 1928-1932 was a member of the community council in Warsaw. In 1932 emigrated to Israel. Was active in the Jewish Agency. From 1948 until his death was director of the press service of the Israeli government.

[Page 39]

Polish-Bolshevik Terror in 1920

by Y. Mitlsbakh (Petakh Tikvah, Israel)

Translated in 2009 by Sylvia Schildt, z"l[1] (1934 -2010) (Baltimore MD)

Reviewed by Frida Grapa Markuschamer de Cielak (Mexico City)

Translation donated by the Historian Enrique Krauze (Mexico City, in 2013)

1.

The house on the Pultusk Street in Wyishkov (Wyszków) known under the name "Epsteyn's (Epstein's) Hotel", fulfilled a not-small role in the history of Jewish social and communal life in the shtetl. But this hotel became sadly famous in the year 1920, when the Bolsheviks, in the short interval of their rule in Wyszków, turned the building into their headquarters, where they also located the "Czeka"[2] and some other of their offices.

But above all, Epstein's Hotel was known for the library and reading room, where the youth would get together evenings. One would come to change a book, one to read a newspaper (not everyone in those days could afford to subscribe to a newspaper and not every parent would allow their children to read a newspaper).

From time to time in one or another locale, they would hold chess evenings and public readings in which their own friends participated: Israel Goldwasser (Goldvaser) the teacher of Nature Science on Shkolna Street, Yekhiel Bz'hoza (Bzhoza/Bzoza), Yurman, Itche Shkarlat, "Der geler"[3] Avraham Ferdman z"l and others. Long winter evenings we would sit at the tables - some read a book or nwspaper and others at the tiny tables would play chess.

Silence reigned in the room so you could hear a fly buzzing. Everyone was absorbed in either a book or a newspaper. The room was warmed by the big white stove, decorated by a pair of lions, painted in gold...

Under the very same roof where the library and reading-room were located, were a group of people who believed that out of the East would come freedom for the oppressed and among them - also for the Jews.

2.

From time to time you could hear outbursts of laughter and singing. But as we said earlier, the entire building, along with its cultural institutions, changed into the headquarters of the Red Army and the "Tcheka." There they condemned many innocent people whom they led out of town and with brutal means carried out death sentences. Among the condemned were two Jewish boys, that were brought (into Wyszkow) by the "Tcheka" from Bryansk/Bransk [4]: Abraham-Yosef ben Eliezer Misharik, leader of the Bransker Zionist Organization and Yisroel (Srulik) Shapiro, Secretary of the same organization. These two boys were led Friday afternoon out of town to the iron bridge and there they were murdered in terrible fashion. The leader's skull was split while he was still alive and they removed the skin off the secretary's fingers as if it was a glove. I got to know of this incident because I had been arrested when the Bolsheviks were driven out and our region was freed. In the town of Ostrow thousands of refugees were gathered who were trying to get to Russia. After the victory of the Polish Army, all Jewish youth had to present themselves to the Magistrate, in order to be sent home to their towns. I too was among the Wishkevers who obeyed the order and signed themselves in. A civilian guard led us to Wyszków, where the fate of each was decided.

Tens of young men were detained for trial. I together with Abraham Rubin (Alter Rubin's son, the heavy-set one), were close friends from childhood - and now each had to be tried in a field court in the gymnasium (high school) in the Senator's Garden. I learned of the sentence of the two Bryansker (Bransker) Jews, because he was in the Militia. (Abraham) Rubin had been sentenced to 10 years in prison. As I was still a minor, they took me to Warsaw. This same court also condemned three to be shot. This sentence was carried out behind the windows of the gymnasium. The three condemned were: Yaakov (the son of the tailor Yisroel who pleaded before the field court: "I will not serve"... The other two were brought from the shtetl Jadów[5]. One of them I knew personally; his name was Yankl Zhelenitz, the only one of the old revolutionary fighters from the year 1905. He wasn't surprised that he had received the death penalty. Those who found themselves in the same room with him he told that he would not let himself be led to the slaughter like a lamb. No sooner had they taken him from the room, he turned to the side as if he wanted to run away and thus with a cry - "I have left my only daughter" - they shot him on the spot.

Gravestone of the two Bryansk(Bransk) martyrs who although innocent, were shot by the Bolsheviks in the year 1920

Standing by the gravestone is at the right: Haim Nosn Vengrov (Wegrow) z"l, thanks to whose initiative the corpses of those shot were brought out from the Christian cemetery to the Wyishkov (Wyszków) Jewish cemetery.

[Page 40]

3.

Before the war broke out with the Bolsheviks, Wyszków had the honor of hearing a lecture by Peretz Markish about Yeshu(Jesus). Because of the recent accusation from the woman Koslowska, who represented the censor, they detained all the men who had attended the reading. A part of those present were active in various institutions and possessed illegal writings. Whoever had on his person lists of names chewed these lists and swallowed them. I then had a list of readers of the youth newspaper "Free Future" - and quickly chewed the list and swallowed it. Yekhiel Bzoza got the idea to dress Markish in a ladies' mantle and led him out the back door.

The previously mentioned Koslowska was also guilty of the heavy sentencing of Abraham Rubin. When we surveyed the proceedings that had taken place in the garden of the firefighters guild, she accused Rubin that he took part in shooting Poles who were buried in the Polish cemetery.

Footnotes

1. The initials z"l stand for the Hebrew words: zikhrono lebrakha or in Yiddish: zikhrone lebrokheh meaning: "of blessed memory," which are added when a person has died and when his name is remembered, written or mentioned.
2. "Czeka, " "Tcheka" or "Cheka" was the Russian name given to the political police.
3. When given the nickname ""Der geler" (Yellow), it referred to a red-haired person.
4. The distance between Bransk and Wyszkow is 94.5 km(58.70 miles).
5. Jadów village is 19 km (abt. 12 miles) from Wyszków.

A Memoir of "That Year"
by Liber Vigoda, Tel Aviv
Translated by Pamela Russ

(In memory of my father Yisrael, my mother Chaya, my brother Yehuda, and beloved Mendel, the Morah Hora'ah [rabbi who can address issues of Jewish law])

The Bolshevik invasion of the year 1920 also reached Wyszkow. The first reconnaissance unit of the Red Army made its appearance on Kosciuszko Street, where we were living. Close by, there was the Polish police force that tried to flee actually moments before the arrival of the Bolsheviks. In order to cover their embarrassment of trying to run away, the Polaks beat every Jew that they found on the road. So, the Jews locked themselves in their houses. In times such as these, everyone followed "Ashrei Yoshvei Veisecho..." [prayer recited three times daily, translation: "Fortunate are those who dwell in Your (God's) house..."].

In those turbulent days, my brother Yehuda was born in our home. My weakened mother remained bedridden, and my father was very concerned: How should he make this child Jewish? My younger brother Reuven and I were thus free from our parents' watch. Through the crack of the slightly opened door, we saw how Russian soldiers, with long hair and dressed poorly, were approaching our home with lists in their hands. We quickly shut the door and soon heard knocking. My father opened the door and they asked him in Russian where was the place of the police force. When he answered that the site they were looking for was a little farther down, the ordered that one of the children should accompany them and show them the place. After they assured him [my father] that nothing would happen to me, my father allowed me to go with the soldiers.

The street was empty and quiet – as in a cemetery. I came home safely. And here they were preparing for the circumcision of the newborn. Truthfully, my father at that point did not know where he would find a minyan [quorum of ten men (as required for the circumcision ceremony)]. Because of the insecure situation in the town it was clear that not everyone would be so ready to leave his home, even to do such a great mitzvah [positive deed as ordained in the Torah]. My mother suggested that we go to Mendel the Rav, who lived not far from us. He readily agreed to come and asked that everything that was required be prepared – and in the merit of the Patriarch Abraham, God would help...

The following day, the invited neighbors and guests forgot about the tense and insecure situation in the town, and they came to our celebration. We drank l'chaim [a toast "to life"], wished each other mazal tov, and – better times. The rabbi (Reb Mendel Bresler) was the sandek [the person who holds the baby during the circumcision]. In the middle of the celebration, we heard loud banging on the door. On the other side of the door, they were shouting in Russian: "Open up!" Everyone remained frozen still. Only Reb Mendel remained seated calmly, and holding the baby he calmed everyone else down. My father did not lose his wits, but went to the door and opened it. Two officers from the Red Army came into the house and asked: "What's going on here, a holiday?" My father pointed to the mother who had just recently given birth and was still bedridden, and explained to them: "Today, on the eighth day after a boy is born, the Jews celebrate a circumcision ceremony..."

The officers calmly listened to the explanation, carefully looked over each person – and then permitted the celebration to continue. Even the behavior of the guest, probably, appeased the officers. Everyone present freely released their breath when the Red Army men left the house, and then praised their fine behavior and appropriate respectfulness.

[Page 41]

Vishkov Remembrances
by Israel Granat
Translated by Abraham Holland

1920

Members of Poalei Zion in 1919

I was ten years old when the Red Army retreated from Warsaw. About 400 Jewish young men who did not want to fall into the hands of the Poles ran off together with them. At Ostrov-Mazovietsk they were overtaken and brought back to Vishkov, where they were triumphantly paraded throughout the city, imprisoned in Senators Garden and there tortured.

I was curious to see what was being done with them. I went up to the Women's section of the small synagogue and from there observed everything that took place in the garden.

All the prisoners were seated on the ground. In the center there was a long table to which each was brought separately. The Jews were beaten from both sides with hoses and sticks, which the Poles had prepared. After three days in captivity almost all were released. The only ones kept were those that had deserted the Polish army. Almost all answered "yes." Only one answered "no." He was **Avraham Yitzchak Shneider**'s son. The court sentenced him to death and he was shot there in Senators Garden and buried there. It was only eight days later that the Chevra Kadisha brought him to a Jewish cemetery.

Three more Jews were killed on the way back from Ostrov. The Bolsheviks had given them explosive materials that detonated on the way and killed the Vishkover Jews: **Reichman**, the son of **Avraham Moshe Brock**, the son of **Nachum Stoller,** and **Sana Shuster**, **Chaya Neshe**'s husband.

1921-1924

In the first years of Poland's separation several political organizations were formed in the town. Worker youth were grouped in the leftist Poalei-Zion where the leader was **Tsembal**, in the Bund under the leadership of **Simcha Yaakov Vengrov** and the Communists. under the leadership of **Shvanek**. There were also organized the parties of the general Zionists and rightist Poalei Zion. The worker youth ran mainly to the left Poalei Zion and the Communists. The aforementioned **Shvanek** afterwards played a noticeable role in the Warsaw Communist organization, where he had an important position. In the year1940 he was arrested, through the Soviets in Manischewitz, accused of Trotskyism and sentenced to death.

Vishkov provided another noticeable activist of Communist leanings, **Chaim Trembelinski**, in the year 1939. At the outbreak of the war he was freed. I met him in Bialostok. Eventually he was arrested in Lemberg and we know nothing more of him. I know that **Trembelinski** was one of Stalin's trusted men in Poland and he helped Stalin to liquidate a whole group of his opponents among the Polish Communists.

1925-1930

On Shkolna Street there was a society that gave evening courses for workers, where young upstanding men from worker families that had hardly any elementary background, were taught. The courses were given in three classes. I was taught in the third class. The courses were given by the teachers: **Rosenblatt** – Yiddish, **Chanah Vistenetski** – Polish, **Israel Goldwasser** – Nature knowledge.

Staff of the Peoples School

This institution was supported by the left Poalei Zion and existed until the year 1928. In that same year a Yiddish school organization was founded, in which the left Poalei Zion, the Bund, and the Communists worked together. The staff consisted of the following friends:

[Page 42]

Polstolski, Shaika

Rinek, Muttel

Rinek, Herschel

Facht, Nata

Tsembal,Aharon

Tsembal, Yisroel Moshe

and Ostroviak, Beinisch.

Sport club "Morgenstern," 1925

A dramatic crisis now existed in the Yiddish school organization, in which the following took part:

Shkarlat, Yisroel

Polstolski, Shaika

Shaiga, Yitzchak

Sapirstein, Muttel

Kraga, Chana

Marcuschamer, Moshe and others.

From time to time they played at theater. The income was set aside for the school organization. The Jewish sports club of the school organization under the leadership of **Baruch Chutnitsky**, ran a lively sports activity. The school organization in Vishkov existed for three years. Because of the inner party conflicts, which more than once brought about the intervention of the area organizers, and with the approval of the Warsaw headquarters, the school was disbanded in the year 1930.

That years the Jewish sports club "Stern" was started, where I was a member. We only played on Shabbos because that was the only day we were free. Because of that, the local Sabbath observing leadership called for an ostracism. In the synagogue a notice was posted that all non-observers would, after death, be buried behind the park.

In the town, there was a baker, a certain **Chana-Yidel**. He was a member of Stern. Once on a Sabbath while bathing in a lake he drowned. Since he was a non-observer of the Sabbath, the Chevra Kadisha decided to bury him in a plot behind the park. All the townsfolk, from right to left, organized to prevent this disgrace from taking place. Police were brought in from Proviat and under a strong watch, the decision of the Chevra Kadisha was realized. He was buried in a back plot. But this was the first and last such episode in Vishkov.

1930-1935

During this period there arose a very strong social awareness among the Jewish youth in Poland and also in our town. To that time I worked as a needle-worker in Warsaw. I would often get away to Vishkov, where together with some friends, organized the first meeting of the needle workers, which took place in the woods.

Around 150 people attended. In the assemblage two separate groups were set up --- a society management and a youth management. In the first group the following were chosen: **Yisroel Granat**, **Yoel Tchervanagura**, **Alter Popovsky**, **Sima Marcus, Sarah Zuzel, Simcha Gershonovitch**, and **Pinchus Sherok**. In the youth group were **Yechiel Shikur, Chaim Garnek, Yosef Zeltman, Faivel Gurshtein, Grushka Kartufel** and **Menusha Kahn**.

The first task was setting the work day. Until then the work day was from morning to night, without counting the hours. Thanks to the actions of the organization the work day became established as eight hours. The second task was a battle against a law which mainly had been passed against young workers and practically made them slaves. Because of that a strike broke out which lasted four weeks and ended with a complete victory. As a result, the law was never enforced in our town.

The organization ran a broad cultural program for the worker youth. Every Shabbos there were readings and other programs. There were discussion groups, where a broad range of problems were dicussed. Many different opinions were offered by the group.

In Vishkov, there existed almost all the political parties. The left Poalei-Zion---at their head **Valman** and **Popovsk**y --- the Bund, with **Avraham Yedvab** --- the Communists with **Frider**. Also active were the Shomer Hatzair and Poalei Hamizrachi. The Chalutz ran their Hacshara (preparation for immigration to Eretz Israel) programs.

The Start of the Second World War

I was then in Warsaw. On the 5th of September, 1939, I arrived in Vishkov. The city was under constant bombardment. There were already fatalities. The first victim was **Chaim Silverberg**, on his way from the railroad station. A great panic broke out. About 60 percent of the Jewish population ran away to Yadov and Vengrov. The rest of the inhabitants hid out in the cellars until the German army took over the city. Right after the Hitlerites marched into Vishkov, all the Jews were gathered up in the town center, where 10 of them were shot immediately. The women and children were sent home and the able-bodied men were sent to Pultusk. The old people were all shot.

[Page 43]

Almost 300 Jews were driven to Poplivess, behind Pultusk. There they were forced to dig graves and were later murdered. Since I lived in Pultusk the last year before the war I went there after Rosh Hashanah. There I was told about the tragedy and the last moments of the Jews of Vishkov.

Martyrs and Fighters

Those Jews of Vishkov that remained alive ran off in all directions. Some to Russia, where they were then sent to Siberia. Others ran off to surrounding cities, like Vengrov, Yadov, and others.

I escaped to Russia and ended up in Siberia, where some of those from Vishkov died.---**Abe Altmark and his wife**, **David Yosef Tsimet, Shimon Altmark and his wife, Beinish Holland and his wife**.

After being freed from Siberia, some of the Vishkov Jews died in Turkistan from various sicknesses. **Faigel-Tsirel Holland**, **Shimon Kiris, Dobres, Sarah-Raiza Holland, Avraham Zuzel**.

Many Jews of Vishkov took part in the Partisan operations --- **Faivel Filler, Rachel Filler, Simcha-Moshe Naiman**, and the **Yanovich family**.

[Pages 43-47]

Wishkov (Wyszków) During Bad and Good Times
by M.Rabin (New York)
Translated by Hershl Hartman (Los Angeles, Ca)
Reviewed by Frida Grapa Markuschamer de Cielak (Mexico City)
Translation donated by the Historian Enrique Krauze (Mexico City, in 2013)

This article "Wishkov in Laydn un in Freyd" (Wyszkow in Pain and in Joy or During Bad and Good Times) does not pretend to consider all of Jewish life in Wishkov (Wyszków) in the interwar period. Wishkov's Jews, as part of Polish Jewry as a whole, shared in the developments and changes that affected all Jews in Congress Poland.

1.

The German occupation of Poland during World War I, destroyed the economic life of Poland and deeply affected Wishkov (Wyszków). Trade ceased, the peasants did not come to the shtetl[1]. There was nothing for them to buy and they feared bringing their products to sell lest the Germans confiscate them.

There was a total ban on transporting of goods, which was considered illegal "smuggling." Prices rose. Those who still had some money were able to pay the high prices and those who had neither reason - nor means - to engage in smuggling endured a bitter life. Malnourishment was a common occurence.

The Germans began to loot Poland. They transferred to Germany anything of any value. Even tree-sap was merchandise for them..., they fell upon the forest in Wyszków like locusts, making large wounds in a great number of trees to tap the tree-sap. The Wyszków forest stood wounded, dying, so that later the dead trees had to be cut down...but it was as though the forest had sworn its young generation, the young trees, to grow quickly, so that the forest would remain here. And wondrously, though forests generally grow slowly, the Wyszków forest was quickly restored...in a few years it was a young, dense forest.

Sport club "Maccabi," town of Wyszków

2.

The Senator's garden[2] could be seen by Wyszków's Jews through openings in the surrounding wall and they had various fantasies about it: about the types of trees and flowers it contained, which had certainly been brought from various countries to be planted there; about the varied birds whose names were unknown and who darted about as though in the heavenly Garden of Eden. The Germans opened the wall, established their command post, and the garden became for the Jews an unholy Gan-Eydn (Gehenna -Garden of Paradise}: it was there that Jewish men and women would come, sobbing and moaning, to seek relief from the orders that the German powers issued daily.

However, even as they were ruling over Poland and enslaving it economically, the Germans instituted political freedoms that were unheard of under Czarist rule[3]: political parties and societies began to be formed legally...

3.

When the Germans halted their advance into Russia at the Pinsk bogs, they evacuated a significant number of Jews westward into Poland. Some of them were sent to Pultusk and Wishkov [Wyszków]. The Germans called them "refugees," but the Jews immediately designated them, properly, as "homeless." I remember the day when the homeless were unexpectedly brought to Wyszków. Within minutes the word spread that homeless Jews had been brought to town and that food needed to be brought for them to the Beis-Medresh (The Synagogue-Big House of Study). Food was carried from every direction. The poorest folk tore bits of their meager food stocks and there was enough food donated to feed twice as many homeless. Wyishkover Jews "grabbed" homeless families to sleep in their homes and later they were settled in dwellings.

[Page 44]

Among the homeless were several educated young people. The homeless Jews, as was true of most from Lithuania and White Russia (Belarus), were dressed in the European style and Wyszków's Jews came to realize that a Litvak[4] is not a "crucifix-head," that one could be dressed as a "German" and still be knowledgeable in a Talmudic tractate...

At that time almost all Wyszków boys wore long (Hasidic) coats. Directly and indirectly, the group of educated young people began to exert an influence on the youth of Wyishkov (Wyszków). A couple of the homeless opened a

modern kheyder (elementary religious training), that was almost like a
school. Some gave lectures in Wyszków homes and the youth began to become
- in both an outer and inner sense - more secular, more mature. "Evenings
Box (called kestl ovntn[5])" were organized for questions and answers, a library
was established, gatherings of young people were organized, and, as usual -
(political) parties and associations began to form.

4.

The first openly public group to appear was the "Maccabi" sport
association. On a bright sunny day, in a garden somewhere, girls in blue-and-
white dresses and boys in "Maccabi" caps began gymnastic exercises and the
shtetl came running, as though to view some weird event, to see this
uniformed Jewish troop that had appeared in public in their "Maccabi"
clothes, risking their ability to return home at night because they knew what
was awaiting them on the part of their parents... But slowly mothers and
fathers became accustomed to this and, willy-nilly, the Hasidic Jews of
Wyszków began to become more tolerant to the developments of the new
times.

Publishers in Warsaw began to become active. (Czarist censorship had
been abolished). Many books began to be published. A Yiddish press of many
(political) leanings began to appear. Some Wyszków young men began to bring
a large amount of newspapers to town every day. When one person bought a
newspaper, it was read by ten others. In this way even the Hasidic cohort
began to become newspaper readers and began to be bound with the (current)
world and time and to creep out of their Wyszków Hasidic ancient ways...

The youth read a great deal of political literature and books and
discussions over various issues became the main content of young people's
lives. Groups were formed, affiliated with almost all the political parties in
Poland. Although Wyszków did not have much of a proletariat, this did not
prevent the formation of organizations with the programs and names of the
various Polish workers' parties.

5.

The formation of parties suddenly led to abolition of the caste-separation
that had ruled Jewish life in general, and particularly in the shtetlekh. A
bourgeoise child would not associate with the child of a craftsman. (A
bourgeoise child was one whose father's hand held neither a hammer nor a
needle. And since most Wyishkov Jews were of that category, bourgeoise
children were in the majority). It was not fitting for such a child to learn a

trade, so most young people hung about unemployed. But the break came on all at once - though the (social) psychology did not change as quickly. But conditions and time did change. Zionist emigration-propaganda and pressure to emigrate to other lands in general made hand-labor "kosher." At first, one might hear a parent's excuse: my son or daughter needs to learn that handicraft for use in Palestine, Argentina, America...This would imply that, if not for those countries, their children would not need to learn handicrafts...Though the gates of all those lands were still locked, the youth began to learn hand-labor skills, or to think about learning a craft.

6.

After the revolution in Germany (in 1918), when the Germans fled from Poland, on a certain day there appeared on the streets of Wyszków Poles with hunting rifles, seeking to disarm any remaining Germans. And, as usual, Jews felt that a change in power would not bode well for them... So, a spontaneous group of Jewish youths came together in a house to plan for Jewish self-defense in the event of danger. But official pronouncements quickly appeared on the streets, signed by the Polish militia in Wyszków, declaring that any act of violence would result in the death penalty. Wyszków's Jews calmed down.

[Page 45]

Upon the formation of the independent Polish state - at first, semi-democratic - life in Wyszków, began to approach normality. But then there occured the pogrom in Lemberg, news of which the Polish government forbade to be published. Nevertheless, all the details became known to us and the mood in the shtetl was bleak.

Later, when the Polish government established relations with other countries, and America became interested in the Polish political situation, Henry Morgenthau[6] came to Poland, partly to report to the American government on anti-Jewish excesses. And because Wyszków, although a small shtetl, with a small Jewish population, was close to Warsaw and had good roads, Morgenthau came to Wyszków. He visited the Rabbi and the entire shtetl came running, filling up the rabbi's house, while those who could not enter stood outside to catch a glimpse of Morgenthau.

The Jews regarded him as an 'American Moses Montefiore'. Characteristically, the youth stood aside, as though immediately perceiving that Morgenthau would not bring redemption to the Jews of Poland (as actually happened, according to the report he presented to the American government).

7.

In 1920 war broke out between Poland and the Bolshevik government [of the Soviet Union]. And though Jews were proportionately represented in the Polish military, all Jews in general and Jewish soldiers specifically were regarded with suspicion by the Polish government. And before the Bolshevik army drew close to Warsaw, Jews were arrested all over the place, including young people in Wyszków - without any charges whatsoever.

The Russian army approached Warsaw and while Wyszków was not a fortified city, its position on the Bug River and its highways made it a target for both armies. Wyszków changed hands regularly and though the town did not appear to have suffered externally - because armies then fought each other, not involving the civilian population - Wyszków was internally shaken up by the war.

Soon after the war Wyishkover Jews took a prominent place in the long lines at the American Consulate in Warsaw. The early 20s saw the beginning of emigration to America. And when the quota[2] blocked the way to the United States, people began heading to South America. Today there is hardly a country in South America without Wishkover from that immigration period, which thinned the ranks of the youth. But soon a new generation arose that found almost all lands barred to them. All that remained were hopes for Eretz Yisroel (Palestine-Eretz Israel) which could be reached through Hakhshoreh [training], Hekhaluts [pioneering] and other Zionist branches - and young people filled the ranks of those organizations.

8.

The youth organizations actually did bring much liveliness to Wyszków - not as much through their (political) programs as through their singing and dancing. And unlike the past, when one could hear the quiet singing of a folk song by a few girls behind closed windows and shutters, now the singing came out onto the streets. Almost every evening and until late into the night, one could hear the songs and dances of the (Zionist) pioneers.

Much of the liveliness was brought onto the youth scene by the newly-formed Maccabi orchestra. It played at various events. During its rehearsals, the quiet Wyszków night frequently echoed with the sound of an instrument, like the call of a shoyfer (shofar/ram's horn). For a certain time, the Maccabi orchestra was an institution in and of itself. And during the honeymoon period of Polish independence, when the First of May was recognized as an official holiday and the Polish proletariat in Wyszków paraded, the Jewish workers' organizations played a prominent role in the May Day demonstration and even the Maccabi orchestra was hired, although it had no relation whatsover with May Day.

The greatest part of the youth belonged to Zionist organizations. But there were also other political parties and each of them would bring in speakers. Almost all the prominent party leaders in Warsaw gave lectures in Wyszków. In addition to the party-speakers, the organizations would also bring literary lecturers, whose readings everyone attended, regardless of party affiliation.

Dramatic groups brought much joy to the young people. Every major organization tried to have such a group. At the beginning, the goal was to self-direct quite serious plays, but later they imported from Warsaw a professional actor to rehearse and direct.

When a performance was held in the firemen's hall, which served as a theater, the long-clothed Jews would not attend the "triyater," but young people would fill the hall to its very last corner. There were exceptions, when Hasidic Jews did attend the theater.

[Page 46]

Once, when (the very famous) Cantor Khazn Sirota gave a concert in the theater-hall, Hasidic Jews also came. I can still see before my eyes the famous cantor standing on the stage in Wyszków's theater-hall, mournfully regarding the low ceiling which caused him, for the first time, to refrain from hitting his highest notes...

Another event was the appearance of Hillel Zeitlin[8] in Wyszków. The personality of Hillel Zeitlin also brought long-clothed Jews to the theater-hall where his lecture took place. The utmost respect that Wishkover youth accorded a famous literary figure can be seen in the photograph that was taken at five o'clock in the morning of a group of Wyszków youth that had not slept all night so that they could accompany Hillel Zeitlin to the Warsaw-bound train - and to be photographed with him. It was in this way that our youth lived with poor food for its body but with a great deal of food for its spirit.

9.

The Hasidic Jews lived in a similar way: they also had their own parties and groupings. He who knew the holy books found his spiritual food in them.

Those who were not as close to the books listened to the recitation of a Talmudic chapter. In addition, they also had their own lecturers - the touring preachers and cantors, with which also involved some curious events. One such case concerned a Jew who appeared in the Beis-Medresh (Synagogue-House of Study) to preach. Suddenly, someone in the audience said that the Jew was not a preacher, but the (convert) missionary whom he had seen in Yadove (Jadów). A tumult arose in the shtetl and some of the porters prepared to take care of the "missionary." He would not have emerged whole from their hands.

However, when it was noticed that a policeman (the police station was opposite the synagogue) was taking an interest in the tumult, things quieted down. The policeman's attention was deliberately drawn elsewhere and it was decided that the Jew be led off to the train station and that his immediate departure be assured. All his arguments that it was a mistake, that he was not, heaven help us, a missionary, were of no avail and the Jew was led to the station like a groom is led to the khupe (hupa, wedding canopy), with guards alongside.

A few weeks later the Jew returned to Wyszków, loaded with packs of letters from rabbis confirming that he was so-and-so, the preacher. His droshe (sermon) was outstanding. And he received more contributions than ten other preachers combined, as an atonement for the sin of wrongly suspecting him.

Another time the incident involved a cantor. A Jew arrived, dressed half-German (modern), half-Orthodox, with a handsome visage, and introduced himself as so-and-so, the Ober Kantor [chief cantor] of a Berlin synagogue, who had fled Germany because of Hitlerism. He was welcomed with great honor, and tickets were sold to an evening service in the synagogue. The synagogue was packed. Experts said that such cantorial singing had never before been heard in Wyszków. A second evening service was demanded. But suddenly the "Kantor" disappeared, after a Wyszków young man happened to recognize him as a tailor from a shtetl near Bialystok...

10.

Thus the Jews in Wyszków lived their unique lives. A large part of the Wyishkover lived physically in Wyszków but in their thoughts - across all the seas! Almost everyone had a child, a father, a husband overseas, and the postman held a very important place in the life of Wishkover Jews. Every morning one could see, at the synagogue, facing the post office, groups of huddled Jewish men and women, waiting impatiently for the postman. When someone received a letter, he ran home in great joy. And those who did not receive letters would stand there sadly, lost in thought...

But it was not only individuals who lived in thought about overseas. The eyes of the Wyszków Establishment were focused on America, and by Hanukeh (Hanuka), they were calculating how much money the Wyishkover in America might send during the following year to help their needy hometown.

There was no lack of people to help in Wyszków. People needed help all year, sometimes this one, sometimes another. This was known to the "cure folk" who spied out a cold oven in winter, or where poverty was covered by a plush tablecloth while the pots stood empty in the kitchen. In Wyszków there were collectors for this kind of secret charity-giving. They were never asked for whom help was needed: they knew that one must contribute.

Wyszków also had many "professional" poor folk (beggars, both local and traveling-through), perhaps ten or fifteen a day. And no one ever left empty-handed, even at the poorest home. Charity was part of the budget of the poorest.

11.

Elections to the shtot-rat (Town Council) were an important part of Wyszkówer Jewish life, because the Town Council was responsible for meeting local needs in the shtetl, i.e.(meaning), the Jewish interests, as well. While the election laws allowed Jews to hold a majority on the Town Council, they did not avail themselves of the right, in order to keep the peace... The Jewish Councillors were composed of representatives of all the larger parties. And despite all the immigration tendencies and discrimination on the part of the right-wing Polish parties, Jews still felt like natives of many generations and demanded, called for, and demonstrated their rights. Characteristically, when a motion was brought to the Council to assign a certain amount of money for Zionist causes, it was not adopted because... not all the Jewish Councillors supported it: some, due to party politics; some, because "what will the Gentiles say..." Wishkov/Wyszków was Jewish. True, Jews did not constitute more than half the population, but its appearance was as if it were 90 percent Jewish. This was because Jews occupied the center of the shtetl. It was different on market days, when many more Christians than Jews were gathered in the shtetl. But even on market days the tumult of the peasants on the babske-barg (Grandma's Hill) could not still the Talmud-chanting of the yeshiva (academy of higher Talmudic learning) and the musical little voices of the children in the talmud-toyre (primary religious school).

[Page 47]

12.

Spring in Wyszków would come rapping on the shutters to announce its arrival. Sometimes - with the crash of melting ice on the Bug River and its echo in the forest; and sometimes - with the groan of the ice as it fought with the warm Spring and refused to surrender. And when the ice moved, the whole shtetl knew about the event - and the mood resembled that of the intermediate days of Jewish festivals. Storekeepers left their stores, craftsmen left their work-benches, and all headed to the wooden bridge where the ice flowed...

The Wyszków Jew was different: even though he appeared no different than Jews in another shtetl, he was still somehow different... Though they were an urban element, and like all urbanites, separated from nature, the magnificent Wyszków landscape brought them close to nature. True, no flowers were seen around Jewish houses, and rarely a flower pot in a Jewish window, as though to say: what need have we for flowers when we have the whole forest...

It was not only the youth who enjoyed the forest, but everyone. On Sabbath afternoons, during summer months, a stroll through the forest would begin. Starting along the whole length of the bridge, the Radzyminer and Lochówer highways, were lined for long distances with strolling Jews: young and old, men and women.

The Wyszków forest heard its fill of discussions about Zionism, Socialism and various world problems. The forest also heard its fill of the singing of various folk songs, love serenades and Hasidic nigunim (melodies), as well as divrey-toyre (Torah elucidations). During the last years another rabbi would come to the Wyszków forest on summer vacation and Hasidim would, with much singing, observe Sabbath suppers and the final Sabbath meals, the "leave-taking of the (Sabbath) queen".

13.

The "daughters of Yaakov" girls played a special role in Wyszków. From the various groupings of the Wyszków Jewish population, the younger ones would study in the Beys-Yakov school after attending the Polish public school. And the older girls had a separate class in the Beys-Yakov school. The curriculum of the Beys-Yakov school depended on the qualifications of the particular teacher. Very often the Beys-Yakov school had teachers of very high spiritual quality. The Beys-Yakov girls were distinguished from other girls by their modest clothing, quieter speech and shy gazes.

14.

In the years preceding the Second World War, during the "stalls[2] epoch" when Jewish-owned stalls in Wyszków were removed from the best spots on the bridge and were moved down into the marketplace, the Endeks (ruling anti-semitic National Democratic Party) artificially created Christian traders with stalls in the marketplace. They brought in peasants, gave them money, and overnight declared them to be "traders." The mood was sombre. Jews feared what might befall the next day - but even then they did not lose their sense of humor. Jewish and Christian market stalls stood side by side, and the newly-minted Christian "trader" wanted to learn something from the Jewish trader... Once, one of these new traders asked his neighbor, a Jewish stall-keeper, why he, the Pole, wasn't making any sales, while the Jew was doing a brisk business, though both were selling the same goods. The Jew replied: "That's precisely why you're not selling anything, because you have the same goods as I; if you were selling something that I don't have, they'd be grabbing it up." Then the new trader asks: "What would you suggest that I stock for sale?" The Jew replies: "Bring in, for example, socks with fingers; I myself will buy them from you at a good profit..." So the new trader folded up his sales table and took the train to Warsaw to buy socks with fingers from the traders on Nalewki Street. The Warsaw Jewish traders didn't mock him, but each sent him to another, until the last one told him that such merchandise could be obtained only on Marshalkovska Street (in Warsaw) from the major Christian wholesalers...

*

Such are my recollections about the Wyszków of the past.

Footnotes

1. shtetl = A Yiddish diminutive term for "town."

2. Senator's Garden (or Park) was the site of the Polish high school building, called gymnasium; those premises were taken by the Russian Army for their headquarters. Under the possession of the Poles, Russians or Germans, access to that garden was forbidden to the Jews.

3. From 1815 to 1915, the major part of Poland, with a large Jewish population, was under the rule of the Czarist Empire

4. Litvak = Lithuanian Jews who did not adhere to the customs of Hasidism.

5. kestl ovntn = During the lectures in Wyszków homes, an "Evenings box" was available for questions on any subject which were written on slips and deposited in a box from which the lecturer drew at random and responded to.

6. Henry Morgenthau, Sr, had been a U.S. Ambassador to Turkey during World War I and participated in the Paris Peace Conference as an advisor on Eastern Europe and the Middle East. His son was Secretary of the Treasury during `President Franklin D.Roosevelt's New Deal.

7. quota =U.S. quotas by nationality established in 1924 that severely curbed Eastern European immigration.

8. Hillel Zeitlin (1871-1942) was an extremely influential critic, a Yiddish and Hebrew writer who edited the Yiddish newspaper Moment. He was killed by Nazis in the Warsaw ghetto.

9. stalls = stands, like vegetable stands, fruit stands, etc., which is the translation most appropiate for this paragraph.

[Page 48]

Pictures of the town
by ... Baranek, (New York)
Translated by Hershl Hartman (Los Angeles, Ca)
Reviewed by Frida Grapa Markuschamer de Cielak (Mexico City)
Translation donated by the Historian Enrique Krauze (Mexico City)

Hillel Zeitlin Won't Come to Wyishkov (Wyszków)

Before Poland gained its independence, a few middle-class boys and girls looked toward Warsaw and decided to schedule a Literary Evening with the famous writer and thinker, Hillel Zeitlin[1]. They actually wrote to him about it.

When the Wyishkover Rabbi, a clever Jew but of the old school, learned that the young people were planning a gathering with a Warsaw writer, he became truly frightened: 'We Jews are in exile, after all. "Fonye" (the police) might think that we're organizing against the regime. Don't we Jews have enough troubles already?!'

So he called in the most distinguished men of the shtetl. At a meeting in his house they considered how they might prevent the young people from becoming involved with gatherings and Literary Evenings, which might, heaven forbid, bring disaster to the community. It was decided that the following shabes (Sabbath), an announcement would be made in all the synagogues warning parents to keep their youngsters from engaging in such matters...

When the initiators of the Literary Evening learned that there were attempts being made to disrupt their plans, they became even more determined. "Look here," they argued, "we're not living in the old days anymore. Why can't they see and hear their beloved writer?!"

A major debate broke out in the shtetl. The parents strove to convince their children, using both kind and stern measures, that they were heading down bad roads. But the youth persisted. They applied to the authorities for a permit for the event. It so happened that at that time a troop of Don Cossacks was quartered in the shtetl. So an agreement was made with one of their officers, by greasing his palm, to send some Cossacks to maintain order at the evening, because they expected the pious Jews to certainly attempt a disruption.

The Rabbi, for his part, was not idle. Learning that Cossacks would be at the hall and it would be impossible to break up the planned evening, he telegraphed Hillel Zeitlin in Warsaw and asked, on behalf of domestic tranquility in Wyishkov, and to avert additional woes for the House of Israel, that he not come for the evening but remain in Warsaw.

Hillel Zeitlin, upon receiving the telegram, understood that it would be better not to go. He immediately notified the Wyishkov youths that he was canceling his visit; perhaps he might come some other time.

The youth replied by telegraph that there was nothing to fear because Cossacks would escort him.

And the shtetl threw all its energy into preparing for the Literary Evening. Everyone gathered at the hall, patiently awaiting the arrival of the speaker. Regretably, Hillel Zeitlin did not arrive. Their waiting was in vain.

Hillel Zeitlin actually did come to Wyishkov - but about ten years later...

If Dowries Will Be Abolished He Supports The Party Platform...

When, after the First World War, the news became known that Polish citizens had the right to vote, great joy and gladness broke out in the shtetl. Everyone was overjoyed. No small thing! From now on they could elect their own people to the town administration!

Every party called meetings and nominated its candidates.

Things grew lively and tumultuous in Wyishkov. But one party seemed to be having difficulty with the matter of elections.

The pious nominated as a candidate their Rabbi – a clever Jew and a good preacher. The Zionists nominated one of their leaders – a man with a silver tongue, an impassioned speaker. The Bundists[2] had a bit of a problem. They were unable to find an appropriate candidate. Almost all their members were still too young to run for office and those who could run were self-employed. And running a candidate who owned a tailoring, shoemaking or carpentry shop – that was something the workers could not abide. "What sense would it be for our candidate to be a...bloodsucker!!"

After several meetings it was decided that their candidate would be the feldsher[3] He is a kosher representative of the workers: he cares for everyone; many of the poor even receive his care gratis. Besides, he is a person of knowledge. He even reads Polish newspapers. It was decided to have a talk with him.

When the committee, consisting of several apprentices, came to the feldsher, he just happened to be sitting in front of his house reading a Polish newspaper from Warsaw to which he subscribed. The apprentices told him that they were sent from the Bundist party and wanted him to agree to be their candidate in the city council election.

The feldsher listened to them calmly and then questioned them as to what the Bund was fighting for, what its program was. The young people began to explain that the Bund combats the evil rulers, the bosses – the bloodsuckers. The Bund wants equality for everyone. That the world be just and equitable, that money be abolished.

Hearing that idea, the feldsher asks: ...

[Page 49]

"If money is abolished, how will one buy what one needs?"

The young people reply that it's a simple matter. Everyone will work and whatever anyone needs will be free. For example: If someone needs a pair of shoes, he would go to a cobbler and order them. And when the cobbler needs bread, he would go to the baker and take as much bread as he needs. In that way, everyone would obtain all that was necessary.

"Well, and when I need to marry off my daughters, how will I obtain their dowries if there's no money?" the feldsher asks.

"Girls won't need dowries then, they'll marry without a dowry," the young people explained.

"In that case, if there will be no need for dowries," says the feldsher, "you may add me to your list of candidates. I like your party very much."

He Earned Himself a Velvet Hat

In Wyishkov there was a khevre-tilim (a self-led psalms congregation). They had their own little synagogue with a gabeh (trustee), distinguished Jews and common folk. It was conducted as were all other self-led congregations.

Avrom-Borukh, the cobbler – the shoemaker, one of the congregants, wanted very much to have a velvet hat. Avrom-Borukh had a good singing voice and often sang the prayers in front of the ark. But earning a velvet hat was difficult for him, because he could go no further than singing the opening prayers at the ark on shabes. He could show his abilities only on rosh-khoydesh (first of the month) and during kholemoyd (intermediate days of peysakh – Passover – and sukes/sukot – Feast of Booths – festivals). Then he would deliver a halell (song of praise) that would thrill the soul. But he was not allowed to conduct shabes or holiday services.

One shabes Avrom-Borukh steeled his resolve and determined to lead the full shakhres (morning service). What did he do? As soon as he had finished singing "in front" – the opening prayer – he proceeded in an exalted nigun (melody), rendering the next prayer, shokhen ad ("He who lives forever"). But at that very same moment he was shoved aside by a "distinguished householder" who had the privilege of praying at the ark on shabes and who proceeded to lead the prayers.

The common folk were shocked at the daring impertinence of the "distinguished Jew." When the Torah reading began a tumult broke out. The common folk protested by preventing the reading. Immediately, two camps developed. Arguments between them arose. Later, a din toyre (judicial hearing) was held.

As a result of all this, the common folk decided to take over the running of the little synagogue. At simkhes-toyre (the Rejoicing of the Law, – ninth day of sukis/sukot), Avrom-Borukh was chosen to be gabeh of the congregation.

And that was how Avrom-Borukh was elevated. And on shabes breyshis (Genesis Sabbath – when Torah reading begins over again), Avrom-Borukh came into the synagogue in a velvet hat with a broad crown – and, before the ark, conducted the entire morning service.

But He Is a Cobbler After All!

A group of Wyishkov cobblers-shoemakers, conducted a khevre known with the name of mesiles yoyshrim (The Way of the Just). They had a little synagogue with their own gabeh and their own shames (beadle – Rabbi helper). They conducted their affairs as did the other self-led congregations in town. They held celebrations, they were involved in politics, and there were disagreements, later ironed out – as among all decent folk.

Once one of the cobblers commissioned the writing of a seyfer-toyre (Torah Scroll), just as was done among wealthier folk. At the siyum ha'seyfer (ceremonial completion of the handwritten copy), when the Torah was finished and it was to be brought into the little synagogue, a great dedication celebration was arranged.

The cobblers did not work on that day. They themselves, along with their wives and children, dressed up in their Sabbath clothes. The seyfer-toyre was carried through the marketplace with great ceremony. It was led by the town band. The klezmer played and cymballed and the cobblers formed a ring around them. They sang psalms and hymns of praise. The cobblers danced with such verve and strength that the houses in the shtetl trembled. Why spare themselves? Need they worry that the soles of their shoes might fall off? No fear – they could later cobble on new ones.

And as they were dancing and celebrating, the circle was entered by the town's gentile cobbler, who grabbed the hands of the other cobblers and joined in the dance...

At first the cobblers were confused: a gentile at a holy Jewish celebration?! The Gentile perceived the confusion and let out a cry:

"It's true, people, that I'm not a Jew – but I am a cobbler, after all!"

Beynish the porter takes a nap in the street

Translator's Footnotes

1.   Hillel Zeitlin, (1871-1942) See footnote No. 8 in previous chapter.

2.   The Bundists, the Jewish Socialist labor party, "General Jewish Workers' Alliance (Bund)"

3.   feldsher(- A barely-trained barber-surgeon, usually the only medical practitioner in rural areas of the Russian empire.

[Page 50]

Romantically, Socially, Idealistically
by by Yekhiel Bzhoza (Los Angeles)
Translated by Ruth Fisher Goodman (Wilmington, DE)
Reviewed by Frida Grapa Markuschamer de Cielak (Mexico City)
Translation donated by the Historian Enrique Krauze (Mexico City)

I don't know exactly how many Jews lived in Wishkov (Wyszków). Certain countrymen estimate the population to be ten thousand. Another old resident told me that 1500 Jewish families lived there. I only know that there was a large and a small synagogue, a Zionist small shul (synagogue), a large Gerer 'shtibl'[1][2], and five or six other Hasidic[3] small 'study houses'. The small 'Bi-leh', as it was called, had its own 'shul' aside from other small shuls and minyanim (groups of ten men) scattered throughout the village.

The shtetl lay at the water's edge of our River Bug (pronounced 'boog') and twenty viarst[4] beyond unites with the Narev River, and together they flowed into the Vistula. In the summer months, they (the Jews) used to send a lot of lumber to Germany and many Jewish families made a fine living from this occupation. The lumber-trade was a big issue for us. The Dan's, the Yakubovicz's, the family Shkarlat and Sokol – with their sawmills, the countless 'subsidiaries' – Vistinetski with the Shrik'es, "der Shvartzer" ("Black") Yitzkhok and his sons and horses and others, that dragged the blocks of wood from the sawmills to the water; the Jewish fisher-men who helped put together rafts and then take them out to the middle of the river.

My father's two-story inn, stood on the hill near the edge of the water, and was the very first house near the wooden bridge. From my childhood on,

Hillel Zeitlin visits Wyszków:

First row -- from right to left (standing): **Epsteyn Alter; Epsteyn Tsinamon/Cynamon Dovid; Novominski; Holtsman/Holtzman Moyshe; Neiman/Naiman/Najman/ Itche; Epsteyn Henekh; Segal Yekhiel; Likhtenshteyn; Hana Malke; Orenstein/Orensztejn Szmuel-Eli; Epsteyn Moyshe;**

Second row: **Funt; Levin Sore; Rinek Yankev; Shkarlat Rafoyl; Orenstein/Orensztejn Perl; Fayntsayg/Feinzaig Pinkhes; Tik; Pitsenik (Teacher); Tchishever Velvl;**

Third row: **Kirzhner; Shkarlat Pesyie; Kohn Blume; Shkarlat Blume; Shkarlat Rifke; Gilbert Shloyme; Zeitlin Hillel; Yungshteyn (Goldman); Ayzenshtat Feige; Grosbard Miriam; Orenstein/Orensztejn Pesie; Ba'harab/Barab Itche;**

Last (lower) row:*_ **Bzoza Alte; Novominski Chaye; Shkarlat Brayne; Mondry Hershl; (The rest of the names - unknown)**

[Page 51]

I was interested in following everything that happened at the river and around it.

On the other side of the bridge, a stretch of the Radzyminer highway (road to Radzymin) started on the right, and on the left – the Lochower highway (Road to Łochów). But the important thing was: that the forest began at that point. Young and old loved that forest, but mostly, the youngsters because there they met girls and went strolling with them. They would sing Hebrew and Yiddish songs with gusto; they would discuss Jewish issues and world problems late into the night.

After the outbreak of World War I, and the influx of homeless from Pinsk and Brysk we were greatly moved by our social duty. Among the refugees, were a number of intelligent people: Hebrew teachers and gifted social workers and with their help we immediately organized a broad literary cultural activity which included concerts, debates, discussions and adult evening courses.

We already had from before, two libraries. The librarian in the "larger" library was Pearl Kuper. I was the librarian two evenings a week. Bella Teff worked in the smaller library.

After the war and with the start of the State of Poland, our youth became more knowledgeable and as a result of this they divided themselves parties and subdivisions (smaller parties).

At that time, we attempted to found a professional general union. Isaac (Itzkhok) Marcuskamer and I were active in this venture. We also organized a cooperative that was very successful the first few years. The dramatic endeavor was also split in two: a general and the workers' dramatic section. I was by then very strongly involved in theater and, therefore, worked with both groups. From time to time I would produce plays for both ensembles. In the general dramatic circle, Malka Shkarlat (Marcus/Marcuskhamer), was "a force." Her brother was truly talented. Abraham Marcuschamer / Markuskhamer was the most dedicated member in the workers' dramatic section and the rehearsals were generally held in his home.

What I wanted to bring out is that: from as far back as our young years, we were romantics, socially (conscious) and idealistic...

Footnotes

1. shtibl (pl. shtiblekh) a religious study-house where the scholars were deeply immersed in the study of the gemore (part of the Talmud) and to studying Torah.

2. Gerer shtibl or shtiblekh, refers to the religious study-house whose scholars followed the learnings of the Hasidic Rabbi Yitzchak Meir Alter (1798-1866) of Ger (the Yiddish name of Góra Kalwaria, a small town in Poland), probably the largest and most influential Hasidic group not only in Wyszków, but in Poland.

3. Hasidic Judaism or Hasidism (the word translates to "piety" or "loving-kindness"): it is a branch of Ortodox Judaism that promotes spirituality through the popularization and internalization of the Jewish mysticism as the fundamental aspect of the faith. It was founded in 18th-century Eastern Europe by Rabbi Israel Baal-Shem-Tov as a reaction against overly legalistic and rigid Judaism.

4. viarst or viars = a measurement of approximately 13 miles.

* Note: According to Mitchell Mondry, from Birmingham, MI (US) the woman on the far right is Adele Mondry, and the man on the far left is Hershl Mondry; these are Mitchell's grandparents

A Bundle of Memories from Days Past
by Chaim Levin, Givat Hashlosha [kibbutz near Petach Tikva, Israel]
Translated by Alan Hirshfeld

So many events and years have passed since I was in Wyszków, that it it is hard for me to remember dates and details. I only remember that our lives there were full of rich content and movement. I lived in Wyszków during the best years of a person's life – their youth. Until I was 24, I hardly left the city from the day of my birth. I will attempt to put something on paper from those years.

During the first world war a group of friends (Klosky, Mittelsbach, Mendel Rosenberg, Yakov Shtellung and others) set up a branch of "Yugent" [youth] in the city. This was an organization of Zionist-socialist youth (of the Poale Tzion party). We devoted much effort to this organization; educational activities, and many-branched cultural work, classes, lectures, parties, and a library. The work was semi-legal; we were always suspect by the government. Nevertheless we also started to organize the youths who were working at the shopkeepers – tailors, shoemakers and carpenters – learning a trade.

The custom then was that these apprentices would work three years without pay and they were also exploited by the shopkeepers to work in their private homes. It was very difficult work for us. Even the parents of the youths objected to our efforts for fear that the youths would be fired. The meetings with the youth would always take place out of doors, in remote corners of the city, in order to hide from the shopkeepers and the police. Nevertheless we often succeeded in improving the lot of one youth or another.

These youths later became members of the youth organization and the parties. For all these projects we volunteered willingly, with the aim of helping these working youths. More than once we contributed our own funds for the expenses. At the same time there existed in the city a youth group of the "Bund" – "Zukunft" [future]. We always had debates with them, for they were opposed to Zionism. But the main debates were in public, following the speeches of lecturers that each party would invite from Warsaw. But besides that we were very active and there were endless meetings in connection with every important incident in Judaism or in the world.

In the city there was a large library in Yiddish and to a lesser extent, in Hebrew. We were proud of this library. We all derived knowledge from it. There were many scientific books there. And when parties arose, each tried to influence the library according to its outlook, and to introduce changes consistent with its spirit. This led to arguments, and whoever had more readers at the library pulled it toward his view. Assemblies of readers more than once pulled in the other direction, towards a different party. Finally a group of us friends arose with the goal of maintaining a proper library, as a general cultural asset, and we worked out a special set of bylaws for the assembly of readers. In it there was a paragraph that all the parties would have equal representation, and that it was forbidden to transfer the library to any one party. The assembly approved the bylaws and from then on the library proceeded to grow. No community board or institution supported this library. There were token charges for use of the books and we covered the expenses by arranging parties, performances, etc. and particularly by voluntary donations. At the end of the first world war it was partly destroyed through removals and confiscations by the Polish government, in whose eyes everything was 'tref' and forbidden.

In those years there was also a clubhouse on Shkolna Street that we called the "Verein" (a special interest group). Actually it was a place for various cultural activities in Yiddish by individuals, members of socialist parties, who could do cooperative work quietly without political debates. In particular, I remember my good friend, Beinush Ostrovyak. I was a Zionist and he a leftist, a communist. Nevertheless together we did almost all of this intensive work. We established a chapter of "Tzisha" (Central Yiddish School-organization). We had strong ties with the central [office] in Warsaw. We organized a school, both in the day and the evening, for poor children.

We acquired books and writing materials and hired teachers. This school existed for several years and the funds for it we got from monthly membership dues and from modest admission fees to lectures. All of the administrative work was by volunteers and the students paid nothing. It must be remembered that the hostile government, particularly the Polish, did not give us rest. Every lecturer that we brought to the city was suspect in their eyes. We had to use subterfuge and all kinds of covers so that they would not interfere.

Once, during a lecture in the "Verein", at 10 o'clock at night, the police surrounded the building and started an intensive search. This was a result of some informer. However, they found nothing suspicious except for one socialist book and some papers, among them a draft of bylaws of a "Hechalutz" chapter that I had. Before the search I had hidden the notebook, but after we had left the hall they overturned everything and found it. The next day, with the intervention of some respected individuals, the police returned the bylaws for they already had suspected that there was an illegal organization. The bylaws were in Hebrew and when it was translated for them they left us alone. However, they held us all night until almost dawn; but that did not prevent us from continuing our work in the succeeding days. The town was like a cauldron over this affair, and for several weeks we were forced to move the school to a different building.

Because of such events we were also forced to arrange our First-of-May meetings in the forest...with a circle of guards surrounding them. Of course only the members of the socialist parties participated. Almost all the parties existed and held activities under some sort of cover. Only the General Zionists, "Aguda" carried on legally and had an open clubhouse. And since the adults among them were not active, we, the Hechalutz youth, used their clubhouse frequently. We even moved the large library there, because that was the most secure location.

I recall a meeting in the home of Eli-Meir Goldman on the "Warsaw Road" (Kosciucsko Street), while the Red army was in the city, at the end of WWI. The meeting was called at the initiative of the Communists, with the participation of an army officer who chaired the meeting. They ordered, in the name of the government, that all the socialist parties disband. The "Bund" then announced that it was disbanding because "socialism has come" and the Jewish question would be solved. We, Poale Tzion, felt and knew that this was not true. We announced, after some discussion, that we were connected to the center in Warsaw and that when the Red army would shortly enter Warsaw an answer would be forthcoming for the country as a whole, since we were only a branch chapter. Our answer was received with disbelief, but the meeting broke up. The army was in our vicinity for a week and when it retreated many communists retreated with it. The next day we heard that the Polish army that entered the city shot and killed two Poles and a Jew of the communists who were caught, without any trial.

The Poale Tzion party of course continued to operate, but the "Bund" for a long time could not raise its head, because they had disbanded. After that our Zionist activity intensified. We collected money for the JNF [Jewish National Fund] and for the KPAI (fund for the workers of Palestine) of that time. We expanded "Hechalutz", etc. When the oppression and the persecution of the Jewish minority in Poland began, emigration to Palestine began from Wyszków, too, naturally from the younger generation.

I remember, however, the emigration of one adult Jew before this. And this was the event: A Jew by the name of Rosenzweig, a simple shoemaker, came to my father in 1920, as I recall, and since he knew him to be an active Zionist, asked that he help him go to Palestine. My father was very surprised and asked the Jew how he would make out in Palestine with his large family? And there were [violent] incidents then in Palestine and only young people, if any, went there, not adults. But the Jew announced that he was travelling to Jerusalem and was taking a pistol. He would bake a loaf of bread and put the gun inside the loaf. My father, when he saw the enthusiasm of Rosenzweig, helped him and recommended him to the "Mizrachi" institutions. The Jew went and later brought his family. And to this day part of the family lives in Jerusalem. This was a unique event in those years. Most of the Jews were either apathetic toward Zionism or opposed it because of their religious orthodoxy. My father had many arguments with these Jews, the Chasidim and the rabbi. He frequently spoke in the "beis medrash" [study] on Zionist topics on behalf of "Mizrachi". The chasidim and the rabbi called him an "apikoros" [non-believer] because of his Zionism. And when my father z"l died, the rabbi and the chevra kadisha objected to erecting the gravestone on his grave because there was a star of David on it.

There was a great conflict in the city between the Zionists and the "misnagdim". This was in 1926. But even before this, in 1924, the first of the "Hechalutz" members from Wyszków left for Palestine and this was a great joy for us. The dancing at the train station went on for a long time. And in 1925 I too went.

[Page 52]

Memories of the old town
by Moyshe Stolik (Tel-Aviv)
Translated by Khane Feigl Turtletaub (Evanston, IL)
Reviewed by Frida Grapa Markuschamer de Cielak (Mexico City)
Translation donated by the Historian Enrique Krauze (Mexico City)

In my mind I see Wishkov(Wyszków)[1] as a small town of great Jewish poverty and happy holidays. On the streets – people are running and hurrying; each person is concerned with his own business, his own worries, problems and hopes.

The years of my childhood in that town, from 1929 to 1939, have been etched especially in my memory. I spent time there with my parents, sisters and brother, uncles and aunts, male and female cousins, comrades and friends. Jews have been here for many, many generations. Most of them – were merchants, businessmen and artisans.

The town also had its social leaders and activists. I am reminded of that inflexible and energetic leader for Jewish rights, the Councilman at City Hall, Khaim-Nosn Vengrov (who died some time ago in Israel), also Doctor Lajcher and the three dentists: Kerner, Leshtshinski/Lesinski, Gutshtat. (There was also) the feldsher[2] (Malowanczyk/ Malovantchik) of whom evil tongues said that he did not always write down the correct prescription. And there were the various merchants: And there were the various merchants: Berish Wilenski/Vilenski, Yoyne/Yone Taub, Czerwonagura/Cherwonagura, Pshetitski, Borukh Krishtal (Kristal/ Krysztal) and others. The artisans were involved in practically every traditional Jewish trade: tailors, shoemakers, bakers, barbers, wagon-drivers, water carriers, woodchoppers, dorozhkazhes[3] and shipping agents. In my mind hover the names Khaim Markhevka, one of the tailors from Warsaw – Shukrin, Shedletski/Siedlecki, Zuzel, the road hewer Ostrowiak, Dovid Lichtman/Likhtman and his sons who traveled to Warsaw twice a week to bring back merchandise. And the (lathe) turner Psheshtshelyenyietz/Przestrzeleniec and his family who also sold milk.

[Page 53]

And who could forget the fabric merchants, who were at the marketplace every Tuesday and Friday and spent the other days of the week – traveling around fairs. The bakers of the shtetl were renowned: Butche Stolik, Pshemyierover, Eli-Meyer Goldman, Lis the lady baker, the widow, who baked black bread with leaves. They called her "Moyshelikhe"[4]. Also in Rynek (market) there was a lady baker, a widow, who baked flat breads of barley and bagels.

On the Sabbath it was joy to see our women and girls carrying home the tcholenter[5]. (To this very day, I still have the taste of a Wishkever tchunt in my mouth...). We also remember

Rabbi Morgnshtern(Morgnsztern), who lived in Rynek and was the moreh-hoyreh (final judge) of rabbinic law from Ostrow Street. My father, Tzvi-Yosef Stulik[6] z'l (may he rest in peace) studied a page of gemore (Talmud) each evening.

And now, the Jewish community led by the Gerer Khosid, President Epsztein; the judges, the ritual slaughterers, the shamoshim[7], the khazanim (cantors), with the head cantor of the large synagogue Malkhiel (the) Shoykhet (ritual slaughterer) and his famous choir. The various businessmen who lead the organization to help the poor (hakhnosas-orkhim), the organization to help marry off indigent brides (hakhnosas-kaleh), the interest-free loan society (gmilas-khesedim), the burial society (khesed shel emet), and many, many more, who worked with greater devotion.

In the other synagogues and shtiblekh[8] the prayer leaders were: Yankl (the) Shoykhet and Itche-Meyer (the) Shoykhet; Khaim-Henakh Shtelung/Sztelung (leader of the prayers at the Gerer shtibl[9]) and cantors of the Otwotzker, Kotsker and Radzyminer khasidim[10]. Besides the minyanim (a minyan, sing., a group of 10 people required for prayers) there was no lack of gabaim[11], beadles, caretakers and... arguments. I am reminded of two teachers who taught me: one from Lodz and Parniarz[12]. The latter lived at the house of the blind Feyge, who sold yeast. This teacher would beat his students with a rope, which had been soaked in water...

The young people in town were, for the most part, from the workers' element and after work took an active part in the social life in town. They were active in the Bund,[13] Communists, Agudas Yisroel[14]. Most of them belonged to the various Zionist groups – general Zionist, the leftist Workers' Zionists (Poalei-tzion), Young Guardians (Ha'shomer Ha'tzair), Young Pioneers (Ha'khalutz Ha'tzair), Mizrakhi, League for Working Land of Israel. They also took part in sports: [the organizations were] H'aPoel and Maccabi (Makabi). In the year 1934, a preparatory kibbutz[15]was founded. It was part of Gush Gerukhov. The pride of the Zionist Movement in town was – the large library.

Zionist life in town was formed by well-known activists: Kaluski, Leybish Pshtitski(Przetycki), Yitzkok-Itche Ba'harab/Barab, Mayer Shtchigel, Ruben Levin, Moyshe Stulik (Stolik), Leyeh Hiller, Leyeh Nudel, Binyomin-Khaim Bruk, Kwiatek, Alte Tchekhanovietska/Tszekhanovietska, Yoysef Leviner and many, many others.

In the year 1935, the Jewish Communists opposed the preparatory kibbutz in Wyszków. They broke their windows and assaulted and beat the members of this group. The writer of these lines even received a threatening letter, because he dared to defend the members of the kibbutz. For a certain period of time, he (Moyshe Stolik) had to leave the city.

These are my memories of Wyszków.

Footnotes

1. The correct Polish spelling is Wyszków, not Wishkov or Vishkov.

2. Feldsher = fake, an un-official Doctor-Surgeon who also was an old-time Barber.

3. dorozhkazhes = Slavic word that translates to road-hewers.

4. Moyshelikhe= from Moyshe= (Perhaps her father or her husband's name was Moyshe).

5. Tschont or tchunt or cholent =Traditional Sabbath stew, a baked dish of meat, potatoes, white beans and legumes; a slow cooking dish, a tcholenter, is the pot for slow cooking. Cholent was kept warm by cooking it the day before Sabbath.

6. The name Stolik is spelled here differently (with a u, Stulik) but as the author of this article is writing about his father, this might have been a printing mistake.

7. shames (pl., shamosim) = assistant to the rabbi in a synagouge; beadle.

8. shtibl (pl., shtiblakh) a religious study-house where the scholars were deeply immersed in the study and discussions of the gemore (part of the Talmud) and the studying of the Torah.

9. Gerer shtibl= a religious study-house with followers, students from what was probably the largest and most influential Hasidic group in Poland, founder of this group was Rabbi Yitzchak Meir Alter (1798-1866) of Ger, the Yiddish name of Góra Kalwaria, a small town in Poland.

10. Hasidic Judaism or Hasidism (the word translates to "piety" or "loving-kindness"): it is a branch of Orthodox Judaism that promotes spirituality through the popularization and internalization of the Jewish mysticism as the fundamental aspect of the faith. It was founded in the 18th century, in Eastern Europe by Rabbi Israel Baal-Shem-Tov as a reaction against overly legalistic and rigid Judaism.

11. Gabe (gabaim, pl.,) = Trustee or warden of a public institution, especially a synagogue; manager of the affairs of a Hasidic Rabbi.

12. Parniarz – It is not clear to what the writer refers, i.e., a person's name, occupation or a town.

13. Bund – A Socialist Jewish labor party organization, "General Jewish Workers' Alliance."

14. Agudas Yisroel – is a Haredi Jewish communal organization in the United States loosely affiliated with the international world Agudath Israel. Both those organizations are affiliated with the Hasidic and the non-Hasidic Mitnagdim/Lithuanian Jewish groups.

15. 'kibbutz' and 'preparatory kibbutz' = Kibbutz is a collective community in Israel that was traditionally based on agriculture. 'Preparatory kibbutz' refers to preparing young people for emigrating to Israel.

A Wishkever Melody
by A. Pat[1] (New York)

Translated by Khane Feigl Turtletaub (Evanston, IL)

Reviewed by Frida Grapa Markuschamer de Cielak (Mexico City)

Translation donated by the Historian Enrique Krauze (Mexico City)

Before the Nazi holocaust descended on the Jews of Poland, Wishkov (Wyszków)[2] occupied quite a prominent place among the well-known settlements. The very name of Wyszków is accompanied by a melody of love and longing for Jewish cultural revival. This deeply rooted love centers around the marketplace, which embodies in it a tradition of struggle to maintain an individual personality for the survival of the nation. In both the old and the new synagogues, Jews made every possible effort to see that the eternal light should never go out.

Wyszków did not arise from the new cultural spirit of the times. The reading circle, several theatrical performances and important lectures connected the generation of young people with the Jews of Israel. Several local and also invited Jewish actors, writers and wordsmiths performed in the Fireman's Hall. In talking about passing one's time pleasurably, one cannot omit from memory the bridge over the Bug River and the gorgeous forest – that listened to the young people's happiness and painful experiences with its eternally secretive rustling of leaves in the summer and the mysterious whistling of the wind in the winter-time.

At the beginning of the 20s, Wyszków had already begun to broaden its horizon with a completely new tune. The awakening young people were proud of their own Maccabi Orchestra, their Dramatic Club and the Jewish book (club). A younger generation to be proud grew up, that with the well known Hasidic[3] fervor, longed for knowledge and felt the necessity of jettisoning backwardness and isolation. There arose new groups and (political) parties – a natural continuation of the lovely Hasidic tradition that the youth of Wyszków had inherited from the previous generation. With the enthusiasm and the Holy Sabbath love for the people there out in the street, the song of liberation and national as messianic redemption was heard. With the spirit of poetic rapture in their hearts and with the new stirrings of the time, there arose a new relationship to language and folk people that recognized the cultural importance of these concepts to the aspirations of the younger generation.

[Page 54]

At that time, the youth of Wyszków invited the great author and thinker, Hillel Zeitlin[4] to give a talk. Although the extremists in the Hasidic movement exhibited strong opposition to the invitation, his talk turned into a true folk gathering. Jews of every persuasion came: those wearing short jackets and shaved chins and those wearing Hasidic garb and beard and ear locks. The patrician's facial appearance of dignity and his piercing black eyes commanded everyone's attention and words conveyed to the beautiful audience a confidence and belief in his own strength. The great scholar spoke about worldliness in the spirit of the old Jewish tradition. His words seemed to come from a modern Sociologist – but they also showed closeness to Midrash[5] and Mishnayes[6]. From that talk, Wyszków felt the great importance and poetic acuity, which was hidden in the Yiddish language. At that time Hillel Zeitlin personified both: the greatness of a Torah scholar and the simplicity of a folk person.

After that festive gathering, which went on long into the night, the guest missed his train back to Warsaw. No one had thought of cutting things short, because everyone was in such a festive mood. When the guest discovered that he would have to wait until the next morning for a train, he settled down in earnest to respond to the questions posed by the gathered audience. Long after the townsfolk were fast asleep behind closed doors and shuttered windows, a group of young people in town remained with their guest. The group that escorted Hillel Zeitlin looked like a tzadik (pious, saintly man) surrounded by his Hasidim (his devotees) that went outside into the street for some fresh air that wafted a refreshing breeze under the dancing stars on the dark blue curtain of the sky. When they neared the woods, a smart elderly man ran over to the guest and heartily embraced him. This elderly man spoke with enthusiasm of Zeitlin's scholarship and mental acuity. In the meantime, the group made a fire and sat around it on stumps of sawed-off trees. The elderly man sat on a crate, close to the bonfire. His face was illuminated with sweet contemplation in those dark woods. He said that many years ago, during the time of Rabbi Shloymele Ayger, the popular, great Torah scholar of that time, Wyszków had been blessed with a Jew, who, although he was not a Torah scholar, devotedly prayed to G-d in his own way. He was ready to sacrifice himself for the Jewish community every minute of every day. Such kind of Jew was Hershele Wasertreger (water carrier). The root of today's songs and tunes can be found, if one will search – in Hershele's melody: "Uru-na, kumu-na, Hito-reru!" " (Please wake up, please get up, awaken you all)!" – (This melody) carried with crystal clarity and pleasurable tremolo over the Jewish houses in the hospitable silence of the pre-Sabbath night. That was his psalm, his song to the Creator. It is said that with the edges of his frock-coat tucked into the back of his belt, he would fly past the closed shutters with the ease of a deer and with great love wake up the Jews of Wyszków, so that they could recite tilim (the psalms) and sing religious song of praise to the Creator of the world. For him it was the most beautiful song. It was one way for him to connect with eternity. "Huru-na, kumu-na, (Please wake up, please get up)" he said through the shutters, and people wanted to get up and wash negl waser[7]. Hershele's melody was full of compassion, and the evil inclination to sleep more could not overcome it. The melody asked: "Lemah ragshu goyim? (Why do nations rage?)"[8] and doors opened; Jews had gotten up to recite the psalms. This is how he earned his place in the oylom-habeh (World to Come). He was girded with sanctity, when he heard the footsteps of Jews on the streets that barely touched the ground.

When it was very dark, very late at night, long rays of light shone from the synagogue. Soon it was full of song and the (words) to the chief musician on negines[9] were like heavenly singing was wafting in the early morning air. The psalms mingled with the rustling of the leaves in the woods and only in the brightness of the early morning light did the birds continue the psalm, and it was just as if the whole world were singing the praises of the Creator and the holy Sabbath. Everything blended harmoniously into one wonderful melody.

When the first rays of the rising sun appeared, Hershele was already standing on the bridge over the Bug River. He was glowing as if G-d's presence itself were his garment. It looked as if the river, the heavens and the sun were embracing each other and kissing. He stood there in awe of G-d as if he were standing before the Holy Presence Himself. The morning was full of secret sounds, just as if the river were saying the morning prayers. In the middle of the river a pillar of cloud arose; it was all the colors of the rainbow, made so by the beauty of the sunrise. The colors changed every moment and dissolved into a sunny stream of light. This cloud column was similar to the cloud of fire that appeared to Moses in the desert as described in the Bible. It looked just as if the ancient fire was hovering here over the river. In these fiery pillars of clouds Hershele saw angels of the heavenly host and heard singing. Soon the sweetness was transformed into mightily resounding melodies celebrating the dawn of the Sabbath.

With joy and awe of G-d in his heart, he stood there as one stands during the Days of Awe and with a still, small voice he sang out "Mizmor shir leyom ha'shabbath (Lets sing (praise) the Sabbath day", in his own odd way. Hershele, by no means was an expert in the holy Hebrew tongue, so he began to sing with the excitement of one possessed in simple mameh-loshn[10], and beautiful, spontaneous Yiddish poetry was formed. And as he was giving himself over completely to his song and his little dance, he felt a hand on his back. Hershele trembled, turned around and, to his great fright, saw before him no other but the great Torah sage of Pozen himself, Rabbi Shloymele Ayger. He knew that this great scholar had stopped in Wyszków on his way back from Warsaw. But he became quite disoriented and frightened when he, Hershele, stood face to face with him.

[Page 55]

Rabbi Shloymele Ayger understood what Hershele was feeling, so he embraced him and calmed him by speaking to him as if he were his equal, telling him what he had seen in Warsaw, the generosity and the greatness of the rabbis there. Hershele, however, did not listen to the meaning of his words, because all of a sudden he turned to Rabbi Shloymele and asked him with a quavering voice:

– Rabbi, is one allowed to speak to G-d in plain Yiddish?

Rabbi Shloymele smiled for a moment and then answered him seriously:

– The language that comes from the heart is the one G-d understands best. Your language, Hershele, is not plain. And even if it were plain, there is holiness in its simplicity. When someone lifts his eyes, looks with wonder at G-d's handiwork and feels a great sense of connection to creation through the song of the wind, the woods and the field: when a Jew can sing like that and with such love inspire people to pray to G-d, his words not only become sanctified, he himself becomes and intercessor for redemption on this sinful earth and brings the Messiah.

When Hershele heard such words from the great sage himself, his face became strangely illuminated. On that Sabbath morning, one could hear and see how a proponent of the enlightenment, who was also one of the great Torah scholars of his generation taught (the people) in Wyszków the relationship between followers of the enlightenment and hasidus[11]. On that morning, before the morning service, Rabbi Shloymele Ayger spent time with Hershele the water-carrier and discussed Torah in plain Yiddish. It became the language of neshama yiseyre[12] and of national importance.

*

This is how the youth of Wishkov/Wyszków spent time with Hillel Zeitlin until the sun came up, and they heard how Hershel's melody, "Hooru-na, kumu-na, Hitoreru! (Please wake up, please get up. Awaken all of you) became the song of national liberation...

Footnotes

1. The name, A. Pat, is printed in the original book. However, the correct name of the author is A. (Aron) Pakht, who is the grand-Uncle of the Historian Enrique Krauze.

2. Wishkov or Vishkov, correct spelling in Polish is: Wyszków

3. Hasidic (Hasidism)= A Jewish mystic movement founded in the 18th century, in eastern Europe, by Baal Shem Tov that reacted against Talmudic learning and maintained that God's presence was in all of one's surroundings and that one should serve God in one's every deed and word.

4. Hillel Zeitlin (1871-1942), extremely influential critic, Yiddish and Hebrew writer who edited the Yiddish newspaper Moment, among other literary activities.

5. Midrash = refers to the compilation of homiletic teachings and stories based on the Hebrew Bible, prophets and other writings.

6. Mishnah (sing.) = there are are 63 tractates of the Oral Law, making up the first part of Talmud. The plural term is Mishnayes Yiddish) and Mishnayot (in Hebrew).

7. negl vaser =Water over the nails (hand). The first thing and Orthodox Jew does upon waking in the morning is to pour water over his nails to rinse off the residual evil spirits that have remained from the night.

8. Psalms 2:1. "Lemah ragshu goyim? (Why do nations rage?)"

9. Nengines (in Yiddish, Neginot in Hebrew), it is the Plural of Nign = a melody, a tune, a song.

10. Yiddish is referred to as "mame loshn" which means "mother tongue" Yiddish as it was spoken in Europe as the first language that a mother taught her child.

11. Hasidic philosophy or Hasidus, alternatively transliterated as Hassidism, Chassidism, Chassidut etc, is the teachings, interpretations of Judaism, and mysticism articulated by the modern Hasidic movement.

12. Neshama yiseyre, the additional soul that one is said to receive on the Sabbath.

The Wishkover Band; Dalekes
by Itzkhok Marcuschamer (Julius Marcus) Los Angeles
Translated by Ruth Fisher Goodman (Wilmington, DE)
Reviewed by Frida Grapa Markuschamer de Cielak (Mexico City)
Translation donated by the Historian Enrique Krauze (Mexico City)

My home has long been burned,

But the wind blows the ashes in my eyes

A nebulous dream

Leads me through a bridge made of cobwebs back to my home.

(by Nakhum Bomza)

...A meeting of Wishkover countrymen, as the two "historians," R'[1] Heri (probably Hershl) and Reb' Khaim – is like a wedding without musicians...

They sit and reminisce about the Jews in the old Wishkov/Wyszków[2]. Between one and another sigh and groan they remember this one and that one, these and those old friends and the organizations; the rich-picturesque nature that surrounded our beautiful shtetl[3]: the Sosnover Forest[4], the green lawns, the wide and deep Bug River, the green orchards with the juicy plums, apples and pears. Today, the red and white karshn (cherries) - which were known far – far beyond the boundaries of our shtetl.

– Today, our younths – intervenes Reb' Yitzkhok, one of the countrymen who overhears the conversation of his countrymen, takes part in it by saying – "the effervescent youths" – as Aron Aynhorn refers to the Wyszkower youths when he became aware of their activities while vacationing in a summer datcheh (country house) while inhaling the beautiful scents from the Sosnover Forest.

– "The effervescent youths' – says Reb' Khaim, – they were indeed effervescent because they lived in poverty. Oh, the poverty!"

– "But because of that," says Heri, "when it was Sabbath or a Holiday, do you remember Khaim, we could hear their loud voices from almost every house. And on celebrations, do you remember? Metch with his fiddle, and Nasele with his clarinet. True talents!"

– "And do you know at least, Heri, how and when the Wishkover Kapelie[5] started? Do you remember the di grobe (the fat) Danchikhe[6]? It happened at her wedding. The fat Leah-Ita, the bride, stubbornly insisted that she would not walk down the aisle under any circumstances unless they bring her the all group musicians from Pultusk and a wedding entertainer."

– "What," yelled her father, – " our Metch and Nasele are not good enough for you? Don't they have to earn a living? Why should we need to get musicians from another city?"

Nothing helped. The bride stood her ground. Her father saw that it was bad (a bad situation, he was not getting anywhere with his daughter), he went to Metch and told him that the bride wanted a full band and a wedding entertainer.

– "What do you mean, she wants?" yelled Metch, – "Will the world disintegrate if she doesn't get her way?" Even so, Metch calmed down and assured that there will be a band and a wedding entertainer – "as I live and breathe".

When the father of the bride left, Nasele said, – "Father, where are you going to find a bass, a drummer and a fiddler, one that can deeply "talk" and touch people's hearts? Oy!, if only you can get Iserl, when he starts playing, all the women swoon."

[Page 56]

– "What?" – The thought catches Metch. – "Iserl?... – He won't play in the band? From the few pieces of parsley and the rotten apples that his wife sells at the stragon [market-barely], does she give him enough to subsist on? He will play for some kerbelakh [money]! Or will he? – he wondered quietly to himself.

– "And what about a bass, a drummer and also a wedding entertainer?" – asks Nasele

– "A bass?" says Metch, – " I have Palukhl."

– "Palukhl? But, father, he has no a hear!" – says Nasele.

– "That doesn't matter," says Metch. "I'll work with him. And I have a drummer, too – Yidl! yes, Yidl has a drum."

– "What?" – yells Nasele – "Yidl, the bottle washer? Oy, vey iz mir (woe is me!) Will this be a band: Yidl with the drum and Palukhl with the bass!"

– "And I have a wedding entertainer, too," – says Metsh, – "Our boy, Khaim Henekhl! I'll send him right away to Warsaw to Big Yosl, and in one day he'll make a wedding entertainer out of him."

And so it happened that at the wedding of the di grobe Danshikhe (the fat Leah-Ita), the Wishkover Kapelie (band) played. – "Hey, was that a wedding! There were head to head, people almost suffocating in the crowd. Young and old, Jews and Gentiles, they came to the wedding not so much to see the bride and groom, but to hear the newly formed Wishkover Band.

Metch, a broad-shouldered, tall Jew, stood very pale and said to Nasele:

– "Listen, my child, when you play, I mean you should play! You know what I mean! Take them to task with your cymbal a 'fa' key and a 'bi' and, do you hear, let the devil take them!"

And to Palukhl, he said, – "The devil will take your father's father if you dare to try any prank with the bass. Start at the same time as everyone and finish with everyone, otherwise one will end with you right after the wedding..."

And to Yidl Falker, he said, – "There, where you wash bottles and you sip from them, that doesn't bother me, but if you take a sip from the bottle while you're playing, I'll make a bottle out of you, you hear? I mean what I say; my word as a musician!"

And to Iser, he says: – "Don't worry, Iserl, it will work. Nasele will keep his eye on them. Khaim-Henekhl, my boy, (and here he starts to cry) – go, show us your stuff. Start talking!"

Khaim-Henekhl puts on his capl [yarmulkeh], steps up on a high bench and begins his spiel, sharp words in rhyme. The women begin to wipe the tears from their eyes, the bride looks straight into the eyes of the wedding entertainer, her mouth open, she laughs. Khaim-Henekhl ends his talk with the following rhyme:

"Oh, dear Bride, dear Bride, cry, cry

You have much charm in the eyes of your mom

And when your groom will see you

He, too, will cry much.

Venehmar (and let us say)..., Amen"

And now he shouts, "Father, Nasele, now play something lively! Play something lively for the bride and for those who led her (down the aisle)."

The crowd becomes tumultuous. Metch and Nasele begin to play and as they play, they dance. Isserl plays the fiddle, but the tones are so thin, so lyrical that they seem to plead 'please leave me alone'. Palukhl shlept (drags) the bass and he screeches on. Yidl bangs on the drum and with every stroke, he gets hit with a snowball from mischievous boys and as he gets angrier, he beats the drum an extra strock harder and yells at them:

– "A cholera will finish you off when we will be done!"

It's dark out now, the wind is blowing and a light snow is falling. The candles that the in-laws are carrying among their fingers go out and in the midst of it all, they hear yelling: – "It's burning! It's burning!" It seems that the kerchief worn by Crazy Leah caught fire from the candle she was carrying. Pandemonium! Yidl and Palukhl take this opportunity to sneak into the kitchen for a snort, "a lekhaim" (a toast "to life").

– "Hey, Yidl, Yidl" says Palukhl, – "If only G-d could send us a juicy wedding like this every week!"…

– "Yes," says Yidl with his nasal twang: – The rolls, the fish, the delicious broth with mandlen [soup nuts]. To hell, it should take!"

– "You know what?" – says Palukhl, – "let's divide: some of the rolls for you; a couple for me. My children have for a long time never seen rolls like this."

– "Let's run, Palukhl" shouts out Yidl, – "the wine glass has already been broken and we will have to play the wedding march."

Palukhl runs, dragging his bass, which is twice his size. Yidl, dragging his drum can barely keep up with him. Soon, the wedding march can be heard and the crowd joins in.

– "Jews who experienced this wedding will never forget it," – concludes Reb' Khaim his memories – This was the Wishkover Kapelie (Musical Band from Wyszków), which had no inkling of what music was, nevertheless, they brought joy to celebrations.....

Dalekes

(a extra stop on the railroad)

For those who were not in Wyszków during the German occupation in First World War (I just won't let it be forgotten and) will the word 'Dalekes' resound loudly like a name in the Haftoireh[7] because, at that time, there wasn't even a stop on the railroad at Dalekes. It was such a rare occurrence that someone in Dlugoshodleh/Dlugosiodlo[8] allowed himself the luxury to go by train through Dalekes and if it ever did occur, the train would stop very briefly to let the passenger off and then race off in seconds to Ostrolenka.

[Page 57]

When the German military boot put its foot down in this area, they made Dalekes a key base where they stored the wealth that they robbed from the cities and villages. From there, they loaded the goods onto wagons; thousands and thousands of wagons, which were then sent to Germany. The wagons were loaded with all good things: wood, corn, wheat, berries, livestock, and anything the Germans could lay their hands on.

The several Jewish families who became 'concessionaires' for the Germans brought in Jewish workers into Dalekes. And this is how this unimportant, little known Dalekes grew in status and became a big stop on the railroad as well as Jewish youths found employment to so that they could earn money to buy a little bit of bread.

In the beginning, the funding for Dalekes was quite pitiful. Food and sleeping accommodations were hardly bearable, but, apart from the physical inconveniences, we were interested in enjoying cultural activities. Among us, youths, was then the yearning for a cultural life which we had had in our hometowns. Later, conditions improved considerably: houses were built; a small store [a gevelb] opened where you could buy foodstuffs and also had the opportunity to buy on credit. But the best thing for us that warmed our hearts was the coming of a man of culture named: Yungshteyn who had been hired there as a writer for the lumber trade.

For us, this started an interesting new life. Thanks to the initiative of Yungshteyn, we organized an evening of culture with song and readings from I. L. Peretz, Sholem Aleykhem, Avraham Raisen. The fellows looked forward to these evenings. After work and a skimpy meal they gathered together. Outdoors a fire was started and we sat around on blocks of wood. First, there was a speaker and then discussions. Later, they had readings and the evening ended very frequently, in a song. Talented youths, who knew excerpts from "Caladonia" and "Salome" by Goldfadn, "inflict" (gave) presentations, with heaven and the stars as backdrops for the theater, with the forest around as decoration and thousands of birds – serving as the orchestra accompanying our songs.

The cultural evenings and the relaxation amidst the beautiful natural surroundings gave us the courage and the strength to withstand the hard work, which was required of us in order to earn a living for our families so that they would not suffer from hunger.

Footnotes

1. R' stands for Reb, which is an honorable way to refer to a person, like 'Mr.' In English.
2. The correct spelling in Polish for Wishkov or Vishkov is: Wyszków
3. A Yiddish diminutive term for "town".
4. Pine-trees are called in Yiddish: Sosne Beymer. A forest of pine trees was called Sosnover or Sosner Vald (Pines Forest).
5. the musical band from Wyszków.

6. the fat daughter from the Dan family (Danchikhe is a diminutive term that refers to the small or young one from the Dan family.)

7. Haftoireh =selection from the books of Prophets of the Hebrew Bible that is publicly read in the synagogue following the Torah Reading.

8. Psalms 2:1. "Lemah ragshu goyim? (Why do nations rage?)"

Theater circle enthusiasts (Hebrew text)   **Amateur-club (Yiddish Text)**[*]

* **Note:** According to Frida Cielak (Mexico City, Mexico), in the top row, the 5th person in from the right, Moishe Markuschamer, is standing sideways and looking at his then wife-to-be, Ethel Saperstein.

[Page 57]

A Day in Town
by Moishe Farbshteyn

Translated by Sylvia Schildt (Baltimore MD)

Reviewed by Frida Grapa Markuschamer de Cielak (Mexico City)

Translation donated by the Historian Enrique Krauze (Mexico City)

When I am reminded of Wyszków, where for generations our near and dear lived, those various types and personages waft before my eyes, those who helped build Jewish national, political–social and cultural life.

Jews from all walks of life who conducted their daily struggle for survival – some by work, some by trade, some… despite lack of work, it was difficult, especially for Jews. In quasi–Fascistic and anti–Semitic Poland, Jews were not able to hold government or municipal positions, or work in factories. They had to find their living within specifically Jewish trades and lines of business. In the last years before the second Word War, this boycott ruined the Jewish trade.

Early in the morning, when it was still half dark, the Wyszkover Jews would get up for morning prayers in response to the call of Hershinke the bahelfer[1] (the helper). He was a dear simple Jew, who "didn't have a mean bone" in his body, always happy with his destiny. Whether to the big or to the small house of worship (Synagogue), Jews hurried thither, got through their prayers, whether as part of a minyan[2], or individually, and someone here and there managed to squeeze in the daily portion of Psalms. Those who arrived a little late had to pray at the second minyan[3] – and rush home for their daily work.

The day began with getting water from the town pump. The clattering of the pails against the carts of the Jewish water–carriers would wake the surrounding inhabitants. Summer for one groshn[4], and winter for two (a couple of pails), the water–carrier would bring the water to the richer households, who could permit themselves this luxury. But most of the inhabitants had to drag the water home themselves.

From the Bug River bank Jews returned, from daily immersion in the river – be it summer or winter. Here goes 'der Shvartzer Yitzkhok' (the dark haired Isaac) with his sons into the Niegrower[5] forest, to get lumber for Shkarlat[6]'s sawmill. They are in a big hurry in order to earn two "yazdes" (short trip/s) for the day – to earn sustenance for themselves – and the horses.

People are rushing to Hershl Holtzman/Holcman who has the concession to take passengers on the Highway from Pultusk in Powiat, in order for them to complete a variety of official business in starosta[7] or in the tax office – personally or through the town representative Haim–Nosn Vengrov. On Dovche´s wagon with white horses, they take slaughterhouse' butchers cart sides of meat to the butcher shops in order to quarter them there, remove the forbidden fat and prepare them for sale.

[Page 58]

Some to school, some to the gymnasium (Polish high school), some to the kheiders[8] – boys and girls are in a hurry –some to 'Geln'[9] Hershl and some to Shimon the Melamed[10], the G–d–fearing prodigy.

The Market Place (Rynek, in Polish) – close to the bridge

Jewishly–clad boys, go to the house of worship to study a page of Gemoreh[11].

The merchants open the shops. The jitnies (shpiliters) hurry to the people who have the concession to conduct passengers to the train for Warsaw, – so they can buy various goods for the shtetl (town) and bring them to the wholesale merchants.

Among the retailers and merchants one can notice the worry concerned with carrying the means of livelihood. They must often seek help from a Gmilas–Khesed (an interest–free loan association) and return the funds in a timely manner. There are philanthropists who help them in the mitzveh[12] of feeding the hungry.

In the pre–noon hours, one already sees Jewish youth with nothing to do, strolling over the Wyzskower streets, without any idea of their future existence. They speak of emigration as the only solution – but where? As long as they are out of there, wherever their eyes carry them. Khalutzim (pioneers) dream of traveling to training camps and then, to Eretz–Izrael. Others, on the other hand, – to North or to South America. Thus the Wyzskowers were scattered over the whole world. But this is said of the fortunate ones who possessed the necessary papers and money. The rest would continue to loiter on the streets of Wyszkow – from the Bug River bank to Pzedmiesztze/Przedmiescie (Street) and later, tired and dispirited/ashamed, they returned home to their parents, in order to eat their suppers.

So lived a part of Wyszkover Jewish youth.

True, there were in Wyszków many houses of worship, shtibelakh and – – – churches, but these did not impede a free life. Who does not remember the Hasidic study houses (Radziminer, Otwotzker, Aleksander, Amshnihover and foremost the Gerer Hasidim[13] – and more and more)? The communal institutions, unions, parties of all directions and shades and at the head – the Zionist movement, the largest, richest and most active party?

Who docs not remember the houses of worship with the old, yellowed Holy Books, from which they studied day and night?

Wyszków also possessed its own dramatic sections or amateur troupes, which produced various plays and actually very serious ones.

The town also had anti–Semitic parties, that always wanted to do us harm. In mostly cases they did not succeed, because of organized resistance from Jews, mostly – the Workers'–Movement, which fought against the Dmowskis[14], Skladkowskis[15] and other enemies of Israel.

Wyszkow also lived through various invasions during the two World Wars – Russians, Germans, Bolsheviks and lastly – the Nazi beasts. These all invasions always brought always trouble for the Jews, until the last Hitlerite flood that annihilated everyone.

And also the Poles of the shtetl demonstrated, that in the trade of spilling Jewish blood they were no better than the German murderers. One remembers a fact from the year 1920, when they brought to Wyszków Jews who had run away and also from the surrounding shtetlakh. They gathered them in the Senator's park, near the firemen's hall. Two long lines of tens of Poles, armed with sticks, laid out – and Jews had to pass through this "obstacle". With sadistic pleasure these hooligans beat the unfortunate Jews. Some became permanent invalids and others took days and weeks to recover.

The Dramatic Group or Circle*

Footnotes

1. Also known as, Hershl der Waser–treger, Hershl the water carrier.

2. A quorum of ten Jewish adults is required for prayer service.

3. A repetition of the morning prayer service done at a later time.

4. a groshn = a cent.

5. The meaning for Niegrower is not clear.

6. Shkarlat's sawmill= The sawmill that belonged to the wealthy family with the surname Shkarlat (Yitzkhok known as 'Itche' (Photo pg.32), Refoyl, Yisroel, Mendl, etc...)

7. starosta = County administrator.

8. kheiders (kheider– sing.) is a traditional elementary school whose purpose is to teach children the basics of Judaism and Hebrew.

9. The 'Yellow' is a nickname for redheads.

10. A religious teacher or instructor.

11. Gemoreh (in Yiddish) /Gemara (in Hebrew) = The Gemoreh and the Mishneh together make up the Talmud.

12. Mitzvah, a good deed, but literally, it means "commandment."

13. Hasidim belonged to different dynasties of influential spiritual leaders, known as Rebbes, and usually were named after a key town in Eastern Europe where the founder may have been born or lived, or where the group began.

14. The followers of Roman Stanislaw Dmowski, a Polish politician who co-founded the right-wing National Democracy political movement in interwar Poland. Dmowski made anti–Semitism a central element in his radical nationalist outlook.

15. Skladkowskis = They were the followers of Polish Prime Minister – Felicjan Slawoj–Skladkowski, President of the Council of Ministers (1936–1939) who at one time came out in about 1937, with the slogan, "to pogrom against the Jews — definitely not. To destroy their stores and stalls – please!"

* **Note:** According to Frida Cielak, her aunt, Feige Marcuschamer, is standing on the right side, in front of the vertical beam.

[Page 59]

Memories of our Young Years

by Shmuel Niestenpover (Montevideo)

Translated by Hershl Hartman (Los Angeles, CA)

Reviewed by Frida Grapa Markuschamer de Cielak (Mexico City)

Translation donated by the Historian Enrique Krauze (Mexico City)

Dzhigan And Shumakher[1] "Reel–Up" A Film In Vishkov/Wyszków[2]

I lived on the fisherman's street (Koscielna Street)[3] at my wife's grandfather, Zelik Fisher's place.

Once, I recall, there was a tumult in the little street. Rokhl, Yosl Binduski (the shoemaker)'s wife, came up to my window and shouted:

"Shmuel, are you sitting at home? The market–place is lively, the whole shtetl[4] is there. They're making a film with Yiddish actors..."

I went quickly to the market–place and saw, Dzhigan and Shumakher emerging from Khaytche Shlizoner's restaurant, feigning drunkenness. The cinematographer keeps cranking the camera and every movement of these two Yiddish comedians becomes eternalized in a film–camera.

At the bridge stood Ester Zelik's[5] with Avreml Farentyazh, Ele Shtoyb, Khayim the fisherman (Khayim Rozenberg), Elye–Mayer/Eli–Mayer the baker and his wife, Elke–Shoshe the wagon–driverin, Knaster the shipping agent, and the old, voiceless baker who smiled contentedly, knowing that "his" Wyszków had been selected for the "reeling–up" of a Yiddish film...

Wolerek the Pole Plays Yiddish Melodies

Even before the start of the Second World War, worry and unease were felt among the Jewish population, a foretelling of the oncoming storm. The Jews of Wyszków, as in other towns and shtetlekh in Poland, suffered from anti–Semitism, economic boycotts and persecution.

The reservists of the Polish military were mobilized a few days before September 1, 1939. I, too, was ordered to report to the 13th Division in Pultusk[6]. Along with many Vishkover, I arrived in the nearby city where we were immediately assigned to dig anti–tank ditches and trenches. We worked from 5:00 in the morning to 11:00 at night.

On the 23rd of August we were issued new uniforms and weapons. Companies are assembled on the large parade ground. At the fence on Chenstojov (Czestochower) Street many Pultusk residents gathered to bid farewell to the soldiers marching off to the front lines. The First Battalion, to which I belonged, marched through the gate toward the railroad station, accompanied by the music of a military band. The streets were full of people. No smiles, no joy – just sorrow and tears on everyone's faces. An old Polish woman approaches me and says:

"Beat the Hitlerites. If you let them go through, they will slaughter everyone..."

The Jewish Wyszkower[7] youth fought well. They fell on the fields of Mlave while mounting resistance to the Hitlerite army. I specially remember Shloyme Burshteyn/ Burshtin, Pepke the cobbler's son.

Among the Wyszków Poles who were in the First Battalion with us, he was the musician Valerek. His family was well-known in the shtetl because they played at the local movie-house until the advent of sound in films. Now, while at the front, Wolerek had brought his fiddle.

Once, sitting in the trenches, he took out the fiddle and began to play... Yiddish melodies. It was so heartwarming, hearing those homey Yiddish tunes. The Jewish and Polish soldiers who listened to those beautiful sounds, momentarily forgot, that death threatened them at any moment. And truly: at the ecstatic moment of that unique concert in the trenches, a squadron of German planes appeared and bombed our positions. Many fell in battle then.

When things calmed down, Wolerek began to play again. This time – Chopin's funeral march...

Another time Wolerek began to play special melodies for... the Wyszkower. "Who knows," – he said, – "it may be that our town has been destroyed and its inhabitants buried under the ruins". Everyone's blood ran cold. We tightened the grip on our rifles...

At evening the soldiers were called to register themselves in the "Death Book". So that in the event of death, the proper family member might be notified. I put down the name of Nekhe Zilberman-Niestenpover[8].

Since I have been on Uruguayan soil (following the end of the war), Valerek's melodies accompany me and remind me of fallen comrades, of the destroyed Jewish population, and of the shtetl where I was born and raised.

Bialystok Street

Footnotes

1. SHIMON DZIGAN(DZHIGAN/) and ISRAEL SHUMACHER were the most famous Yiddish comedic duo of all time, who worked together as "Dzigan & Shumacher", one of the most famous Yiddish comic duos in the 20th century who made many films, stage shows and records in Poland and later, in Israel and the US. In 1935 they founded their own cabaret company (the "Nowości Theater") in Warsaw. The filming of a movie in Wyszków was one of a kind event of great importance mainly because these so well known artists had chosen, among all the Polish–Yiddish shtetls, to do their film in Wyszków! Shimon Dżigan (born,1905 in Lodz – died, April 14, 1980 in Tel-Aviv). His father was a soldier in the Russian military. After the outbreak of the first world war Dzigan was apprenticed to a tailor to help the family, but he could realy do so when he became a succesful comedian. Izrael Shumacher or Szumacher (born, 1908 in Lodz – died, May 21, 1961) He met Dzigan at Ararat literary cabaret company and then in Warsaw with the troupe Yidishe Bande, their succes was impresive and become then the famous Yiddish comedy pair "Dzigan & Shumacher". After the outbreak of WWII the duo Dzigan & Shumacher were in Bialystok, in 1941 they were evacuated to Tashkent, where they were performing in the so–called artistic brigades of the Red Army. They were trying to reach the Anders Army but they were arrested on charge of desertion from the Red Army and exiled to Kazakhstan. They returned to Poland in 1947. They were performing in a variety theatre in Lodz. They moved to Israel in 1949. In 1952 they stopped performing as a duo and 9 years later, in 1961, at age 53, Izrael Shumacher died in Israel. They 2 were the last masters of Yiddish comedy created for a Yiddish–speaking audience.

2. The correct spelling in Polish for the town of Vishkov or Wishkov: Wyszków

3. Koscielna Street in Wyszków was the street where the fisherman placed their stalls to sell their fish.

4. shtetl =The Yiddish word (a diminutive term) for "town." shtetlekh, in plural

5. When a name is said with another name in a possesive form, e.g., Ester Zelik's, it means that Esther was the daughter of Zelik.

6. Pultusk, is 28 kms./18 miles away from Wyszków.

7. Vishkover or Wyszkower = citizens from Wyszków.

8. Nekhe Zilberman–Niestenpover = It is understable that the author of this article, Shmuel Niestenpover, used in this case, the 2 surnames of Nekhe, to denote that he was a member of his family one of those who had died during the German attack.

[Page 60]

Our train station, the Poremba settlement
by Yankev/Yakov Palukh (Buenos Aires, Argentina)
Translated by Hilda Rubin (Rockville, MD)
Reviewed by Frida Grapa Markuschamer de Cielak (Mexico City)
Translation donated by the Historian Enrique Krauze (Mexico City)

A (Alef)

Wishkov/Wyszków[1] didn't have any places where the local population could go to relax and enjoy themselves after a hard day's work. The Jewish young people who were aspiring to a new and better life used the bridge over the River Bug to stroll along with their friends. The bridge was the meeting place. It was there that one could hear various discussions. Or if one preferred, simply chat or even do some singing.

However, there was another spot in Wyszków where one could go to soak up the fresh air and enjoy views of the pretty surrounding countryside and that was — the railroad station.

The lovely and sweet memories of our shtetl[2] are concentrated around that station. It was there that the rendezvous between the boys and girls took place. But it was at the bridge that each one of us felt truly comfortable, just as if we were in our own homes.

As opposed to that feeling, the stroll to the train station brought forth a more refined character and a sort of proper behavior. It was at the station that our youthful dreams appeared to have the possibility of breaking through the daily routine drudgery. There, we felt, even for a short time, that it was possible to rise to a higher level in our dreams of a better tomorrow.

One can't say that our shtetl didn't present signs of better times to come for our young people, even though the older generation appeared to be anchored to its place, unable to move from it. The young people who were already finished the kheyder[3] and away from the study from Beis–Hamedrash[4], had a broader outlook on life. They felt that their position in the shtetl was like being trapped in an immobile situation. This feeling drew them all the more to struggle to become emancipated from the suffocating small shtetl atmosphere.

And so, those strolls to the railroad station really satisfied a sort of far off yearning, even if it were only for a few hours. The young people were freed from their daily grind and were able to shake off depressing moods. There, at the station, in the fresh air— they could look through a "window" to the wide world.

B (Beis)

The Wyszków train–station was to be found not far from the shtetl's main–street, Pultusk Boulevard. The way to the station was through a small, narrow garden, which ran between two espaliered, or trellised walkways. This walkway served as both an entrance and exit to the station.

At the sides of the walkway stood wooden benches with armrests, deeply embedded in the ground. These benches were painted green and served as resting places for the train station personnel, when they were off duty, and their friends. These benches were also not off limits to the shtetl's inhabitants and so they used them to sit and enjoy the fresh air on the walkway. One could also frequently encounter people using these station benches to catch little catnaps.

In general, the station house made a good impression. It looked like a church, but without a bell tower or bell. Stone steps led to wide entrance doors with large glass panes. This area gave the impression that one was standing in a princely palace.

The way to the station was not terribly long and so provided a fine place for a stroll. It also provided a living for about ten families of Dorozhkozhes (cab operators, jitneys), who would drive you to the station. They had skinny, old horses harnessed to wagons, at the ready, in the middle of the market place, which were for hire at a moment's notice. The pathetic look of these horses cried out with a thousand mouths the poverty of their owners.

These Dorozhkozhes would frequently go days on end without earning anything. The horses stood and whinnied pleading for some hay while their owners wandered about the shtetl looking for some way to earn money. They were ready to take on any trip, no matter how far they would have to travel. Without any work, they had time on their hands and would always fool around and tell jokes. If a fare or a passenger should suddenly appear there would be such shouting from all sides from the Dorozhkozhes, that the passenger would get completely confused. Their best times for earning money came when the merchants and suppliers returned from Warsaw and the surrounding cities and towns. These business folk brought their packs full of merchandise and boxes wrapped around with iron bands and needed the services of the jitneys. All the wagons were then full and busy delivering goods and people.

G (Gimmel)

The station looked very different at daybreak. The local important agencies had prevailed to have the train wait for passengers all night long. When a train arrived in the evening, the locomotive would stop belching smoke from its chimney and would rest over–night. It would be restocked and powered up the next day.

In the early mornings, the passengers traveling to Warsaw or other destinations would start to gather. The Polish passengers stood out with their pleasant and polite behavior. They arrived early and waited calmly for the time to board the train. On the other hand, the Jewish (Yiddish) passengers always arrived in a great hurry. They always seemed to be a minute late for the departure. The Jewish men and women would rush in, breathing hard, barely managing to shove their way to the ticket counter to purchase the needed ticket.

At the same time, the ticket agent, nattily dressed and thoroughly rested would slowly and phlegmatically sit himself down behind his barred window and get to work. It was as if the train were miles away and not at the station ready to depart. The agent would very deliberately open the ticket window at a very precise minute. And then would begin the pushing and shoving at the window as people tried to buy their tickets. Finally, with tickets in hand, the Jews would grab their packs and bundles and willy–nilly run to the train which had already begun to belch fire and smoke, ready for departure.

[Page 61]

In the afternoon hours the Wishkever[5] train station was full of Jewish young people. They would be waiting for someone to arrive by train from Warsaw. Some hours before the train was to arrive, the young people would congregate around the station and amuse themselves in various ways.

I also remember times when the stroll to the station was full of danger. These were times when there were anti–Semitic waves surging in Poland. However, our Wishkever young fellows didn't walk away from a fight with the anti–Semites. In fact, they gave their attackers a good drubbing and even broke some bones. And all this fighting was done in a way that the police wouldn't catch us Jewish young people. We were not the guilty ones – it was the anti–Semites who were "heroes" attacking our young girls and boys, as well as older Jews. But, there was the constant fear that the police would arrest the ones attacked and not the attackers, so we Jewish young fellows developed a tactic. We would beat the anti–Semites up well and then – simply disappear into the populace.

The times were constantly getting worse. After some time of indecisiveness, I decided to leave my hometown Poremba. After Sukes[6], I went by foot over two unpaved, muddy little streets to the one avenue in our community in order to get to the autobus. This bus ran on the Bialystok–Warsaw line.

I waited on that avenue a good two hours. Overhead the stars twinkled in the night sky. A cool autumn wind was blowing that could be felt in ones bones... My waiting for that autobus was in vain – it never arrived. I decided that I had better get myself to the Wishkever train station from Wyszków, quickly. So I went directly to a peasant named Loyek[7] that I knew, who used to make "yazdes"(voyages)[8] for a few zlotes[9], or (sell) a cigar, or a herring with a fresh roll. I asked him to harness his horse and take me to the train station in Wyszków.

The trip from the avenue in Poremba to the station took a good bit of time. We had to travel about 20 kilometers. I and Loyek(Łojek) got frozen through and through. We hoped to warm ourselves up at the Wyszków train station. But to our great disappointment, when we got to the station, everything was sort of in half darkness. In one corner of the station there was a peasant on a bench sleeping cozily. It was cold in the big hall of the station and we had to warm ourselves by running briskly back and forth and slapping our hands to keep the blood flowing. Loyek(Łojek) was cursing his fate and the world.

Bit by bit, the station started to fill up with people. It really became somewhat warmer. For the last time I was a witness to the Jewish crowd hurrying to the train. These Jews were half asleep dragging their huge packs. In their haste, they seemed to be tripping or falling into the brightness of the lit station. For the last time I parted with the beloved and well–known places of my youth and went forth into the wide unknown.

I had left Poland forever !

Footnotes

1. Wishkov– the correct Polish spelling is: Wyszków
2. shtetl = "town" in Yiddish (in diminutive); shtetlakh is the plural.
3. kheyder is a traditional elementary school whose purpose is to teach boys the basics of Judaism and Hebrew.
4. Beis–Hamedresh translates as: "House [of] Learning", a study hall.
5. Wishkever = from Wyszków.

6.   Sukes (in Yiddish)/Sukkot (in Hebrew) is a seven–day harvest holiday that arrives during the Hebrew month of Tishrei. It starts four days after Yom–Kippur. Sukes is also known as the "Festival of Booths (or Huts)" and the "Festival of (Autumn) Harvest."

7.   Loyek = Łojek is the correct spelling in Polish. In Polish, the "j" is usually pronounced as an "i."

8.   "yazdes" = This is a Yiddish–Polish word for rides or voyages The Polish word "jazdy" is the plural, whereas jazda is the singular form.

9.   zlotes = It refers to the still current Polish money or currency. The modern złoty is subdivided into 100 groszy (singular: grosz) and Złoty is used alike in plural and singular.

The Poremba Settlement
by Yankev/Yakov Palukh
Translated by Pamela Russ

A rich, social, Jewish life flourished not only in the larger Jewish settlements in Poland, but also in the smaller and even very small areas, practically in all districts.

The stamp on the town came primarily from the religious sector. The small and more significant rabbis had spiritual influence, each in his own stiebel [small place of prayer], that bore the name of the city where the holy tzaddik [righteous man] conducted his tisch [literally "table," but also referring to the gathering place (at a table) of the followers around their Rebbe (rabbi or spiritual leader)]. Suffice it to remember the Holy Shabbath, when the Jews discarded their weekday essence [physical lives] and devoted themselves to the spiritual, accompanied with passionate dance and song that reached great distances, first with the third Shabbath meal, and then with the melave malkes [literally: "escorting the [Shabbath] Queen," referring to the festive meal that takes place after Shabbath has ended; hence escorting out the Queen]... No one wanted to part from the Shabbat Queen and return to the weekday grayness and its problems and worries.

Jews were busy – some on the shoemaker's stool, some at the tailor's machine, some as blacksmiths, and some as small merchants. Everyone worked hard to earn a living, but not always with success. Everyone celebrated Shabbath and yom tov [Jewish holidays] in his own way.

A (Alef)

In our town, there was also the younger, more enlightened generation, along with their organizations, factions, and parties that wanted to save Poland, the world, and the Land of Israel. We also had periods when we forgot about the daily worries, being busy with community issues. These were the times of community elections, or Sejm [Polish parliamentary] elections, or arguments about the gabbai [beadle] in the shul, or in the stiebel [small place of prayer], or if there was an issue of importing a new shochet [ritual slaughterer] or Rav [rabbi].

Did anyone hear of such small towns? Was anyone interested in these small settlements around Wyszkow, such as: Poremba, Dlugosiodl, and others, with their residents and flowering Jewish life?

Or even, Jewish villages such as: Kamienczyk, Branszczyk, Szczonka, and many, many others, where some Jewish families lived?

And who heard of such places as Back and Ostrowieck, where Jewish life flowed – a play of general Jewish life in Poland? It was enough to observe the local youth on a Shabbath day when we were free from the daily tasks and so had the opportunity to dedicate ourselves to organizational life within the four walls of the party's location, that was either one of two political directions: Under one common roof, there were discussions around the same problems that were listed on the daily roster. Discussions – stormy, that more than once ended in arguments.

Now I want to mention the town of my place of birth, Poremba, and remark on some interesting details:

There were about 60 Jewish families living there. The only Jewish main street, not paved, was intersected in the middle by a half stone, half steel cross, that stood on the fork [dividing road] that led to several villages (also with the same name), where there was also a small number of Jewish families. The town boasted a beautiful, large Beis Medrash [House of Study], that was also a place for all kinds of squabbles because of private or community issues. There were also two individual stieblach [plural of "stiebel," small synagogues], that did not have any designated rabbi. The teachers did not have real livelihood from the two cheders [elementary religious schools]. Poremba had its Rav, a shochet, and a ritual bath. There were sharp discussions around whether the local shochet should be relieved from his position and be replaced by a younger shochet who could also be a baal tefila [lead the prayers].

[Page 62]

B (Beis)

The town also had a large church with sometimes a good and sometimes a bad priest. In the post office, often, they took out from the letters that Jews would receive from their relatives from America, some of the dollars that would be sent from time to time to save them from their difficult financial situation. There was a telephone connection, a pharmacist who would dispense medicine without a doctor; two barber–surgeons who did not get along with each other, both had to help themselves [augment their incomes] with haircutting. There was a Polish municipal office, a local prison, where, along with the drunks, there were also honest homeowners who had to do their time there for not having kept clean their places in the courtyards; there was a police commission and a commandant who was easily bribed. This commandant was friendly with everyone. He used to remove the lint from the beards of Jews who would pass by. There was a fire brigade that did not hire any Jews, but would often sound their alarm to frighten the local Jews. There was also a fair once a month, a very special event in the whole region. Here, as in the other areas in Poland, there were anti–Jewish activities and picketing in front of the Jewish shops. Understandably, the "friendly" police commandant went into hiding [at that is time]. There was also a Polish "spulke" [cooperative] that urged the local farmers not to purchase from the Jews.

And in spite of all this, one lived anyway, raised children, married them off, and lived to reap some joys from them... There were also times of sadness among the Jews: a mourner in a Jewish home, or just a tragic event. There was an energetic youth with a lot, a lot of hope for a more beautiful world, a better world, and a world that was friendlier to the Jews.

C (Gimmel)

My small settlement had the same good and bad features as every other settlement in Poland. We actively participated in all events – large and small ones, important and unimportant ones, which from time to time stirred up the general and Jewish open minds. We excitedly followed all the important events, read with interest the reports of the Sejm [Polish parliament] meetings, as they addressed Jewish issues.

At the time of the Beilis trial, in the year 1911, we were all under the strong influence of the publicity of both sides. In the Beis Medrash [House of Study], in the streets, in the baths, in the homes – everywhere that Jews gathered, this trial was the central topic, and in the year 1913, when Beilis was freed, the joy among the Jews was boundless. We received weighty ammunition against our enemies.

At the same time, the incident with the priest Mateusz took place. He was sentenced by the courts for having stolen the bejeweled eyes of the holy icons in the church. The Christian young boys would shout after us: "Beilis!" And we would reply: "Beilis is alive and Mateusz is rotting!"

D (Daled)

Our joy was great at the time of the Balfour Declaration. Jews were prepared to leave everything and go to the Land of Israel. The youth was prepared to leave their warm homes in order to build up the old–new home.

There was a library of several hundred books in Poremba. This serviced the youth from all directions in the town and the surrounding villages. Very frequently, there were literary evenings, informal talks, concerts, discussions, and science lectures. Also, the writer of these lines was one of the speakers. This useful institution was later split by the members of the so–called leftists.

With the establishment of Hashomer Hatzair [socialist Zionist group], our youth was caught up in the new way of thinking. We spent every night in song, dancing the Hora [Israeli dance], while listening to speakers. The site was decorated in blue and white, and on the walls were pictures of the prominent Zionist leaders.

E (Hei)

Many books have already been published describing our last destruction. But, in general, these types of small towns, such as Poremba, were wronged [in their omission]. In truth, even in these small towns, Jewish nationalist life also sprouted, thanks to which we were able to withstand such a long road of exile. There, in the small settlements, a significant number of the Jewish kibbutz in Poland, was concentrated. There is insufficient energy to describe the history of the heroism of the Jewish youth in the small settlements, and their battles with Hitler's murderers. How much collective heroism revealed itself in the times of the destruction of the third temple [referring to the Jewish people themselves as the "temple"] – and particularly in these small settlements?

Chaval al deavdin [Aramaic: "We long after the great people who are unfortunately lost to us"], you small settlements, with the thousands and thousands of Jews. Remember, who will eternalize the story for you?

[Page 63]

From Wyszkow To Kibbutz Dafna
by Yehuda Ilan, Kibbutz Dafna
Translated by Chava Eisenstein

My childhood years I spent between the walls of the "Kheder" and continued at the Yeshiva of the Rabbi of Radzimin. I come from a ramified khassidic family of the great Rabbi of Ger. I received a Jewish traditional education. My family – Family Olleshker – was outstanding for its social public activity for the Jewish communities and was very involved in caring for the daily needs of the Jews in Wyszkow.

To my great dismay and sorrow, I was not privileged to know my dear mother, Shaina–Fruma–Malka – a righteous clever and good–hearted woman, as I was told by others. She had the combination of everything: identical to her names: (Shaina) she was beautiful, (Fruma) fervently religious, and (Malka) a real queen. She was adored by everyone and highly regarded. She would be wherever she was needed and offered her help to poor and depressed people as well as to brides in need of funds. She always assisted people in a hidden manner, with money – and once, before Pesach, she went out to collect money for people that couldn't afford the extraordinary Pesakh expenses and she caught a cold. On the first day of Khol HaMoed Pesakh, she passed away at the young age of 32, when I was only 2 years old. What a pity, it was such an unforgotten loss.

As I said, I am from a khassidic family and my father, Yitzkhak Yoseph, didn't spare any effort to bring me up in the "right" way. The same way of his forefathers. I studied diligently at Yeshiva and was deeply engrossed in the various Talmudic topics. The Talmud, the Gemara were constantly in front of my eyes, day and night I would pore over my studies. My adolescent years passed in Yeshiva. But one bright day a spark of another life embarked within me, a life of a generation that envisions the yet to be born, of a generation that sees its future in the land of Israel. In the land where he will feel free like any other nation in its homeland.

At that time was founded in our town Wyszkow, the "Ha'Khalutz" (the Pioneer) organization. In spite of my Yeshiva upbringing, I sharply envisioned the "Ha'Khalutz" as the way I should lead, but it wasn't that simple for me to go to "Ha'Khalutz" since my parents were entirely opposed to this movement, where girls and boys would gather together, something that my father considered intentional apostasy. My father's view was that I am to walk the same path of our ancestors, to be fervently religious at home and a human being outside, and not to go astray from the treaded path. Indeed, my father was very religious and a fervent khassid, every day he awoke at dawn to study the "page of the day" Talmudic Page. Later in the day, between the afternoon and evening prayers he learned a page of Gemara with its commentaries. He was popular amongst the Kharedi Jews, his place in the shtiebel was upfront at the mizrakh side, and he spent much of his time for public affairs, but together with that he was also accepted by the gentiles. As a proud and well–established Jew, on behalf of his dealings in the wood trade, he possessed forest lots and was a partner in the sawmill where tens of workers worked. He also managed the book keeping with the Polish lords and noblemen, and bought plots in the woods for the saw–mill. My father (unlike other Jews in his times, which acted as sycophants and boot lickers of their Polish landowners), by his visits to the noblemen, did not flatter them, he knew how to be proud and emphasize his Jewishness with his aristocratic appearance he was Jewish to the full sense. At the shtiebel he was from the organizers and also served as manager at affairs. He was a member of many Jewish institutions and acted on their behalf. Every Shabbat it was customary for each khassid to invite khassidim for a "Kiddush" where they made the Kiddush blessing over a small glass of whisky and added some cookies and enjoyed the gathering before each dispersed to his home for the meal. To our home too, khassidim came and drank "L'Khaim". Between one whiskey and another, they sang a moving khassidic melody continuing with a shoulder–to–shoulder heartwarming dance. Life was full of enthusiasm and every year father traveled to the Rabbi of Ger for a few–day visit. This is how my father wished to give me the upbringing and education that he received. Nevertheless, as I already mentioned, in me, an inner revolt has begun, that pushed me out into the open space, to fresher air and to not stay most hours of the day and the night amid the Yeshiva walls.

Quietly, in "underground" I began to be active at the "Ha'Khalutz". Where I was able to vent my desires and have cheerful get–togethers with friends and mostly with girlfriends, which were afar from me up to then. True, also when I was in Yeshiva I would peep out of the window, to see the girls of which many of them I liked, but that was only in my mind, I did not show anything in open and it was unmentionable to meet a girl – something most forbidden. At the "Ha'Khalutz", I started to act with the full excitement. My meetings were of course, without the knowledge of my parents, but I continued to study even more enthusiastically at Yeshiva, I didn't want to awake suspicion from the Leaders of the Yeshiva or the students, that my heart is already somewhere

else. And I am planning for my future to finally reach the land of hope –
the Land of Israel.

I devoted myself to the "Histadrut" and worked for the "underground" for
the idea of Eretz Yisrael. The head of the Yeshiva knew completely nothing
about it, and so was my father, he knew nothing about my leading a dual life.
In 1923, between Purim and Pesach, I was appointed amongst other fellow
exceptional yeshiva students to have a trip to Warsaw, to the Rabbi of
Radzimin that will test us on the issues we have learned during the year. My
father was overjoyed that I was to go to the Rabbi and will be tested. For a
week I stayed there, the attendant watched over me as of a treasure, and
finally I got admission to the Rabbi. The Rabbi tested me on 20 pages of the
PsaKhim tractate. I knew the 20 pages by heart with all its commentaries, the
Maharsha, and Tosefot – supplements and more, and I emerged from the
exams, which lasted a few hours, fully successful. The Rabbi gave me a slight
pinch on my cheek and told me I should be an assiduous good learner. But at
that time, my heart wanted otherwise, my ideas were already far from this
fashion which I followed until then. I returned home and the head of the
Yeshiva delivered to my father the excellent results of the tests I passed, he
was very satisfied with me. But I stood before my father and let him know of
my final decision, that I am not able to go on with my studying in Yeshiva,
without telling him my ideas about the new way I have chosen. His pleads to
me to continue learning after such good marks were in vain. I told him that I
want to help him in the sawmill with the measuring etc. after a long dispute
he agreed to my ideas, but he asked from me, so I will not forget the Talmud I
learned, to study every night one page of Talmud in the shtiebel. And, of
course I did that for not much time.

Participants of The Young Khalutz

Young Zionist's in 1918, with Dr. Gotlieb

[Page 64]

Then it happened. My father's good friends reported to him about my going astray and gave him the information about my meetings at the "Ha'Khalutz", that after the Shabbat meal I go with the gang to the woods, beyond the bridge over the Bug River. That in itself is a transgression of surpassing the "Shabbos Boundary," and other things, which are forbidden to even mention. One time, my father decided to give up his noontime nap and went to the bridge to meet me and bring me back to the "right" track. The balloon busted and the matter became known. Indeed, that day I returned home with him, but then after there was a change: instead of acting in hiding, I went openly. After stormy arguments, he complied with my way, clearly – with a heavy heart.

My transformation from Yeshiva life to dealing with my father's business affairs went smoothly, the same goes for my public activities.

On the 25th of Tamuz 5,685 (1925) my father passed away after suffering a cold, as he visited landowners in hard weathers and didn't notice his cold until his conditioned worsened and doctors were not able to help him. The tragedy hit us very hard, my brother Yaakov was already married with two children and lived in Ostrow–Mazow. At home were left me, and my brother Buch'e (Baruch). My brother Shmuel left to Argentina in 1921, and I was not able to continue with the partners at the sawmill, because the times were hard for the wood trade, the Polish government asked for higher taxes then the business was able to tolerate, at the end the government confiscated the sawmill for the tax we owed, and we barely managed to liquidate and sell the wood. Thus I began wandering to Warsaw, where Hersh Yoseph Sokol, son of a partner in the sawmill, opened a wood business and invited me to work for him as a clerk. My brother Buch'e, who was 5 years younger than me, remained in Wyszkow with my mother and aunt Malka, there he continued his studies in Yeshiva.

For 5 years I was in Warsaw, 1926–1931, those were turbulent years. In the beginning, I continued activities at the "Ha'Khalutz," until they split, when one part turned more left, me amongst them. That was when I encountered the Communist party, there I was popular and valued, until they trusted me with the printing machine, where I was to put out publicity leaflets in favor of Communism for the ammunition and weapons manufacture in Warsaw. I did this secretive work in the summer nights when I boarded at the office of the workplace where I worked. Students came to visit me by day to give me craft books to read and at that occasion, I inserted packages of booklets that I printed during the nights, into their bags. I hid these anti regime leaflets beneath layers of wood that were laying there. For two years, I worked in this style and my boss knew nothing about my activities. As time passed, I was excused of meeting party members and I didn't have to visit the cells of the leftist divisions, so not to arise suspicion. I visited the clerk–union of my profession, which was under Communist influence, a rich union where members of the Communist party lectured and held speeches. Until one meeting, when the building was surrounded, all those that were present were questioned, and their names registered, and so, they also came to investigate at my boss, they searched and explored my belongings, but didn't find anything, they didn't say what is the purpose of the search of my possessions, but the boss began to keep an eye on me, until it came to his ears, a fellow employee that desired to take my place, and he tattled. He would help me occasionally to print and it didn't dawn on me he would do that. That is when I took the machine that was in hiding, and without saying a word, I gave it back to the one that has given it to me. On that occasion I resolved, after heavy afterthoughts I had with this issue, and the second thoughts I had of the management and their conducting's and ideas with which I was unable to make peace. I let a final notice that I am stopping my membership in the party and I promised that whatever knowledge I possessed, would not leak out, and everything will stay within my heart. They treated me with remarkable understanding, they even wanted to help and give me the means to settle, but I rejected it and so I came back to by home, to "Ha'Khalutz."

I did not continue much time in Warsaw and I went over to the city Sokoly, where my mother's family resided, I threw myself attentively into Zionist activity and raising money for funds. Along with that, I began to think of self–fulfillment to which I always strived. In 1933, I decided to join a "Hakhshara" – a training structure, and to prepare myself for finally immigrating to the land of Israel. I spent 5 years at the training Kibbutz Borokhov at Lodz, and in those years very few certificates for immigrants were given. For 300 members, only five certificates were issued, so I really didn't have much of a chance.

In that time, began the illegal immigration, Immigration B, and that involved much endanger. But I was absolutely determined on immigration, no matter what and how much risky the charge. But, also illegal immigration had a waiting line. In one of the nights of 1938 it came, as I slept the secretary whispered into my ear, to leave early morning to home, and to prepare to immigrate illegally, not to part with my friends with whom I lived together for years. What will I not do that thinks should pass "smoothly"? I traveled home to Sokoly, there I also didn't tell friends, except for those closest to me. When I started out, only close family escorted me. We traveled by train from Warsaw via Nazi Germany, they checked us in search for money or other suspicious items. We passed the contaminated land to Italy, we traveled for 3 days until we reached the port in Italy, where our ship was already standing, a nameless ship. We got on the ship and crammed together like sardines. The ship was suitable for 40–50 people, but we were 320. Water for bathing and even for drinking was very scarce, the food was awful but my mind was only on the destination, all the hardships and obstacles were minor in my eyes.

[Page 65]

After 5 days on sea, we were able to see the shores of the land. But we were not allowed to arrive prior to the set time, so we wandered on the water until the ship received (there were a few Israelis working on the ship too) signal that we can go ahead, and the ship immediately speeded towards our homeland, and came to a stand not far from the shore, facing the city of Netanya. Under the darkness of night boats arrived with members of the "Ha'Poel" movement and we jumped on them. When we came close to the shore, they let us down into the water that came up to our waist and higher. With our few belongings, we walked the water until we reached shore, "Hagana" members, veterans of the settlement welcomed us warmly, and encouraged us to advance fast towards the hill, accompanied by Jewish armed guards. We walked for a few hours until we reached the Kibbutz "Maavarot," now, upon reaching safety, we were able to have a calm and fearless rest. A nice party was arranged in our honor; we sat around set tables and in spite of being tired and drenched, broken and depressed we were happy that we made it to the shores.

These were the years of the Arab revolt in Mandatory Palestine 1936–1939. Drivers traveled in armored cabins, busses too were armored, so to avoid bullets from Arabs in ambush. We would hear about daily attacks of Arabs on Jews. I came to the Kibbutz "Ness Ziona" (Givat Michael), and worked at the citrus plants, besides, I would do night shifts as a watch guard at the posts against Arab attacks. The work at the plants was arduous, especially the turning over of the soil and other tasks that were unbearably hard. The Kibbutz existed from hired work at a daily budget of 28 millim (1000 millim equaled one pound). We existed scarcely then, without excessive demands. We didn't need more than a bed, mattress and quilt in a tent, no chair or table, and of course not a closet that was needless, for we didn't have what to put inside. But life was good, happy and lively, filled with constant song and dance, until the year of 1939. During those years the Settlements Department of The Jewish Agency was in search of a place for a permanent settlement for the kibbutz Givat Michael and they offered Rukhama (a girl was born and she was named Rukhama). Thereafter they offered "Kadesh–Naphtali" and this too ended with nothing, until we reached the settlement in the Dafna grounds, which is near the Dan River, on May 1, 1939, we went up there after a few months of preparations. A thousand people with many vehicles from all over the country were enlisted, and in one night the new settlement was put up – "Khoma Ve'Migdal," a number of sheds and a clinic, a lunchroom, a shower. In the morning the colony was standing; the British could not take it down, because of the law that if a house is roofed, it is exempt from being taken down. These territories were not allowed to be settled with Jews and enthusiastically we began to prepare the bare ground to qualify. The grounds were separated and with our joint effort, we built a great model of a colony. Whoever visits it nowadays cannot believe that in such short time we reached such accomplishment.

On September 1, 1939, at the outbreak of World War II, I was then at the Dafna Kibbutz, we worked energetically to put up the new settlement.

At that time, I was sent by the Kibbutz to work in Sodom, where there was a grouped company of the "United Kibbutz." In 1941 the Palm"akh was founded (the strike forces of the "Ha'Hagana"). At the beginning of 1942, I volunteered at the Palm"akh – at the same time, many enrolled with the Jewish Brigade, and our colony too had volunteers at the Brigade. Me and some more members left to the Palm"akh camps which were spread over the farms that belonged to The Labor Settlement.

Palm"akh, an un–uniformed army, soldiers – pioneers, where labor and training was combined at the Kibbutz bases, lived in tent camps, and would be ordered to be transferred from one side of the land to the other. We did our activity and worked below ground. We were a Jewish army based on estate labor and training, but we didn't receive payment for our work – we did get food, meager clothing, lodging in tents and some pocket money. We were all volunteers of free–will. We practiced with any device we got hold of. We only had few tools for operation. We went through almost every type of profession, with not only weapons but First Aid too, how to prepare bombs, sea rowing etc. and most important – to be acquainted with the paths of the land. From time to time we would go out on a two–week voyage: walking by foot in uncertain routes, we passed upon fields and wadis, valleys and hills. Once we walked by foot to Jerusalem, to the north of the Dead Sea and all the length of The Dead Sea, Jericho, Ein Gedi, Massada, Sodom, Machteshim, Maale Akrabim, the lone Arava lane until Revivim. And a different time – to the west Galilee, the Efraim mounts and more.

                    *

For general public property, in addition to my private wealth – a wife and three lovely children – "Sabras"...

The Zionist Labor committee (z.s.) in Wyszkow

(standing from R. to L.): **Chaim Shlomo Levin, Tschechonowietski, Laibel Bresler**

(sitting): **Shlomo Newmark, Moshe Perle, Israel Kaluski, Chonna Appelbaum**

The "Ha'Chalutz" committee

(from R. to L.): **Israel Grossbart, Shaike Gorni, Israel Kaluski, Malka Epstein, Yaakov Mittelbach, Leib Bresler, Chaim–Shlomo Lewin**

[Page 69]

Establishment of the
Zionist Association In Wyszkow
by Mordechai Kronenberg, Tel Aviv
Translated by Chava Eisenstein

In 1910, (Jewish year) 5670, at the ninth day of Av – Tisha B'Av in the afternoon, the entire youth, including Beth Midrash scholars, were called to a meeting in the forest (on the route to Radzymin). The purpose was of setting an organization that should help assist immigration to the Land Of Israel. At the head of the organizers were R. Itsche Skarlet and Israel Asman.

The initial activists were:

R. Itche Skarlet, Israel Asman, Rephael Skarlet, Abraham Mordechai Esthersohn, Leibel Rosenberg (Leibel, Joshua Chaim's son) Chaim Bialystok (son of R. Isaac Hirsch the blind, currently: Chaim Bialas, Los Angeles), Jechiel Meir Altman (owner of the iron shop, later became a big dealer in the city), Jaakob Judel Kasche–Macher's, Samuel Elya Orenstein (one of the founders of Kfar Khassidim) and me – Mordechai Kronenberg (Mordechai, Joshua Winemakher's son), and some more, whose names I don't remember.

At the opening of this rally, R. Itche Skarlet read to us "In The City Of Killing" by the poet Kh.N. Bialik, and Dr. Z'lenow's declaration for the benefit of the Jewish National Fund, named "Keren Kayemet L'Israel." Israel Asman lectured about the significance of organizing Zionist societies, with the purpose of practicing fulfillment of Zionism by settling in the land of Israel, for which only the youth can qualify to build a new nation with a new future in the land.

This assembly left us with a deep impact. Immediately we began doing propaganda in the city, for joining this society. And the result – many youngsters, girls and boys, joined us enthusiastically.

With Israel Asman's assistance, classes were formed for these purposes: The Keren Kayemet, for learning Hebrew, foundation of the "Tarbut" school in Wyszkow and selling Shekels (coins) for The Zionist Congregation, for actual realization, immediate coming to the Land Of Israel, and for building settlements and laboring in the land.

And me, the writer of these lines, merited to be sent as first emissary of The Youth's Society, to the land of Israel, in 1910.

A course of Hebrew, 1919

Zionist committee in 1918

The First Pioneers in Town
by Yisroel Kaluski, Tel Aviv
Translated by Pamela Russ

Alef (first letter of Hebrew alphabet)

The first years of Poland's independence in Wyszkow, just as in the entire country, were under the mark of a stormy slope in the socio–political and cultural development of the Jews. All the parties, organizations, and unions that grew like mushrooms after a rain in the small and larger settlements in Poland, did not leave our Wyszkow behind. The Jewish population in town threw themselves passionately into their raging lives, searching for an ideological path.

The parties did what they had to do: [they had] meetings, open readings, circles, propaganda work, organizations, and the like. There was a great selection of political or social addresses for the Wyszkow Jewish youth.

The Jewish struggle was not only with those who were already established, but it was mainly with those who had not yet tasted partisanship, primarily the young boys in the Beis Medrash [House of Study] and yeshivos, the working youth, and the older generation. The main disagreement was between the Zionist and the anti–Zionist groups. Also, even though the Zionist movement was colorful enough and numerous in its various formats, nonetheless the organizational framework for practical activities and preparation of the youth for Aliyah to the Land of Israel was missing.

The Zionist youth in Wyszkow, therefore, felt the need for a pioneering, Chalutz–type [pioneer] of organization that would, in the town itself, undertake to produce a youth that now was very distant from physical work or in general did not have a defined vocation. In the year 1922, some youth gathered together to establish the first pioneer organization: Yeshaye Gurner (now in Tel Mond), Yisroel Grosbard (Tel Aviv), Shlomo Levin (Kibbutz Givat Hashlosha), Aryeh Bresler (Einat), Yakov Mitelsbakh (Petakh Tikvah), and the author of these lines. Our goal was clear: begin to work in Wyszkow in order to be productive people in the Land of Israel.

[Page 70]

Beis (second letter)

I was eighteen years old at that time. My education, as was the complete atmosphere in our home, was absolutely Zionist. My parents dreamt only of Zion and would correspond with and receive mail from Artur Ruppen, M.M. Ussishkin, and other Zionist leaders. Thanks to this Zionist atmosphere in our home, the path to this movement was easy for me, a path that many of the youth in town had to experience with many stumbling blocks.

Being prepared for Aliyah, and understanding the importance of the work over there in Israel, I and Shlomo Lewin and Yisroel Grosbard learned metalworking in the repair shops for the agricultural machines of Moshe–Dovid Jaskowycz (now in America). Everyone in town knew Jaskowycz because of his modern dress and long whiskers, and also because of his Zionist attitudes. In addition to his eight workers, whom he kept regularly in his workshop, he was always ready to take on more young men who were preparing for Aliyah.

The movement also took care of several Hachshara [organization that prepares for Aliyah] points, especially for girls, whose dreams and hopes for Aliyah and practical efforts for becoming productive, were not any smaller than for the boys. Therefore, the efforts of the first Hechalutz [pioneer organization] committee were great in Wyszkow, to which the following people belonged: Chaim Shlomo Lewin, Aryeh Bresler, Yakov Mitelsbakh, Yisroel Kaluski, Yeshaye Gurner, Yisroel Grosbard, and Malka Epstajn.

Our location was in partnership with the Poalei Tzion Party [Social Democratic Labor Party] (Tz.S.), and was on the central Skolne Street in the house of Eli–Meyer Goldman. The multi–faceted cultural activities of Hechalutz, first included lessons for learning Hebrew that took place in special evening courses, Yediat Haaretz (Palestina Grafia), and actual lessons or speeches on various topics, including Jewish history. In the beginning, there was no marked growth of this organization because we came a little too late, because the town was already filled with all kinds of diverse youth movements from each party. This was also the case because Hechalutz took in young members from the age of eighteen upwards, while the other organizations gave fifteen–year–olds the opportunity to become their members.

And, the view on Aliyah was weak at that time, especially in a place such as Wyszkow.

Gimmel (third letter)

In the first period of pioneers in Wyszkow, there was a strong connection within the membership. The newly arrived element, the majority of whom were chassidic youth, who had no tradition [background] of organization membership, was not inclined to remain in a movement that required of each member both their physical work and patience and perseverance while waiting for their certificates. For those youth who were from the Beis Medrash or the

Yeshiva, their belonging to Hechalutz was for the most part illegal without the consent of the parents. Sending such a young man to work would be a total conspiracy against the mother and father, and this would cause the organization much harm. All these moments contributed to the fact that at the very beginning of the establishment of Hechalutz, there was not a strong following.

In the year 1924, the Wyszkower Hechalutz received its first certificate [emigration license to Israel]. Fate had it that this valuable piece of paper which thousands of pioneers in Poland wanted so earnestly, came into my hands. Thanks to this, I was the first Oleh [person moving to Israel] of Hechalutz in town and the first to merit moving to Israel legally since the end of the World War of 1914–1918. With great emotion, I remember now how I merited having this certificate:

In November 1923, the center of Hechalutz in Poland received an allocated 35 certificates. When I learned of this, I left for Warsaw to Eliyahu Dabkin and pleaded with him to allow me to make Aliyah to Israel. My interlocutor, however, did not indicate any interest to accept my pleas, indicating my unlabored hands and young age that disqualified me as a candidate for Aliyah. But in midst of our discussion, Eliyahu Golomb, later the chief commandant of the Hagganah [Jewish Defense Organization] came into the room. At the time, he was staying in Poland as an emissary from a settlement in the Land of Israel. Golomb had a conversation with me in Hebrew, and after more than an hour of explaining myself, he said to me the following words:

– Go home to Wyszkow and work out a passport for yourself ...

It would still be some time until I would be of age to acquire a foreign passport. But the joyful moment arrived – and I made Aliyah to the Land of Israel.

A group of pioneers from Wyszkow in Yaffo, 1927

[Page 71]

Daled (fourth letter)

For personal reasons, and mainly – for health reasons, after being in Israel for four years, I returned to Poland. In Wyszkow, I now found a broad, extensive organization of Hechalutz, that had many members and a larger number of active, devoted, committed chaveirim [members "friends"]. Tens of pioneers from the town at that time were located at the important Hachshara sites in Czestokhowa, Klosow, Wloclawek, Mlawa, and in a series of other places in the Warsaw area. The movement had established its own location that became an important center for all Zionist youth organizations in Wyszkow. Hechalutz had become the general vehicle through which members of the Zionist youth groups received their certificates.

In the years 1935–1936, in Wyszkow, there was a Hachshara point of the central Hechalutz in Poland. The Hachshara had not set up any steady work places and therefore had to be satisfied with sporadic work by individual Jews. This work entailed, for example: washing laundry, chopping wood, carrying water, and the like. There were many incitements by the local Jewish communists against those who with their difficult toil and poor lives were preparing themselves for Aliyah. And the terror was even greater: constant attacks at the site, on individual chaveirim, and on work sites. Once, one of our pioneers was so beaten up, that he had to be taken to the hospital in Warsaw.

The atmosphere in the town was tense. The movement felt that with our own energies we would not be able to withstand Juskowycz's terror, and therefore, we were forced to bring down two "fighters" from Warsaw – the famous Yidel Prager and Aryeh Treger. We even foresaw the eventuality that we would need to be armed – and to that end, there were some revolvers hidden in my home.

The Jewish communists were not asleep either. They knew that with their own strength they would not be successful at breaking the Hechalutz and liquidating the Hachshara site. So, to deal with that, they brought in a group of Polish shoemaker "khalupnikes" ["cottagers" (those who lived in huts but didn't own the land)] from the nearby town of Branczszyk, who worked for the large shoe stores in Warsaw. These shoemakers were communists and they considered it a mitzvah [positive command from the Torah] to help their Jewish comrades in the town in their struggle against the "Zionist danger." One Sunday evening, the Hechalutz site on the Rynek [market square] was surrounded by Branczszyker khalupnikes and local Jewish communists. There was a mood of a pogrom in the town. The henchmen did not let anyone go in or out of the locale. In this situation, when a little bit of communist and Jewish blood would be spilled, the police did not get involved.

But our chaveirim did not allow themselves to be provoked. Our position was dignified, without fear, without panic, but also not confrontational, so that no one could point at the Hechalutz chaveirim as the guilty ones in the eventual happenings. Later, our tactic appeared to be the correct one. Early Monday morning, the shoemakers from Branczszyk had to return home to work. It was the local Yevseks [Jewish members of Communist Party "Yevsektzia"] who later besieged us, but not with the impetus of chutzpah [defiance], when their Polish chaveirim were in Wyszkow. The rest of the Zionist groups saw the danger that lurked because of the Jewish communists – and united to stand up against the Red hooliganism and terror.

Hei (fifth)

Some time later, it was once more necessary to unite all the Jewish powers; included in this was the Yevsektzia, local Polish communists, and the PPS ["Polska Partia Socjalistyczyzna," Polish Socialist Party] – against the dangers of the NDK [Polish police] thugs and NARA [Polish anti–Semitic Party] bandits and their pickets by the Jewish stores, attacks on Jewish passersby, and widespread Jewish, anti–Semitic hatred that poisoned the air in the town. A general committee was established to fight against Fascism and anti–Semitism, that ran successful activities for about a year's time. The committee held its meetings in secret. Most of the meetings were held in my home, as I was the chairman of the above mentioned committee. At that time, I represented the Poalei Tzion Party [Jewish Social Democratic Labor Party] in Wyszkow, and the Polish representatives (communist agents and PPS), just as the Jewish parties, agreed to give over the chairmanship of the committee to the director of Poalei Tzion. We collected money, primarily from wealthy Jews, prepared arms, and set up special combat groups to fight off the eventual attacks. Collective guards of Jewish and Polish workers would patrol the town at night, in order to give the anti–Semites the feeling of an established strong, united, Jewish–Polish resistance. Aside from that, there was education work in the local villages and in the town itself. Two communists were even tried for these acts and sent to prison. In this wonderful act of solidarity, the following two Polish activists were exemplary: Cytrinek (of the Polish communists), and Drozdowski (from the PPS – Polish Socialist Party).

[Page 72]

Vav (sixth)

Finally, some memories about the Poalei Tzion Party and its youth organization "Freiheit" ["Freedom"], where I was active for a short time.

The Poalei Tzion movement in Poland dug down deep roots within the Jewish settlements, and did not forget our town. I remember that already in the year 1917 (I was twelve years old at the time), that on its own a strong youth organization grew out of the party, and the older members were quite astounded by this development. At that time, we were able to allow ourselves to bring down a special counsellor from Warsaw, teacher Freint. Until the split (in the year 1920) the organization recorded a constant growth. The site on Koscuiszko Street, in the home of Avrom–Yosel Joskowycz, buzzed with the livelihood and incessant singing of the youth. The most active individuals in this movement were: Yakov Stelung, Laya Malczyk (his later wife), Mendel Rozenberg, Bzhezhinski, Chaim–Shlomo Lewin, Yakov Mitelsbakh, and I.

For evening courses, the Wyszkow Jewish youth sat and studied Hebrew, general education, Graetz's history of the Jewish nation. An honorable place in the culture work was occupied by the presentations from the most respected lecturers in Warsaw – writers, journalists, party activists. The beautiful Wyszkower forest and the surrounding areas were a fine place for country houses for Warsaw Jews, particularly for the businessmen who would spend the hot summer months in town. So we used them for recreation in Wyszkow, and our youth enjoyed the readings of a Peretz Markish, Alter Kacyzne, the Dark One [a pseudonym for Yosef Tunkel, Yiddish humorist, 1881–1949], Gottlieb, and others.

Zayin (seventh)

In the year 1921, the Bolsehviks entered Wyszkow and ruled there all of eight days. This was the period of the "honeymoon month of the world's revolution," as we would describe it. The Jewish communists were then "on their high horse." The majority of the then Jewish parties were sympathetic to them at that time – somewhat out of fear, and somewhat out of respect. Almost all of the workers' parties received expansive locales at the time, with many rooms. During the week of Russian rule in Wyszkow, the locations were over–filled, especially the Poalei Tzion club, because they had to create a certain legality for being affiliated with the workers' movement. Each evening there would be passionate discussions with some from the "Politruk"[a] from the Red Army and communist youth, who while present urged us to join their camp. But the majority of the Jewish youth decided not to identify with the communists, but to remain loyal to the Zionist ideology.

After expelling the Bolsheviks from Wyszkow, the communist youth went underground, and the reaction to this was delivered with a strong hand. Many activists were locked in prison and the movement was weakened. Right after the split of the Poalei Tzion (that took place at the end of 1921) in Wyszkow, a large number moved to the leftist Poalei Tzion, and a smaller number remained with the right wing. The rest were neither here nor there.

Only two years later, the organization was given the name "Freiheit" ["Freedom"], and wrote a beautiful page in the history of Zionist activity in Wyszkow. Freiheit experienced many rises and falls. The movement became particularly weakened when the majority of the activists immigrated to America and to the Latin American countries.

The activities of Freiheit, organizationally and ideologically, were tightly bound to the work of Hechalutz. Many activists, myself among them, did not see any conflict between the work of the two movements, only a straight, total consonance.

In the year 1936, my wife, my son, and I made Aliyah (for the second time) to the Land of Israel.

Being torn away from the movement for years because of making Aliyah twice, does not allow me to describe the total picture of this heroic chapter of the Jewish history in Wyszkow that carries the name "Chalutz movement." With the selected fragments of the above mentioned memories I wanted to draw the beginnings and later development of an idealistic and creative Jewish youth in a small Jewish settlement in Poland, that gave its important contribution to the Chalutz vision and deeds, both in Poland and in the Land of Israel.

A group of sportsmen from "Morgenstern"

Original Footnote

a.   Political commissar; an official of the Communist Party who was assigned to teach Party principles.

[Page 73]

The Left Poalei Zion ["Workers of Zion"] and Its Youth

by Yankev Shtelung, Buenos Aires

Translated by Pamela Russ

1.

1917. It's more than three years that there is an ongoing bloody war on the European killing–fields. Millions of dead and wounded. In the so–called hinterland, in the cities and towns in Poland – hunger and hardship, typhus and waves of refugees. The powers are constantly changing. Nonetheless, we are hoping that there will be an end to the slaughter. Is there no limit to the suffering?

And how to express this yearning, if not through ideals and organizations! Where do you find comfort and calm if not in the party clubs, in a society with a common goal? The year 1917 was really the inroad to the " Sturm und Drang"[a] period in the large cities, and also in the smaller settlements. No wonder that already in the year 1917 in Wyszkow, a Worker's Home [club] was established, which the chaveirim [friends, comrades] Jurman, Czembel, Dergycz, Rokhel Malina, and others wanted to decorate beautifully, but also wanted to fill with ideological content. And according to their deepest convictions, it was only the Borochovitch ideology that was totally appropriate for the Wyszkower workers and general population. According to their levels they set up circles for education. They spread literature and dreamed about a better life in a liberated world and in a redeemed Land of Israel…

Along with the parties, that also included elderly people, the city youth began to search for their ideals. At that time, the Bundist youth organization "Zukunft" ["Future"], already had a strong influence in Wyszkow. Their location was the meeting place for the youth in the town. There is an opinion that the "Zukunft" would have remained the only organization in town for many years if not for their opposition to Zionism and the Land of Israel. Their denial of the nationalist freedom thoughts caused a portion of the youth, including some of their own members, to rebel against such an establishment. Therefore, I and Binyomin Tik assembled a council of those dissatisfied with the Bundist program. If my memory serves me correctly, the participants of that first meeting were: Kaluski, Kh. Sh. Levin, Y. Mitelsbakh, M. Brzhoza. At that time, I expressed my doubts about the program of "Zukunft," that although it did please me, but why without the word Palestine? … Since there was an elderly friend in Wyszkow (meaning – Jurman), we should go see him, and maybe he would answer all these questions for us, the ones that were troubling the youths' minds.

Poalei Tzion youth in Wyszkow

[Page 74]

At this meeting, it came out that chaveirim [friends] Kaluski and Levin had the same thoughts, but did not take enough initiative [to resolve the issue]. Now they grabbed hold of the idea of establishing a youth organization in Wyszkow that should also have a place in the program called the Land of Israel… But they said that in order to be "enlightened," we should go to chaver Segal. (You should know that while Jurman belonged to Poalei Tzion, Segal remained ideologically connected to Tzeirei Tzion.) Understandably, we met with these two Jews more than once, had discussions day and night, and were educated until a verdict was reached: When Kaluski, Levin, and Mitelsbakh left for Tzeirei Tzion, Brzhoza, Tik, and I decided to go with chaver Jurman (that is, with Poalei Tzion).

Both groups were organizationally weak and had few people. There was a lot to be done, and the main thing was that the anti–Zionist "Zukunft" should not take over the town. We came to an agreement that both groups, although ideologically not in synchrony, should begin a joint project, first of all – the recruitment, then there should be secret elections that would determine whom to follow. Meanwhile, each group remained in close contact with the older chaver, who gave them direction. Both sides prepared for a fight.

In passionate discussions, the details of the elections were worked out. How to run the electioneering, how and where to distribute the ballots, and so on. At that time, we lived in Khelenowski's house, that was identified by its wide gate. On the day of the elections, none of my family members were at home, so we used the opportunity to stick on election material of both parties on the wide gate. The arrangement was that the elections would be respectful, no one could tear down any proclamations, or upset or disturb any electioneering. Nonetheless, one of the Tzeirei Tzion chaveirim did not restrain himself and tore down a poster of his opponent. I couldn't stand this type of offense that broke our agreement. So I gave him a slap. Don't forget that at the time we were all of fifteen years old, and we took all these issues very seriously – and the tendency to slap had come from the chassidic environment where we had grown up.

Lecturers group of Poalei Tzion

The result of this? The Poalei Tzion got the majority! This increased our motivation, and with renewed momentum we got to work.

Self–education group of Poalei Tzion

2.

At the Dergycz house, we rented a small room as an office. The work and the membership grew. The room became too small to fit the growing needs. A private home no longer was appropriate. It was time to rent a location. We found a fitting place for our needs on Kosciuszko 5. Soon, a library was opened there, with socialist books and brochures. There were also courses for reading and writing, talks about political and literary themes, where we also provided a buffet so you could have a glass of tea and a bite to eat.

Wyszkower youth began to stream to the site because of their thirst for general knowledge and their interest to follow the actual political events in the world and events on the Jewish street. The site was full every night. In town, it was known that the youth of Kosciuszko 5 was hard to win over in discussion. We did not have many older chaveirim, because many had to go serve in the Polish army, while at the same time, others tried to get out of this service – because of the unwillingness to fight against the Bolsheviks, and for other reasons.

The entire burden of the party's work therefore fell onto chaveirim Jurman and Czembal (the latter had come back from Russian prison after the end of World War I) and onto some of the youth.

A contact was established with the youth center in Warsaw which at that time was directed by Lehrer ["teacher"] Avrohom Freint. I remember how we shivered [with excitement] when we held in our hands that first publication of the "Jugend" ["Youth"], "Der Junger Kempfer" ["The Young Fighter"], which was copied [with a hectograph machine]. The movement prepared for the first "youth" gathering.

[Page 75]

3.

In the year 1919, there was the first country wide assembly of the Poalei Tzion youth. Wyszkow already had the right to send a delegate. Since the assembly was semi–legal, the author of these lines had to use a pseudonym in order to be able to represent his organization in Warsaw. From Shtelung, it became Chait [name change].

Meanwhile, a new war began – between Poland and Soviet Russia. As the Bolsheviks neared, persecutions began against the workers' organizations. Especially, against the Jewish ones. Our place was locked up and with that, any organizational and cultural activities. But this did not stop us from putting out an illegal appeal, where the general situation was clarified, and the youth was cautioned to be more vigilant.

"Borokhov Group" of the Poalei Tzion, for the release of Kh. Czembal (16.7.21) [July 16, 1921]

On their march to Warsaw, the Bolsheviks took over Wyszkow. They permitted us to go back to work, and the Revkom [Russian; Revolutionary

Committee] even gave us a place – a former elementary school on Kosciuszko Street.

This good relationship, however, did not last long. At the first meeting, the delegation from Revkom appeared, and ordered that ... we dissolve and register in the communist party. In that delegation, there was a chaverte [comrade, female chaver] Dzhbanek from the Bund, that had already disbanded itself, and from which the majority of members actually did go over to the communists. We, however, were not in such a rush to do so. The answer was: We are waiting for directions from the Central committee in Warsaw. With that, we reminded them that the Poalei Tzion was also a legal party in Soviet Russia. Interesting, the Russian officer agreed with our point, while chaverte Dzhbank was required to renege [on her membership with the Bund]. But they didn't accept what she said ...

Within the eight days that the Bolsheviks were in Wyszkow, we worked together with them, and even helped create the citizens' militia.

4.

As soon as the Polaks became the bosses in the city again, repressions began of those who worked or sympathized with the Bolsheviks. They particularly persecuted the Jews. In the Senator's Garden there was a military court. So the Polish press described our town as the "Red Wyszkow." The military court did not even prevent the carrying out of a death sentence against the young Rubin – but thanks to his young age, the sentence was changed to ten years of imprisonment.

The Polaks also arrested me. After spending six months in the famous "10th Pavilion" [renowned for its political prisoners] in the Warsaw prison on Dzhika, in Mlawa and Pultusk – they released me on bail until there would be a new trial. Returning to the town, I found renewed activity, and a strong, evolved youth organization that met on Kosciuczko Street 5. We became the largest organized power in the town – until the split in 1921.

5.

The rip in the Poalei Tzion movement on a worldly scale, did not forget Wyszkow. After long and stormy discussions, we called a meeting in the forest, with the participation of the chairman of "Tzukunft" ["Future," socialist youth organization of the Bund], Ch. Karol. After a lengthy exchange of opinions and a vote, only a small group (Kaluski, Levin, Mitlesbakh,and Rosenberg) left the meeting. Interesting, that these were the same chaveirim who in the year 1917, were oriented towards the Tzeirei Tzion group, and now they moved to the right Poalei Tzion.

[Page 76]

There was a new committee formed at the leftist Poalei Tzion (Yseof Czembal, Brzhesinski, M. Brzhoza, Moshe Sokol, and I). The large number of members was divided up into groups that held their meetings in the homes of individual chaveirim, because the new government bothered us. In our place, it was difficult to do the politically enlightened work. At least the place was used by the mother of chaver Czembal – and that's why, the Poalei Tzionists in the city were called "Czembalists." ...

At the end of 1921, some chaveirim returned from military duty. This brought a revitalization to the party. The newly elected committee worked to spread the Warsaw "Arbeiter Zeitung" ["Workers' Newspaper"], with which the city library actively collaborated while not neglecting the activities of the "Youth" organization.

6.

In the year 1923, Dr. Eisenstat from Warsaw visited us in order to set up a division of the "Socialist Evening Courses for Workers." True, this name served as a badge for Poalei Tzion to conduct its party and political activities. But the name also obligated us to conduct authentic courses for young workers who couldn't even write a single letter. Particularly, in Wyszkow, there was a large number of illiterates. As soon as we started the courses, 150 young people registered. The first teachers were: for Polish – the young women Wistinyeczka and Malawanczyk; for Yiddish – Ch. Zor, sent from the Central. In these courses, they learned reading, writing, arithmetic, Jewish history, literature, political economy, knowledge of Israel. In the first election, the following were elected: Yisroel and Aharon Czembal, Avrohom Popowski. After the institution grew, and there were already 50 adult, active members, there were new elections held for a new administration, in which the following were elected: A. Czembal – chairman; Wistinjeczka – secretary; Moshe Sokol – treasurer; Yisroel Czembal, Chana Skarlat, Chameneshe Khiles, A. Popowski, and Velvel Popowski. After that, these were the teachers who taught the courses: Zar, Lisman, Plukalowski, and Czuker (all sent over by the Central).

Thanks to the social evening courses, we also began running extensive cultural activities. The library and reading room complemented the work of the courses themselves. These were the library functionaries: Velvel Ruzhe, A.

Czembal, Yankel Stelung, M. Jazhemski, Velvel Popowski, Velvel Nowogrodski. Because of the increased activity, we had to rent a new location where there was a large hall and a stage. This was the largest party location in the city, where every Friday night, there were political and literary events, "box talks" [informal "soap box" presentations], and speeches, with the participation of local speakers and some from Warsaw: Dr. Eisenstat, J. Zerubabel, N. Buksboim, Y. Peterzeil, Val, Yosef Rosen, Yitzkhok Lew, Dr. Refoel Mahler, Dr. Emanuel Ringelblum, the teacher Bratmakher, Kh. Glat, Loifer, Z. Segalowycz, Dr. Y. Kruk, Yoel Mastboim, Laya Finkelstajn, Shloime Mendelson, Dr. Weinreich, Dr. Krasucki, Mina Abelman, and others.

Our society was the first to invite entire troupes to perform in the Wyszkow theater, and especially Friday night, though a bitter clash broke out because of this, with those who kept the Shabbath. From time to time, we also invited down reciters from Warsaw.

At the expense of Poalei Tzion and the social evening courses, we should also describe the establishing of the workers' sports club, "Gwiazda – Stars" that had several hundred members and boasted different levels of gymnastics, football, and ping–pong, and organized contests in the local towns, such as: Ruzhan, Pultusk, Jadow, Bock. The gymnastic exercises were directed by Aharon Czembal.

A part of the Poalei Tzion in Wyszkow

[Page 77]

Under our initiative, a volksschulle ["people's school"] was established in Wyszkow, with the consent of the Central Jewish School Organization (Tzesha) in Warsaw. The administration was a collaborative one between the parties – and Poalei Tzion was represented by the chaveirim: Yisroel Moshe Czembal, Aharon Czembal, Yankel Bronstajn, and Velvel Ruzhe, and others.

"Youth" group and their leaders

7.

At the location of the society's evening courses, the Poalei Tzion party and its "youth" also met there. The two movements held some intense political discussions, especially among the youth. The youth circles carried the names of Borochov, Surek, and Marx. We studied: political economy, historical materialism, the Erfurt Program[1], Borochov's "Class Interests and the National Question," as well as real political and social problems. In the inner circles, we used our own speakers. The chaveirim: Yosef Czembal (until he left for the United States), Moshe Sokol, Yisroel–Moshe Czembal, Yankel Stelung, Aharon Czembal, Yankel Wolman, Moshe Jazhemski, and Feivel Ernstajn. The Borochov academies had a special place. They were organized every year to be held in December with the participation of a speaker from Warsaw. The Central also sent speakers to open meetings. Our goal was also to spread the newspapers and publications that were printed in Warsaw.

The only professional union in Wyszkow – of the needle trade – was composed of all these political factions. The Poalei Tzion in the administration of the union: B. Yismach, V. Ruzha, V. Nowogrodski, and Feivel Ernstajn, who actively worked there.

With great effort, they organized the porters. They were a thoroughly religious element and therefore showed a distrust for the parties who wanted to bring them into the professional union. Once the transport union did get established, the chaver Stelung worked there as a technical secretary – without remuneration!

The Poalei Tzion was particularly active in the election campaigns of the Polish parliament (Sejm). Thanks to the campaigning that we held in our homes, we always received several hundred votes. The open meetings also attracted many people. At the last Sejm elections, the Tz.K. [Tzukunft] decided that we should bring the district list of Poalei Tzion – and we respectfully fulfilled this directive.

We had a particular success in the elections for the Wyszkow city council. The 226 votes on List 2 (leftist Poalei Tzion) resulted in more than one councilman (Yisroel Moshe Czembal). The spokesman of the list was Aharon Czembal.

In the later elections the same chaver was re–elected. The second place candidate was the author of these lines. Spokesman, Moshe Knaster. For the eight years that Poalei Tzion was represented in the city council, and participated in the work of several city commissions (such as for the unemployed and others), we were always active for and kept in mind the interests of the Jewish workers and general population, not fearing the chicanery of the Sinatzia [fascist party that ruled pre–war Poland] and other anti–Semites.

8.

At the First Pro–Palestine Workers' Congress, the Poalei Tzion organization of Wyszkow carried out major education work. And the result? More than 600 votes and ten delegates: Czembal Aharon, Czembal Yisroel Moshe, Stelung Yankel, Knaster Moshe, Jazhemski Moshe, Popowski Velvel, Yismach Boruch, Bronstajn Yankel, Starowiecki Moshe, and Ruzhe Velvel. It is important to mention that the above–mentioned congress took place in the sessions chamber of the Wyszkow city council. This was the first time that a Jewish assembly held its meeting in this room.

The elections to the World Congress of the workers for the Land of Israel, that took place in 1927 in Berlin, led to an incident with the police who sealed the ballot box in the middle of counting the votes. Only when the village chief in Pultusk intervened, did they allow us to reopen the ballot box and finish counting the votes did we take first place.

The party also put forward its candidates for the community elections, with the chaveirim Y.M. Czembal and Dovid Sredni at the head, and spokesman – Y. Stelung. Interesting, that in this very area, we had to withstand all kinds of repressions and even subversions from the Agudah, which was in the very least worried about the success of our list. Because of their behavior, we postponed some of the community elections for several months, until they showed that they had prepared an election list with many names of – deceased people.

Thanks to that, they were assured continued governance in the community. Despite all of this, our list received more votes than the manual laborers and the Zionists.

Several years before the outbreak of World War II, the Polish governing organizations began their persecutions and oppressions against the Jewish population, and especially against the Poalei Tzion. This was an angry message of a far–reaching changing relationship vis–`–vis the largest national minority in Poland. In the spirit of the Hitlerist politics, the economic boycott covered itself completely with the political extermination – until the bloody year 1939 came and destroyed the Jewish settlement in our town.

Translator's Footnote

1. The Erfurt Program was adopted by the Social Democratic Party of Germany at Erfurt in 1891. The program declared the imminent death of capitalism and defined its immediate task as working for the improvement of workers' lives rather than for revolution. (Wikipedia)

Original Footnote

a. "Storm and Stress"; figuratively, refers to 'a period of turmoil.' "Sturm und Drang" was a German literary movement of the late 18th century characterized by works containing high action and emotion that often deal with the individual's revolt against society. (Encyclopaedia Britannica)

[Page 78]

Along the Lines at the Shomer Hatzair In Wyszkow
by Leah Goldstein, Ramat–Gan
Translated by Chava Eisenstein

It was on a Shabbos in May, 1927. Two girls came running and happily announced that they were invited to a meeting at the cell, which is taking place in the nearby woods at the back of the bridge. To be truthful – I wasn't enthused with the idea and of course – didn't participate. I considered myself a very serious girl, and most of the activity there was dancing and singing. That did not appeal to me, but to no avail, the girls didn't leave hold of me until they succeeded to take me one evening to my first meeting with the group in the cell.

We got together, 14 girls, elementary school–girls, part of us in seventh grade and some in eighth grade. We were very impressed with the meeting. Chana Deutsher, of blessed memory, was the head of our group. After only one meeting, I realized that these activities are really very meaningful. We began to work energetically, various committees were elected, in other words – we were given the courage to practice independence. And so, we began to prepare our own actions, since Chana was very busy, she attended high school which was obviously opposed to the fact of students belonging to youth movements. Above all – to Zionist Youth movements. They were forced to hide and disguise themselves when they came to the cell, so not to be recognized, otherwise, they would be dispatched from school that was a Polish school with few Jewish students. The Jews were in any case unwanted, and tuition was so high, that only few were able to allow themselves to go on, and attend school.

The "Shalakhnes" group of HaShomer Hatzair, 1927

With no other choices, most youths were forced to make do with elementary studies and continue to complete studies on their own. And I can say with much satisfaction, that only the Shomer Hatzair movement enlightened the path for us to do so. Moreover, from the song and dance – as it appeared to the outsider, we took upon us a heavy burden. The cell went through a crisis, the high school graduates decided to carry on the studies whilst another part wasn't considering pioneer fulfillment, since the gates of the Land were shut, and without chances of immigration – they left the movement. At the wheel remained, those that were youngsters only a year and a half ago. Responsibility weighed heavy, a few young groups remained and the question: will we be able to go on? We debated a great deal. Looking for solutions, for it was a pity to destroy such a wonderful plant.

I remember when I was invited to a meeting of the group's leadership and was told that I have to start managing the administration. I didn't know then, what exactly that is, but very soon everything became clear to me. The elder group decided to break apart and to attach slowly the young forces, something they wouldn't do in ordinary times.

At one bright day, we were informed of our new roles: a number of girls were dispatched to the pedagogic council, they understandably received groups for guidance, and all this progressed in a dizzying speed. Within 3 months, we remained the responsible regiment over all that is done at the cell. At the start we felt downhearted, we were bereaved. All the older members and the counselors had left us, we felt as though we are afloat. Apparently, the main management knew this, and hurried assistance to our cell in Wyszkow. The emissaries began to come to us. The first was Judeks, after him – Jacob P., Jechiel H. and many followed. These visits were crucial for us. After long discussions we concluded, that together with the few locals we have a full right to existence, that gave us much courage, the main management promised us maximal help. Since Warsaw was only 50 km away from Wyszkow. This encouraging gave us wings and we decided: we are going on!

[Page 79]

We had a hard time with the budget, not having steady income – it was all built on a monthly tax that each group and individual was to give every month. I must say, that we passed the test. The children abdicated on candy, every penny was spared for paying the needed tax.

From children we grew into adults. The first thing we wanted to do – was to go to a summer colony in spite the fact that we didn't have the required funds. The wealthier parents did not agree that their children should leave, and time was short. We made a collective moneybox, and we undertook various jobs as, mending socks, creating paper bags and mostly, packaging candy. We carried heavy sacks to the cell, where we worked energetically all night, for weeks on. We succeeded in gathering a nice sum and together with our private savings, we arranged at Dlugosiodlo a scout's colony of over 20 girls. This colony provided us with many experiences, and even more, encouragement. We learned that our movement is mighty and there is good reason to fight for its existence even in Wyszkow. After the colony, we returned to work and to our studies, more mature, stronger, and more convinced that we are doing the right thing.

We got over the initial hardships, we exercised being head of groups, for each group and regiment. We began to work steadily, we even brought a teacher to teach Hebrew. (There wasn't a Hebrew school in our city). We ascended step after step, a short while later, a delegate from the main management visited to hand out to the most of us, symbols of graduate scouts, of which we were so proud... we certainly deserved it, if we succeeded to overcome the crisis.

Meanwhile, new problems crept up. The proprietor was not willing to keep us any longer. The neighbors urged her, and she too, was an anti–Semite. To add to this, the nearest neighbor was a professor of Theology at high school. The neighbors (all Polish) did every attempt to get rid of us – and at the end, they succeeded at their scheme. We were left outside, with no possibility to find a place so comfortable and nice, like the place at Kosciusko street, in Kopc'ikowa.

During the summer we continued our activities outdoors, our meager belongings were stored at all kinds of private homes. Our home, in spite of my parent's resistance, ended up to be the only home, to where I transferred the cell's archive. We didn't give up so easily with the loss of our cell. At the end, we found a different house with a surrounding garden that was at the end of the street. We had three rooms, one, was – a large hall, where 3–4 groups were able to lead their activities without disturbing one another. We also had the garden and the porch, the big tree in the garden shaded us in the hot days. I loved the cell, it served as a real home, where we found meaning in life that made us feel very good. Here we learned to get to know humanity and see the beauty in each person. To this home, we dedicated lots of concern and devotion. We cleaned the place thoroughly every month, the floor was wooden, we would coat it with oil, and kerosene so there wouldn't be dust when we dance. We polished the windows and decorated the walls and doors with all sorts of pictures and colored glass. The groups competed with each other; after a thorough cleaning, we would spend hours in the cell, observing the fruit of our labor, this was an inseparable part, and we didn't even feel to what degree we are connected to the idea and to this new way of life.

And time did its own – from minor concerns, we "rose" to major problems. The older group was supposed to be leaving and joining Hakhshara. The tasks were many and the sources were few. I was the first to decide on going to Hakhshara. No one at home knew about it. It was clear to me that I won't get my parents approval. Slowly and quietly, I readied myself, and one nice day, I received notice, to go to the periodical Hakhshara in Khins'ini. After much arguing, I was freed from my duty at the cell. This step was to serve as an example for many others. I left the cell for three months in the summer.

I left our unit singlehanded and reached a small faraway place, 10 boys and two girls were there. My first encounter with reality was difficult. I realized that the girls jobs are only washing, cooking, housekeeping etc. but I imagined the Hakhshara – Training for immigration very different. Still, I accepted my job immediately, without hesitating, and I even found meaning in this nature of life style.

The Hakhshara season passed, I came home and went back with more energy to activity at the cell. Meanwhile we found a room that fit barely to be a cell. Then after, we changed to a different apartment, of two rooms outside the city. Here we began to characterize the place, but the creativeness at

Kosciusko street, we just didn't succeed to restore. We tried trying our best to reestablish the cell once more, we made a work schedule, we involved new strengths, and we made progress.

Every year we would go to the summer colonies of all levels, and we stabilized into a normal cell. We felt an inner drive to make an effort and make our immigration materialize. Sure, many laughed at us, but we proved that we have the right outlook at life. We worked a lot for the Zionist Idea and its movement. We distributed Shekels and collected the sum that they themselves picked. This we continued to do for a few years. We, activists, were well-known throughout the city. First, because we made sure to wear our uniform of which we were so proud: the gray blouse with the black tie – and take walks all over the city.

We became famous, the best of youth joined our lines, and with united strength, we filled ourselves, and the many amongst us, with Zionism and progressive contents.

Anti-Semitism began to spread. In many cases, Jewish youths were afraid to pass quiet side streets. When we complained to the Police, they would say: "Who asked you to walk there?!" I remember well a few episodes, which I witnessed by myself: one day I put on a new pink sweater, which my sister Rachel'a z"l gave me. I was in a good mood and walked to my friend Rivtcha Altman z"l to do homework. She lived in a Polish area, I think they were the only Jewish family there, all of a sudden, a fellow appeared holding a full kettle of soot, he came near me – – – and let out all that soot on my new sweater. I was left in shock, all my life I will remember this encounter. This guy was a known hooligan that wasn't able to see a Jew on his way...

The second experience, which I remember so vividly, happened on the day that Simcha P. was leaving us upon immigration. We gathered at the "Khalutz" club to part with him, and say a few words one to another. The club was at the end of Stodolna street. After all blessings and wishes with all that it entails, each of us parted to go home. About 20 steps before my house, that "Sheigetz" appeared again, he gave me a mighty slap over my eye, that I felt it for a month. Of cause I didn't go the next day to the train station. I stayed home many days, I was embarrassed to be seen with my multi-colored eye...

[Page 80]

That is when a new perception overcame me: there is no future for Jewish youth in Poland. Times really changed, and the entire Jewish population is getting to feel it more and more.

I left for the second time to the Hakhshara at Lavlozlawek. I began working seriously on materializing my dreams. I received from home letters and reports about all sorts of oppressing decrees: Jews are forbidden to set up stands at certain parts of the city, they are not allowed to sell a certain product, to visit the main park. Restrictions on every move and step.

I returned home from the Hakhshara, immigration was down to zero. I had to wait for my turn. I wasn't finding my place in our town, I was not able to go back to activity at the cell, I have already lost contact. Besides – others replaced me. Over the years, we infused the pupils to be dedicated and aware to continue practice.

A year later, in 1934, I immigrated to our Land. Little by little, the other activists came too. Relatively, they were only a small amount of all those that were supposed to come. Many of us didn't imagine that the end has come to Polish Jewry – in particular, and of European Jewry – in general...

The "Khabibi" squad

[Page 80]

In the Youth Movement Hashomer Hatzair
by Bina Jakubowycz–Tabak, Ramat Gan
Translated by Pamela Russ

Until today, the song rings in my ears – the song that was carried across Kosciuszko Street, and the dances in our nest [center or clubhouse] in Wyszkow. Many years have already gone by. The youth is gone, but I feel that I am still the young Wyszkower girl from Hashomer Hatzair who dreams of Aliyah to Israel. And it's no wonder: My best and most beautiful years belong to that period when I was in that movement.

Council from the nest ["kein" in Hebrew, meaning "clubhouse"] of Hashomer Hatzair

I came to Wyszkow with my parents in the year 1922. My father was a Wyszkower.

After the few large cities in which we had lived in Russia, this little town seemed strange to me, revolting. But after a short time, when I began to attend the gymnasium, and I befriended the boys and girls in school, I became a whole–hearted Wyszkower. Later, when they would ask where I came from, I answered proudly: from Wyszkow!

On the main street (Kosciuszko Street), in an orchard, there was a tall, white building, surrounded by a wall. This was the gymnasium. The majority of the students were Jewish girls.

Wyszkow was a chassidic town, and you had to attend classes on Shabbath. That's why very few Jewish parents (a total of 3) sent their children there.

But the Wyszkower youth looked for ways to live with their culture – politically and socially. Therefore, various youth organizations were established.

A group of female students from the sixth grade in the gymnasium: Chana Jakubowycz (today in Tel Mond), Faige and Esther Rosner (today in Haifa), Refoel Gurni and Chaim Barab (both in Tel Mond), Esther Bzhoza and Chana Deutcher (both murdered by the Germans), Berl Bzhoza (today in America), as well as the author of these lines – assembled the first group of Hashomer Hatzair under the name "Avodah" ["Work"] which the nest organizes. As the head of the nest, Refoel Gurni was elected. Over time, other members of "Avodah" were also elected as heads of the nest. I managed the nest "Flowers" to which the following belonged: Chana Jakubowycz, Chana Shpira, Bina Holczman, Chaya Neumark, and Chana Kawe. These were all gymnasium students, but one class lower than me.

We were in tight contact with the main leadership in Warsaw and received instructions for our ongoing work from there. Chaveirim from the Central would visit us as well. The Wyszkower nest was exceptional with its beautiful cultural work, the Hebrew courses, and with living together with one another. The gymnasium students began befriending the "Shomrim" [those from "Hashomer Hatzair"], simple working boys. There was also a group of boys only, called "Hagiborim" [the mighty men, heroes], (the head of the group was Refoel Gurni). I still remember a few of the groups, how "Shibolim" ["sheaves"], (head of the group was Faige Rosner); "Chilot" ["bravery"] (head of the group – Berl Bzhoza).

The group "Giborim" [mighty men, heroes]

[Page 81]

What were our activities?

At their meetings, the group "Avodah" would work out a work plan appropriate for each group. Meetings of each group were held once a week. They would study Jewish history, sociology, have literary discussions about all kinds of books, particularly about Peretz's and Frishman's novels [both famous Yiddish authors]. I would prepare myself for one of these meetings just like a teacher of a class, and work through a thesis. The girls would also prepare themselves – and we would hotly and enthusiastically discuss the theme at hand.

We also set up laws for a larger forum of several groups together. I remember one such open law about school "thieves" that we passed together with the older group. Thanks to the cultural activities, we implanted a knowledge into the youth that the gymnasium did not give them.

Very often, we organized trips in the nearby forest that was on the other side of the river. The road to get there required crossing a long, wooden bridge. When we arrived in the forest, while singing, we set up tents, lit bonfires, and danced the hora [Israeli folkdance].

The first Lag be'Omer [holiday on the 33rd day between Passover and Shavuot] remains fixed in my mind, as we organized our nest. We marched through the Wyszkower streets. At the front, was the head of the group, with a blue and white flag, and then the other groups, dressed as scouts with the multicolored ties that indicated the groups, with their heads at the front. Then the flutists and drummers. We marched to the tempo and our singing echoed through the streets. The whole town admired our parade, and even the parents who, because of religion prevented their children from visiting the nest, had tears in their eyes from joy and pride at how Jewish youth were marching so beautifully and with such discipline.

Dear, beautiful, unforgettable years! I see you again, my beloved and dearest chaveirim, and I dance the hora with you again, and sing romantic songs with you.

That is how the town of Wyszkow and its youth lived and breathed – filled with ideals and yearnings, for a trusted and better tomorrow, for a freer Aliyah, spirited and bred by "Hashomer Hatzair."

At the Religious "Ha'Shomer Ha'Dati" Youth Movement
by Menakhem Nagel, Bnei Brak
Translated by Chava Eisenstein

As a member of one of the Religious Zionist Organizations in the pre–war era, I feel an obligation to mention the movement and its members, with whom I walked together hand in hand, during my childhood, living in Wyszkow.

The Jewish youth scout association "HaShomer Ha'Dati" was about the great idea of the Jewish Nation returning to its homeland. Its flag carried the slogan "The Jewish Nation in The Spirit of the Torah and the Land of Israel." This movement didn't make do with empty slogans, but implied a personal obligation on each of its members. Just as was demanded from all traditional Jewish youth.

The "Shomer Ha'Dati" was started by a few teenagers of our town. Amongst its main initiators, whom I would especially like to mention, are: Simon Pazor (secretary at the branch of the Mizrakhi Youth and the Mizrakhi Khalutz). Samuel Chaim Wonswer, Moshe Shedletzki, Shalom and Joseph Koplowitz (all perished). Shmull Zotorski, Menakhem Bronstein and myself, may we live long.

As a main task, while having to struggle for our ideals, we approached various youth circles in the city, we didn't skip any members of different movements, like: Beitar, Ha'Shomer Hatzair, Bnos Agudat Yisrael and the Aguda Youth Yisrael. In a short time, our influence developed progressively. From a handful of members at the beginning, we grew in only a few months to 40 brothers and sisters, which declared allegiance to the Religious Zionist Movement. In conjunction with our numeral growth, we expanded the fields of activity, we were active in the various committees in town: the Keren Kayemet – The Jewish National Fund, and Keren Ha'Yesod – the United Israel Appeal, and all other Zionist foundations. We ran extensive cultural activity, which steered leftist and rightist youth to join our lines. Our membership doubled in a very short time, and we were admired by all types and walks in life. Many youths left their squad at Beitar or HaShomer Hatzair, even girls from Bnos Aguda and Agudat Yisrael left their clubs to join us. The secret of our success was the religious Zionist atmosphere united with exuberant spirits about applying the ideal of Jews returning home in our time.

In addition to our cultural doings, we also lead fitness activity, combining soul with body.

The club was too crowded to house all the members of "Torah and Avoda" (Torah with Work), so we split the cell into groups, each group managed its own educative activity on a limited scale. Besides, there were general meetings and free discussions for all, led by counselor Samuel Khaim Wonswer and Simon Pazor. At onset, our meager means didn't allow us have our own hall, we wandered from place to place. At the beginning, we met at the Mizrakhi hall and Wistnizkis z"l home on Kosciuszko street. From there, together with the elder movement we transferred to the shul place of Elli–Meir Goldman z"l. Frequently, we ran our meetings in the yard that belonged to Zalman Felner. Finally, thanks for our own effort, and donations of members, we ended up buying our own hall.

The next thing was to dress all members of the cell in uniform, with the scout's shades and blue and white stripes on the hat. This was accomplished in a short time and we appeared dressed in them at Lag Ba'Omer, and on the 20'th of Tamuz, (memorial day of Theodor Herzl) when we appeared at the colleges.

In honor of dressing all club members in unison, we made a party that carried on until dawn, we danced and sang Israeli songs. For this occasion delegates of the Shomer Ha'Dati headquarters paid a visit to Poland. We were flabbergasted upon hearing all the praise and compliments, the other branches looked up to us with envy for our success in mastering discipline and order. For only two years after opening, towards the end of 1934–1935, we arranged an assembly for all the religious Ha'Shomer clubs in the vicinity. It was made in our own hall, we decorated the place with blue and white flags, and pictures of the worldwide Zionists and Mizrakhi leadership. On the facing wall were the pictures of the founders of the World Mizrakhi – Rabbi Reiness zt"l and Rabbi Zvi Hirsch Kalisher, Elliahu Gutmacher. At the right were the pictures of Herzl, Bialik, Sokolov and Osichkin, and diagrams of the new Jewish settlements in the Land of Israel.

A short while thereafter, we traveled to a regional conference at Makow – Mazowiecki. We sent our delegates, for which we voted at a general get-together. How happy was I, when I found out, that I and Menakhem Rosenberg were elected as representatives of the club for summer camp, which will be in one of the forests of the area. We felt so respected upon receiving the admission permits from the main leadership at Warsaw.

After returning from the conferences and summer camps. We went back to activity at the movement with renewed energy, since we acquired essential guidance of how to lead the activities.

The headship at our cell organized educational get–togethers on various topics:

World history, Jewish history, the story of Zionism. Talks on nature topics, Exploration and the Bible. We put out an oral weekly newsletter – entrance was free. We set up a "Noah's Ark" and made trips to places surrounding the Bug River. Sometimes, we would personally have emissaries come from the Land, they would describe life at the religious Kibbutz as perfect. Each of us strived with all our might to materialize this ideal, of Torah and toil. But, that's when it began to storm... a disastrous storm which bombarded tragedy on us Jews. Unfortunately, most of us didn't merit to materialize the idea.

I remember one famous event, at the funeral of the Marshal Pilsudski, which was to pass Warsaw on its way to Wilno. Even then, the Polish scouts were envious of us. They couldn't believe their eyes; Jewish youths marching in uniformed dress and disciplined mode, just like genuine scouts. Obviously, that upset them, those Polish scouts, but we were proud of our conduct and appearance.

My heart aches for the many that marched together with us, and didn't live to march at our own land, on Independence Day of the State Of Israel. That horrendous war brought a bitter close to almost all Jewry in Europe, with our town's brethren amongst them. It is not known to me, how, and where, were killed our dear brothers and sisters. Only few were left, scattered all over the globe...

I do know that Menakhem Bronstein, the secretary at the Shomer Ha'Dati in Wyszkow, is living in the USA. And the others are in Israel: Menakhem Rosenberg, Samuel Zotorski, Feivel Ostry, Sima Markhavka, Sara Holland, Brakhc'a Ostrowik, Phaya Brama, Mottel Farbstein.

At completion, I will allow myself to commemorate my annihilated friends: Simon Pazor – secretary at the Mizrakhi, Samuel Khaim Wonswer – office member at the Mizrakhi Youth and the Mizrakhi Khalutz, and instructor at the cell. Moshe Shedlecki, Shalom Koplowitz, Joseph Koplowitz, Khaim Jagoda, Moshe Meir Novgrocki.

May their memory be blessed!

The leadership of Hashomer Ha'Dati

L to R: **Moshe Shedlezki, Mendel Nagel, Simon Pazor, Samuel Zotorski, Shalom Koplowitz, Chaim Jagoda**

[Page 82]

On the Eve of the Jewish Community Elections in the Year 1931

Translated by Pamela Russ

There is a buzz in the town with the supervision elections. Our city totals up to 800 families. There were six lists:

A handworker list (number 1), with Mr. Moshe Dovid Jaskowycz at the head.

Radzimin chassidim – with Chaim–Yehoshua Frishman (teacher) at the head.

A handworker list (number 2) – with Yehoshua Pastalski at the head.

Zionists – with Messrs. Chaim Noson Wajngrow, Janis, Shmaye Rappaport.

Poalei Tzion – with Mr. Yisroel Moshe Czembal at the head.

Agudah – with Mr. Chaim Meyer Lys.

All these six lists were compiled in the election meetings just as in any other large city. Thank God, speakers are not scarce for us even today. The crowd learned how to speak, and that Sunday during the day, the Gerer chassidim organized an "evening" in their own shtiebel [small, informal synagogue] and some parties went there to vote, until they jabbed a knife into one of the young boy's hands.

I will write about the results of the election separately.

(According to a public correspondence in the weekly "Dos Neue Blatt" – a newspaper for Praga and the vicinity; number 4, Sivan 5, 5691; May 21, 1931 – confirmed by a Wyszkower.)

[Page 83]

Non–Profit Fund with the Socialist Handworkers Union
The Wyszkower Loan Fund in the Year 1935
by Paul A. Kramer
Translated by Pamela Russ

(From the article "The United Jewish Relief," printed in "Der Landsman," and published in honor of the 40th jubilee in Wyszkow Support Union ..., 1896–1936, New York, 1936.)

Before me lies a complete report from the Wyszkower Loan Fund of the year 1935–1936. According to this report, the Loan Fund gave out loans in the year 1935, to the following skilled workers:

41 tailors, 50 shoemakers, 12 carpenters, 6 butchers, 102 from other vocations.

9 from manufacturing and from haberdashery, 24 – leather works, 16 – food stores, 79 – market sellers and street merchants, 6 – village goers [merchants on the road, traveling to villages], and to all kinds of other small businesses – 170 loans.

In total, 523 people used the loans from the Wyszkower Loan Fund in the year 1935.

That same year, the following loans were given out from the Wyszkower Loan Fund:

> 40 loans of 25 zlotys
>
> 20 loans of 30 zlotys
>
> 9 loans of 40 zlotys
>
> 172 loans of 50 zlotys
>
> 8 loans of 60 zlotys
>
> 70 loans of 75 zlotys
>
> 316 loans of 100 zlotys
>
> 2 loans of 200 zlotys
>
> 13 loans of 150 zlotys
>
> 14 loans of 20 zlotys

In total, throughout that year, 50,529 zlotys were given out as loans to individuals.

Taking into consideration the small Jewish population in Wyszkow, these numbers give a good idea of the difficult Jewish situation. The main thing – was how important this Loan Fund was for the poor Jewish population in Wyszkow.

Administration of the Free Loan Fund, 1935

Standing from right: **Borukh Khutnicki, Berish Haldak, Yakov Gamre, Zalman Felner, Bromo**

Seated: **Yehuda Yosel Malczik, Moshe Zelig Ostry, Shaike Postolski, Yakov Dovid Pseticki, Borukh Ciwiak, Yitzkhok Babek**

[Page 84]

Interest–Free Loan Fund
for the Socialist Handworkers' Union
by Y.M. Czembal, Buenos Aires
Translated by Pamela Russ

Celebration of the five–year jubilee of the Interest–Free Loan Fund, 1935

Seated from right: **Yosel Polocker, Yankel Jakubowycz, Dr.Gutstat, Dr. Leicher, Director Giterman (from the Joint Central), Yisroel Moshe Czembal, M.Z. Ostri, Shajke Postolski, Yekel Dovid Przeticki, Zundel Elboim, Chaim Jonasowycz**

In the first years of Poland's independence, when poverty among the Jewish masses was huge, and in the public soup kitchens that gave out free soup there were long rows of people who needed help – Joint, American Jewry's most important aide–institution for European Jews, decided to provide assistance in more constructive means as a support for the Jewish population in Poland. Instead of helping once or twice in the form of a soup kitchen, product distribution, clothing packages, etc. – they decided to open interest free loan funds, [that is] people's banks or interest free loan funds, to distribute loans under favorable conditions for those who needed the aid, in order to put them on their feet. The intention was that the non–productive elements that showed that they needed support, should be able to infuse their lives with productivity – in business, handwork, and small trade [small retail business]. This was one of the nicest and most wonderful activities in the history of Joint: They forced social cases to turn into productive people.

At that time, in the entire Poland, and within Wyszkow too, various institutions, organizations, and societies were set up to service not only party politics, but also the social and material [needs]– of the various classes within the Jewish population. Unfortunately, I don't have the necessary material for all of this, because the main facts in the publishing of this Yizkor book, already speaks enough about the fate of Wyszkow. Therefore, according to my memory, I will describe the establishment and actions of the Interest–Free Loan of the Socialist Handworkers' Union in our town. Aside from that, I left Wyszkow in the year 1936, and the only memento that I have with me to this day is a small calendar from the Fund – one that was given out in the year 1933 ...

At the end of the 1920s, a Handworkers Union was established in Wyszkow as a local unit of the citizens Handworkers' Central in Warsaw. At the head of the newly established organization were: Eliyahu Meyer Goldberg, a baker–entrepreneur, who did not stand at the oven but hired other workers to do so: Moshe Dovid Joskowycz, the technician; a certain Khzhan, Fishel Bronstajn, and others. They rented a room in Goldman's courtyard, created a stamp and when they received several hundred dollars from Joint, they opened a fund.

[Page 85]

Sadly, it must be said that this new institution did not show outstandingly great activity and wide–spread work. After distributing some smaller loans to an insignificant number of handworkers, the activity of the fund almost came to a complete halt. This caused Joint to also terminate its support. There was now a pressing danger that Wyszkow would remain without a source of effective and constructive aid for handworkers, small merchants, and general needy people.

Under these conditions, it is no wonder that the requests to our compatriots in New York were more frequent and more urgent. Of the 2,000 souls in the town, half came for assistance for Passover to their compatriots on the other side of the ocean. Our brothers in New York were not sparing with their help. Each Passover, they would send $1,000 to be distributed. The Wyszkower aid society in the suburbs, however, also knew that Joint supported interest–free loans in Poland, and so posed the question as to why such a fund did not exist in Wyszkow. An answer came from Joint that they actually did send money and that such a fund was opened, but it was not active. Joint's policy was that the city itself had also to raise money for a loan fund. So, just as the necessary funds were put together, Joint added the same amount – and the fund was opened. But Wyszkow did not do so. So the compatriots in New York ran a campaign for constructive help and that's how they reassured that Joint would contribute even a larger amount.

When a group of handworkers in Wyszkow from various areas found out about this, they decided at a meeting to send out a delegation to Joint in Warsaw. But here they explained to the delegation that if the existing fund would not be reorganized, then they themselves would do nothing.

When [the delegation] came back to Wyszkow, the messengers, as well as the other handworkers, asked the administration of the fund to renew their activity, call a general assembly, and elect a different administration – but this went without heed. They explained to these activists that to activate the fund also meant acquiring increased support from the compatriots in America and from Joint.

Unfortunately, they could not come to an understanding. Now everyone felt that there was no other way than to establish another handworkers' union. An appeal to the Warsaw Central of Socialist Handworkers' Union quickly gave these results: A unit of this union was established in Wyszkow.

In the first administration, these were voted in: Postolski, Czembal, Wengrov, Ostri, Malczyk, Brome, and others.

The fund was opened in the year 1930. Until the final minutes, efforts were made to activate the old union – but without success.

In Wyszkow proper, we set up a small chapter and began giving out the first loans. The later administration was set up as: Yitzkhok Rajcyk – chairman, a simple Jew, a smith by profession; vice–chairman – Yisroel Moshe Czembal; secretary – Shajke Postolski; treasurer – Moshe Zelig Ostri; elected members – Chaim Yonasowycz, Yehuda Yosel Malczyk. Shmuel Brome, and others whose names I cannot remember now. Every member of the fund had to pay a minimum fee of ten groshen [coins, pennies] a week.

Some time later, we received money from our compatriots in America and also from Joint in Warsaw. The number of people who received loans increased each day. These were not only handworkers, but also small merchants. There was never enough money to satisfy everyone, and they had to wait in line to receive the loans. The most difficult time for the fund was before the Jewish holidays. The tailors, shoemakers, spat makers, and small merchants who ran their business in booths, would always go to Warsaw before Passover to buy their raw materials and accessories to work on their items and sell them on market days – Tuesdays and Fridays.

I will never forget the Tuesday evenings after market day, or after a fair day (every Tuesday following the first of the month there would be a fair day) when our Jewish handworkers and small merchants would count and calculate the profit of the day and then plead with the fund to give them a needed loan so that the next day, Wednesday, they could go to Warsaw and once again get the required materials for themselves so that they could continue their business and work. But more than once, someone left the site of the non–profit organization upset or embittered because the available capital was not sufficient for everyone's needs. More than once, there were tears in the eyes of one Jew because his entire existence depended on one small loan...

The administration struggled with this problem – how to increase the capital funds? It was decided to turn to the wealthier Jews in Wyszkow and ask that they lend a certain amount of money to the fund, interest free, in order to relieve the needs of those who required a loan. In part, this plan worked. We say in part, because the majority of the wealthy Jews did not want to reveal the amounts of monies that they had to the fund.

Some time later, I was elected chairman of the administration. The goal was that our fund should provide for all ranks of the population, particularly the Jewish population in the town, for whom a small loan, under favorable conditions, would be able to put them on their feet. To that end, an extended council was formed with representatives from all ranks. The Rav and other delegates from the religious sectors participated, although the majority of the members of the administration of the Non–profit Loan Organization of the Handworkers' Union were worldly Jews. At the meeting, we informed them of the activities of the institution, and with numbers and facts showed who received services from the fund, and discussed the challenges and means used of connecting with the wealthy Jews.

[Page 86]

The report, as well as the fact that the administration comprised people from other ranks and groups, provoked the council to apply more earnestness to our institution. At that point, a "Social Friend of the Non–Profit Fund" was established. Dr. Leicher, the city's doctor, was elected chairman of this society. He was also chairman of the Merchants' Union fund; Dr. Gutstat – dentist; Yakov Jakubowycz, Yosel Ploczker, Yitzchok Epstajn – chairmen of the community; and others. (Dr. Leicher was later the commandant of the uprising in the death camp Treblinka. As Yankel Wiernik writes in his book about the uprising of Treblinka, he erroneously states that Dr. Leicher came from Wengrow. He actually did come to Treblinka from Wengrow, because Wyszkow was destroyed very early on in the first few days of the war – but Dr. Leicher is originally from Wyszkow.)

Establishing such a committee gave our institution much importance. Even the wealthy Jews began to show more interest in supporting the fund. More actions were taken to increase the monies in the fund. And therefore, the Joint also increased their subventions.

In the year 1935, in conjunction with the fifth year of existence of the fund, we held a great celebration, which was attended even by the general director of Joint in Poland, Dr. Giterman. This also proved to be a "good name" ["Giter man" means "good man"] for us in the Joint and in the relationship of the institution and the fund. (At this point, I would like to mention this fact: I went to Warsaw to bring Dr. Giterman to our celebration. On the way back to Wyszkow, in the same train, he had a first class seat while I had a seat in the third class. But as soon as the train began to move, he came to me in the third class, and we talked about our issues for the entire rest of the trip.)

The celebration took place in the large hall of the fire department. After a report of the author of these lines and greetings from Dr. Leicher, a friend of the Society of the Non–Profit Loan Fund, Director Giterman reported on the aide funds in Poland. After the celebration, we prepared a beautiful dinner for both administrations and for the delegates from Jadow, Serock, Dlugosiodlo, Goworowo, and so on. After the meal, everyone escorted Dr. Giterman to the train.

Joint in Warsaw gave authority to our administration to set up non–profit funds in the surrounding towns. The friends Postolski, Elboim, and Czembal, visited the neighboring settlements, held open meetings, and helped them with practical means to set up their work.

My report will not go completely until the tragic year of 1939, because I left Wyszkow on January 26, 1936, immigrating to Argentina. At the farewell banquet in honor of my leaving, the chairman Dr. Leicher, as if sensing what was coming, declared the following, among other things, in his greetings:

"I am envious of you that you are leaving Poland. If I could, I would do the same thing..."

After presenting me with a gift and praising my dedication, I was asked to stay on with this work, and told that the fund was prepared to pay me a salary (until now, all the work was done without remuneration). Understandably, I did not accept the offer.

As far as I can remember, 800 families received loans at the beginning of the year 1936. The following were members of the administration: chairman – Y.M. Czembal; secretary – Shajke Postolski; treasurer – Yakov Dovid Przeticki, Chaim Yanosowycz, Bins Burstyn, Yehuda Yosel Malczyk, Berish Aldak, Yankel Wolman, and others. The bookkeepers were Zindel Elboim and Yakov Yakubowycz – the bookkeepers were volunteers.

The following belonged to the social committee, "Friends of the Fund": chairmen – Dr. Leicher, Dr. Gutstat, Yosef Plocker, Dovid Sredni, Moshe Stern, Yitzchok Epstajn, and others. If someone is not mentioned here, note that there is no ill will, only simply – no memory, and should not feel left out.

When I was already in Argentina, until 1939, I maintained continuous correspondence with Dr. Leicher and Postolski, who informed me of the ongoing work of the fund.

After I left, Mr. Zhepka was elected as chairman of the administration.

On the first of September, the busy social life of the Jews in Wyszkow terminated forever. Along with that, the short but fruitful activity of the Wyszkow Non-Profit Loan Fund of the Socialist Handworkers' Union also ended.

[Page 87]

Sports Clubs and Self Defense
by Baruch Yismach (Buenos Aires)
Translated by Abraham Holland

Donated by Howard. B. Orenstein

Sports Club "Morningstar" ("Morgenstern")

In the year 1925, the idea arose to create a sports club. Understandably, the need to organize such a club was another link in the chain of societal activities, such as early-morning school, evening courses and professional groups. The first was the woodworking section. Afterwards, it was broadened to include many other skills. This ambition then included forming libraries. Almost every party and organization took upon itself the initiative to create its own library. Understandably, the availability of books was not very great---but people did read. Every library put up its best person as librarian. It was also decided that a reader could not keep a book more than 15 days. When a reader returned a book, the librarian had the right to test him to see if he had actually read it. And if he did, whether he understood it.

Many times there were strong and passionate discussions about the heroes of one or another book. The most requested books were those of: Sholom Aleichem, Sholom Ash, Y. L. Peretz, Avraham Raisen, Peretz Hirschbein. We, the young readers, barely out of school, loved the Jewish writers.

The second most requested were the works of Tolstoy, Dostoyevsky, and others. Understandably, there were not many copies available. Sometimes there were many weeks of waiting for a requested book. Because of this the librarian had to accept the complaints from all, because it was, of course, his fault.

I volunteered to be the librarian because in the bylaws of the three sports clubs that were organized at that time, the first task was to find a librarian.

The sports movement started with two clubs. "Maccabi" formed from the secular elements of the city with the active participation of the "Chalutz" and "Shomer Hatzair," and the United Worker Sports Club, "Skala." But the union did not last very long---only a few weeks. The main reason was ideological. From "Skala," there left the whole organized movement of the leftist "Poalei Zion" who then immediately formed a third sports club "Gviyazda" ("Shtern"). After that the ambition to overtake each other broke out. Each club formed a football team and in the town it became lively because of the competition. At the beginning the matches were strictly of a local character. The victories were varied. It goes without saying, the atmosphere in the town was tense because a victory in a match also meant the victory of one club's ideas over another.

I have commented earlier about the political affiliation of the "Maccabi" and "Gviyazda" clubs. The "Skala" club belonged to the Communists. Known as "Yevsektziyeh," they also enticed a certain element, politically undecided, under the slogan, "If you are a worker, then you must belong to this club." In this way, almost every club became entrenched in a party. Although the battle between the Jewish clubs was a bitter one, yet there were certain individuals with a greater understanding. When one of the clubs had to travel to another town for a match they would borrow players. There were also moments of farat (?) when, for instance, "Gviyazda" had to play the town club of a different town, and they borrowed a player or two, the last ones played especially weak so that their "idea club" should win. However, it was different when a Polish club called for a match, then "Maccabi" and "Gviyazda" were in full understanding that they would play with full earnestness and win.

[Page 88]

There was also a time when two clubs made an agreement to hold a common gymnastic exhibition. The only club that organized a full array of sports sections was "Gviyazda." They even had uniforms for each section. It was imposing when the club would march from their location, through the town, to the places where gymnastics were held. Our elders were not happy. There were already those who were spreading all kinds of rumors. However, when the idea of an organized self-protection was brought out, and that gymnastics made the muscles strong, these people became sadly quiet.

Two moments stand out from that nice era. One: The sports club "Gviyazda," made up of a men's section, a women's section, and a youth section, each in their representative uniforms and sports insignia, marched from the center of town to the train station "Puflaves" and after that in full dress into the town of "Ruzan." Our arrival in Ruzan caused a whole revolution. An orthodox town, it was not accustomed to seeing such a group of young men, women, and children, dressed as soldiers---although not soldiers. The Jews ran to their Rabbi and asked what to do with us, The Rabbi ruled that since it was Sabbath eve, the town had to welcome us. We felt very good that Sabbath and Sunday. Monday evening, when we returned, there was waiting for us a large mass of people and our parade into town was a beautiful demonstration of Jewish strength and organization.

The second moment was: The 13th Peoples Army, which was famous in Pultusk with their football section made up of officers, challenged the club "Gviyazda" to a match in Pultusk. The parents of our players did not allow them to travel there. The population was known as the worst sort of anti-Semites. Knowing that our team would not allow them to win easily, it was a real fear for the lives of our players---but the challenge had to be accepted. After a bunch of discussions, in which most of the Jews in town took part, it was decided that the team would travel and allow the others to win, but with honor.

There were also moments when the Jewish club had community problems.

Outing for the Wyszkówer Sports Club "Stern" in the town of Rozan

There was in Wyszków a habit (difficult to tell when it started) on Friday evenings, after the meals, of almost all the young Jews strolling back and forth in pairs and in groups. We talked, had discussions, gossiped about this one or that one. There was enough time for this. The stroll lasted from about 9 p.m.

to 11 p.m. The street was full of people. The laughter and happy voices made the stroll very pleasant. As it turned out, our Polish neighbors couldn't take this, and they hired street youths, got them drunk, and sent them out to chase the Jews off the street. When such a "goy" showed himself among the strollers and started yelling: "Jews to Palestine," there was a commotion in the street, a panic, people fell. One person stepped on another. At one edge of the town there was running away and at another edge there was yelling that Jews were being killed. After such a panic, the center became empty. There was a fear of going out of the house. These occurrences took place fairly often. The hired hooligans received much help from volunteers who took pleasure in the activity, and their nerve got greater each time. One goy was able to chase a thousand Jews. The leaders of the Jewish sports clubs got together and agreed to form a self defense. They chose the healthiest and most daring young men and formed them into pairs. The first task was to put an end to the panic---to stop the running away of many from one---to defend the Jewish honor and prevent possible serious happenings. The second---not to allow the "Shabbos" strolls to end. It was not a small task to demonstrate to the membership of the "Skala" club that the first priority is to remove from the streets the hired bullies---mostly wood workers--- that belonged to the same professional group and let them know that for a little whiskey they don't have to sell out the Jews. In that area we did not accomplish much. But the strolling Jews knew that among them there were strong hands that were prepared to beat off every attack. There were instances when we allowed our fists to be used against those hooligans that refused to move off and go home. Our tactic was this: At the start we told of our plight and begged them to stop---because today their work would not succeed. Sometimes we were able to prevent a fight, and other times we had to carry out our threat and force them to taste gutter water, where we let them lay to sober up.

[Page 89]

The anti-Semitic group also did not rest. Even if their strength was not up to it they were able to receive help from the police. Behind them were always the policemen. In this way they were the innocent ones and we --- the guilty. In a well-organized manner, they started a war against individual people in our organization who were pointed out to them. A warning arrived: Either leave the town or receive a knife in the back. Many of the youth left, mostly to Latin American countries---the only places where one could emigrate in the years 1929-1930.

The Jewish situation became worse---the self-defense had to stop. Against hooligans we could defend ourselves but against the police we were too weak. Besides that we were informed that any self-defense could lead to a Pogrom.

[Page 89]

The Sport Club "Maccabi"
by Sh. Sh., New York
Translated by Pamela Russ

The nationalist attuned youth in Wyszkow understood that other than [doing] general political, educational, and Zionist work, it was also necessary to attract the younger generation into their own sport society. To that end, the sport club "Maccabi" was established in the spring of 1927, where the youth, who had the Zionist ideal close to their heart, came.

Under the chairmanship of Shaul Stajnberg, the founding meeting was held in the home of Mendel Stelung. The meeting was conducted by the secretary Binyomin Brok. As I can remember, the participants were: Yitzchok Nudel, Esther Kurnet, Mendel Rosenberg, Yehuda Olshaker, Faige Bronstajn, Gitele Hiler, Bluma Zuzel, Khava Edelman, Shaul Grosbard (all now in Israel); Dina Rozenstajn (in Costa Rica); Yisroel Tenenbaum (in Argentina); Surtche Bzhuzha (in Cuba); and the holy martyrs Shimshon Erlikht, Yisroel Malina, Mikhal Holand, Zundel Elboim, Avrohom Banakh, Majcze Paniatczyk, Nekhama Bulmstajn, Yisroel Skarlat (the son), and Gitele Najmark. Of those who died – Khana Jakubowycz, Feivel Grinberg, Khava Krystal. I hope those whom I did not mention here because of my poor memory will forgive me.

The call of the founding meeting was taken up with enthusiasm by many of Wyszkower Jewish youth. Within a very short time, Macabbi grew into a large sports club that benefited from the moral and financial support of the majority of Zionist groups in the city.

From right: **Yisroel Tenenboim, Goldman, Gurner, Zeltman, Mesing, Rotenberg, Lewiner, Blumstajn, Domb, Jagoda, Prager, Miera, Tandeczsat, Bzhuzha**

Seated: **Alenberg, Rotenberg, Zeltman**

The friends [chaveirim] Shimshon Erlikht and Yisroel Malina were hired as instructors and accomplished their work with great enthusiasm and commitment. The chaver Erlikht also successfully set up his own choir that appeared at almost all Maccabi events with great success.

[Page 90]

The football section practiced regular activity and the athletic groups earned themselves a name in the region and were acknowledged by the Polish union of sports clubs in the Wyszkower circle.

The union [sports association], known by the initials W.O.Z.L.A. (Wyszkowski Okrennowy Swiedzek Lekkoatletyczny), which, other than Wyszkow, also included Pultusk, Makow, Serock, and Czekanow, approached Maccabi about registering in the association. The invitation was accepted and the Wyszkower Jewish sports club took active participation in all the region's competitions.

The athletic group of the Maccabis

First row: **Mikhal Brama, Khana Jakubowycz, Nekhama Blumstajn, Bluma Zuzel, Yisroel Malina**

Second row: **Avrohom Bahrav, Shimshon Erlikht, Zundel Elboim, Jan Wiernicki (a Polak, chairman of W.O.Z.L.A.), Tenenboim, Dina Rozenstajn, Esther Kurnet, Mirtche Paniatczyk, Feivel Grinberg**

The surviving Wyszkower Jews still remember that Lag b'Omer[1], when Maccabi and their blue and white flag appeared on the streets of the town and marched with the resonances of the orchestra that played Zionist songs. The enthusiasm of the Jews was boundless. Even the non–Jewish population did not scrimp on their compliments of the beautiful performance.

The activity of Maccabi was not limited to sports exercises and competitions. Very often, readings, concerts, classes, balls, and entertainments were organized. In the inner circles and groups, they studied Jewish history and delivered anatomy lectures.

Deeply etched in my memory is the successful Herzl–seminar of the 20th of Tammuz [Hebrew month, generally in July], that took place in the largest hall in the city – in the firemen's hall. Almost all of the different strata of the Jewish population participated in this successful evening, with the contribution of local and outside energies. Many Jews were left outside because of a shortage of space.

Also, all the various celebrations, evening dances, and balls in conjunction with certain Jewish holidays, were always very successful in a holiday mood.

In general, Maccabi did not miss the opportunity to celebrate the Jewish holidays. It was clear that all profits were designated toward the Keren Kayemet fund of Israel.

Thanks to the sports and their general activities, the club evolved quickly [greatly]. New sections were created, and the life of the Jewish youth acquired a completely different appearance.

Our sports club was also invited to various other activities in the surrounding towns.

Football players of Maccabi during a match with Ostroleka

Once, on a chol hamoed Sukkos [intermediate days of the Sukkos holiday, between the third and sixth day, a lesser holiday], the football section of Maccabi, along with the orchestra, went on the road to Pultusk. After the match, there was a great ball with all kinds of attractions. The profits from the event went to Keren Kayemet.

In general, there were no Zionist events in Wyszkow in which Maccabi was not an active participant.

Unfortunately, I am not in a position to describe purely from memory the all–around and broad–based activities of the Maccabi club, especially because I left Poland in the year 1932.

"Hapoel" Wyszkow, 1936

Translator's Footnote

1. A Jewish holiday celebrated on the 33rd day of the Counting of the Omer, days between Passover and Shavuot, which occurs on the 18th day of the Hebrew month of Iyar.

[Page 91]

The Worker's Sports Club "Skala"
by Mayer Leyb Holczman, Buenos Aires
Translated by Pamela Russ

In about the year 1925, the Worker's Sports Club "Skala" was established. At that time, there also existed all kinds of social, cultural, and sports organizations.

Three members of the cyclist section
(from the right): **Khaim Ayon, Shayna Ayon, Mendel Stelung**

"Skala" was the first Worker's Sports Club in Wyszkow and included the more mindful youth which actively participated in the exercises, surveys, and performances of the club.

In the evening, after a hard day's work, we assembled in the forest for all kinds of sport exercises, hiked for a few kilometers on the Radzyminer highway, until Kamenczyk, all the while singing all kinds of songs. Our instructors knew their jobs well, they served in the Polish military.

We had all kinds of courses on cultural and political themes. In the summer of 1926, when a number of chaveirim [friends, colleagues] born in

1905 had to present themselves for military service, we organized a bicycle excursion to Pultusk in the sports dress of the club. We were welcomed warmly by the Pultusk youth.

There was a very active cyclist section in the club founded and managed by chaver Mendel Stelung. Wearing white hats, green belts, and black lacquered caps, in an organized manner, and as representatives, we went out to exercise on the Serock highway. After completing the exercises, we strolled back to the city via the wooden bridge. While the Jews were watching us with pride and joy, the Polish youth demonstrated their envy and displeasure with the Jewish cyclists.

All this existed until the Hitler beast attacked Poland and also destroyed our home town of Wyszkow.

Membership card of "Skala"

[Page 92]

Worker's youth at a gathering in the forest, 1929

[Page 95]

Religious Life

Religious Institutions and Shtiblakh
by Motl Wenger (Montevideo)
Translated by Judie Ostroff Goldstein

in Honor of Rabbi Szmul Cywiak

Wyszków was renowned as a Jewish and Hasidic city. This name was absolutely right. To catch a glimpse was enough, especially of the market place and main streets during shabes [the Sabbath] and yontoyvim [religious holidays] in order for every Jew's heart to be filled with pride. Everything was closed. The Jews, dressed in their best and finest clothes, with tales [prayer shawl] bags under their arms streamed in large numbers to the bes hamedresh [synagogue, study and meeting hall], to the Hasidic shtiblakh [small Hasidic prayer house] and minyonim [groups of ten men needed to make a prayer quorum]. However the progressive youth quietly strolled and chatted about world, polish and local events. When people arrived by train in Wyszków, Jewish porters were there to offer their help.

The shtetl was rich in religious institutions. The seat of honor was occupied by the large bes hamedresh located in a large building with a courtyard. The Jewish kehilla [community council] was also located there (president, Icchok Epsztejn). Among its many functions was overseeing the permits for slaughtering animals...the Talmud-Torah [free schooling until age 13 for poor boys] was located in the same building, under the direction of Reb Boruch Cywiak hy"d [whose death god should revenge-used for Holocaust victims]. The shtetl's poor children studied there in four groups. There were people coming and going all day and during the evening. Members of various khevras [societies]– ein yankev [Ein Yakov-Jakobs Spring. One of the best knows works of rabbinic literature-collection of legends, fables, moralistic passages and commentaries by Rashi], medresh [Midrash, homiletical exposition of the scriptures], mishnayes [and others studied on their own or with melamdim [teachers].

The gabe [synagogue trustee] of the large bes hamedresh was Reb Jechiel Mejer Domb. The shamosim [sextons] were Reb Tuwia, Reb Szmul and others.

Assistant shames – Reb Herszynke also woke everyone for slikhos [morning prayers said during the High Holidays]. There was a large bookcase in the bes hamedresh containing religious books which were used by those who came to study – from the well versed in Torah to the simple artisan. The tables were overwhelmed with tallow candles. To the left and upstairs was the women's section which was full every shabes and yontef [religious holiday].

One floor up was the Yeshiva Bes Yosef. During the summer, the tasty sound of their studying carried forth from the open windows. Their speech was Litvak and they studied musar [morals, ethics studied by Misnagdim, the opponents of Hasidism]. The yeshiva director was Szymon Chafetz, a very religious, good-looking man who inspired repentance especially during the month of elul [Aug/Sep – last month of the Jewish year], the month before rosheshone [Rosh Hashanah – New Year]. For a while the yeshiva director was Reb Szymon Srebrnik. He married in Wyszków and became a resident.

The list of religious institutions located in the bes hamedresh building does not end here. The mikve [ritual bath] was in the courtyard. The female bath attendant controlled all the Jewish wives, making sure they observed tares hamishpokhe [laws of cleanliness that applied to the family]. The men had to furnish their own brooms to beat themselves. As the water in the mikve always had to be moving, the last bather was Jechiel Mejer Rampa. During the first days of the Second World War, the Germans shot him near the mikve.

Against the mikve was the poultry slaughterhouse. Every erev [eve] shabes and yontef, especially erev yonkipper [Yom Kippur, Day of Atonement], the courtyard was full of women who arrived with a fowl to be killed. More than once a slaughtered hen, with its last strength, had stood up and even walked around flapping its wings...

The hakhnoses-orkhim [free room and board for poor travellers and the impoverished] was also in the same courtyard and had two rooms – one for men and one for women. The overseer was a small, blond man who also had another job: shoemaking. He and his family lived there. Next to him lived the town shames, Szmul with the nickname "mvaz" (Yiddish"red") ["speak"] because the rabbi didn't know any Polish so once he was called to speak for the rabbi during a visit by a government official. Szmul shamas also had another job. He had a stand at the exit of the bes hamedresh courtyard where he sold cooked beans, peppered chick peas, candy and apples, by weight, measure and by the piece...the majority of his clients were yeshiva students and boys from the Talmud-Torah.

Neighboring the courtyard was Rabbi, Reb Jakob-Arja Morgensztern's house. He was the Wyszkower rabbi. Every year at sukes a long suke was put up in the long courtyard. Wyszków was certainly worthy of it as our rabbi filled the place of the Lomozer and Radzymin rebbes. During yontoyvim a great number of Hasidim would come to him and a large suke was necessary. There is a story that when the Wyszkower Hasidim wanted to build a brick suke [Sukah, wood hut with branches for a roof where Jews eat and sleep on Succot, the Feast of Tabernacles], a rich Jew donated the roof, another the windows, a third the walls and still another the floor. But they couldn't find anyone to donate the foundation – so the suke was never built...

Management of the Wyszkower Talmud-Torah

From right: **Mordchai-Mendl Domb. Icchok Epsztejn, Icchok-Ber Rozenberg, Morchai-Mendl Olenberg**

[Page 96]

The so-called small bes hamedresh was on Strarzatke Street next to the town fire station. There was a custom there, upheld by the khevra tilim [Psalm society] that before praying the men gathered to say tilim [Psalms], and then they prayed together. Abraham melamed taught his grammar students there all day long. Reb Zysze Kaluski taught there between minche [afternoon prayers] and maariv [evening prayers], along with the khevra tilim. There was always a large crowd.

A lesson in the Talmud-Torah

Every erev rosh hodesh [start of new month] the khevra kadisha said yonkipper kotn [eve of the new month was a fast day for religious Jews]. There was a women's section in the small bes hamedresh. The gabe was the gravedigger and the shamas drove the hearse. Every day the shamas rapped with the pushke [charity box similar to the blue and white box for Keren Kayemet] and begged for several groschens [pennies] to be dropped in...he kept the black hearse in the bes hamedresh courtyard.

The wealthier Jews prayed in Eli Mejer's bes hamedresh – on Kosciusko Street – but only on shabes and yontoyvim. There had been a modern heder there previous where modern Hebrew was taught.

2.

The Hasidic shtiblakh are a separate chapter. A large number of Hasidim travelled to their rebbe for yontef. Often there were divisions of opinion between the Aleksander and Gerer Hasidim. The Gerer shtibl, neighboring the small bes hamedresh had its own building with two large rooms and a large number of followers. Every day several minyonim prayed there. Men studied there the entire day and there was no shortage of religious books. The Radzolower melamed also taught his heder [grade school for boys] there. The Lubowiczer Hasid, Reb Chaim Lis gave lessons while another group studied a page of gemore [gemara part of the Talmud that comments on the Mishnah] led by the Dean of Yeshiva Chochmei Lublin, Rabbi Reb Mejer Szapira. The Gerer shtibl was also known for beautiful melodies heard there especially when they celebrated shaleshudes [third meal eaten late in the day on the Sabbath].

Above the Gerer shtibl were the orthodox organizations Agudas Yisroyel, Poeli Agudas Yisroyel [Orthodox Zionist organizations-established later than other Zionist groups] and the political party Agudas Yisroyel. Each organization had its own room and its own library. The men went there every day to read the daily orthodox newspaper that was published in Warsaw ("Togblat"). Poeli Agudas Yisroyel also sent its young men to Hakhshara [trained Jewish youth for life in Israel for all Zionist groups] and then to Israel.

Another Gerer shtibl was located on Kosciusko Street, in Szolom Zysman's courtyard. The split among the Gerer Hasidim occurred due to honest differences of opinion. The Kosciusko Street group was more progressive.

The Aleksander shtibl was on Senatorska Street at Reb Fajwel Szron's house. They were a small group of Hasidim, but were like one family. They studied the entire day and all of them were acknowledged scholars.

There are still other shtiblach to enumerate: the Warker or Otwocker shtibl in Fiszer Street. Open all day long, men studied regularly from religious books kept in the large hall. The Amszynower shtibl was on the market place at Fefke Szuster's. The well-to-do, dear Jews and scholars studied and prayed there. The Radzyminer shtibl was the rabbi's neighbor, located in the same house. They were large in number. Among the Hasidim who studied there was Reb Symcha Sznek – murdered during the first days of the war [Second World War].

In Gdalia shokhet's [ritual slaughterer] courtyard there was a Bes Jakob School for girls from religious families. Many volunteers such as Jakob Josef Plonczak, Bercze Oldak, Boruch Cywiak hy"d, Chaim-Benjamin Wiernik (died in Israel in 1961) and others made sacrifices in order to establish this school.

3.

Among the community organizations one must mention the Merchants' Union on Strarzacka Street, opposite the fire station, where people could borrow at discounted interest rates. The Secretary was Mosze Josef Abramczyk and the President, Zelke Rozenberg. People said that he was a most honest man and gave generously to charity. The gmiles khsodim [loans without interest], bikur holim [visiting and caring for the sick-there wasn't a hospital, people were taken care of at home] and other philanthropic institutions helped a great deal in providing for the needy Jews and they attracted a large number of volunteers especially women, who worked for the good of the community.

The Aleksander Hasidim were famous in the city, not only as scholars but also as people who behaved as if they were one family. They made sacrifices for each other and offered help regardless the cost to themselves. Unfortunately I don't remember all of them, but every one of them should be inscribed in the Memorial Book.

[Page 97]

I would now like to share with you what I do remember.

The first I would like to immortalize is my father Jechusza a"h [olev hasholom – may he/she rest in peace]. My father's family had been Wyszkowers for many generations. His father, Icchok Hersz Wenger played a large role in building a lot of religious institutions. There was a hakhnoses orkhim for impoverished men in his house. My father grew up in this environment. My father married the Sterdyn rabbi's daughter, my mother Rywele a"h. Reb Eliezer haLevi Ajbeszyc was a rebbe of the last Aleksander rebbe, Reb Menachem Mendl. He took my father to Aleksander to teach him Hasidus. What I remember is that every shabes, summer and winter, in the morning after the mikve, the majority of Aleksander Hasidim gathered at our house, drinking tea from the shabes kettle which was prepared Friday before sundown. They told Hasidic stories about helping one another. The first to arrive was Reb Benjamin. People called him that because he was a "stutterer". He lived across from the large bes hamedresh and was the gabe for the khevra mishnayes and the first to open the large bes hamedresh. Reb Benjamin gave away the last of his money as an anonymous gift and then became a great man at hakhnoses orhim. (His wife's name was Basia).

The second was Reb Szymon Srebrnik (Szymon melamed). He really studied day and night and learned everything by heart. He was a great Jew. Before his death I met him in Bialystok running from the German murderers. One of his cheeks was bandaged. He told me that the cruel murderers had ripped off half his beard.

Then comes Reb Mordchai Kaufman (Reb Mordchai, Chone's [son]). He was always the khevra medresh rebbe and Dean of the Hasidic yeshiva. All questions concerning religious law were referred to him. When Reb Mordchai died in Warsaw a eulogy was given for him in the large bes hamedresh as he was a great, poor man. He took care of everyone. I would also like to mention his son Israel who was truly a simple human being and also a great scholar and teacher. He only knew the way from his house to the Aleksander shtibl.

The Aleksander Hasidim's Cohen, Reb Wilenski a"h, arrived later. He was a great Torah scholar and loved by the entire community. With his patriarchal beard, calm pace and behavior in general – he gave the impression of being a high priest who cared for all of the Jewish people. He always said that men must always help one another. He wife Bejla, a woman of valor, helped him in his dry goods store. She also took part in his anonymous donations to help Jews. That is how their sons and daughters were brought up and how the entire city was reflected. They grew up to be scholars and community activists and they continue even today.

Then Zysze Kaluski, Motl blacksmith's [son] arrived. His pleasant way of teaching attracted a lot of Jews. He studied with the khevra tilim in the small bes hamedresh, neighboring the Gerer shtibl. A lot of Hasidim came to study with him. I would like to add that in his old age the wealthy Wiszkower, Dawid Gurner studied with Reb Zysze and began attending the Aleksander shtibl and gave large amounts of money to Jewish charities.

Our neighbor Reb Fajwel Szron, a brother-in-law of Reb Szymon Srebrnik, also came [to our house]. Reb Fejwel's wife argued with him about why he devoted himself to providing for every Jew except those in his own house. He brought all the Aleksander Hasidim to his house and it became the Aleksander shtibl. He took care of everyone. Fate wanted that this Jew, Reb Fajwel live his entire life as a Hasidic Jew, even in Russia. His son was a high-ranking officer there who provided him with kosher food. He had the privilege of coming to Israel and lived there to a very old age.

The Porember rabbi arrived after. He was the moyra-hoyra [rabbi who decides matters of rabbinical law] in Wyszkow. His lesson in Hasidus was – help one another and the Most High will also help. The Lord of the universe wants only good hearts.

Langer [tall] Lejbl also came [to our house]. (I've forgotten his family name). People called him the Warsaw genius. He was a Hasid who never thought about earning a living. His wife drove to Warsaw to sell poultry (already dead), while he sat in the shtibl studying, went to the rebbe's and sniffed a lot of tobacco.

A group of "Tzairi Agudas Yisroyel"

[Page 98]

Then Reb Leizor Sapirsztejn arrived. He lived near the railroad station. He was one of Zelman Grosbard's neighbors. People called him the Rebbe of the Wyszkower Aleksander Hasidim. When there was a leisure day [a holiday], a Hasidic yontef, or a yahrzeit [anniversary of a death] for a rebbe, a rosh hodesh, shushan purim [celebrated only in walled cities, Purim is when Queen Esther saved the Jews from Haman] the men went to Reb Leizor's. He was a very charitable man. My father a"h told me that before Reb Leizor died he called together his closest hasidim and begged by father, who was a shoykhet, to kill a fowl for him so that he could perform a mitzvah before dying. It was as if he wanted to fulfill the entire Torah. Then he asked for nine measures of water to immerse himself in, then ordered the great genius to say a chapter of mishnayes with him – and quickly died. A remarkable thing: his wife the rebitzin [rabbi's wife] (as people called her) went in the same way.

One must also add Reb Icchok Hersz Rotbard, Reb Szlama Frydman, Reb Henech Brzoza, Reb Jechiel Kaluski (one of Zysze Kaluski's sons who died in Acco [Israel]), Reb Zelman Felner, Reb Jechiel Szulc and Herszl Szulc (the Szulc's decided to go to the Gerer shtibl when the Aleksander Hasidim were without a shtibl for several months) and Reb Berl-Dawid Kwiatek.

All the Aleksander Hasidim were distinguished scholars, studied with khevras, were active in public service, were sextons, rebbes, etc.

When the moyra-hoyra (the former rabbi in Poremba) was alive, for shaleshudes the men sang shabes hymns at his table and listed to Torah. After his death, the shaleshudes was celebrated in the shtibl.

I have written only about the Hasidim I remember.

Wyszkow - A religious town
by Velvl Olenberg (Haifa, Israel)
Translated by Sarita Zimmermann (Bethsheda, MD)
Reviewed by Frida Grapa Markuschamer de Cielak (Mexico City)
Translation donated by the Historian Enrique Krauze (Mexico City)

Wishkov/Wyszkow[1] was a religious observant-Hasidic[2] city, which in the course of hundreds of years, was ruled by various "good Jews," "observant-Hasidic Jews" and their followers. Like in hundreds of Polish towns, there were also widespread wonderful and amazing stories in which the people looked for comfort, hope and a place for their suffering and happiness. I will not stop here for the various legends, which were widespread by the different religious Hasidic groups, about the greatness of their Rebbe[3]. In every religious house they told about them during the "three Shabbat meals," "Melaveh Malkos" (meal at end of Sabbath) or on the anniversary of the Rebbe's death.

The most distinguished shtibelakh[4] from the Hasidim were: the Gerer, Alexander, Otwotzker, Amshinower and Radzyminer. Wyszkow also had its own Rebbe (on Pultusker avenue) who used to accept "kvitlekh"[5] and "pidyoynes."[6] He used to gather two prayer quorums of Jews for the daily prayers. He was an itinerant-Rebbe. He used to travel for the most part of the year.

The "Khevre Kadisheh" (Burial Society) had a municipal character and did not participate in political issues. The gaboim(wardens)[7] of the synagogue were: Butche "the baker" Stolik and Moishe-Aron Olshaker/Alshaker. They were held in high esteem and had everyone's acknowledgment.

The main "Khevres" (groups of scholars) were the Khevre Talmud, Khevre Mishnoyes[8], Khevre Toireh (Torah), Khevre Khok L'Israel (laws of Israel), Khevre Midrash[9] , Khevre Mesilas Yeyishorim (dedicated to Justice and Equity), who used to pray in the main synagogue. The small synagogue belonged to the Book of Psalms Group. The said groups used to "buy a Rebbe" for themselves, for him to study with them and be their spiritual leader. Each small Hasidic house of prayer and study(shtibl) and society-group used to elect the wardens(gaboim) who were in charge of the budget, pay the monthly dues, sell "Aliyahs" (the honor to be called to the Torah) and established special cashbox of funds for "gmilas-khesed" (good deeds). They used to help the "downhearted or fallen" with a single action, to help them "stand on their own two feet."

A big change took place with the creation of the "Zionist Beis-Medresh," (a gift from Eli-Mehyer/Eli Meier Goldman) under the management of Henekh Kaluski, Yakov Yakubovicz/Yakubovitch, Dovid Gurni/Gurner, Leybish Pshetitzki/Pszhetitski, Yitskhok "Itche" Ba'harab/Barab, Yakov Nayman/Najman/Neiman and others. They were in charge of "Keren Kayemet" and "Keren Hayesod", helped create the organizations and clubs: "Ha'khalutz", "Hashomer Hatzair", "Maccabi", "Gwiazda"[10], "Betar"[11] -- and hereby received great support and backing from the population.

The Jewish Community was made up of representatives of all sorts of circles. President - Yitzkhok Epsztein/Epsteyn; Vice-President - Mordkheh-Mendl Olenberg/Alenberg; Secretary - Moishe-Yosef Abramczyk; Management committee group: Yitzkhok-Ber Rozenberg/Rosenberg, Yitzkhok Mondry, Shmuel Elboim, Bertche/Bercze Oldak, Henekh Kaluski, Dovid Gurni/Gurner ande Haim-Nisn (Natan) Vengrov. The community did not provide for a Jewish school. All children received a religious education in kheydorim[12] or had private teachers (girls also used to study with private teachers). With the founding of the Tarbut School by the Zionists, the "Agudah" society established the "Beis Yakov" school (for girls). The government used to support the elementary schools (powszechnej)[13] with Jewish teachers.

For the poor families that wished to give their children a religious upbringing the city established a Talmud-Toireh[14]. About 120 children studied there and also received bread and hot cacao every morning, a lunch at midday - and holiday clothes and money. The Talmud-Toireh-school committee was made up of Mordkheh-Mendl Olenberg/Alenberg (President); Yitzkhok-Ber Rozenberg/Rosenberg Yitzkhok Epsztein/Epsteyn; Mordkheh-Mendl Domb. And the first founders of the Talmud Torah: Shloime Fridman (Alexander-Hasid resides today in Canada) and Mendl Epsztein/Epsteyn/Epsztejn/Epshtein, today (i.e., in 1964) in America. In order to support the teachers and melamdim (learned-men; teachers) the committee established dues to be paid by the Jewish community. The expenses for the kitchen at the Talmud Torah and clothing for poor and needy children was taken care of by the "Joint[15]" and the Wishkever Committees in America.

[Page 99]

The more important of the institutions (in Wyszków) was the General Gmilas-Khesed Kasse (philanthropic cashbox of funds), (President --- Shaike Posztolski/Postolski, who emigrated to Eretz Israel in the year 1943 after long wandering thru Russia with his family, he died some time later. He took part in the founding of the "Irgun Yoitzeih Wishkov b'Israel)[16]. The members of the administration of the Gmilas-Khesed Kasse were Borukh "Benny" Dobres, V. Grabina, Henekh Kaluski, Yakov-Dovid Pshetitzki/Pszhetitski (from the founders of the "Irgun Wishkever Organization in Israel" and cashier until the year 1957), Mordkheh-Mendl Olenberg/Alenberg and others.

In Wishkov/Wyszków there was also a Yeshiva[17] "Bais Yosef," a Novorodker Yeshiva lead by Rebbe Shimon Arie Heifetz/Khofets. Over 50 students from Wyszków and its surrounding area, studied in this Yeshiva. The out of town students used to eat "teg"[18] in the homes of different wealthier members of the community. But the main support for the Yeshiva, the Talmud-Toireh (school system) and the Gmilas-Khesed philanthropic fund came from America. Also the Wishkover Committee in New York, under the direction of Mrs. Rokhl Radziminski/ Radzyminski, sent every year $1,000.00 dollar for Passover, from this - $100.00 went for the Talmud Torah, $100.00 - for the Yeshiva and $100.00 for the Gmilas-Khesed Kasse The remaining $700.00 was distributed among the poor for the Holiday. The people who belonged to the Wishkover Committee that distributed the money received from New York were: Yitzl/Itzel Radziminski/Radzyminski; Mordecai-Mendl Olenberg/ Alenberg, Yitzkhok-Ber Rozenberg/Rosenberg and Henekh Kaluski. This Passover aid had a great meaning for the poor citizens.

The Zionist Organization revived the town. The young people were mostly Zionists. Also the religious jews began to prepare leaving for Eretz (the Land of) Israel (then called Palestine), specially with the tide of the third aliyah[19](Yisroel Itzhok Tik and his family, the Shenberg/Szejnberg's and others). Tik was an Otwotsker (from Otwock) Hasid, and the Otwotsker Hasidim sent with him letters for the Warker (from Warka) Rebbe, to the grave of the old Otwotsker Rabbi Reb Mordechi-Melakhem Kalish ztz'l[20] in Tiberias whom they used to call the Rebbe from Eretz Israel, one of the founders from general "Kolel" in 1863.

The great Zionist (Movement) revival, the Ha'halutz[21] movement and the third aliah were the main initiatives of the "Agudah" (association). Also the Bund (Union of the Jewish Labor Party) was at that time a big force and its adherents used to travel thru the Americas, instead of Eretz Israel.

After the death of the Wishkover Moreh Horeh (the decider of matters of rabbinical law), who was a Hasid of the Alexander Rebbe, the Gerer Hasidim wanted to install one of their Hasidim as Moreh Horeh. This started a difficult struggle of the selection of the different candidates, who needed to give sermons. The Otwotsker Hasidim presented their candidate, the Alexander supported the Otwotsker candidate, and their opinion decided all the issues.

The Gerer conducted a bitter struggle against such said candidate. The Otwotsker Hasidim took advantage of the oportunities from the Gmine-President Itzhok Epsztein/Epsteyn/Epsztejn/Epshtein (a Gerer Hasid), when he travelled to Ciechocinek[22] for health reasons, and the Vice President of the Jewish Community (Kehileh/Kheila) Mordechai-Mendl Olenberg (Otwotsker Hasid) proceded with the election of the Otwatsker Hasid as an enlightened teacher and received the confirmation of the position as the person in power.

At the same time the Aleksander Hasidim put forth their candidate as a Shoykhet (kosher butcher- slaughterer) Reb'[23] Yoshua Vengersh, a popular man, who also had the support of the Zionist prayer group, so therefore the Gerer Hasidim decided not to allow him to win. This struggle of the Aleksander Hasidim which continued for a long time was backed by the Otwotsker Hasidim and by the enlightened people. All these Hasidishe Group dealings had deep reverberations ...

Footnotes

1. The correct spelling in Polish for Wishkov or Vishkov is Wyszków.

2. Hasidic (Hasidism)= A Jewish mystic movement founded in the 18th century, in eastern Europe, by Baal Shem Tov that reacted against Talmudic learning and maintained that God's presence was in all of one's surroundings and that one should serve God in one's every deed and word.

3. Rebbe = Is the honorific title or term that refers to the leader or founder of a Hasidic movement or dynasty.

4. shtibelakh = is the plural in diminutive of the Yiddish word "Shtibl"- a religious study-house/es of the Hasidim.

5. "kvitlekh" = notes with petitions to the mystical Rebbe and G-d.

6. "pidyoynes" = payments to the Hassidic Rebbe for advice.

7. Gabeh (sing) Gaboim (plural) Trustee or warden of the synagogue; manager of the affairs of a Hasidic Rabbi.

8. Mishnah refers to the collection of post-biblical laws and rabbinical discussions (plural term is Mishnoyes in Yiddish, and Mishnayot in Hebrew).

9. Midrash refers to post-Talmudic literature of Biblical exegesis (explanation or critical interpretation of the Bible) which refers to the compilation of homiletic teachings and stories based on the Hebrew Bible, prophets and other writings.

10. Gwiazda (Polish word, pronounced: g'viaz.da) meaning: Shining Star (a sports club in Wyszkow, similar to Maccabi)

11. Betar = Jewish youth organization of the Revisionist Zionist movement founded by Vladimir Jabotinsky.

12. kheyder (sing.) kheyidorim (plural in Yiddish) = Traditional religious school for boys younger than 12-13 years, where they learn the Hebrew-Yiddish alphabets, the Khumesh (Pentateuch), traditions, etc.

13. (powszechnej)= Polish word for universal.

14. Talmud-Toyreh is a tuition-free Jewish elementary school maintained by the community for the poorest children.

15. Joint = refers to the Joint Distribution Committee in U.S, which aids Jews in distress overseas.

16. Irgun = organization. "Irgun Yoitzeih Wishkov b'Israel" translates to: The Organization of Wishkow people who went out from Wyszków and are (now) in Israel.

17. Yeshiva = A Jewish educational institution that focuses on the study of traditional religious texts, primarily, higher Talmudic and Torah learning.

18. "teg" (days; but some use the term "oyf teg", i.e., on days) = When a student went to study at a Yeshive in another city, he could sleep on the yeshiva premises. For dinner, a student, would be invited to someone's home on a pre-established day that the community gabetes (women caregivers) committee, used to arrange for each student that needed it.

19. aliyah = (Hebrew word whose literal translation means: ascent) It refers to the immigration of Jews from the diaspora to the land of Israel. It is one of the most basic tenets of the Zionist ideology.

20. zt"l = (zekher tzadik livrakha) stands for honorific words used when referring to a very religious, a righteous or pious deceased person; it translates to "May The Memory Of The Saintly Be A Blessing."

21. Ha'halutz = the Pioneer - (a Zionist organization).

22. Ciechocinek a Polish spa town located on the Vistula River about 182 kms (abt. 114 miles) from Wyszków.

23. Reb or R'= is an honorable way to refer to a person, like 'Mr.' in English.

My Children Are Not Agnostics
by Freyda Kaplovitch, Buenos Aires
Translated by Pamela Russ

Published in memory of my parents and sister who were killed by the Nazi murderers.

In memory of my uncle Mendel, the morah ha'raah [chief rabbi of the city], who died in the year 1922.

1.

This happened in the year 1916. I remember it as now: The youth in Wyszkow had started to become less religious, crawling out of their daled amos [small space, literally "four cubits"], freed themselves of fanaticism, established clubs, libraries, and all kinds of organizations and parties. Among the activists were – also my sister Hinde (killed by the Nazi murderers).

One day, one of the youth organizations decided to invite the world renowned cantor Gershon Sirota for a concert. They rented a hall on Strazhaczka Street, right opposite the Gerer shtiebel [small, informal synagogue] where my father prayed. A tumult broke out in the town: What was this! Such heresy! In those times, in the eyes of our parents, this seemed to be worse than conversion.

That evening of the concert, all the Gerer chassidim set themselves out on both sides of the street that led to the hall. They wanted to see the children who were prepared to don the heresy so that later their parents could give them their dues. My father was not of the terribly fanatic ones. But he knew that if we children would go hear Sirota then the Gerer chassidim would chase him out of the shtiebel, and maybe even excommunicate him... So he quickly went home where he found the children preparing for the concert. After his pleas and calm explanations we decided not to make any trouble for our father. We did not go to hear Sirota... Our father was greatly delighted. He said:

[Page 100]

"Now I can say in the shtiebel that my children are not heretics, like those which have recently flowered in our town..."

2.

I remember Yom Kippur of the year 1919. At that time, our town already boasted all kinds of cultural institutions and youth organizations, among them – the Bundist "Zukunft" ["Future"]. For musaf, [early afternoon prayers], when the religious and even the free–thinking Jews filled the synagogues, study halls and shtiebels in Wyszkow, a rumor spread that in the Zukunft location on Rynek (market place), there was smoke coming out of the chimney. That's what it was. They were cooking there on Yom Kippur.

The town was in a storm. My uncle Mendel and another few Jews went immediately to the Bundist club to determine whether it was really true that Jewish youths were moving to lessen the holiness of the day. They found some youths there and admonished them strongly for this behavior. In addition, he spoke to the conscience of the elder chaver Smietanka (now in America). He demanded of them that they not do this sort of thing again.

The following day, when I came to my uncle, he – usually quiet and reserved, turned to me and said in these words:

"Yesterday, when I went to the Zukunft location to see if they were cooking on Yom Kippur, I had a heavy feeling and an embittered heart. God forbid, maybe I'll find my nephews there. My joy was great when I came there and did not see any of you. I am proud that my nephews did not shame me ..."

The First Kheyder Metukan [Proper School]
by F.M.R.
Translated by Pamela Russ

1.

When the new educational institution was established in Wyszkow, the so-called Kheder Metukan, our parents' intention was not only to give Jewish children a religious education, but also to light a fire in their hearts to be proud Jews, soaked through with the love of Israel.

The Kheder Metukan was located in the small building on Wonske Street (near Retken), where in the spring the tree blossoms were fragrant, and in the summer the apples with the red spots whetted our appetites.

The dear teacher and unforgettable resident Yitzkhok Skarlat, of blessed memory, learned Tanakh [the books of the Torah, Prophets, Writings], and aroused a love for the Land of Israel and for the People of Israel. He would always direct us into a dreamland. We soared to somewhere in the blue skies... With wide open mouths, we swallowed up his interpretations about learning and practicing the virtuous behaviors which we received on Mount Sinai, about the heroic fighters in the Tanakh, and about all those who beautified and enriched our history.

2.

Who can forget our dear teacher Yosef Peczenik, with his Jewish aristocratic demeanor, when his tar black forelocks would sway in rhythm to the Hebrew songs that he taught. Each of his words rang with love and conviction.

I don't remember one sad day in the course of those several years studying in the Kheyder Metukan, except for one that reminded us of the destruction of the ancient Temple. That day, tears ran steadily from my childhood eyes. Other than that, it was when our dear teacher Shapiro with his graceful figure, bid farewell as he was returning to his family in Pinsk. My childhood heart sensed that this goodbye was forever ... In a short time, he actually did die.

Thanks to these types of parents and educators, our town was a ripe field for Zionist activity. The sports club Maccabi was established, thanks to which we marched on Lag b'Omer [a Jewish holiday celebrated on the 33rd day of the Counting of the Omer between Passover and Shavuot, which occurs on the 18th day of the Hebrew month of Iyar] with the blue–and–white flag across the streets Stodolne, Wonske, Kosciuczko, Rynek, and the bridge, until Skusew. In our eyes, this was ... a march to the Land of Israel. As I was at the head of the children, my mother dressed me up in a white dress, a blue band, and blue–and–white beads.

The worldly and nationalist–Jewish education of Kheyder Metukan left visible impressions on the spiritual development of a part of the Wyszkower children.

Women's committee of the Wyszkow Bikur Cholim [non–profit organization that takes care of the sick and the families' needs]

(Right to left) **Elke Goldman, Nekhama Stern, Rebbetzen Morgenstern, Faige Male Abramczyk**

[Page 101]

Student at "Darkhey Noam" Yeshiva Recalls
by Khaim Umyal
Translated by Chava Eisenstein

1.

A year prior World War I, the Radzymin Rebbe, who served as dean of the "Kollel Polin" announced the opening of a yeshiva in Wyszkow with the name "Darkhey Noam." The students were promised two entities: "Wedding Saving" while studying the full term: and in case of immigration to Eretz Yisrael, they will land a position, at the "Kollel Polin" office in Jerusalem. He even sent out special messengers to various Polish provinces with the appealing offer, and Jewish youth came flocking to the yeshiva in Wyszkow.

At that point, I was residing in Zyrardow, and it happened that the Rabbi of Klimontow, Simkha Gelernter came to our town, which was famous for its fabric industry. At a fiery speech he held, the Rabbi turned to all with the following words: "The voice is the voice of Jacob – and the hands – are Esau's... At the time when Jacob's voice will go strong with Torah, the hands of Esau will fall weak". Who better than us, Zyrardow's youth, knew and felt Esau's hands?! Our parents held on to those promising words and enrolled us in yeshiva.

One evening in the spring, we went on a ride with the "Omnibus" hitched to horses, on the Radzymin – Wyszkow lane. At dawn, we reached the wooden bridge over the Bug River. That's where the Jewish part of the city began. Instantly we had our answer to the enigma, why is a gentile called "Klipa" – the shell? For they reside on the outskirts of the town, whilst the Jews live inside the town, they are the kernel inside...

Our yeshiva was on Przedmiescie street, within an orchard, the Polish guard strictly ensured that none of the fruit dare go along with us. Therefore, the garden rightfully earned its name we gave it "Hanukah Candles"... that are to be seen but not to be used. That served us as a great lesson to overcome our inclinations. Besides this gentile with his hands of Esau, we didn't encounter more of this species in Wyszkow, and we repeated the Rebbe's words: with our Torah voice high, we will diminish the wicked hands...

Our accommodations at the yeshiva were strictly modest, the boys ate "Days" meaning, they ate every day at a different home. I remember favorably the Tuesdays, when ten of us ate at the home of Mr. Joseph Jacobowitz the lumber trader. After supper, he would give each of us one "didke" (3 kopeks) for pocket money.

On the first day of Elul we traveled again with the wagonette to the Radzymin Rebbe, he will test us, and after that, we shall enjoy a festive meal and receive our diplomas. Upon receiving our certificates, the Rabbi requested from us to bless him with a son, that shall serve as successor after him, in exchange, he would bless us to elude being drafted to the Czars army. That's when the Rebbe and the boys including me, burst out at once: we shall all be soldiers in the army of the Messiah... and not only once did it happen, standing at duty for the "Haganah," weapons in hand facing the hooligans, I thought to myself, perhaps our prayers at that time, were accepted. But there wasn't a son to accede the Rebbe...

2.

I remember an incident that happened in those days: in Wyszkow lived a very wealthy Jew, he owned the biggest house at the market place. Rabbi Morgenstern, too, lived in the house, which stretched over two or three streets. It so happened that this Jew fell ill, and was about to die. Being childless, he bequeathed the entire house for the Radzymin Rebbe. The end was that the man became well again and his wife gave birth to a son. The woman and the child demanded the Rebbe should return the house to them. Since the reason for the inheritance has abolished. The issue went from one court to another. How shameful...

3.

On the Shabbat prior the ninth day of Av, we were visiting in the late afternoon at Jacob-David Zatorski's home, not far from the synagogue, we were enjoying chickpeas and beer when we were alarmed to hear yells and the bell siren of the fire engine. "Fishke with the kishke" (rubber hose) - the only Jew in the fire department, was running at the head of the team towards the shul to save the woman of the woman's-section that was collapsing. Three woman were injured heavily, and we gained a new joke, of the "Shlosha Imahos Nizokos" - three wounded women, since we were studying at that time the tractate of "Arba'ah Avot Nezikin" – the four chief (fathers) of damages...

The town's medic was rushed over, to save the wounded women, that all too familiar medic, Mr. Berel Kerner, who once plucked off my tooth... in the center of the market was his clinic. On the door, he hung up three copper plates. "Medicine" was his occupation: he plucked teeth, shaved beards, laid fire-cups, dressed fractured bones, softened wounds, etc., a private practitioner in small...

The Yeshiva "Beis Yosef"
by Paul A. Kramer
Translated by Pamela Russ

In the yeshiva "Beis Yosef" there were about 84 students. The largest percent were from Wyszkow. The rest were those who came from cities and towns around Wyszkow.

Harav Reb Shimon Aryeh Khafetz, as principal and head of the yeshiva, conducted the classes along with four other teachers. They all had to live [make a living]. Their payment for the year was a total of seven thousand six hundred and eighty zlotys. That meant, for each individual teacher fifteen hundred and thirty six zlotys per year. A set sum of three hundred and seven dollars in American exchange; approximately six dollars a week. With that, one can be sure that these teachers would be the happiest if they would receive these meager wages regularly each week.

Aside from supporting the poor boys with clothing and food, there was also the cost of rent, heat, light, and other small expenses.

From the city of Wyszkow, an approximate sum of one thousand seven hundred and twenty zlotys was brought in; from tuition throughout the year – one hundred and fifty zlotys. A few paid ten zlotys, a few five groshen weekly. There were also those who could hardly pay even one zloty, or those who paid fifty groshen a month.

[Page 102]

The Wyszkow women's union of the yeshiva annually raised about fifteen hundred zlotys.

In total, the yeshiva Beis Yosef had an annual income of 3370 zlotys.

According to this calculation, not only was their meager salary of six dollars not enough for the poor teachers, but even half of the lamentable profits was not either. So – how does one survive?

The answer: "This is the way of learning the Torah. Eating bread and salt, drinking measured amounts of water, and sleeping on the bare ground."

But to buy bread and salt one also needed to have the means; and to sleep on the bare ground you still needed a place to live, and not be on the street.

There was really a holy obligation on the residents of Wyszkow to support the Wyszkow Torah institution Beis Yosef and to support them [the boys] to their best abilities in their need, so that they [the boys] shouldn't live a life of difficulty as they studied Torah.

Jewish Chains[a]
(A gratitude poem)
by Rabbi Shimon Arie Kheyfetz
Principal of the Yeshiva "Beis Yosef" in Wyszkow
Translated by Pamela Russ

In the golden country –
Thanks to the Wyszkower,
For your noble hearts filled with love,
Support the children
Who are learning with eagerness
In the Wyszkower Beis Yosef yeshiva.
The only ray [of light, hope]
In these dark times,
Has always been our Torah.
Armed with belief,
Anchored with faith,
[As we] wandered in exile without fear.
There were times
It was thought that this was the end,
With depression and confusion we remained.
But suddenly there appeared
Help from New York,
To chase away the needs of the yeshiva.
You gave shoes and clothing,
Provided and gave them new,
You sharpen Jewish minds,
So that if a storm erupts
We can conquer our enemies
With spirited energies.
So, continue to help us,
Residents of New York,
To strengthen the Jewish chains
The chains of generations
Who teach us emphatically
To spread compassion and justice.

Wyszkow; May 5, 1936.

Original Footnote

a. A thank–you letter (in person) to the Wyszkower in New York for their help provided to the Yeshiva Beis Yosef, from the collections of "The Landsman [Compatriot]"; published for the fortieth jubilee of the Wyszkower support union (1896–1936), New York, 1936.

My Memories of the Yeshive[1]
by Shimon Zakharia Malowanczyk (Tel-Aviv)
Translated by Hilda Rubin Rockville, MD)
Reviewed by Frida Grapa Markuschamer de Cielak (Mexico City)
Translation donated by the Historian Enrique Krauze (Mexico City)

Our Yeshive, although it was to be found in Wishkov/Wyszków[2], it was supported by the (big) city. It bore the name "Nevordiker Yeshive[3]" and was run in the spirit of the moral teachings of Rabbi Yisroyel Salanter[4], according to an ethical way. There were about 200 young men students in six classes.

From 5 in the morning till 9 at night the students were immersed in learning. From very early in the morning their learning took place till 7:30 am, then the students would davn shakhres[5] (pray the morning prayer) with much enthusiasm. A group of students would stand a good half hour saying the shmone-esreh (the 18 benedictions). After their praying the students would go and eat breakfast in the kitchen, which was supported by a group of Wishkever[6] householders and was run by a special women's committee that was very active in this field. To the householders' committee belonged: R'(eb; i.e., Mister) Eyli Rozen, who worked day and night for the good of the Yeshive; R' Avraham Lerman, R' Borukh Stolik (also known as Butche), and R' Alter Szukegnik. In the women's committee were active: Khaveh Markushjamer/Markuschamer/Marcuschamer, Leyeh Ostrovyak/Astroviak and Dvoyre, the rope maker (knitter). Their worry was, that the Yeshive-bokherim[7] should have where to eat substantially and also have a bed where to lay their heads. They (these ladies) decided in which Wishkever household the boys would go "esn teg"[8]. The members of both committees, the men's and the women's, truly served as "fathers and mothers" for the Yeshive-boys.

From 9:30 till 2:30 the students studied with intensity.

[Page 103]

The walls from the Yeshive and from the Beis-Hamedresh[9] absorbed the scholarly words of the Torah over the many long years that the Yeshive was housed there. It also happened that, for a group of Yeshive fellows who also studied through the long winter nights, the "outside" world was only an antechamber for them - as compared with the spiritual world of their Yeshive. If a Wishkever Jew wanted to experience the feel of the spiritual life, he would enter the Yeshive and would experience complete fulfillment.

At 1:30, psalms-lessons were recited at the classrooms. From central Bialystok through the auspices of Rabbi Avrom Yafo Shlit'a[10] very special brilliant teachers and scholars were sent to Wyszkow such as: Rabbi Nakhman-Dovid Landinski, Rabbi Leyzer Levinsky, Rabbi Aron/Aharon Stolner, Rabbi Noyekh Stolner, Rabbi Yosef/Yoysef Lomzher, Rabbi Abraham/Avrom Tsitrin/Cytrin/Cytryn[11]. They were all fine lecturers and taught with much scope and vision.

The spiritual head of the Yeshive was the Rabbi Shimon Heifetz our headmaster, and Rabbi Avrom Tsitrin/Cytryn served, too. Rabbi Shimon was absolutely a saint, who was unconcerned with the outside world. He could live on bread and water. His major teachings were concerned with "Midas Toibes"[12]. Rabbi Shimon would lead discussions twice a week, after which each student would select two more fellows and in threes, they would stroll back and forth discussing what it took to be good Jew. They would talk about how to avoid doing evil and how to perform only good deeds. These strolls were called "birzshes."

Every day for one hour the students learned how to look at themselves with an eye for self-criticism. And each time before Rosh-Khodesh (Beginning of the Month) a committee was formed to work on self-critique. The leaders would conduct interesting discussions. Then afternoon prayers were said with much enthusiasm and strong feelings. The "Our Father-Our King" (special Rosh Hashone, i.e., Jewish New Year prayers) also were recited.

In its early years the Yeshive was conducted in the Beis-Hamedresh. Later on the synagogue a special building was added to serve as the Yeshive. That entire building served as a temple for the people of Wyszków. It was people from our city in America, who sent money for this endeavor.

Also, Rabbi Abraham/Avrom Tsitrin/Cytryn gave fine lectures with appropriate moral teachings that had a lot of influence on the local townsfolk who would come to hear them. One of the local landlords very much wanted Rabbi Avrom as a son-in-law - and he succeeded in this. He took him into his home and treated him as he would his own son[13]. The Germans murdered Rabbi Avrom. It is told that before he was shot he was able to accuse them in a speech and threaten them with terrible consequences for the deeds they were committing against Jews. He died (as a martyr) on Kiddush-Hashem[14]. May his memory be blessed!

On Shavues[15], at night, the entire Yeshive would be on alert. Everybody would be studying intently and saying the special Shavues prayers. At 4 in the morning they would all go to the mikve (the ritual bath) and then davn (pray) with much enthusiasm. After the praying, there was a repast with the blessing of the wine. And then, there was Hasidic dancing done with such enthusiasm

that everyone felt at that moment they were able to communicate with
the creator himself... From 12 noon, till 5 in the evening everyone rested. Then
there were evening prayers in the Yeshive and all enjoyed themselves studying.
These Shavues celebrations were conducted by: Rabbi Avrom Tsitrin/Cytryn,
Rabbi Noyekh Stolner and Rabbi Shimon Heifetz.

When the month of Elul arrived the spirit of holiness truly entered the
Yeshive. The students attacked their prayers with great devotion and the
learning intensified. All sorts of prayers were recited - much repentance
sought. After an awakening of a spiritual morality, the lights would
extinguished so that each person could take a self reckoning and weep quietly
as he communed with the creator... One could truly feel the approach of the
Yom-Hadin (Day of Judgment) and that the holy sparks were flaring with more
power.

"Beis Yakov" School from Agudas Israel (political arm of Ashkenazi Torah Judaism Org.) in Wyszkow

With a particular loyalty feeling to the Yeshive a group of community
activists, among them Avrom/Avraham Lerman Avraham z"l (of blessed
memory), distinguish themselves by looking after the families of the teachers
and the master teachers who taught the students. A. Lerman organized some
groups of religious Jews who used to collect weekly-money for the Yeshive
from the different stratum groups from the population. If someone couldn't go
on his collecting shift, Avrom Lerman would take his place. Not only would he
go on the rounds collecting from the homes, but also if the collecting were
"short" he would give from his own pocket the missing sums. And of course,
extra money was always needed...

He would deliver the collected money to the wives of the heads of the Yeshive so that they could prepare the Sabbath meal. Not once, but many times did the he, the principal from the Yeshive, Rabbi Shimon Heifetz say:

-"Reb' Avrom, G-d should give you strength for what you do for us. If not for your devotion, who knows how we would manage. In all our dire moments you come to help us. We shall always remember what you have done for us!"

Thanks to the loyalty and devotion of those Jews, it was possible to continue and maintain, without interruption, the teaching of Torah to the students at the Yeshive in Wyszków.

To hear, test and examine the students at the Yeshive, would come the Rabbis: Reb' Dovid Bodnik, Reb' Khaim Stetchiner and Reb' Hillel Vitkind. For the testing, everyone prepared himself day and night for weeks. It was the ambition of all to receive an outstanding certificate.

Such was the life at the Yeshive in Wyszków.

Footnotes

1. Yeshive (in Yiddish, Yeshiva in Hebrew) A Jewish school of high Talmudic learning. The Wyszkower Yeshiva was very well known, and lots of students attended from other shtetls, many from un-wealthy homes. The Yeshive's women trustees cared for and provided necessities like food and shelter; some times, they even gave them some extra groshns to spend.

2. Wyszków = Both words Wishkov or Vishkov are how they sound in Yiddish, the correct Polish spelling is Wyszków.

3. This Yeshive was later named, Yeshive Beis-Yosef.

4. Rabbi Yisroel ben Ze'ev Wolf Lipkin, the father of the Musar movement of Orthodox Judaism.

5. Shakhres (Yiddish; Shakharit, in Hebrew) is the daily morning prayer of the Jewish people, said, to have been established by the patriarch, Abraham, when he prayed in the morning.

6. Inhabitants, people from Wyszków.

7. The boy-students from the Yeshive.

8. "esn teg" literally mean "eat days." When students went to study at a Yeshive in another city, they had breakfast at the Yeshive, but for dinner and for overnight, the women's committee made arrangements for the boys to stay at homes "for a day." This was called "esn teg" or "oyf teg."

9. Yiddish for "House (of) Interpretation" or "House (of) Learning"); it refers to a study hall, whether in synagogue, yeshive or any other building.

10. Shlit"a is an acronym occurring with the word Rabbi, meaning "Rabbi of leadership."

11. There are 2 or more ways of writing various surnames.

12. Good Virtues and Good Behavor, Trait of Goodness.

13. It is known now that Rabbi Abraham/Avrom Tsitrin/Cytrin/Cytryn's father-in-law probably was Yakov-Arie Shtaynman/Steinman, originally of Amselof. Avrom's wife, Bella/Beyle, born in Wyszkow, was the daughter of Yakov-Arie, and Rabbi Avrom ben Shamai Ha'leivi

Tsitrin/Cytrin, who was the son of Sarah Rivka Gelman, later became recognized as a Rabbi in a larger city (in Rowno) and was famous for his interesting work there, too. (See pg.193, "Sefer Wyszkow".)

14. Kiddush-Hashem means "sanctification of the name." It refers to a religious or moral action by a Jew that brings honor, respect, and glory to God. It is considered to be sanctification of His name, that causes a person to die for one's Jewish beliefs and reverence to God. On pg.193 ("Sefer Wyszków"), you can read "The last request of a martyr," the last letter found in a pocket of Rabbi Avrom Tsitrin/Cytrin/Cytryn's jacket. He wrote it just before the Nazis killed him. He was the Rabbi of Rowno after he had served for many years as Rabbi and teacher at the Yeshive "Beis-Yosef" in Wyszkow. In the letter he asks "not to be forgotten together with all the other Jews killed unjustly.

15. Shavues (in Yiddish), the religious festival of Shavuot (in Hebrew). The word Shavues/Shavuot means weeks, and the festival marks the completion of the seven-week counting period of the Omer (a measure of grain) begun during Passover. Shavues commemorates the anniversary of the day G-d gave the Torah, the 10 commandments, to the entire nation of Israel assembled at Mount Sinai.

[Page 104]

The Keepers of the Sabbath in Town
by Arie Shtelung Sokol (Buenos Aires, Argentina)

Translated by Hilda Rubin (Rockville, MD)

Reviewed by Frida Grapa Markuschamer de Cielak (Mexico City)

Translation donated by the Historian Enrique Krauze (Mexico City)

The Society of the Keepers of the Shabbes (Sabbath)[1] was founded in 1922 in the shtetl Wishkov/Wyszków[2]. My father, Khayim-Henekh (Shtelung/Sztelung) was one of the most active members in the society. Their purpose was: to make sure that no one in the shtetl would defame Shabbes.

At that time I was living and working in Warsaw. From time to time I would visit my parents and family. The most inconvenient way to get there was by train because there were only two departures a day: morning and evening.

Once, I arrived in Wyszków on Friday evening. It was already 5 minutes after the candle lighting. My father knew that I would arrive with a "shtokh in Shabes" (a "stich" in Shabes) and so he had warned my mother that she should feed me immediately upon my arrival and not wait for him. The reason for this was so that he would not have to eat with a defamer of Shabes when he arrived from his prayers. He did not want to sit at the same table with such a person.

My mother (Esther-Mindl Sokol) was delighted to see me since we hadn't seen each other in a while. She wanted me to sit down and eat. As she put out the food she told me about my father's decision not to eat with me. In no way did I agree with this attitude. After all, a son comes to his parents for Shabes and the whole family would not sit down together at one table?

Seeing that I was so adamant, my mother gave this advice -- that I should immediately stand and davn(pray) and finish my praying just as my father would arrive from shul[3]. I should then greet him with a "shalom" and that he would then forgive me my transgression.

However, my father was a stubborn man and additionally was a devoted member of the Society of the Keepers of Shabes. He couldn't allow himself to go back on his decision not to wish me "shalom" nor to sit at the same table with such a one who would defame the Sabbath.

I finished praying the 'Shmone'esreh'[4] as my father came in I held out my hand to him. He ignored my hand and stated that according to the law he could not extend a "shalom"[5] to a defamer of the Sabbath. And he ordered my mother to serve my food to me, separately.

This infuriated me and I left he house. But -- where should I go?

My two older brothers lived in shtetl[6]. Both were married. Moyshe (the older one) and Yakov, the younger. I decided not to go to either one of them. I wandered silently around the street for a while and then headed for Avruml Markuschamer who had a restaurant. His restaurant was a meeting place for members of various groups and organizations-- mainly the Bundistn, (because Avruml himself was a Bundist[7].

Entering Avruml's place at a time when everyone else in the shtetl was sitting down to their Friday-eve festive meal, was a puzzle for Avruml. But I quickly explained the reason for my "visit". He and his wife[8] greeted me warmly and insisted that I sit down and eat together with them. When I wanted to pay them for the meal, (after all this was the way they earned their living), but they wouldn't take any money. (Today [i.e., in 1946], he lives in Mexico (Monterrey) and I send him my thanks!)

After that, I went into the street looking for my pals - Zindl/Zundl Elboim, Avremke Burshteyn/Burshtin, Itche Shayke and others. (They were all killed in the years 1939-1945)[9].

A stroll on the Wyszków bridge on a summer's night was really quite wonderful. However, that was something that disturbed the Shabes Keepers Society. The Society members would follow every one of us like shadows watching to scc if wc wcrc smoking cigarcttcs. Oncc I was caught smoking on a Friday night. The next day, on Shabes morning, it was reported to my father as he was davening (praying) his morning prayers in the Gerer Shtibl[10] that I, his son, I was smoking on a Friday night. My father denied the accusation, because he thought, that I did not smoke at all...

On Saturday nights after the Sabbath there was theater in Wyszków. It seems to me that it was Yakov/Yankev Vayslits and his troupe. The performances were held in the fire-fighters hall and the tickets were sold - in the fire-fighters "salon" that was located across from the Gerer Shtibl.

One Shabes in the morning I met my friend Sorotche Bzhoza (Khil Bzhoza's sister). We both went to the "salon" to buy tickets. There was already standing a Shabes Society member - a former teacher of mine. He stopped me with a question:

- "Where are you going Arie?"

- "I'm going to find out what's playing tonight," I replied.

But he didn't let me go in. He grabbed me by both of my lapels and held on tight. I really had to struggle to get out of his grasp.

Of course, this incident was reported immediately in the Gerer Study House, where my father was to be found.

This was the way Shabes went on. The Shabes Society Members were dogging my every step.

For the second night I still didn't sleep in my parents' home, but at my brother's. Quite early Sunday morning, my father arrived and waited for me to get up. As I awoke he came over to me and extended his hand in "sholem"[11]. At this point I teased him saying that I really couldn't shake his hand, because it was... Sunday. The two of us went home. As we walked he tried to get me to understand that he couldn't have acted differently.

My father obeyed the learned books. He was a smart man and had strong feelings for his family. He was never silent about any injustice. That entire incident really bothered him. My mother Esther-Mindl, was also upset over the fact, that her son, coming all the way from Warsaw as a guest, had to eat at a stranger's table. At the end of my visit, my father took me aside and entreated me that I should do him a favor in the future and please not come on Shabes to Wyszków...

Footnotes

1. Dih Shomrei-Shabes (in Yiddish) was a group of Orthodox Hasidim in Wyszków, concerned with the correct religious observance of the Sabbath. Beginning with sunset on Friday evening until sunset, Saturday, Sabbath meals, rituals, prayers, rest, etc., had to be observed (whereas certain activities were prohibited). The group was expected to fulfill such commandments, and have other Jews do so, as well.

2. Wishkov = Wyszków is the correct spelling in Polish for the town.

3. shul is the Yiddish word for synagogue.

4. 'Shminesre' (in Yiddish) = It is the central prayer of every Jewish service that translates as the Eighteen Benedictions ('shmone' = is eight and 'esreh' is ten)

5. "shalom" = Customary greeting of "hello" which literally means "peace".

6. shtetl is the Yiddish word for "town" (plural is: Shtetlakh).

7. Bundistn & Bundist (plural and singular) was the word given to the people who belonged to the socialist organization: Bund - A Socialist Jewish labor Party Organization (or "General Jewish Workers' Alliance").

8. Avruml's wife, née Khayeh-Nekhe Goldstein.

9. Zundl Elboim was the son of Peshe and Shmuel Elboim. In a chapter in "Sefer Wyszkow," Yitzkhok Baharav/Barab writes about the tragic moment that Zundl was cruelly murdered by the Nazis in front of his mother, his 2 brothers and Yosef Meyer and Shloime Grapa who had given them shelter in their home in Sadowne after escaping from Wyszków when bombarded by the Germans.

10. Gerer Hasidic house of study. Gerer Hasidim followed the teachings of Rebbe Yitzchak Meir Alter (1799-1866) from Gur (Góra Kalwaria), probably the largest and most influential Hasidic group in Poland.

11. In this specific case the "sholem" greeting was used expressly with its literal translation of "peace"

[Page 105]

The Excommunication (der kheyrem)
by Borukh Yismakh/Ismaj, Buenos Aires
Translated by Pamela Russ

One autumn evening, in the year 1925 (or 1926) in the large Beis Hamedrash [Study Hall], beside burning black candles, an excommunication was declared against a respected Jewish businessman in town. This event caused a great uproar. This was the first occasion of an excommunication in the history of Wyszkow; second, this Jew had made great contributions in many social areas: He was the chairman of the committee to support the yeshiva of the Lithuanian youth, who in the time of the years 1914–1918, were chased from their home towns. They stayed in Wyszkow. The abovementioned Jew provided the yeshiva boys with whatever they could possibly need.

"Tze'ir Mizrachi" [Mizrachi Youth]

In the town, people far and wide commented on the event. It was difficult to believe that Rav Morgenstern would elicit such a harsh judgement.

The story began with a ... marriage match. A son of the mentioned Jew married a girl from the neighboring city of Malkin. The bride was very beautiful. In the beginning, the young couple lived happily. But after that, peace in the home was disturbed. The arguments became more frequent and sharper, until finally the young man left the house. Actually left everything behind. The wife, understanding that her husband had run away from her, alerted her relatives in the town who were close to the Rav. The Rav decided to summon the father of the fugitive husband to Jewish court of law. They demanded that he bring back his son. Despite his objections that he did not know where his son was and that the son was already an adult, and on top of that a married man over whom a father no longer had any influence – the judgement was passed nonetheless. In the course of eight days, the father must return his son and at the same time pay the daughter–in–law a large sum of money. And if these demands would not be filled in all details, they would take severe measures against the father.

It was impossible to carry out the judgement simply because the son was already in another country.

After the eight days had passed, there was a gathering held with the Rav, where it was decided to deliver the harshest punishment for a Jew who did not carry out a Rabbi's judgement. If, in the course of the next three weeks he would not carry out the verdict, he would be excommunicated …

The sentenced Jew, just as the majority of Jews in town, did not believe that this harsh judgement would be carried out to its fullest. So, Friday night, as the overseer, he went to the large Beis Hamedrash to welcome in the Shabbath. Just as he was approaching his usual place (called "the city"), he suddenly heard three bangs on the podium, a sign that they wanted to announce something important. And immediately, the voice of the beadle was heard:

"Today we will not welcome in the Shabbath because the excommunicated one is here in the Beis Hamedrash. One is not permitted to stand in his daled amos [immediate space]!"

The terrified congregation ran off to their homes. The Jew, broken and downtrodden, went home alone. That Shabbath in the town was a disrupted one not only for the judged victim, but for many, many Jews. There were two factions: one that sided with the Rav, and another that protested against the unfair judgement. There were also people who tried to find a way to annul the excommunication and to appease both sides. They even tried to assemble a minyan [quorum of ten men for prayers] in the home of that Jew, and after the prayers there that first Shabbath and after drinking a le'chaim [a shot of whisky with blessings to life] – the excommunication decree was withdrawn...

Gershon–Borukh, the milk and chicken tradesman at the market

[Page 106]

Buried behind the Fence …
by Y. M. Tzembal/Cembal, Buenos Aires
Translated by Pamela Russ

1

In the year 1926, those who were Shabbath observant, along with the local chief rabbi, realized that they had to go out and do battle with the heretics [those who renounced their religious beliefs], because if so many Jews were dying, or if so many young children left this world early, that would certainly be because of these heretics....

A meeting was called in the Rav's home where it was decided that on the first Shabbath Khazon ["Shabbath of Vision"; the Shabbath before Tisha b'Av] the Rav would give a speech expressing opposition to these heretics. And that's exactly how it was. Before they took out the Torah scrolls for reading, the Rav arose to the podium, banged on the table, and shouted out:

"Jews! There is a fire!"

With this call, a great tumult arose. The Jews quickly put away their prayer shawls and began rushing to leave. But the doors were locked. The first gabbai [sexton, beadle] in the town, Yekhiel Meyer, calmed the frightened Jews:

"Don't run! Yes, it is burning, but not on the ground, only in the heavens. Listen to the Rav's speech. Where are you running?"

And the Rav? Standing on the podium, repeated these words:

"Jews! There's fire! It's linked to a plague! It's already invaded kosher Jewish homes. What should we do? The heretics are enjoying themselves as they are spreading their plague at every step. I don't want to lie in the cemetery next to such heretics. We don't have to have such neighbors in the cemeteries. You can't even allow them into the cemeteries. So we have to enclose a special place in the cemetery for these may–their–names–be–erased ones. And that's where they should be buried. Tomorrow, Sunday morning, right after prayers, you must come to the cemetery, where we will put up this enclosure. In this merit we will all be helped and live until the Days of the Messiah, speedily and in our days. Now let us take out the holy Torah from the ark and read the portion of the week."

The following morning, after prayers, the Rav, along with his congregants and several of the gabbaim [beadles] from the Khevra Kadisha [Burial Society], went to the cemetery. They made a circle not far from the fence, dug out small ditches, and hammered in some poles. They enclosed this place with some wire and placed a small board with this inscription:

"This is the place for those who desecrate the Shabbath."

After reciting several chapters of Psalms and the Kaddish, they all left with the conviction that they had done holy work, and that the honored Jews, who were already in the ground, would not have to be neighbors with these heretics...

Now there was a real danger that these worldly Jews would actually lie outside the fence. So they decided... not to die. Time passed peacefully. The grass on the separated area grew taller and completely covered the board that was nailed in with the inscription. The Burial Society unfortunately remained without work...

2

A group of friends used to come to my home, activists for the "Society's Evening Classes" and from the Sports Club "Stern" [Star]. I was chairman at the time of the abovementioned Society, administrator of the Sports Club, and instructor of gymnastic exercises. Within this group there was also a member of the Ruzhiner Sports Club who worked as a baker for a Wyszkower Jew.

At these meetings we would discuss many different social issues. Once, we also discussed the issues of the separated place in the cemetery. A Ruzhiner Jew says:

"If there will be a conflict about where to put you, Comrade Tzembal, I will give my head and not let them bury you in the separated place." (The Ruzhiner comrade was a tall and physically strong man.)

I answered jokingly, that if he would die, then I, as chairman of the Society, would arrange a beautiful funeral and not permit him to be buried behind the fence.

3

Again, weeks and months passed. The heretics completely forgot that there was a separate section in the cemetery for them. The activities of our "Society's Evening Classes" continued to expand. Every Shabbath morning, when the religious Jews were in their synagogues praying, we went into the forest, had discussions, and did gymnastic exercises. After eating, we went to the place of the Society, where we held meetings and debated all kinds of issues with cultural, social, and economic character. There were also lectures. After that we went into the woods, had discussions, and at the end we formed rows and marched back into the town.

Once, on a Friday morning, when it was very hot, after working all night the abovementioned baker decided to go for a swim in the Bug near the bridge where the road split into two directions: one to Warsaw through Radzymin, and the other – to Łochów–Bialystok.

At the same time, I went to my mother, who at that time was in her summer house in a village not far from Wyszkow. She was a religious woman, but since she was a working woman, she actively participated in all the discussions that we had in our home. For that reason, they called her "the mother of the Tzembalists." More than once, the Rav would reproach her for her participation in our activities – but she didn't listen to him.

[Page 107]

I stayed over at my mother's in the village, and only returned to the town in the evening. As I approached the bridge, I noticed a large number of people who were looking down at the water. Soon I realized what this was. Our comrade, the baker, had drowned. Jewish fishermen were searching for his dead body. Meanwhile, a messenger from the Rav had arrived, and he told the fishermen to stop their search because searching for a heretic did not warrant desecrating the holy Shabbath...

I immediately summoned a general meeting of the administration of the Society's Evening Classes and Sports Club. We decided to find the body as quickly as possible and to turn to the professional unions about declaring a strike at the time of the funeral – a strike that would go across town. We also had to get our comrade's family's consent. The family lived in our town – the sister and brother–in–law. We decided to conduct the funeral ourselves and not allow the Burial Society to deal with it. It was clear that the Rav was waiting for the first heretic to fall into his hands in order to bury him in the separated plot, behind the fence...

We made an agreement with the Polish fishermen in the village of Rybniki, that on Shabbath morning they should spread out their nets so that the dead body should not float too far out. For that, we promised them payment. In fact, we found the dead body not far from that fishing village.

After Shabbath [Saturday night] the Rav summoned a gathering. He thought that because the deceased did not have family in the town, no one would oppose the burial behind the fence. But he forgot that we, the baker's friends, would not allow the Rav to carry out his plans.

Sunday morning, we paid Dr. Weikhart and sent him off with a wagon, along with the police commissioner, to write out a death certificate. We made an agreement with the sister of the deceased that she would permit us to do the burial. We explained to her that if the dead body would be given over to the Burial Society, they would bury him in the cordoned off ground. But at the same time, we would give him a nice funeral and put him with all the other Jews. She gave her consent.

We also turned to the police commissioner about permitting the funeral to take place. The county official was in Pultusk – and Sunday no one worked there.

The Rav from his accord called the sister of the deceased and promised her financial support and a lot of … place in the World to Come. He also called the police commissioner, gave him some money, and asked that he not permit the funeral wagon to cross the town because that could cause a plague since a dead body was being carried on a bed! For hygienic reasons, a dead body must be in an enclosed wagon belonging to the Burial Society (and he was certain that the Burial Society would not give him the wagon).

But the commissioner did as the Rav requested. When the funeral wagon approached the city, the commissioner stated that he did not permit the wagon to cross town because this endangered the residents, unless the dead body would be taken in an enclosed wagon. The funeral procession stopped and a delegation went over to the Burial Society to ask for a wagon. They refused, and demanded that we give them the body – saying that they would bury him. So we demanded one of two things from the commissioner: either he forces the Burial Society to give us a wagon, or he permits us to go across town. The commissioner became a little scared, because it was the first time that he'd ever seen such a large funeral in Wyszkow, with the participation of so many people. So he ordered the Burial Society to give us the wagon.

Meanwhile, the Rav received news of this large funeral. He went out on his balcony to see this with his own eyes. We passed his house with the wagon – with raised and clenched fists…

At the cemetery, we found the gates locked. Two people from the Burial Society were in the purification house [where they ritually prepared the body for the burial]. We asked them for the keys to the gate. They refused. Once again we were forced to turn to the commissioner, and on his order they opened the gate. A few of the comrades from the funeral committee entered the cemetery, selected a place, and began to dig the grave. We knew that once a grave was dug out, you were not permitted to replace the earth unless there was a body buried in there.

Meanwhile, the commissioner ordered the police that were present to hold off the burial, and along with the Burial Society, he went to see the Rav. Once again, they summoned the sister of the deceased and told her that they would perform the appropriate purification rituals, even though you did not need to do this for a drowned person – and in this merit, he would fly straight up to Heaven … She had only to agree that they bury him where they want. And if not – she and her husband and children would lose their place in the World to Come.

In the end, she broke, and signed the agreement.

There were waiting for the police commissioner at the dug–out gravesite. The Rav's judgement was that since those "whose–names–should–be–erased" had dug up the grave – then the grave is not really a grave, only a ditch, and you are permitted to refill a ditch.

[Page 108]

The commissioner returned from the Rav and told us that the sister of the deceased gave full consent for the Burial Society to bury her brother. He did not know what to do, so he ordered them to seal up the body until Monday morning so that he would be able to ask the mayor what to do...

The mayor's decision was: to give the body to the Burial Society in accordance with the will of the sister.

Under heavy police guard, with bayonets on their guns, the baker was buried behind the fence.

This was a victory for the Shabbath observers.

Cantorial Singing and Choirs in Wyszkow
by Eliyahu Y. Brukhanski, Tel Aviv
Translated by Pamela Russ

In the year 1921, under the initiative of five head synagogue wardens – president Yisroel–Yitzchok Wystiniecki, vice–president Shloime Bamasz, and Eli–Meyer Goldman, my father, Reb Khaim Malkhiel, of blessed memory, who at that time live in Zakroczym, was brought down to Wyszkow as the khazzan [cantor], shokhet [ritual slaughterer], and mohel [circumciser].

One day after Sukkos, Eli–Meyer Goldman, of blessed memory, came to Zakroczym, and completed the negotiations with my father about accepting the position. The negotiations did not take long. Eli Meyer left my father a large sum of money for the travel expenses of the choir that he was to bring with him to Wyszkow. It was agreed that on the Shabbath of the Torah portion reading of "Lekh Lekha" ["Go for you," Book of Genesis; Abraham travels to Canaan], he would come and assume his new position. Until that time, my father was to prepare the choir in Zakroczym, 12–15 people, youths and adults.

Not everyone went at the set time. But the most important members of the choir did go. Among others, were: my uncle (my father's brother) Reb Menakhem Brukhanski, of blessed memory, who at that time was the khazzan in Serock. He had a beautiful baritone voice; my other uncle from Lomzhe, Reb Moshe Brukhanski, of blessed memory, who was a wonderful singer. In the later years, my uncle Moshe would come for the High Holidays to participate in my father's choir.

That first Shabbath, there were 13 people in the choir. We were living in the home of Reb Moshe Bamasz. The first appearance of my father's choir made a wondrous impression on the Wyszkower Jews who were not accustomed to such singing. They were like hypnotized. The young and old kept on singing and repeating the melodies they heard that first Shabbath. It is worth mentioning that it was the same in the town of Zakroczym. Children of wealthy, aristocratic parents became part of the choir and sang with them for many years. Khazzanut [cantorship] evolved into a fashionable item. Among others, Reb Avrum Bzhaze from Makow remained with the choir for a long time. This was a Jew with a beautiful tenor voice. A wonderful soloist, he did not leave the choir until they were able to train new singers.

After the first Shabbath, it was decided to hold a Khanukkah concert in the Wyszkower synagogue. The choir rehearsed with an orchestra in which

Henokh Ihrlikht and Yakov Jakubowycz performed. Both were very talented violinists. Henokh Ihrlikht completed music conservatory and studied with famous violin maestros.

At the Khanukkah concert, Wyszkower singers who participated were: Shimshon Ihrlikht, who had a beautiful baritone voice, and sang with his heart. The crowd was captivated by his solos; Berele Bzhaze, with his alto voice, was exceptional with his singing from his childhood years on. Later he sang as a tenor; Yeshayahu Gureni was of the first to sing (tenor).

Of the Zakroczymer, two children remained: Nakhman Dorembus and Yehuda Esterzon. The older singers from Zakroczym used to come to Wyszkow and from time to time would join the choir whenever necessary. There was also a Naszielsker young man who would join the choir, a student of my father, Reb Moshe Binyomin Zhepka. He had a baritone voice and was an excellent soloist (today he is a khazzan in Argentina).

The two abovementioned children in the choir stayed in Wyszkow. They were registered in the Tarbut school [secular Hebrew language school] and ate at the homes of respected people of high standing. These two children were well taken care of, even with pocket money. They sang with the choir for a few years, until their voices changed – and then were forced to stop singing. These were two gifted, musical children.

The first Khanukkah concert was not able to take place at the set time. It actually did start on the designated time, but it was not possible to continue because of the huge crowd. The city's curiosity of the concert was so great, that young and old came to the synagogue to hear. The synagogue was too small to hold such a large crowd. There was a terrible frost outside, but inside it was so hot that the violins were actually soaking in water. Because of the pushing and chaos, it was impossible to continue the concert. It was even worse in the women's gallery. All the women wanted to stand near the window and peer into the men's part of the synagogue. Wigs [of the married women] flew off many women's heads, and there was no shortage of slaps, arguments, and loud women's voices. There was no other choice, but to interrupt the concert and continue another day. It was decided to empty out the synagogue. All the benches and tables were removed so that there would be more space for the crowd to stand. The women's gallery was locked up because most of the disturbances had come from there.

[Page 109]

The concert actually took place on that next day in a tightly packed hall. Everyone was standing, but all were charmed by the beautiful, heartfelt melodies of the choir.

This concert was the beginning of my father's cantorial activities in Wyszkow. From that time on, there was always a choir in town that consisted of Wyszkower and Zakroczymer youth. Among others, there were: Itche Holand, who had a beautiful tenor voice and was a fine singer; Avrohom Markuskhamer, tenor, sang with his heart and with emotion; Yisroel Beharav, tenor; Krystal Khaim, soprano; Avremel Beharav, soprano.

In the later years, others joined: Yisroel Grosbard, baritone; Yisroelke Bronstajn, tenor; Simka Nowominski, tenor; Mashke Toib, tenor; the young Motele Ihrlikht, the younger brother of Henokh and Shimshon, was already singing in the choir at that time. He had an alto voice, and was very musical. At that time, there was also a young man from Pinsk in the choir, Kohanowycz (homeless, until his departure to America); my brother-in-law Mikhel Brame also sang in the choir; Yitzkhok Nodel, tenor; Yisroelke Rotbard, baritone; Yitzkhok Aron Holand, tenor.

Of the first singers, there should also be mentioned: Mendel Stelung, alto; Shultz Pinkhas, alto and later baritone.

During different times, the Malczyk brothers joined. As children, they began singing as sopranos, then later as tenors.

Notes to the chapter in the Book of Psalms, "Mizmor Le'Shir"
["Psalm for the Song"] composed by Eliyahu Brukhanski
[second line is Hebrew, same as Yiddish]

[Page 110]

Leybtche Stajnberg sang as a soprano as a child, and later as a tenor. Moskowycz, soprano; the Mondry brothers, altos; the scribe's son Yakov Yosef, alto; Velvel Jakubowycz, soprano; Daniel Jakubowycz, alto.

When a Hechalutz [Jewish pioneer movement for settling in Israel] organization was established in Wyszkow, I created a youth choir that gave concerts at all kinds of events. Now there were also girls who participated in the choir. We performed on Herzl evenings [evenings of recitations], at Chanukkah evenings, Lag be'Omer celebrations, and other Zionist events.

In this choir, among others there were: the sisters Yokheved and Golde Fromowycz, sopranos; the three Bzhoza sisters (Esther and Rivka sopranos; Yocheved, alto), all three musically talented girls; Khava Blum, soprano, had a beautiful voice and sang well; Yisroel Kaluski, baritone; often there were some men who also sang in the choir, members of my father's choir. Among others – also Henokh Ihrlikht.

In these times, when I was working in the Tarbut school as singing teacher, I would organize Herzl and Lag be'Omer evenings with the students of the higher grades. The profits of these types of evenings were designated to the Tarbut school.

The Guardians of the Sabbath Were Not Successful
by Yosel Popowski, Buenos Aires
Translated by Pamela Russ

In the market square [Rynek], on Kosciuszko Street, stood a one–level house where Rav Morgenstern lived. In that same house was the barber shop of Khaim Bursztyn – a small, narrow, and long shop, with three armchairs for the customers and a narrow, long bench for those who had to wait.

After Khaim Bursztyn's death, Moshe Avrohom, his son, took over the business. But the widow, Mindel, saw that the son was unable to manage the business, so she took in Markus Szwarcz as a partner. He used to work for the medic Malowanczyk.

Once, on a Friday morning, Shmule the beadle came to the barber and asked if he could go to the Rav and give him a haircut. At that time, I worked as a tutor. Szwarcz told me to pack up the utensils in a small sheet and go. I felt very proud of myself. In honor of the Shabbath, I, myself, would cut the Rav's hair! Reb Khaim the polisher!

When I came upstairs, I was met by Shmule the beadle, and he directed me into a room near the kitchen. Through the open kitchen door, I saw how all kinds of foods were being prepared, from which came wonderful aromas. In my whole life, I had never smelled such wonders. I remained intoxicated from the smells. Suddenly I heard:

"Why are you standing there? Get to work!"

This awoke me from my stupor, and I saw how my client, the Rav's son, was sitting and waiting for me to service him.

I began working with the machine, and did not notice that his peyos [sidelocks] started at the top of his head, taking up half the head. When I saw, long twisted hair laying on the small sheet, my hands began to shake. The client already understood what had happened, and he began to scream:

"My peyos!"

With this, the Rebbetzen [Rav's wife] came running. Seeing the peyos in her son's hands, she covered her face and gave out a moan:

"My eyes should not see this. My son's peyos! What did you do?"

I trembled like a fish, unable to respond. After completing the cut, the Rebbetzen said to me:

"Come after Shabbath and I will pay you."

When I returned to the barber shop, my boss asked that I give him the few groshen [coins] that I had earned. I told him that the Rebbetzen did not pay me. So one of the customers who was sitting being shaved, said:

"The payment is lost. The Rebbetzen has a heavy hand..."

B

At that time, the Shomrei Shabbath group [Guardians of Shabbath] was created. One Friday evening, it was already ten minutes after candle–lighting time, a Jew came to the barbershop and ordered him to lock up – It's Shabbath. Szwarcz replied:

"We'll finish up our work and then we'll lock up the shop."

The Guardian–of–Shabbath left. I shut the outside door. Soon another Jew came, and screamed:

"You are non–Jews! You have no shame! You are desecrating the Shabbath!"

He kicked the door and left.

A short while later, a group of Jews came, at the head of which was Rav Morgenstern. Some remained standing at the entrance; others along with the Rav, came inside. All of them were talking at the same time, screaming, some even threw up their fists. We heard a loud voice of one of the Jews: "In our Rav's house, you dare to desecrate the Shabbath?"

[Page 111]

In the small barber shop, chaos broke out. Markus Szwarcz tried gently to calm everyone, but without success. They did not let us finish our work. Szwarcz, now angry, ordered that the police be called in. I barely pushed my way through the people, out onto the street, and called the tall Sobolewski who was just then staying right near Mondry's tavern [inn]. When Sobolewski came over, he told everyone to leave. Szwarcz asked him how late he could keep the shop open. Why did they come to bother him at work? Once again, there was chaos. The police saw that he would not be able to calm down the Jews with easy methods, so he took out his book to write down punishments. He asked: "The Rabbi also?" And Szwarcz answered, "Yes."

That very minute, the door opened and a Jew looked in. When Szwarcz saw him, he called him in and turned to Sobolewski:

"Write him down too!"

When the Jew heard this, he began to tremble and pleaded:

"Mr. Szwarcz, I did not come to disturb, only to look!"

"Having a look costs money," replied Szwarcz.

Sobolewskyi wrote down his name as well and told him to leave. We completed our work peacefully.

A few days later, every "Guardian–of–the–Shabbath" had to pay a fine: eleven zlotys.

The following Friday evening the "Guardians–of–the–Shabbath" did not bother us but went to the Tenenboim brothers who had a barber shop on Yatke Street. They disturbed the work there too. The third Friday, the "Guardians–of–the–Shabbath" group hung up a note in in the Beis Medrash [study hall] with a black border, where it was written that the Tenenboim brothers are desecrators of the Shabbath and so they should be boycotted...

When the youth in town found out about the note, they went to the Beis Medrash and tore it down.

All week they were talking about the Tenenboims and the boycott. Some followed the call of the "Guardians–of–the–Shabbath" while others went to get haircuts at the Tenenboims – but through the back door.

On Shabbath day, after the daytime meal, the "Guardians–of–the–Shabbath" gathered in the marketplace near the bridge, and disturbed the youth who were out strolling. They also found out that Jewish young boys were playing football in the horse marketplace. So they went over there with the Rav and wanted to disrupt them. When the players saw them coming, it became almost festive. Some of the young boys even invited them to play...

The "Guardians–of–the–Shabbath" expanded their work but had no success. There was already a well– advanced youth in Wyszkow.

The large Beis Medrash [study hall] in Wyszkow that was burnt down by the Germans along with several hundred Jews who were burnt alive

[Page 115]

Personalities, Businessmen, Figures, and Types

[Page 117]

Postcard sent by M. Anielewicz from the Warsaw ghetto

Mordekhai Anielewicz,
Commander of the Ghetto Uprising in Warsaw –
Born in Wyszkow

Translated by Pamela Russ

(Excerpts from Yisroel Gutman's book, "The Revolt of the Besieged" – Mordekhai Anielewicz and the war of the Jews in the Warsaw Ghetto, "Sifriat Poalim" ["Library of Writings"], Merchavia, 1963.)

(From the chapter "The Childhood in Powiszla")

The family Anielewicz were not original settlers in the city of Warsaw. Mordekhai's parents came to the main city of Poland at the end of World War One from the small town of Wyszkow – which, in an unusual manner, was connected to Mordekhai's fate. He was born in this town, and with time this town was of the first to be a victim of the war. At the end of the great resistance in the Warsaw ghetto, the remaining fighters assembled in the forests of Wyszkow, and here they even created a unit of Jewish partisans that bore the name of Mordekhai Anielewicz.

In truth, only Mordekhai's mother Tzirel (maiden name Zlatman) was from Wyszkow. His father, Avrohom Anielewicz came here by chance. Avrohom's parents, Mordekhai's grandparents, were from Galicia. During the events of the First World War, they left Galicia, as did many other Jews, but not as part of the main flow of refugees who left Galicia for Vienna and for the other side of the ocean. The Anielewiczes settled in with their relatives in Wyszkow, that was close to Warsaw – until the rage would pass. Here, Avrohom met Tzirel Zlatman, a young girl, who with her red cheeks and strong stature, completely resembled a village girl. Their acquaintance was brief, but Tzirel did not have to think long. Avrohom was really far from the knight-like figure that this girl had dreamed of. And, on the other hand, he was also not a young man of religious studies, a Torah scholar. Nonetheless, Tzirel knew that the house of her step-father was drowning in poverty and her three grown sisters needed to find husbands and be provided with dowries. When the family Anielewicz found out about her means, and rumors circulated that their son was appropriate – they withheld nothing.

[Page 118]

A short time after their wedding, important changes took place in the big world and in the intimate, small world of the Anielewiczes. The war in Europe had ended, and the marching of armies through Europe across Poland's ground, ended as well. When the war broke out, the Czarist soldiers were stationed here, the well-known and despised "Fonyes" [nickname of Russian name Ivan, to Vanya, to Fonye]. When the Czarist soldiers fled, the Germans arrived – tall in stature, polite, and well dressed. Jews, who are always waiting for salvation and appeasement, welcomed the new conquerors with hope and good will. With their uniforms, the soldiers that came from Germany symbolized the countries of progress and tolerance; a land where Jews had equal rights and economic well-being. Other than that, the Germans spoke a language that was close to the Jewish people's Yiddish, and every Jew could understand the new rulers. But it quickly became clear that those who used the "close" language were also close to Jew-hatred. In the marketplace and in other open areas, inscriptions appeared, saying, "Dogs and Jews are not welcome." In the end, the Germans also wore themselves down, and with a flurry, independent Poland was declared. After 150 years of subservience, dreams, and unsuccessful uprisings – Poland again rose up with life. The Polaks were drunk with joy and whisky in honor of this event. The Jews understood that everything would leave – armies, regimes, languages – the only thing that remained was the hatred for the Jews.

Avrohom's parents did not return to Galicia, to the south of the country. They went to Warsaw and opened a food and colonial goods shop on Tamki Street in Powyszlye. In contrast to this new group, the new couple were provided with "kest" [full room and board] by the parents of the groom – and not of the bride. In about a year's time, the Anielewiczes provided a generous sum as a basis of income for the young couple. This couple also settled in Warsaw. But very quickly, Avrohom was drafted into the commanding Polish army and Tzirel went to live with her mother-in-law. The Anielewiczes in Warsaw, after a forced detention in Wyszkow, returned to a regular and normal life. Here, everything was buzzing with business, trade, and even the regular conversations circulated around this central axle. But Tzirel did not feel comfortable with this dizzying tempo of the large city. She very soon became ill, being in the first few months of her pregnancy. The doctor found spots in her lungs that foretold bad things. He recommended special foods and fresh, village air. That's how Tzirel was forced to go to her relatives in Wyszkow for a period of time. For a long while, she had already missed the town, surrounded by forest. She missed the crooked, wooden houses, and the quiet, G-d-fearing Jews. In Wyszkow, she freed herself from her yearning and her difficult moods. Tzirel strolled by the edges of the forest, picked blueberries and wildflowers, and ate dairy products. Her sisters, particularly the oldest, Faige, took care of her with devotion and love. In the old, wooden house that was surrounded by shrubs and that belonged to the family of her parents, Tzirel gave birth to her oldest son that was called Mordekhai after the name of her deceased father. The newborn opened a pair of small, blue, lively eyes that looked with concentration and understanding, and whose skin color was pale and fresh. Tzirel would often repeat that her son who was born during wartime (between the Polaks and the Russians), and who experienced needs – would be a lucky person in his lifetime.

(From the chapter: "Press in Action")

Janos Turkov, an old actor and the son of a famous performing family, was active in the ghetto in social assistance, and in his memoirs he told about his encounters with Mordekhai.

"I met Mordekhai Anielewicz during the German occupation at the beginning of 1940. At that time I was chairman of the Refugee Department and of those who had suffered fires for the Independent Social Assistance (Rimorska 20) program. Mordekhai Anielewicz came to me (together with Laya Saperstajn) about the house on Leszno 6, that was occupied by the group of Shomer Hatzair [socialist Zionist youth group]. Because the apartment was on the fifth floor, we wanted to move it to another location. Mordekhai wanted to leave the group because they had organized a kitchen there and the expenses were very high.

"Thousands of people would go through the office of social assistance, and it was difficult to remember all the visitors. But as strange as it was, from the first moment that Mordekhai Anielewicz spoke to me, he left an incredible impression. He was a young man, tall in stature, strong build, and refined behavior. His face showed understanding, kindness, and a lot of energy. His smiling eyes twinkled with a suggestion of strength.

"He began to speak to me in Polish. When I asked him if he knew any Yiddish, he replied that it was easier to express himself in the Polish language. Each of his words was weighed and measured. He supported his speech with an iron logic. To each of my counter-arguments he reacted quietly and calmly, but with so much confidence that you knew that the bottom line was going to be his way.

[Page 119]

"He really made me understand that they would not leave the house on Leszno.

"I really felt that this young man possessed a strength that was impossible to defeat. A fleeting thought crossed my mind, that this young man would fulfill an important mission for us. After some time, when I had discussed with Dr. Ringelblum what sort of an impression this young man had made on me, he commented: "Yes, this young man will yet give us much nachas [make us proud]."

(From the chapter "Mila 18," a letter from M. Anielewycz to Yitzchok [Antek Zukerman])

[Translation below from JewishGen Yizkor Book site, "The Terrible Choice, Some Contemporary Jewish Responses to the Holocaust," Yitzchak Zuckerman.]

Shalom Yitzhak.

I don't know what to write to you. I'll waive personal details this time. I have only one expression to convey my feelings and those of my comrades. Something has occurred which is beyond our wildest dreams. Twice the Germans fled from the ghetto. One of our squads held out for 40 minutes, and the second - for more than six hours. The mine which had been buried in the brush makers' area exploded. On our side only one victim has so far fallen: Yechiel, he fell as a heroic soldier beside his machine gun.

When the news reached us yesterday, that members of the P.P.R. [Party Directorate of the Jews] attacked the Germans and that the Shwit [underground radio station] radio station broadcast the wonderful news about our self-defense, I had a feeling of completeness. Although we still have much work to do, everything that has been done so far was done to perfection.

The general situation: All the workshops in the ghetto and outside it were closed, except for "Werterfassung," "Transavia" and "Dering." Regarding the situation with Schultz and Toebbens, I have no information. Communications have been cut off. The workshop of the brush makers has been in flames for three days. I have no contacts with the units. There are many fires in the ghetto. Yesterday the hospital was burning. Whole blocks of buildings are in flames. The police has been disbanded, except the "Werterfassung." Schmerling has reappeared. Lichtenbaum has been released from the Umschlag. Not many people have been taken out of the ghetto. This is not the case with the "shops." I don't have details. By day we sit in our hideouts.

From evening on we change to the partisan method of activity. Three of our units go out at night - with two objectives: to search out armed patrols and to steal arms. You should know - a revolver is of no value, we have hardly made use of it. What we need are: grenades, rifles, machine guns and explosives.

I cannot describe to you the conditions under which Jews are living. Only a few chosen ones will hold out. All the others will perish sooner or later. Our fate has been sealed. In all the bunkers where our comrades are hiding, it is impossible to light a candle at night for lack of air...

Of all our units in the ghetto only one man is missing: Yechiel. Even this is a victory. I don't know what else I should write to you. I can imagine to myself that you have one question after another, but this time please let this suffice. Be well, my friend, perhaps we shall meet again. The main thing: The dream of my life has been fulfilled. I was privileged to see Jewish self-defense in the ghetto in all its greatness and magnificence.

Mordechai.

(From the chapter "Until the End" – About the death of Anielewicz in the bunker, in the Warsaw Ghetto)

"... and this is what we learned about the events from those who survived:

"Yesterday, in the middle of the day, when they were still lying on their cots half naked, the guard suddenly informed us that the Germans were closing in on the bunker, and you could hear their steps. In these cases, the Jewish fighters used two systems. Since the Germans usually first ordered all the Jews to go outside, then our group would go out first with their borrowed weapons and after a few seconds would suddenly begin shooting at the Germans, and in the chaos, they would scatter everywhere. Some would save themselves. The second system, was not to respond to the Germans' order of going outside, remain inside, and if they would try to force themselves inside – to welcome them with gunshots. During the day, you could still hold out – the Germans would not dare to come inside – and for the night, we would have to find a hideout. We knew that the Germans also used gas, but this didn't bother us. Someone said that if your face was in water, the gas did not have an effect.

"When the Germans ordered the people out, the civilians and bunker inhabitants left, and gave themselves up. The Germans said once again that those who gave themselves up would be sent to work, and those who refused to come out – would be shot. Our friends fortified themselves against the invasion of the Germans. The Germans once again repeated that nothing would happen to those who would come out, but no one tried to leave. In the end, they let in the gas, and all 120 fighters died.

"The Germans did not sentence [the fighters] to a quick death, but let in a small amount of gas and then stopped in order to depress the mood and implement a slow and prolonged suffocation. Aryeh Wilner was the first to call out to the fighters: 'Come, let's all commit suicide and not fall as the living to the Germans.' And so began the chapter of the suicides. Shots were heard inside – Jewish fighters took their own lives. It happened that the shot of one gun was not heard, so its owner, tragic and devastated, asked his friend mercifully to kill him. But no one came forward to kill their friend. Lyutek Rotblat, who was there with his mother and cousin – shot four bullets into his mother who was still shaking with wounds and pouring with blood. Beryl Broda, who had been wounded several days earlier in his hand and could not hold a pistol, pleaded with his friends to end his life. Mordekhai Anielewicz was certain that water would deflect the dangers of the gas, and suggested for all to try this. Suddenly, someone came in and announced that they had discovered an escape route that the Germans did not see. But only a few left through this opening and the rest suffocated slowly.

[Page 120]

"That's how the life energy of the Jewish rebels was snuffed out, along with the struggling Warsaw. Hundreds of Jewish fighters met their fate here, and among them - Mordekhai Anielewicz, beloved by the fighters, the courageous commander, the kind one, who, even in the hours of terror, carried a smile on his lips..."

Admo"r Rabbi Jacob Aryeh of Wyszkow–Radzymin

(Admo"r is an honorific meaning: Our Master, Our Teacher, and Our Rebbe)

From "The Rabbi of Kotzk and His Sixty Hero's" monumental book about the Torah, Account, and achievements of the Rabbi, his great followers and descendants up to the very last generation. Written by Jeheskel Rotenberg and Moshe Scheinfield. Published by "Netzah", Tel–Aviv, 1959. Volume 2.

Translated by Chava Eisenstein

The Kotzk Dynasty, which is ramified with sons and disciples, was founded by Admo"r, the Elder Menakhem Mendel. And continued to blossom for many years after the Zadik's departure. His disciples have developed existing dynasties, which continue to spread brightness and purity all over the Khassidic world. The descendants of the dynasty were nearly completely annihilated by the Nazis,

Wyszkow, a small town in Poland. It was here that Rabbi Yaakov Aryeh began serving as rabbi. Since then, his life was a continuous chain of doings for his followers–children. In those few years that he was rabbi in Wyszkow, he acquired reputation for his distinguished piety. His devotion to his people, caring and worrying for each one of them in all aspects of life. (It was told of him that if one of the Khassidim fell ill, he would be beside himself with worry, and did everything in his power to have him cured.)

Rabbi Yaakov Aryeh was openly admired when his father, the Admo"r of Lamaz was still alive. When his father, the late Rabbi, passed away on the third day of Elul, year 5,686 (1926), the community appointed the Rabbi's son, Rabbi Yaakov Aryeh to take over and become the rabbinical authority. Word spread that the Rabbi will begin his leadership the following Shabbat, in spite of still being in mourning of his great father.

The first Shabbat was a hit! Thousands of followers arrived from afar to participate. His uplifting Torah talk was exceptional. From that Shabbat many people, seeing his high personality, joined his leadership, complying with his every word of advice.

Aside being their Rabbi, his people found in him a fatherly figure who cares and thinks devotedly about each one of them, he would take interest in their general and financial life and offer help and empathy with good advice.

His home and courtyard were swarming with Jews from all over Poland, who came to seek his advice, or were in need of heavenly relief and mercy.

With his constant smoking–pipe between his lips, his noble appearance and clever eyes claimed awesome respect from all who saw him.

The home of Rabbi Yaakov Aryeh had a unique blend of the Kotzk and Warki Khassidic movements. The Rabbi was the grandchild of Rabbi Menakhem Mendel of Kotzk, on the other side he was son–in–law of Rabbi Menakhem Kalisch of Amshinow – Warki so that the pure love of a fellow Jew was deeply implanted in his heart and permeated his personality.

A large amount of his followers, resided in Lodz. The Rabbi made a point to leave his home in Wyszkow, for one Shabbat annually, and come to his followers in Lodz. While being in Lodz he hosted at the home of R. Zysia Hendlis. This R. Zysia published the sefer "Toras Ha'Cohen" written by Rabbi Zysia of Plock, and Rabbi Yaakov Aryeh wrote a recommendation letter upon printing it.

In Lodz, he encouraged and strengthened the community and his influence was felt long, long after. This annual conduct caused love and unity amongst the Khassidim.

Years passed and the community in Wyszkow became larger as more and more Jews were drawn to Rabbi Yaakov Aryeh. Every Shabbat the courtyard crowded with Khassidim that gathered to pray, and then dine with the Rabbi. During the meals, he spoke deep thoughts of Torah that penetrated heart and soul.

In the year 5,692, the old Admo"r of Radzymin passed away and the Khassidim were left without a lead successor. They turned to Rabbi Yaakov Aryeh who was also a grandchild of the Radzymin Admo"r. The people of Wyszkow begged him to stay with them, but finally, the Radzymin Khassidim won, and the people of Wyszkow accompanied him respectfully out of the town.

[Page 121]

Now that the town was left without a rabbinical authority they turned to the son of Admo"r Yaakov Aryeh, whose name was Rabbi David Shlomo, and he took over the position at Wyszkow.

Before World War II, Rabbi Yaakov Aryeh felt the threatening danger that was looming above Jewish Europe. He wrote a special appeal from the depth of his heart, calling his followers to strengthen their contact with G–d and the Torah, and shouldn't fall weak in their faith. The letter was spread all over Poland and echoed strongly between the Khassidim in Poland

His sons who perished as well, as martyrs:

Rabbi Israel Isaac – Rabbi of Rotzk, Rabbi Elimelekh Jehuda – son–in–law of Admo"r Rabbi Joseph of Amshinov, Adm"r Mordekhai – Rabbi of Skrazisk, Rabbi Berisch – son–in–law of the Admo"r of Grokhow

Itta Tova Kalish, wife of Admo"r Rabbi Meir of Amshinov (May he live for many good days, amen), is the sole survivor of the complete distinguished rabbinic family.

Reb Khaim Henekh (Shtelung),
the Baal Tefilah [Prayer Leader]
by Menakhem Shtelung, Tel Aviv
Translated by Pamela Russ

(Dedicated, to the memory of my father, mother, sisters, and brothers)

Who in Wyszkow did not know Reb Khaim Henekh – the Czerwiner Baal Musaf [the afternoon prayer leader from Czerwin]? He, along with his five sons, the accompanying singers, would give vitality to the souls of those who would hear his Kol Nidrei [primary prayer on Yom Kippur eve], and afternoon prayer on Rosh Hashanah and Yom Kippur, or simply a Neilah [final prayer at the closing of Yom Kippur]. His "G–d, He is the Lord," tore open the Heavens.

When it was time for Neilah, people from the other synagogues, study halls, and congregations left their places and came to the Gerer shteibel [small house of prayer], in order to enjoy Khaim Henekh's sweet voice. Even our neighbor, the mohel [ritual slaughterer] Cziwiak, of blessed memory, who was the khazzan in the large synagogue (until the arrival of Khazzan Malkiel Brukhanski, of blessed memory), also came over for Neilah, to her Khaim Henekhs's prayers...

My mother tells...

My father's success as a khazzan, and the frequent briefings to me in town as one of his sons and assistants, made me curious to know how he had achieved this career. I gathered up my courage and once asked my mother, Esther Mindel, may she rest in peace. To my great surprise my mother sat down with me and gladly began to tell the whole story:

"When Khaim Henekh was a fifteen–year–old boy, he came from Czerwin to study here in the local yeshiva. Every Friday night, he would lead the prayers, and soon his singing became famous in town. Many young girls would stand under the window and they would enthusiastically listen to the beautiful singing. I too would be one of the frequent guests under the window of the Wyszkower yeshiva, from which the prayers of Kabboles Shabbath [the beginning of Shabbat] of the Czerwiner young man would be carried. I, along with other girls, would wait a long time after the prayers were ended to see him leave. Now, there is nothing to hide. I very much liked this khazzan and my parents felt this. As was done in those times, my mother left to see her father, Reb Moshe Sokol, a wealthy, Jewish man. After several words, my father sent over a matchmaker, and in a blessed time, we were married.

Since Reb Khaim Henekh came from Gerer khassidim, he started to pray in the Gerer shteibel. Once, on a Friday night, they asked him to lead the prayers – and the Gerer could not praise him enough. From that time on, he became the regular prayer leader there...”

Reb Khaim Henekh Shtelung

[Page 122]

Why not a shokhet [ritual slaughterer]?

I remember as if today, even though I was just five or six years old then. In a bureau drawer I just happened to find a shokhet's knife wrapped in a scarf. I left with the find to my father and asked him why there was a knife in the house if he wasn't a shokhet? He mumbled some words, of which I understood nothing, but I felt that he wanted to hide a secret from me. I was very curious, so years later when I asked my mother, Esther Mindel, may she rest in peace, the same question, again she did not hide anything and said:

“After the wedding, Khaim Henekh was “oif kest” [had daily room and board] with his father–in–law, as was the style then, and was there for several years. But he also composed several compositions to “lekho dodi” [Friday evening prayer, “Come My Beloved”] and composed several other cantorial melodies. At the same time, he also studied how to be a shokhet – and was also successful. He would always take the sharpened knives to the Rav, and after, when the Rav had checked them all, the decision was made: He would be given the right to be a shokhet. But, he did not become a shokhet... He was simply too gentle. He had a weak nature, could not look at spilled blood and at slaughtered chickens that wanted to live ... His breaking point came in the slaughterhouse where they killed livestock. He came there with a properly sharpened knife and was prepared to do his job for the first time. Everything was ready, but – all at once, the cow raised her head and gave a sorrowful look at your father, so it seemed as if she was asking: Why do I deserve to be slaughtered? – – –

He put away his knife back into its sheath – and went back home with a strong conviction of never becoming a shokhet...

New Compositions

After forgoing shkhita [slaughtering], my father completely turned to khazzanus [cantorial music]. He used to compose new melodies that quickly became popular in the town, and then travel far, far beyond the border of Wyszkow. When we the children grew up, he would teach us the new melodies. On Shabbath, when we would sing zemiros [special songs in honor of Shabbath], it was very festive in our house. We not only sang, but harmonized together, learning new compositions. For shalosh seudos [the third meal, Shabbath evening], we would partake at the home of the chief rabbi of our city. My father would take me there along with him, where I would help him sing his new melodies. I remember that once, at such a shalosh seudos, Reb Khaim Henekh requested such a new melody, and the crowd remained glued to their seats. They spoke about this for a long time afterward, and I was especially proud of my father's accomplishment. The chief rabbi himself called out: "Strength to you!" ["thank you"].

A few weeks before the High Holidays, it was very festive in our home. There was a whole choir of singers, directed by our brother Avrom Moshe, of blessed memory, who for hours, day in and day out, prepared for those days. My father's "Unesane Tokef" ["Let Us Speak of the Power..." solemn prayer of the High Holidays] or the "Hineni He'oni" ["I Came before You..." another solemn prayer of the High Holidays], are to this day deeply engraved in my memory. When I go to hear a khazzan today, I always try to compare them to my father's new compositions or his interpretations of famous melodies. It is always evident to me that the Wyszkower prayer leader Reb Khaim Henekh takes first place...

After we completed our prayers on the High Holidays – the reward came quickly. Gerer khassidim almost had a "war" among themselves over having the honor of inviting us to their table for Kiddush [light lunch after services, beginning with prayers recited over a cup of wine]. They wanted very much to express their acknowledgement and gratitude for having had the pleasure and enjoyment of our leading the prayers.

And that's how our family – along with the entire town – lived until the outbreak of the First World War.

In Warsaw

As soon as the Germans took over Poland, we decided to leave Wyszkow and go to Warsaw where our sisters Khaya and Brokho'tche lived. We dragged ourselves with horse and wagon for several days to the capital of Poland. The traveling was very difficult and exhausting. We were attacked by bandits, and I don't remember exactly if my father gave them money to save our lives. One thing I do remember: The thieves terrified me and in their presence I cried and screamed bitterly. Nonetheless, we arrived safely to our sisters.

With the permission of the Gerer Rebbe, my father became the prayer leader for Musaf [the afternoon Shabbath prayers] in the Gerer shteibel in Warsaw on Gensze [see Gęsia note below[1]] 19. Here too, my father, along with his sons as the choir, was very successful. But Reb Khaim Henekh missed home very much, missing the Gerer in Wyszkow. He also knew that one was not permitted to resign so easily from a fixed job [referring to his cantorial job back home]. He prayed for a quick end to the war so that he could go home.

An opportunity for this arose – but from a different, indirect, and tragic way. Our sister Yokheved, aged 15, while standing in line all night waiting for bread, received a smack in the head from a German with butt of his gun. She died from a brain infection. In great distress from this tragedy, my father said this was probably a punishment from G–d, because he had broken off his fixed time of work [back home], even though the Rebbe had allowed him to do so. So he returned to Wyszkow for the High Holidays and led the prayers there. And from that time, wherever he was, he would always come back to Wyszkow for Rosh Hashanna and Yom Kippur, even when he lived in Ostrolenka and other places.

[Page 123]

A Seder [Passover Ceremony] Night

At the end of World War One, we were back in Wyszkow, and we lived on Stodlana Street in the large wooden house of Jakubowycz, where there was also the home of the shokhet Yankel Bursztyn.

Our home was large, and especially the huge dining–room which is etched in my memory, which was set and prepared for the seder night. But this is what happened. Right in Passover eve, the Russians took over the city and some of the officers went into homes to demand requisite lodging for the army. That night, when my father recited Kiddush [blessing over a cup of wine] with his strongly melodious voice, the door opened and a Russian officer entered. He wanted to begin to speak and certainly demand to have the house for himself or for other military personnel, but my father did not interrupt his Kiddush, and the officer, excited and upset, instead of making his demand, simply placed his hand on his cap, saluted, and quietly left. All of us saw an extraordinary miracle in this. On that seder night, my father and his sons as the choir, surpassed even himself. Until the early hours, we sang and celebrated. Particularly festive, was our father's reply to our question of "Ma Nishtana...?" ["Why is this night different...?" one of the "Four Questions" that begins the seder recitation]...

Don't forget that these types of visits of Tzarist officers to Jewish homes would generally end tragically. According to the mood in town at that time, there was the danger not only of losing one's home, but also to punish, to mock, the residents. An officer from Nikolai's army did not demonstrate exemplary politeness towards the Jew, especially during wartime, when Wyszkow was not far from the front. I remember how at that time my childish heart pounded from fear and my entire family waited with terror for the judgement. And because nothing happened to us that night – it remained engraved in our memories. Our large home was one of the only ones that was not requisitioned by the Czarist army. As a memory of that night, we would arrange and celebrate every seder night with exceptional singing and ceremony. Beneath our windows there stood many residents of the town and listened to my father's compositions.

At the beginning of the 1930s, when I made Aliyah [moved] to the Land of Israel, in his letters to me, my father asked if I remembered that Passover in Wyszkow and his seder. In the year 1935, instead of responding to his letter, I sent him the following lines:

My Father's Seder

My father sits today at the seder table

And my mother at his side.

Both are thinking, as was done,

About the children far away.

Once Passover holiday was so festive,

The entire house filled with laughter

My father – an authentic king

Among his sons and daughters.

To each child, a second question

Would be asked by my beloved father

And now, each has flown off

Across distant, wandering roads.

Now my mother sits at the seder table,

Just as I am doing here.

He is there and I am here,

Both lonely as a rock.

That's how, in these helpless lines, I expressed my yearnings and ties to my mother and father, whom I wanted to bring over to Israel, but was not successful because of the political certification of the mandating government, and because I myself had entered Israel illegally (with the Second Aliyah).

Death in Warsaw Ghetto

On his final High Holy Days, in the year 1940, Reb Khaim Henokh led the prayers in the Gerer shteibel in the Warsaw ghetto. This time he did not have his choir and not even his congregants. The two quorums of Jews [20 people] were not Gerer khassidim. The few that managed to save themselves from under Hitler's nails, tell how heartrending and anguish–filled these prayers of Reb Khaim Henekh were. He too, with the example of Reb Levi of Berditchev [great khassidic leader 1740–1809], complained to the Creator: "What do You want from Your Nation of Israel?"

He merited to die a natural death and had a large funeral in the Warsaw ghetto. He was buried in the Gęsia*cemetery where our dear mother was buried in the year 1935.

May their illuminated memory be honored!

Footnotes

1. Gęsia (pronounced Gensha/Gensze) means Goose (Street) in Polish. Before World War II, it began at Nalewki Street (its extension to the east was a street named Franciszkanska) and ran west to the gates of the Jewish Cemetery at Okopowa Street. It no longer exists.

[Page 124]

Reb Khaim Malkhiel (Brukhanski),
the Khazzan [Cantor]
by Y. Brukhanski
Translated by Pamela Russ

My father, Reb Khaim Malkhiel Brukhanski, may he rest in peace, came from Lomza. My grandfather, my father's father, Reb Eliyahu Brukhanski, of blessed memory, was also a Khazzan [cantor], shokhet [ritual slaughterer], a fine singer, and a pious Jew. In his younger years, he sang for Nisen Belzer, the renowned Tzadik [righteous man]. The famous Tzadik Reb Zalmele Khosid, the first Lomzer Rebbe, was his great–uncle.

As a child, my father displayed great musical talent and already at that time he would be an accompanying singer in the largest synagogues. He sang for Pinye Minkowski in Odessa, and also in Kherson, where he also studied music. Because he was a religious Jew, he chose to be a khazan [cantor], shokhet [ritual slaughterer], and a mohel [circumciser].

His first position was in the small town of Serock. He lived there for not more than one year. It seems that he did not have any great earnings from there, so he left for Nowy Dwor, and remained there for two years. Here, his earnings were not so great either, so he left this position as well.

There was also another reason: This happened in the year 1905, when the Jewish socialists warned him that if he would continue to make a "mi se'beirach" [blessings for someone's wellbeing] for the Tzar – they cannot be held responsible for his life...

He left Nowy Dwor and went to Makow, and here, too, his earnings were little. My father always made sure that the level of prayers or of blowing the shofar should always be the highest. He was always exceptionally fastidious in these areas. Recognizing that the Makower Rav, Reb Reb Yisroel Nisen Kuperstok, was, other than a religious man, also an outstanding baal tefilah [leader of prayers], my father helped him. Especially – during Neilah [closing prayer for Yom Kippur], when the Rav prayed in the famous Makower synagogue. My father would also take pleasure in the pure blowing of the shofar done by the abovementioned Rav.

The roaming did not end in Makow. The next town – Goworowa, which was almost entirely destroyed in World War One. Of the Jewish community, half remained. Here he met the renowned Torah–reader Yenkel Klepycz. He went especially to hear him read [the Torah portion] when he still had time. In Goworowa, there also lived a family of nobility, scholarship, and multi–branched – the family Grudko. One of the family members – Reb Khaim Ber Grudko, along with his wife Brajna, later became my in–laws. Reb Khaim Ber was an excellent baal tokeah [the man who blows the shofar], and my father always selected him to blow the shofar wherever he [my father] was praying.

After Goworowa, we went to Zakroczym. Here, doing the ritual slaughter was already too difficult for my father, because he still had to service the local fort with ritual slaughter. So, he went to Wyszkow where he stayed until the end of World War Two.

The praying, blowing of the shofar, and Torah reading were all holy work for my father. If the blowing of the shofar on Rosh Hashanah was not done properly, he would not continue with the Shemoneh Esrei [the "Eighteen Blessings," central part of prayers] but would signal with his hand to repeat the blowing of the shofar.

Reb Khaim Malkhiel died in Lomza as a refugee, in the year 1940.

May his memory be honored!

Yisroel Asman
by Yosef Zajdenstat
Translated by Pamela Russ

He came from Wyszkow. In about the year 1906, he came to Lomza and took private classes. He was drawn to the intellectual Zionist circles because he was a man of letters. He wrote stories of khassidic life in Zeitlin's "Yiddishe Wokhenblat" [Jewish weekly]. He would participate in illegal meetings; speak in synagogues about Zionism; study "Ein Yakov" [commentary on Talmud] with the youth, and explain the "agudahs" [legendary material] of the Talmud according to science and logical thought. He immigrated to America (Los Angeles) in 1909. There he published his pedagogical and literary works in the "Zukunft" ["The Future"] and in "Hadoar" ["The Post," Hebrew weekly]. He translated Carlyle's "Heroes and Their Hero–Worship" into Yiddish. He also published stories in Hebrew in an exceptional style.

In his house, which served as a club for the skilled and for writers, he would always mention Lomza where he himself learned a lot and studied with others. He prepared himself to go to Israel – but he did not merit to do so. He died of a lengthy illness in the year 1950 [5711]. In Lomza he had many friends and admirers.

(From the Lomza Book, Its Rise and Fall, New York, p. 8)

Yisroel Asman's Folk Legends and Folklore
by Sh. Ernst
Translated by Pamela Russ

The Jewish folk–treasure was for generations like a sealed well. Inside, it fought, thrashed, and stormed – but it did not reach being investigated.

Who ever looked at old wives' tales? From generation to generation, old treasures amassed of true folklorist richness:

[Page 125]

... tales which the folk–people weave "without knowing," without skilled inspiration, but in the spirit of the people's soul, until the rise and sprouting of the Jewish folk story. In his "Popular Stories," Y.L. Peretz drew rich panoramas and pictures that describe the "past" with rich, dramatic elements, and awoke the interest in other writers and artists.

After him came Mikhah–Yosef Berdiczewski, who broke a window in the ghetto wall of the Middle Ages. In his work "Tzefunos Ve'Agudos" ["Secrets and Tales"] and "Me'Otzar Ha'Agudah" ["From the Treasures of the Tales"], he gave us important folklore material.

Yisroel Asman – Dr. Khaim Zhitlowski described – followed in their footsteps. At that time each week he would publish his stories from the cellar – old sheimos [tattered papers with holy names on them, etc.] in the New York newspaper "Tog" ("Daily")." Asman, more so than Berdiczewski, saw "36 Tzadikim" ["36 righteous men"[1]] not only in the craftsmen, but also among the vagabonds and people from the dek (?).

Zhitlowski writes that in Yisroel Asman's stories and tales the simple Jew also was "repaired" [given prominence] for the entire year.

Jewish Folk–Fantasies in the Middle Ages – Some of Asman's Publications

Y. Asman's book "Sefer Ha'Nisyonos" ["Book of Trials"], that was published in Yiddish and Hebrew, is only a small sample of his large treasure of folk–stories that he published over the years in the New York "Daily," and in this book he only gave samples of all kinds of stories, some of which he had prepared handwritten and which did not merit to be published in book form.

In his weekly folktales in the "Daily," he also published "mystical folk fantasies." "Rabbi Yosef Dela Reina" [Tzfat, 1418–1472; story of how he wanted to invoke the coming of the Messiah] was not an exception, a rarity, but an expression of people's life and stormy inner tension for generations. He describes these moments in many variations.

The Messiah Idea in Folk Legends

The "Messiah idea" smouldered in the people's soul, and the longing for "salvation" broiled up from time to time, and with the events [of the time], they affected the folk legends. The false Messiahs, Shabtai Tzvi [1626–1676, rabbi and kabbalist, self–proclaimed Messiah, Turkey, Europe] and Yakov Frank [18th century Poland, claimed to be reincarnate of Shabtai Tzvi], had a rich resonance in folk fantasies – and Yisroel Asman describes several interesting folk legends about Shabtai Tzvi, as he meditated at the sea and how, using Holy Names of G–d, he sank a ship of pirates …

Also, about the discussion that Frank had in the year 5519 (1759) with Reb Khaim Kohen Rappaport, Asman has a story: They go out, and along the way the horse does not want to continue going. So they remain there for the Shabbath and they miss their trip to Lemberg. Later, it becomes known, that during that same time, the Frankists [Frank's followers] had organized a "fire" of Talmud books on the non–Jewish street in Lemberg that was being prepared at their [Frank's and Rappaport's] arrival. They [the two men] merited not seeing this great desecration with their own eyes because the horse was obstinate and did not want to continue.

Yisroel Asman in Los Angeles

About Yakov Frank and His Followers

The majority of legends about Yisroel Asman are based on historical fact. His portrayal of Yakov Frank, the False Messiah, was taken from Frank's own handwritten "Biblia Balamutno" [Frank's own manuscript called "Book (Bible) of Disturbances"] in red ink, is based on the famous book by Alexander Kraushar in Polish, "Frank and His Frankists," and on Zalman Shazar's "Ikvot Akhim Ovdim" ["Footprints of Laboring Brothers"], publications of Offenbach, and others.

Also, his stories of Frank's follower Baron Wolf von Eibeschitz, the son of the Rav of Prague, the Gaon [genius] Reb Noson Eibeschitz, how he becomes repentant after the death of his father, Reb Yonosel Prager, who would not allow him to sleep with his disturbing dreams.

Popular Fantasies Are Unified

When reading Y. Asman's "The Book of Challenges," you would think this is a real Jewish creation. But according to the Jewish mystical inclination in the Middle Ages, Sh. Pietrushka writes in the Warsaw "Today" about Asman's book that his stories are migrant motifs of folklore, because the Jewish ghetto in the Middle Ages was actually not isolated from the influence of the local people. Also, Sh. Prager shows that Asman's story "David King of Israel" is similar to the story of " Fligan and Troles," who lived in the second century, and also to "Haribhadra," according to Johannes Hertel's Indian stories.

[Page 126]

Y. Asman once wrote about his folklorist work himself: "I easily take a story that demonstrates the sensitive Jewish spirit that is soaked with migrant folklore. Jewish folklore resembles worldly folklore. With the popular motifs, while having his own productions from his inner well of life, old Yiddish had as its beginning the "Artur Roman" [novel] and a book about Prince Bobeh that later became the familiar "Bobeh Maaseh" [old wives' tales]. Also – "Ulenspiegel" and the "Spilman Richtung" ["Spilman Way"] – all rooted in worldly folklore.

"In its unique setting – writes the famous essayist Khaim Liberman – Jewish literature could not keep going in the direction that European literature experienced. For that reason, the unique Jewish folk spirit evolved, which shows us in the folk story the eternal human questions, and the relationship with G–d, the world, and the human being."

We find a new approach to Jewish folklore with Yisroel Asman. While we find in the folktale book "Oseh Peleh" ["He (G–d) does Wonders"], or "Maasim Pelaim" ["Acts of Wonder"], "Niflaos Tzadikim" ["Miracles of the Righteous"], and others, we always find a moral or religious thought, then Y. Asman's stories have a worldly depth. If other folktales cannot be separated from the current thinking of those who created them, then Asman's fantasies are free, not tightly bound to any limitation, while stylistically maintaining the authentic folkloristic characteristic.

Reports and Lectures about His Productions

When Yisroel Asman was in Israel, I went with his compatriot Motel Wenger to Asman's lecture about his productions:

"I always searched in the soul of the people," he said, "the stamp of the folk spirit, and distanced myself from every story where I recognized the fingerprint of an individual signature, without the fingerprint of an individual – This is the absolute sign of a true folktale."

"I searched for the "36 Tzadikim" [righteous men] in the folktales of evil men, of a spiteful person, a sinner without any respect for rabbis. You would think that this person is an outcast, but in his heart he has a deep love for the Creator. Beggars, who are everywhere across the country, and those begging for money – they were in the folk–fantasies of the "36 Tzadikim," for whom the world is being sustained.

"If I searched for that which is really Jewish and for that which originates from foreign nations, I had the sign that Sh. Ansky gave: "The eternal concept, " not the passing one, but that which remains, which lasts, that which is a piece of eternity – that is truly Jewish.

"In the Jewish folktale there is the cycle – of faith in the Creator. Nowhere, not with anyone else, is the motif of faith stronger.

"If Khoni Hamagel[2] sees how a Jew is planting carob tree that will bear fruit only in about 70 years, that too is the theme of "faith," since that Jew, who lives in constant fear of having to move to another place, is offering assurance to his grandchildren, since he has faith that they will benefit from his work.

"A gray day was always a corridor to a bright tomorrow.

"King David, the young shepherd, was triumphant over Goliath, who was armed from head to toe – is once again a victory motif, as the Jewish spirit will be able to defeat the physical strength that to him is abhorrent."

In "Hatzofe" ["The Observer" newspaper] the author of these lines wrote about Y. Asman's lecture, that he reflected the romantic charm of the Jewish world–conduct with the complete fantasy that is unique to the Jewish mentality. A Jew has a "World of Legends," living with the memories of previous generations that were also carried over to the "Next World." The Jewish spirit in the course of time has distanced itself from the circle of time.

"The association of time and place does not exist for the Jewish story. They would put children to sleep with stories of long ago. The theory of relativity existed for us Jews long before Einstein, in a romantic way.

"I would like now to cite Sh. Niger's appraisal of Y. Asman's stories:

"Yisroel Asman is the master of the legend of long ago. He does not search for world ideas, as Y.L. Peretz, but he wants to show us how the tattered, ragged Jewish pauper bathed in the ritual bath of the large folk well. His stories do not always have a romantic character; in fact sometimes it's the opposite: abrasive, coarse, or a helpless creature. But even such a creation is G–d's creation, part of the higher regions of the cosmos."

Yisroel Asman was the master of the Jewish folktale. He used his own fantasy in order to clothe each legend in literary robes. His talented descriptions are not only narrative, but bring the reader into the fantasy of the magic realm, around which the persecuted Jewish masses wrapped themselves as an armed circle against different demons that arose against their existence. The people's soul always searched for G–d's mercy in the baggage of generations and dreams of the future. His intellectual baggage greatly enhanced his talented strengths. It is unfortunate that he took to his deep eternity a large part of his viable creations.

[Page 127]

In one of his stories, he once described the magic, dark gate of the cemetery, which he later went to, dying before his time, not being able to publish his works in book form.

May these lines be a memorial tombstone for his honored memory!

Footnotes

1. It is said that in every generation there are 36 ("Lamed Vav" in Hebrew the letters are numbers) righteous people for whom the world is sustained.

2. Jewish scholar of the First Century. It is told that on one occasion, when there was no rain well into the winter (in the geographic regions of Israel, it rains mainly in the winter), Khoni drew a circle in the dust, stood inside it, and informed G–d that he would not move until it rained. When it began to drizzle, Khoni told G–d that he was not satisfied and expected more rain; it then began to pour. He explained that he wanted a calm rain, at which point the rain calmed to a normal rain. (Jewish Virtual Library)

Yisroel Asman in Los Angeles
by Yekhiel Bzhoza
Translated by Pamela Russ

We, the Wyszkower in Los Angeles, were very proud of our landsman [compatriot] Yisroel Asman when he lived here in this city for a few years, where he was respected and beloved by the entire Jewish population.

He ran a refined home, and was known as a great host. Understandably, when a Wyszkower came here, Asman's home was the address where we met, asked about other landsleit [compatriots]. His home was also the address of other Jewish writers and social activists who would come to Los Angeles. Whenever a needy Jewish writer had to sell his books, Yisroel immediately went to work, drove around with him in his car from morning until late at night, not only to help the writer, but mainly – to spread more Jewish books in Jewish homes.

Yisroel Asman was the book master par excellence, raised by a father who was an intellect and a great scholar, all his life Yisroel did not cease to dig and research old Jewish books. He was in love with Jewish books and in the Jewish nation – the People of the Book.

Years ago, he was a teacher in a Jewish Talmud Torah [Hebrew school]. He never stopped being interested in Jewish education. He was one of the initiators to create the "Bureau of Jewish Education" in the community, and then later became one of their directors.

He also belonged to one of the founders of the local "Jewish Culture Club" that does important culture work in the Jewish street.

Within a few years, Yisroel was a contributor to the New York newspaper "Daily" where he wrote interesting khassidic stories. He was also the representative of that same paper for the distant western states. Each year, he would travel for a few weeks across the Jewish cities and towns, in the interests of the newspaper. He was welcomed everywhere with respect and love. Other than the social matters, he also was occupied with readings of literary themes. He particularly enjoyed speaking about Y.L. Peretz.

Yisroel is also the author of an important book built on khassidic legends and kabbalah [Jewish mysticism]. The book was also published in Hebrew, in his own translation ("Sefer Hanisyonos"; "Book of Trials").

Another characteristic stripe in Yisroel's personality was his close tie to our tradition and his keeping of the Shabbath and Jewish holidays. Every Friday, he was very busy preparing for Shabbath. He himself used to prepare the gefilte fish [traditional Friday night food made of ground fish].

On Friday night, for the festive meal, he always had guest. They recited the Kiddush [blessing over wine], sang zemiros [special Shabbath songs], discussed Torah issues, and recounted khassidic stories until late in the night.

His Passover seders were something to talk about. It was considered a sign of recognition to be invited to participate in conducting the seder at Asman's home. Each year, before Passover, he himself would prepare the kharoses [mixture of apples, nuts, and wine to use as part of the seder ritual] for all his friends and neighbors.

Yisroel Asman was a deep thinker and researcher, but at the same time – a quiet, calm, and humble man.

In the year 1949, Asman went for a visit to Israel with the intention to settle there. But he became sick there and had to return home.

After a long and difficult illness, he died on June 8, 1951. He left his wife Penina, a son Shlomo, and his sister Laya.

May his memory be honored!

Community Activists
(Wyszkower Personalities)
by Yitzkhok Baharav
Translated by Pamela Russ

Five Wyszkower figures: Dovid Gurni, Eli–Meyer Goldman, Moishe–Yosef Abramczyk, Dovid–Leyb Holdak, Velvel Kronenberg

Dovid Gurni. He helped many needy Jews, paid them weekly monies. He himself took money to some of them personally for Shabbath. There were some who were embarrassed to tell anyone about their need – but they trusted Dovid Gurni, and he supported everyone, even beyond his own capabilities... May these few lines be an honored Kaddish [prayer for the deceased] for this holy martyr.

Eli–Meyer Goldman. He and his wife Elke discreetly gave a lot of charity. Not everyone knew that he was sustaining several families with financial support and other charitable deeds. As president of the "Kupiecki Bank" [founded in 1920, it allotted funds to Jewish credit co–operatives], I would often call him over, because he endorsed the exchanges of many Jews who later did not have the money to repay. On the spot, he brought in the papers, and tore up the promissory notes. These kinds of events did not prevent him from endorsing others again...

[Page 128]

Moshe Yosef Abramczyk. An Amshinower khassid [follower of the Amshinower Rebbe], prayer leader on Rosh Hashana and Yom Kippur, community secretary and secretary of the merchants' union, bookkeeper in the "Kupiecki Bank." Since he managed the registry of those who needed social help, he knew everyone's situation. He knew the status of each small merchant, artisan, market traveler – in a confidential and discreet manner he would get money from the community and the bank for the needed support as loans that put them back on their feet. One Friday night, very late, I met Reb Moshe Yosef, and he was carrying a heavy basket. When I asked about this, he told me that just before candle–lighting time, just as he was closing up the administration office, a Jew came over to him (he did not want to say the name) and confessed that he had nothing for Shabbath and asked to borrow ten zlotys. Abramczyk immediately gave him the requested amount, but it was late and all the stores were already closed. The Jew could just about buy candles, bread, and herring. Reb Moshe Yosef was worried that, Heaven forbid, a Jew and his children would be hungry over Shabbath – so from his own prepared food, he took half, put it into a basket – and now was taking it over to him...

Dovid Leyb Holdak. He was better known as the Branszczyker baker. He lived and had his bakery in the marketplace in the medic Malowanczyk's house. He gave a lot of charity, worked very hard, but each night, after completing the baking, took down four breads and divided them up among the poor. In the same way, each Friday, from noon onwards, he would go to stores and homes and call out: "Jews, please give a few groshen [pennies] to poor Jews!" He was a sick man, heavy, and his walking was difficult. Nonetheless, he did not forego a single Friday to do this mitzvah. His words were well–known in town, when he asked someone for monies: ...: "jak posmarujesz, to pojedziesz..." ("that you grease (my palm), then you will go" (i.e., "travel").

Velvele Kronenberg. Better known as Velvele Yehoshua Wajnmakher's, a Gerer khassid. He lived off what his children sent him from America. He was always satisfied, would always sit in the Gerer shteibel, and only thought about how and for whom to do a favor... Because there were children in the Talmud Torah who came from poor households, who didn't even have the funds to pay school fees, Reb Velvele (without being rewarded for this!) arranged for Wyszkower businessmen to pay weekly funds to the Talmud Torah. Everyone gave, poor and wealthy, as much as they could. He considered it a great mitzvah for Jewish children to learn Torah and to be able at the same time to have food to eat. Three times a week, from Wednesday to Friday, summer and winter, he would collect these weekly payments going up stairs and into cellars.

These are the kind of Jews that Wyszkow had.

Henekh Kaluski
by Avigdor Mondry
Translated by Pamela Russ

One of the most popular figures in town, a respected Zionist activist, to whom the ideologies of Hertzl, Hesse, and Pinsker were dear and beloved, he believed that we were approaching the realization of the establishment on Zion [Messianic times].

Henekh Kaluski possessed a great capacity for persuasion, and it was easy for him to attract new people into the movement and have them become active in the fundraising for Keren Hayesod [United Israel Appeal], Keren Kayemet [Jewish National Fund], and for laboring Israel.

In town, it was also known that Henekh Kaluski was always ready to help a friend with any advice or support, and warmly be there for each person.

His deeds in the area of culture were particularly significant. He established a library, evening classes for teaching Hebrew, and the founding of Tarbut schools [Hebrew language schools] – is one of the undeniable assets of Henekh Kaluski.

There was a time when the Zionist movement conducted a campaign to buy a small farm in Israel. Kaluski was very preoccupied with this project. He dreamed of sending his children to Israel in order to settle his entire family there later on. In 1924, he sent his son and daughter–in–law there. Despite the difficulties because of the mandating government and the opposition of the Arabs, he believed with all his faith, that the Zionist ideal would be successful.

As secretary of the United Zionist Committee in Wyszkow, I remember the sacrificing, tireless activity and initiative of Henekh Kaluski.

Sadly, this idealist and fighter did not merit to see the State of Israel. He was dealt the tragic fate of the Jewish people at the time of Hitler's occupation and died in sanctification of G–d's Name.

May his memory be honored!

[Page 128]

Dr. Laykher[1]

by Shimon Malovantczyk[2]

Translated and funded by Frida Cielak nee Grapa Markuschamer (Mexico City)

He was an intelligent, able, and very respected person in the city (Wyszków). He was in close contact with the Polish local intelligentsia [intellectual group], but he always considered himself a national Jew. It happened more than once that he did not charge a visitation fee from a poor, sick person. As an elected member of the city fund, Dr. Laykher took personal interest in Jewish poverty and provided aid there where it was really needed.

[Page 129]

When the Germans occupied Poland, Dr. Laykher, along with other Wyszkower Jews, was deported to the Wégrow[3] ghetto. There, he set up extensive medical and social activities among the depressed, dejected Jewish population. All his strength was devoted to help the suffering, and he sacrificed himself for the sick.

In the Wégrow ghetto, Dr. Laykher was the head of the underground movement.

A separate chapter of his life was his active participation in organizing the uprising in the Treblinka death camp, about which Yankl Wiernik,[4] who was able to escape, wrote: It is a pity that we have so little knowledge and information about Dr. Laykher's activities during the occupation years.[5]

Italics in parentheses are translator's remarks

Translator's Footnotes

1. Dr. Berek Laykher's surname was registered officially as LAJCHER in Polish. In Polish, the letter 'J' is read as 'I' or 'Y' and the 'CH' is pronounced like 'J' (as in Jim). The Lajcher surname transliterated from Yiddish, according to Yivo transliteration rules, is written as 'Laykher.' Before this, and because of the absence of vowel signs in some Yiddish printings, the name would sound like 'Leikher' or 'Leykher.' This could certainly be why, when his surname was transposed phonetically into Roman letters, authors would use various spellings of the name, such as: Leycher, Leicher, Leichert, or even Leichera and Laycher. Many survivors of the Treblinka camp where Dr. Lajcher spent the last days of his life, wrote their memories after their escape in August 1943. Different versions of his name were used in these records, as were names on registered lists of survivors and prisoners of Treblinka. From all the writings reviewed, we know that the camp inmates often used nicknames among themselves to avoid becoming too friendly with newly arrived inmates. They feared too much intimacy since the SS Nazi camp commanders could shoot any of them just for fun on a daily basis. The use of nicknames or only surnames was customary in Treblinka, as in many other camps. Therefore, when referring to Dr. Berek Lajcher's activities, we can find his name and surname written in many different ways, including Leicher, Leycher, Leichert, etc. Also, he was referred to as: Dr. Beck, or Beniek, and even registered as Dr. Marius Leichert.

(In Yitzhak Arad's book "Belzec, Sobibor, Treblinka," chapter 28, p. 219, he was registered as Dr. Beck. Among the list of names at Yad Vashem, and at the Alphabetical Listing of Treblinka Survivors and Victims site "Treblinka Remember Me," the three different given names contained descriptions coinciding with Dr. Berek Lajcher. Similarly, his name was registered as Dr. Leichert by Stanislaw Kon in his "Revolt in Treblinka and the Liquidation of the Camp.")

2.   Shimon (full name: Shimon Zakharyeh) Malovantczyk, the son of the Wyszkow hairdresser on Rynek, F. Malovantczyk, a hairdresser and a popular city *feldsher* doctor ["fake" doctor, rural practitioner of medicine without medical degree, an old–time barber–surgeon; a doctor's assistant). F. Malovantchik/Malovantczyk was considered to be the top in his field, and enjoyed talking with the Jewish doctor Leykher (Berek Lajcher). Malovantczyk used to say that doctors could not tolerate intelligent *feldshers*… (p. 156 Wyszkow Yizkor Book ["*Der Feldsher Malovantchik*"] "The Rural Doctor Malovantczyk").

3.   Wegrow is about 27 km from Wyszkow, and it is there that Dr. Berek Lajcher moved when the Germans invaded Poland. (*Note: Because he arrived with the Wegrow ghetto people, he became known as the doctor from Wegrow. Dr. Berek Lajcher was born on October 12, 1893, in Czestokhowa, Poland, studied in Warsaw where he also served in the Polish Army as an officer, moved to Wyszkow where he married and had his only child, and became one of Wyszkow's prominent citizens and a popular doctor among Jews and non–Jews. He moved to Wegrow with the sole intention of helping the Wegrow ghetto Jews, and was, from there, deported with all of them to Treblinka. There he was commonly known as the doctor from Wegrow, where he worked at the camp infirmary replacing the late doctor Julian Chorazycki who, until his death, was the commander of the Camp Underground Organization, in which Dr. Lajcher actively participated. (Stanislaw Kon, in his "Revolt in Treblinka and the Liquidation of the Camp," wrote: "Dr. Leichert from Wegrow was selected by the Germans from a new transport, and replaced Chorazycki.")

4.   Yankel Wiernik /Jankiel Wiernik, is the author of a Yiddish manuscript titled "A Year in Treblinka." Wiernik was born in 1890 in Biala Podlaski, Poland. He belonged to the Bund Socialist Jewish Organization in Eastern Europe, was arrested and sent to Siberia. After completing a term of service in the Tsarist Army he settled in Warsaw, where he became a building contractor. On August 23, 1942, he was deported to Treblinka. Almost a year after his deportation, he escaped from Treblinka during the uprising of August 2, 1943. In 1944/45, he wrote his memoir in order to let the world know what went on in Treblinka. Wiernik was also a witness at several trials against the German Nazi commanders who were captured. Wiernik's manuscript was translated from Yiddish to English, and it can be found at: http://www.zchor.org/treblink/wiernik.htm

5.   The "Biography of a Martyr: Dr. Berek Lajcher (Leicher)" manuscript is being prepared by the historian Enrique Krauze, assisted by his researcher Frida Cielak (nee Grapa Markuschamer).

———

Reb Motl Broder
by Shimon Malovantchik
Translated by Zulema Seligsohn

A great God–fearing man, who bore all pains and suffering without blaming anyone, and least of all, the Lord of this world. He never parted with his Book of Psalms. No one ever heard a bad word out of his mouth toward anyone. He found something to say in everyone's favor and was very careful and considerate in his speech

Reb Motl Broder was the trustee of the Hevrah Kedisha (Burial Society) and everyone said that he was the right man in the right place.

His wife, Reitse, the daughter of Reb' Shloime, official slaughterer of Nasielsk, was truly a holy woman, always with good traits and joy. They both were able to raise their children in their own spirit. One son–on–law was Reb Mendl Kolner, a slaughterer and great Torah scholar and God–fearing man.

When the Germans came in to Wyszkow and led many Jews to the outskirts of the town to shoot them, among them was Reb Motl Broder. Soon afterwards, the other members of his family were also martyred there, except for his two sons, who had emigrated before the war.

Reb Yakov Dovid Pszetitski
by Shimon Malovantchik
Translated by Zulema Seligsohn

He always sacrificed himself to help the needy, and had the rare virtue of listening to other people's sorrows and worries. His ear and his heart were as open to others as his purse, For everyone who came to him for help or for advice, he tried to think of the best means to help them. Meanwhile he never delayed taking care of whatever came to him. In such a case he left all his own occupations and any business; did not think about his own family, and brought the help that was needed – but with respect and in a discreet manner, so the recipient would not feel embarrassed or ashamed.

Yakov Dovid Pszetitski, like a father, showed his interest and concern for those who needed a one–time loan to greet the Sabbath or a holiday, or to prepare for the winter with appropriate clothes and a quantity of coal.

He was a counselor to the congregation and chairman of the treasury of the free–loan institution in Wyszkow. In these two realms he was able to develop his philanthropic and social activities, and those who benefited from his help will always remember him.

With the breakout of WWII, his wandering life began. After many years of suffering and wandering, he was granted the joy of realizing his dream; to migrate to Israel. There also he undertook his social aid activities and again became the address for the survivors from Wyszkow, who had begun to reach the Jewish land. He immediately contacted the residents from Wyszkow in America. He was active in the local aid organization on behalf of Wyszkow. He was one of its founders and treasurer until death took him in Tel Aviv in 1956.

May his memory be blessed!

Mordkhe Tchekhanov
by Tch. (Khane) Appleboim
Translated by Zulema Seligsohn

Mordke Tchekhanov

Mordkhe Tchekhanov was a warm person and a wonderful Jew. A quiet, calm, polite speaker, but every one of his words was spoken wisely. Thus quietly with no unnecessary loudness, he accomplished a great deal of work. His house was an institution in itself. There was no important organization on the Jewish street that was not connected with him and with his life's companion, his devoted wife Molly, who with a generous hand supported all those who came to them for help.

Mordkhe was a cultured man, with a fine demeanor, heeded and loved by everyone. He founded and built the compatriots' organization in America. Everyone came to him for advice. His whole family looked up to him, held him in high esteem, and he had full authority over them.

[Page 130]

With his death, not only his whole family found itself orphaned, but also his Wyszkow compatriots everywhere.

His whole activity was – benevolence. For years he led the Wyszkow relief works. He sent tens of thousands of dollars to Wyszkow for the maintenance of kitchens, institutions, schools, etc. On his own, he gave a great deal to charity, even when he himself did not have very much. As a dedicated Zionist from early times, he was a generous supporter and believer in the land of Israel, and he was fortunate to be able to visit the Jewish land and see the realization of his dream. This visit gave him a push to increase his activities on behalf of Israel.

Mordkhe died with a smile on his face, knowing his physical sufferings were over, and with the certainty that his dear wife and his children who were brought up in his own national spirit, would continue his noble work.

Honor to his memory!

R. Simon son of Yehezkel Serbernik
by Yerakhmiel Wilenski
Translated by Chava Eisenstein

R. Simon Serbernik Z"L

With high regards and much respect, I wish to bring up the noble figure of my teacher and Rabbi, R. Simon z"l. he was one the limited "Elevated Souls"in our times. Beloved and admired by all folks from every type, in our city Wyszkow and the surrounding towns, where he was well known as a great scholar, that many rabbis throughout Poland obtained Torah from him.

With esteemed awe, I envision his bright image at events or different occasions. His glowing face and passionate words resembled a divine figure, a serpent. His sayings, thoughts, permeated fiery Godliness, his whole self, seemed to reflect the Divine Presence itself.

I remember him standing in prayer, at his steady corner, his eyes so clever, as if penetrating with beautified fear, as not from this world, he didn't move as he turned his prayer to heaven. Only his lips whispered, as if his soul has returned from the highest spheres. Indeed, whoever witnessed him praying was convinced that "Heart Labor is Prayer".

In our city, he was known as R. Simon Hezkel's, or R. Simon the melamed – The Teacher. He fully reflected the saying "He Teaches Torah to His Nation Israel". He was teacher and educator for youngsters as well as for adults. In his heider, he had teenage boys learning Gemara with commentaries, with the poskim - earliest and later allocations. He would also devote several hours a week to teach Hebrew grammar and Tanakh. The classes would usually count up to 40 students. They took place at the small synagogue of the "Hevrat Tehillim"– Psalms saying group. He never raised a hand or even scolded his students for improper behavior; a glance at the boy was a sufficient reprimand for the pupil who lowered his eyes in shame. He implemented in their hearts care for the fellow Jew and his needs. Every week he would sent two students to collect money for a poor student. R. Simon didn't hesitate to challenge his excelling pupils, he would assign them to be up Thursday nights and restudy all they have learned over the week.

His schedule was crammed with various studies for the public. In the evening, between prayers, he would learn in the main Bet Medrash with the working folks, and members from the "Mesilat Yesharim"society. Many people would gather around the table, and listen eagerly to his captivating words. Being many years the steady manager of the Alexander synagogue, he would make on occasion melave malka feasts on Saturday nights for the fellow Hassidim, he would then bring up interesting Hassidic anecdotes. Things that happened in the Rabbi's room while he was present. Hassidic tales from back in the days of the "Baal Shem Tov". He also started the circle of learning "Likutei Torah"of Rabbi Schneor Zalman of Liadi. In the wee hours of the night, he would be engrossed,learning Kabalistic studies. In the morning, after immersing in the Mikveh, he and his people would go to the main synagogue and recite psalms.

On holidays or festive days as well as at days of mourning, R. Simon stood at the center of the life at the community, serving also as spokesman.

I recall the night of Yom Kippur, when Rabbi Simon took out the Torah scroll from the Holy Ark, and encircled the pulpit saying excitedly: "Or Zorua La'Zadik"– Light is implemented for the righteous, and the honest will deserve happiness.

And, when you looked into his bright blue eyes, you acknowledged the light and the joy of the zadik. This repeated itself on the day of Simhat-Torah, when he called out "Atta Horeisa"and when he danced with the Torah in his arms while surrounding the pulpit, his eyes beamed with joy, faith, and love.

The night of Rosh Hashanah, those sacred minutes when the New Year was about to settle in, his whole being, said love and favor for the Jewish youths that approached him for a blessing upon the coming year. He would hold the hand of the youth and slowly let go of him even after wishing him the best. One would imagine that this is not R. Simon, but rather the lad's biological father who cares for his son and his future; he was entirely burning with excitement, thus, enticing the whole crowd with him.

Journey of His life

As a youngster, in the 1890's, R. Simon's father sent him to learn Torah at the yeshivot in Poland. The most of his Torah knowledge, his great proficiency, and wittiness, he acquired being a pupil of Rabbi Avrumele from Sochaczew z"l, and obtained his Rabbinic Authorization from him. He inherited from him many handwritten of Torah findings, rabbinic discourse, alike the notorious "Noda Be'Yehuda"has composed. His father of blessed memory, was an ardent Hassid of the Rebbe of Alexander, Author of the "Yismah Yisrael". For the holidays, he would travel with his son Shamele to be by the Rabbi. The Rabbi had a close relationship with him. In his young years, he would stay at the "court"so that the Rabbis own children should learn and be educated by him. When he married the daughter of a prominent Alexander Hassid, he came back to our Wyszkow, where he built his home. The Rabbi directed him, to accept his status as "Torato Omanuto"meaning, Torah - is his profession, nothing otherwise. That, until he receives a job. Occasionally the Alexander Rabbi would request him to accompany for several months newly appointed rabbis, to various communities in Poland, and guide them with halacha issues and religious customs. For two years, he was head of the Alexander Yeshiva, but he needed to support his large family, and make sure to their Torah education, he returned to his family, and despite all the many trouble and concerns that bothered him, they didn't leave their imprint on his personality. He was always happy with whatever he had. His aware and vital approach impressed everyone that was in touch with him. When there was disagreement between the Ger and Alexander Hassidim, he would say, that his concern is not the ruling of the community, but the young generation, which is growing up under the influence of modern literature, which began infiltrating the Agudat Israel youth. His spiritual influence was great; no one had the ability to sway him. He was simply admired and honored by all.

[Page 131]

His Final Way

In those horrendous days that befell the Wyszkow community, when the city was aflame, he ran with his family towards the Bug River, heading to Kamienczyk, where the Germans reached him. They physically abused him; shaving off parts of his beard together with the flesh. From there he continued to Bialystok where he encouraged the remaining survivors, advising them not to return to occupied Poland, and go on traveling to Siberia. The Russians exiled him together with a large group to Arkhengelsk (city in Russia).

He was taken to a labor camp in the forest, and in spite of it being of forced labor, he was the only one to be exempt from labor, as the N.K.V.D. realized that he is a prominent Rabbi. Nevertheless, his life was still very difficult. His inventive devoted wife found how to sustain the family. His older sons too, worked and helped financially. He would encourage the distraught people. Some of those who were with him in the labor camp convey, that the N.K.V.D. was on constant watch of him, still, he succeeded in finding a hiding place in a shack, there he conducted cultural activity and communal prayers. Therefore, they were eyeing him. Together with Cantor Griniski from Kielcz, Jews said "Kol Nidrei" prayers on Yom Kippur eve. Jews would awake at 5:30 and pray, at 6:30 they were already at work. Here, they were "encouraged" by the whip to work faster. Once, in middle of prayers, the bullies showed up, wending straight ahead to R. Simon. They locked him in a tiny dungeon, for 10 days he laid there shivering from frost. When they took him out, he was unconscious, people alarmed a doctor, but his tormenters would not allow him treatment. Doctor Tzarkin hid medicine on him to save him from pneumonia; the doctor himself succumbed later to Typhus.

On Sunday, the thirteenth of Nissan, 1941 at 9:00 in the morning, when his follower Huna came to see him, he opened his eyes, called Huna, and returned his soul to his creator. The inhabitants bought shrouds and obtained a burial issue. A quorum of men, Cantor Grinski amongst them, brought his coffin up to the hill; there he was put to rest under a fresh tree.

Our heart aches upon the loss of this precious soul. inadvertently we cry out: "Is that the Reward for such Sanctity?" in my ears still reverberate the eulogy of the "Ten Martyrs" recited by Reb Simon, all orphaned and engulfed in bereavement, in the dark night of the ninth of Av.

This same vicious fate awaited him too. For ten days, he was confined, covered by snow, quivering between life and death, nourished by dry stale bread and some water. Still, his sense remained undeterred, when he was drawn out of the hole, semiconscious, he whispered a prayer, or was it the prayer of David, psalms composer: "G-d, strangers have entered your estate..." his[1] strong spirit and deep rooted faith infused him with the strength to withstand the Pneumonia, and last for another six months. Until the night before Pesakh 5711.

What a great unforgettable loss.

From his family are left:

His wife Feiga

His sons: Rabbi Zadok Silver – N.Y.

Menachem and Israel Kaspi – Israel

Translator's footnote

1. Here comes a phrase: למים בשרם נתנו - which doesn't appear in Psalms. Instead it says: נבלת את נתנו עבדיך

Motl and Sore Baharov
by Yitszkhok Baharav/Barab
Translated by Zulema Seligsohn

Reb Motl Baharov was a well–known personality in Wyszkow. For more than 50 years he was the slaughterer in the town (therefore his name Motl Shoikhet [slaughterer]), a respectable, true Khasid. His father, Reb Faivel Baharov, had been a rabbi in Wyszkow for fifteen years. Afterwards, he held the rabbinical chair in a larger town, Nowy Dwor, for 25 years.

Sore Baharov, Motl's wife, was well–known in Wyszkow for her honesty, modest behavior, and religious devotion. Her father, a learned man and a scholar of the Talmud, was well–known in Warsaw by the name, Reb Yosele Kaftal.

Motl Baharov (*Shokhet,* Ritual Slaughterer)   Sore Baharov

[Page 132]

A Very Ramified (Well–Branched) Family
by Yitszkhok Baharav/Barab
Translated by Zulema Seligsohn

Motl and Sore Baharov had ten children, nine sons and one daughter, Gitele, who married Khaim Leib Kliger from Pultusk. He was the slaughterer there until WWII broke out. Motl and Sore's sons were Leibl, Yosef, Moishe, Faivl, Barukh, Velvl, Itche, Hershl, Yisrolyk. Leibl and Yosef had died before the war. Perished among all the saints and martyrs, either at Treblinka or in the Ghetto, were:

Yosef Baharov, a true Khasid, president of many institutions in Serock. (He and his wife, two sons and two daughters, perished. One daughter lives now in Israel).
Faivl Baharov and one of his sons perished. (Two other sons were rescued: one is now in Israel and one in Argentina)
Hershl Baharov perished with his wife, two sons, and one daughter.
Yisrolyk Baharov perished with his wife and one son.
Gitele Baharov perished in Treblinka with her husband, Reb Khaim Leib, two sons and a daughter. (One son is now in Israel)

In 1930, Motl Shoikhet died. All shops in the town were closed as the funeral cortege passed on its way to the cemetery. The coffin was carried the whole way. In the middle of the street, for the first time ever, the eulogy was delivered by the Rabbi, Reb Yaakov Yehuda Morgenstern; the second eulogy was delivered at the open grave by the deceased's son–in–law, Reb Khaim Leib Kliger. Nearby following were his children and their mother Sore, who was muttering during the whole walk "Motl, Motl, I envy you. I wish that some day I could have such a funeral and my nine sons and my daughter and their families would be able to accompany me..."   Unfortunately, Sore Baharov was not fated to be buried in a Jewish grave. At the age of 83, she, together with her children and grandchildren (27 in all) perished in martyrdom.

The survivors

From the far–flung family, the following survived: Velvl Baharov with his family (in Israel); Itche Baharov with his wife Feige (Israel); Rivke Baharov and her family (Argentina); Yehoshe Baharov (z"l), who died of a heart attack in 1961 at the age of 39 in Buenos Aires, survived by his wife, two sons, and his parents; from Barukh Baharov, a son in Israel; from Leibl Baharov, a son in Argentina.

R. Hanok (Heinoch) Kornet
by Moshe Kornet (son)
Translated by Chava Eisenstein

I was an infant of two months when my father passed away. Many people told me about his personality, he also bequeathed me a book he composed – "The Citizen in Israel,"which had Torah notes, interpretations on the Gemara, Psalms etc. He published his book in 5,688 (1928) at the print shop of R. Isaac Meir Alter of Warsaw, carrying the approval of the famous figures: Rabbi Joseph Lewenstein z"l of Serock, Rabbi Asher Gershon z"l of Rypin, and Rabbi Menahem Mendel Albek z"l of Zyrardow.

He has also written a commentary on Genesis. It is worthwhile noting, that the name of his sefer "The Citizen in Israel"is not incidentally, in spite of being famous in our town as a khassid of Ger, who was authorized as member in the Rabbinate, he was Torah observant, and even an ultraist – yet, he did consider immigration to the Israel. In those days, a Zionist was regarded as a heretic. Father said, "Perhaps these Zionist youngsters are a G-d-send... like when there is a wedding, the first to run ahead are the children, they can run fast, then come the parents and the high esteemed guests... maybe, the youngsters should make ready the ground for immigration."

*

My dear pious mamma, Miriam, was the daughter of Mendel Mizlutz z"l from the town Ostrolenka. By only forty she was widowed and left with six children, the eldest, Hana'le z"l, was seventeen, and I – a two month infant. Yet, Mamma, being modest and well educated, knew to speak and write six languages, had dedicated her life for her children, she never remarried and has undertaken the complete financial burden of the family and brought us up as loyal Jews. She didn't merit to enjoy her children for long because she was murdered by the Nazis in the Warsaw Ghetto.

Grandpa, R. Israel-Isaac
Grandma, Freida-Perla
by Isaac, son of Nahum Weisman (Perla)
Translated by Chava Eisenstein

R. Israel-Isaac Perla, so tall and straight, his whole appearance called for honor. Indeed, everyone, Jews and non-Jews alike, accepted and revered him. Therefore he was elected as City-Council member of Wyszkow.

He volunteered to be active for the public voluntarily, but it took up most of his free time, often it prevented him from being at home with his family, but the family was accustomed to perceive him almost as a guest at home. Despite that, we had much honor for him, because we knew how much he cares for each one of the entire family, we felt, that inside him is a warm fatherly heart that loved us all fervently. And with this heated love, his heart burnt out untimely.

I still remember Grandma Frieda in her prime years (in Wyszkow she was called 'Frieda R. Shaloms'). Nevertheless, the passing years didn't erase all the natural beauty from her radiant face. We grandchildren were drawn to her and loved her to pieces.

Grandma Frieda served as a motherly image with rare noble characteristics and a receptive good heart. Although life didn't pamper her, she suffered plenty sorrow and pain, twice she was widowed, and most of her life she had to solely provide for her family. And yet, she cared relentlessly for them, being for her children both, mother, and father.

[Page 133]

Grandma Frieda was known for her special affection to the Land of Israel and to the Zionist idea as a whole. Although she was very religious and observant (religion and Zionism didn't necessarily go together). She did whatever she was able to help her children who were then planning to immigrate to the Land of Israel. When she received mail from the Holy Land she was so very happy, she would read them with joyful tears a hundred and one times. How proud she was with her Israeli children, and for her share in inhabiting the Land of Israel!

She craved to join her children in Eretz Israel, but to our dismay she didn't merit that. Yet she did virtue to play an active role, and see part of her family settle in Israel. Besides, thanks to her, the rest of the family immigrated after her death, thus, escaping the Nazi hell.

No doubt, Grandpa Israel-Isaac and Grandma Frieda z"l can fit the words of our great sages: "Tears shed over a worthy person, the Almighty counts them and stores them in his treasury."Those tears we cast upon remembering them, will not be in vain. Their memory will serve as an ideal model of love and compassion for humanity.

———

To the Memory of my Father, Simkha Mushkat

by YH. Mushkat

Translated by Zulema Seligsohn

Dedicated to my parents, sister and brothers, who perished in the Warsaw Ghetto.

At the edge of the Senators' Garden, on the western side, there, was a road that led downhill to the Bug River. Near there, there was a house where two families lived: ours and our neighbor's, Velvl Fisher, who had grown sons and two beautiful daughters.

The boys from the Beth–Hamidrash would often come there in the summer, enjoy a swim and, perhaps, catch sight of Fisher's daughters. My younger brother once got into a small boat, pushed off from the shore with the oars and went off into the middle of the river. Fortunately, a few of the boys had just come over to swim in the river, and seeing the boat, swam out with the current and saved my brother. Another time, my father, Simkha Mushkat, rescued a little boat. But he was not a swimmer, and barely made it out alive himself.

This happened about 60 years ago, before Passover. The warm spring breezes had already arrived. On a certain evening, our house needed water; and as usual, when this happened, my father took the bucket and went to the still frozen river to knock out a hole in the ice and thus bring the water home.

After a good while, as my father had not returned, my mother went looking for him. Her voice cut through the quiet of the night: "Simkha! Simkha!" But there was no answer. She gave the alarm to Velvl Fisher and his sons, who also came down to the river to call for my father. To our great misfortune, we saw that the ice was moving. Desperately, Mother began to call even louder "Simkha, Simkha," and broke down sobbing. With each shout, its echo reverberated all the way to the forest, on the other side of the river. But this time, because of the roar of the breaking ice, there was no response from the echo. Everyone was sure that my father was no longer among the living.

Disheartened, my mother lit candles and placed them in the windows, so that the lit up house could be seen from the distance. We, the children, walked around all night on the shore crying. As dawn came, we saw that Father had suddenly appeared. Full of joy and fear we pelted him with our questions: "Where were you? What happened to you"?

And then Father told us:

When he bent over to fill the bucket, the ice began to break up and move away, dragging with it a little boat that was standing there. Father, realizing that it was too late for him to jump to the shore, got into the little boat as it was carried away in the current. There was the risk that the boat would be destroyed by the ice that pressed and squeezed it on all sides. Father sought a chance to catch on to a breakwater, and he finally was able to, but he was by then quite far away, past the Lord's palace. With his greatest last effort he pulled himself up unto the rocky shore and also pulled the little boat out. This was a tremendous physical feat, because the ice was pulling at the boat. After getting it to higher ground and securing it from the ice, Father sat down to rest for a while.

All this happened on a very dark night.

———

[Page 134]

Defenders of Our Land
Zvika Musberg
by Penina Musberg
Translated by Chava Eisenstein

These were the days... Not long ago, and yet eons ago. He was a boy of just 25, "A man without a biography..."

His path in life seemed smooth and blissful, with nary an obstacle. Throughout his childhood and adolescence, he lived at home and eventually found a job as a clerk. Simultaneously, he devoted his time to the study of Torah and science, and only when he reached the age of twenty did he determine to make it on his own.

He married, and with generous financial support of his father-in-law gained social and financial stability. From then and on, his life indeed resumed its smooth course. He supported his family in a variety of capacities, taking whichever road seemed best at the time, always trusting Fortune as his guiding hand. His exploits and successes came and went.

When he was 25 years old, following the Massada incident, he joined an aerial reconnaissance unit searching for the murderers. As a talented scout, he was familiar with all the paths of the Negev and wide open spaces which he so loved. It was also here where he met his tragic end when his plane crashed into a stone cliff.

Throughout constant activity and intensive daily action, he inscribed his autobiography, which is worthy of being published in his memory.

*

Zvika was born on May 25, 1934 in Wyszkow, Poland. He was an attractive child of average height, and constantly growing. Well-built and slightly round, he was laughing and good-natured, always bringing smiles to the faces of others. He loved music and song, listened and told stories wherever he was, both at home and on the road.

From early childhood, he displayed a flair for drama, and he acted and entertained those around him at every opportunity. His early life heralded his later years. By the time he was five, he began manifesting independent, logical thinking. When playing with friends, he was ever the leader, marching ahead of the rest. Tragically, his blissful childhood was cut short by the outbreak of World War II.

The world was in upheaval, and we escaped along with everyone else. Our first hiding place was in the Polish cemetery in Radzymin where we lay motionless among the graves. Zvika cried out, "Mamma, Tatte! Don't pick up your heads, or the Germans will kill you!"

When the tempest settled somewhat we remained in Radzymin for another three weeks, but the situation there was unbearable. Determined to escape, we joined another family and hired a gentile wagon driver named Kortzkedi to transport us to the border in the middle of the night. On the way, we were stopped by the Germans who stripped us of all our wealth and belongings. Zvika wept hysterically when the Germans reached to search him physically, and pitying him, they let him be.

Throughout our journey, Zvika constantly peppered us with questions such as, "Why are we escaping? When will we return home?" The child couldn't fathom what was happening around us and throughout our world. He listened intently to the men discussing and arguing politics, and he enjoyed expressing his own opinion about these matters. We suffered the throes of war, yet still could not fully fathom the meaning of the word: War. To hunger for bread... Every time we bit into a slice of bread, our joy knew no bounds.

The following image rises before my eyes: I sat with Zvika, playing with our bread and occasionally taking a bite, because it was such a shame to have to eat and finish it. It's impossible to recall or count the nights when we went to sleep hungry and thirsty, or to forget that awful sensation of hunger. Mamma would stare at us with tear-filled eyes and comfort us. The war will end tomorrow, and everything will be good again. We won't be hungry again...

1945. The World War ended, and Zvika was 11 years old. We came to Poland to the city of Szczecin and joined the "Ichud" group. For two weeks, we were without our parents, but we were heartened by the kibbutz's promise to us that we would soon be reunited in Berlin.

Reaching Berlin, we were certain that our parents were awaiting us. To our chagrin, they were nowhere to be found, and we were deeply disappointed. For six months, we lived without them. Living conditions in Berlin were quite good, as the kibbutz provided for all our needs; yet we sorely lacked parental love. After the terrible suffering that we'd endured during the war, we kept close watch on each other since, we really liked each other. The Kibbutz moved from Berlin to the town of Muhldorf in Bavaria, Germany. We learned, danced and sang, Zvika participating in every show, being a natural performer, he always featured the head figure. One evening the counselor came to tell me that Zvika is ill. I ran over to him, he laid in bed helplessly, writhing with abdominal pain. I ran to bring him a hot water battle, luckily, I didn't find hot water, it was an inflamed appendix. At night, he was brought to the hospital and was operated, without my knowing. That night, I didn't stop crying and shedding tears until the counselor took me to the hospital to see him. I found him in bed, white like the sheet and I burst into tears, but he calmed me saying not to fuss "over a small infection, you will see, tomorrow I will be back on my feet."

Zvika with a jeep, descending from an airplane...

Zvika Musberg in the Israeli Military

Over Zvika's grave

[Page 135]

In a short while, he was back to himself. We would obtain permission and leave the camp to go out window shopping. We would buy small gifts from our meager allowance we received from the counselor, hoping to surprise our parents shortly with our purchases.

I still remember our bitterness, watching from far a couple coming to take home their children, they were all so happy and excited, kissing their children all the time. How we envied them, but Zvika would always console me: you'll see, they too will come.

Indeed, in 1946 we found ourselves in our parents hugging arms. We traveled along with them to Munich, there we lived in a big apartment house for two weeks together with thousands of people.

Towards the end of 1946 the American patrons opened a new camp in Bavaria, named "Trauenstein,"we stayed there till the beginning of 1949. At the Hebrew school there, we learned to write and read. Overall, we had a good time there, for us it was sort of a deliverance after all the suffering and the trouble we encountered during the entire war.

Here we learned of Jewish customs, the Jewish holidays and of our wonderful Land, Israel. We heard about the Kibbutz and the settlements and of our right to fight for our land. People began immigrating to Israel, and Zvika too has had enough of it. At a violent encounter with the shkotzim (gentiles), one of the gangsters titled him the popular farfluchte Jude – cursed Jew.

That's when Zvika came to me with an idea: tomorrow we will go on strike, we'll stay in bed and cry we want to go to Israel (our parents were not yet keen on immigration). That is what we did, we sat and cried for hours, until our parents gave in and promised to begin to move about it.

In May 1949 we arrived in Israel on the "Independence"ship. Zvika adapted right away, he knew Hebrew from school in Germany, so he was considered a natural "Sabra."He began studying in the evenings, high-school studies, while serving as municipal clerk at the engineering department of Netanya, a job he received from "The Youth Labor,"and excelled at it. Truth is, he didn't really enjoy this type of work, he always claimed that office work is not his destination, "I cannot sit and warm the chair"he would say, anticipating the moment he will join the Israel Defense Forces (IDF).

That happy day soon arrived. Zvika, with his good friend Naphtali, who was also joining the army, arranged a farewell party, not neglecting to print invitations. They enlisted in the army, and after some training Zvika came home for a short leave, his face was shining with happiness, and excitedly he unfolded his training encounters, expressing his opinion, that the army provides essential schooling for everyone, and sets one off for life.

Zvika was transferred to the "Givati"section, in the infantry he found the right place for his many ambitions. He took part in some retaliation acts, and was wounded a few times, without our knowing. He would always say to mamma: "Ima, don't worry for me, d'you know what the army means? I don't know when I will come again."His happiness knew no bounds, coming home for a break as lance corporal.

Whenever he came home, he would tell us that he passed well this course or another. He would show us proudly his diplomas as a master trainee. I recall how I would iron his uniform; he stood near me and instructed me exactly how each pleat should be ironed. Saying that he has to serve as a model for his co-soldiers. Indeed, he always appeared tidy and immaculate, with an optimistic air.

Soon his military service was over, and he was about to be released as staff sergeant. He came home, but expressed his desire to stay in the IDF to join the active forces. Mother didn't want to hear about it and so he discharged from the army.

Again, he and his friend Naphtali arranged a party, this time upon their release.

Zvika returned to his old job at the Netanya municipality. If he would be bored prior to his army service, now he was bored sevenfold. He would reprimand mamma, stating that in civilian life he won't get anywhere, but in the army he can make his career. Occasionally he would attend various courses on account of the reserve duty he owed the army, which he was glad to face and accomplish faithfully.

At the end of 1957 mamma gave into him, and Zvika enlisted in regular service, straightaway he passed the officers course successfully, he was the happiest man as an officer. He took part in the Sinai Mission although he was in middle of the officers course. In one of those evenings, our door opened, in walked an unexpected guest. At the first moment, we didn't recognize him.

[Page 136]

He was dressed like an officer. Only after he said a heavy "Shalom"exposing two rows of smiling teeth we recognized Zvika! We asked him, aren't you at the course? and he answered: "with so much work waiting, you expect me to sit around and study? Do you want to wait for the Arabs to come in and slaughter you"? He slept for two hours in which we heard him imagining he is at battle, shouting orders, "Fire, fire, guys!".

Later, Zvika asked to be shifted to the open space of the Arava, since he was familiar and knew all the ways of the Negev (south), he felt he was needed. His wish was met, and now he was a solo ruler, undisturbed by orders and regulations, he and his people following him, roamed for days and weeks the arid desert, guaranteeing security for the travelers in those difficult routes. I recall him being nicknamed "Popski,"for after long days not being able to track him in that terrible desert, his commanding officer reprimanded him "Do you think this is your private army?", since then, he was named and known as "Popski."

Yes Pop, you featured a special image amongst your friends, of a lively clever fellow, fully aware of all the goings-on.

At that time Zvika suffered pain in his foot, he needed surgery. He had a slipped disc in his leg, although the leg was injured a couple of times, it healed smoothly and he even went to rehabilitation for two weeks, where he was treated and recovered, his physical fitness was limited for one year, but Zvika laughed off that order, insisting to continue as regular. One day he came home announcing: "Mamma, I'm getting married!"his girlfriend Mira whom he got to know in Eilat, we had known for a year. His decision was so sudden that mamma spontaneously called out "Mazal Tov."

Zvika set his mind on Beer-Sheva, where he received a nice apartment. He arranged, repaired and decorated with his own hands, until it looked like a beautiful museum. He hung beautiful paintings he painted himself on the walls amongst other original items. For 5 months joyousness reigned at the young-couple's home. But one day that terrible tragedy occurred, also now, while writing these words, I can't bear the terrible thought, that Zvika is no longer here...

*

Yair Biberman (Jerry), Zvika's commander-in-chief, writes about him:

Courageous, with a stormy character of always heading forward... he was put through the wringer serving at a short assessment, at one of the unobtrusive places in the region, he did well, and later he was sent to Nitzana – the challenging spot in the region. In no time he put order to the place and to the whole zone, serving at a short assessment, at one of the unobtrusive places in the region. He set order to that place, serving as an excellent model for his soldiers with his assiduous devotion, his cleverness and daring... his intensive energetic activity kept the Bedouins away from the boundary, to the second side of the Sinai border...

At headquarters too, the man was incapable of building and ordaining patrol missions on others, without taking an active part in them. That's how he went out on part of the tasks as an observer or chief... but he met death on a patrol which he attended, being pulled by his inner sense of responsibility...

*

Mr. Shalom Baukman of Netanya wrote about Zvika in the "Herut"journal, for his first annual memoir:

...your life-song was interrupted in the midst, while life was fully ahead of you, only a few short months passed since you married your heart's choice, and you built a Jewish home. The home, to which you were so connected, has become bereaved together with all of us, from our beloved, good-natured Zvika, the lively and model-commander. Your associates – admirers and subordinates attributed to you honor and respect, for the strength and audacity you always displayed.

Your sudden death spread heavy mourning on all your acquaintances. How can I comfort your parents? There is no exchange and no words either...

May you find peace in the soil of your land, which your young blood has saturated.

Your blessed memory will remain with us.

Prime Minister and Defense Ministers announcement, upon the death of Zvi Musberg:

State of Israel

Sorrowful, we wish to bring up the memory of 236198 lieutenant Zvi Musberg z"l who fell on duty, on the 19'th of Nissan 5719 (27.4.1959). The State of Israel, the Israel Defensive Forces and the Jewish Nation will forever carry with pride and love, the memory of Zvi who performed faithfully his mission at protecting the State.

D. Ben-Gurion
Prime Minister

Zeev Holland
Translated by Chava Eisenstein

Zeev Holland was born in Wyszkow in 1928 to Moshe and Rivka Holland. Since childhood, he aimed for immigration and help build up to the Land of Israel. He attended traditional kheder and then elementary school. He was smart and intelligent, so he excelled academically, and everyone liked him.

The war broke out when he was eleven years, and was forced to drop school, he and his parents fled to Russia, Siberia. There too, his care and awareness for others in need was outstanding. In 1941, upon returning from Siberia, he joined a youth group which was preparing to immigrate to the Land. Indeed, in 1942 the opportunity came, his parents pleaded with him to wait, and not go by himself until they too will be ready, but to no avail, he reprimanded them that the mothers "Don't wish to part with their children, and who will build the land? By the time you will decide to go, the Land will be already in our hands, but the youth must pave the way for the older generation, for we have wandered the world more than enough..."that is how we parted from him, not knowing that it's forever.

Upon immigration, he joined a Kibbutz where he volunteered for the Palm"akh, he was only 18 when he married and his daughter was born.

At a military operation in 1948, on the third day of Adar 5708, Zeev fell on duty, by the young age of twenty.

We shall remember him amongst his fellow State Defenders.

Abraham Tenenbaum
by Hana and Borukh-David Tenenbaum (parents)
Translated by Chava Eisenstein

Our son Abraham-Haim was born in Wyszkow on the first day of Elul 5658 (1925). At the outbreak of the war, our whole family fled to Russia. After much trouble and wandering we arrived in Siberia. Life there was unbearably difficult. If not for our Abraham-Khaim, he literally saved our lives, doing hard labor, thus devotedly providing for our needs. In 1942, he volunteered for the Polish army that set up in Russia, and very soon, he reached the rank of Sergeant. For his self-sacrifices in combat, he was awarded medals of Honor. After the war, he came with us to Germany, with Argentina as our destiny, our son Abraham, refused to go along with us, and he immigrated in 1948 to the Land of Israel.

When he arrived, he was taken to Atlit, where he was recruited to the IDF. After a short training, he took part in conquering Beer-Sheva and rose to become staff sergeant. He participated in the "Horev"operation. In the action the Abu-Agila post was conquered by the Palm"akh regiment no. 7, division 12. At the onset of the battle, on 28.12.1948, Abraham was killed.

[Page 137]

In his last moments of life, he mumbled to his friends: "I am dying in battle and won't merit to enjoy the freedom of this land. I will remember my parents." He was buried in Revivim, but in 14.8.1950 he was relocated to eternal peace at the Nakhlat Yitzhak cemetery.

Isaac Zamir
Translated by Chava Eisenstein

(Excerpt from his book "Divrei Yemei Isaac"– Isaac's encounters. A year from the heroic death of Isaac Zamir z"l. Kibutz Evron – 5710 [1950] – Tel-Aviv)

Isaac Zamir

Isaac, son of Rahel and Abraham Zamir from Wyszkow, was born in Warsaw in 5684 (1928). He came to the Land of Israel in 5693 (1933). Amongst others, he founded the Evron Kibbutz near Naharia. He served at the Palm"akh in the year 5708 – 5709 (1948-1949) as patrol officer in the Negev segment.

On the 26'th of Kislev 5709 (28.12.1948) while on aerial patrol over the Negev frontier, he was attacked by the enemy and his aircraft crashed...

The combat staff of section 12 announced upon the death of Isaac:

"Horev"action combat segment, Section 12

Daily Combat Summary no. 5

Wed. 26 Kislev 5,709
Third day of Hanukah, 29.12.1948

Our brigade will memorialize its members who fell in battle to free
the Negev (south). They were not anonymous; together with us, they grew up,
together we fought shoulder to shoulder. They gave to the best of their ability
for the benefit of the brigade and to enhance its fighting skills, while being
fully aware of the huge goal and the heaviness of the task.

With great sorrow, we are parting from the best of our scouts, Isaac Zamir
who found his death while being fully dedicated to duty. Honor for those who
fell upon fighting for the Negev.

Prime Minister D. Ben-Gurion, too, announced a special statement upon
Isaac's death:

The State of Israel

With deep sorrow, we announce that

Isaac Zamir z"l

Fell on duty on the 26'th of Kislev 5709 (28.12.1948) at an air combat in
the Negev. The Government of Israel and the Hebrew nation will forever carry
the memory of Isaac who found his death upon defending the state, and at an
assault for her liberty and independence.

D. Ben-Gurion
Prime Minister

These Wyszkow former residents fell in duty at defending the State of
Israel.

Their Memories Must be Forever
by YH. Mushkat
Translated by Zulema Seligsohn

Whenever we speak of Wyszkow, we always recall the magnificent natural beauty surrounding the town: the large forest, the quick–flowing river, the iron bridge, the meadows on its shores, etc. Indeed its natural beauties is one of the glorious recollections we took with us from our town, but it hurts when we think we should spend more time remembering the people among whom we lived and spent our youth—the movements that were created and added so much to the economic, political, and generally cultural development of our generation.

There exists a world of material waiting for a hand to be put to it to create something out of it –to spite our enemies who wanted to erase them, not only from this earth but even from our consciousness.

A whole literature could definitely be created from the Fishkes, Polukhlekh, Djuvags, Metch and his orchestra, the grass–goose, Ershinke the water–carrier (he recited psalms), Shie Kalatz, Urke with the clans and others. This is, of course, a very small percentage, from the hard worker to the most needy sort in our little town. And then the so–called middle class, the well–to–do Jews, the Deges, Jakubovitches, Shkarlats, and Eli–Meirs.

And why should we not mention our leaders, cultural promoters like Henekh Kalusky – Mizrakhi; Israel Asman, Itche Shkarlat – General Zionists; Yurman – Poale Zion; Israel Goldwasser – People's Party; Shimen Malavantchik, Sholem Shidletsky, Mordekhai Fridman of the "Bund"; Dzbanek and Motl Rinek from the Workers' Cooperative?

All of this must by any means possible be eternalized! I would like to bring out some of these people's types and their characters.

Yekhiel–Meir Dzbanek

Whoever in Wyszkow knew Srulke the gaiter–maker's son, and even those who did not, could not believe their eyes when they saw him on a clear morning walking around the market, dressed in a Russian military great–coat, sporting highly polished varnished boots, and on his head with its black forelock, a military hat.

Yekhiel–Meir Dzbanek could not be recognized. He had grown into a tall man with long hard hands, and a sun–burnt face with large brown eyes under a broad three–cornered hat. This was not the same Dzbanek who had joined the tzar's army at the outbreak of the First World War, with an open–cut coat, under which one could see the ritual four–cornered garment. But one thing was true: instead of a Talmud under his arm, he was surely carrying hidden on his person The Communist Manifesto. This was now a man with a sure step and a voice that could give orders rather than obey them.

[Page 138]

From his first few meetings with the Wyszkow young people and the workers, Dzbanek immediately won their trust. These were the young people, whose names I will here incorporate as a memorial: Motl Rinek, the painter; Benyumin, Isroel–Mendl Becker's son; Mordkhe Loketch; Urke the driver; Leyzer, the ropemaker's son; and a few other Jewish workers, who comprised the first underground circle Dzbanek founded in Wyszkow.

In the town something was moving. On a clear beautiful morning, they distributed proclamations that called the Jewish workers to a meeting where a workers' cooperative was to be organized, and where Dzbanek would deliver a report about a committee that would help with the work. The meeting was a great success. After long discussions a managing group was chosen, comprising representatives from the "Bund," "Tzukunft," Poale–Tzion, and from the Jewish section of the Communist Party.

The tasks the cooperative undertook were as follows: to come to the aid of the suffering unemployed population by purchasing food products that they needed at discounted prices, such as bread, herring, potatoes, sugar, and others that were being sold at extremely high ones. The problem was where to get the first thousand zlotys for the first purchase. Dzbanek had a certain plan: to put together a list of wealthy property owners in town, who would contribute a specific amount every week until the cooperative could stand on its own feet; that is, until they had enough products to sell and didn't need their help any longer. Well, how were they going to be against this? And so, on the Sabbath, at the reading of the Law, they would play them such a merry tune that they would never forget it.

And so there came a Sabbath that all of Wyszkow could not forget for a very, very long time A few groups from the cooperative came to the great synagogue. Urke and Motl planted themselves by the doors. Some other young people went up to the reading–desk (bimah). The rest spread themselves out in the aisles, and didn't allow the prayers to continue, until the Rabbi promised that that very evening, after the Sabbath, a few of the more prominent property–owners would meet with the spokesmen of the cooperative to discuss the matter.

Zisha pot merchant

After the first meeting with the property–owners, no practical results were achieved. But the victory of the cooperative seemed assured. The property–owners bound themselves to call a conference of all the wealthy Jews in the town. At the conference, which took place in the Jakubovich's house, it almost became a physical confrontation; but a few of the property–owners, whose hearts were "broken (poor dears)," just had to contribute a few hundred zlotys, for which a whole wagon of potatoes was immediately bought.

This was in Winter. Around February 1918, on a frosty day, the first potato wagon arrived. But it was a pity to look at, as the potatoes were … pieces of ice. Because of the horrendous hunger that the population was then suffering, it is no wonder that the frozen potatoes were quickly grabbed and the wagon was soon empty.

The potato wagon showed the practicality and the possibilities of such an undertaking and gave a push to the work around the cooperative, so that it became the one great help for the indigent, starving Jewish population. And let us make it clear: the people of Wyszkow give honorable mention to the name of Yekhiel–Meir Dzbanek, who thanks to his indefatigable work, the dedication of his honest worker/fighters to the poor and to the alleviation of their needs; thanks to his wise leadership in founding and further direction of this undertaking, made possible the great success of the cooperative.

Dzbanek did not limit himself to the work involving the cooperative. Through his zeal and dedication, he became one of the most renowned leaders of the General Polish Communist Party, where no kind of work was too difficult for him or too menial. He was seen in Warsaw befriending the pavers that worked in the streets. He would sit on a rock or on the ground to talk to a worker, then move to another. He asked about their lives, their pay, their homes. He earned their trust and tried to organize them.

[Page 139]

The last news about Dzbanek were horrifying for his friends and companions. It was a terrible blow for us to find out that a murderous hand put an end to this hero, and especially in the Soviet Union.

Honor to his Memory!

[Page 139]

Enda, the Lady-Butcher (Katzfke)
Translated by Milly Hock

Wearing a plain cotton dress, wrapped in a large linen-like apron, runs Enda the lady-butcher in her men's slippers, self-absorbed and talking to herself.

What do they mean? she thinks, – and if they owe me a few gulden, would I let them go to their Shabbos table without a little soup, without a piece of meat? No, dear people, Oy Veis Meir!! She moans.

It is late and Enda runs with a little package of meat wrapped in white paper. She arrives at a poor family on one street, and immediately is reminded of another housewife who didn't come today to buy meat, being too ashamed to borrow.

"What is there to be ashamed of?" she would argue with the women, as she laid the package on the table. "When you will have the money, you will certainly pay me."

"Meanwhile, why should the children suffer? I am in a hurry," she would say as she stood in the doorway. "Don't be offended. Have a good Shabbos!"

She runs further, her wig blowing in the wind, with a pale, tired face.

Berish Taharness, her neighbor, teases her. "Why do you run, Enda? You are losing your apron."

While running further, Enda would respond to him. "Stop your foolish talk, Berish. Better go in and help your Yideneh get ready for Shabbos."

And Berish would talk into his red beard. " Let there be already such a year, what a dear person she is!"

And the people of the shtetl, from one border to the other, know well this special woman who lives among them.

It was about time for the stores to close, when Enda turns around, tired and smiling. In the distance, one could already hear from afar the cry of Yitschak-Jacobs. "Jews, close the stores!"

She sits down for a while to catch her breath. Chana, her daughter, stands over her and murmers impatiently.

"Mama, let's close already."

But Enda is absorbed with again counting the merchandise, and her customers, to determine whether she had forgotten someone.

"Wait, don't nudge me!" she answers Chana and continues to count on her fingers.

"Chinkeh-Rachel. Yidl Polker. Ezri-elkin. Paluchi. Chatskel, the teacher. David Volvishes-"

And thus counting, her face lightens and becomes more restful.

"It seems to me, nobody is forgotten, thank God. Now, Chana, we can close the butcher shop and make Shabbos."

Enda and Chana go home, wash themselves, dress in their Shabbos garments, and set forth to the synagogue. On the way people greet Enda with a cordial "Good Shabbos," as was proper to a distinguished person in the shtetl. On the steps to the women's synagogue she meets Chaveh. They greet each other. Chaveh's "Good Shabbos" strikes a chord in Enda's heart. She stops Chaveh.

"Tell me, dear Chaveh, why have you not bought any meat from me for Shabbos?"

Chaveh blushes a little.

"In truth, dear Enda, a piece of chicken has remained from yesterday, and we managed somehow."

In the synagogue, Enda stands in her usual place, opens her prayer book to Kabalas Shabbos, and when the cantor begins the "L'chu n'ra-nan"ah," a question arises in Enda's mind. How did Chaveleh get a hold of a chicken? She wants to go to Chaveh but her mind speaks again. Here, we can't talk. And what good would it do? The dear Chaveh couldn't possibly have cooked for Shabbos.

"Oy, veis meir" exclaims Enda. "What will they eat today? I am thinking of her sick husband and their dear children?" she murmers.

"What's the matter with you?" asks the wife of the Shamus quietly.

"I am very warm and my head is spinning. I must go out and catch a breath of fresh air. I'll soon be back," she answers, softly.

Enda slips out of the synagogue, goes home, takes out the hot pot with the Shabbos soup, wrapped with a cloth, and runs breathlessly to Chaveh's house. Upon her arrival she doesn't even knock, but goes into the kitchen and places the hot, covered pot on Chaveh's cold stove.

"Children," says Enda, "I have brought your mother's soup which she had cooked in my oven. Tell her it is a bit tight in my oven, so I brought it here,"

And without waiting for a reply, she goes back to the synagogue.

When Enda arrives the praying is already over and the people of the congregation are heading for home. She doesn't find Chaveh.

* * *

The children in America had written Enda more than once that she should go to them. They had even sent her a ticket for the ship, and the necessary papers. The children often begged their mother to leave the butcher shop, make them happy, and go to America. Enda would read the letters from her children, look at the ship's ticket and cry. How could she leave the shtetl, her dearly beloved people? So many years to be together, in joy and in sorrow! How can a person just travel away, never to return?

[Page 140]

In the evening Enda goes to Mendel, the scholar, to counsel with him. He knows Enda quite well. She lives not far from him and she goes to him often with her bitter heart. He knows well how difficult it is for Enda to tear herself away from here, and her longing for her children. Mendel speaks to her as though he is her brother.

"How long, Enda can you hold out here alone, in your butcher shop? The competition in Poland is affecting the Jewish trade, and you carry more and more packages of meat on loan. The poverty here cries out to heaven. True, you have the heart of a saint, but you have children, may they be well. Be a mother to your children! It is a great mitzvah. Go Enda. Go to America, in good health, and help them prosper."

The time comes for Enda's departure. The shtetl is saddened as in the Nine Days of Tisha B'Av. People come to the butcher shop and to Enda's house, for the farewell. In these days many tears are shed by the women, neighbors and friends, There were those who owe Enda for meat and had nothing with which to pay. Enda cries along with them, comforts them, blesses and thanks them.

Nighttime, in her bed, Enda is not able to sleep. Her sole thought is, how can I convince the Ribono shel Olom to feed his people Israel? She had already read all the books of prayers for women but she is not satisfied. She must talk it out with God, in her own words.

She goes away to the large Bays Ha-midrash, falls to her knees with eyes closed, clasps the Ark, and these are Enda's words, her own prayer!

"Thank you, dear Gottenu, loving heart, Father, for the kindness you do to me and my children. Forgive a sinning woman, who comes to you, not for herself, but for all of Israel. Master of the Universe, you know the truth, that I did not want to depart from our shtetl. These are your plans, that you have sown like seeds, and spread my little calves, my little children over the seas.

Now I order and command You. You shall, trustful Father, nourish Your children of the shtetl. They should have, at least, a little piece of meat for Shabbos!"

Enda clasps her face with her hands, which had held the Holy Ark, and cries and moans bitterly.

Thus does Enda depart painfully from her shtetl. We shall remember her name with great love, esteem, respect and faithful memory.

Noyke (Noakh'ke)
by Yitzkhak Markuschamer
Translated by Pamela Russ

How the simpleton Noyke merited having two jobs – to suddenly become an assistant [in kheder, religious school] and also a water carrier – is really a miracle. In actuality, anyone can become a water carrier, but an assistant who doesn't know even a line of Hebrew – was unusual in Wyszkow.

But the story was straightforward for those who knew Yakov–Yisroel the teacher and his daughter who was mute, deaf, and on in years...

On Shabbath, Noyke would come to the Otwocker shtiebel [small, informal synagogue] to have at least one meal a week. And Yakov–Yisroel the teacher, also a very poor man, quickly snatched up Noyke, thinking: Maybe God Himself had sent Noyke to be a match for his daughter? And, in fact, it did not take long for Noyke to marry the deaf–mute daughter. So what did he do for an income? The father, the teacher, gave Noyke two jobs: to be his assistant in the kheder, and also to carry water for the people in their homes.

Being a water carrier was what it was. Once, he forgot about someone, and so brought someone else water – twice. But everyone survived. Because of this [behavior], being this type of assistant [in kheder] was a complete failure. There were a few older boys in Yakov–Yisroel's kheder, thirteen– and fourteen–year–olds, who knew the simple Noyke well. When the Rebbe [teacher] presented Noakh as his helper, the older boys exploded with laughter. Following them, the entire kheder went into gales of laughter, so much so that even Noakh'ke laughed along with them. That was the beginning, and no one had to wait too long for the end of the assistant's career.

The boys discussed among themselves that they would have to study the Torah portion of "Balak" [Book of Numbers, story of King of Moab, prophet Bilaam, talking donkey, and God's intervention]. Abba, Faivel Moishe's, and Kudak, Urke Parkh's young son, worked out a plan. And this is what happened. Once, when the Rebbe went to the shtiebel for early evening prayers, and Noyke sat in a corner and swayed back and forth over the empty buckets, the group of boys suddenly befell him. They lay him out across the bench, twisted him as if with a rope, and gave him a real one–two, and warned him that if he dared say anything to the Rebbe, then next time they would take their revenge in an even stronger manner.

When Yakov –Yisroel returned and found Noyke with a scratched up face and torn frock, he immediately fell into a teacher's murderous [mood], pulled out his whip from somewhere, and in a hoarse voice, began to ask who had done such a horrible thing. He shook up Noyke's shoulders, and shouted: "Tell me, tell me. Who beat you?" Noyke became very frightened in front of his father–in–law, and began mumbling: "Tell you? Tell you? They told me not to say anything! They'll give me more for saying anything." Yakov–Yisroel challenged the older troublemakers. He understood that this was their doing. But his whip found my shoulder, upon which he released his entire wrath... The reason for that was, as the other businessmen said – was that my father could not pay any school fees.

As Noyke saw how the whip was beating me he ran over to me trembling, then put his arms around me to protect me from the blows, and shouted:

[Page 141]

"Father–in–law! Do not beat him, father–in–law! Do not beat him, father–in–law!" And then he turned his head and sobbed with me. I cried because of the pointless beatings, and as the entire kheder watched, they all cried as well.

It was already dark in the kheder, other than the thick yahrzeit candle that burned on the shelf, lighting up a small space on the long table. The children sat quietly over their seforim [religious books]. A frightful silence reigned in the kheder, all you heard were the sharp steps of the Rebbe, who was going around upset, with his hands behind his back, holding a whip that dragged along the floor.

From that time onwards, no one ever lifted a hand to Noyke, but he was no longer the assistant.

Noyke prayed close to his father–in–law in the Otwocker shtiebel. One can say: prayed. But how can you call that praying if the person did not even know one single letter [of the Hebrew]? But he would sway back and forth with great intensity, repeat after his father–in–law, or connect to a few words which the leader of the prayers sang out, and with great devotion he would say them again and again, until the words would be lost in a strange muttering. Sometimes he would make the most unusual sounds, which only he and God could understand.

Yitzkhok–Ber the khossid [pious man], a scholarly Jew, for whom everyone had great admiration because of his humility and warm–heartedness, would go among the people during Shabbath and Jewish holidays, to have some conversation, make a l'khaim [blessings (toast) on some schnapps, brandy, etc.], and then he would ask Yakov–Yisroel about his kheder, and then go over to Noyke and say with great respect: "Good Shabbath to you (or Good Yom

Tov) Reb Noakh!" At first, shyly, Noyke would shake Yitzkhok–Ber's hand, and quickly snatch his hand back, not lifting his eyes from the floor. But later, when he felt that Yitzkhok–Ber really wanted to get closer to him, Noyke's face would light up with a smile because Yitzkhok–Ber himself had come to greet him with a grand hello.

Once, it was the holiday of Simkhas Torah [last day of Sukot, celebrating with the Torah scrolls], at the hakafos [dancing with the scrolls], when Yidel Kashemakher had already called upon all the wealthier businessmen and ordinary Jews [for the privilege of carrying a Torah scroll during the dancing], and Noyke was standing there distracted. It seems that the hakafos were ending, and he had not been called upon [for the dancing]. At each hakafah, he followed along, singing and dancing with great emotion. But it was almost time to replace the Torah scrolls into the Holy Ark. I was just standing near him, and saw how his face was changing to many colors: Now it is red, and soon it is pale, and his eyes were filled with tears. Suddenly we heard a smack on the table and Yitzkhok Ber's clear voice sang out: "Come forward, Noakh son of Tzvi the Levite, to the hakafah!" Everyone in the shtiebel was stunned. Noyke tore himself from his place and ran forward, embraced a Torah scroll with both arms, pressed it close to his heart, and began to dance around the table, singing in a wild voice: "Please save us! Save us, please!" And huge tears ran down his cheeks. Soon Yitzkhok–Ber embraced Noyke and both danced a fiery dance. The whole crowd joined in and everyone was in a circle of dance, singing and dancing so joyously that the entire shtiebel was broiling with the fiery ecstasy of Simkhas Torah.

*

It is told that when the Nazis, may their names be erased, attacked the town, shooting and throwing fire bombs, and when Wyszkow began burning, and when murdering airplanes began flying low and shooting the people, Noyke ran through the streets and shouted: "Jews, save yourselves! Jews! Jews! Save yourselves!"

And when the city was already in flames, and people began running to Ostrowa Street, Noyke ran with them. But he suddenly stopped, as if he had just remembered something, and ran right back to the town. He was running against the flow of people. Everyone screamed at him from all sides: "Noyke, go back! Save yourself, Noyke!" But he listened to no one. He ran back to the burning town. He reached the Otwocker shtiebel, rushed in against the flaming walls and burning, ripped up religious books, grabbed two burning Torah scrolls out of the Holy Ark, and ran with them, although he himself was already engulfed in flames. Pieces of the Torah's coat and of his own clothing, as burning doves, flew over him. That's how he ran until Ostrowa Street. And when he fell, one of the Torah scrolls opened, and rolling, completely covered him with its parchment.

That's how Noyke gave up his life. As a hero – in sanctification of the Holy Name.

Hershele the Water Carrier

by Yisroel Osman

Translated by Hershl Hartman (Los Angeles, CA)

Reviewed by Frida Grapa Markuschamer de Cielak (Mexico City)

Special thanks to Pamela Russ (Montreal, Canada)

Translation donated by the Historian Enrique Krauze (Mexico City)

Who is it who disturbs sleep during quiet Friday nights with his arousing singing? What sort of voice is it that descends from afar, opens doors and shutters, bores into deafened ears, pries open sleep–sealed eyes, infiltrates tired hearts and fills them with strength and freshness? What is the source of the passion of the Jews, exhausted by a week's hard labor and care, who awake before dawn on Shabbath and rush off, refreshed and joyful, in frosty winter dawns and in the sleep–inducing breezes of the last moments of short summer nights – to dash ecstatically to the old Beis Medrash to recite Psalms? It was neither the rooster nor the alarm clock that awoke them, and they were not torn from sleep either morosely or resentfully, but in holy anticipation, lively, fresh and full of joy, as though for a mitzvah tanz,[a] ready to sing and to praise God and his beloved, holy Sabbath. It is the voice of Hershele the water carrier (Hershele, der–wasertreger) that tears the deathly silence of the night, arousing and calling:

[Page 142]

"Please wake up! Please awaken yourselves! Please stand up! Yidelech [literally, "little Jews," endearing term], arise to the service of God, rise up to recite P–s–a–l–m–s!"[1]

Hershele awakened the shtetl to Psalms for many years, every Friday night; the task was his by right, all his long life. He was young when he began to awaken the town, the town was young and small when it began to stir to the voice of his waking. Hershele the water carrier and his generation are gone, and there is almost no remnant left of the old town, and to this day the same awakening call is heard every Saturday morning from the midst of the old market place where once the old pulley–well stood, awakening and interrupting sleep – and parents tell their awakened children the story of Hershele the water carrier.

The shtetl was young and small and it had just begun to grow. The first Rav arrived, Reb[2] Aba'le, at a salary of 50 kopecks a week plus two bundles of firewood. He began to develop the community, to convert it into a Jewish town. He provided for everything, but was unable to find a place for the dead. The fields and pastures surrounding the town belonged to an evil priest, who would not sell land for a consecrated Jewish cemetery for any amount of money. So a corpse had to be taken to a nearby little shtetl that Jews were in the course of abandoning.

A major epidemic struck, may we be spared, and people died like flies. Other cities and towns did not allow entry [burial] of those corpses, and that town itself [where the epidemic was] did not allow delays. Some Jews died, and they did not know what to do. So, Reb Aba'le took the most prominent businessmen with him and they went to see the priest to plead that he sell them a piece of land. The priest was not in town, and his representative responded to them by saying he would sell them a piece of land on one condition: If the priest would return and not agree to this, they would not have their money refunded. They would also have to disinter the bodies and return the land. They had no choice – and they agreed.

When the priest returned, he wanted nothing other than to keep his word. He did not help at all. He did not allow anyone to speak to him, and sent out the dogs. Reb Aba'le took charge, and went on his own to the villain, spoke to him kindly and angrily, but it did not help at all. The villain said that if they wouldn't unearth the bodies on their own, then he would order them to disinter the bodies and throw them to the dogs. Reb Aba'le went home and sobbed. A stranger, a young boy, carrying a small sack on his shoulders, approached him. He stopped the Rav, and asked why he was crying. Reb Aba'le poured out his whole heart, and told the story. The young man became incensed and cried out: "I'll show him, that villain! A thunder will penetrate his intestines even on this very day!"

The Rav looked at this crazed young man, embarrassed that he had poured out his heart to this uncouth young soul.

Later, when the Rav and his congregants were in shul, and in their great need they cried and pleaded to God, suddenly heavy clouds gathered and a storm broke. There was thunder and lightning, and then in the middle of the lightning, they heard the news that a thunder had struck and killed the priest.

When the Rav heard this, he cried out in great wonder:

"Aye, oy, oy, oy!"

But he did not say anything to anyone. That night he found the unknown young boy, strolled with him in the outskirts of the city, almost until daylight, and whispered discreetly with him. That next day, there was a wedding between that young boy Hershele and the town's orphan Khinke–Rokhele. The wedding was in the cemetery. The Rav and the congregants were the parents and in–laws. As a dowry, they gave him all the Jewish homes in town; the wedding gift was the "poverty"and "buckets" [i.e., the poverty and empty buckets of the Jewish homes]. The Rav himself took him into the group of Psalm sayers, and gave him the position of "weker."[3]

And the epidemic died down.

From that time on, Hershele's voice was heard every Friday evening. An unsettled voice, that awakens, tears one apart, breaks the heart, and brings you closer to the Father in Heaven.

And still, such a wild illiterate, such an uncouth soul.

The genius, Reb Shloimele Eyger, may his memory be blessed, traveled from Warsaw home to Pozen. He left from his son's engagement celebration. The road was terrible, an axle [of the wagon] broke, and other reasons. He barely made it to Wyszkow, and had to remain there over Shabbath. The wealthy man, Reb Eliezer Karpel, gave him his entire home. There was a buzz in the town. The surrounding towns found out about this, and the local Jews came together for Shabbath. The crowd was large, and the "tish"[4] went on until late hours.

They had just about gone to sleep, when the voice of the Psalms weker was heard. Reb Shloimele Eyger heard the voice, and was very surprised. The voice did not permit him to remain in his bed, so he got up and went to the Beis Medrash and recited the Psalms with the other congregants, with great passion and dedication. The melody of the Psalms weker rang through the Beis Medrash. Everyone praised him in his own manner. He had never heard such a heartfelt recitation of Psalms. He felt that King David himself, with his entire chorale, the Bnei Korach, Asaf, Yedusun, Eitan Ha'Ezrachi, and all the rest, were here with him in the Beis Medrash reciting these songs.

He understood that it was not for nothing that the twists of Heaven had brought him here to this foreign town for Shabbath, and quietly, he undertook to figure out this situation. And he discovered who this Psalm weker was. But from the Rav, there was not a word.

[Page 143]

But he was not finished with this.

Some time went by, and there was wonderful news in town: Rebbe Shloimele asked from his son's father–in–law to be, that the wedding be held in Wyszkow – Warsaw is just too large and too spread out. The father–in–law agreed, and people were sent over to prepare for a wedding that was appropriate for such esteemed people.

Reb Shloimele Eyger arrived in the town, and once again took up with Reb Eliezer Karpel. Learned and distinguished Jews rushed over to him, wanting the honor of becoming his sexton, but he would not allow it: It was not right for a simple Jew to act as the sexton for a Torah scholar or a Torah student. It was an honest illiterate whom he wanted. So the lot fell to Hershele the water carrier.

He instructed that a pallet be installed for Hershele in a corner in his own room. In this way Reb Shloimele Eyger could closely observe his behavior. But he saw nothing. He monitored him by day–nothing; at night he would fall into a deep sleep. One Friday night, after the first sheva brochos,[5] he felt he had to learn the secret. He feigned a bit of tipsiness, and fell back into bed as though in a dead sleep. However, he peered through the slits of his eyelids and saw all that occurred in the room. This time, he did not fall asleep.

In the middle of the night he heard Hershele sighing on his pallet and tossing from side to side. A light flared in the room's darkness–it was Hershele's face, his eyes were twinkling. He sprang up like a lion, gathering strength for God's service. He quickly left the house, having performed the ablutions, and his voice was already heard in the outdoors. A strong spiritual awakening is felt in all worlds.

The next morning Reb Shloimele Eyger confronted him and he had to confess.

And before Reb Shloimele Eyger departed from the town, the leaders of the community asked him to bless the town so that they would not suffer as much from fires, since no year had passed without several house fires. So he said to them:

"The Lord of the Universe has created a spiritual remedy for fire–water. The Bug River flows here; you have a very good water carrier. Buy him a barrel and a horse and cart, and He Who Rules Over Us will do His part. When one is careful with water, fire does no damage."

Sixty years went by, the entire generation passed. Only one of them remained, Hershele the water carrier. He lived all alone in his half–collapsed shack on the outskirts of town. The town was old and its houses bent in old age. No fires burned there and no floods carried the houses away. No one accurately remembered the words of Reb Shloimele Eyger; they knew only that he had blessed the town and that old Reb Hershele had been there.

Old Hershele continued to carry water for the town. A barrel of water always stood ready at his house.

On Friday nights he would awaken the residents for Psalm–reading with his singing. His voice was young and fresh and the melody resounded ecstatically. The entire town would arise and fill the old Beis Medrash.

He refused to renounce his right to the task; they could not get him to give up carrying water in his old age.

Hershele died suddenly on a mournful winter's day. Almost no one in town knew of it. They became aware only when several saintly men in the area unexpectedly arrived for the funeral. They eulogized him and interred him with great honor.

A short time later, the shtetl burned to the ground.

Yisroel Osman

Footnote

a. At the end of a chassidic wedding, there is a mitzvah tanz, i.e., a dance held because of the law of God [mitvzah], where the most respected guest or religious attendees dance solely with the groom and then, accordingly with the bride, but holding onto a long belt [gartel] or other item so as not to have direct physical contact with her, according to Jewish law.

Translator's Footnotes:

1. P–s–a–l–m–s: Written in this manner to indicate that Hershele used to stretch out the word as he uttered it.

2. Reb: This is the Yiddish honorific term commonly used as a formal prefix and respectful way to refer to or address a male, similar to Mr. in U.S., or Sir in England, etc.

3. Der Veker was the person who went from house to house early mornings, knocking on the shutters to awaken the men in time for reciting Psalms and early morning prayers.

4. A tish, literally "a table," refers to a gathering of chassidim who sit at a large table with their Rebbe, chassidic leader, celebrating a particular event or auspicious time.

5. Sheva Brachos are set of seven blessings recited every evening, for seven evenings after a wedding, thus continuing the marriage celebrations for one week.

Hershele Kurlap
by Yisroel Asman
Translated by Pamela Russ

Short in stature, heavy, with a short neck: the wide, cloth hat with a creased crown [of the hat] – pushed to the top of the head; from the front, dull blond, short hair sticks out, and from the back – the edge of a feathered and greasy skullcap. A high forehead, with several deeply–etched creases, from which peek out a pair of glassy gray eyes, red cheeks. A red, haughty nose with a pair of thick lips, from which hangs a pipe with a short stem [shank of pipe]. A thin mustache with a small, two–pointed beard, dull blond, and here and there green from snuff tobacco and pipe fluid, dressed in a fat–stained, cotton frock [black coat], and girded with a green belt.

He really did not know any Hebrew. On Shabbath, his wife used to read the translated khumash [Five Books of Moses] with him, and still he would toss out verses and wisdom of the Torah which the town would carry around. Scoffers would often drink with him and bet with him over a glass of whiskey, that he could [or could not] find where his verses are quoted [in the original khumash]. They would wait for his mistakes; such as when he had a yahrzeit; on Passover, they would stand under his window and listen to how he would recite the Hebrew, and try to catch him in a mistake. On Yom Kippur, they would drive him mad and frighten him by telling him his memorial candle had gone out. When he would be called up for a Torah reading, they told him that the portion was about the Tokhekho [Torah portion describing punishments G–d sent to the Nation of Israel, a portion that is read quickly because of its negative content], and then tease the sexton, who would shout, curse, then laugh. And he [Hershele] would wholeheartedly laugh along with them. When they would roll in laughter because of him, "I, Hershel Kurlap," he would say, pulling back his forehead, shutting his right eye and shaking his beard, "can still recite Torah better than all you [so–called] scholars."

Hershel did not have great respect for any teachers. Wealthy and prestigious people did not receive much regard from him either. More than once, a fine Jew would hear from him, "I am Hershel Kurlap. I consider you with your head deep in the ground [something like "I wish for you to drop dead"]. He loved the poor people and as was his way, he dealt with them with love and respect.

[Page 144]

He was a fisherman – and according to the billboards – he was the Rebbe of the fish market. His curses were reputable in the whole area. On Fridays, his voice was heard across the entire fish market, teasing and cursing the women, who themselves took to select and toss back the live fish into the tubs. Very often, they would see him fulfilling the command of slapping a housewife's face with a fish as he caught her by the hand just as she was about to steal a fish. With curses, he would delineate the entire ancestry of this Jewish woman. He didn't spare anyone. Even his wife was careful about starting up with him. Because of that he would always hold her in great esteem.

Everyone knew that Hershel would give away his last for a poor man. In town, they would say about him: He has a mouth like Bilaam [from Book of Numbers, speaks in a rough manner, trying to curse the nation of Israel] – but with that, a heart – a Jewish one, not to be criticized. No one felt insulted by him. People knew that he had to curse and tease. People also knew that he occasionally took a little too much whiskey.

Deep down, everyone loved him. His Torah teachings were often repeated in the Bais Medrash and in the khassidic shtieblech [small, informal synagogues]. Jews who were scholars or khassidim, would laugh at his ignorant ideas that always contained a spark of humor. His original voices and humorous words were also often repeated with a good–humored smile.

They called him Reb Hershel, and very often you would see the finest businessmen strolling across town with him. On Shabbath, he would stand in shul [the synagogue] in the place of the wealthy man Eli Dans, opposite the Rav. In the hot summer evenings, Friday night after the meal, when the finest Jews sat on the walkway of the bridge, watching the silver rings of the Bug River, and paying deep attention to terribly sad stories which Bunim–Leyb recounted – Hershel would approach, begin shouting and making a tumult and ... then pour out his Torah learnings. Everyone walked away from Bunim–Leyb and paid attention to Hershel's speech, and laughter was heard right across the bridge. Then they would escort him home and drink cold water with juice.

Everyone knew that there was never an extra ruble in Hershel's house. If someone needed money for business, then Hershel would take him to a gemilas khesed [non–profit loan organization]. He didn't wait until the person came to ask money of him, but cursing and teasing, he went to the person's home and gave him ten ruble, and then to another one. He knew that the next day was market day and they needed money to go to the market. Now it seemed that he argued with Velvele Shia's and cursed him with death curses – and now you saw Hershel going to his house and saying to Velvele's wife: "May you have a black year ... give this to your husband the scholar, that he should have something to use at the market." And not waiting for any thanks, he left, sometimes without even a "good day."

Hershel was allowed to do things that no other was allowed to do. He wasn't held accountable, not even for a hair. He was allowed to talk during prayers or during the reading of the Torah, even to wear his tefillin [phylacteries] at an angle. Even Zachariah Kopolovitch and Mendel Kalb, who, along with the entire town, would argue about this (that's why they were called "inspectors"), would also not say a word to him. No one said a word to him even when he would come to the large table in the morning, where along with the voices of the prayers, the sweet–longing gemara melodies were carried – and here he tossed out his verses and translations, not allowing the young boys to study. Not one of the young boys said a nasty word to him when Hershel called him "scholar" [in a teasing manner] or "bench presser" [meaning, sitting on the bench and studying all day]. All of them laughed, and Hershel laughed along with them. Often, he would approach them and they would quiz each other about Hebrew words. They asked: "How do you say onions and fat in Hebrew?" And they themselves would say: "Kaafikim banegev ["like streams in the Negev," overflow of streams or water in the Negev]. When they would burst out laughing, he would shout loudly: "Why are you laughing, you [fake] scholars, you bench pressers? I wish you a black year! On the other hand, tell me, gluttons, gluttons and drunkards, who sit all day over the holy books, tell me, really, what is the meaning of Kaafikim banegev? Is it only to laugh at Hershel Kurlap? Scoundrels, vermin, pests! Because Pharoah is just like you! You belong in the ground, along with Pharoah!"

With that, everyone would laugh very hard, and finally, he would laugh along with them. But because of that, they knew that when they would go collecting charity for a Jew, Heshele contributed with his generous hand and whole heart.

Hershel never went to his Shabbath meal without a guest. In his language, this was called "a Jew." Often he would take two guests, and the poor would say about his house: "This is like Abraham the Patriarch's house. May G–d give him blessings – and all his curses should be turned to blessings."

He would be very conscientious about having a "Jew" [guest] for Shabbath. On Friday mornings, he would give an extra fish to the wife of the sexton and then say to her: "Here, tell Yitzkhok–Yakov that he should choose a good Jew, one that eats a lot, you hear, a pike – not a tench [cheaper type of carp]..."

When he would come into shul, dressed in the outgrown, satin frock, with his wide velvet hat on his head, he ran directly over to Yitzkhok–Yakov to collect his guest, not leaving him [the guest] for the entire Shabbath. If it happened that in the large Bais Medrash there was no guest to be had, then he would also run to the other Batei Midrashim [plural of Bais Medrash, Study Hall] to look for someone. He did not have a particular interest in taking someone from the khassidim shiebelech. "They are not worth it," he would say. "Tenches [carp, cheaper fish]. A Jew from a khassidim shtiebel – only Torah and Torah. Even the fish remains untouched..."

Once, there was no guest in town. Hershele had already searched through all the Batei Midrashim and minyanim [prayer quorums], and found no one. For some time, he ran around and cursed. Everyone had already left shul, and he was still running around, cursing the world. He already convinced himself to take in a "tench," a Jew from the khassidim shtiebel. He went to the Gerer shtiebel but all he found there were some local khassidim. They told him that they thought there was a guest but they did not know to whom Meier–Beinish had sent him.

[Page 145]

Filled with hope, Hershel went to Meyer–Beinish. Breathless, Hershel ran towards the open window. Meyer–Beinish was sitting comfortably at his table, concentrating on his fish. Through the window, Hershel threw in a swallowed "Good Shabbos!" and before Meyer–Beinish even had a chance to ask why Hershel had come so suddenly, in a pleading voice, as was his way, Hershel called out: "Reb Meyer–Beinish, my crown, tell me, where did you send the Jew? I've already run across the whole town and could not find even one Jew to invite for Shabbath! It's as if all of them have sunken into the earth." Meyer Beinish, surprised, looked at him. He had never seen Hershel so upset. He creased his high brow, patted down his long, silvery beard, and said: "There was one, and I asked Sholom Mikhalkes to take him in."

It was as if Hershele became alive. He threw back a quick "Good Shabbos" to Meyer–Beinish, and ran over to Sholom. He met his wife en route, and in her way, she gave him a mi shebeirach [a tongue lashing, figuratively]. Hershel did not react, but said to his wife: "Come, Rochel," he said with a pleading voice. "Let's both go to Sholom and ask him. Maybe he'll have mercy on us and give us the Jew so that we do not have a bleak Shabbath... Maybe he'll do that. He was once a good neighbor..."

Rochel was silent and followed her husband.

Sholom Mikhalkes was sitting comfortably at his table with his sons and sons–in–law, and was singing zemiros [special Shabbath songs] in his shrill voice. The men of the house sang along. The burning candles and the silver candelabrum lit up the shtreimlech [fur hats] and satin frocks of those men around the table. In a corner of the table, there sat the guest, embarrassed, and he did not even join in singing the zemiros. They guest seemed pre-occupied, maybe because he was thinking about years ago, before he became so downtrodden – and blood ran from his heart. At the other table, there was Kaila Shloime's with her daughters and daughters–in–law, all dressed in their Shabbath finery. The pearls and diamonds from the earrings shone and winked in the light. Quietly, they enjoyed the zemiros that were being carried from the men's table.

Suddenly, the door opened, and Hershele appeared with his half-embarrassed "Good Shabbos!" Behind him, quiet as a thief, Rochel, Hershele's, stepped into the house. Everyone suddenly stopped singing and, surprised, looked at the unexpected guest.

Pale, half–terrified, with a trembling voice, Hershel blurted: "Reb Sholom, I wanted to ask for your respect. I mean – I've been left without a Jew. I've run through the entire city. I'm going to have a bleak Shabbath..."

Hereshele couldn't say more. His voice was stuck in his throat. He tossed a pleading look at Sholom, and his glassy eyes filled with tears. Sholom threw a pair of eyes at him, and the entire household watched the scene with amazement. They had never seen Hershele in such a situation. They could never imagine such a thing. For a few minutes there was a painful silence, a heated stillness. Finally, Reb Sholom patted his beard, and said:

"So, now, what do you want, Reb Hershel?"

Hershele hardly spit out the words:

"The Jew, Reb Sholom. Give me the Jew..."

With a broad smile, Reb Sholom replied:

"Let's ask the Jew – if he has no problem, then you take him!"

"Reb Yid [Jew], come with me. You'll have a mitzvah [fulfill a religious commandment]," Hershele pleaded with the Jew. "With me you'll eat in royal clothing and be in the company of angels. Come. Reb Sholom will forgive you...."

Moved, the Jew widely nodded his head and stood up from the table.

Hershel and his wife wished Reb Sholom everything good, thanked him, said "Good Shabbos," and went home with the Jew ...

[Page 145]

My Teachers

by Motl Wenger [or Venger]

Translated by Hershl Hartman (Los Angeles, CA)

Reviewed by Frida Grapa Markuschamer de Cielak (Mexico City)

Translation donated by the Historian Enrique Krauze (Mexico City)

When I reached the age of three, my father took me to study with the Broker' Melamed.[1] He lived on Wanska Street. I do not remember his family name. He was a widower who lived in a single large room with a foyer. The greatest space was occupied by a long table and its large pointer.[2] In winter, we would sit inside near the large stove and play; in summer – in the corridor on the wooden floor and carry on. The Melamed would call each of us and point to the poster with its large letters. In this way we learned the alphabet by the end of the semester, because one went to kheyder[3] by semesters. In the second semester we already began to learn biblical Hebrew. My parents were very impressed by the Broker' Melamed.

Later I was taught by the Hebrew–Melamed, "the hat maker". Apparently, his previous employment was as a hat–maker. His dwelling was in Ita Mates' courtyard, near the drainage ditch and he lived in one large room. He shared the dwelling with his elder daughter and his son Mendele. The last was an older boy, but quite short – and he helped his father as an aide. All the children sat on the floor. Each boy was called up by the large pointer. The boys, on leaving the Rebe,[4] would almost always be crying. The Melamed was a very angry man while Mendele, his son, would play with the children. The joy among the children was very great when the Rebe would let us go for lunch, or at night. It had the appearance of prisoners escaping a jail. But, for all that, he taught Hebrew well.

[Page 146]

Then I was assigned to the Dodzhilover' Melamed.[5] I remember that he came to our house during the intermediate days (of a festival–trans.) to talk about me. The Dodzhilover' Melamed had his kheyder in the Gerer[6] prayer house. The Melamed, with twisted legs, may God preserve us, was an angry man and often talked to himself with his fingers...This Melamed also taught us khumesh.[7] (In kheyder there were two groups of boys: one studied only Hebrew, and the other was already studying khumesh. And in the time between one subject and another, we played at cards...).

Later I was taught by the Melamed Mendl Trane's,[8] a Gerer Hassid[9] who lived at the drainage ditch, in Shloyme Dlugashodler's courtyard. Mendl

Trane's was a tiny little Jew with a large beard, who possessed a large pointer. He lived in a room with an adjoining kitchen. All day long his wife, Trane, would berate the boys for their carrying on. Luckily, there was a large area there in which to play. The greatest punishment a boy could get was to be forbidden to go into the courtyard to play. Reb Mendele taught the entire Bible and a bit of Gemara.[10] Every Friday we would review the portion with "a great spreading and raising" to a sweet melody that resounded through the entire street. On Sabbath eve in kheyder, we also studied the Sayings of the Fathers.

There dwelt in the same courtyard another children's teacher, Reb Aaron with his goatee. There was a legend told that his students once glued his beard to the table while he was dozing and then lit papers under the table and shouted, "Rebe, fire!..." He had to tear off one side of his beard – which remained thus.

Sometime later I was placed with a higher Melamed, who was called the Lodzer' Melamed.[11] He lived with his two daughters near the Bug River in two rooms and a kitchen. He was a tall Jew with spectacles, a Gerer Hassid but somewhat modern. He taught us Gemara with Rashi's[12] commentaries and the whole Bible. At midday, his daughter Ratse, would lecture us in writing Yiddish and a little Polish.

And every week there would be a visit from Reb Borukh Cywiak, the son of Itche–Meyer the slaughterer, who would hear us recite and issue awards. To a certain extent this encouraged the kheyder boys in their studies.

Later I was taught in a kheyder in the small House of Prayer, where older boys studied Gemara and its added commentaries. There were times when we played "21" with cards under the table. Reb Shimon would teach by rote. When he noticed us playing cards under the table, he would ask one of the boys: "What are we up to in our studying?" The boy, confused, would place his whole splayed hand on the Gemara, so that his fingers would point to every part of the page... On the first occasion, the Rabbi would forgive the miscreant; the second time – he would be expelled from the kheyder. Most of us had great respect for Reb Shimon.

This is how I recall some of the melamdim[13] of our birthplace.

A House and Its Inhabitants

At the corner of Strazacka Street in Yiddish: Strazhatske) and Senatorska, across from the Senator's garden on the bank of the Bug River, there was on a hill the large corner-house of Isaac–Hersh Venger, a part of which belonged to

Jacob–Ariye the butcher. The house was famous for its inhabitants of all classes: the great wholesale merchant Yekhiel–Meier Rubin, who provided food for the town and environs. Day and night wagons would arrive to unload and take on merchandise. He owned large food warehouses. Porters found employment there. Reb Yekhiel–Meier and his wife were childless and lived very modestly. Characteristically, if a child happened in to buy something for a penny, they would wait on it. They would say that a business is built on pennies.

In the first fore–house [it probably refers to the front section of the house], at the right, lived the town's miller, Itche–Meier Wysocki/Visotski and his family. He supplied the town with flour, conducted an orderly home, prayed in the second Gerer prayer house, and helped any needy Jew with a full hand. Their nearest neighbors were Zilke Rosenberg and his family; a bit of a banker (cashing checks on commission for traders), he was the representative of the leather business in Warsaw. A good man who did favors with his heart and soul. Later his dwelling was added to by the ladies' tailor Yoynish from Warsaw, who married Sheyndl, the sister of Khaye the baker's wife. In that same fore–house, on the first floor, lived my family, the Venger family. The proverb says that another should speak of you, but since my family was martyred in Glorification of The Name, one wants to say something about the house, whose walls had absorbed Torah and hymns of Hassidim and good Jews. Ours was a spacious house, open to all. There was a canopy in the house. During Sukkes/Sukkot[14] they would remove the covering and replace it with skhakh[15] – and all the neighbors would take their meals in our suke.[16] Almost the entire second night was celebrated there in song, at the Festivity of Water–Drawing.

In the next fore–house lived the family of the fruit merchant, Brodatch/Brodacz. In recent years his wife contributed to their income by conducting a tailor shop in their dwelling. They raised good children.

[Page 147]

Near them lived Itche–Meier Zuzel/Zuchter and his family. He was a Hassid in shtibl number 2. He worked in the lumber exchange as a broker and was an excellent Talmud–student. In the same fore–house, on the first floor, lived Abremele, the son–in–law of Yankef–Aryeh the butcher, and his family. He studied night and day, striving to become a Rabbi, and did achieve the rabbinic post in a shtetl.[17]

On the other side of the house, one descended stone steps, where the windows were low. In the third fore–house of the building lived the carpenter

Hershl Brak [possibly written Bransk in the Polish Census] and his family. He had his workshop in the apartment. Lived modestly, was an honest person, belonged to the Psalm Society; raised good children who were social activists. His grandson, Benyomin–Khayim Brak/ Bransk, was the leader of the "Young Pioneers" in Wyszków [Vishkov in Yiddish]. In next door lived Khane the widow. Later, the dwelling was occupied by a Jew from the Wyszków–region, a simple person. His demeanor drew everyone's respect. Characteristically, he died in the Little Synagogue while removing the Torah Scroll from the ark for study – collapsed with the Torah Scroll in hand and died...

A bit farther on one entered the gate of the house, which led to the courtyard. There one immediately encountered a surrey and a coach with rubber wheels. These belonged to Shmuelke Ostrowiak, who lived in the house with his family. He had one large room as well as stalls for his horses. He was a fine Jew, a man of the people, and had well–raised children. Reb[18] Shmuelke had a son during his later years. The Wyskower/Vishkover Rabbi held the child at the circumcision. That event is well remembered. Reb Shmuelke, the man of the people, drew respect for his honesty.

The courtyard was redolent with history: It heard the joyful laughter of the small children who played there. Half the yard was paved with stones. In earlier years grandfather Yitskhok–Hersh had wanted to build a health spa in the yard, because doctors had confirmed that the nearby water source had high mineral content. A wall had been erected for the building, but a flood washed everything away.

Entering through the gate one encountered Fore–house number 4. At the left side of the fore–house lived the Brama family, the pouch–makers. They created paper pouches and sold them to many businesses in town. The Bramas were honest folk, reflecting the town itself. Across the way lived der Geler Hershele [literary: Yellow Hershele, probably a read head] who sold lottery–tickets and other things, such as palm branches and citrons (carried during Sukkes ceremonies). His wife was very nice and had two little children. They lived on very modest means. The dwelling also lived through tragic times.

There were two neighboring dwellings on the first floor. Moyshe Rynek and his family, produced homemade cigarettes that sold for five for three pennies. Though he and his family barely eked out a living on his earnings, he was always jovial. The other neighbor, the Lodzer' Melamed and his two daughters, conducted their teaching in the modern style. His daughters added to the family's income by teaching Polish and Yiddish reading and writing to the pupils. He was a Gerer Hassid. In his free time he was absorbed in his Hassidic books and studied aloud.

The bestial Nazis, wiped out the house, which was exuberant with Jewish life and absorbed with the joys and sorrows of its inhabitants.

By Motl Wenger

Translator's Footnotes:

1. Melamed– stands for teacher of children, boys, in a religious school. When the teacher was called Broker' Melamed – it was done as so o denote its birth place origin, the town of Brok which was about 31 kms (or 19.34 miles) away from Wyszków.

2. pointer– This word refers to a Jewish ritual pointer which has the shape of a hand with its index finger extended like pointing out, which is also known as a "Torah pointer" used by the reader to follow the text during the Torah reading from the parchment Torah scrolls. Beyond its practical usage, the "yad" [the hand] ensures that the parchment is not touched during the reading.

3. Kheyder– the elementary religious school for boys.

4. Rebe–The Melamed was also called 'Rabbi' whether or not he was officially ordained. By saying that: 'on leaving the Rebe (who used the pointer on his students), the boys would almost always be crying.'

5. Dodzhilover' Melamed–This religious elementary school–teacher of children was nicknamed so because he arrived from the Dodzian town which was about 6 or 8 hours away from Wyszków.

6. Gerer– A person that follows the learning of the Hasidic Dynasty originating from of Ger, or Gur (or Gerer when used as an adjective), Ger, is the Yiddish name of the town of Gôra Kalwaria, a small town in Poland were the founder of this dynasty of Torah–students, Rabbi Yitzchak Meir Alter, lived, preached and taught.

7. khumesh (khumash or Chumesh),the five books of theTorah.

8. Melamed Mendl Traine's– Literally translated to "Mendl, Traine's husband" this was because in the shtetls, [the small towns in Europe], it became customary to use this inflexion of names as almost no surnames were used in daily life. For a man– the first name of his wife was used (or from the father). In order to identify a woman, – the first name of her father was the one most often used.

9. Gerer Hassid a follower of the Hasidic dynasty, an orthodox and mystical religious interpretation based on the interpretations of Rabbi Yitzchak Meir Alter.

10. Gemara–Is the name given to a vast collection of Jewish laws and traditions of the Talmud which is infused with vigorous intellectual debate, humor and deep wisdom.

11. Lodzer' Melamed– This religious school–teacher of children nicknamed so because he arrived from the city of Lodz (Lódz) 180 km (abt.111miles) away from Wyszków.

12. Rashi– Rabbi Shlomo Yitzchaki (1040–1105 Troyes, France) known as Rashi was the outstanding Biblical commentator of the Middle Ages, He was a fantastic scholar and studied with the greatest Torah connoisseur Rabenu Gershom of Mainz.

13. Melamdim– The plural for the noun Melamed– [religious school teacher or teachers of boys].

14. Sukkot (or Succot) – Literally "Feast of Booths", is commonly translated to English as "Feast of Tabernacles".

15. ss'khakh (or ss'chach) – Name for the material used as a roof for a Sukkah, an organic material, such as leafy tree overgrowth, mats or palm fronds.

16. sukke [in Yiddish], or sukkah [in Hebrew], is often translated as "booth", a temporary hut constructed for use during the week–long Jewish festival of Sukkot It is topped with branches and often well decorated inside with autumnal, harvest or Judaic themes and it is where the family eats their meals all week.

17. shtetl– (plural=shtetls, the small towns in Europe so called in Yiddish.

18. Reb'–In this case it is like the honorary pronoun noon Sir. or Mr., it does not refer to the pronoun Rabbi.

The Blind Rabbi
by H.Mushkat

Translated by Hershl Hartman (Los Angeles, CA)

Translated by Hilda Rubin (Rockville, MD)

Reviewed by Frida Grapa Markuschamer de Cielak (Mexico City)

Translation donated by the Historian Enrique Krauze (Mexico City)

This happened at the very beginning of the current (20th) century. I was already working in Warsaw, but I would return home to Wyszkow for the holidays. I was then a frequent visitor in the home of Motl, the kosher slaughterer, who lived in Aplboym's house. Across the way was Wenger's[1] house, in which lived an old Rabbi, known as the Blind Rabbi. It was difficult to determine whether he was completely blind or partially sighted. The Rabbi shared the dwelling with a son–in–law (or son), and the latter's wife and children. No one knew where the Rabbi had come from. But it was well known in the town that he was extremely poor and still more needy.

So the Jewish women in the shtetl[2] did not forget the hungry Rabbi. Especially on Wednesdays and Thursdays, when shopping for Shabes,[3] they would bring to the Rabbi's home: a home–baked khale[4]; a piece of meat; a fish; produce. No Hasidim[5] were to be seen coming to the Rabbi's–only women.

At a later time, rumors began to spread in the shtetl that the Rabbi helped sterile women to conceive and that he aided many women. Understandably, the number of his women supporters grew significantly–and with them, his income. It was no longer necessary to collect items for the Rabbi for Shabes. The rabbi's household members were now, better dressed.

It was told that the Rabbi put a separate price on the birth of a boy and another for a girl...His household kept elaborate books, because the Rabbi agreed to have his fees paid out in installments.

A middle–aged couple that lived in Aplboym's house had no children. He was a dyed–in–the–wool Litvak[6] who did not believe in (Hasidic) Rabbis and who laughed at the supposed wonders performed by the Blind Rabbi. The couple dearly wanted to have a child, but the husband refused to believe in the rabbi's miracles. Suddenly, sensational news spread through town: the Litvak's wife had become pregnant. It was said that she had visited the Rabbi secretly and, as was usual, had signed up for installment payments for the fee. She probably told her husband about the fee agreement with the Rabbi–and he strictly forbade her to make any further payments.

[Page 148]

When the woman's time came to give birth–the child was dead. The shtetl had grist for its conversational mill for many weeks thereafter. The authority of the Blind Rabbi grew still greater...

Translator's Footnotes:

1. Wenger– The surname in Polish begins with the letter "W," but is pronounced as a "V" (Venger).

2. shtetl– It is common to use this word in Yiddish when speaking or writing about a town in Europe. (shtetls, plural).

3. Shabes– Sabbath, which begins Friday evening.

4. khale– The typical braided bread (or loaf) used for Friday night dinner for when the Shabbath is welcomed and the food blessed.

5. Hasidim– The term (in plural) refers to religious men. (Hasid or Hassid is the singular form).

6. A dyed–in–the–wool Litvak– Here the phrase is used to mean 'strong opponent' of the behavior of the Hasidim.

Ayzikl, the Teacher
by M. Rabin

Translated by Hershl Hartman (Los Angeles, CA)

Reviewed by Frida Grapa Markuschamer de Cielak (Mexico City)

Translation donated in 2013 by the Historian Enrique Krauze (Mexico City)

Ayzikl[1] Melamed[2] was known to all in Wyszkow, but only as much as could be seen visually. The real Ayzikl, the inner, invisible to human sight, was known to no one but his Creator. His appearance to others was as follows: A medium–height Jew, with a modest–sized beard, more grey than black, always clean and well–combed. Though poorly dressed, he was so meticulous that he always seemed to be wearing his Shabes[3] clothes. I would see him going by several times a day to, or from prayers, or also sometimes on business–to and from the marketplace–and was astounded that he never failed to say "good day." He was an expert at saying "good day." No sooner than someone looked him in the eyes than he responded with "good day," adding "a good year" as a bonus...

When I knew him he was no longer a melamed. Whether he had ever been one–I cannot tell. One thing is certain: he was called Ayzikl Melamed.

He had a kreml (a small store) and lived next door to Christians. Among them he was known as "Panye[4] Isaac." When I would come to his store to buy something, though he did not have much of a selection, I would always find him sitting over a holy book. Though he was not a great scholar, he did know his obligations to God. And as to his obligations between man and his fellowman— these were dictated by his simple sense of justice. I never saw him angry. A loving smile always played on his lips. This was true, even when I would happen into his shop, while his wife was in the midst of one of her wild tirades. But he, Ayzikl, bore her no grudge. To the contrary, he would insist, that she was truly saintly with a heart of gold. That she doesn't shout at him as much as she should, because her life with him, pitifully, is very, very bad. Is she then not right? How can one earn something from customers, when the store is empty. So, she shouts: "You do get money–loans, so why must I stand in front of empty shelves?"

Ayzikl the teacher did really often require an 'interest–free loan'[5] –and did obtain it. When borrowing he would specify the date on which he would repay with the aid of the Blessed G–d. He would chose the specific day according to the Torah portion of the week: Monday of the tenth or Tuesday of the eleventh, and he would repay on time. However, he did not use the interest–free loans to buy merchandise, but–to lend to others.

At times, the ways of the Creator of the Universe seemed perverse to Ayzikl: "the evil prosper – while the saintly suffer?!" But it would not pay to pose questions. His daughters, for instance, who were called "enlightened," did actually attempt to show how much injustice there was in the world. And it was rumored that they even had ideas about how justice could be made to blossom on all the earth. But it was difficult to convince Ayzikl of this. He would listen to them pleasantly and agree that perhaps more justice was needed in the world, but as to their solutions, he would say:

"–Children, that is not the way! Believe me, the Master of the Universe knew those plans before you did. If HE doesn't institute yours, he probably has other and better plans."

I once tried carefully to determine to which Hasidic[6] sect he belonged: –to the Gerer[7], the Radzyminer[8] or maybe to the follower of another Rabbi. He cut me off and quickly replied that he was a follower of the Master of the Universe, just a Hasid. Once, in a conversation he almost let fall that the mitzve[9] of charity might remain even if there were fewer poor people and perhaps, who knows, no poor people at all. That another, a profound mitzve might be created "in place of" charity. He quickly caught himself, knowing he had gone too far in his thoughts and that one dare not offer advice to the Creator of the Universe.

Ayzikl Melamed was soft–hearted by nature. He was unable to bear someone's pain. And not only the pain of a person, but of any living thing. When he would notice that a Christian neighbor had a hen that limped, he would cry out:

"–Oh what a pitiful thing! After all, as it is written, –the pain of living creatures!"...

To say nothing of when he would see a neighbor throwing a stone at a cow to drive her away from the garden. He would certainly be beside himself and cry out to himself: "–cut–throat hearts". In summer, when he would sit over a holy book and a fly would annoy him, he would not drive it off in anger, but with a barely–noticeable move of his gentle hand.

This is how Ayzikl the teacher spent his life until the murderous Nazis entered Wyszkow. Then Ayzikl became an entirely different person. He no longer smiled. He ran about earnestly and lost in thought, murmuring something to himself. From time to time he would wave his hand, as though he were arguing with the Master of the Universe for permitting the Nazi bestialities. He felt his own helplessness to do anything. What could he do with empty hands against a loaded Nazi gun?

[Page 149]

Once, standing near his house frozen in thought, he saw a German pointing his rifle at a small Jewish boy who was darting from one tree to another, seeking protection from the Nazi murderer. The cries and terrible sobbing of the boy carried to the heart of the heavens. Nevertheless, the German carelessly followed the boy with the snout of his rifle. Any moment, one thought, he would squeeze the trigger. Ayzikl understood that he dare not lose any time. He bent down, picked up a heavy stone and sprang upon the German, splitting his skull. The German fell like a split oak, holding the gun and its unfired bullet. Arriving Germans carried off the dead Nazi and took Ayzikl, in manacles, and threw him into a dark prison cellar.

He lay there, captured, and reviewed his life:

"–A life lived and never raised a hand to anyone–and now I've killed a person. Ha? A person? Can such killers be called by the name people?"

He recalled that Moishe Rabeinu (Moses, Our Teacher and patriarch), had also killed an Egyptian. But he was Moses, after all, God's messenger–something he could not say of himself. Because if he were doing God's work, he would not have killed only one. He would have had to smash thousands and thousands of Nazi heads in that way. That means that he did it of his own free will and that he will therefore have to answer for it before the Master of the Universe?

At dawn, when one could not yet distinguish between night and day, the door of the cell opened and several armed hangmen entered. They threw themselves upon him like wild animals and dragged him out to a wide plaza. Here there awaited a detachment of German soldiers. Two of them ran up to Ayzikl, dragged him to a post, placed his hands behind him and bound them tightly with a solid rope. An officer issued a command and the murderers came to attention. Another command and...they raised their rifles, aiming at him.

Ayzikl Melamed kept moving his lips and quietly murmured, "in Your hands is my spirit." His entire life flashed before his eyes, from the first moment he had begun to understand the world up to the moment when he had raised the stone and killed the German–and the doubts that so tortured his mind: "Was he justified or not in having killed a human being?"

The officer raised his sword and opened his mouth to issue the third and final order. Ayzikl saw before him a line of rifles. He heard a shout, then a fire and smoke with fluttering letters in the air that flamed like bloody suns:

"It is well to have crushed the brain of the snakes!"

Butchers conferring in the market

Translator's Footnotes:

1. AIZIKL Melamed– AIZIKL is the diminutive of the name ISAAC or, as in this case, it is a loving, kind way to call a person.

2. Melamed is a term for a teacher in a religious school.

3. Shabes– Sabbath

4. Panye–is the Polish word for Mister (Mr.)

5. The Interest free loan association in Wyszków and in other shtetls was known as "Gmilas–Khesed."

6. Hasidic Judaism (meaning "piety" (or "loving kindness) is a branch of Orthodox Judaism that promotes spirituality through the popularization and internalization of Jewish mysticism as the fundamental aspect of the faith, and was founded in the 18th century in Eastern Europe. In Wyszków there were many houses of Hasidic–worship, that were called shtibelakh [small houses] like the Radzyminer, Otwotzker, Aleksander, Amshinover and foremost, the Gerer. Each group of Hasidim (plural of Hasid) belonged to different dynasties of influential spiritual leaders, known as Rebbes, (Rabbis), and usually each group was named after a key town in Eastern Europe where the founder may have been born or lived, or where the group began.

7. Gerer is the name of a Hasidic dynasty based on the learning's and interpretations of Rabbi Yitzchak Meir Alter and his followers.

8. Radzyminer refers to followers of the Radzyminer Rebbe.

9. mitzve–(in Yiddish; mitzvah in Hebrew) a good deed, but literally, it means "commandment".

Itche–Metch der Klezmer (the Musician)
by Yankl Mitlsbakh
Translated by Hilda Rubin
Reviewed by Frida Grapa Markuschamer de Cielak (Mexico City)
Translation donated by the Mexican Historian Enrique Krauze

One of the most popular people in Wyszków, known to all— young and old, recognized by his round, shorn brownish beard and half–round belly— was Itche Metch, der klezmer.[1] He was there playing at all the weddings and at all other happy occasions. He was always there with his band of musicians.

Both of his vest pockets were connected by the silver chain of his pocket watch from which hung a little key. Itche used that key to wind the watch and he always made sure that the watch was fully wound so that the hands never stopped. The dangling key also served another purpose for his group of wedding–musicians, namely— they kept their beat by the bouncing movement of that key.

He spoke with the accent of a Litvak[2], but the most notable thing about him was the fact that he knew many trades and had various kinds of knowledge. However, his specialty was — music. A separate weakness (if one can call it that) was that he raised and was involved with— goats! Another talent of his was that of barbering. But he would never shave a person's beard because of his religious beliefs.

Itche Metch was not simply a musician; he ran his own music school in town. His highly developed musical ear could immediately identify a false note one of his students made and poor playing would really cause him misery.

Itche took great pride in his talented sons. And the most talented of them was the eldest Khaim–Henekh who was a true artist and badkhn.[3] Khaim was a tall young man with a full round face. He wore a black skullcap with a wide brim from which dangled two silk buttons. It was said that he wasn't always able to do well with the liturgical poems. However, the experts in these matters said that he could always bring the women to tears when he performed.

[Page 150]

The second son, Nisele, had his specialty— the cornet. His playing, the tones of his cornet, it was said, could be heard echoing way off in the distance. In addition, the last three sons were also musicians. And, so this entire family was celebrated in Wyszków and the surrounding towns.

Understandably, besides his five sons, Itche was blessed with a few daughters. But who even remembers their names today?

However, it isn't difficult to understand that with such a large family, Itche would have to find other means of earning money besides just his music. Is it such a wonder that he would turn to—— veterinary medicine? He would tend to heal all the sick goats in Wyszków, using his own concoctions and herbs. And if he couldn't cure a little bearded goat with his ministrations, well— the matter was in God's hands.

When the beloved spring season arrived, our musician brought into play his agricultural skills. He would sit himself down in the market place and sell all sorts of seeds. He would share his knowledge and experience and deliver advice to the peasants.

His living quarters consisted of one room. The kitchen was found in one corner of the room where there was a big flue or chimney to draw off the cooking smoke. However, there wasn't enough wood in the town for such a stove so, in the summer the cooking was done on a three– footed small stove.

As a rule, the dwelling was white washed before Passover, which was the custom in Jewish households at that time. And, so the chimney would become caulked over and the smoke and soot settled over everything for the entire year. The darkness in the room, caused by the smoke and soot, permeated everything.

And as it was in most of the towns and hamlets in those days, so it was at Itche's— he kept some hens. Needless to say it was more frugal to keep a few hens because they could be fed the table scraps which otherwise would have been thrown out. He would go straight from his table as he was saying the blessing, tossing the crumbs to his hens.

Now here we must describe another of Itche's special skills— that of an eye doctor! He would say, "I can wash my eyes out with a newly laid egg— and I will see better and more clearly."

As for his orchestra— he invited the renowned violin–cellist, Khaim Palyukh, to join the group. Palyukh's instrument was twice the size of this musician. Khaim was a little Jew with a beard. His every day trade was as a porter. He would wait all day with his heavy rope (used for tying the loads on his back) for a job— but at night if there were a celebration and the band was needed— he would be off with Itche and the players.

To add to the earnings of Khaim (Palyukh)'s family— his wife would hire herself out as.... She could do this because she was frequently pregnant and after her deliveries, she sold her milk.

Translator's Footnotes:

1. Yiddish, "klezmer" refers to a professional Jewish instrumentalist, a musician.

2. Litvak translates to: a Lithuanian Jew or a man from Lithuania. The Litvaks are well known for the different dialect that was spoken by Jews in Lithuania and in the Suwalki region of northeastern Poland.

3. An entertainer at weddings, specializing in poetic improvisations.

Reyzele – Di Zogerin[1]
by Yakov Mitlsbakh

Translated by Hilda Rubin (Rockville, MD)

Reviewed by Frida Grapa Markuschamer de Cielak (Mexico City)

Translation donated by the Historian Enrique Krauze (Mexico City)

The town of Wyszków lay in the midst of tall, slender pine woodlands[2] that had for hundreds of years provided shade and coolness for the town. These woodlands were witnesses to the comings and goings of generations – some of whom lived in happiness and satisfaction and others that lived in sorrow and suffering. Nearby was also the small hill called the Tuczyner Hill[3] where the town (old) cemetery was located, it was there that the town's dead were interred in their graves, together with their secrets for their journey to the world after death...

The living ones were also drawn to the Tuczyner Hill. There were those who went simply to go for a stroll with a friend or others, for a more intimate encounter with a lady friend. Others went to weep at a grey gravestone at the time of a yortsayt[4]. And still others went to invite a dead relative to a family celebration or to have the relative intervene in behalf of a female relative having a difficult delivery.

Today, this holy Wyszków site sits shamed and silent. The cold stones that had absorbed so many hot tears over centuries have been ripped out by the hands of vandals. These stones have been used to pave sidewalks. The small sand hills have been leveled and the holy tombs of the Rabbis destroyed.

One has memories now of all those holy graves on the Tuczyner Hill where our Rabbis, pious people and important men were buried. Many notes had been placed on those graves– notes that were soaked with tears and that held requests for– health, a good living, a decent marriage for a daughter, healing for a sick child– and more and more...

The German murderers also had a hand in not leaving a trace of those holy bones, which had been placed there for their eternal rest. Those bones have been plowed up and mixed with earth and fruit trees were then planted. Now those trees are producing fruit for the very people who perpetrated these crimes and even for those who simply looked on and did nothing.

At the Wyszków cemetery: an "Askore" (a memorial service)

[Page 151]

At the entrance of the cemetery, which was at the beginning of the small hill, one had first to enter through an "ante"–house[5] that was opened by two tall half–doors. These doors had been cobbled together with discarded boards and odd pieces of wood. This particular door most certainly was hundreds of years old. On its Eastern–wall hung two large black frames with letters of gold written on parchment that had various appropriate prayers and psalms for honoring the departed. The "professional women criers" would instruct the others when and how they should "chant" these prayers and psalms and at the appropriate times...

Amongst these "professional women–moaners," the most well known was – Reyzl, di zogerin. She was a small, wizened little vaybele[6] with a lined, shrunken face, who seemed to be able to absorb all the sorrows and laments of those who came to mourn on the Tuczyner Hill. This Reyzl couldn't read or write, and even the alphabet was unknown to her, – but, she knew just where every departed soul was interred for its eternal rest.

A soon as a relative of a departed one appeared at the cemetery, Reyzl with her skinny arm, would hit a few times on the door. This rapping of hers would create a pall of fear upon all those at the cemetery. It was as if with her rapping she was causing the dead to come back to life. However, it was her words – that impressed more than her rapping. Her words caused all of the seekers of comfort to start unburdening themselves of talking about what was in their hearts. When Reyzl, di zogerin, began to talk one could trust her instincts. Each person was drawn into her words and prayers. One felt that one's soul was calmed and comforted

Reyzele had her "tomb–inspired language" all down by heart. She knew every verse from the holy books by heart and she knew which to use for the proper occasion and when to use it. She had a verse for every situation: be it the illness of a child or the son who had to present himself for the draft of the Czar's army or for example, –earning a decent living.

She would intercede for all her "customers" so that they should have enough to live on and yet, she herself, lived a very impoverished life.

Translator's Footnotes:

1. zogerin is a woman who is usually more educated in prayers than the other women in the community and she, therefore, says the prayers for other women or leads them in prayer in the women's segregated area of the synagogue. Some were also professional women criers at burials.

2. slender pine woodland– those slender high pine trees were called in Yiddish in Wyszkow: "Sosne beymer;" in this case, the forests were called Sosne velder. Aaron Pacht, in the book "Tzvey Shtiber," mentions the pines several times. Also, in articles and poems written by Jewish citizens of Wyszkow, this definition of the pine forests is often used.

3. Tuczyner Hill– The correct Polish spelling is Tuczyn but in the shtetls Jews used to name streets or places with words that sounded more familiar to them, therefor in this case, they added the ending letters 'er'.

4. yortsayt– the yearly anniversary of a person's death.

5. ante–house– in Yiddish 'a for–haizl' – A small room before the house, also called antechamber; it is a smaller room or vestibule serving as an entryway into a larger one. The word is formed of the Latin 'ante camera' meaning: "room before"

6. vaybele– a thin little woman or, also used as: wifey, a lovable way of referring to a condescending or lovable man's wife or girl friend.

Hershl Melamed
by Yankl (Yakov) Mitlsbakh

Translated by Hilda Rubin (Rockville, MD)

Reviewed by Frida Grapa Markuschamer de Cielak (Mexico City)

Translation donated in 2013 by the Historian Enrique Krauze (Mexico City)

Hershl Melamed[1],[2] was better known by his nickname, "the Black Hershl." He was a short fellow, somewhat nervous — but, always neat and clean. Apparently, this neatness was one of the main principles he lived by. His black beard was always neatly combed and his rubber summer shoes as well as his winter boots never failed to be neatly polished.

He lived in a large room, which was divided into two areas. One half served as a bedroom and the other half as his school, his kheyder[3] where he taught about fifteen students. In this particular half of the dwelling could also be found a small bakery. The bakery was run by his wife, Esther— a tall, thin worn out woman— exhausted from much hard work and raising a batch of children. In a large oven she baked loaves of black bread. Her baking was done to help her husband with expenses. However, neither the bakery nor the kheyder brought in enough income, so Reb' Hershl sold whiskey for the Sabbath table and Esther also dealt in cereal grains. Twice a year Esther did very well with her cereal grains: once in the summer during the "nine days" observance when the people ate a lot of cereal with milk; and then again in the winter during Khanukeh[4] when the women baked "gritshkelekh" (a delicacy for which they needed a grits–like flour[5]).

The business that had to do with the "bitter drop" (the whiskey enterprise) was conducted in a corner of the room. There stood a cabinet with various flasks of whiskey and utensils for measuring— half and quarter cup measures. After all, a Wishkover[6] Jew whether rich or poor, really enjoyed raising a glass after eating his Sabbath fish. These tasty Wishkover fish were harvested from the nearby river, River Bug, where they were very plentiful.

Clearly, the kheyder (the school), the bakery, the grain–cereal enterprise and the liquor "dispensary" were carried on without the proper authorization and so Reb'[7] Hershl was constantly under stress. He was always in fear of a visit from some "unwelcome" guests.

When our melamed went to eat a meal, we, his students had to leave the house. He couldn't stand being observed by his students as he ate. He couldn't bear it if a drop of anything should stain or wet his thick, white tablecloth. We, his students, really hoped that our melamed would keep stuffing himself at his table so that we could continue to enjoy ourselves outdoors. Opposite our melamed's house was a courtyard that belonged to a fellow called Joseph Pakht/Pacht who owned a small "food processing plant." Even in those days he had adopted somewhat modern procedures with which he could mill various grains and press oil. For this purpose he had a machine, which was run by (real) 'horse–power'. A horse was harnessed to a span and had blinders on so that he wouldn't get dizzy going round and round as he powered the milling machine. Our pleasure was, when our studies were interrupted, to hop rides on the "arm" of his horse driven "contraption" if Joseph Pakht would allow it. We considered this great fun. We'd go round and round under horsepower as long as Reb' Pakht didn't get rid of us. But usually our fun was interrupted by R' Hershele in person who'd call to us to return to the kheyder. It was then that we'd become very heavy hearted because we had to get back to our studies. It was a particularly bad time if it were Thursday, because on Thursday, R' Hershele would proceed to question us about the Torah portion of the week and the commentaries concerning that portion of Rashi[8]. Woe to that fellow who couldn't give his answers quickly and correctly. A flood of curses would come pouring out of our Rebbe's[9] mouth. But luckily, this torrent stopped flowing when his liquor–buying customers would come on Thursdays to buy their whiskey for the Sabbath. However, our Rebbe felt justified with his punishments of cursing and even blows because of our transgressions.

R' Hershele also had an important reason to be uneasy. It was necessary to obtain a permit to operate a school. Clearly, our Rebbe did not have such a permit. Actually, it wasn't so necessary to own a permit, as it was necessary to also teach "worldly" subjects in the government approved schools. And our religious, orthodox parents did not approve of this. They wanted their children exposed only to a religious curriculum and not a worldly one. The government appointed observers would come frequently but R' Hershl would be tipped off about their visits – and we boys would be allowed to run off and play until the visits were over.

[Page 152]

And another situation kept R' Hershele in constant upset and agitation: he had a batch of daughters! And daughters had to be provided with dowries and bridegrooms and then, there would be weddings. It was because of this that he was involved in so many "businesses." And because of these problems he would direct… his anger at us, his students.

And we boys were delighted to get out of the kheyder whenever our Rebbe gave us the opportunity. We were happy to escape his whims. When the

government officials came to observe – we boys would "escape" even
before R' Hershele gave the signal. During these off times, we had games we
would play such as a hide and seek sort of game and a button game. We
would get these metallic buttons that had a satisfying metal sound when
bounced against a surface. The game consisted of slamming these metal
buttons against a wall and seeing how far they bounced. Then we measured to
see whose button had bounced the farthest. These were our summer games.
In the wintertime we went sledding on the small Striga River[10] that flowed
from the upper far fields past the Rebbe's courtyard. With home made gliders
and sleds we "flew" down that little frozen river. Or we would hike up to the
church with the green copper roof, whose gilded cross could be seen from way
off in the distance – and from up there we would go downhill so fast that the
snow would spray from our runners. These good times would last as long as
the government observers were conducting their official business at the
melamed's dwelling. Then it was back to our studies.

During the winter the daylight hours were short and we learned till well
after dark. When we were dismissed from class we walked home in groups of
boys. Each boy had a lantern made of colored paper which he decorated
himself with cutout decorations and designs. The candle burning inside the
lantern made patterns in the dark... (We bought the colored paper at Bertshe
Oldak's[11] who lived on Ostrower Boulevard)

Bagel salesman

Translator's Footnotes:

1. Hershl Melamed– Hershl the teacher. A teacher from a religious school for small boys called "kheyder". Melamed is used to describe his occupation, teacher.

2. Hershl Melamed– Hershl the teacher. A teacher from a religious school for small boys called "kheyder". Melamed is used to describe his occupation, teacher.

3. kheyder – Traditional Jewish religious school, where younger boys, at about the age of 5, 6 used to come to learn "Khumash" [the beginning of the five books of Moses]. Kheyders were widely found in Europe before the end of the 18th century. Lessons took place in the house of the teacher, known as the Melamed.

4. Khanukeh (Hanukkah or Chanukah) refers to the Jewish "festival of lights." The holiday commemorates the miracle of the oil in the Holy Temple that burned for eight days although there was only enough to burn on a single day. This holiday represents the triumph of the Maccabeans over the religious persecution of the Greeks around 165 B.C. E.

5. grits–like flour– was needed to bake "gritshkelekh". Grits are small broken grains of corn.

6. Wishkover– term used to denote those born in Wyszkow.

7. Reb' or R'– is a term used by Jews when addressing somebody with respect like SIR or Mr., for example:: R' Hershl, here Reb' does refer to a Rabbi either to Mr. Hershl.

8. Rashi– Rabbi Shlomo Yitzchaki (1040–1105 Troyes, France) better known as Rashi, was the outstanding Biblical and Talmudic commentator of the Middle Ages.

9. Rebbe–The Melamed was also called 'Rabbi' or 'Rebbe' whether or not he was officially ordained so.

10. Striga River (?)– There is no river called Striga near Wyszkow. However, there is the small Rega River, which, could be the one mentioned here. The Jewish citizens of Wyszkow often changed the Polish names of streets and avenues into Yiddish– sounding names, so probably this was the case with this river.

11. Bertshe Oldak's who lived on Ostrower Boulevard" (In Wyszkow the Jews gave "Yiddish names" to many streets, probably this was Ogrodowa Street ....) *Note –>As per the Business Directory from 1929, we know that Oldak Bercze had a Bookstore on Bialostocka Street (where she could probably sell paper products) and she is registered also with a Leather Shop on Dluga Street.

[Page 152]

Mates–Faivl der Kremer (the Storekeeper)
by Yankl Mitlsbakh
Translated by Hilda Rubin (Rockville, MD)
Reviewed by Frida Grapa Markuschamer de Cielak (Mexico City)
Translation donated by the Historian Enrique Krauze (Mexico City)

Even the poorest young kheyder–yingl [school–boy] would now and then, get a penny to spend from his father and mother. We, kheyder–yinglakh [school–boys], as well as our parents knew just where that penny would end up— with Mates–Fayvl, the storekeeper. It was at his place that we would buy the nash (snack). Every Friday evening, before sundown, the wealthier Jews would congregate at his store to buy some castor oil to smear on their boots. In the summer time you could refresh yourself with a cool drink of sour brine. That brine came from the barrels of pickling cucumbers that Mates–Fayvl kept. At the beginning of every month, the Bobes (the grandmothers) and the mothers would buy Mates–Fayvl's "worm–kraut" which was used as a purge to rid the bowels of worms.

Mates–Fayvl would greet all of his customers, whether they were grown-ups or children with a smile. He was a small man and was always decked out in a greasy apron. He always had a good word for one and all.

Hersh–Leyb, Shingle–Maker[1]
by Yankl Mitlsbakh

Translated by Hilda Rubin (Rockville, MD)

Reviewed by Frida Grapa Markuschamer de Cielak (Mexico City)

Translation donated by the Historian Enrique Krauze (Mexico City)

During wintertime the kheyder–kinder[2] were busy with constructing dreydls[3] for Khanukeh.[4] The pewter[5] they needed was found at the train station. The pewter was collected from the discarded metal seals of the uncoupled railroad cars. After the gathering came the more difficult job of melting the pewter and pouring it into molds. More than once did the hot pewter burn a hole in the boys' pants and sear their flesh. And if so it was with the dreydlakh[6] –then why not do the same with graggers[7] at Purim? Of course, they had to form these graggers themselves, so this also became a problem to solve. It just so happens that in the same house where Reb' Hershl–Melamed lived, there also was to be found Reb' Moishe[8], the "second rate"–tailor[9]. From him the boys collected the empty, used spools of tread, which they then used for the graggers. However, the most important part of the gragger was the klapper[10] and that piece of merchandise was found at Hersh–Leyb's, the shingle–maker. He lived on Koleyove Street[11] which was on the way to the train station. Hersh–Leyb was not a rich man but in the shtetl[12] he was looked upon as a kind of miracle man because in his seventies, with his second wife, he had a son... Hersh–Leyb was a tall, strong Jew, with a yellow tangled beard[13]. He didn't dislike or turn his nose, up at a glass of real 95% proof whiskey. His main business was to lay shingles on rooftops, but he also did lumbering in the woods around the shtetl. He chopped down pine trees[14] that grew around their shtetl and also produced kindling wood from them. In addition, he made forms to insert in boots that the "bargain" shoemakers used.

[Page 153]

The clappers or tongues of the graggers which we (the boys) formed at Hersh– Leyb's, made a great noise and din at each mention of (the name of) Homon–Haroshe[15], (when the (Purim)–Megileh[16] was read. When everyone got home from synagogue, we were rewarded with a delicious, fresh "three–sided homentash"[17]. filled with poppy seeds and slathered on the outside with fresh, pure honey, which were bought at Pinye–Mates' store.

Translator's Footnotes:

1. Shingle–Maker– a person who cuts lumber, wood, in the forest; or, that shapes the wood in the form of shingles, or who covers the roofs with shingles. Hersh–Leyb, did it all.

2. kheyder–kinder– the school–boys that studied at a "kheyder". Kheyder (or Cheder) was the elementary Jewish religious school in which children were taught to read the Torah (Five Books of Moses), and some other Hebrew books.

3. dreydls or dreydlak (plural in Yiddish, (singular, Dreydl) The translation of the word means "to turn around." This device is a four–sided spinning top played during the Jewish Holiday of Hanukkah which has a different Hebrew letter on each of its 4 sides The 4 letters stand for the saying: "Nes Gadol Haya Sham," meaning: a Great Miracle Occurred There.

4. Khanukeh–(in Yiddish); (Hanukkah or Chanukah, transliterated from Hebrew). This is the name of the Jewish Holiday of the "festival of lights" in reference to the miracle of the oil which, at the Second Temple, it had only enough to burn on a single day, but it burned for eight days. The Holiday commemorates the triumph of the Maccabees over the religious persecution of the Greeks around 165 B.C.E.

5. pewter (cley in Yiddish– which is translated to cooper or rather to a metal like pewter).

6. dreydlakh((in pl. in Yiddish) same as dreydls (*see footnote 3)

7. graggers– (word in pl. in Yiddish – In sing: gragger) Noise maker devices, typically, fitted with a handle that when turned around, they make a loud noise. They are used by children who, whenever the name of evil Persian minister Haman is mentioned, they turn them around so not to hear the hated name of someone who wanted to destroy the Jews. His name is mentioned several times during the reading of the Book of Esther on Purim.

8. Reb'– is a term used by Jews when addressing somebody with respect, like SIR or Mr. like in the 2 cases here of calling the 2 personajes: Reb' Hershl–Melamed or Reb' Moishe (the tailor).

9. The "second rate"–tailor– A tailor that produced cheap goods.

10. klapper– clappers or tongues, or a metal tab with a gear that produces the noise of a gragger . a rattle that makes a loud noise when turn around.

11. Koleyowe Street– The Jews in Wyszkow had the habit of converting many of the street names in Polish, uttered in a mixture of Yiddish and Polish like the ulica (street) Kolejowa, the Kolekhowa street, which they called 'Koleyowe gas', or street.

12. shtetl– The Yiddish popular name for the Europe Villages, small or big.

13. with a yellow tangled beard– refers to a readhead person.

14. pine trees– The Wyszkow forests grew pine trees which in Yiddish were called "sosne beymer" of which many 'Wyshkever' wrote poems or stories.

15. Homon–Haroshe – (In Yiddish.) The name of evil minister "Haman– the Bad One", who wanted to destroy the Jews, is appointed during the reading of the Book of Esther on Purim and the children make noise when his name is uttered.

16. Megileh– A story told in the Torah is called Megileh ("Megilah" in Hebrew), this citation refers to the reading of the story in Purim, of the Queen Esther when she was married (around 400 B.C.E.) to Ahasuerus, the Persian king, and she and her uncle Miordekhai were able to save the Jews from the bad intentions of Haman the 'bad&38217; minister who wanted to convince the king to kill them.

17. homentash– A special Purim bread called so in Yiddish, which is a filled–pocket cookie or pastry recognizable for its triangular shape, usually associated with Purim recalling the triangular shape of bad minister Hamman's hat, Homentashen(pl.) are made with many different fillings, mainly poppy seed (this is the oldest and most common and traditional, variety), or: prunes, dates, apricots, etc..., etc....

[Page 152]

Mates–Faivl der Kremer (the Storekeeper)
by Yankl Mitlsbakh
Translated by Hilda Rubin (Rockville, MD)
Reviewed by Frida Grapa Markuschamer de Cielak (Mexico City)
Translation donated by the Historian Enrique Krauze (Mexico City)

Even the poorest young kheyder–yingl [school–boy] would now and then, get a penny to spend from his father and mother. We, kheyder–yinglakh [school–boys], as well as our parents knew just where that penny would end up— with Mates–Fayvl, the storekeeper. It was at his place that we would buy the nash (snack). Every Friday evening, before sundown, the wealthier Jews would congregate at his store to buy some castor oil to smear on their boots. In the summer time you could refresh yourself with a cool drink of sour brine. That brine came from the barrels of pickling cucumbers that Mates–Fayvl kept. At the beginning of every month, the Bobes (the grandmothers) and the mothers would buy Mates–Fayvl's "worm–kraut" which was used as a purge to rid the bowels of worms.

Mates–Fayvl would greet all of his customers, whether they were grown-ups or children with a smile. He was a small man and was always decked out in a greasy apron. He always had a good word for one and all.

Hersh–Leyb, Shingle–Maker[1]
by Yankl Mitlsbakh

Translated by Hilda Rubin (Rockville, MD)

Reviewed by Frida Grapa Markuschamer de Cielak (Mexico City)

Translation donated by the Historian Enrique Krauze (Mexico City)

During wintertime the kheyder–kinder[2] were busy with constructing dreydls[3] for Khanukeh.[4] The pewter[5] they needed was found at the train station. The pewter was collected from the discarded metal seals of the uncoupled railroad cars. After the gathering came the more difficult job of melting the pewter and pouring it into molds. More than once did the hot pewter burn a hole in the boys' pants and sear their flesh. And if so it was with the dreydlakh[6] –then why not do the same with graggers[7] at Purim? Of course, they had to form these graggers themselves, so this also became a problem to solve. It just so happens that in the same house where Reb' Hershl–Melamed lived, there also was to be found Reb' Moishe[8], the "second rate"–tailor[9]. From him the boys collected the empty, used spools of tread, which they then used for the graggers. However, the most important part of the gragger was the klapper[10] and that piece of merchandise was found at Hersh–Leyb's, the shingle–maker. He lived on Koleyove Street[11] which was on the way to the train station. Hersh–Leyb was not a rich man but in the shtetl[12] he was looked upon as a kind of miracle man because in his seventies, with his second wife, he had a son... Hersh–Leyb was a tall, strong Jew, with a yellow tangled beard[13]. He didn't dislike or turn his nose, up at a glass of real 95% proof whiskey. His main business was to lay shingles on rooftops, but he also did lumbering in the woods around the shtetl. He chopped down pine trees[14] that grew around their shtetl and also produced kindling wood from them. In addition, he made forms to insert in boots that the "bargain" shoemakers used.

[Page 153]

The clappers or tongues of the graggers which we (the boys) formed at Hersh– Leyb's, made a great noise and din at each mention of (the name of) Homon–Haroshe[15], (when the (Purim)–Megileh[16] was read. When everyone got home from synagogue, we were rewarded with a delicious, fresh "three–sided homentash"[17]. filled with poppy seeds and slathered on the outside with fresh, pure honey, which were bought at Pinye–Mates' store.

Translator's Footnotes:

1. Shingle–Maker– a person who cuts lumber, wood, in the forest; or, that shapes the wood in the form of shingles, or who covers the roofs with shingles. Hersh–Leyb, did it all.

2. kheyder–kinder– the school–boys that studied at a "kheyder". Kheyder (or Cheder) was the elementary Jewish religious school in which children were taught to read the Torah (Five Books of Moses), and some other Hebrew books.

3. dreydls or dreydlak (plural in Yiddish, (singular, Dreydl) The translation of the word means "to turn around." This device is a four–sided spinning top played during the Jewish Holiday of Hanukkah which has a different Hebrew letter on each of its 4 sides The 4 letters stand for the saying: "Nes Gadol Haya Sham," meaning: a Great Miracle Occurred There.

4. Khanukeh–(in Yiddish); (Hanukkah or Chanukah, transliterated from Hebrew). This is the name of the Jewish Holiday of the "festival of lights" in reference to the miracle of the oil which, at the Second Temple, it had only enough to burn on a single day, but it burned for eight days. The Holiday commemorates the triumph of the Maccabees over the religious persecution of the Greeks around 165 B.C.E.

5. pewter (cley in Yiddish– which is translated to cooper or rather to a metal like pewter).

6. dreydlakh((in pl. in Yiddish) same as dreydls (*see footnote 3)

7. graggers– (word in pl. in Yiddish – In sing: gragger) Noise maker devices, typically, fitted with a handle that when turned around, they make a loud noise. They are used by children who, whenever the name of evil Persian minister Haman is mentioned, they turn them around so not to hear the hated name of someone who wanted to destroy the Jews. His name is mentioned several times during the reading of the Book of Esther on Purim.

8. Reb'– is a term used by Jews when addressing somebody with respect, like SIR or Mr. like in the 2 cases here of calling the 2 personajes: Reb' Hershl–Melamed or Reb' Moishe (the tailor).

9. The "second rate"–tailor– A tailor that produced cheap goods.

10. klapper– clappers or tongues, or a metal tab with a gear that produces the noise of a gragger . a rattle that makes a loud noise when turn around.

11. Koleyowe Street– The Jews in Wyszkow had the habit of converting many of the street names in Polish, uttered in a mixture of Yiddish and Polish like the ulica (street) Kolejowa, the Kolekhowa street, which they called 'Koleyowe gas', or street.

12. shtetl– The Yiddish popular name for the Europe Villages, small or big.

13. with a yellow tangled beard– refers to a readhead person.

14. pine trees– The Wyszkow forests grew pine trees which in Yiddish were called "sosne beymer" of which many 'Wyshkever' wrote poems or stories.

15. Homon–Haroshe – (In Yiddish.) The name of evil minister "Haman– the Bad One", who wanted to destroy the Jews, is appointed during the reading of the Book of Esther on Purim and the children make noise when his name is uttered.

16. Megileh– A story told in the Torah is called Megileh ("Megilah" in Hebrew), this citation refers to the reading of the story in Purim, of the Queen Esther when she was married (around 400 B.C.E.) to Ahasuerus, the Persian king, and she and her uncle Miordekhai were able to save the Jews from the bad intentions of Haman the 'bad&38217; minister who wanted to convince the king to kill them.

17. homentash– A special Purim bread called so in Yiddish, which is a filled–pocket cookie or pastry recognizable for its triangular shape, usually associated with Purim recalling the triangular shape of bad minister Hamman's hat, Homentashen(pl.) are made with many different fillings, mainly poppy seed (this is the oldest and most common and traditional, variety), or: prunes, dates, apricots, etc..., etc....

[Page 153]

The Fishermen
by Yankl Mitlsbakh

Translated by Hilda Rubin (Rockville, MD)

Reviewed by Frida Grapa Markuschamer de Cielak (Mexico City)

Translation donated by the Historian Enrique Krauze (Mexico City)

Thanks to Pam Russ

On the little Koszcielna [Polish word for church; aka "Fisherman's"] Street that was on the other side of the wooden bridge that crossed over the River Bug, in a little house whose walls and roof were covered with green moss, the melamed [teacher] Yankev [Yakov]–Yisroel lived and taught little school boys [kheyder yinglekh] their kometz alef "O".[a] With his long pointer he would point to the letters on a much erased board that was rubbed out from age and stains...

There in those small wooden houses, also lived a number of fisherman–families. Among them were two well–known fishermen: Zelik – a tall Jew with a trimmed black beard and a roundish stomach decorated with a thick silver chain attached to the silver watch which he had received as a gift when he became a bridegroom.

The second fisherman family with the name Rozenberg, was called by the name of the wife and mother of the family Nekhtshe, the fisherwoman. The Rozenbergs were blessed with many daughters and only one son [Khaim].

Before the Sabbath and before the days of the holidays, the small street would be crowded with benches upon which were placed many wooden tubs in which all kinds of lively fish were swimming. One could hear all kinds of curses and name calling, because it seemed that one fisherman was earning more than the next. The wealthy, religious Jews in their long black coats, wanting to obey the commandment of honoring the Sabbath, would come to the street on their way home to buy fish for the Sabbath, place the fish they bought in one of the folds of their coats, and so would also honor their wives in this manner of dress, by bringing fish into their home...

Nekhtshe, the fisherwoman, was the real type for this line of work. She came from many generations of fisher–folk. Her one and only son was called Khaim, who from infancy on, grew up on the River Bug.

Khaim and Feige Rozenberg

At the shores of the river were anchored all kinds of small boats and canoes, and it was there that he grew up.

Opposite Koszcielna Street, was another small street called Senatorska Street, where the Gerer stiebel [small, informal house of prayer] was situated, a little study house, where the two well–known deaf mutes prayed – the tailor and the baker [Mendl Brodakh was known as "der shtumer beker," "the mute baker"]. Each night, between mincha [the late afternoon prayer] and maariv [the evening prayer], they would meet in the study house and "chat" with their special deaf–mute language and hand gestures [sign language].

On that same street lived the distinguished Holcman, a dyer, not a poor man, rewarded with talented daughters and sons. His oldest daughter [Feige], who was exceptional in her beauty and abilities, was betrothed to Khaim, the only son of Nekhtshe, the fisherwoman. And that's how they led their family lives for many years, until the onset of the Second World War. In an attempt to escape from the Germans, Khaim Rozenberg and his family crossed to the other side of the River Bug in one of the little ships, to the village of Brzoza [distance around 18.24 km, 9.86 miles], to a fellow they knew, a Christian. He greeted them in friendship but then murdered them like a fiendish enemy, such that to this day it is not known what has become of them.[1]

The figures discussed were like part of the landscape and in tune with Jewish Wyszkow. And all this went up in smoke, burned and destroyed by the Hitlerist murderers, with the active aid of the local Polish population, and particularly with the (skusewer zavuzhnyokes)? who were known as murderers and anti–Semites.

Footnote

a. Kometz = vowel "o"; alef = first letter of Hebrew alphabet = A. Basically, meaning he taught them their ABC's. The phonetic sound for kometz alef is "uh."

N.B. Translation Coordinator:

1. To find out what really happened to the Rozenberg family, read this book by the surviving Rozenberg child : A Daughter's Promise by Helen Rothstein, Montreal, Éditions du Marais, 2008 (**ISBN** 9782923721019).

"Der Sfas–Emes"[1]
(The one who speaks: The Language of Truth[2])
by M. Rabin

Translated by Moisés Mermelstein (Columbus, OH)

Reviewed by Frida Grapa Markuschamer de Cielak (Mexico City)

Translation donated by the Historian Enrique Krauze (Mexico City)

You will agree that he earned in a kosher way[3], the nickname Sfas–Emes (the "Language of Truth" person), after you have listened to, at least some, of his extravagant stories.

I was traveling, at night, from Warsaw to Wyszkow on the last scheduled train. The railroad cars – unfilled, almost completely empty. With the business situation as it is nowadays, Jews travel very little.

And if you do have to travel, you look for a familiar face with whom to have a chat, to expel the sadness.

So I roam, from car to car, looking to find a well–known like you search for a light.

To my delight, after a short time, I ran unto the half asleep Wishkever "Sfas–Emes", bundled up in a corner of one of the cars.

With quick steps I swiftly approached and I sat beside him and, as if by accident, I poked his ribs because, it seemed to me, that "Sfas–Emes", was only pretending to be asleep.

He immediately let me know that my suspicions were justified, because he started to speak right away and suddenly asked me a question:

[Page 154]

–"You were probably wondering, why I was so sleepy at such an early hour of the night" –and added, – "last night I did not sleep a wink."

–"What was the reason?" –I half–played the fool.

–"Oh",– he said,– " only business, business and business. There is not even time to sleep. One night here, another night there! You have to be constantly on the move. For example, last night, a very important professor from the Music Conservatory in Warsaw, came to visit my son. He did not let go of my son, not even a minute, he wanted him –that is my son– to play for him, –that is for the professor. He is very much in awe–in admiration–of my son's violin playing. He said, he has never heard anybody playing in such a wonderful manner, and do not forget that the Professor is not an ordinary man and has heard many violinists playing in his life."

–"Is that so?" –I go on pretending to be impressed, – "I didn't know that your son was such a virtuoso of the violin, and if he is, excuse my asking, why is your son a simple drum player in the Maccabi Orchestra of Wyszkow, instead of being a first rate violin player?"

–"It is strange that you should say that",–and I sensed that "The Language of Truth person" was offended, – "What did you expect? That my son, the gifted violin player, who very soon will be known throughout the whole musical world, should play the violin for the people of Wyszkow? Can the people of Wyszkow even appreciate such a performance?... A drummer, on the other hand, is something else: a good drummer can be appreciated by everybody, even by an army horse...."

In order to keep the conversation going, I address the Sfas–Emes again:

–"So you traveled to accompany your guest, the professor?"

–"Yes and no. You guessed correctly, but you are not completely accurate. I traveled with the professor to Warsaw, but not for that reason alone. I also traveled to Warsaw because last week I received a wire from a bank there, advising me that they had received the sum of fifteen thousand pounds in my name. I am a very busy man, so I would not immediately rush, rush to Warsaw because of this... However, since I did accompany the Professor of the Conservatory in Warsaw, I took the opportunity to go to the bank to find out who had sent the money. It so happens that the fifteen thousand pounds were remitted to me by my cousin, an electrical engineer in Palestine. We have been at odds with each other for many years and this bothers him very much. He questions why we should be angry at one another and suddenly decides to send fifteen thousand pounds to me, and he wrote to me: –'Dear cousin: I am sending fifteen thousand pounds to you, and, please, stop being angry at me."

–"So",– I say, pretending to be surprised and giving my Sfas–Emes a brotherly pat on the back like you do to a good sibling "–So, my good friend you became a wealthy, rich man all at once. It is no small matter –fifteen thousand pounds cannot be found, nowadays, lying in the streets."

–"So",– he says with contempt, "–you seem to think that I cashed that money. You know what? Who wants that money? Who? As soon as I found out, that the money was sent to me by my angry cousin, I immediately ordered to the bank to send it back".

Sensing that everything is going exactly as I had planned, I take my "Sfas–Emes" to task:

–"I understand"– I said–"that you have close relatives in Russia?"

–"Anything can be called close relatives",–he stimulated answers "– I certainly have a dear brother in Russia; and he is there, listen carefully, he is the chief engineer of all the trains in the whole of Russia".

–"If so", –I say, – "if your brother is in such an important position in Russia, he must be showering you with gold".

–"The problem, hear it, is that you cannot send money from Russia. Otherwise, he would have sent me, at least, a couple of million rubles. But go and send if it is prohibited".

–"Truth, yes I know it is not allowed", –say I, trying to corner the Wyszkower Baron von Munchausen[4] –"but since your brother is such an important person in Russia, he could surely find a way to do it".

–"Yes, –the "Sfas–Emes" tries to extricate himself from this one – "as a matter of fact he did try it once. Not long ago, I received a parcel from him in which I found a used overcoat with a fur collar. He writes to me that as soon as I will receive the overcoat, I should, carefully rip open the collar, where I will find, some very expensive diamonds hidden inside".

[Page 155]

–"Nu,"[5] I say rather indifferently, "–a collar with priceless expensive diamonds should bring in a quite high sum."

He becomes enraged and starts yelling in loud tones. "–What diamonds, which diamonds! Panie Ganev [6] got suspicious and in the post office he took out all the diamonds–till every last one."

–"That was still okay"–, I said trying to console him. "–That at least you got a winter overcoat. Nowadays, a warm winter overcoat, even a used one, is also useful."

A youth group "Tzukunft" (Future)

With my reasonable, but careless remark, I hit the center of his pride. My interlocutor the "Sfas–Emes" became immediately indignant and upset because I had not taken him seriously and forced him straight from his high illusions down into the grim reality of life. That is why he locked up his truth-language lips and would not utter another word.

During the remaining way to Wyszkow, already, I sat by myself immersed in my own thoughts. Such thoughts that pierced holes in my weary, poor soul.

Images upon images, one worse than the other, floated in front of my half closed eyes in the dimly lit wagon. "He is, ultimately, right",– I was thinking, "– our "Sfas–Emes" from Wyszkow, with his extravagant and exaggerated lies he interprets, without realizing it, this actual dejected life we have in Wyszkow, where helpless shadows stroll around instead of people. Shapes of businessmen from the past and successful artisans walk around aimlessly, preoccupied, upset, resentful and humiliated, thrown out of their livelihood, without any security and without hope for a better future; they can only dream, fantasize, build up mirages in their dark thoughts: that their son, the drummer in the 'Maccabi'–Band Orchestra in Wyszkow, should, by a miracle, become the next day, a violin virtuoso, famous all over the world. Another one fantasizes that if he could send his son to Palestine, he would surely become, with his talents, the most important engineer in the Rutenberg Electrical Station.[7] The third one imagines how wonderful it would be if his brother in Russia would become a very important person in the railroad organization...?"

...So people console themselves with such false hopes, wavering and clutching to spider webs in order to stay afloat. And to such false hopes clings the majority of the actual population of Wyszkow.

—"W Y S Z K O W   S T A T I O N!"– the loud scream of the train conductor, interrupted my thoughts ...

Translator's Footnotes:

1. Sfas Emes–in Yiddish, (Sfat Emet–in Hebrew)–This was a nickname given by the Jewish town-people to that someone who "spoke the truth." But many times this nickname was ironically used to describe a "person" who does not exactly have the quality of being truthful or who does not speak with honesty].

2. Language of Truth– The language of honesty.

3. in a kosher way– The author, by using the word kosher (meaning proper according to the Jewish dietary laws), intended that such a nickname be given to his interlocutor (a correct, honorable, proper person), with irony to emphasize how big of a liar he could be.

4. Baron Von Münchhausen (1720–1797) was a German baron who supposedly told a number of outrageous tall tales about his military adventures. German writer Rudolf Raspe, in his 1785 book,"Baron Munchausen's Narrative of his Marvellous Travels and Campaigns in Russia," mythologized the baron as the world's greatest liar. The author (M. Rabin) uses the adjective Wyszkower to describe the local "Baron," taunting him while he compared him with the famous liar.

5. –"Nu..." a very popular well known used Yiddish word to start a phrase alike to –"Well..." – in English.

6. Panie Ganev– Master thief (Panie –in Polish, is master; Ganev– in YIddish or Hebrew, is thief).

7. Rutenberg Electrical Station – The author might refer here to a similar Electricity Factory "Elektrowna Miejska" that existed on Pultusk Street in Wyszkow, a reference to what was known there, as the best electrical power station.

The Two Mutes[1]
by Yekhiel Bzhoza (Brzoza)

Translated by Khavele Ash & Chana T (San Jose, CA)

Reviewed by Frida Grapa Markuschamer de Cielak (Mexico City)

Translation donated by the Historian Enrique Krauze (Mexico City)

If a stranger would have stopped a Jew from Wyszkow and asked him "where does Mendel Brodach live?" – the citizen of that town would have looked at the stranger with a surprised look and with raised shoulders answered: "Never have I heard such a name." However, if the person asking would have added, "I believe that people call him here "The Mute Baker," – then the homey Jew would smile and good naturedly say:" Come, dear man, I'll take you gladly to the mute baker's house."

You must know that the mute baker was very famous in the town of Wyszkow. Young and old knew him. Everyone, even the gentiles, loved him.

He was of average size, not heavy, straight as a musical string, and as strong as an ox. He used to stand up the whole night kneading dough and snoozing only when the bread or rolls were in the oven... Before sunrise, he would run to the small Beis–Hamedresh[2], for the first Minyan[3] together with the coachmen and the workmen. He didn't know how to pray (because he was born deaf and dumb), still he used to put on the prayer shawl and tephilin[4] rocking in prayer and with fervor concluding the "Shmoneh Esrei[5]" prayer together with everyone.

He also used to sit together with the group of friends between Minkheh (the afternoon prayers) and Maariv (the evening prayers) when the Rabbi was explaining a chapter from the Mishneh[6] or the Torah[7] portion of the week.

He belonged to the group studying the Tehilim (Book of Psalms), and to the Burial Society.[8] And at each funeral he used to run around and shake the big box with the inscription on it: "Charity Saves us from Death."

[Page 156]

Every morning he used to meet the mute tailor at the small Beis–Hamedresh and after praying they used to "talk" in sign–language about the news and events in shtetl.[9]

Just when they found out about a poor cobbler whose wife was sick and that there was no money for the Sabbath, they agreed where to meet later. The mute baker brings a couple of Khallehs[10] and the mute tailor brings wine for the Kiddush[11] blessing. But first, they go to the fisherman–alley to Nakhum, the fisher. His wife, Nekhe the fisherke[12] mumbles something under her nose as soon as she sees the two mutes – but they don't hear her, of course. The mute baker pulls up a sleeve, and from the tub, pulls out a shaky fish. (The last time, they took a carp from Zelig the fisher). Nakhum, the fisher, scratches under his short and thin beard and uses both of his hands as if talking in sign language: "Go, in good health".

From there they go to the market, into several richer food stores. Freyde, Sholem–Mehkhel's[13] tries to protest; with all her might she tries to pull them out the door, trying to convince them that there are other food stores in the market. But the two mutes have their own calculations, as according to their calculations, it is now her turn to help a needy family.

After some bargaining, they finally receive the necessary food. Then they turn to the butcher's street to Yoneh, the butcher. He receives them with a very kind–male reception: "–Look who has shown up!" But he softens and offers them a nice piece of meat.

They check once more to see if they have everything needed for the Sabbath – and they head to the poor cobbler who lives in a basement, where his sick wife is bedridden. The cobbler is repairing an old pair of peasant's boots.

Seeing the two mutes with the food, he looses his composure, wants to thank them, but he gets choked in his throat with tears.

The (now temporarily) mute cobbler makes strange sounds, he tries to say something...The mute baker points with his finger towards the sick woman, as if to say: –"You, brother, better take care of your wife, so that she should get healthy soon!" And before the cobbler is able to compose himself, the two mutes leave the poor basement.

Sometimes it happens that an old, overtired horse belonging to a poor coachman, dies away, and there isn't any money to buy another horse. So what is there to do?

Then our two mutes take a red handkerchief and head to the homes to collect a little money. They haggle with every one, if they don't receive enough money. After counting the collected sum of money, if it turns out that it is still not enough to purchase a horse, and then the two businessmen make an effort, and go to the charity treasury[14], where they meet a few owners sipping hot tea. The mute baker has brought his son Avreml as an "interpreter." He tells them really how much money they had collected and that they want to borrow from the treasury the rest of the money in order to buy a horse.

The treasurer, a well to do gentleman, with a beautifully groomed beard, explains to Avreml: –"Tell them that we will consider the matter at the next board meeting and that the coachman needs to find a guarantor".

The two mutes can't understand this, and don't want to know this...they need to have the money right now, so that the coachman can earn money for bread, for his wife and children.

After each member of the existing management committee was able to explain his expertise in matters of loans, and after long discussions, they assure the mute baker that when he guarantees the loan – then the mutes will receive the demanded sum of money.

The mute baker was also an exceptional swimmer. He used to stay under the water longer than anyone of us. His bakery was located near the wooden bridge. If someone drowned in the river, then they would run immediately to call the mute baker – and he really saved scores of people from death.

Yekhiel Bzhoza

Translator's Footnotes:

1. The Two Mutes in Wyszkow, were known by the names of their occupations not by their own names.

2. small Beis–Ha'medresh= synagogue of prayer

3. Minyan= In Judaism, a minyan is the quorum of ten Jewish adults required for certain religious obligations, mainly to start the religious recitation of certain prayers.

4. tephilin=phylacteries, black boxes with scriptures in them, that Jews wear on their heads and left arms during weekday morning prayer.

5. Shemoneh Esrei (eighteen) is perhaps the most important prayer of the synagogue. This prayer is recited while standing and facing the ark that houses the Torah scrolls. Shemoneh Esrei consists of eighteen blessings, but an additional "blessing" was added later, so now there are nineteen.

6. Mishne–(Mishnah–in Hebrew) are commentaries on the Torah written in the 12th Century, by Rabbi Moses Maimonides whose real name was Mosheh ben Maimon (born 1135, Csrdoba, Spain–died 1204, in Egypt). Among the Jews, he was called Rambam, and Maimsnides by the Latin world. He was a Jewish philosopher, scholar, jurist and physician, the foremost intellectual figure of medieval Judaism. Maimonides's major contribution to Jewish life remains the Mishneh Torah, his code of Jewish law.

7. Torah= The Bible, the Jewish Written Law, which consists of the five books known by the Jews as the Torah (and to non–Jews, as the Old Testament).

8. Burial Society= in Yiddish: Khevreh–Kadisheh.

9. shtetl= little town

10. Khallehs. Yiddish word for the Shabes–bread, khalleh (khallehs plural). In the Jewish tradition the Sabbath meal (on Friday night), starts after the blessing of wine followed by the meal itself, which begins with the blessing of a braided bread (Khalleh).

11. Kiddush blessing= It is customary that the Sabbath meals start with the blessing of a small glass of wine.

12. the fisherke or fisherin, the Fisher–woman.

13. Freydl, Sholem–Mehkhl's Frida, the daughter of Sholem–Mekhl: –The common way to address the daughters in Shtetln was done by adding to her own name, her father's name. This custom persisted even after women were already married.

14. charity treasury, in Yiddish: "Gmilas–khesed–kaseh".

The Rural Doctor Malowanczyk[1]
[Der Feldsher[2] Malovanchik[3]]

by Yosl Popowski

Translated by Hilda Rubin (Rockville, MD)

Reviewed by Frida Grapa Markuschamer de Cielak (Mexico City)

Translation donated by the Historian Enrique Krauze (Mexico City)

The feldsher Malovanchik/Malowanczyk never completed his medical studies at the university– in spite of that he healed the sick and was much loved by his patients. Wondrous tales were told about him. Even when other doctors had given up on a (person's) life – Malowanczyk would take over, he would prescribe a remedy and the illness was removed as if with the wave of a hand...

Malowanczyk knew how much his patients were devoted to him even though he didn't enjoy working in this manner. What he really enjoyed was the pursuit of medicine as a science, as knowledge– not as a profession, not as a way of earning a living. That is why he set up a hairdressing establishment (a barber shop). To help in the business he brought a Mr. Marcus Schwartz from Warsaw.

A good friend of Malowanczyk's once entrusted him with his idea of taking the "feldsher–exam." Malowanczyk warned him that this was a foolish thing to do– that he would be sorry for the rest of his life (if he pursued this). He himself had fought with all–the–energy he could muster for the interests of the feldsher even though in his private life he was an enemy of the feldsher occupation. "Doctors without the proper certification of a medical doctor, should not exist," he stated... "(People) required from us (the feldshers) as from a doctor– perhaps, even much more——However, the attitude toward the feldsher was pretty dismal. We are not given a free hand with our patients. Even though we may have a good understanding of the illness– we're not permitted to be independent (make our own decisions). The doctors hate us because we present them with competition."

[Page 157]

Malowanczyk was considered to be on the highest rung in his field. He used to enjoy testing himself with the Jewish Dr. Lajcher[4], who used to tell him that doctors couldn't abide intelligent feldshers...

Malowanczyk was also a good barber–hairdresser and an outstanding "tooth extractor." He would often tell funny stories about his peasants patients and also describe how he pulled their teeth.

Once, from the house on Rynek (market, in Polish) where Malowanczyk lived, cries could be heard. A woman, Khaye–Surkele's[5], was walking by and asked, – "What's' all this crying about?" They said to her, "Malowanczyk is terribly sick." "Oy vey! He makes everybody well but cannot help himself! What kind of a feldsher is he?"

But, he did get well in a short time – and once again went about healing the sick in the town and in the surrounding rural country.

Translator's Footnotes:

1. The rural doctor Malowanczyk– This is the translation in English done to the original title from Sefer Wyszkow, edited in 1946. The original title in Yiddish reads: Der Feldsher Malovanchik

2. Feldsher – (literally: a fake), a rural practitioner of medicine without a doctor's degree: an old–time barber–surgeon that was seen as some kind of doctor, like this one in Wyszkow or in any other shtetl.

3. Malovanchik– This was the Yiddish pronunciation for the surname, which, in Polish was Malowanczyk.

4. Doctor Lajcher– The Jewish doctor Berek Lajcher (pronounced Laykher) graduated from the University of Warsaw, and spoke perfect Polish and Yiddish. He served in the Polish Army during WW I. He was born in Chestokhowa, emigrated as a newlywed to the Jewish community of Wyszkow that had requested a real doctor. Dr. Laycher was well liked and respected in Wyszkow, where he became fully integrated. His only son, Yosef, was born there. After the Nazi destruction of Wyszkow, he was called to the hospital in the neighboring town of Wegrów to help cure patients of the typhoid plague that developed in Wegrów's Ghetto. From there, he was taken by bus transport, to the Treblinka Murder Camp. In Treblinka, he was selected to work again as a doctor and he participated in the underground organization involved in an escape at Treblinka. He died as a hero protecting the camp's youngsters so that they could invade the weapons–room in their escape.

5. Khayeh–Surkele's– In the Shtetlakh (pl. for Shtetl), it was common to refer to a daughter using a parent's name, either from the father or the mother, e.g., Khayeh the daughter of Surkele (i.e., Sarah, in the diminutive form).

Reb Sholom Refoelkes
by M. Federgreen
Translated by Pamela Russ

From the novel "The Mill on the Mountain," by M. Federgreen (whose real name is M. Greenfeder). The book was published in the original "Kokhos" ["Strengths"], in Warsaw 1939 – and was sent to us by our friend Byalus of Los Angeles. In this book, the story carries the name "Dawn" and is based on a real occurrence in Wyszkow with Reb Sholom Mikhalkes.

Through the closed shutters, a thin string of light shone in.

Old Sholom Refoelkes stirred in his bed. He pulled out a thin, steamy hand from under the feather cover, yawned loudly, and began to rub his eyes, still half-shut from sleep.

He wanted to turn toward the wall, and allow himself to continue weaving through his dawn's sweet half sleep, half dream, but he suddenly remembered the same as yesterday, the same as the day before yesterday, as every day for the past fifty years: that Leizer Avraham's had certainly already opened the faucet and he was definitely already standing and "stuffing" his pockets with money for bran and wheat [which he collected] from the peasants who came.

Quickly, energetically, he stood himself up on the floor. The cat on the chimney got quite a scare and quickly hid himself under the bed.

Sholom Refoelkes quickly washed his hands with negel vasser ["nail water," washing hands in predefined religious manner upon awakening], pulled on the white, rubbed-out pants and the floured coat, and quietly began "swallowing" [quickly reciting] a few words from the "front"[of the prayer book] …

It was very peaceful in the house. Daylight, with all its strength, cut through the closed shutters in the pre-dawn darkness that was settled in all corners of the house. Sholom's wife, Kaila, was still sleeping soundly, and rhythmically, leisurely breathing. Across her face, there was a tranquil calmness, as if nothing bothered her, as if she had completely forgotten that they had to open the store, that they have to earn a few groshen [pennies].

A fly hummed on the window and tore around in the pale outside on a bright gold spot on the window pane.

Swiftly, Sholom grabbed his long, dried-out pipe from the night table, packed the tobacco box into his pocket, and quietly, with small steps, he went out into the street.

A fragrant, early morning breeze, mixed with smells from the nearby river and the green meadows all around, greeted him.

In the large, four–cornered marketplace, it was quiet and empty. The small wooden houses were still dreaming and cuddled up to the large, two–floor house of Moshe'l the baker. Only the local he–goat was already awake, and quietly and proudly, he strolled across the marketplace, shaking his long beard.

Sholom went to his store, took out his keys, and turned the lock. The clang of a pole that had fallen rang through the empty marketplace. The local goat raised his head and looked around confused, as if he was surprised.

Sholom opened both store doors and sat down on the staircase.

"Oy vey," he thought to himself. "I've made such a mistake. I thought it was already the middle of the day outside and it's really only just begun. The street itself is still sleeping. Ha, ha, to make such a mistake! ... The first time in my life."

He lazily pulled out of his pocket the smokey, dried out pipe that was greased with tobacco fluid, and his tobacco box, and began to smoke.

From his pipe, there came balls of thick smoke clouds. He tried to see far, far over the bridge, from where the farmers always came into town in their wagons, but there was nothing to see. The entire long road behind the bridge that stretched like a long, silvery ribbon deep into the forest, was empty. There was no shadow of a person or a wagon.

Sholom laughed to himself. His grey, half–yellowed whiskers lifted themselves nervously. This is the first time in his life that this sort of mistake happened. To get up so early! He never looks at a clock. Just like that – for all the fifty years. He wakes up himself, and always – at the right time. His sense is the best clock. Fifty years! This is no small thing... And now suddenly something like this ... So, yes, he's not a young boy any longer. A little bit more than seventy, he already passed it with just a little bit. There was almost no time ever to think about this... Always occupied with the store. Two small people – two alone. She and he, he and she. Struggling for a little livelihood. As the donkeys. The children, spread out across the seas... There was no time to think about tomorrow... To have gotten up so early. What a mistake he made...

[Page 158]

Suddenly, he heard something, from a distance, on the opposite side, he heard steps. He took a strong puff of his pipe and turned his head to see who was there.

It was YItzkhok–Yakov the shamash [sexton]. He was walking slowly and softly, with a quiet gait, supported by his thick cane that had an ivory handle. He was going, as he went every day, to open the synagogue.

Sholom was happy. At least he was finally seeing another person before his eyes. But why did YItzkhok–Yakov suddenly stop? He was standing still, looking at Sholom with a curious gaze, with disturbed eyes, and did not budge from his place. Maybe he wasn't feeling well? He was an elderly Jew, this Yitzkhok–Yakov the shamash, a lot older than Sholom, and a frail man too. He remembered exactly the year when... But why was Yitzkhok–Yakov going back? Didn't even say a "good morning," and was actually going back? So who would open the Beis Hamedrash? A strange Jew, this old man.

No, he reconsidered. He was once again going toward him [Sholom]. What kind of tricks was he doing here? Why was he looking at him so frighteningly? Why was he not saying a "good morning"? ...

Suddenly, Sholom stood up from the staircase. He did not believe his own eyes. The elderly Yitzkhok–Yakov was not coming towards him, he was running towards him. And running quickly, with all his strength and energy, wringing his hands, as if something terrible had happened...

What does this mean? ... Now, another Jew appeared on the other side of the marketplace. And another two Jews. All of them were running towards him... They were gesturing something with their hands. What was going on? Yitzkhok–Yakov was gasping, he could hardly catch his breath ... He was shouting ... What was going on here? ...

Nervously, Sholom took a puff on his pipe, and frightened, he looked at the shamash. What was going on with him? ... It's not possible! ... It is not p–o–s–s–i–b–l–e!...

Yitzkhok–Yakov was running with his last energies. He was wringing his hands.

"Reb Sholom!" he shouted. "G–d is with you! ... What happened here? A tragedy. Terrible. Reb Sholom!! It is Shabbos today! ... Woe!! Why are you in the store today? A pipe? .. Jews, scream! Look at what happened here!" ...

A cold sweat poured down Sholom.

Jews were running in all directions. Where did they all come from? What? Today on Shabbath? They were all running to him. What? Today is Shabbos? –
— Terrible! Such a dark tragedy on his head, in his older years. What a mistake! ... So why was he still smoking his pipe? [Smoking is prohibited on Shabbos]... Why was he not throwing it away? ...

Now, all the people surrounded him. Jews in their Shabbath frocks. They looked at him strangely. They were speaking and gesturing with their hands. What should he do? Scream? Cry? Excuse himself? Whaaaat?...

The smoke covered his eyes. He could hardly see anyone. As if on purpose, the pipe billowed with smoke... clouds of smoke ... He did want to say something, but he did not see anyone. Where were all the people?

With all his strength, Sholom jumped out of his seat, lifted his hand, but somehow his teeth stubbornly locked, so that he could not open his mouth.

Suddenly, he staggered, and lost his balance. He clutched his heart and fell down in his entire length.

In his unconsciousness, he still heard a deaf screaming as if from many throats, and then everything became terribly still.

When the astonished Jews came over to the collapsed Reb Sholom Refoelkes, the peacefulness of death already rested on his face.

[Page 160]

Translated by Pamela Russ

The tombstone on the grave of the bones of the 12 Jewish heroes who fell in battle with Hitlerist occupiers in the Wyszkower forests. This tombstone was put up in the year 1946 in the Genshor cemetery in Warsaw after the disinterment of the bones.

Same text follows in Hebrew.

Here lie the bones of the 12 Jewish heroes, who in the final minutes fought in the Warsaw ghetto—— against the Hitlerist enemies—— for the honor of the Jewish people, they [too fuzzy to read]

Their eternal rest, their memory

[Page 161]

In the Wyszkow Forest
by Binem Heler
Translated by Pamela Russ

The road stretches to Bialystok
Through the sunny village and the forest.
In the auto, in the middle of the way,
I felt – that I detained someone.

Did I hear a scream?
Or was that an order?
In the middle of the asphalt highway
The auto quickly came to a halt.

The light air vibrated
The sun burned the tree trunks.
Who is calling into the empty stillness?
Who recognized me on the road?

A moment, another, I hear:
The forest magically awoke.
In the echoes of the distant guns
The noise of battle is growing.

My heart is constricting from the waiting
A joy and anxiousness befalls me.
The echo of the ghetto in battle
I hear in the Wyszkower forest.

These are the heroes of May
That came out of the fiery days.
They are leaving the ghetto again
Away towards the enemy and battle.

The fire did not choke them
The resistance was not disrupted:
They were sent out of the ghetto
They chased the enemy off the earth.

The last and thin row
Of fighters was counted –
A part of the large army,

Part of the "Gwardia Ludowa." *

The road to the village is closed –
SS takes the group into its grip.
They fall until the last one in the slaughter –
And that is the noise that I hear.

After a while – the vision disappears
A stillness envelops the forest
And solemnly, into the wind,
The eternal rest begins to speak.

* Gwardia Ludowa or GL was an underground-armed organization created by the communist Polish Workers Party in German occupied Poland, with sponsorship from the Soviet Union.

[Page 162]

To Remember and Commemorate
by Menachem Kaspi (Serbernik), Kfar–Uno
Translated by Chava Eisenstein

We are obligated morally and humanly, for those who remained alive. To remember and to remind those dark days of the Holocaust.

It is a life command demanding and crying out – do not shut your eyes and ears and do not ask to escape the pain, which is yet yelling out loud!

The shadow of the torn apart, burnt, and afflicted city Wyszkow is still hovering over us. They still are straying, upon the slaying fields, the gazing eyes are still penetrating our hearts. Those furious sounds, the last minutes begging for mercy before the silence of death – are still echoing in the emptiness of our world. The silent shouting of babies clinging to their crying mothers mixing with bullet shooting on the heads of the infants are still ringing in our ears and accompanying us forever. Their anger, pain, grief, and wrath are ignited into a fiery blaze. We must never ever forget! And if we will forget you, for only one day of our life, the way we have seen you Wyszkow, in those terrifying days, obscene and lawless exposed to annihilation – forgotten shall be our right hand!

"Not a thing should be lost to memory – for ten generations, until my affront will be calmed – until they are all, all wiped out. I vow if in vain this nightmare has passed, I vow If in the morning I will go back to my evil and nothing will I learn this time too!" our Wyszkow, you calm and lovely town, you attracted us with your remarkable charm, surrounded by forests with an ancient splendor stretched over you. The Bug (*River*) flowing calmly at its edges bringing from time to time a refreshing breeze. The Jews dwelling in her for ongoing generations were known for their tirelessness, diligence and toil at the difficulty of life battle. Religious Jews, Torah scholars in long black garb, their entire life encircled the Torah and its observance, their whole being was to sanctify God and serve him with all their might. Witty merchants, resourceful and energetic always prepared for a good deal, their livelihood they make from one trade–affair to another. The unpretentious folks – the blacksmiths, carpenters, cobblers, tailors with coarse hands and wretched expressions. Only the shine in their eyes conveyed faith and hope for a better future.

This town was the first to be crushed by the cursed oppressor. It happened in the first days in the month of Elul – September 1939, right by the onset of the German invasion of Poland, the word went around that wherever the Nazi beast appears he scatters ruin and loss. Before we had a chance to comprehend what is occurring, the town woke up to the deafening explosion that killed tens of people, woman and children, a big part of the city was destroyed. The Germans continued to disperse death on the roads which swarmed with people fleeing for life. The great synagogue went on fire, all the towns people, amongst them the youth came running to extinguish the fire. The month of Elul is the time of huge awakening, the sound of the *shofar* scending from the great synagogue calls for purification prior the High Holy Days. A deadly serious overall; each one is awaiting the Day of Judgment. In the *shul* (*synagogue*) many many men would gather to thank, praise, admire, beg forgiveness, pardon, and atonement from the Lord. Now, broken–hearted, desperate, hopeless, they put life and soul to extinguish the fire in the *shul*! At least this sanctified place shall be left, so they can pour out their bitter heart, and bitter pain to the almighty! Alas! only eight days after the blood thirsty beasts, the Nazi army came in, and we didn't expect such bad fortune should await us, days of dreadful horror and genocide has come on us. We are a suffering–trained nation, our history is filled with persecution, oppression, pogroms, degradation, and massacres and the almighty saves us. Again, the spirits calm down and life goes on. Now too there were Jews who thought at the end of the struggle we will continue with normal life, therefor they advised against escape. "Jews, do not run" – and who was able to predict such annihilation? Even the most hellish Satan himself is not capable of the extermination that awaited us.

Friday evening, at the time of candle lighting, the Germans began setting on fire Jewish houses; the burning houses looked like the Shabbat candles. The Nazis killed and murdered whomever they came across. Jews were walking to *shul* to sanctify the Shabbat, the Beth Midrash and the almighty. Nevertheless, the Germans surrounded the *shul* and began shooting inside. Hundreds of Jews meet death at this night, whoever manages to escape is slaughtered the next day, on Shabbat, September 9, in the death march. You can fully feel how an entire town is marching to obliteration. My dear town! Your pain, your enjoyments come to my mind; I remember the entire city celebrating the admission of a new Sefer Torah for the big synagogue. All and everyone, the whole city rejoiced and paraded happily with the holy Torah scroll.

My mind brings up images of the High Holy Days; the whole town is heading to the synagogue, pace is slow, each individual seems self–concentrated, engaged in reflecting, enveloped in thought, yearning to elevate, striving for soul heightening. Our mothers walked faster, dare they not miss the prayer of the upcoming year's fate – *U'netaneh Tokef.* The Ger khassidim hurry fast to their *shtiebel*, the Alexander, and the Radzimin khassidim rush to their *shuls*. The Yidden (*Jews*) from the large and from the small synagogues gather together at the edge of the river for "*tashlich*," to cleanse and purify their souls from any wrongdoing and sin. I recall the youth marching joyfully on Lag B'Omer to the woods, happy to hold the blue and white flag. They also march with the red flag believing in human equality and peace among nations. Now, in this terrible dreadful moment, the whole town: Ger khassidim, Alexander khassidim, famous Jews, ordinary Jews, Agudists, Zionists, Revisionists, Bunds, Communists – people, women and children – forsaken, deserted, ostracized, battered and humiliated, despised at the death march, led by monsters, wild beasts. No one is here to shed a tear, to cry for you Wyszkow, because not even an orphan or a widow is left, all are being put to death – you, your wife and son, the whole family. The sun rays are fondling pleasantly and indifferently the butchers and the victims alike. Who bears the courage to justify the verdict, to whisper "Baruch Dayan Emet" – blessed is he the judge of justice?

It is our obligation to remember, not to forget, until ten generations not to forget. We will painfully remember with wrath the souls of our brothers and sisters, so holy so pure, which fell in the bloody hands of contaminated murderers that lack any emblem of humanity. We will remember the great loss of Torah treasures and Jewish wisdom of the crown of humanity, the noble and knowledgeable, the best of the ancient and new culture. We will remember our massacred sons, victims of a cruel and evil kingdom, who were tormented horrendous tortures in the ghettos and death camps. We will remember our dear ones who were deported to a lawless land and their whereabouts are unknown. We will remember our dear brothers and sisters that were murdered on the streets and on the market places, who were brought to slaughter by death wagons, were buried alive, were burnt together with holy Torah scrolls, and the flag of freedom in their hands.

Remember all, those that were slain, drowned and choked, their dignity was desecrated, and murderous contaminated hands shed their blood.

Nation Of Israel, remember our adorable children who were plundered from their parents' lap and brought as herd to slaughter, who were scorched and put to various weird cruel deaths, and stacked on tall piles exposed in the open.

Remember the infants, the sucklings, whose life were plucked by brutal hands, their scalps were smashed at the brick wall and were thrown alive into deep water of rivers.

[Page 163]

Remember Israel your children, their pitiful moans from the fiery flames of the gas chambers.

Remember the groaning of the fathers and mothers, their bleeding torn apart hearts, witnessing their dearests shredded to the ground.

Remember! Do not forget!

———————

The First Air-Raid of Vishkuw
by Yosef Gurni
Translated by Jane, Mikhail Freider and Vladimir Fronton

Vishkuw is a Jewish shtetl. It's the whole world. It's a lost world that was destroyed so that nothing and nobody is saved for the future existence. For most of those who lived through this flame the disappearance of this world wiped off memories about the family home, manner of living, community, language, soul, about the childhood and youth, and about other values that connect people with their motherland. But even after becoming dead this world has risen in a new body and became a different one. Young people hold only imprecise, unclear childhood memories that are difficult to distinguish from fantasies.

Between those memories there are events that were imprinted in our memory in spite of their distance. They could not be forgotten; they are part of our feelings. Maybe only now, after many years it's possible to define a level of unexpectancy and fear during a first bombing attack, first sign of war.

During that summer of 1939 when I was a sixth year old boy the surrounding world was changing. In one day it has changed from a world of tenderness, spoiling and joy to a dark, angry world full of worries about the father who was being on the war front.

I didn't understand completely what is a war and during first days of the war I was in the ignorant state, full of despair and fear. Though I listened patriotic songs playing on a radio and I, a boy, really believed them. The war front was still far and I believed that there was no power that could break great Polish soldiers.

Adults thought differently. They packed stuff in boxes to leave to Warsaw. They thought that a miracle would happen in 1939 the same way as it was twenty years ago in Warsaw. This way I first understood what is the war on the bright fall morning. I still don't know how German pilot decided to drop a bomb exactly on our calm street. Our world woke up from the ringing sounds of breaking glass. My first reaction was to hide under the blanket that was a defense from the surroundings. That morning my mother woke me up earlier to finish packing our stuff. At that moment my mother was very much like a tigress than a home chicken. She ran to men and cover me by her body and then we embracing each other hid behind the commode and we heard the sound of dropping bomb from there. After that there was heavy silence, suspicious silence. Besides the fact that we are still alive we didn't know whether it was the end or just the beginning of the bombing. After that voices of people asking for their children and relatives resounded around. There were a lot of cries and tears. Desire to stay alive hurried us away from this place. We left together with grandfather. Last part of the family had to join us near the bridge over the river Bug. I, full of fright and curiosity, squeezed to my grandfather body. House walls were like witches with black faces, there was smell of burning, sounds of cries from the center of the town.

Nothing surprised and shocked me anymore. Neither crying wounded people that were lying here and there, nor died people who were at least covered, not even a Jewish cabman who abused a goy in the fireman clothes. He was standing on the cart, pulling the horse reins by one hand and beating the goy using a whip in another hand.

This goy was trying to push the cabman down from the cart (surely he wanted to take a cart for himself). "Jew beats goy!" a thought fast as lightning came through my head and I even felt a pride for a moment. My childish wounded pride was very satisfied by this fact because of continuous pursuit by the goy gang.

There was another world after the bridge. Blue waters of the river Bug flew in the eternal calmness. Fields were green and a sky was blue. Smoke didn't cover everything in the black color yet. We were lying near the road and waiting for a cart.

In Warsaw we arrived at the evening. It admitted us with alarm sounds, guns fire and discharges of air defense artillery.

Beaten and wounded Poland was still defending.

[Page 164]

In the First Days of the Destruction
by Moyshe Venger

Translated by Jane, Sofia, Mikhail Freider, Mikhail M., and Vladimir Fronton

Friday, September 1, 1939. I arrived in Wyszków. I had to be with my family during the most difficult times. In the morning radio announced that Germans attacked Poland. All people from Wyszków ran from the town. But journalists found out last news in the town. At the same day people from other places near the border arrived. They told about mockery of Jews by Germans. It was said that polish authorities are going to leave Wyszków. We were left without passports. Germans were bombing the railroad bridge and other locations. On Sunday and Monday everything was silent. On Tuesday, September 5, German planes were bombing Wyszków. In our house my sister Khletche was sick of lethargy for 8 months already. That's why my brother Moyshe and I created a stretcher to carry on the sister to the house of Moyshl the Baker at the market plaza. There were many families on this plaza because they thought it was safe there. All the time planes dropped bombs on the town and all people went through wooden bridge and ran into the forest. My mother Rivele, brother Moyshe, little Sorele and I decided to stay because of sick sister. Later she woke up, kissed everybody and asked: "Let's take me underarms and run to save ourselves".

We passed the bridge and entered the forest with many other families from Wyszków: Malkhiel the Ritual Slaughterer, Pshetitski and others. Planes fired on the running people and spread death. Every couple minutes we were lying on the ground, once going up we found that my coat has got holes from bullets. We were running through the forest in the direction of Jadow.

Wanders During Voyage

At the end of forest on the way to Jadow we met wounded people after the bombing. Among them there was Rokhele Shkarlat. She was being taken on the cart to a doctor. At that time everybody ate together in one common because Leybish Pshetitski had taken some food provisions from his bakery shop. We arrived in Jadow in the early morning. Immediately we were bombed by planes. A lot of people hid in a grocery store but I don't remember the name of this store. One rich and kind Jew invited us and gave us food, drinks and beds. There were no authorities left in Jadow at that time. Polish army ran and Germans were expected to arrive in the town. All of us left this town and hid in trenches from guns' firing. Someone shouted that it would be better if Germans had come already because our fear was too big. Next day Germans came in the town and found hammered doors and gates. It took them half a day to do all their affairs and they started goods requisition. Some families from Wyszków stayed too long in Jadow that time. Leybish Pshetitski went to look at his house and didn't come back ever. Germans killed him on the way.

[Page 165]

During those days Germans and Poles killed all Jews in Wyszków and burned everything. People told Germans occupied Wyszków in vengeance because Poles killed fifteen German spies there. We saw a lot of Jews from different towns in Jadow; they passed me this hard news. My mother's sister and all her family Youngsteyn were killed in Karlishem.

Under Soviet Rule

There were rumors that Soviet Army was coming. In the beginning when Soviet authority just settled everybody was glad. People prepared to meet the ones who would be walking through the town. When we were going through Wengrow we've spent a night in Reyzman family and visited our acquaintances there. We met the Rubin family and also Fayvele Shran with his wife Ite who was in a dangerous condition (her leg was injured with bomb's splinter). Fayvele Baharav, their father of son-in-law, a very good Jew, never left them and helped her all the time before she died.

We arrived in Kosow at night and Red Army detained us. In commendant's office we explained (with arms and legs) that we ran from Germans and now we have families and jobs here. Later we were freed. First days in Kosow we felt very free. Red Army showed movies on the streets. They propagandized how to behave in foreign country. Red Army didn't stay in Kosow for long.

We were allowed to go with the army. The border was opened for about two weeks. A very small number of people went with army. But we wandered with a hope to find a better life those days. My sister Khletche prepared to go in Wyszków. In days of wandering she recovered and hired a cart to go to Lochow and then to Wyszków by train. Her speech and appearance wasn't similar to Jewish woman. Her travel lasted ten days and she came back with bad news. We found out that Wyszków was occupied. Our house was destroyed. And we had to think of place to live. These days Germans came in Kosow. A lot of Jews didn't come back there and tried to find a job.

Our family had important discussion and it was decided that my brother and I had to cross the border, find some job and later the whole family will come to us. We and many other families hired a cart to go to the border. We went through the forest avoiding any bands of robbers. This was we arrived to the German border. We were examined and all our things were taken away. Every Jew received ten golden coins and we were taken to the river so that we can swim through the border under gun's fire. We had to pay two golden coins per a person for this. When we reached another bank a few soviet people with rifles came to meet us. And they clearly ordered us to go back. My brother Moyshe told them something in Russian and explained that we can't go back because we would be killed there. Soldiers told us to go to the commendant's office. There we were examined again and we were told to wait in the yard. This night we were taken somewhere. On the way we met other groups of Jews that were convoyed too. We arrived in neutral zone near Malkin. There were people from special services. Near Malkin station Soviet soldiers gathered together about six thousand old people, children, parents. There were staying on the open field in rain and cold. Speculators sold bread for big money. A lot of people died without medical help there. We sent a delegate to ask to free us but it didn't help. After that we decided to explode a bar and free ourselves. We waited for a moment when there were fewer guards. Mothers with little children were moved to the front and old people stood behind them. On the predefined time the bar was exploded and a mass of people went out. Young girls began to kiss soldiers. Some people were so excited because of these events and then all people were singing "International". Soldiers who sat in trenches near border greeted us. We arrived to Zareby Koscielne station. At about two o'clock at night there were several thousands people from Poland in the forest. Together we moved forward to Tshehanovcy where we've been met and given a cargo train to move to Bialyastok.

[Page 166]

In Bialyastok

In Bialyastok we came to town committee. They gave a half loaf of rye bread to everybody and told to go to Folvark that is about 15 km from Bialyastok. We came to the town committee of Folvark. They didn't admit us and we came back to Bialyastok under a heavy downpour. Nobody admitted us again. Then we decided to come to Jewish baker.

You can't imagine how bad was our situation at that time, we took off our boots, dried them our and sold them to buy bread. Then we spend horrible days when we had no place to sleep. Even synagogue was completely full of people. There we met the Farber family who wanted to give us a place to sleep for a night but they had many louse. Then we ran to the rail station but there was no place too. We were wandering around this way until we get a job in the bathes where we could wash ourselves. My brother Moyshe knew this job before from Israel. From this time we slept at our workplace. In Bialyastok we met with many families from Wyszków: Asti and his family (I've heard they died from hunger in Russia later), Tchekhanogura and his family, the Shults family, Srebnik and his family, Shran with his son and daughter, Itche Baharav, Nayman with his son, Frayman and the Segal family who had a place to live. Many people from Wyszków found each other. We gave a place to sleep to others together with Moyshe Stolik. All were glad about this meeting. Ours from Wyszków were working and trading buying old clothes on the market and then selling them. Everyone who was from Wyszków let in others in the lines. My brother Moyshe couldn't be in Bialyastok any more and was pursuing every possibility to return to Kosow to my mother and sister. At this moment I've got a postcard from my family to return back to them. Also at this time Soviet authorities started registration. Everybody who wants to get a passport must stay in USSR and move forward because they didn't allow to stay in Bialyastok; others had to go back to Germans. Most of people signed to go back to their families who were left in Poland. Many families who went together with echelons further into Russia couldn't live there and came back to Bialyastok. These families signed to return back to Germans. Many people thought that it would be better in Poland in the end. But the end came actually. We were not allowed to go back. We started to grow accustomed to the new life. Everyone lived as one can. Some tragic night around 12 o'clock, everyone who didn't have a soviet passport was arrested. Immediately they were taken in the echelons to Siberia, into the jails and concentration camps.

Opening of Fire, September 1939
(Memories of a soldier in the Polish division)
by Naphtali Kretsmer, Tel–Aviv

Translated by Chava Eisenstein

The soldiers of our division, young people trained as bragging heroes at the expense of the Germans testify to meet them in occupied Berlin, deride and mock the Jewish citizens who encounter them at the stations.

However, already in Malkinia we witnessed with our own eyes the Germans air raiding: the soldiers turned solemn, many of them were injured, the laughter, the bragging was over, we neared the front.

Our First Fire Encounter

We reached Wyszkow in the evening, the streets and alleys were pitch-dark, there was great army clamor, civilians were loading quickly their possessions on wagons in order to leave the town. Only several Jews remained home locked up, peeking from the tiny holes in the shades with deep concern and fear. Only armed military groups are still active at protecting the city. It is a Polish September night, the cloud–covered moon appears suddenly out of the dark and lights up the town streets looking so calm and clean. It's chilly and cold all over, the autumn night dew appears as tears covering the entire ground. It seems, the names on the posters of the Jewish shops too, are shedding tears. What does the next upcoming day have for the owners of these Jewish names?

[Page 167]

After wandering for hours on, we were posted at the end of the street leading to Pultusk. We moved into one of the nice–looking houses, it was surrounded by a well–groomed garden with fruit trees and flowers, this house probably belonged to a Polish clerk who fled with his family. In a short while, the beautiful gardens turned into communication trenches and a unit for munitions and anti–tanks. Day and night, the Germans bombed the entire city, they only refrained from blasting the bridge. We would go out to secure the rail tracks, and the whole length of the road. The German army proceeded from Pultusk slowly and cautiously. For days the city reverberated from the raiding, aircraft thunder and the Polish anti–aircraft, at the end the order was announced: "to retreat"...

We had to draw back fast, then after, the Poles will blow up the bridge over the Bug. I was one of the heavy artillery machine section and before leaving the city the soldiers ravaged the Jewish homes and shops, in the shops remained empty boxes, matches, combs and mirrors. The soldiers boasted happily of the goods they seized. I too, entered one of the houses at the street corner, by the square leading to the bridge, I thought I might meet a Jewish face. I searched the store where everything was scattered on the floor. From the store, I went into an apartment, in one of the rooms stood beds and a crib, in the second room family pictures were strewn all over, only the wall carried the picture of the imposing figure of the grandfather gazing at the grandmother in the hanging picture. The table was covered with a white tablecloth, on it was salt, butter and bread scraps. Obviously, the family had left the house just now. My parents' home came to my mind, the room I was in, transformed into a mini–temple. I left the house in awe and looked on painfully at the room where life came to a sudden halt. The quiet was deafening, forecasting awful proceedings.

Our troop with all its outfit hurried towards the bridge, but soon after we were directed to the shore of the river, there we alighted on boats, crossing the sea under canon fire, about 50 meter before the bank we jumped into water and swam to the shore. The German "Messerschmitt's" showered us with fire, the bullets fell amid us in the water. Arriving at the banks we recovered somewhat and crawled with our weapons towards the high road. We made our way through overturned wagons on their cargo, dead human bodies mixed with wounded horses, we leaped and crossed the road into the woods.

Inflicting Death on the Running Civilians

After entrenching and taking placements in the forest, I was able to pause to observe what the Germans did to the population. This, even before setting boot in the town Wyszkow and its surroundings. It appeared that most Wyszkow Jews managed to escape two days earlier, some of them I met in the forest at the roadside, suffering hunger, shattered and exhausted, rumors came around saying, that the Germans crossed the river, and are encircling us. Towards evening, the pressure increased and the Germans began a non–stop raid on the fleeing civilian population and on the armed forces. The commotion of horses going wild, women screaming and yelling, crying children that lost sight of their parents, the racket of trees cracking and falling, and military commands, all mingled together. At last, the Poles realized - when many of them secretly awaited the Germans to come and save them from what is awaiting them. In the midst of all this chaos, a soldier told me, that he noticed a Jewess with her little girl, she is very weak and is barely alive. I looked for her and found her laying in a pit hungry and thirsty, I gathered some toast and water from my group and brought it to her, she said she hadn't eaten for two days, adding, her elder parents are in the forest exhausted and running out of strength. I gave her my ration of iron and advised her to run eastwards, she should not stay here.

At night, the forest began to burn. The shelling came stronger and closer. We were all losing our mind in the chaos and confusion.

Past midnight we were commanded to retreat towards Kaluszyn. For two weeks, day and night we were engrossed in combat whilst escaping from one "pit" to another. At the end of September, I found myself amongst thousands of Jews from the area, with a few Wyszkow Jews between them on a long cruel and failure of a journey to Prussia, around us were corpses, battered and abandoned all the way on the road and in the ditches.

May their souls rest in peace.

———————

The "Black Friday"
by Leibel Popowski, Buenos Aires
Translated by Pamela Russ

It is the first day of World War II. We had no idea what sort of catastrophe was going to come about. It was only on Shabbath in the evening, when darkness fell on our town, that the German planes flew overhead and dropped several bombs on a nearby gypsy camp. They had noticed a fire there. And this was only a taste [of what was to come].

Sunday morning the first refugees from western Poland appeared. We no longer went to work or to do business, but only listened to the radio and accompanied friends to the army. The shutters were covered with paper – but after the first explosion, the [the shutters] fell off. Ditches were prepared so people could protect themselves from the dropping bombs – but the ditches ended up not being used. We prepared food for two weeks – but we did not even have a chance to eat the provisions.

On Monday morning, we had the first air attack; there were not many dead and wounded. At around eleven in the morning, I went to Pultuski Street. The flow of refugees increased. Then the second air attack happened. When I ran back, yellow [blond?] Chaim (the gaiter maker), who was speaking to me a few minutes earlier – was already lying dead on the sidewalk. Next to him was lying another old man. The wounded were pleading for help.

After lunch, another air attack was repeated. Shaul Dan found his sister who was wounded. He ran to the infirmary and found no one there. Near their house there was a policeman lying on the ground. He died from the same bomb.

Tuesday morning, the Germans began to throw fire bombs. Everything was burning. People were running from one place to another. My father and I ran into the cellar.

[Page 168]

The bomb that exploded in the church square ripped off the door to our cellar. We left the cellar, and together with our mother went to Yankel–Dovid Shuster. In the afternoon, it became quiet. The fires spread. There were only a few people in the streets. The police had run away. One policeman told me: "It's time to run away!"

I quickly said to my brother Velvel, who was standing at the fishermen street:

"Tell our parents that I am running to Jadow to bring my cousin's horse and wagon. Then we will all go to Jadow, because it is quiet there."

I left, crossed the bridge, and went on my way. On the road, everything was on fire, even the grass. In Skuszew, I met Pulye Skarlat with his wife and daughter. Her neck was scarred with burn wounds. I helped them take her over to a farmer. They got into a wagon and left.

When I was halfway to Jadow, I met Yozef Krawczik. He told me that Jadow was also bombed and we decided to spend the night in the forest. In the morning, we went to search for food from the surrounding farmers.

In the forest, I found many Jews from Wyszkow. It seemed to me that the entire Jewish community had come into the forest. I didn't have the courage to ask about my parents. They told me that they had been here the entire night. In the morning, they had gone to Jadow. My heart was overjoyed, and I left to Jadow. On the way, there was another bombing. When we came to Jadow, I found out that my parents had gone to a more "secure" place. I came to them at night, with a few other men. We slept in an attic with hay. We saw burning fires at a distance.

We arrived to Jadow very early and "settled in" at friends' homes. Here there were also many Jews from Wyszkow and Pultusk. The very friendly Jadower Jews gave us a roof over our head. The bakers worked by day and night in order to provide the Jews with bread. If they were missing flour, they ran to the farmers in the surrounding villages, putting their lives at stake.

The Germans came into Jadow and took over the city without even one shot. Because of that, nothing was destroyed. The Germans announced that they had to leave because the Russians would be coming soon. We learned about this by reading a German newspaper. By that time, the Russians were already in Bialystok, Brisk, and were approaching the Bug River. For us, this was the best news.

In Jadow, we, a group of Jews, discussed among ourselves about running off to Wyszkow in the hope of maybe rescuing ourselves. On the way, we met Beryl Koval, who warned us:

"Come right back if you don't want the Germans to torture you as they did Leybish Pszeticki and the butcher. They too went home from Jadow. And more, there was nothing to find in Wyszkow. Everything there was destroyed. It was all one mountain of ash, mixed with dead bodies. The air was so fetid that even the German horses did not want to go through those places.

In Jadow, the Germans kept us in perpetual fear. They robbed, cut beards, and raped.

Finally, we received news that the Russians had arrived in Stok and in Kosow, but they were not coming to Jadow. I and my friend Motel Gzhende went to Stok and there found no Russians and no Jews. So we left to Kosow, and there was great joy there. The Red Army was already there. We went to a friend's home, and tired from the road, we went to sleep.

In the middle of the night, we heard the marching of the military. Our friend went out into the street and soon returned with the bad news that the Russians were retreating across the Bug River where the new border was going to be set up. So we also left during the night, because in the morning it might be too late. On the way to the Bug, we were drenched by the night's rainfall. In the morning, when we came to the Bug, the sun was shining. It was much easier for us; the Russians smiled at us ...

In the town Denir, on the other side of the Bug River, it was all happiness and celebration. Jews felt more secure because the Red Army would stay there. There was rumor that the border would stay open for a short time. You would be able to go back and forth. My friend did leave for Jadow in order to bring back his parents and my parents.

Meanwhile, I stayed with strangers, and I did not have any money to pay for their hospitality.

On the third day, not being able to wait any longer for my parents, I left for Bialystok to my cousins where I stayed until my parents and my brother Velvel and my sister's daughter also arrived. Then all of us left to a settlement not far from the city.

All the open halls [salons] in Bialystok, as well as the synagogues and *Batei Midrashim*, were packed with people from across the border who had run away. People slept on the bare floor. I went out to look for my acquaintances.

In about a week's time, the Russians announced that whoever wanted to go deep into Russia – could enlist. And immediately, those who had registered were in splendid wagons, with steel ovens, and cots for sleeping.

We arrived in Toloczyn, White Russia [Belarus], and began to acclimate to our new lives.

About a year and a half later, Germany already attacked the Soviet Union. I was drafted into the Red Army. I had to separate from my parents. Soon the German army invaded Toloczyn where my parents had remained. I never heard from them again.

[Page 169]

I took part in the fight with the Hitlerist mobs, and was wounded. In the Moscow hospital, where I was in the spring of 1944, I heard the news that the Red Army had liberated the city of Toloczyn. I immediately sent a letter to the city administration with a question about the fate of my parents. The answer was that they knew nothing...

With my parents were: my brother Velvel; my sister's son and daughter. Their parents had likely died in Warsaw. My oldest brother Moishe and his daughter, who lived in Luniniec (Kressen), where they went after leaving Wyszkow, were also killed by murderous hands.

Honor their memory!

The Nazi Murderers in Town
by Kh. A.
Translated by Pamela Russ

Wyszkow was taken over by the Germans soon after the fall of Warsaw. Their first job was to – rob from the Jews, and then take everything they could get their hands on, even furniture. In particular, they very much liked the bed linen. From almost each house, they took the pillows, blankets, bed covers. It was difficult to understand for what purpose they needed so much bed linen.

Then an order was given that no Jew was allowed to be out in the street. The order applied for several days. Later – a new order. All the Jews should assemble in the middle of the marketplace. Armed Germans ran through the houses like wild beasts, and herded the Jews together. When all the Jews were in the marketplace, they were chased behind the city. No one knew where they were going. Finally they were told to stop so that they could be chased into stables that were there. When the Jews filled up the barns, the murderers set fire to one of them. Huge flames flew up from all sides and thick clouds of smoke, mixed with the screams of the victims, flew up to the heavens. The Jews who were locked into the other stables tore open the gates and began to run. The Hitlerists opened a murderous shooting on those who were running. Many fell to their death, others were wounded. During that massacre, 77 Jews were shot and burned to death. Among them – eight Christians.

From the "V" "A" Materials in New York, Number 1140 Wyszkow

———————

Wyszkow in Flames
by Tzvi Yakov Gemora, New York
Translated by Pamela Russ

Friday, September 1, 1939, when the war broke out, Nazi airplanes appeared over the town. They didn't throw bombs, but we felt the tragedy in the first days of the war. On September 5, at five AM, Wyszkow was already in flames on all four sides. The city was shot up by machine guns. There were already many dead and wounded. Sadly, one person could not help the other. Everyone had to help himself as much as he could. Men searched for their wives; desperate women were searching for their husbands, and together, they searched for their children. A terrible wailing carried across the entire city – and everyone was running.

I am running through the street that held the large *Bais Medrash*. I see how the *Bais Medrash* is in flames, and the old sick people who were inside are screaming with desperate shouts:

"Save us!"

Tragically, they all died. The souls of the holy martyrs, along with the letters of the holy Torah, were carried by flames directly to heaven.

We are running again – and we look around. Many of our Wyszkower Jews are already gone. We run into the house where our Rav, of blessed memory, lived. We discuss with him what to do. It was hard to think of a way to save ourselves.

Later, a government official came to take away the Rav. When he left the city, he said goodbye to us, and tears were running down his face. He wished us that we should be helped. This scene with our revered Rav is difficult to describe.

We decided to leave Wyszkow. A crowd of Jews were leaving in the direction of the wooden bridge, to go into the forest, so that they could continue to run from there. When we were already on the bridge, in the middle of this terrible situation, we saw how the German airplanes were flying overhead and throwing down bombs.

[Page 170]

Fortunately, the bombs fell into the water. A few hours later, when we were already on the ground in the forest, we heard how the bridge was blown up. Later, people who were running out of the city had to take boats to cross to the other shore. In the forest, they said that the Nazis were already rampant in the city. The *Batei Midrashim, Batei Tefilos* [houses of prayer], *khassidim shtiebelech* [small, *khassidic* synagogues], were all burned down. A few days later, almost everything was destroyed by bombs, artillery shootings, and fires.

After four days of wandering in the forest, we arrived to the town of Jadowa. After about three days, the Nazis also arrived in Jadowa. The city was full of Jewish refugees from the surrounding areas. There was a great panic. There was nowhere to sleep at night. The streets were also filled with refugees. Because of the crampedness, everyone pushed themselves into attics and cellars. There was not enough food, no ability to wash oneself properly. Epidemics began to spread in Jadowa. Meanwhile, the Days of Awe [Rosh Hashana and Yom Kippur] arrived.

We received horrifying news. On Yom Kippur, the Wengrower Rav, of blessed memory, was killed. We decided to leave Jadowa right after Yom Kippur, and with great difficulty we struggled to the border.

Struggling with Death
by Lemel Rubin, Paris
Translated by Pamela Russ

The First Days

Tuesday, September 5, 1939, on the fifth day since the outbreak of the war, Wyszkow was bombed. Almost the entire population of the city ran across the bridge into the forest to seek protection. My family and I, as well as our neighbors – Rochel Frumowycz and her two daughters Chava and Faige, together with the Holdins, who had their own horse and wagon, stayed in hiding in the Wyszkower forest. You couldn't go any farther because there were too many people on the wagon. By chance, we met a Polak in the forest, from Przasnysz, who had two horses and a wagon. He did not want to go back, because the Germans were already in his town. So we agreed that he would make available to us his wagon and the horses, and for that we would take care of him and his four–footers [horses] all the way, and at the end of the trip we would pay him well.

Once again, we went on the road, but with a larger number of families: Asher Golanski with his wife and children; my brother–in–law Yosel Holand and his wife, and also my dear mother Liba–Roiza Rubin, who later died; Rochel Frumowycz, with her two children; Holand with his wife and children; Szniadower with his wife and children.

We left at night, but we were thinking: Maybe it would be right to go back? We knew that the city was almost completely burned down. The only thing left was the teacher Domb. Many residents left to Bialystok, Grodno, and to the small towns.

We rode at night, rested during the day, and remained in hiding. Eating became very difficult, and finding water was even worse. We drank from the puddles in the forest, fetid and filthy. These treks lasted eleven days.

As we went through Wengrow, we met the Wyszkower wealthy man Eli–Meyer Goldman, and took the opportunity to complain about the worth and worthlessness of the amassed possessions and estates that become nothing during times of war... At the same time, I told him that on the way, I had met another wealthy Wyszkower man, Yechiel–Meyer Rubin. He and his wife were roaming on foot, and looked like all the other refugees who had left our city.

We arrived in the town of Lachowicze. Since this place was actually on the border, it was impossible to remain here. Asher Golanski had his fellow businessmen in Lachowicze, with whom he did business, and they set us all up in a neighboring village. After staying there for three days, we happily decided to go back to Lachowicze, because the Red Army had entered the town. Now our sufferings had come to an end. We were freed.

At that time, we did not yet know what the new border would look like between Germany and Russia. All kinds of rumors were circulating. So, we stayed in Lachowicze, but thought that it would be right to send out a few people to Wyszkow. I had a particular interest in doing so because I had buried a lot of leather in my stall, and this was still a very valuable article, particularly for the Russians. My son had to go back to Wyszkow. But how, if there were no trains or buses traveling? Because of that, there were always groups of Soviet military on the highways. A pair of boots and a piece of leather enabled my son to board a Soviet military car and drive in the direction of Wyszkow. Other children and families, who were with us, went along with him.

[Page 171]

One week passed – and we had no news from the children. Our worry and unrest grew. We even had complaints about ourselves. We may have wanted to save our possessions, but with that we risked the lives of the children. Suddenly – great joy! The children had come back, but they recounted their terrible experiences. When they came to Ostrow, the city was already taken over by the Germans who dragged out several hundred Jews from their homes and began shooting. The children survived with their lives and ran off to Zombrowa, where the Russians were. There could no longer be any discussion of going to Wyszkow.

To Baranowicze

Later, the Wyszkower resident Yankele arrived in Lachowicze. He used to trade old things; he was the son–in–law of blond Faige the fishmonger. He said that a bomb had hit my stall and revealed the hidden merchandise that was then stolen by the Polaks. Now, there was no longer any interest in thinking about our possessions in Wyszkow. We decided to leave Lachowicze and go to Baranowicze.

In Baranowicze, I looked for familiar tanners and took to selling their leather, and I was assured of some income. Some time later, I began working in my own vocation, sent the children to gymnasium, and we lived with the hope that the war would end and we would return to our homes.

Meanwhile, the Soviets announced that whoever wanted to return to their homes could register with the Germans. But those who did not want to return had to get Soviet passports and become Russian citizens, and they would no longer be allowed to return to their original homes. This announcement evoked great upset from the refugees. It was difficult to decide. Meanwhile, the designated amount of time had passed, and as is usual, a part decided to stay, and a part – to return home.

Since I was working as a tanner of leather and skins in a government company that was active in the entire province, and which was able to support its fifteen families; being assured of an income and a home; and also because of the fact that the children were studying in a gymnasium – we decided to stay in Baranowicze. On the other hand, my family decided to go back. But what happened then is today known to everyone: Those who had registered to return, on one dark night were told to put together small packages for themselves, and in specially prepared echelons [transport trains], they were taken away ... deep into Russia. The letters that we later received from those unfortunate ones told of hard labor and work camps with thugs, about starvation and inhuman treatment. And for those who survived, they were envious of those who had registered themselves to remain on the other side of the border. From Poland, that was occupied by the Germans, news arrived as well as tragic information about persecutions, starvation, pain, and suffering. With these terrible reports, we, those who were set up and secure in Baranowicze, felt very lucky and optimistic. But here too, things came to an end.

Summer 1941, the Germans attacked the Soviet Union. Now we were in the same situation we were in Wyszkow in 1939: bombings, fires, panic, roads filled with refugees, homes that were destroyed. Where to hide?

We left the city and we began to go on foot, with the others. The roads were bombed, and only at night was it safer to move. We were not far from Slonim. We heard that there was fighting around the city, bombing, artillery shootings. For a few days, we lay in the fields, without food or drink. We were terrified to even lift our heads. The city was burning. Only when it calmed down and it seemed that the people could return home – that was when we left the fields and all the other hiding places. Now the Germans already occupied the city.

In Slonim

In the first days of the German occupation, there was relative quiet. The impression was that despite the war operations, everything was returning to normal life. But one night, those remaining from the Soviet military, who were hiding in the surroundings, conducted a surprise armed attack on the building where the German military headquarters was housed. Many officers and soldiers of Hitler's army were killed, the building was blown up, and the Red Army retreated. The following day, the Germans decided to avenge the night attack. Hundreds of soldiers invaded each house and ordered each man to leave the house immediately. With raised hands, running, he had to get to the assembly place at the edge of the city. The Germans were convinced that the attack had been conducted by the civilian residents of the city – and for that all the adult men would be punished.

I and my son Yankel, with raised hands, also ran to the assembly point – a large place at the edge of town, enclosed with barbed wire, where there were already 20,000 people gathered. Among them were many Russian soldiers and officers. They said that even a Russian general was among the prisoners.

This large crowd of people were kept under the open sky, without food or drink. Everyone had to sit on the ground. Standing up risked being shot on the spot.

The day passed, night arrived and dawn foretold of the arrival of another day. It seems that some women managed to successfully convince the German commandant to allow them to bring food to their husbands. In the morning, some women and girls appeared with baskets of food. My daughter Manya, who came to me together with my son – was not allowed in. Only when she pleaded with the priest who was close to that place (he came as a matter of interest in the fate of his faithful Catholics, the detained Polaks and White Russians), she was able to give us the food.

[Page 172]

Another twenty–four hours passed, and finally they released people one by one. Each person was carefully searched and any valuables were taken away. Each person who was freed was badly beaten by a "blaze" of soldiers set out in a row.

Now, so–called normal life began in the city. The Germans exhibited interest and understanding of my work and even offered me the chance to be a broker for leather and skins, as I had done for the Soviets. The tanners were permitted to do their work, and it was declared that my overseer was a German. The company, where I now worked, had grown and now had 175 workers and employees who regularly received a salary.

When the Germans set up a *Judenrat* [Jewish council], an unrest befell the Jewish people in town. It became apparent that after the various decrees and dictates, the day of killing all the Jews was not far. Meanwhile, all the Jews were forced into hard labor, from darkness to darkness. When we came back from the slave labor camps, there was not enough food to satisfy us and no place to rest because there were several families living in each room. The Germans had made sure that there would be hunger in the ghetto, neediness, overcrowding, sickness, and demoralization, and on top of all of that, the terrible, the unwanted, the unknown that hung in the air about which everyone talked and which everyone sensed...

Once, the *Judenrat* was ordered to assemble 60 capable Jewish young men and they were taken away in an unknown direction for labor. A rumor spread in the city: that they were now digging huge, deep ditches. It might be – against tanks, and could be – who knows. Maybe these were common graves for the Jews of Slonim?

Some information reached us that not long before, 200 Jews had been removed from a small neighboring town. They were shot and buried in large ditches. We believed that our fate would be the same.

Suddenly, a decree was put forth about special permits that would be given out by the German military headquarters. And those who will not receive these permits – will be deported. A wild rush for these permits began in the city. Some with money, some with *protekzia*, some who could have made themselves useful to the Germans – these received the papers. The unfortunates, who did not receive the papers – and there were many of these – began to live in deathly fear. I, as a skilled laborer, received the permit. Dangerously, I took in another seventeen people into our small room. They apparently were not able to get the permits. Among these people were the Wyszkower Rokhel Frumowycz and her two daughters.

One month passed like that. Twenty–two people slept like that in one room on the floor. In the morning, those who were hiding went to their houses, but they spent the nights with us.

The First Roundup

October 14, 1942, the ghetto was surrounded on all sides by Germans and Ukrainians. Chasing out the Jews – the elderly, women, children, unemployed men – was done in a very brutal, cruel manner. Even before the unfortunate 10,000 Jews were taken away to the ditches, Jewish blood already flowed in the streets from the shootings and murders. We, those remaining, knew what happened to our unfortunate brothers and sisters. The mass graves, in a few days, shifted, those Jews who were not shot or those who were half dead were breathing under the heavy earth covering ....

Nine people were successfully able to come back into the city – heavily wounded. They had lost blood, and we gave them first aid and set them up in the hospital. The Germans found out about those who were saved, and then in the morning they came and took those out of the hospital, back to the ditches, shot them, and buried them.

After that, everything returned to the "normal" way. Those Jews who remained were once again herded off to slave labor. In the German newspaper, there was news that a few thugs had killed the Jews in the city, but they, the Germans, chased away the thugs...

Several weeks later, the Jewish population was given an order, that they would have to raise 100 kilo of gold. The entire *Judenrat* was completely mobilized for this action. With great efforts, they managed to put together the required amount... Again, we lived with the illusion that now they would not bother us anymore.

Nine months passed after that great slaughter. During that time, Jews began building all kinds of hiding places, bunkers, shelters, organized cellars and attics, and built double walls.

Every morning at six AM, all the Jewish workers and skilled laborers were assembled at a roll call in Zhabinka Plaza. After counting the shoemakers, tailors, tanners, carpenters, mechanics, and other vocational workers, they were placed into separate groups and taken away to work. Often, the Germans themselves put out rumors that the ghetto would be liquidated on a specific day – but did not carry this out. The goal of the Germans was to confuse and disarm us so that we should never really know how we stood in the world. For the residents of ghetto, the life of fear and hunger was already long ago made awful, and more than one looked upon death as a liberation. But the majority fought death, wanting to conquer it and remain alive.

[Page 173]

The Second Roundup

The murderers had already long before placed a death sentence on the Jewish nation. One day (I cannot remember the date), they surrounded the ghetto and through loudspeakers they called out the group leaders of the Jewish skilled workers and after that, all the ghetto dwellers. They were told they would be left alive as long as they appeared in the roundup. All they had to do [they said] was to count, calculate, and estimate. The Jews felt that now the murderers really had in mind to finally liquidate the ghetto. Those who were sitting in the bunkers decided not to move from there.

Nonetheless, the Germans succeeded, especially with the help of the group leaders, to lure out some of the Jews from their hiding places with the intention to include them – but my daughter blocked my way, and categorically stated that she would not allow me to go. "*Tateshi* [Father], don't believe them. They just want to fool the people and take them to their graves..."

I gave in ... and returned to the bunker where seventeen people were hiding, among them – the Rav of Kozlowszczyzne (?).

From outside, we heard the choking sounds of the roll call that had begun. The Germans and their helpers from the local population systematically searched each house. Wherever there was a thought that Jews could be hiding – they set fire to that place. We also heard shots, wild screams of the thugs and wailing of the victims. The air was constantly being sliced through with shooting and screams.

This mass murder of Jews lasted for eight days – these were Jews who had been saved from earlier roundups and from other horrifying deaths that the Germans thought of in order to destroy our nation. There was no food in our hiding place, no bread, and the main thing – no air to breathe. I couldn't tolerate it any longer, so I decided to go out to breathe some fresh air. I went onto the roof and from there looked out. In front of me, there played out a terrifying picture. The entire street and Zhabinka plaza were completely burned down. Some people were still walking about, but there were no Jews. The Jews were taken in cargo trucks – likely to clean up the dead, and probably these cleaners would also be shot. By that time we were well versed in the ways of the murderers.

I went back down into the cellar and recounted what my eyes had seen. Meanwhile, one of the women there had given birth to a child. Everyone there understood that such a newborn little bird threatened us all. The mother, weakened and exhausted from the birth and from the difficult conditions in the cellar, gathered her last energies and – suffocated the child. At night, she carried it into the yard.

Once again, I could not stand being in the cellar – and went out into the fresh air. I decided to go to the engineer Paskornik, who was my chief. He worked with all the tanneries in the city. In his house, all I found were dead bodies that had not been cleaned away. The city looked dead. When I returned to the cellar, I bumped into an armed Ukrainian who pointed his gun at me and then arrested me. Then he asked me to remove my new, good boots. He took them away, and told me to go to the police commander ... But on the way, he told me to tell him where I had hidden money or gold, and to reveal the hiding places of the Jews. If I would do both those things, then he would allow me to live. Well, I thought, you won't seem me do this... But how will my wife and children ever know that had happened to me? "You know what," I said to the Ukrainian, "I don't live far from here. I have a pair of gold earrings hidden there. Come, I'll give them to you."

He came into the house with me, where the hiding place was under the floor. Really, I did look for the earrings and at the same time was speaking to the Ukrainian in a loud voice so that my wife and children would know that I had been captured. Understandably, I did not find any jewelry – and he took me to the commander. And from there, to prison.

There I met many people. Jews that I knew, who were discovered in all kinds of hideouts. Their fate, exactly like mine, was clear: to be shot near the ditches. I strongly regretted that because of one thoughtless misstep I had fallen into the hands of the murderers. Everyone had warned me not to go out!

Eight o'clock in the morning, some cars drove by and some officers began to take away the Jews who were over fifty years old. Suddenly, among the Germans, I see the head man of our business to whom I would often give from our tannery the best leather for boots, for a coat, and for other things. I went over to him and said:

"*Herr* Shifman, I have to go to the slaughterhouse to get the skins for salting..."

"Yes, *Herr* Rubin, go right ahead," he replied, measuring me up with an expressive [understanding] glance.

[Page 174]

"Your chief Paszkornik is waiting on the other side of the fence and he will take you to work..."

Who can describe my joy and deep relief at such an enormous switch? I left the prison yard where the unfortunates were already loaded up to be shot. Paszkornik was actually standing at the gate, and when I reached him, I laughed and cried for joy. The first thing he told me empowered me even more so: My son Yankel was alive and well! I asked Paszkornik that he go to my bunker and tell my wife and children the news, and also that I was saved from a sure death. Paszkornik had the right to go about freely around town. I, along with a group of others, marched off to work.

The following day, the Germans ordered the one hundred Jews who were still alive to sleep in the house where I lived and where the hiding place was under the floor. Only men were allowed in that room. So, we organized the women in the cellar while the men, in cramped quarters and filth, had to squeeze themselves into one room and sleep there after a day of hard labor.

Return to Bialystok

Suddenly, they no longer are assembling anyone for work. No other reason, but now they were keeping us only for murdering. What to do? I found out that there was a Polak in town who, for payment, took people over to Bialystok, to the local ghetto that was still standing. With great difficulty and challenges, I looked for the Polak, and for the price of $5,000 we agreed that first he would take my children there – my son Yakov Ben–Tzion and my daughter Miriam. When we received a note from them that everything went well, we too – the parents, and our youngest daughter Itka, decided to go there as well.

For ten nights, we wandered across fields and forests, because during the day we had to be in hiding. With our last bit of strength, we finally arrived in the Bialystok ghetto. Conditions here were exactly the same as in the Slonim ghetto: hunger, need, sickness, shooting in the street, roundups, and on top of everything – the unknown of the following day, because even today was always filled with chaos. Here they also spread all kinds of rumors and news, from so-called certain wells of information, that had one goal: to disorient and disarm the already downtrodden Jews.

In the Bialystok ghetto, we met Chaim Shlomo, Golde, and Baltche Frumowycz. Together we set ourselves up in a bunker and agreed to hide ourselves there, since we already had behind us the experiences of the Slonimer ghetto. After being here for nine months, notices appeared in the streets that all residents should appear in a designated place in order to register and be assigned to work. We already knew what this registration meant and we warned the Bialystok Jews. But they did not believe us. "What do you mean? They'll just go ahead and shoot people or burn them? They need us as workers." That tragic day repeated everything that had happened in Slonim. They really did count the assembled Jews, sorted them, but also beat them and tortured them – until they were loaded onto the prepared trains that took them away to Treblinka...

In the evening, the Jews, as shadows, crept out of the bunkers and saw the emptiness because of the bareness of the houses and deported residents. With broken hearts, we returned to our bunkers. A few times a day, and a few times at night, we heard over our heads how the Germans and Ukrainians were searching for Jews that were hiding. Our bunker, especially the entrance, was well disguised. In the evenings, sometimes we allowed ourselves to go out for air.

Once I had an upset when I was outside. I bumped into the Polak Janek, the same one who had taken my children to Bialystok. He was in contact with Jewish partisans who were in the forests. He knew where my children were hiding. He was ready to take me, my wife, and my cousin to the partisans on the condition that I would dig out a radio station in our hiding place with which one could send information, and then take the information into the forest to the partisans. I agreed, even though I knew the huge risks involved. Janek came to me that night and took me over to his house on the rooftop. I waited there until three AM, when Marila would come, the contact for the partisans, and together we would have to carry out the work of digging up and transporting the radio station. But instead of Marila, the Gestapo came. The arrested Janek and took him away. I remained on the roof, and my only thought was: How will I get back to the ghetto, to my dear ones?

It was already daybreak when I jumped down from the roof, and with fearful heartbeat, from side street to side street, I managed to get back into the ghetto and sneak into my bunker. I knew that we could not stay here much longer. I knew the address of my children, so all three of us decided to sneak out to the children, and then after that – to the partisans.

On the second day, we left the ghetto through the same small door, through which Janek had already taken me...

The Tragic News

All night, we moved with the greatest caution and terror. The goal was: to reach the children and stay with them. At the designated place, about twenty kilometers behind Bialystok, there was no one. So we went into the forest, sat down at a tree, and considered the situation. Our hearts beat more quickly and nervously, but still we did not lose hope. We knew that my son should have been hiding at the farmer Malinowsky, who did not live far from the village. But how do we get there, if there are so many dangers on the roads? I decided to risk it. I took a pair of boots under my arms to give the impression that I was a shoemaker who was carrying his work to the farmer – and I left to the village.

[Page 175]

The farmers who knew me and who met me on the way advised me not to go to Malinowsky. But the desire to see my children was greater than anything else – and I knocked at Malinowsky's door, gave all the right signals, and asked for my son, daughter, and another two children that should have been with him. And now came the terrible news: All four children were shot by the Germans near the bridge...

After that, I do not know how I went back into the forest, to my wife and children. Instead of calming them down, in my anguish I said that I did not want to live anymore, and the best thing would be – to hang myself on a tree. But both women cried and pleaded that I not leave them to themselves. Without me, they too had nothing to live for. We decided to wait until nightfall and I would once again go to Malinowsky. When I came to him the second time, he became angry as to why I was making him crazy and making him risk his life. I begged him, asking if he knew where the farmer Milewsky lived, because once my son had prepared a shelter there. Malinowsky agreed to take me to Milewsky, but with the condition that I not say who showed me the way.

When I knocked at Milewsky's door, a tall, strong farmer answered the door. I was frightened simply by his appearance. In answer to my question about whether he knew where my son was, he said that he did not know, and he also confirmed that at the bridge in Zlotegorje four Jews were shot – two men and two women. Once again, my heart constricted at this tragic news. Now there was no hope of ever again seeing the children. I asked the farmer if he would consider taking us in since he had a prepared bunker. He did not want to hear of it. But seeing my determination he told me to come in and then said he would ask his wife what to do. I told him I would pay him well for the hiding place – and finally, they agreed to take us into the attic over the barn because the bunker was already filled, and they agreed to prepare the attic within a few days.

Once, in the middle of the night, I decided to go out of the bunker in order to stretch and get some clean air. I saw light in the hut of our rescuer, and through the open door, I heard all kinds of voices with the worst, cruel words: "So, where are you hiding those three Jews? You've got one man and two women. If you give them up, we won't do anything to you." And again, curses, taunts, and ugly words. They are pushing the farmer with the worst, but Milewsky declared categorically that there are no Jews in his place. On the contrary, let them go and search. Truthfully, a while ago there was a Jew here – but he chased him away.

I quickly ran back to the bunker and told my wife and her cousin about the uninvited guest. We were quiet in the hiding place, filled with anxious expectation and tension. Soon, over our heads, we heard noise, speaking. They took out the horse, and someone banged with a stick at the entrance to the hideout. Later, we heard how the voices were carried outside. There too – there was a search, talking, threats, abusive talk. Finally, it was quiet. In the bunker we were frozen from this experience.

In about a quarter of an hour, our cover was lifted, and Milewsky said:

"I'm sure you heard what happened here. I don't want to experience such a thing again. I'm very sorry, but you'll have to leave here. I will no longer – keep you..."

We asked him where to go; to whom to turn? His answer: He has no suggestions for us. He does not want to risk his life.

There was no other choice but to leave his bunker and once again to be homeless. The dark of night enabled us to go to the forest nearby. There, the three of us sat all day, without food, without drink. Everyone shivered with cold.

Once again, it was night. We decided that I would go to Milewsky to ask for help. When the farmer saw me, he began to scream; why am I playing with his life. I should never come back to him. But my excuse was that three people were in the forest without food, without shelter, exposed to all the dangers. He was a good person. Until now, he did not disclose us to the murderers. Why this sudden change? I asked him to take us to a certain Szimanka, a good peasant. She was hiding a Jewish girl (her name was Bialystocka). Also, I asked him if first he could go to Szimanska alone and tell her about us. We would wait for the results of the discussion. The farmer agreed to partially fulfill the request: only to find the peasant. He told us meanwhile to go back into the forest and then the next evening he would bring her address and then take us there.

[Page 176]

Milewsky kept his word. He appeared in the forest the next evening, bringing bread and milk, and then after our hearts were revived from the bit of food, he told us to come with him. After traveling for a few kilometers, we came to Szimanska's hut. I knocked at the window. Her son appeared and did not want to talk to us. I told him that there was a Jewish girl in his place, Bela Bialystocka, and that we brought money from her parents. When he first heard these words, the young peasant denied everything, saying no one was hiding there. But after some reconsideration, he decided to call his mother.

She too at first denied the fact that she was hiding a Jewish girl, but once we said that we would give the money only to Bela, she finally allowed us to go into her house, and from there she called out to the cellar for the girl to come. She was very happy to see us, and she already knew the tragic fate of her mother and sister who had died together with my son and daughter (all four were hiding in one bunker).

Now I began to plead with the Christian to have mercy on us and hide us in his house. Understandably – for payment. But all talk was for nothing. Szimanska and her son would not hear of it at all. I went out to my wife and cousin and told them that staying here was not even a thought. So we began to plead with Milewsky to have mercy on three fugitives and again show his humanity by taking us back. But the farmer would not even hear of it. He left quickly, leaving us outside, in a dark, cold night.

In Grobnik

Our confusion was great. Only our cousin did not lose herself. She said that we could not allow ourselves to fall apart, but we had to find a way out. "Let's go to Janina. She once promised to hide your son. Who knows, maybe the children are with her!" On that cold night, we left to go to the village Grobnik, but as we approached a small forest, both women declared that they would not go any further because their exhaustion had depleted them. In fact, they soon fell asleep on the ground, under a tree. But the entire night, I stayed near them and could not shut my eyes. In the morning, just as daylight broke, we began our long trek.

When we encountered a peasant, I asked how to get to the Wiezna main road. In order to reach Grobnik, you had to cross the bridge in Wiezna – a small town not far from Lomze.

The trek to Grobnik took two nights. We could not go during the day, and even at night a thousand dangers lurked. Nonetheless, we arrived in the village safely, and only now did a dangerous inquiry about Janina Wendilowska begin. They told us that she lived at the edge of town, around swamps. It was very difficult to get there. One peasant allowed his son to take us there. We thanked him warmly, and finally reached the hut. The woman Janina did not want to open the door right away, but while talking through the window, I reminded her that we had been here about nine months ago, had left some pyjamas and shirts here, and then she had allowed the children to stay with her. Tragically, the children had died, and now we asked to stay with her for a little while. Her first question was whether anyone knew that we had come here. Because we knew that a young boy had brought us here, she categorically said no to us. Her reasoning was that we were already sentenced to death, so why should she risk her own life and hide us? The Germans burn down any huts where they find Jews, and the peasant and his family are shot on the spot. I answered her:

"Listen here, *Frau* Janina. I'll tell you the whole truth. We told the peasant that allowed his son to show us the way here that we had come from Jedwabne where all the Jews had been killed. We want now to go to Wendilowska to get a few things that we had left there. We are living in the forest, and in order to survive the winter we have to come into the village from time to time. I understand your situation, but we also have to live. So, I propose this plan to you: We'll leave for a week and go into the forest, and during that time, you'll look around the village and decide whether you want to hide us or not."

She agreed. It was midnight, and she told us to come into her house. She gave us food, and told us to rest before we continued on our way. It seems that this Christian did not want to completely abandon us and at about four in the morning, she awoke us and told us that she had another plan. In the morning, she would send her brother Julik into the village Rostek, to see how it was going there. When he would return, she would decide whether we could stay or whether she would tell us to leave.

She took us into the attic of the barn. We stretched out on the hay, and at that moment we are the happiest people. More so, that the peasant woman brought us food and that her words were very sincere and compassionate. She appeared again in midday and reported that the news from Rostek was good, and she said that we could stay. Our joy was indescribable. But she became very frightened when we heard a warning from below to hide in the hay and lay perfectly still because the Germans were coming. The murderers did come, but this time they were not looking for the three Jews in hiding. They were just conducting a raid and grabbing the men from the village for work. When the Germans left, they let us know right away, and we breathed freely. Our lives were saved. Especially since now the good-hearted peasant said we could stay with her.

[Page 177]

That's how we were in hiding in the barn for two years. I am not able to give all circumstances of this long period of time that was rich and stormy with events, inner battles, fear of death, and also – many comical moments. I only know that thanks to Janina Wendilowska and her children, three Jews were saved from certain death. Right after the liberation, and also in later years, with all my strength, I tried to show my gratitude to the children, helped marry them off, rewarded them with everything, and to this day, I maintain a correspondence with them, and often send them gifts from Paris. I still hope to visit Poland in order to once again express my gratitude to these Christians who in those dark times demonstrated humaneness and refinement.

About the Fate of Other Wyszkower

In the town of Inzewycz, as refugees from Wyszkow, there were: Moishe Stelung with his wife Esther and their little Itzele; Mindel Feinzeig and her two children from Grajewe; Skarlat Fulje, Rivka, and their son. They all died there, glorifying the Name of God.

In the Slonim ghetto, the following died glorifying the Name of God: Itche Najman, Binek Branstajn, Avremel Zawiszanski (Yankel Katzav [butcher]'s son–in–law), Bunim Branstajn. In the period of the ghetto in Slonim, once Henoch Kaluski came to me and told me that he, his wife, their son and daughter–in–law and small child were hiding in a large forest not far from the town of Biten. The joy of meeting Kaluski at that time was tremendous. He was particularly happy about the hearty meal that he ate. When I asked the question about where were the drops [for medical purposes] that he always carried with him, he replied that because of the conditions in the forest, he could not avail himself of drops or medication. I offered that he remain with me, but he declined with the reasoning that everyone would die in the ghetto, but in the forest he might still have a chance to live. We parted with great emotion, and I put twenty breads, meat, and products on the sled, and together with Itche Najman, who was with me the entire time, we went into the forest to those Jews who were hiding. Kaluski told me that his wife died in the forest.

[Page 177]

In the Years of Misfortune and Anguish
by Khana Srebro – Lod, Israel
Translated by Pamela Russ

1.

My current memories are but a small portion of the sufferings and pain that I experienced in the days of Hitler. Their beginnings – in the days of September of the year 1939, when the German airplanes on the Pultusk highway were shooting at the fleeing Jews of Pultusk and other towns. They were running to Wyszkow with the hope that here they would be more secure. A young Polish boy shot at the airplanes through a window.

It seems that it was not enough for the Germans to bomb Wyszkow from the air. As they entered the city, they set fire to it from all sides. We did not know where to run. Tongues of fire spread all around. Everything was burning. How could we save ourselves?

I, my mother, and two sisters, ran out of our house and went to the brick house of Yankel–Duvid Pszeticki, and hid in the cellar there. From the street, you could hear the screams of the wild Germans:

"Cursed Jews! Who fired those shots?"

The Polaks told the Germans that it was the Jews who had shot. The brown–clad bandits grabbed hold of the fleeing Jews, herded them together on the marketplace and there shot all the men, women, and children. This was the first mass slaughter of the Wyszkow Jews. At that time, they died either from the flames of fire or from the German bullets. And those who were not killed instantly by bullets were buried alive. Innocent Jewish blood flowed in the town.

The group of residents that was then in Pszeticki's cellar heard in deathly fear, or sometimes even saw what was going on in the streets. The men had donned their tallis [prayer shawls] and tefilin [phylacteries] and were praying to God. Outside, children were searching for their parents, and parents called for their missing children by name. But even that lasted only until a murderous bullet reached them.

The shooting and fires lasted until late in the night. When it got dark and things calmed down in town, those many who were hiding in the cellar began to crawl out and run. I, my mother, and my sisters, went out into the streets where many dead bodies lay. We did not recognize anyone. The darkness was lit only with the flames of the burning town. They followed us with shots, yet we were successfully able to reach the bridge – and from there, the open highway. The overcrowding there was extraordinary. Fugitives with horses and wagons, entire families on foot, some with parcels, some without any baggage, were wandering in the dark night. From many, you could hear shema yisroel [prayer recited when pleading for help from God or when facing death], and that's how it went the entire night.

[Page 178]

A group of partisans and those living in the forest:
Shloime Szlyzaner, Khana Wengel, Khaya–Soroh Szczanko

Also, at dawn we saw these masses of people roaming around without a goal, without a direction. I could hardly walk. I was exhausted and when I fell down depleted, my sisters would pick me up and beg me not to show any weakness at this time, but said I should muster all my energies and keep going. Beaten, starved, and thirsty, we dragged ourselves to Wengrow. In one Jewish house, they gave us some food and also a place to spend the night. In general, the Wengrower Jews received us warmly. Here, we found many Wyszkower families in the same situation that we found ourselves. One person asked the other if he had seen his father, mother, sister or brother, because many families were lost or separated. And when the answer was negative, people cried terribly and poured out their bitter hearts.

Our situation was a terrible one – without money, without belongings, because everything was burned along with the house. In Wengrow, we found our brother Avrohom Wengel. He did not know where his wife and children were. They disappeared and he did not know anything about them. We begged him to come with us, but in his determination to find his lost family, he refused our request. He must find his wife and children. He left us – forever. He too, died as a victim of the bestial murder that the Germans threw over our nation.

My mother had a sister in Komorow, near Ostrow–Mazowieck. We decided to get ourselves there. Maybe it would be calmer there. So, we took to the road. We moved at night, and during the day we stayed in the forests. When we came to Komorow, we found our family who took us into their home and helped us with whatever was needed. But the Germans were already here, even in this small town. They gave an order that all those who had come from another place should leave immediately. So once again, we had to take our walking staff in hand and leave. Now we went to Zambrow which, according to the German–Soviet entente, belonged to the Soviets. After a strict interrogation, we crossed the border point and safely came to Zambrow, and from there – to Bialystok.

2.

In these large cities, the refugees were set up in the Batei Medrashim and in the synagogues. Each family had its corner. Once, a Jewish Bialystok woman came into the Beis Medrash where we were, and she took a liking to me as a tutor for her child. She hired me, and then also sent me two more families, who also hired my sisters, but none of them permitted us to bring along our mother, even though they did provide food for her.

Later on, the Russians began to register people for work deep in Russia, and also for receiving passports. After standing in line for many hours, I was able to register to go to Russia. In a huge train, I arrived in Chelyabinsk in the Urals. We were given lodging and work. I – in an office, my two sisters – carrying bricks. Later, they took me to a school to study. It would all have been fine if not for the fact that at night we had to stand in line for bread and food, and then during the day – work.

My friend Leybel Januszewycz remained in Bialystok. He later came to Dereczin, because they did not permit refugees to remain in Bialystok. In his letters to me, he always asked that I come back, and he even sent me money for traveling expenses. He assured me that later I would even be able to bring over my mother and sisters. Then, we, along with another Wyszkower, Mordechai Jagoda, decided to leave Chelyabinsk at the time of school vacation. And that's exactly how it was.

When we arrived in Kiev, they detained us for three weeks and then finally sent us to Dereczin. I set myself up with the family Januszewycz. I had not yet rested from the far and difficult trip, when the NKVD [Communist Secret Police] arrested me and sent me to Slonim. It appears that there was an informer. I sat in the Slonim prison for several weeks, and when my case came up, I defended myself [so emotionally], that my speech could have moved even a rock. In fact, it worked. Almost all of the accused were sentenced to exile, and I was lucky to be let free. When I returned to Dereczin, it was already 1941.

[Page 179]

3.

On June 22nd, 1941, the Hitlerists invaded Russia. Immediately, we felt the war in Dereczin. Here too, as in Wyszkow two years earlier, the airplanes continually circled over the town and threw their devastating bombs. Again, dead, again wounded, terrified, and helpless people with children. Once again, days and hours of fear, confusion, hunger and pain. Until – the Germans entered.

The created Judenrat [Jewish Council] had to collect the number of Jews that had registered earlier for all kinds of hard labor and demeaning work. The young men were sent to dig deep ditches. (Among them – the Wyszkower were: Leybel Januszewycz, Duvid and Leybel Flude, the Aldok brothers.) But then no one knew that these would be our graves. The young girls cleaned the streets. For this, you received a few grams of bread.

There were a few Wyszkower families in Dereczin: Chava Elboim and her elderly mother, Yankel Grinberg's children, the Aldok family. I lived with the family Januszewycz. At that time, I became acquainted with a family Rozenzweig. He was a doctor in the Derecziner hospital. He was able to get me in to work in the hospital – and I no longer had to clean the streets.

It was only in the hospital that I was finally able to see the full horror of the war. Not far from Dereczin, there was a terrible slaughter between the retreating Soviet military and the German army. In the slaughter field, there lay hundreds of dead, wounded, without hands, without legs, with wounded limbs or ripped open bellies. Doctor Rozenzweig received an order to collect the wounded German soldiers and to take care of them in the hospital. We, a group of Jewish girls, assisted him in this difficult work.

In the same hospital, there were wounded Soviet officers and soldiers. You have to remember that this was just at the beginning of the war when the Germans still permitted you to collect the wounded enemy soldiers after a battle. Doctor Rozenzweig worked day and night, operating on and taking care of all the sick, without exception. Once he operated on the two Soviet officers, Boris Bulak and Fiedja Komarov. For the first, a piece of shrapnel had torn off a finger until the bone. I assisted in the operation by handing the instruments to Doctor Rozenzweig. Everything turned out well.

I was busy in the hospital almost twenty–four hours, each day. My earnings allowed me to assist the Wyszkower families.

In the German prison there was also a Ukrainian nurse with the name Tonya [later in this chapter referred to as "Sonya"]. She behaved very poorly toward the sick, and was even very stingy with the little bits of food. It seems that because of that, the Germans had placed her as the head nurse. When I asked her for some food for the sick people, she answered me in Russian: "They can all die!" Obviously, she meant the Russian sick, because she would not have dared to speak like that about the German sick ones. When there were peasants and their families from the surrounding areas in the hospital, from time to time they would also give me some food products. With those, I helped the wounded Soviets, and for that they were very grateful to me. But as soon as they became well, the Germans sent them off to the concentration camps for hard labor and – their death.

4.

At the beginning of 1942, the ghetto in Dereczin was created. All the Jews were closed in there with strict orders not to leave that designated region. From the rumors that circulated in the town, and also from the German indications, we understood that this ghetto was the beginning of the liquidation of the Jewish population. We began to think of fleeing. Without mercy, the Germans shot every Jew who was found outside the ghetto. But you had to leave the ghetto. We suffered from hunger because of the amount of food the Germans gave each Jew. Because of that, we risked our lives and snuck out to the farmers in order to exchange the last shirt or the last dress for a piece of bread. But many of those who risked their lives died from a bullet shot by a German.

The Hitlerist cruelties increased. In the town, we felt as if the rope around the throats of the Jewish population kept getting tighter. Also, the Soviets wounded from the war were becoming restless. I helped them as much as I could. But now it became a reality to try to help them escape, because the Germans would always control the conditions of the sick with Dr. Rozenzweig. As soon as someone became better, he was sent away in an unknown direction. We were worried about the fate of Boris Bulak and Fiedja Komarov. So it was decided that they should run away at night. The hospital was guarded by Germans. They shot those who tried to escape – but these two were successfully able to reach the forest that was not far from the hospital. When they were still in the hospital, the escaped officers promised me and Dr. Rozenzweig help if we would ever need it. But for now, we did not know where they had disappeared.

[Page 180]

The dug out ditches not far from Dereczin waited for their Jewish victims. The Germans would always take groups of Jews – and no one ever saw [these groups] again. When a few weeks passed, and those people did not come back, their fate was clear. People began to escape from the ghetto. When the Germans found out about this, a strict order was given that those who had run away should return. Many actually did come back to the Derecziner ghetto. Among them – was Duvid Fluda from Wyszkow. They were taken to the ditches and shot.

Esther Dvoira Fluda, wife of Duvid, all the years, did not have any children. On that day when they took away her husband, she gave birth to a little girl. The happy grandparents, Hershel–Mechel and Lieba Fluda, with great joy and excitement, went to the German administration and begged to be taken to their son to tell him the news. The murderers led the elderly couple to a separate room, stripped them naked, and shot them. The new mother was left with the newborn child, without her husband and without her in–laws.

5.

A rumor spread in the ghetto, that the two Soviet officers who had escaped – Boris Adamovitch and Fiedja Komarov, had created a partisan unit in the region that operated in the area of Ruda Jaworska and Ruda Lipichinska. The farmers in the area helped the partisans and told them what was happening in the Derecziner ghetto. The officers decided to save me from the ghetto. That night, a farmer came to the house with his wagon, and after inquiring about the whereabouts of Anetchka Wengel, he gave me a letter written in Russian:

"Anetchka, soon they will slaughter everyone in Dereczin. Not one Jew will remain. We want to save you. Run away with Vanya Pilidovitch, the one who is delivering this letter. He is one of us, I promise you. Do not be afraid. Boris."

The family Januszewycz, however, did not let me leave alone. So I remained, and the farmer left with nothing. Our situation later became worse and worse. The Germans, along with the Ukrainians, locked up the entire city and did not allow anyone to come in or leave. The ghetto inhabitants now looked for hiding places. A group of us, about thirty people went into a house where there was a large cellar. In this group, there were the following Wyczkower Jews: Borukh and Civia Januszewycz, Zlate Winzber, Leybel and Roza Januszewycz, Soroh and Volf Kaufman, and Khantche Wengel. The family Kaufman had an eight–month–old child with them.

From outside we heard suffocating echoes of the Aktzia [roundup for murder] being carried out. The Germans' wild calls of "Heraus! Heraus!" [Get out!] were mixed with the confused Jews' "Shema Yisroel." The many shootings made it clear to us how many Jews were being murdered in the actual ghetto. The Germans went from house to house, and with brutality and terror, grabbed out the tragic Jews and sent them to the assembly point. Through a small opening in the cellar we even saw how they ordered some of the Jews, dressed in their prayer shawls, to dance.

Suddenly, we heard how the bandits entered the house that was above our cellar. "Jews, get out! Jews, get out!" the Germans bellowed with their Ukrainian helpers. The young child in the cellar began to sob. I froze with terror. The murderers over our heads would surely hear the cries. One of those hidden with us continued to try and calm the little bird. We stayed in the cellar for three days and three nights, without food, without water, and heard the shootings and murders of our tragic sisters and brothers. After that, they were loaded onto trucks and taken away to the prepared graves.

On the fourth day, everything quietened down. Even the ground of the darkened mass grave, into which they had thrown half–dead people – stopped its tremors...

As we were lying in the cellar, after three days we heard the Germans calling through loudspeakers that the remaining Jews should leave their hiding places. Those who were still alive – will remain alive. We did not believe the Germans. As we were in the cellar, we knew exactly what happened in the town and in the ditches. How?

On the second day of the Aktzia, we heard someone was knocking on the cellar and a weak voice called: "Jews, open up!" We did not respond immediately to such a call, even if it was in Yiddish. But the knocking and the pleading did not stop. And when we opened the entrance to the cellar there was a small girl, wounded and bleeding profusely, completely black from gunpowder. She said that she had been shot in the foot, and lay in a corner like that in the yard for more than a day because the Germans thought that she was dead. Only when things became quieter, did she drag herself with her final strength, to the cellar because she knew that there were Jews hiding there. The young girl told us what she had seen and heard during this Aktzia.

Unfortunately, we could not take care of her as needed. All we did was tie up her wound with a torn shirt. There was no food or water to give her. Feeling faint, like the rest of us, she remained in the cellar.

We all realised that to remain like this in the cellar was pointless – we would die of hunger and thirst. So, slowly we began to go out of there, when the darkness of night would wrap itself around the town. We also knew from this young girl, that there was no danger of being shot. The Germans were short on bullets – since they used so many while liquidating the ghetto.

[Page 181]

6.

As we left the cellar, we breathed some fresh air. Spending these three days cramped and suffocating, without bread or water, had completely depleted us. Now we ran outside of the town as far as possible from the very place where our dear ones had just these past days been murdered in such a cruel manner. Individuals began crawling out of other hiding places and when we met them everyone began sharing the news that each one knew. I found out that in the last Aktzia these Wyszkower Jews died: Izak Wonsewer, his wife and children; Soroh Wonsewer; Chava Elboim, her mother; the Aldok brothers and their families; Duvid, Hershel–Mechel, and Lieba Fluda; Esther–Dvoire Fluda and her mother (the youngest son, Leybel Fluda, saved himself at that time, but later died in the forest).

Now, I ran with Roza Januszewycz. I was carrying a small bag with a few things, among which was a watch and a pair of earrings that my mother gave me at the last minute. Suddenly, I bumped into a German guard post. They didn't ask anything, but one soldier gave me a smack on the head with his gun. He did not shoot. Did they really not have any bullets? I dropped to the floor, bloodied and shocked. The German grabbed my bag away from me. Roza Januszewycz pleaded with the German: "Shoot me, but leave her alone! She is still a young child..." She lifted me off the ground, and with the greatest efforts, we went on running. We passed by some sort of body of water, and then came into the forest. There we met many of those who had come out of the cellar with us.

I and another person ran across the forest, without a goal – but hungry, bloodied, thirsty, filled with terror and shock. I hardly heard what is going on around me. Finally I saw a hut and heard the barking of a dog. I didn't even consider that there may have been Germans there. I fell against the fence and begged for a piece of bread. A woman peasant appeared and she gave me something to eat and a little water to drink. She then warned me that I should run away as quickly as possible because the Germans were close by. Once again, the wandering began, the running and getting lost in the forest.

Suddenly, I heard shooting. It must have been heavy shooting because even with my deafness I was able to hear strong echoes of the shooting. At the same time, the Germans and their helpers discovered the few Jews who had rescued themselves and now killed them in the forest. This was surely the end of the Derecziner Jewish community and of those refugees who found shelter during the first years of the war.

My friend and I made the greatest efforts to remain standing. The most important thing was to keep moving, not to remain in one place. Maybe we would be able to get ourselves out of our surroundings. Would anyone have pity on us and would we be able to save ourselves? Now we went out into the open field. It was dark. I took off my shoes that were torturing my feet. The cut wheat bore hard into the soles, and they became bloodied. But we could not stay in one place. But maybe, over there, in the unknown and thick darkness, we would be saved.

Suddenly, shooting and screaming: "Jews! Stop! Cursed Jews!" The dogs' barking got louder. We started to run, fell, and continued to run. Who knows – maybe we would fall directly into the murderers' hands? But thoughts now were to save ourselves. My friend encouraged me: "Khanale, come, don't fall.

... You cannot be weak now!" The bullets were flying over our head. "Jews! Stop!" we heard them again very close by. I kept running. But where were my sisters? My mother? ... Right in the middle of this danger, I thought of them. I didn't know about them, and surely they didn't know about me, if they were still alive. But still the danger pushed me to go into the foreign, cold fields and forests.

[Page 182]

From a distance, we saw small fires burning. Probably there were people living there. But what kind of people? Would they welcome you or would they chase you away? Would they hand you over to the Germans or would they murder you themselves? With these thoughts, I dragged myself forward with my last energies even though I felt that the road was far, the dangers were real, and my feet could barely carry me.

That's how, from the year 1939, I wandered and ran to maintain a little bit of life. The surrounding world was hateful, wanting to swallow you like angry animals. I remembered the old Yiddish folksong:

With the wandering staff in hand

Without a home, without a land,

Without a redeemer, without a friend,

Without a tomorrow, without a today.

Not with patience, only harassed,

Wherever you spent the night – you did not spend the day.

Always walking, moving and moving,

Always pained, pain and pain;

Always stepping, steps and steps –

As long as the strength remains.

That's how it is, year after year,

That's how it is, generation after generation –

Without any hope, without a friend,

Without a tomorrow, without a today...

With these thoughts I approached the fires. Now I knew: These were the villages of Ruda Lipiczanska and Ruda Jaworska. The residents here sympathized with the partisans, helped them. From here stretched the forests in which we saved ourselves. A miracle happened. We were among good people. The peasants received us warmly. Among them was – Vanya Filidovitch, the same one who was sent by the Soviet officer to take me into the forest.

Meanwhile, more Jews that had fled arrived here. In the village, they were all given food and then led away into the forest where we remained all night.

Early in the morning, the peasant went to the partisan headquarters where he was connected. Going with the partisans, Boris Adamovitch Bulak and Fiedja Komarov found out that some Derecziner Jews had saved themselves and were nearby. So they sent out two messengers on horseback to find out about the group. Their first question was if Anetchka Wengel had also been saved. They said yes, and now she was sleeping on the ground – very sick, swollen, and deaf. The messengers left food for those Jews who had been saved and went immediately to the commander to deliver the news.

I remained in the forest – sick with fever, sick and broken from all these experiences. Angry dreams and hallucinations did not let go of me. I imagined that the Germans were here on their horses. I got up and started to run. But suddenly there was shouting in Russian:

"Sisters and brothers! Do not run. We are not Germans, we are partisans! We want to help you."

I felt how someone lifted me off the ground, kissed me, and there was extraordinary joy. The people got off their horses and began to take care of the Jews who were saved. As if through a fog, I recognized my two saviors: Boris Adamovitch Bulak and Fiedja Komarov. They asked me: "Anetchka, are you alive?" But I was not able to respond. They offered to drive me to the headquarters but my friend resisted. They assured him that nothing bad would happen to me and that he would yet see me as healthy and happy. I trusted the Soviet commanders and agreed to be driven to the headquarters.

7.

We approached a small river that flowed through the forest. At the commander's whistle, some partisans appeared dressed as Red Army men. They threw some boards onto the water and we crossed over to the other side. Here we encountered a partisan camp. Dugouts, well disguised with trees and greenery, kept hidden in them people, food, animals, and even a hospital. There lay badly and mildly wounded partisans, parachutists, and also peasants who were shot by the Germans. Coming into this underground hospital, I felt how someone grabbed me with great joy, kissed me, and screamed without stopping: "Anetchka! Anetchka!" Now my joy and excitement were also great. None other than Dr. Rozenzweig was standing before me, dressed in a white coat, and he told me how he once saw how Germans and the chief Ukrainian nurse Tonya went up to the third floor of the Derecziner hospital where he was. He sensed that they had come to take him away. This was after the slaughter in the Derecziner ghetto, where Dr. Rozenzweig's wife and child were killed. He now had nothing to lose – and left the third floor. He was able to successfully escape into the forest, find the partisans, and now he was managing the partisan hospital. So now, I wanted to stay and help with his work.

At that moment, my personal fate did not interest me. I knew that on the other side of the river there were some Jews that were rescued, who if the partisans would not protect and give them the opportunity to set themselves up in the forest – they would be lost. I tell the doctor of my last experiences and also tell him about the rescued Jews who were waiting in the forest for the partisans' help. The two Soviet officers did not want to assume the responsibility of taking care of part of the civilian population on top of the conditions of the forest and partisans. But they told me sincerely, that they remembered what I had done for them when they were lying wounded in the Derecziner hospital, and that they understood my present action of risking myself for the rescued Jews. Thankfully, they were ready to take on the burden and responsibility. The following day, those few Jewish families, remnants of broken families, were brought over to the partisan camp.

[Page 183]

Slowly, the men were integrated into military units, and as the first large military action, it was decided that: a large attack would be conducted in Dereczin, to clean out the German powers, and in that way, avenge the innocent spilled blood of an entire Jewish community. We did not have a lot of ammunition. Armed with guns, revolvers, knives, axes, and even sticks, we snuck out to Dereczin at night. The first attack was on the police offices. After killing the guards we took the ammunition and set fire to the building. After that, we left for the central office, threw in some hand grenades, killed the oldest and a few soldiers. After taking their arms, we set fire to the supply rooms, but emptied them out first. Laden with cases, we returned to the forest. We took a few prisoners with us. Among them: the nurse Tonya. On our side, there were only a few wounded.

Proud, happy, and empowered, we returned to our partisan camp. There was great joy, especially for the Derecziner Jews who had somewhat calmed their thirst for revenge and also strengthened their commitment to the partisans. The following morning, after the onslaught, the chief of the headquarters set everyone out in rows, and held a speech in Russian, in which he greatly praised the Jews – the new fighters. He shook everyone's hand [congratulating them] for their heroism.

8.

Our partisans were in touch with Moscow, and thanks to that, the dissidents provided us with everything necessary, including medicine and medical instruments. I worked in the hospital and each of the rescued Derecziner Jews had work or tasks to do with the partisans. We started a new life, even though it was filed with tension, but still, we were like free people who would resist and die with arms in hand if necessary.

A radical change took place on the front. The governing German army began to receive one smack after the other, and their stronghold began to crumble. The German retreat had started. On Radio Moscow, we always heard about liberated cities and entire regions. The Hitlerist army had begun to retreat. But in order for them to ensure a secure withdrawal, it was necessary to liquidate the partisan units that had strongly harassed the Germans in the back lands. Special divisions were thrown into the struggle with the partisans. They used to capture peasants from the surrounding villages and force them, through torture and threats, to show them the partisan hideouts. There were some peasants who were willing instead to give their lives rather than tell on the partisans. But there were also some who assumed the role of informer rather than give themselves up.

Once we heard a dog's loud barking and soon we heard shooting and explosions. This was it – the Germans had discovered our camp and were now attacking it with their full power. The screaming and echoes of the shooting were getting closer. The hospital was in the so–called "family camp" where the rescued Jews were kept, along with the elderly, women, and children. I saw how the sick are beginning to run around in confusion. The Germans were screaming: "Cursed Jews, surrender! We will slaughter you like dogs, regardless!" I was also grabbed by fear and began running, not knowing in which direction. I saw how Roza Januszewycz was hit by a bullet. Other residents of the camp also fell dead. The murderers cut off the lives of women, the elderly, and children. They set fire to the camp after that.

Running away from that hell, I suddenly see three figures approaching me. For sure they were Germans. It was already night in the forest and it was particularly frightening in the dark. I felt these were the final minutes of my life. Nonetheless, without thinking, I cried out:

"Who is that?"

It was Dr. Rozenzweig, the nurse Sonya ["Tonya" in other places], and her elderly mother. They were very happy to see me and embraced me, caressed, and comforted me. They felt that I was very distraught and overwhelmed with this last experience.

The four of us took to the road. We crawled into another forest.

"Where are we going?" I asked Dr. Rozenzweig.

"Come, and be quiet," he replied.

Suddenly, in front of us, there was a large river.

"This is the Njeman," explained the doctor.

We removed our shoes and outer clothing and went into the river. The "stroll" in the water went on and on, without end. More than once, I felt that I was drowning. Suddenly I began to shout: "Mama! Mama! Save me! I am drowning!" Dr. Rozenzweig calmed me down and warned me at the same time, saying that this sort of behavior would bring tragedy to everyone.

[Page 184]

Only when it began to dawn did we reach the other side of the shore. We went to rest and dry our wet clothes. From a distance, we heard a dog's barking. Surely there was a village close by. But who knows?

Maybe there were also Germans here. Again we took to the road, not in the direction of the village, but toward the forest – the deeper, the safer.

Suddenly, we saw two youths. These were our partisans. They were happy to see us, but because of their sad faces we saw that something was not right. We asked what happened, and they told us that the headquarters, that was not far from here, had put out a death sentence on us four because we abandoned the hospital. True, the hospital with those who were rescued was saved, but we did not maintain our care and we left our positions.

In spite of this gloomy news, we asked to be taken to the headquarters and there we found many of our friends and acquaintances. My friend Leybel was also there. And they were all looking at us with great pain and regret because of the sentence on our heads.

They took us to the headquarters. The sole fact that they gave us food to eat and told us to remove our wet clothes and put on dry ones – awoke hope. The commander Boris Adamovitch did pronounce this judgment, but he added that they would ask the sick and the wounded in the hospital for their opinion. Special messengers were sent to them, and they returned with the verdict:

"Dr. Rozenzweig, the nurse Sonya and her mother, should be shot. Khantche Wengel – not..."

We are all put into isolation. No one was permitted to come to us. We were traitors. A few days later, a military court was set up in accordance with all the details and procedures. I defended myself strongly, sensing that with my defense I might make the judgment lighter for the other three. My excuse was that because of the attack I lost myself. I had experienced and lived through too much to maintain my spiritual equilibrium when the German murderers so heavily armed, and with their dogs, attacked. And if I was saved it was only thanks to Dr. Rozenzweig. He found me in the forest and brought me here.

Boris Adamovitch presented that the tribunal carry out the death penalty – but for me, in gratitude that I helped him in the Derecziner hospital, he was ready to grant amnesty. I fell to his feet, kissed his hands, and began to plead for Dr. Rozenzweig. I reminded him that the doctor did much for him in the hospital in Dereczin, and he needed to show the same degree of gratitude. At that same time, I thought the officer carried a grudge against the doctor because he felt the doctor had too lightly and quickly amputated a piece of his hand in the Derecziner hospital when, according to his own estimate, there was no need to cut, and they could have left the wounded hand intact. But I didn't want to leave it that because of a feeling of personal revenge, the hardworking doctor and compassionate person should be shot as an informer and coward. It seemed that Boris Adamovitch did not really have the courage to carry out such a verdict, and the end was that all four of us were sent back to the sick in the hospital. Our joy was great since a few Jewish lives were saved.

9.

Now a difficult period began. The retreating Germans were pursuing the partisan detachments, and we always had to run with our camps from place to place. We were hunted and chased. More than once we thought: Who knew if more of these experiences would tear us apart from the living, even at the end of the war when victory was so close?

The peasant Vanya Filidovitch helped the partisans again. Dressed as a woodchopper, with a saw and axe, he came into the forest and informed the partisans about the Germans and also brought food. Thanks to him and to other good peasants, we were saved from a sure death.

Sadly, not all merited the same. Leybel Fluda, with another five partisans once went out to scout around. They belonged to the razviedka ["reconnaissance group"]. In a few hours, we heard shooting. After much time – the scouts did not return. I, along with a group of partisans, went to search for them. The following day, we found them, shot dead in the forest. The Germans had been hiding in the trees and shot them from up high. Leybel Fluda was still in a reasonable state, but he died in my hands.

We dug out a grave in the forest for all of them and then cried for the fate of the cut off lives of these young people.

Victory could already be felt in the air. But the road to that was still filled with incidents, victims, and terrible events.

Once, Boris Adamovitch announced that the front was already far away in Poland and that they were abandoning the head office of the partisan units. The headquarters would go to Moscow and the partisans, as well as the "family camps" were free to go where they wished. The headquarters did leave, and we were left to God's care. The people ran off in different directions and everyone tried to find some salvation for themselves. I, along with the doctors

Rozenzweig and Miasnik, went to the village that night, to Vanya Filidovitch. He set us up in his stable where we hid for several months, until the end of 1944, when the Russian army entered the village.

[Page 185]

Now I was free. I was very grateful to Vanya Filidovitch. He also received distinction from the Soviet army for his service. I, and others who were rescued, were sent to the town of Szczecin, near Grodno. There we were placed in the city's plaza. The mayor gave a speech, told about our war experiences, and asked the people to welcome us warmly and give us whatever we needed. Then I got sick in my head because I fell down some stairs. It was difficult with food and medication. It seemed that we had not yet completely emptied the goblet of problems. But even these difficulties soon ended.

Later, I went to Dereczin, and from there – to Lodz. The uncertain situation of the Jews in liberated Poland caused us to continue wandering: to Walbrzych, and after that – to Israel.

Hitler's Murder of Children
by Leah Direktor (Lerman), Tel Aviv
Translated by Pamela Russ

1.

When the war broke out, I was in Warsaw. Since part of my family lived in Wyszkow at that time, I decided to go there with the thought that a small town would be safer and quieter than a main city. Together with Yakov Pienik and a few other Wyszkower we went on the road. But it took a lot of time and energy until we arrived there. The roads were filled with refugees, there was no communication, and the German airplanes were continuously bombing the civilian population.

When we arrived in the town, the civilian guard mobilized us to bury the dead. Wyszkow already had its first war victims. On the Ostrower main road, not far from the toker ["turner" – i.e., one skilled in turning wood on a lathe] Przestrzeleniec, where all the neighbors from all around were hiding – a bomb had fallen. The number of victims was very high. With shovels and steel bars people were searching for their dear ones among the victims. Maybe someone had saved himself. This image, how living people we knew well, were searching in confusion for their dead relatives, made a frightful impression on us when we first arrived to the town. A certain Zelig Litera found his dead children there; another person, without a hand, discovered his wife and parts of his children's bodies.

When I calmed down after witnessing this terrible scene and after helping to clean up the dead bodies, I began asking around for my family. I found them hiding in the Wyszkower cemetery, together with Yakov Wajntraub (a comfit maker), his daughter, son–in–law, and children. We decided to leave Wyszkow and go back to Warsaw. But it was not easy to follow through on this decision. My father, may he rest in peace, my sister, and the children, were sick. How to get to the main city – there was also no means.

Having no choice, in the evening we ran to the benzene station and there waited for a cargo truck that took everyone to Warsaw. We arrived there several days before Rosh Hashana.

On Rosh Hashana, the terrible bombings of Warsaw began – especially of the Jewish quarters. In the court of Francziszkansker 31, where my sister lived, a murderous bomb fell and wounded all of us. Fortunately, we all managed to save ourselves. You could see the real destruction on the streets.

A fire bomb fell close by and killed and wounded scores of people. Charred, burned people, gushing blood, roamed in the streets and in the courtyard.

Afterwards, when Poland was losing the war, and it became calmer in the occupied country, again we decided to return to Wyszkow. I came to Radzymin and found familiar Wyszkower Jews there, who were able to tell about the destruction of Wyszkow. Hundreds of Jews were assembled into the brewery and there they were shot by the Germans. My brother Mordekhai was burned to death by a bomb. Those who survived, escaped to Jadowa and to other cities. With this tragic news, I returned to Warsaw – where the brutal fist of the Germans already ruled.

Since my sister's home in Warsaw was destroyed, we had nowhere to live. Therefore, my father decided that because of the strong anti–Jewish persecutions, I and my brother Shloime, may he rest in peace, should go to Kovno where my brother had lived for many years. We took to the road again, and now for a long time. On this new path, we found many familiar Wyszkower in Jadowa, Czyzewo, Bialystok, Vilna, and Kovno.

2.

This is what happened. As we Jews were running – our tragic fate followed us. In January 1940, we, four family members, arrived in Kovno and for about half a year, we lived under the Soviet government with relative calmness and hope that with time, we would still see our dear ones who had remained with the enemy. But June 22, 1941, the brown power began to spread again.

[Page 186]

The first day that the German murderers entered Kovno, they, along with Lithuanian civilians, carried out a pogrom in Slobodka. Innocent Jewish blood ran in rivers. In this blood bath, our dear friends from Tluszcz died: Devoira Goldvasser, her husband, young child, and brothers–in–law, along with many Slobodker Jews who were literally slaughtered in the cruelest manner... From that day, the horrors and agonies of the Jews in Kovno began. Raids and arrests were in all the houses. My family and I were taken on the seventh transport. The men and women were separated there. The Lithuanians learned how to aim at the men. It became an amusement for them. Tens of innocent Jews were murdered like that. Among them, my brother from Kovno, Yitzchok Lerman, of blessed memory. We women experienced tremendous fear, but they let us go after that in order to witness and be victims of more terrifying experiences.

3.

August 15, 1941, we were herded into the Slobodka ghetto. This is where the real road to hell began. We were terrified of the dark of night just as of the light of day. The growth of the Slobodka ghetto was tied to the Aktzia [roundup] of 10,000 Jews. The so–called "Great Aktzia." The orders stated that all ghetto inhabitants without exception must assemble at a designated place. They wanted to count us and send us to all types of work. But the murderers did not rely only on this order. They raided every house, room, cellar, and attic, and in the most brutal way, they dragged out all the elderly, sick, women, and children. The guns and pistols worked without stop.

At the assembly place, the sorting began – to the right and to the left. The families where there were no husbands – went to the left. My niece and I went there too. As long as I will live, I will never forget that horrifying night when they were sorting the people. Such animal brutality you do not see even in the jungle...

We were of the first to arrive in the so–called small ghetto. In a small room, four–by–four, other than us, they crammed in mothers and small children. The crowding was so terrible that it was impossible even to stand. The cold was crackling outside, it was freezing, there was no food. The shooting did not stop, and the children's whimpers fill the small room. The mothers were moaning and sobbing bitter tears about their dark fate. Suddenly, the quiet of the night was ripped open by a malicious bang on the door. Soldiers and armed Lithuanians stormed into the room and all of us are ordered to go out and march in an unknown direction. We try to figure out what this decree meant, but one brave person dared to ask an armed guard, "Where are we going?" To which there was the cynical reply: "To work." This was a bold lie. Sick, drained and hungry women, with little children in their arms or holding the children's hands – are not working elements. Would these elderly, these unfortunate children and the broken women be ready for work?

At that moment, I remembered an oath that my father used to use for especially important issues. He used to say: "May I merit to come to a Jewish burial." For our parents, having a Jewish burial was one of the most important requirements after death. Now, my feelings were that we would not have a Jewish burial. If this was a wish for Jews in normal times, under these current conditions, this was a distant, distant dream. My niece and I decide to run away. We told those nearest to us of our plan, but they were too tired, drained, and resigned, to risk such a plan. They continued on and we were able to successfully escape the Angel of Death.

... Later, for days and weeks they carried the clothes of those who were murdered. Christians later said that the mound of the accursed mass graves rose and moved for a few days. Those who were not dead, and those who were half alive, still breathed under the cursed ground. Some who died in the Name of G–d had a prolonged Gesisah [state of being a "dying" person, on the last throes, agony]...

The beaten remaining people in the Slobodka ghetto now asked: "Where are my children? Where is my wife, my husband, my father, my mother?" They knew the answer – but these questions filled the narrow, tragic vacuums of Slobodka. There was not a single house where several family members were not missing.

4.

Life in the ghetto proceeded in a "normal" fashion. Human skeletons wandered in the streets (Jews were not allowed to use the sidewalks), with two yellow patches (one if front and one in back). This went on until the second large Aktzia [roundup], the so–called "children's Aktzia."

Even though official numbers were not public, they said in the ghetto that the large mass Aktzia killed 10,000 Jews. Another factor was added to the already tense mood in the ghetto – hunger. There was nowhere to buy a little food, even those who still had the means to buy something. Since we no longer had the means to send a food package to Poland, there remained a few food products for us, and these were used in a very sparing and rationed manner.

The remaining men and women who were able to work were herded daily to the work of building a flying [airplane] field. This type of work, the hunger, cold, and torture, that resulted in many deaths, weighed heavily on everyone and caused great depression. But on top of all this, there was always the main worry – food. Where can you get a piece of bread, a potato, a little fat?

[Page 187]

One group of Jewish workers was working in an outlying district of Kovno, where they could buy food with their money. By chance, I worked with this group and when I thought no one was looking I went to buy food. A Lithuanian secret agent in civilian clothing recognized me and arrested me. My pleas and cries that he let me go were useless. He delivered me to the German commandant and I was sure that this would be the end of my life. But they locked me up in prison, in a room where there were other Jewish women.

Among those other detainees, were: a well–known children's doctor, who even before the war, was already serving in the Kovno prison where she was now. The doctor's entire family (she, her husband, their son, and a Christian housekeeper), were reported for using Aryan documents. In this cell were now also two sisters and two Christians who wanted to help hide the sisters; a girl who had left her possessions in a Christian home, and when she came to get her things – they arrested her; a woman who worked on a farm and hid her two children elsewhere. Out of jealousy, the wife of the farm owner, informed on the Jewish worker who was thrown into prison. Every day, she would come back from the investigations beaten and bloodied because they wanted to find out from her where was the hiding place of the others. But she did not betray her children despite the intolerable pain that she had to tolerate. In "my" cell there was also a history teacher who, a student to whom she had given a low grade, reported her as a communist...

5.

When I came into the cell, all the detained women there wanted to know the news of the city and of the fronts. Unfortunately, my reports were horrifying because that period was marked by Hitler's wartime victories on the Soviet front and an increased terror towards the Jewish people.

Now I am sitting in a corner of the prison cell and my thoughts are ... about freedom. My dear ones were certainly worried that I am no longer among the living. They waited for my return with hope and that I would bring the piece of bread that I was supposed to bring. They had separated us, and who knew if this was not to be forever.

But sitting in prison, brings strong people closer. The women in the cell became one family. If one person was summoned to an investigation, everyone lived through it together and was sincerely interested in the fate of that person. Worse was when the cell door was opened in middle of the night and one of us was summoned. For sure – someone was being led to her death. And everyone accompanied her with compassion and choked tears. That's how, from day to day, the number of detainees decreased.

The women who had already been in prison for a longer time, after hearing the story of my arrest, did not want to believe that because of that reason I would be locked up and detained without an investigation. For these types of sins – they argued – one is immediately released. They advised me to go to the prison warden during the evening roll–call when the prisoners were allowed to present their requests to the prison administration. So I asked to have a talk with the warden. The result was that there was no guilty verdict against me. The warden then "comforted" me that I should be happy that I was there because in the ghetto the situation was much worse. People were going around barefoot, with torn clothing, starving, and beaten. My answer was that even a bird locked in a cage, even though he has everything, tears himself to his freedom. Other than that – I did not commit any crime.

Spring arrived. I also found out that soon it was to be Passover. Having been raised in a religious spirit, I decided that, even in these prison circumstances, I would not eat any bread, and I began to collect beets for the holiday time. There was already a large collection of this food in my coat – but suddenly they summoned me to an inquiry. I was afraid of a consequence with these beets, so I grabbed the coat of another prisoner and left the cell. They took me to the Gestapo commando, pushed me into a room where other men and women were detained. All of them stood with their faces to the wall. They told me to stand that way as well. They asked me if I had gone to buy things myself or did I take one of the others who works with me. What did I buy and from whom? Then, a Gestapo office took me into the cellar, tied my hands to two steel rings that were hanging from the ceiling, and with a leather whip, they began beating me across my entire body. Bloodied and beaten, I was returned to my prison cell, and on the evening of the last day of Passover, I was released into "freedom" – back to the ghetto...

6.

One day, the wild Gestapo murderers and Lithuanians tore into the ghetto with large cargo trucks and from the all the hidden places, they managed to drag out the elderly people and young children. From behind mill–stones, bricked walls, from cellars and attics, from bookcases and ditches, from closets and canals, these murderers dragged out their victims. The screams and cries of these little birds were able to move stones – but not the stone hearts of these murderers and sadists. In order to subdue their own senses, or to outcry the wails of the tragic ones, they played festive music through the loudspeakers...

[Page 188]

On the mothers who did not want to hand over their children and who struggled with the murderers, they [the murderers] unleashed specially trained dogs. The dogs tore pieces from these terrified mothers. And when they fell down impotently, the German or the Lithuanian threw himself upon the child that was just torn from its mother's arms and threw it on the truck. Some of the mothers allowed themselves to be shot on the spot, if only not to be torn away from their child; others jumped onto the trucks in order to share the fate of their little son or daughter...

After this child Aktzia, I found myself in the Jewish hospital. Afterward, a mother came into the hospital. She had not wanted to be separated from her two children. One of the hospital staff told me that the Germans did not allow her to go along with her children. The woman resisted and they let the incited dogs loose on her. She was so bitten up that when she lay in the hospital, as one wound closed up the other soon opened. She continually screamed to the doctor: "It won't help you. I won't live without my two children. Your energies are wasted..."

This organized child murder lasted for two days: the 27th and 28th day of March, 1944. But despite the fact that these murderers searched and beat with such zeal, tore open and destroyed all hiding places, a few children still remained in the ghetto. But they moved about like shadows, having lost all expression of joy and hope in their dulled eyes. They had terrible dreams at night, of being taken away from their parents.

One night, I head the cry of my nephew, a nine–year–old little boy. I went over to him and saw how his mother was clutching him close to her. Both were crying, and the child related his dream, that they had taken his mother from him. "I begged the murderers to leave me, but they dragged me and dragged me, without end..." And the child asked:

"Dear mother, promise me that if they come to take you – you will not leave me here. If we will be together it will be easier."

The mother promised the child not to leave him – and kept her word. Both of them died later in a concentration camp. This little boy shared the fate of the million Jewish children who were cruelly killed by the hands of the Nazi murderers...

Some time later, with a transport of Jews, I was sent to a concentration camp. Here, a new chapter of horror began. Pain and lack – until the liberation. But about that, we will have to write separately.

[Page 188]

My Experiences during the Occupation
by Fanya Hertz, Akko
Translated by Pamela Russ

Dedicated to the holy memory of my family that died sanctifying the Holy Name of God.

1.

When the war broke out in 1939, I was eight years old. Maybe that was young in years, but it was rich in experience for having worked in Warsaw for three years. And when the main city in Poland was bombed, and a mass fleeing from there began, I also left the city with a determined decision that now my home was – Wyszkow. In that house near the train, that is surrounded by fruit trees, flowers, and green meadows, there were my mother, my brothers and sisters. That was the house of my grandfather, Avrohom Leyb Rubenstajn, of blessed memory. My goal was – to run away from the bombed out Warsaw and run to Wyszkow, to be together with my dear ones and to share their fate. I had a bad feeling just as I came to the town. I was advised to leave my home right away. And that's what we did – but it was already later on, after the first victim of the family had fallen, our oldest brother Fishel.

One bright September morning, the Wyszkower sky became dark with German airplanes. Bombs and bullets from machine guns fell onto the city without stop. Just a few minutes before the German attack, my brother's father–in–law, the elderly Reb Yisroelke Szlanczik, said to Fishel:

"Come, let us go and pray."

And this was their final road. A bomb tore them both apart. Soon they let us know about this tragedy. We went into the street and began to collect the still warm pieces of both bodies and put them into an abandoned wagon that stood not far from us. Despite this horror and tragedy of both victims, and also despite what was going on around us, we still had a feeling that we were doing what were the final rights for the two. But just as we completed this work, once again airplanes flew overhead, threw bombs, and one of them hit the wagon that began to burn.

[Page 189]

Fiery flames tore apart the wagon. The whole town was burning and an infernal fire also burned in our hearts.

Now we had to run – but to where? I still thought about taking along a few things and going into the house. But a fire bomb fell near the house. They were still able to drag me out through a window.

We left a Wyszkow that was wrapped in fire and smoke. The tragic inhabitants ran in the chaos and terror, with wide–open eyes. Their screams and tremors, as sharp knives, sliced into the voids. Small children were searching for their parents, and the parents, with confused broken hands, called out to their children. Wild cows and horses ran through the flames as if they would find salvation there...

The tongues of flame meanwhile did their work, swallowing up almost the entire town. That night, the ashes of the destroyed homes were already smouldering. The bombs stopped falling, and as always – night fell. Then I was very disturbed by the fact that on that very day my two brothers, Motel and Gavriel, had left for Pultusk to fetch a sick woman from there and bring her to her husband who was in Wyszkow.

They returned safely at night. We were now standing in front of our grandfather's destroyed house. The house where we were born and raised was no longer, where thousands of stories arose in our memories – good and bad, happy and sad. The unforgettable home of Wyzkow was no longer... These thoughts suddenly overtook my mother:

"It's too bad that we did not listen to you," she said to me, and then pointed to the horse and wagon that was the only thing remaining after the bombing.

We left on that wagon, without anything. There was nothing to take with us. The horse lazily took himself into the dark night. We left behind the destroyed town and its tragic inhabitants.

2.

Now we were homeless. The creaking of the wheels tore through the night. I was sinking into my thoughts. Why did my oldest brother have such a death? When my father died, I was six years old. Fishel became the sole provider for the entire family, concerned for each one of us, buying shoes and clothing. He had a warm word and kisses for every one of us. That's also how he was to others. He was prepared to remove his own shirt and give it to someone else who needed it. He well knew who in town needed a piece of bread, and saw to it that the person should not suffer from hunger. He lived more for someone else than for himself.

One night earlier, before death stole him away in such a grueling manner, someone knocked at the gate of our house. My oldest brother went down, opened the gate, and the entire yard filled with children. They filled up the barn and the rooms. We found out that nuns and the children from a Christian orphanage had come to us. They had been evacuated from western Poland. Fishel already gave them some food and fresh hay for sleeping. In the morning, the guests awoke well fed, having had drinks, and having slept, and one of the nuns blessed my brother:

"May you never know any sorrow because you helped tragic orphans..."

I cried at the thought of what happened to him just hours earlier. He was also very religious. My father–in–law, a Jew with 96 grandchildren, loved him more than any of his own children or grandchildren. That's why he had asked Fishel to go and pray with him. And then he met his end. Why? Where is justice? Tears ran down my cheeks. And maybe – I thought – this was from God. It was just barely better for him now than for us (later I thought about this many times). May these words serve as his tombstone that was never placed...

3.

The road that left behind so many victims, began. Even today, I still think about how I, the youngest and weakest, remained alive, the only one of a large family that was destroyed in the fires of war. We rode and walked, walked and rode. Going uphill, we had to push the broken–down wagon that was completely dried out. We had no grease, even though my grandfather had a factory of that. So the axles and wheels were greased with butter – anything, as long as it would be easier for the horse.

Small Jewish children were roaming, lost on the roads. Hungry, barefoot, alone. We sat them in the wagon and went on foot ourselves. We only rode at night, during the day we rested in the forest. But we needed to eat. It was already evening, when I and Moshe Leyb Gunter's grandson, ten years old, went onto the highway that divided the Sokolower forest into two. Suddenly, tanks were coming towards us and stopped. Two Germans jumped out of a tank, and with aimed guns, they asked us:

"Where is the Polish military, spies?"

We were silent out of fear. This was my first encounter with Germans. Suddenly, there began a shooting from the other side. We dropped to the ground and began crawling back into the forest. Bullets flew over our heads shot by Polaks who tried to put up a resistance to the shooting of the Germans.

[Page 190]

But that shooting [of the Polaks] saved our lives.

4.

I knew the Germans better in Wengrow. I still shudder when I remember those times. There were many Wyszkower in Wengrow at the time, but I can, t remember who. The days were dark, and the nights – filled with a deathly fear. I cannot forget the German cruelty in Wengrow. They ordered the Rav to tell the baker to bake bread on Yom Kippur. When the baker filled their orders, they tortured him in front of my eyes.

Once, they herded thousands of people into one place: priests, rabbis, soldiers, civilians. It was raining all day, and they stood with their hands dropped to the ground. Whoever raised his head or moved, was shot or was beaten with a club. We knew that these people had not eaten for a 24–hour period. In a large laundry tub that we had brought to our new quarters, we cooked food, and my brother Gavriel and I went to the needy to bring them a little cooked food. As we approached the first guard post I received a whack with a rubber stick. Gavriel ran away and they shot after him, but thankfully they only got him in the heel of his boot. They turned over the tub with the food into the mud, and screamed at us: "Cursed Jews!" I went back home.

Once they allowed us to take coal residue and coal dust. As the bags were filled and the happy people put these bags on their backs, and were allowed to go home, the Germans assaulted them with horses, stomped on them, beat and shot them. Blood flowed in the streets.

There was no shelter here in Wengrow. We had to keep going. But to where? The somewhat rested horse and the greased wagon once again drove us across fields and forests – in rain, in sunshine, during the day, during the night. Hungry and barefoot, we made it through this road.

I will never forget Sadowne and the place where the sons of Moshe Elboim (of the inn) the Wyszkower lay. They were buried alive there. Afterwards, the Germans ordered their mother to sing and dance on their graves – and then later tortured her as well.

In Sadowne, they said to us: "Jews, why did you come here? Today is our last day. By the middle of the night, we have to be packed and be at the church. The roads around Sadowne are walled in by the Gestapo."

Gavriel knew that area well. We left there at night, and again: Stok, Bruk, tens of settlements, villages, and towns whose names I have long ago forgotten. With each step – hunger, pain, German murderers, lonely children, sick elderly, upset women. We took several orphaned children onto the wagon, and managed with difficulty to reach Ostrow.

5.

There were thousands of refugees in Ostrow – lying, sitting, waiting for a miracle. Armed Germans were roaming around in the sea of people. Rumor said that in a certain place in Ostrow where there is a low gate, people were registering to go to Russia. You went in there one at a time – and no one came back out through the gate. You just bent your head down, and were pulled in one at a time. The gate worked day and night. What could we do?

Several children were sitting cramped in our wagon. A cold rain was ripping into their faces without mercy. There was nothing more to eat. I saw a German at a distance. I didn, t know what possessed me to approach him, I heard my mother's question as if in a fog. "Where are you going?" But I kept going. The German stopped, and we looked at each other. "My sir," I said to him. "What time is it now?" He measured me from head to toe, and boomed, "Three p.m." "The children have not yet eaten," I continued to say, and pointed to the wagon – and I saw no sign of acknowledgement on his face. These few minutes seemed to time to be an eternity. "Follow me," I suddenly heard him say. These two words could have had several meanings, more bad than good. But I followed him. I was in the guard' post, it was small and drab. I stood opposite the heavyset German. "Bread for the children," I said. He said nothing, but took four loaves of bread off the shelf, along with a piece of butter and a package of cigarettes. He gave all this to me. I was still standing there, and he asked me: "How many are you?" "Fifty," I replied. He began to write on a piece of paper, put stamps, and then put the document into my hand. "They are changing the guard in an hour. I will give you a sign, and then you can ride off." The hour dragged on for a year. But we waited for the signal and began to leave from that place.

I went in front – behind me, the wagon with the children. My mother, brother, sister, and others went behind the wagon. The road from Ostrow to Puszkow, where there were Russians, was open to us. Thanks to the German's paper, each guard post let us through undisturbed. The Germans from the last guard post even helped push the wagon up a hill, not far from the new border.

6.

The Russians were also surprised when they saw this unusual paper that I had.

[Page 191]

Until this very day, I cannot understand what happened to that German who saved us from certain death. It seems that we were saved in merit of the children.

I remained alive – in order that I suffer more. Long after that incident, I would very often wake up from sleep with a scream, and then wake up the others. It seemed that I dreamt that the branch upon which I was sleeping in the forest, broke, and I fell; or that I pulled out my foot from the entrails of a dead body – but the dead person held onto me and did not let me free. I cannot forget the singing of the mother Elboim on the graves of her murdered sons. More than once I would erupt in wild laughter. Also not forgettable, was the scene of how the Germans forced a religious Jew, with a beard and side locks, fill up an empty bucket with water from a pump – but he had to do this with a cap that had a hole in it. The Germans enjoyed themselves at the expense of the victim before beating him to death.

We did not rest for a long time, because the sky once again was covered with airplanes and the entire area was shuddering from the explosions. Again, we were forced to leave this place. That same moment, my mother called me over, and moaned: "I cannot continue." And she died in my hands.

My dear mother! To us, she was both a father and a mother. Her devotion to us was limitless. I remember an episode when my oldest brother Fishel was in the military in Pultusk. It was a very difficult winter. The road to Pultusk was – completely snowed under. It was dangerous to even stick your nose out of the city. So she packed up some food and went on the road to Pultusk in order to see with her own eyes how they chased her son out into the cold to wash himself behind the faucets.

May these words serve, for my mother, as a tombstone which I could not put up myself.

7.

We took to the road once again, crossing fields and forests. Tears choked us in our throats. The tired bodies could no longer carry us – but we had to continue. Many times, it happened that when I was lying down during the day, my brother Fishel was coming on a white horse and gave me wine to drink from a small bottle. Then we got up and continued on. Soon we saw, that in the place where we were, a bomb fell. I lay down and closed my tired eyes, never to open them again. People thought I had died. But a few minutes later I opened my eyes again and continued on the road. My tired feet carried me not with their strength. It seems that this is what my dead mother did for me, and my murdered brother ...

***

After the war, I tried to find my close relatives in America and England – but did not find them.

These words are a comfort for me and a balm for the pain that I suffered by the Germans.

In the Forest with the Partisans
by Fayvl Fular, Born in Wyszkow in 1931
Translated by Pamela Russ

In September 1939, the Germans took over Wyszkow and herded all the Jews into a stable behind the city. They ordered some to dig ditches, some to carry hay. They said that they were going to set fire to the Jews in the stable. They placed the men in rows and shot almost all of them. They told the women and children to go east to the Bolsheviks. We went to Bialystok on foot. And from there we were taken over to Krasnaya Sloboda, a town in White Russia. There were 300 Jews there.

I studied in school until the year 1941, in the second grade. On the third day after the city was captured by the Germans (June 1941), all the Jews were assembled in the raizpolkom [city district executive committee]. They read out some orders for those who were assembled. Then they beat the Jews. The Germans, who did the beating, wore skull–and–crossbones symbols on their caps. In the evening, they let the Jews go. The next day, they grabbed Jews to clean the cars. After doing that work, they set out the men in rows of ten, and shot them all. They told the women and girls to go home. My mother wrapped me in a scarf and took me out as a girl. The next day, the women buried the dead men in the cemetery. There were no policemen yet in Krasnaya-Sloboda. The Germans gave weapons to the peasants and told them to find the Jews and shoot them. The peasants hunted the Jews as they would hunt rabbits. That's when they killed my father, even though he put up a resistance. I heard how an elderly Jew pleaded that they kill him as quickly as possible because he could not watch [the goings on] any longer. We buried our father and once again, my mother dressed me as a girl. We left for Czajkiewicz, a central region. We found out that they were digging ditches there - and in fact the next day they murdered all the Jews. We managed to hide ourselves. Only a few Jews remained in the entire province, skilled workers, among whom we were also included. All lived in seven or eight houses surrounded by barbed wire.

[Page 192]

We heard that in Rejowiec there were active partisans. The policeman Karzin had a Jewish girl, his bride, in the ghetto. Even though he was a policeman, he was actually connected to the partisans. He advised us to run to the partisans because there was going to be another Aktzia [roundup] in another few days. My mother and I went into the forest along with an 18–year-old young man. Because of my non–Jewish appearance I was able to go around freely and beg for bread and milk from the surrounding peasants. We went to a large forest, Smolniki. One day, I was confronted by two armed men. They asked me who I was and where I had come from. When they found out that I was Jewish, they told me to get my mother and the young man, and they took us over to a group of Jews, among whom there was a beautiful girl. One of the partisans said that if this girl would agree to become his wife, he would take all of us over to the partisans. The girl did not consent. So they left us and went deep into the forest. At a distance, we noticed a fire burning. When we approached, we saw a group of armed men who told us to go over to the Towarne forest.

When we got to the forest that the partisans had shown us, all we found were traces of the abandoned camp. The partisans had left. I took a pair of polished shoes with a bag and left to the village to trade them for food. The peasants liked the items and wanted gladly to buy them. I told the peasant that if he would tell me where to find the partisans then I would sell the items to him. He told me that the partisans are accepting only those who have arms and he could sell me a gun. The following day, he gave me the gun and some bullets for the polished shoes and bag. We left for Woleszczyn(?) and found the partisans there and some other Jews from Kopiec and the surrounding area.

A Jew by the name of Gilczik began to organize the detachment. They let us know that the Germans were coming to the village Rejowski(?) to requisition the cows. When the Germans were already in the village, the partisans blocked all the roads, surrounded the farmhouse, and opened strong fire on the Germans. After a brief resistance, they hid in the ditches. The partisans threw grenades into the ditches, killed them all, and took their arms. When I wanted to take a gun for myself, the others did not allow this, and they said: "You did not fight, so you have no right to take arms."

In a few days, 182 Germans came to retrieve their dead comrades. They set fire to the village.

Gilczik was designated as commander of this partisan unit and he soon acquired arms for his detachment.

Although I was in his unit, Gilczik did not allow me to be part of the fighting saying I was still too young. Only in September 1942, without permission from Gilczik, I took part in a "bombing," meaning in an "economic" operation that was very successful. We brought a pig into the camp, with cheese, butter, bread, and eggs. The commander screamed viciously at me about why I had left without permission, then he assigned me as his adjutant [orderly].

In March 1943, once again I went on a mission. On the way, we encountered Germans who had come into the forest for a manhunt. We ran in all directions. Later, I could not find my unit because they had already changed their place. I cried and was very sorry that I had not listened to my mother and gone on the "exercise." I was also terrified of wolves. I wandered in the forest for a few days, becoming familiar with all kinds of herbs. Finally I found traces of the partisans who were so familiar to me.

Through binoculars that I had with me, I noticed a nine–year–old child who also lost the unit. I approached him. He cried bitterly to me. Together we continued looking for clues. On the second day, I found our partisans. They surrounded us both. My mother hugged and kissed me, and cried loudly. I was embarrassed by my mother's affection. They brought me a full bowl of food. I thought I would eat it all, but I ate almost nothing.

The unit left to Szczyrk. The German guard ran away from us. Then we changed the commander of our detachment. Instead of Gilczik there was Baranow. He allowed me to partake in all the fighting and war operations. I did not miss even one action of our unit.

Summer 1943, I put dynamite under train tracks. As a scout, I went to spy out the gypsy camps, attacked and exploded the train line of Warsaw–Moscow. I also lay in ambushes.

Once, we lay in ambush on the road of Miedzywodzie–Krzyzanowice. Before daylight, twelve policemen patrolled the road. They walked, singing: "We will pass over mountains and heights, we will stab Jews and Communists…" At that time, I was standing at the first post. With a hateful shooting, we killed eight of them. I already owned my own machine gun.

After the liberation, I received a signet, a rank, and a medal.

(According to the YIVO documents number 643)

[Page 193]

The Last Request of a Martyr
Translated by Edward Jaffe
Donated by Rona G. Finkelstein

In a pocket of a perished Jew from Rovno, who was the head of the Vishkov Yeshiva and later became the Rabbi of Rovno, the following letter[1] was found:

To our Jewish brothers:

Our time has come. Like all other Jews subjugated by the Evil Empire, we give our lives to God, blessed be he.

I am Abraham, son of Shmai Halevi Tsitrin, born in the town of Trachenbad. My father was Shmai Tsitrin, born in Vald, the son of the exalted Rabbi Meyer Zeev. My parents lived in Rovno. My father with his son-in-law Itzchak Chekhnizer, the ritual slaughterer and congregational messenger, were killed last year in Rovno. My mother Sarah Rivka, daughter of Eliokem Getzel Gelman of Trachenbad, together with the entire family were killed by the murderers in Rovno. We have relatives in America. My mother's brother, Joseph Gelman, my wife Bella, daughter of Yakov Arye Steinman of Viskov near Warsaw, member of the large family Steinman of Amselof.

I am leaving behind in Pobrusk two houses with many things hidden in the walls. Furniture and other things are left with the Ukrainian clergymen. Find our relatives and see to it that our bones will not be scattered and our names not forgotten.

Our relatives should say Kaddish and observe annually the day of our death. I Abraham, son of Shmai Halevi and my wife Bella, daughter of Yakov Arye, who has a brother in Russia – Zvi Steinman, say goodby to this foolish world. My dear son Meyer Zeev, 9 years old, my daughter Chaya, 6 years old, my daughter Masha, 3 years old, my mother-in-law, Chava Ziatah and her son Moishe, and daughters Chaya Sarah and Yentah Hadassah, her daughter-in law, wife of the above mentioned Zvi who is in Russia with her three small children and her mother – all of us are being sacrificed in His Holy Name, together with the 70 families of Pobrusk, and 15-20 families from Piasetchny.

Don't forget us, the murdered innocent.

Hear, O Israel. The Lord is our G-d, the Lord is one.

Abraham son of Sarah Rivka

Abraham, son of Shmai Halevi cries out at the threshold of death to search for his relatives and requests that his and his family's bones not be scattered, and that they be remembered. He also asks that relatives say Kaddish (prayer for the dead) and observe the annual day of their death.

———

This letter was brought to the USA by Rabbi Moishe Steinberg of Brod, who visited Rovno after the liberation in order to once again organize a Jewish community. This is a reprint of the letter which was published in the "Day" (Tog) of December 16th. This is a document of the awful period. The letter conveys a cry from a life that refuses to give up and disappear without a trace, and wants to be remembered. It describes what Abraham, son of Sarah Rivka, felt in the last minutes of his life when he saw no escape from the hands of the murderers. This was also experienced by thousands, hundreds of thousands of other Jews.

Avraham Tsytrin, head of the Yeshiva in Wyszków, with his wife, both died in Rovno.

———

The Polacks Helped Kill the Jews of Wyszkow

Hebrew newspaper

Translated by Pamela Russ

We arrived in Wyszkow, which, before the war, was a typical Jewish town. Now it is destroyed. The center and Warsaw Street are completely ruined. There, where houses used to stand, the inheritors of the Jewish belongings are putting up wooden huts and cabins that serve as stores. Together with the officer, I go into a kiosk to drink some tea. I ask a Polish worker about the fate of the Wyszkower Jews. He answers me naively:

"In 1939, the Germans liquidated all the local Jews, and to my great sadness, our own people helped with this. Now there is not even one single Jew. Our town, that once blossomed financially, has now become a cemetery."

The Jewish officer of the Red Army becomes enraged when I translate the content of my conversation with the Polish worker.

"If so, then I am right when I compare them to dogs!"

[Page 194]

When once again, a crowd of Polish men and women gather around his car, and ask that he take them with him, he shouts:

"Get away from here, you bandits, pigs, Hitlerists!"

Only we two continued to ride in the direction of Ostrow–Mazowiecka.

Here too you can see traces of the war. The main street, that used to be a Jewish street, around the beautiful magistrate building, is completely destroyed. In the place where the houses were, it is now empty, covered with rocks and grass. We meet several of the twenty Jews who live in the city. Among them – a woman and her son, whose husband was murdered three weeks earlier in the street, in middle of the day. They only wounded the son, and miraculously, he was saved from death. Understandably, they did not catch the Polish murderers. The Jew, the owner of a mill, was murdered for two reasons: because of his khutzpah that he dared remain alive, and the khutzpah that he asked that his mill be returned to him.

(From a Hebrew newspaper)

We Succeeded to Escape
by Velvel Elenberg, Haifa
Translated by Pamela Russ

It was the ninth day since the Germans invaded Wyszkow. The city was burned down. The people ran off into the forest. But many families were still hiding in cellars. They dragged out many families, and ours as well, from the cellars and about 350 people, men women and children, who did not try to escape, were herded into the marketplace, and forced to go on the road to Pultusk. The SS men who went with them kept shooting at them. My uncle, Hershel Elenberg, had his talis [prayer shawl] and tefilin [phylacteries] with him, so an SS man gave him a smack with the butt of his gun, telling him to throw these things away.

He had terrible pain from the blow. My sisters Krasse and Naomi Elenberg took out a bottle of whisky from their coat, and rubbed my uncle's hands so that he could continue running. With the rest of the whisky, Reb Yitzchok Ber Rozenberg made a "l, chaim," so that he would have the energy to go on running. Many times on the road, people were taken aside and shot. At the last minute, the orders were stopped by higher up officers who just happened to be driving by. We now remained a small group, and at the opportunity that the SS were busy with themselves, we were able to escape to the Russian side.

Partisans and Ghetto–Fighters in the Forest of Wyszkow

Translated by Chava Eisenstein

Diary and anthology of "The Book of the Encounters – Between the Ghetto Walls, In the Camps, and Forests", edited by Isaac (Antek) Zukerman and Moshe Basok. Published by United Kibbutz Movement, Beth Lohamei Ha'Gitaot in memory of Isaac Cazenelson Tel–Aviv, 1954

Shlomo Alterman – "Dror" activist in Warsaw ghetto. Fighter at the brush-makers area and at the central ghetto. He was from those that left the ghetto on May 8, 1943. Served as Partisan in the Wyszkow forests. Fell in combat with the Germans. At the age of 23.

Haim Arbuz – born in Warsaw. A Shomer Ha'Zair cadet and member of the Resistance in the Warsaw Ghetto. Took part in putting on fire the manufacturing works of the German industrialist Hollman. By the April Revolt, he battled at the Tebens–Schultz area. After that, he served as partisan in the Wyszkow woods. Haim was murdered together with Mordechai Grobams entire detachment by the A.K. (Armia Krajowa). At age 22.

Eliahu Erlich – born in Warsaw. Activist at the leftist Poalei–Zion. Member of a resistance group in the Warsaw Ghetto. Battled at the brush–maker area and at the central ghetto. After exiting through the sewer canals, he was a partisan near Wyszkow. Perished at the Polish Rebellion.

Mordechau Grobas (Mardok) – born in Warsaw, Shomer Ha'Zair member. Chief of a resistance unit in the Warsaw Ghetto. Carried out together with Eliahu Rozhanski the death verdict on Jacob Leikin. He was amongst the defenders in January 1943. At the April Revolt he was head of his detachment in the central ghetto. On the tenth of May he was among the ghetto departures to Lomianki. Served as chief of the detachment in the Wyszkow woods. Was persuaded by the A.K. to collaborate and was murdered by them together with his entire detachment at the summer of 1943, at the age of 22.

Wotsak (name and surname unknown) – member of the Shomer Ha'Zair that crossed to the Aryan side of Warsaw to join a resistance group, and helped save the remainder of the ghetto combatants. Was partisan in the Wyszkow area, shot by the Germans during a patrol.

Julak Jungheiser – A "Bund" member. Belonged to the resistance in the Warsaw ghetto. At the time of the April Revolt he fought against the Jurak Blonas's unit in the brush–maker area and then after at the central ghetto. On the 8'th of May 1943 – he exited the ghetto via the sewage canals to Lomianki.

Was partisan at the Wyszkow area with Mordechai Grobas's unit. He was murdered by the A.K.

Izzieu Levsky – was a P.P.R. (Polish Worker's Party) fellow, member of the resistance in the Warsaw ghetto. At the time of the April Revolt he fought at the Tabens–Shultz area and was with those who exited through the sewer canals to Lomianki. Was partisan in the woods around Wyszkow, in the Mordechai Grobas's detachment. Was murdered by the A.K.

David Novodvorski – born in Warsaw, one of the organizers of the Shomer Ha'Zair movement in the Warsaw underground. Chief of a resistance unit in the Tabens–Shultz area and from those who exited through the sewer canals to Lomianki, and afterwards – to the Wyszkow woods. In the summer of 1943 he and some friends decided to break through their way to Hungary. He returns to Lomianki and tries with the help of the Polish Kiszczak to connect with the chief of the Warsaw resistance in the Aryan district. At the age of 27 a "Folksdeutche" woman that showed them the way to Kiszczak handed him over to the Gestapo.

[Page 195]

Jewish Partisans in the Wyszkow forests in autumn 1943. Janek Bilak (left) and Jacob Putermilkh, participants of the Jewish Camps Organization (ZC.A.B.) in the Warsaw ghetto, which fought later with the partisan unit "Gwardia Ludowa" in memory of Anilewicz. Bilak fell in combat at the time of the Polish uprising in Warsaw, 1944. (From photo–album "Martyrdom. The killing of Polish Jewry 1939–1945 published in the Polish language by the "Ministerial for National Self–Defense" – Warsaw 1960)

Stephan Sawiski – Polish, a cadet of the "Toor"(?), and the youth movement of the P.P.S. (Polish Socialist Party). Was active in the resistance unit in Warsaw on the Aryan side, helped transfer the remaining fighters from Lomianki to the Wyszkow forests. Was murdered in June 1943, in a restaurant in Warsaw, by the German Gendarmerie. His aunt was Anna Wenkhleska.

Abraham Stolak – member at the left "Poalei–Zion", and of the resistance in the Warsaw ghetto at the Aryan side. Battled at the brush–makers area and then after at the central ghetto. Amongst those who exited the ghetto through the sewage canals. Partisan in the Wyszkow woods. He drowned in the Bug River at the age of 25.

Pnina Papier – member of the resistance of the Warsaw ghetto. At the time of the April revolt, she fought at the Tabens–Shults area. April 29 she was from those that exited the ghetto via the sewer canals to Lomianki, and then after, she was in the Wyszkow forests. She survived, and lives in Israel.

Jacob Putermilkh – member of the resistance of the Warsaw ghetto. At the time of the April Revolt he fought at the brush–makers area with the detachment of Jacob Feigenblat. Was amongst those that escaped through the sewer canals to Lomianki, from there, to the Wyszkow forests. He resides in Israel.

Jacob Feigenblat – born in Warsaw. Member of "Gordonia" (Zionist youth movement). Chief of the posse of the Warsaw ghetto resistance. At the time of the April Revolt, he fought at the Tabens–Shults area. At April 29 he was with those that exited through the sewer canals to Lomianki. Partisan in the Wyszkow forests, in January 1944 he returned with Gutta Kavenaki to Warsaw where they have been set up with Jablonski, a Polish civilian from the A.K. and janitor at Proszana St. no. 14. A couple of days later the house was encircled, and both of them were killed during self–defending. Jacob was 23 years old. The fighter Sigmund Igla too, fell with them. Jablonski was arrested and deported to a concentration camp.

Haim Primar – an activist at "Akiva" in the Warsaw ghetto, and member of the resistance. By the April rising he battled at the central ghetto. From May 10, 1943 he was in Lomianki and then after in the Wyszkow forests. He joined the Russian Partisan units in the woods across the Bug to east. He lives in Israel.

Israel Kanal – born in Bydgoszcz. Member of "Akiva". In the war he was in the Warsaw ghetto and was from the first to engage in combat by joining the resistance. On August 20 1942, he shot and wounded Jusaph Sherinski, chief of the "Ordnungsdienst." On January 20 1943, he and a few comrades took defense at the Tabens–Shults area. From the beginning of April, he served as commander–in–chief of the central ghetto. On May 10 he was amongst those that exited the sewers to Lomianki, and then after to the forests surrounding Wyszkow. In August, he returned to Warsaw and

[Page 196]

left as a South American citizen to Bergen–Belsen. In October, 1943 he was deported to Auschwitz where he was murdered, at the age of 23.

Heniak Kleinweis – born in Warsaw, member of "Gordonia" and of the Warsaw resistance. By the April revolt he fought with Jacob Feigenblat's detachment, in the Tebens–Shults area. He was amongst those that fled the ghetto to Lomianki and afterwards to the Wyszkow woods. By the end of June, he joined David Novodworski's group. The group attempted to break through to Hungary but was murdered after being betrayed in the village of Lomianki, asking to connect to headquarters of the Warsaw resistance. He was 26 years old.

Michael Rosenfeld – was one of the P.P.R. activists, and was one of the people in chief of the resistance in the Warsaw ghetto. By the April rising he battled at the central ghetto. From May 10, he joined those that exited from the sewer canals to Lomianki, then he joined the partisans in the Wyszkow forests, where he was until he collided with Germans and they killed him. He was then 30 years old.

With My Wandering Stick in Hand

On the dirt road Wyszkow –Bialystok –"Posziolek" [Posziolek Czarny, Dark Village] —Samarkand –Wroclaw –Prague –Paris –Buenos Aires –Tel–Aviv

by Yitzchok Baharav/Barab, Tel Aviv

Translated by Pamela Russ

1.

Until the outbreak of the Second World War, I was in Wyszkow where for many years I was active in various Jewish organizations and institutions. I left the town along with all the inhabitants after the terrible bombing in the first days of September 1939. That vandalizing attack on a peaceful city, without any military objective, forced the entire Jewish population to take the walking stick in hand and run. That's when the wanderings began, that lasted several years for us even after the war. Not everyone went where they wanted to go. The wandering of the Wyszkow Jews, from September 1939, stretched across eastern Poland, across the steppes, taigas [snow forests], which are the fields of the great Russia, and then back to Poland. Some went to Israel at the time, some continued on with the wandering. But not all who left Wyszkow at the time were lucky enough to be saved. Our path was also marked with many deaths, losses, tortures. This writing, even though it is closely connected to the experience of the author, is characteristic of the majority of the Wyszkower Jews who on that chaotic day left the city. And although many Wyszkower will be mentioned here, I felt it was necessary to relate my experiences during World War Two and beyond, so that the readers should have a picture of what happened to almost an entire Jewish community during those terrible years of the war.

2.

Friday, September 1. The whole country already knows about the war that Hitler's Russia declared on Poland. We in Wyszkow knew that after 4 a.m. police already carried mobilization notices to all the reservists ordering them to be at the magistrate's office by eight in the morning, and from there they would be taken to Pultusk. It's difficult to describe what kind of scenes there were each early morning. Hundreds of mothers, fathers, sisters, and brothers, with cries, screams, moaning, whimpering, said their farewells to the reservists. They felt that this present parting meant separating forever...

It was dark in the town in the evening. The lit Shabbath candles no longer burned in the windows. Everything was hidden and covered out of fear for the night attacks. Shabbath in the morning, when some of the Jews were returning from prayers at the Beis Medrash [Study Hall], others evacuated – some on foot, some on wagons. These were the refugees, Jews and Polaks from the western areas of Poland where the German army had already put down their bloodied boots, or destroyed a series of places by air bombing. We told the Jews to get down from their wagons and then set them up in various houses. They were given food and then they rested. We felt very sorry for these people who were suddenly torn out of their home nests. Who could have imagined that in about four days, we too would be in their situation....

That Sunday passed calmly. Only those refugees who were passing or driving through did not allow us to forget for one minute that the war was on. On Monday and Tuesday, the small merchants from the villages Porembe, Brajnszczyk, Joszcolt, and Kamenczyk, came to me to buy things in my wholesale shop. On Tuesday morning, when I was standing and packing up the merchandise for a line of merchants from Wyszkow and the surrounding areas, a loud siren and shrillness was heard. Later –the explosion of two bombs. Everything in the shop shuddered. I ran into the street and saw that one bomb had fallen in the outskirts, near the house of Motel Nowogrudski. And the second bomb –on Stodolny, by Reb Yitzchok Epstajn. They were already carrying the wounded. Blood is running in the streets. The screams are reaching the heavens. The stores closed immediately. The town was upside down. People were running –some in foot, others on horse and wagon. Whatever they tried to take with them, they carried on their backs, in their hands, but no one is forgetting the children. Some were still at their mothers, breasts, others are being led by their fathers, hands, some are running and screaming: "Mother! Father!" Within a few minutes, the bridge across the Bug River was completely destroyed. People are going in the direction of Jadowa, Wengrow, and to the Ostrow main road. People were running away from Wyszkow.

[Page 197]

3.

But where to go? You saw fear in everyone's eyes, and there was great panic. People were afraid of the bombs and of the Germans who were coming soon; of the unfamiliar and unknown road with all its dangers and shocks. The refugees saw how several hours later, after those two bombs had been dropped, another bomb fell in a corner of the Ostrower main road where Reb Avrohom Fajncajn lived (he had a steel shop). Now everyone felt there was no way back, so they ran into the forest. It was cool there, shaded, and more secure. But it was only words –we were running into the forest ... The German air pirates were chasing the fleeing civilian population and with machine guns and shooting the refugees. The main road became covered with the dead and wounded.

I, my wife Faige and my eight–year–old daughter Rivkele ran to the Ostrow main road. Since my son Yehoshua was in Warsaw at the time, I went in the direction of Radzymin, to get to the main city. But the trains were no longer running. It was treacherous to go anywhere during the day, so you could only go at night.

My wife, with a group of Wyszkower, left to Poremba. In the group were the following: Peshe Elboim and her sons Zundel, Leizer, and Nachman, her daughter, and daughter–in–law and grandchild. After staying few days in Poremba, Peshe Elboim went to Sadowne to my cousin Reb Boruch Grapa, Sokol's son–in–law. A few days later the Germans invaded Sadowne.

One German patrol once came into Grapa's house where there were nine men and women. They ordered the women to leave and the men (my three brothers and some Jews) were taken outside, ordered to dig ditches –and then shot. Zundel Elboim was holding his child in his arms, so the German told him to give the child to the mother...

After this tragedy, Peshe Elboim, with her daughter and daughter–in–law, returned to Poremba and told my wife what had happened since their separation. She said that her son Zundel, who was shot, had their money with him and now they did not have a single groshen [penny] (my wife helped her out.)

Good fortune had it that after two weeks of being separated from my wife, we met each other in the village of Sieczka, near Wyszkow. In those times, a parting –probably meaning that you would be separated forever –was not hard to imagine. There was no thought of staying in the village, because as soon as the Germans took over Sieczka, they chased all the Jews into the street, put them into a circle, checked each one, and took away valuables and money. Later –we were ordered to run, and then they shot in the air as we ran. The Germans had already reached Ostrowa, the new demarcation line between Soviet Russia and Germany.

Even though the border was open, and you could still go freely into the Russian zone, the Germans still searched us and took away everything. I cannot forget the wildness of one German soldier who demanded the wedding ring that he saw on my wife's finger. Every effort to remove the ring from the finger ended uselessly. It seems that the ring had grown into the flesh of the finger. The German did not think for too long, then took out a knife ready to cut off the finger and take the gold. But after great pains and efforts, we managed to remove the ring from the finger, but my Faige was hurt. Nonetheless, we were able to get to the other side of the border, but beaten and upset because of the German sadism. At that time, a 75–year–old Jew from the village of Sieczka was also beaten. They also cut off his long beard leaving only one corner. They told him to keep going like that .... We arrived in Zombrowe late at night.

4.

The city was filled with Polish refugees, particularly –with Jews. Almost all the houses and residences were full. There was a strong, continuous rainfall – and there was nowhere to find shelter. We managed to find someone to take in our eight–year–old daughter under their roof, while at the same time, I, my wife, and my unforgettable son Yehoshua remained outside all night.

The following day, many Jews went to Tiktin –so automatically, we went too, without having a goal or knowing the way. We spent the night in the large Beis Medrash [Study Hall] that had a history of several hundred years behind it. In the morning, we went into the street to look for a kilo of bread.

Under these conditions, we spent two weeks in Tiktin, and then continued on –to Bialystok.

The first "address" was: the large synagogue. But here everything was crowded with refugees. Even the anteroom was full, crushing one body to another. Without a choice, we spent the night in the street. A Bialystoker Jew had mercy on us and set us up in a small house. At four in the morning we went to a bakery where they were giving out bread. There was already a line of hundreds of people. We stood there for half the night and half the day and everyone in my family managed to receive a kilo of black bread. It seemed that we were now so poor that we would not have money the following day to pay for the kilo of bread. I went to the bazaar to see if I could earn some money. There, I found my good friends and acquaintances, formerly successful merchants in Wyszkow: Itche Najman –holding three pieces of soap in his hands; and Yisroelke Dzenkiewicz –with a pair of boots to sell; Pula Skarlat –

with a pair of new bootlegs [spats]; Henoch Kaluski and Mordechai Mendel Holenberg, and other Wyszkower, such as: Meyer Prager and Fishel Koplowicz. I too was dragged into this business, because there was no other way to earn some money. Almost every day, the Russians did round–ups, confiscated merchandise that was to be sold, and then arrested the owner for two days.

[Page 198]

Life in Bialystok was difficult and not tolerable. For each thing, from a small piece of bread to slippers –you had to stand for hours in line. This waiting "queue" was spread everywhere, but there was no choice. You had to bargain in order to maintain yourself and the family.

5.

Once, important news was heard, that registration of the refugees who wanted to become Soviet citizens and receive passports, was beginning. Either that, or they could go back to Warsaw to the Germans. This news got everyone excited. Because everyone now had two choices it was difficult to decide. Other than that, no one wanted to go back to the Germans, from whom we had run away not long ago, but taking upon yourself the burden of Soviet citizenship – no one rushed to do that either. We, the refugees, knew that many Bialystok Jews, former merchants and factory owners, were sent to Siberia. Was the same fate waiting for us?

Before the news appeared on the streets of Bialystok, many of the youth took the risk and went over to Warsaw to bring merchandise from there and sell it in Bialystok. These youth said that in Warsaw at the time (1940) the situation was not so terrible. In general, it was quiet, and trade was continuing. With that information in mind, many Jews registered to go back to occupied Poland. But the majority was confused and undecided. Our Wyszkower in Bialystok –Henoch Kaluski, Mordechai Mendel Elenberg, Khaim Ring, Refoel Skarlat, Itche Najman, Yisroel Dzenkiewicz, and others, once got together and discussed the issue of registration. Henoch Kulaski was of the mind that it was better to get Soviet passports. That meant –not yet becoming communist. On the other hand, with the Germans in Poland, it would always be getting worse. Jews should not go there. Unfortunately, the majority of the Jews in Bialystok registered to go back to Warsaw. A minority decided to take on Soviet citizenship, and these were permitted to live under the Soviet rule in small cities.

Today, I remember with regret, that I too had heeded those who registered to go back to the Germans. Of course, at that time there were many reasons for this. First, the Molotov–Ribbentrop Pact and the amicability between Germany and the Soviet Union. We did not hear about anti–Jewish persecution on a large scale. At that time, many of our Jews returned to Bialystok who seemed to already have been in Russia for several months, and the greetings they brought from there, were not too happy. In addition to the hard work, there was real need. And the frequent deportations to Siberia and judgements against the Jews, certainly did not encourage the refugees to become Soviet citizens.

Once, a rumor spread in the city that many NKVD [Soviet secret police] were coming to Bialystok. Only late at night did I feel on my skin the real meaning of such a police invasion. Three armed NKVD knocked at the door of our house, and after asking if four members of the Baharav family were living there –they told us quickly to leave the house and go behind a convoy. I was hardly   able   to   take   along   our   "fortune":   my tallis [prayer shawl], tefilin [phylacteries], and a few small things. In front of the house was a cargo truck with more detained Jews. We were taken to the freight station, where there were freight trains with benches and prepared boards for sleeping. After each car was filled with people, the doors were locked, and an NKVD with a loaded gun posted himself at the entrance.

We rode like this for three days. We thought that all those who had registered to go to Warsaw were now being taken there. But after they gave us a loaf of bread for another four days, and then at the larger stations they gave us a plate of soup, it became clear that we were being taken deep into Russia.

Now we know where we are. Barges and cargo ships took us across the Dvina River to the city of Kotlas in the Arkhangelsker Oblast (region). This is where enemies of the Soviet regime were sent, prisoners with long sentences and with many years of jail behind them .... and ahead of them. There were thirty people in one barrack, all together –men women, and children.

6.

The slave–labor of chopping down forests stretched for fourteen months. The hard labor, the meager food, the difficult and unsanitary conditions, the inadequate clothing during the days of bitter cold and frost, made our group less in number. These conditions gave rise to sickness and decline. We would get up at five a.m., march on foot for six kilometers into the forest, and here begin to saw, chop, and drag the trees and wood. I, as an older person, worked in the actual "camp" gathering the wood. My Yehoshua collected the wood on the Dvina River and with a float, sent them across the river.

[Page 199]

In the "eating hall," we received food twice a day on ration cards given only to those who were working. Therefore, women, even elderly ones, also had to go work. Otherwise they would have no food cards. The lunches were very meager, without meat, which we had only one day per week –Sunday. My family and I did not eat in the eating hall, because everything was non–kosher. We sustained ourselves with bread, tea, and potatoes that we cooked ourselves. It was difficult to get the potatoes for ourselves because the camp residents did not want to sell anything for Russian rubles, but wanted to trade –to give them shirts, shoes, boots, and so on.

In the year 1941, there was the so–called Sikorsky–Stalin Pact between the Polish immigration government in London and the Soviet government. According to this agreement, all former Polish citizens arrested or interned in Russia were freed from their place of exile or from prison. Since the realization of this pact came during the winter months, the majority of freed Jews, among them –also those from our camp, went to warmer places. We arrived in Samarkand, in the Uzbek republic.

7.

In the Uzbeki cities and towns, there were many Jewish evacuees from the occupied Soviet provinces, freed from the camps and exile places, as well as the so–called Bukhari Jews. The years of prison and the camps, inadequate food and hard labor, now, after changing climate and places, left behind tragic consequences. The raging typhus made the numbers of freed Jews less. The dead and devastated lay in the streets of Uzbekistan.

And those, whose feet were still carrying them, slowly began to set themselves with work. The youth was mobilized in the Polish army of General Anders or in the Red Army. The older Jews went into trading. That's how we waited for the end of the bloody war that left its deep marks in the distant hinterland of Soviet Central Asia.

My son Yehoshua took a job as train worker, because the bread ration for such a category of worker was 800 grams a day instead of 400 for the children and non–working family members. Also, every worker could have a midday meal in the eating hall of his work place. But I, who was careful not to eat non–kosher food, would sell my bread quota at the bazaar and for that would get potatoes, onions, vegetables, in order to taste a little bit of cooked food.

This regime led to an overall depletion and I became sick with brain inflammation. I was in bed for an entire year and the doctors were not optimistic about my life.

In the year 1943, our situation improved as a result of receiving packages from Israel and from America, from friends and relatives through the "Joint" (American Jewish Joint Distribution Committee) organization. In the years 1944–45, "Joint" sent many boxes of clothing and food to Samarkand. This eased the need of the Polish Jews there and in other cities in Russia.

8.

In the year 1946, after the agreement with the Polish government, Moscow permitted all former citizens of Poland until the year 1939, to return to their former homes. The great repatriation began. The Soviet government set up special trains, gave the repatriates money for the trip, and every one of us, even those who knew of the great tragedy, still lived with the illusion that if he returned to Poland he might find a family member in his city or town, or his former home or some other possession that was left behind seven years earlier. Tragically, Majdanek, Treblinka, Auschwitz, and Sobibor told of the destruction of the Polish Jews, about a murdered nation that died in glorification of the Name of God. There was no thought of returning to the former places of residence. Anti–Semitism was broiling everywhere –in the large cities as well as in the smaller places. A thousand perils hung onto the surviving Jew.

The majority of the repatriates were sent to Lower Silesia that had emptied because of the Germans who were chased away from there. My family and I arrived in Wroclaw, and here the Polaks cynically and shamelessly sent us to "Palestine" and then asked themselves with surprise, "Where do all these Jews come from?"

Once again, the great aid activity took place from "Joint" in Poland of that time. Not only was food and clothing distributed to the needy, but they also set up cooperatives, work places, kibbutzim, and financed immigration to Israel. We did not stay long in Wroclaw and then left (understandably, illegally) to Prague. Here we also felt the comforting hand of "Joint" that after staying for six weeks in the capital of Czechoslovakia, they sent us to Paris.

After staying for a half a year in a kibbutz of Poalei Agudas Israel behind Paris, through written correspondence, I successfully managed to contact my brothers–in–law in Argentina. They were; Velvel Rotbard and Yisroel Sokal.

Since we were the only survivors of their families, they strongly urged us to come to Buenos Aires. They welcomed us there and even set us up with a colonial shop, but sadly I could not make a living there because the shop had to stay open on Shabbath. For a Jew such as I, who under the terrible conditions of wandering across countries and among different nations, still kept the Shabbath, I did not want now, after the liberation, to desecrate the Shabbath in my own store. The merchant who sold me the store, was surprised. "But," he argued, "on Shabbath you have the most business. And if you are not here then you might as well be a sexton in a synagogue...."

[Page 200]

Broken, I returned home that Friday night and decided to become a worker in the factory of my brother–in–law Velvel Rotbard. When my two children –my son Yehoshua and daughter Rivkale –married respectfully in Argentina and set up their lives, I no longer had to work. They completely fulfilled the mitzvah [positive commandment] of honoring their mother and father. (My son Yehoshua married the daughter of the big forest merchant and sawmill owner from Rifin –Reb Shlomo Brun; my daughter married Yakov Szaiman, the son of the big factory owner and home owner on the Nalewka [?], Reb Moishe Szaiman. My daughter–in–law and son–in–law, as I, experienced the wanderings during the war years.)

9.

On Hoshana Raba [seventh day and culmination of Sukkos holiday] 1961, a terrible tragedy happened to me. My very beloved and dearest son Yehoshua died of a heart attack at the age of 39. He left behind not only his wife Rochele, but also his two sons Shlomo (10 years old) and Mordechai (five years old). My wife Faige and I also felt very desolate and shocked from the unjust loss. He was of the rare few of this generation who so devotedly and loyally took care of his mother and father.

My daughter–in–law, daughter, and son–in–law, seeing the great pain of the death of Yehoshua, managed to get us a tourist visa to Israel so that in this Jewish land, we could forget our tragedy for a little bit. When we came to Israel and saw what was going on, my wife and I decided the following: We are staying here! This is how our great dream came to reality after many, many years, at the time, still in Wyszkow, when a longing for Tziyon [Israel] stirred in us.

At the beginning, we were filled with the deep impact and experiences of that which our eyes saw and our ears heard. The Jewish country opened before us in its dynamic way of taking in and setting up the Olim [immigrants coming to live in Israel] from different countries. At the same time, we had a positive experience: seeing the activities and liveliness of our Wyszkower organization. Here we found our compatriots –the first Khalutzim [pioneers] from Wyszkow, who now had gray hair, and the survivors of the terrible, destructive war, who had already come to this country right after the establishment of the state.

It should be said that the Irgun Yotzei Wyszkow in Israel [Organization of those from Wyszkow] remained true to the most beautiful traditions of the Jewish social life in Wyszkow. When the "Beis Wyszkow" ["House of Wyszkow"] was established in Tel Aviv, in the best way possible, they perpetuated the memory of the Jewish town on the Bug River. The work and preparation of the Yizkor Book, from the onset, allowed me to believe that we would successfully publish a book–monument for the destroyed Wyszkow. The same is true for the Gemilas Chesed fund [non–profit loans organization] that helped put many compatriots on their feet, those who needed constructive help. The loans were distributed without requiring interest. There was also an active women's committee that displayed a lot of initiative and activity.

At the head of the Irgun in Israel was the president, Menachem Stelung, the son of the holy martyrs Reb Khaim Henokh and Esther Mindel Stelung; secretary –the quiet and humble Yerakhmiel Wilensky, the son of the holy martyrs; with the financial administrator Pinkhas Shultz, the son of the holy martyr and an Alexanderer khassid [follower of the Alexander Rebbe] Reb Yechiel Shultz, the construction businessman Avrohom Wilner (Wilensky), under whose direction the Beis Wyszkow was built, the vice–president –Yakov Mitelzbakh, son of Michel Mitelzbakh, of blessed memory.

In the women's committee, particularly active were: Rivka Bismanowski, Liza Stelung, Tzipora Kahan, Khava Yechieli, Khaya Ostri, Sarale Pzieticki, and others. May those I did not mention please forgive me. I wanted only to give over my first impressions of the way I found the Wyszkower compatriots in Israel.

Dead Shadows Walk in the Marketplace ...
by Dr. Khaim Shoshkes
Translated by Pamela Russ

(Reprinted from "Der Tog–Morgen Zhurnal" ["The Daily Morning Journal" Yiddish daily newspaper in New York, 1901–1971], New York, November 15, 1959: "My Trip across Former Jewish Cities and Towns in Poland.)

... And already we are in the city of Wyszkow. Oh, oh, how many memories are forming of the first time I came here 35 years ago in order to set up the cooperative bank.

I was not alone in the car at that time. Accompanying me was, at the time still unknown among the Jews in Poland, the engineer Adam Czerniakow, later on head of the Warsaw ghetto, who went to his own death when they demanded of him that he send the first transport of Jews to the gas chambers. Now his name is famous and his place in Jewish history secured.

But then, during our first trip on the Warsaw–Bialystok highway, he was very distant from Jews and Judaism. His father already spoke only German and Polish. And the same for the son. He did not even know any alef-bais [Hebrew alphabet]. As a building specialist, he was appointed by "Joint" to build a series of settlements from the ruins, and that's how we traveled together for several years. He – to help build houses, and I – cooperative banks.

[Page 201]

When we drove into Wyszkow, we stopped at a Jewish restaurant that was famous for its fish.

And years later, when I visited Wyszkow once again, I stayed overnight at the baker's, whose bread had a good name in the entire area.

And now, after the destruction? The Wyszkower market has a few government shops: of leather, electric tools, food. Also, round, black breads, similar to those that my baker had baked, are loaded onto a wagon and a few people are walking around the market around farmers' wagons. Everything is new, everything is strange.

A sign near the gas–lamp in the middle of the market invites us for food and whisky to the restaurant in the small street, under the somewhat foreign sounding Italian name in Poland, "La Bella Donna" ("The Beautiful Woman"). The house is actually there, in which Czerniakow and I once ate gefilte fish. The driver goes to get gas, and I turn into the small street.

The same small gray house is still there among the autumn trees, and on the window sills there are small vases holding red flowers. A shaggy head appears, one with badly dyed blond hair that hangs in strands, with a rosy, fresh and smiley face. The "head" asks me: "Who are you looking for here, please, mister?" I reply: "The La Bella Donna is what I am looking for." "Please come in, don't keep looking. I am the "beautiful woman," says the modest head.

I excuse myself and continue on. I know that what I am looking for is no longer. Dead shadows stroll around the marketplace, drink here in the taverns, and I look back at the years when together with Czerniakow we ate gefilte fish in the khassidic Wyszkow.

Rabbi (Tzvi) Borenstajn Visits Wyszkow in 1961
Translated by Pamela Russ

HaRav [the Rav, prominent rabbinic leader] Borenstajn, former student in the Novardok yeshiva in Wyszkow, and now the rabbi in the Lebanon Hospital in the Bronx (New York), in the years 1958 and 1961, visited a series of Eastern European cities (Russia, Poland, and others), as part of the religious team commissioned by the American Agudath Israel.[1] In Poland, Rav Borenstajn performed circumcisions on 200 Jewish children and young people.

When he was in Poland, our compatriot HaRav Tzvi Borenstajn considered it as his holy obligation also to visit Wyszkow. We see him here in the photograph at the entrance of the city. In the background – the old–time Wyszkow church.

Photo: no caption, HaRav Tzvi Borenstajn

HaRav Borenstajn came to Wyszkow with another compatriot, Nakhum Ciwiak, who today lives in Warsaw. In the picture below: N. Ciwiak is burying the bones that were strewn about, in the Jewish cemetery in Wyszkow (summer 1961).

Photo: no caption

In one of the running rivers in Wyszkow, in the so–called "Struga," HaRav Borenstajn found a tombstone with Yiddish script, which he is pointing at with his finger (picture on page 202). He brought a piece of the stone to Israel and, gave it over to the ownership of "Beis Wyszkow" ["The House (Association) of Wyszkow"] in Tel Aviv.

[Page 202]

ב"ד בי"ת
לי' לי"ת
לי"א לי"ת
ו' ם לי"ת
ני"א לי"ת

ועד הקהלות הקדישות בפולין

Związek Religijny Wyznania Mojżeszowego w P.R.L.

Warszawa ul. K R N. 6   Tel 6-75-25   K-to P K.O. Warszawa 1-9-120721

Warszawa dnia ...

ב"ה יום ג' י"ם לח' אדר תשכ"ב

אל כבד הנהלה אגורת ישראל באמעריקא

ולהרב ר' צבי ברענשטיין

דער ועד הקהילות הקדושות בפולין וויל דא אוסדריק ... אין נאמען
פון פולישן אידענטום איהר האַרציגן דאַנק אוּן ברכה צו דער ...
פון דער אגודת ישראל פון צום חשבון הרב בראנשטיין פאר דער היילינער ...
כשירה נסאדיקער ארבים אין פולין אין דער שלימות פון כל זיין אידישע
קינדער אוּן דאס אויסטולין פוּן ... יונגעלייט אלץ פוהלין...
הרב בראנשטיין האט ביז הידנט פל.געוועץ הנערים ... ...
קינדער אין פארשיידענע שטעט אין פולין אין פלעטר פוּן 6 חדשים ביז 18
יאהר. פים ווארגעקערבאָרץ רעזולטאטן אוּן אין אייגקלאנג פוי ... ...
פסורחדיגן דין.
פיר ווילן דא קאנטסטאטירן דאס הרב בראנשטיין האט געטאן זיין ארבים
אונטער אוּיסטעדגעוויייגליץ שווערע באריגגונגען אלביריסענדיג גאנצע סעג
אוּן רייצענדיג ביינאכט.
פיר ווילן אבער דא פעסטסטעלן דעם פאקט דאס עם עם איז משום חידוש
ניט געווען פעגליך פאר הרב בראנשטיין צו פל זיין אלע קינדער יתלכע
עלטערן האבן דאס פארלאנגט צוליב דעם פאקט ... ...
גאענגען אוּן אזוי ווי עם זיינען שוין פארהאן נאר איבער 400 רעגיסטרירטע
פארלאנגען פוּן עלטערן פאר מילה - אפעלירן מיר צו דער אגודת ישראל אין
אמעריקע אוּן צום חשבון רב דורכאויס צו זעהן צו קימען נאכאמאל קיין
פולין נאך פסח אום צו ערלעדיגן דעם היילינן ענין.
דאס פולישע אידענטום וועם דאס קיינמאל ניט פארגעסן וויל דאס איז אן
היסטארישער אקט פוּן גרעסטן אוּן היילינסטן באדייט.
פים דער צרווארטונג דאס איהר וועם אונדזער בקשה ערפילן פארבלייבן
פיר פים די בעסטע וואוּנשן אוּן דאנק.

דר מ. ליבא   סרעזעם י. פרענקל וויצע פרעזעם
הרב רוב בער פערצאווילים

The photograph above shows the building of the current Wyszkower magistrate (official city hall), photographed by HaRav Borenstajn.

In order to cmphasize that the Polish government offices and the Committee of Communities of Martyrs in Poland provided HaRav Borenstajn with extensive help and understanding of his mission, in Legnica, with excellent mobile equipment, he was able to perform the act of circumcision on children and youths – the majority repatriated from Russia.

For this accomplishment, the union of religious Jewish communities gave him a special letter of thanks, signed by Dr. A. Liba and Y. Frankel. The letter describes in detail the self–sacrificing work done there.

When he visited Israel, HaRav Borenstajn met with the committee of the "Irgun Yotzei Wyszkow" ["Association of those who came from Wyszkow"], and reported about his visit to the old home city in which there is no trace today of any Jewish life.

Translator's footnote:

Agudath Israel of America is an ultra–Orthodox Jewish organization in the United States that aims to meet the needs of the Orthodox Jewish community, through charitable, educational, and social service projects across North America. Wikipedia

[Page 204]

Committee of Association of Those from Wyszkow in Israel and the book committee. From the right: Yekhieli Pinkhas, Ostry Khaija, Kovitz Khaim, Shtelung Liza and Menakhem, Farbsztejn Moishe, Wilenski Yerakhmiel, Bitmanowski Rivka, Mitelsbakh Yaakov and Caspi Menakhem.

[Page 205]

The Beginnings in Israel
by Moishe Farbsztejn, Los Angeles
Translated by Pamela Russ

Until the establishment of the State, the Wyszkower came to Israel with the third and fourth Aliyah, and also as individuals. Each one of them, with his own capacity and temperament helped form national Jewish life and participated in the struggles of settling, with the mandate government. Our compatriots would get together from time to time, but these were gatherings with personal interests, even though memories of Wyszkow were not lacking.

Presidium of Irgun Yotzei Wyszkow b'Yisroel ["Association of Those from Wyszkow in Israel"] during the memorial in Tel Aviv, 1950.
From right: Khaim Nosson Wengrow, Bina Holcman–Rakhman, Yakov–Dovid Przeticki, of blessed memory, the cantor, director of the Union of Those Who Came from Poland, Moishe Farbsztejn, Yakov Mitelsbakh.

Only after the end of World War II, and with the strengthening of flow of Aliyah with the surviving refugees, did our hearts begin to bear more strongly: Did any of our close ones manage to be saved? Will we merit to see in the Land of the Jews a saved member of any branch of Wyszkower families? And if they will come here beaten and downtrodden from the horrors of their war experiences – who will take care of them? Why should they not feel the brotherly, warm hands of their compatriots?

It was only in 1950 that we saw that of those who were saved from the sea of blood in Europe, our compatriots, Wyszkower Jews, were also coming to the established State, and they would have to be welcomed with brotherliness and warmth. The first official gathering of almost all the Wyszkower was held in the home of Y.D. Przeticki, of blessed memory, in Tel Aviv, with the participation of the well-known Yisroel Osman of Los Angeles. The elected administration put out a notice to all Wyszkower in the country and outside the country, that reported on the establishment of our organization and that urgent basic help was needed from the Wyszkower around the world. The needs were tremendous at that time, and the potential of help – very limited. The small capital was not sufficient for the ongoing expenses and loans. So, from time to time, the administration members would tax the fund and in that way would be able to help those who were in need.

In the first year of its existence (1950), the established loan fund gave out loans for minimum conditions. For those newly arrived, this provided financial and morale help at the first level. That same year, the Wyszkower in Los Angeles sent us $6,000 – and thanks to this money contribution, it was possible to extend the aide work in many areas. We also began to distribute assistance for the Jewish holidays twice a year for the needy – on the eve of Rosh Hashanah, and the eve of Passover.

Material aide also came from Argentina, and in the same way, all the compatriots over the world responded to the needs of the Wyszkower in Israel. In 1950, the first loans were distributed at more than 75 Israeli Lira – and later, in the year 1953, thanks to the help from foreign countries, the loans went to 200 Israeli Lira, which at that time, was a very significant amount. With this sum, every new immigrant to Israel was able to help himself with his first steps into the State of Israel.

The work grew. Our goal became: to put out a Yizkor Book and to build a permanent monument in memory of the Jewish community of Wyszkow. As the secretary of the Irgun Yotzei Wyszkow b'Yisroel for the first seven years, I was pleased that our organization had grown so beautifully. Both the aide fund, as well as the Beis Wyszkow, and the Wyszkow Book, can fill each of our compatriots, wherever they are, with real pride.

Memorial service in Beit Hachalutzot [Pioneer Women's Home] in Tel Aviv
From right: Moishe Farbsztejn, Yakov Mitelsbakh, Brama, Director of the Hitakhdut Olei
Polan ["Union of Those Who Came from Poland"], Menakhem Shtelung, Yakov Dovid
Przeticki, Yisroel Kaluski.

[Page 206]

Fifteen Years of the Irgun Yotzei Wyszkow b'Yisroel [Organizaton of Those Who Came from Wyszkow]

by Rabbi Yerakhmiel Wilenski – Grapa, Tel Aviv

Translated by Chava Eisenstein

Fifteen–years of the Wyszkower Association in Israel is certainly a modest amount of time for the many tens of years of existence and activities of our landsmanschaften [compatriot associations] in foreign countries. Nonetheless, our organization became the center of Wyszkow activity in the entire world and a central address for all our compatriots in Israel and in foreign countries.

One of the main objectives of the Wyszkower Association in Israel was and still is: to stretch out a warm and brotherly hand to each compatriot, a new immigrant who crosses the threshold of this Jewish State; help him to free himself from his experiences in the countries of exile, and to speed up the process of his acclimatization and organizing himself in this country in order that he live his life here in a warm environment. And one more thing: to eternalize the memory of the Wyszkower martyrs and pure souls who died in the Name of God – through memorial events, "Beis Wyszkow," a memorial room, a Yizkor Book, and so on.

How effective we were to accomplish these important tasks – the following report of our activities will tell.

The Establishment of the Organization

The Association in Israel also has its history until the establishment of the State [of Israel]. There were Wyszkower in Israel in a respectable number, about one hundred souls. Their main problem was – to create a new form of life. Without having a difference between life with an ideology or belonging to a [political] party, all strove towards "...And lead us upright into our land, and we will plant for us in our borders..." [recited as part of daily morning prayers], which connected the hundreds of Wyszkower in Israel to their new lifestyles and conditions. Whether these were new members of a kibbutz [collective farm] or moshav [settlement], or in a workshop and factory – they carved out their governing independence in their own land.

But everyone was tied to his town, and tried to bring over his close ones from the old home town. Understandably, in those circumstances it was not possible or necessary to create a landsmanschaft. A change came about with the tragic outcome of the Second World War.

At the end of 1946, we received the first reports of the tragic deaths of the Wyszkower Jews: From over 10,000 souls, only hundreds were saved. We did not know the full force of the tragedy. Then, the first group of Wyszkower orphan–children from Tehran* [*translator's note: The "Tehran Children" is the name used to refer to a group of Polish Jewish children, mainly orphans, who escaped the Nazi German occupation of Poland. This group of children found temporary refuge in orphanages and shelters in the Soviet Union, and were later evacuated with several hundred adults to Tehran, Iran, before finally reaching Palestine in 1943. From: Holocaust Encyclopedia] came to the land. Also, older immigrants, adults, who came to Israel from Teheran at the beginning of 1947, told about the destruction of our city. Not understanding the horrors of the tragedy, Wyszkower in Israel ran in great confusion to the Jewish Agency or to the Red Cross to learn about the fate of their own families. At the beginning of 1948, when they were already awaiting the establishment of the State of Israel, it became clear that the only way to save the survivors of the Holocaust was only by having them immigrate to Israel. But who would be the lucky ones, whose close ones were still alive – no one knew yet. Sporadically, committees were formed to help those survivors by sending food packages and providing first financial aid to the new immigrants. Mrs. Orensztejn (Goldwasser) Pesse, then in Haifa, assumed the responsibility at that time of taking care of the new immigrant children through Aliyat Hanoar ["Youth Aliyah"]. She came to Tel Aviv and together with Zamir (Bzhozha) Rokhel, Osenholtz Dvoshe, Baharav Zev, Brama Shmuel, Lieber Wigoda, and others, they turned to our compatriots to raise financial aid and any other means of assistance.

In 1948, smaller meetings of compatriots took place, where letters of saved compatriots were read, filled with tragic news and horrifying details. They requested from us that we establish an aid fund that would send help to the foreign countries and welcome the newly–arrived to the country. When the War of Independence broke out, the organization could not maintain the system that it wished: that there be representation of the Wyszkower youth in Israel; and to position the aid committee in a primary position. At that time all were preoccupied with securing a victory over the Arab aggressors. With the arrival of the first group of Wyszkower families from the German camps in the American zones, we learned many of the details of the tragic outcome of the Wyszkower Jews. The families that arrived were: Rosenberg, Przeticki, Wengrow, Postolski, Najman, and others, all community activists in Wyszkow for many years (councilmen, inspectors, and so on). They called meetings of other compatriots and requested overall activity and no involvement with small aid work.

The first official founding meeting was held on March 4, 1950, at the home of Reb Yakov–Dovid Przeticki, of blessed memory. The most important resolutions that were made at that time were: to establish a loan–free financial aid fund for constructive help; to distribute support for the needy. A committee of the friends was established:

Khaim Wengrow, Simkha Farbshtejn, Pesse Orensztejn–Goldwasser of Haifa,

Yisroel Kaluski, Rokhel Zamir (Bzhozha), Avrohom Kwiatek, Yakov–Dovid Przeticki,

Shmuel Brama, Yitzkhok Nudel, Moishe Farbsztejn, Yakov Najman, and Khaim Cembal.

Two main points underline the activities and path of development of the organization in Israel: a) the aid work in many different forms; the efforts to expand the activities, and set up the organization on a larger social/economic level. b) to contact the Wyszkower compatriots around the world. The mutual aid and collaborative work, as well as the common guidelines that were planned and realized during that time also provided partnered achievements. I will describe these activities chronologically in order to give an exact view of the active deeds and accomplishments.

[Page 207]

Renewed Activity

On May 8, 1950, the plans of the new committee were accepted. These were already the first sums, thanks to the donations and loans of the wealthier friends in Israel. Moyshe Farbsztejn, together with Yakov Dovid Przeticki, were designated to create a money fund, to take care of the accounts of membership fees of all Wyszkower in Israel, and to connect with the landsmanschaften [compatriot organizations] in America and Argentina, in order to acquire the required funds for a gemilas khesed [non–profit] account. Najman Yakov was assigned as the one responsible to collect the members' fees.

At the end of 1950, Mr. Yisroel Osman was elected – a Wyszkower who came from Los Angeles, known as a prominent literate, and researcher of legends and folklore, employee of the New Yorker "Tag" ["The Day,"] and author of several books. He becomes familiar with the work of the committee, and participates in a larger gathering of Wyszkower in Tel Aviv. He says that the active Wyszkower group in Los Angeles (Yekhiel Bzhozha, the Teffs, Markuskhammer, Rotblat, Byalis, and particularly the devoted secretary Muskat, and others) were prepared to help realize the economic and cultural plans of the Association in Israel.

In the months of October–December 1950, the following were co–opted to the committee: friends Moyshe Pakht, Rakhman (Holcman) Bina, Yakov Mitelsbakh, Yerakhmiel Wilenski, Laya Goldsztejn (Nudel), and Meyer Postolski.

The committee's work is extended. The treasurer, Yakov Dovid Przeticki, reports on the loans distributed and the greater number of requests for new loans. The secretary Moishe Farbsteyn reports on the capital of the loan fund that contained $500 at that time (then only 170 Israeli pounds) in Los Angeles; 85 pounds from Argentina, and the collective loan fund in Israel – 265 Israeli pounds. He also reports on the foreign food packages that were received from Buenos Aires, New York, and Los Angeles. M. Farbsztejn tells about the development of the Association in Los Angeles, and that they should provide them with the names of those who received the food packages; and also about the letter from the compatriots in Israel to the American committee with criticisms of this committee, with the request to send them food packages directly. At that time, there was a period of "austerity" in Israel. You only received food according to your cards. Our committee could not meet all the demands and persuade the needy ones that there were those even needier than they.

At another meeting, Secretary Farbsztejn reported that Los Angeles would soon send another $500 to the loan fund, and that the New Yorkers were asking for a list of the needy compatriots for Passover support. This type of aide was given to each compatriot that presented himself to the committee, and also to those who were embarrassed to come forward, even though they needed the help.

Constructive and Social Help

In the year 1951, the activities of the Association were reorganized. Separate committees now were responsible for their own resources of their activities. On the loans fund committee, the following were designated: Yisroel Kaluski, Moyshe Pakht, and Moishe Farbsztejn. The secretary's job is expanded with taking on Mr. Yerakhmiel Wilenski as protocol secretary. The idea of a Yizkor Book has not yet been actualized, because the economic situation in the country is still difficult. The steady stream of new Olim [immigrants to Israel] is occupying the committee with many demands and applications. We are looking for ways and means to address all these demands. Then we receive another $3,000 from Los Angeles. The loan fund is set up in the "Discount Bank." Then we look for ways to increase the loan possibilities for the compatriots. We adopt the recommendation from the bank "Otzar Amomi" ["People's Treasury"] to keep our capital there, and therefore we receive loans from them for double the sum. The regulations of the loan fund are: "Loans are given for a maximum sum of 100 Israeli pounds (then $300). There have to be two guarantors for every request for a loan. Each week, the loans committee reviews the requests, and the bank guarantees it with their own deposit, and they also decide who should receive the loan first, and who second." The loan committee borrows the designated sum from the committee, only for social needs and for those in difficult need. The social aid will be provided within the realms of possibility, primarily – from the support that we receive for this purpose from the American landsmanschaften or from individuals.

In the years 1952–1953, the activity of the Association is expanded. We receive another $3,000 from Los Angeles and a promise to send more annually in order to increase the monies in the loan fund in order to meet the needs of the hundreds of new Olim and help them establish their lives in Israel. New friends take on positions on the committee: Khanina Stolik, Berish Sapersztejn; Control Commission: Yosef Yanisz, Avrohom Kwiatek. The Association receives acknowledgement by all compatriots in Israel. Khaim Noson Wejngrow (from Haifa) requests that a branch of the loan fund be set up in Haifa. The treasurer Yakov Dovid Przeticki claims that compatriots in Haifa have received loans for a sum of 2,000 Israeli pounds over the last year and they are not being wronged for this. The decision is made to ease the load of the Haifa compatriots so that they should not have to go to Tel Aviv especially for this.

[Page 208]

Then, the suggestion of several friends is raised, that the loan fund should become a non–profit fund. Instead of the loans coming through the "People's Treasury" bank and the "Discount Bank" the loans should be allocated through a non–profit fund that would use the same percent that the bank uses. Also, our compatriots from distant areas would not have to come especially to these banks in Tel Aviv. This suggestion is accepted in principle, but with the condition that the fund is increased to 20,000 Israeli pounds in order to be able to meet the demands of the requests for loans. We negotiated with the Wyszkower committee in New York that they participate in this loan fund, aside from their yearly aid and individual assistance. That year, the "Building Club" was established in New York, that invigorates the local Wyszkower compatriots, but also causes disappointments and misunderstandings with the longstanding Wyszkower Associations. The "Building Club," which carries youthful energy, also connects with us, and, in a limited form, sends us support, disregarding that they are busy with local issues and challenges. In the American tradition, they make an effort to help the compatriots. We turn to all the Wyszkower Associations in New York, asking that they unite under one Association that would serve all the same interests. Our call was accepted only a few years later. The secretary of the "Building Club," Kh. Apelboim, to our joy, became the secretary of the united Wyszkower committee.

Also, the Association in Argentina sends tens of food packages annually for the needy in Israel, according to the list that is compiled by our special commission.

Plans for a "Beis [House of] Wyszkow" and a Yizkor Book

In the year 1954, the activities of the Association are increased by electing the following friends onto a committee: Menakhem Sztelung, Avrohom Wilner, Yakov Pakht, and Henja Goldbarszt. They generate new plans for greater tasks, such as putting up a monument for the Wyszkower martyrs: 1) publishing a Yizkor Book, 2) the plan from Los Angeles to put up a "Beis Wyszkow" in Tel Aviv that would provide for all the activities of the Association: the loan fund, a public hall for all the gatherings, and a Yizkor Book.

At the end of 1953, our secretary Moyshe Farbsztejn leaves for America. He receives full authorization to arrange for establishing the two memorials in Israel. In the year 1954, we receive another $1,000 from Los Angeles for the loan fund.

In the new administration, Menakhem Sztelung is elected vice–president. The committee for the "Beis Wyszkow" is: Avrohom Wilner – chairman; Yisroel Kaluski and Menakhem Sztelung – members. Yakov Pakht is coopted to the treasury committee (Kaluski, Farbsztejn, and Przeticki). The Yizkor Book committee: Yisroel Kaluski, Menakhem Sztelung, Yerakhmiel Wilenski, Laya Nudel. Chairman, secretary, protocol secretary, and others – as before.

According to the reports of Moishe Farbsztejn, there is important material for the Yizkor Book in New York, in the YIVO Institute [Jewish Research Institute], and elsewhere. A lot is accomplished in Los Angeles about "Beis Wyszkow": They collect a sum of $10,000. They have already collected a sum of $3,900. After sending the plan of "Beis Wyszkow" over to Los Angeles, it seems that they already have $4,000 for this goal, and they are in touch about this with the Associations in New York and Argentina.

The administration next addresses the issue of legalizing the organization. A lawyer is working out the regulations that are discussed at great length. The committee for the "Beis Wyszkow" suggests buying building sites with good conditions. All the suggestions, prepared and presented by Mr. Avrohom Wilner, are confirmed and afterwards – are put aside because of shortages in funds. In the years 1954–55, the loan fund gives out loans of sums more than 18,000 Israeli pounds annually (more than a hundred loans per year).

At the annual Yizkor evenings, there are more than 400 participants. With increased activity, opening our own office becomes a reality, since the work of the Association becomes very challenging. Reb Yakov Dovid Przeticki takes compatriots into his home because of debts and all kinds of other issues. Others are also taken into homes of other committee members. There are administration meetings every week at another member's home. The question about building or buying a house becomes pressing, and at the same time – close to reality. According to the reports that we receive from all the landsmanschaften, special committees are formed for the "Beis Wyszkow" in Israel. In the year 1955, the Association in Israel begins to work out the plan of "Beis Wyszkow" and negotiate plans for purchasing a building plot or old house. Also, the regulations of the Association are decided by us and are sent to the government for legalization.

A special committee addresses special need situations and social requirements of the Wyszkower in Israel. From the New York Ladies Auxiliary, we receive the first sum of $50 as social assistance. Also, the Building Club sends significant sums for special projects, indicating the persons who should be given the aid.

January 16, 1956 – Shevat 3, 5717. Reb Yakov–Dovid Przeticki, of blessed memory, our long–time, commendable community activist, and in his last years our capable treasurer, took his final leave from us. His devotion, activism, and self–sacrifice for our compatriots served as a symbol of brotherly assistance and reciprocal commitment. At the meeting of the administration on the 23rd of January, 1956, his memory is honored, and on his shloshim [30 days after death] – a memorial takes place at his gravesite.

[Page 209]

Reb Pinkhas Yekhieli (Shultz) is invited to a special meeting and he is elected as treasurer of the Association. When his father–in–law, may he rest in peace, is still alive, he would assist him with managing the loan fund.

February 28, 1956, at a meeting about the loan fund, Mr. Yekhieli reports that the fund's capital consists of:

In the Bank "People's Treasury"	8460.80 Israeli pounds
In the "Discount Bank"	875.74 Israeli pounds
Change	2342.75 Israeli pounds
Total:	11679.29 Israeli pounds

We recently received 1000 Israeli pounds from Los Angeles.

In the month of February, twelve loans totalling 2431 Israeli pounds were given out.

The last annual report by H. Przeticki, of blessed memory, stated:

During the year, until September 1955, 116 loans were given out, with an approximate sum of 20,900 Israeli pounds. The capital in both banks, after dealing with old debts, is 9,000 Israeli pounds. Understandably, the needs are much greater.

The administration has decided to create an internal fund to increase the capital of the loan fund. The friends of the administration, on the spot, give 105 Israeli pounds and it is confirmed that a tax would be added with an annual due.

In April 1956, the editor Mr. Dovid Sztokfish, was assigned to begin collecting material for the Yizkor Book. Then we also decide on the mission of the "Beis Wyszkow" that should address all the needs of the compatriots in Israel – both as a memorial and for the activities of the Association. The income will provide for the loan fund and for the social expenses. The plan of the "Beis Wyszkow" committee, with H. Wilner at the head, includes: The costs will be $10,000, the construction $8,000. In August 1956, old debts are paid off. The friends of the administration create a special internal fund.

The report of the seven months of 1956 (February – September): membership dues – 371 Israeli pounds; special find – 1230 Israeli pounds; loans – 10,400 Israeli pounds.

In July 1956, Mr. Farbsztejn travels to Los Angeles for the second time. He deals with the Association in New York and Los Angeles about the Yizkor Book and about acquiring material from YIVO. At the annual general meeting, September 1956, Reb Dovid Sztokfish describes his steps to gather material and preparations for publishing the "Sefer Wyszkow." At the constituents meeting, a special committee is elected for the Yizkor Book: Kaluski Yisroel, Sztelung Menakhem, Wilenski Yerakhmiel, Yekhieli Pinkhas, and Farbsztejn Moishe. Chairman – Kaluski Yisroel; vice chairman – Sztelung Menakhem. Treasury committee: Kaluski, Sztelung, Wilner. Secretary – Farbsztejn Moishe. Treasurer – Yekhieli Pinkhas. Building committee – Sztelung, Wilner, Mitelsbakh. Protocol secretary – Wilenski. Control committee – Yonisz Yosef, Rakhman Bina.

In the months of January – April, 1957, many Wyszkower immigrated to Israel. The committee decided to give each of them 20–40 Israeli pounds. The Book Committee addresses the issue of money, paper, editing. A special internal collection is established for the book, so as not to overtax the expenses of the loan fund. A special circular is sent to all the compatriots requesting they send material and dues. Mr. Yekhieli takes the responsibility upon himself to collect the debts of the loans that were neglected all this time.

Because of Kaluski's illness, M. Sztelung is elected chairman. Because of the absence of Secretary Farbsztejn, Yekhieli replaces him, and later – Wilenski. June 26, 1957, Mr. Farbsztejn returns to Israel. In a special meeting in the house of Mr. Sztelung, he reports on the Wyszkower Associations in New York and Los Angeles: They already have $6,000 in the bank, and another $4,000 will be added in the near future. The Wyszkower in New York will finance the Yizkor Book, and the "Beis Wyszkow." The Building Club already has a few hundred dollars for the Yizkor Book.

July 4, 1957, an administration meeting takes place in the home of Bina Rakhman. Moishe Farbsztejn reports that he is going back to America for a longer period. He asks that before he leaves to America, we should buy a plot of land for the "Beis Wyszkow." We also have to elect a secretary and a treasury committee because of the departure of three members of the administration: Kaluski to Europe; Sztelung to Argentina; Farbsztejn to America. Leyb Holcman (from Argentina), who attended the meeting, assured the representatives of both Wyszkower Associations of establishing the memorials in Israel.

A treasury committee is elected: Wilner Avrohom, Rakhman Bina, and Postolski Meyer. As secretary – Wilenski Yerakhmiel. Mr. Farbsztejn is coopted on the building committee, and they take on the responsibility of purchasing land within the next two weeks. But the Los Angeles group wants to wait for the participation of Argentina and New York for this plan. From New York, they write that the local Khevra Tehilim absolutely wants that in the "Beis Wyszkow" there should be a place for praying. Then they would commit to paying into this plan. We decide to wait with the "Beis Wyszkow" and increase the work on the Yizkor Book.

July 1957, we organize a farewell evening in honor of the departure of M. Sztelung to Argentina. He receives the mandate of the Association to work with the Association in Buenos Aires with the Yizkor Book and "Beis Wyszkow," and also to describe the efforts of Secretary Wilenski for the unification – so that they should collaborate in the questions of the Yizkor Book (that has no political bearing)...

[Page 210]

He feels that the trip was successful, even though it had a personal nature. At a reception in his honor, a $5,000 commitment is made for the book and for the House. Also, his efforts for a union were fruitful.

Beginnings of the Realization

The year 1958 marks the beginning of the realization of the two large projects. March 1958, our compatriot HaRav Bronstejn comes to Israel as a delegate of the American Jewish Rescue Committee, on his way to Jewish children in Poland, born during the war years. He reports to us about the excitement of the Wyszkower in New York regarding the memorials in Israel, and that the New Yorkers would collect a lot more than the Association in Los Angeles. Then, a larger delegation of leaders and founders of the Association in Los Angeles comes to Israel. We have several meetings with them, dedicated to the treasury reports that contained:

During the year 1957, 120 loans were distributed for an approximate sum of 23,000 Pounds. The capital:

In the banks	10,020 Israeli pounds
Exchange	1,811 Israeli pounds
Postponed debts	97 Israeli pounds
Yizkor Book	111 Israeli pounds
Support in the form of loans	350 Israeli pounds
Total:	12,389 Israeli pounds
From taxes and membership fees	2,306 Israeli pounds
Expenses and support	2,306 Israeli pounds
Formal debts	401 Israeli pounds

These figures do not satisfy the compatriots, since their requests for loans have not been acknowledged. The administration takes on the action of increasing the loan fund by another 5,000 Israeli pounds, possibly with the help of New York. The Building Committee holds several meetings with the delegates and the same for the Yizkor Book committee. They familiarize themselves with the many arms of the work and needs of the Association in Israel. April 29, 1958, we organize a festive event for them in "Beis Sokolow" with greetings honoring the founders and activists of the Wyszkower landsmanschaften [compatriot associations] in America. A discussion of the goals of our activities followed. In closing, all the delegates of Los Angeles enthusiastically agreed to facilitate the building of the "Beis Wyszkow" and to send over $10,000 for that goal.

The activity of the Association is lessened, after canceling the contract to buy the "Beis Wyszkow" on Brenner Street. Mr. Kaluski became very ill at that time and did not participate in the weekly meetings. The treasurer, Mr. Yekhieli, is in Europe, and Mr. Sztelung also acts as the official for the loan fund. The work for the Yizkor Book encounters great difficulties. We call a larger meeting of the active compatriots. The coopted members receive a mission, each in his own area: Alenberg – in Haifa; Mrs. Goldbarszt – in Netanya; Mitelsbakh – in Petakh Tikva. The point – to collect material and money for the Yizkor Book. Wilenski is assigned to organize the money collections and create a fund for the book. Mr. Bruk Binyomin Khaim, former secretary of "Hekhalutz" in Wyszkow, is assigned as vice–secretary. A special account is opened in the "Bank Hapoalim" for the Yizkor Book fund and for the "Beis Wyszkow." We also receive new material for the book.

We come to an agreement with the Association of Polish Jews and they make their place on Ben Yehuda Street 100 available to us. We hold our meetings there. The secretary welcomes compatriots there twice a week in the evening hours.

The Goal – Our Own Non–Profit Fund

The reorganization of the committee, under the chairmanship of Menakhem Sztelung, brings in a vitality and expansion of the activities in all areas.

The program for the year 1959 includes:

1. An increase to the loan fund and the creation of our own non–profit fund in order to improve the deficient activities of the loan fund that had losses because of the bank expenses, displeasure of the compatriots, for whom each inaccurate payment of the rates incurred great costs (each letter cost 2 Israeli pounds) for them, other than the percentage, and so on). All of this was taken off the capital of the Association, which was responsible for each loan. Many times it was impossible to collect on the debts, because they informed us when the person was already out of the country, or for other reasons. Also, the loan fund did not allow the compatriots to leave part of their loan in the bank as membership fee, as a bank percentage, or as other expenses. Instead of that, they pay their membership fee to the Association – 10 Israeli pounds from that loan for 200 Israeli pounds. When they turn to the treasury committee to delay repayment until later, this does not cost any money. The treasury lender, Mr. Yekhieili, receives the assignment to work through this new program and be in contact with the Postal–Bank, and then to transfer the money from the People's Treasury to the Postal Bank.

We create the women's committee, which helps us in the work of the Association, such as: social aide, collection activities, welcoming compatriots, all kinds of technical work, organizing welcomes for guest, and all kinds of celebrations.

We receive more work for the book from New York, Los Angeles, Argentina. Mr. Wilenski gives the sum of 3,000 Israeli pounds (for the necrology) from New York, Los Angeles, and from Israel – over 2,000 Israeli pounds as a contract for increased responsibility. For this money, we buy paper for the book, for a reasonable sum of 5,000 Israeli pounds.

[Page 211]

The Building Committee renews its activity, receiving guarantees from Argentina regarding sending over the first $1,000 to Los Angeles, and that in time, they would send an additional $4,000. Los Angeles agrees immediately to send over the $10,000 for the "Beis Wyszkow."

March 29, 1959, these foreign guests are welcomed: Mr. Radziminski and wife, Mr. Tzimerman and wife, HaRav Bronsztejn, also Mr. Leybel Rozenberg and wife, who came at that time to settle in Israel, participated in the meeting of the administration. After the greetings and the addressing of the requests for Passover support and loans, Mr. Radziminski donates 1,200 Israeli pounds for Passover support and 1,000 Israeli pounds to create the non–profit fund. This guest relates that these past few days he had received favorable information about the work of the Association in Israel. HaRav Bronsztejn talks about the accomplishments of Mr. Radziminski and his wife Rokhel in New York. Also, Mr. Tzimerman reports on the many years of activity in all areas of the "Society" and the new interest of the compatriots in New York to help the compatriots in Israel. Mr. Wilenski greets the guest and briefly talks about the accomplishments of the Association in Israel. The committee members have given their time voluntarily to the committee, but the needs are much greater than the means. Mr. Yekhieli gives a report about the activity of the loan fund. Mr. Radziminski assumes the responsibility to place the tombstone on Har Tzion in Jerusalem (which the Association in Israel had decided to do, according to the secretary's report), and he hopes to meet a greater number of compatriots in order to hear their requests and reports about this in New York. This type of gathering took place on khol hamoed [the interim days] of Passover. In the reception hall of the "Association of Emigres from Poland" and with the participation of 200 compatriots, Mr. Radziminski promises to establish the non–profit fund earlier, and after that the "Beis Wyszkow" and the Yizkor Book. During his visit, they set up the marble memorial plaque on Har Tzion for the Wyszkower martyrs.

In June 1959, we receive from them 2,400 Israeli pounds for the non–profit fund (which they promised during the farewell banquet for them at the home of secretary Mr. Wilenski). Then we receive about 5,000 Israeli pounds from Argentina for the projects of the Yizkor Book and for "Beis Wyzkow." Meanwhile, we decide to borrow this sum from the non–profit fund and remove the funds from the "People's Treasury." We begin to manage the non–profit fund according to the new regulations.

February 13, 1960, the women's committee organized a "Tu b'Shevat festival" [15th day of the Hebrew month of Shevat, celebration of the new fruit, usually mid–March], with a rich program. Hundreds of compatriots from the entire country participated, being so happy that they had the opportunity to get together in warm, friendly evenings. The income was directed towards social assistance and support for the holidays.

July 26, 1959, with the help of the Association in Argentina, the Wyszkower Association in Montevideo is established. They immediately connect to us. We ask for their collaboration with our work on the Yizkor Book and "Beis Wyszkow." March 21, 1960, we receive from them the first $100 as a contract for the book, and for materials and pictures.

June 1960, Mr. Biales and his wife come to Israel from Los Angeles, along with guest from Argentina and Montevideo. At a larger meeting, the ongoing activities and the relationship between the two compatriot associations are addressed. Mr. Biales guarantees that the purchase of "Beis Wyszkow" will be realized.

October 1960, the book "landsmanschaften in Israel" is out, with a description by secretary Y. Wilenski, about the activities of the Wyszkower Jews in Israel. Unfortunately, some entries in the article were changed to refer to the Association in Argentina, instead of in Montevideo.

Guest from Argentina

The delegation of Wyszkower landsmanschaften to the World Congress of Polish Jewry, was in Tel Aviv, January 1961, represented by: on the organizational committee – Aryeh Sztelung – chairman; Moishe Kwiatek – member. On the social constructive committee – Menakhem Sztelung – member. They participate in several meetings of the committee and various other committees, such as: the loan fund, Yizkor Book, and "Beis Wyszkow." January 28, 1961, a large "Tu b'Shevat festival" in the reception hall of "Beis Hasofer," with the participation of more than 400 compatriots. The delegation from Argentina was energized by the Wyszkower Association in Israel.

February 12, 1961, at an extraordinary meeting of the committee, the purchase of "Beis Wyszkow" was confirmed as a house that was being constructed on Bugrasow Street 25.

The committee gives over the full rights to the chairman of the building committee, Mr. Avrohom Wilner. At the same time, we hold gatherings of compatriots, and within a few months, over 2,000 Israeli pounds are collected.

Mr. Wilner devotes a lot of time to establishing the "Beis Wyszkow." Thanks to his expertise, the hall of the "Beis Wyszkow" was extended and he saved some necessary expenses.

The Wyszkower center in Israel – "Beis Wyszkow," becomes a reality. Participating in this memorial, are Wyszkower in

Los	with 20,000
Angeles	Israeli pounds
New York	with 9,500 "
Argentina	with 6,000 "
Montevideo	with 500 "
Israel	with 3,000 "

In September 1961, the annual Yizkor evening is already organized to be in the hall of the "Beis Wyszkow." More than 400 compatriots participated. The hall is not yet completed. There are no chairs to sit on, no tables. But the joy of our compatriots is great.

[Page 212]

Presidium of the "Khanukas Habayis" celebration [for new home], May 12, 1962. From right: D. Sztokfish, editor of "Sefer [Book of] Wyszkow"; Yerakhmiel Wilenski, general secretary of the Wyszkower landsmannschaft in Israel; Menakhem Sztelung (speaking), chairman of the landsmannschaft; Pinkhas Yekhieli (Shultz), treasurer; Y. Mitelsbakh and M. Kaspi – administrative members.

Along with the mood of the sad evening, hope is expressed that the house will provide for the spirited health of Wyszkower Jewry. The words of Cantor Brukhanski (Malkiel's son): "velo yosefu ledaava od," ["May we know of no further harm"] take on a profound meaning...

On December 5, 1961, we organized a welcome for Rav Silver, newly-elected president of "Khevra Tehilim Anshei Wyszkow" ["Group (Congregation) of Psalm Reciters, People of Wyszkow"] in New York. After learning about our activities, he offers several suggestions to expand the activities of our Association by establishing a special fund for constructive help. He takes on the responsibility for this objective to help raise money in New York, and offers a donation from the Khevra Tehilim for "Beis Wyszkow."

At the beginning of 1962, the inner furnishings of the hall are completed. March 22, 1962, a welcoming is organized for the secretary from the Los Angeles union for the Wyszkower – Moishe Farbsztejn. The guest also participates in several meetings of the administration and committees. Issues of the Yizkor Book, the non-profit fund, social aide, and other topics are discussed.

The Festive Opening of "Beis Wyszkow"

May 12, 1962, with 500 compatriots and foreign guests present, the celebration took place, along with the celebration of the 15th Yom Ha'Atzmaut ["Day of Independence of the State of Israel"]. The representatives of the Wyszkower foreign Associations are honored with lighting six memorial candles in memory of the martyrs. In his opening speech, the chairman of the Association, Menakhem Sztelung, underlined the importance of our own "house'" in Israel for our survivors of the destruction, and then he thanked the Wyszkower around the world for their open willingness and interest to establish the "Beis Wyszkow" in Tel Aviv. The chairman of the evening ended his impressive speech with a "shehekheyanu" [blessing over a new home].

The secretary of the Association, Yerakhmiel Wilenski, reports on the tasks and the accomplishments of the Wyszkower landsmanschaft in Israel in the past, and the plans for the future. He tells of the compatriots' joy all over the world in relation to this festivity, and the blessings that they sent. He ends with the wish that this joyous event, that is mixed with sorrow, in memory of our dearest, the martyrs of Wyszkow, should in the future come to full joy, " oz yimo'lei s'khok pinu ... ve'hoyinu semeickhim" ["our mouths will be filled with laughter ... and we will be joyous": Book of Psalms, 126:2]...

The following gave greetings: Engineer Anshel Reiss, chairman of the Union of Polish Immigrants to Israel; the well–known Borukh Yismakh, Bronsztejn, and Yakov Palukh – from Argentina; Rotblat – from Los Angeles; Sholom Grapa – Uruguay; Mrs. Mondry – Detroit; Mr. Khashmal – New York; and also guest from Mexico and Canada.

[Page 213]

Further greetings from: Margalit – from the landsmanschaft Ostrow-Mazowieck; Warsawski – from the Association out of Serock; director – from Pultusk, Asher Ben–Ono (of blessed memory) – from the Association out of Mizac.

The artistic program, the dances, the entertainment, and bright cheer, left a wonderful impression on all those present.

After the Khanukas Habayis, there was new energy for completing the work of the book and the printing. The editorial committee meets often and presents their thoughts about the material gathered. The clichis [printing plates] are ordered. Also, in September 1962, for the annual memorial event, other compatriots brought more material for the book.

Now, with our own place, the work grows. Also, the non–profit fund acquires a lot of activity. Because of a shortage of time and money, we put off for later the organizing of the memorial hall. We think that sales of the book that will be published at the end of 1963, will help take care of the future investments of our place, which include: a synagogue with an ark for the Torah scroll; a library, and the memorial room. "V'osu li mikdash v'shokhanti b'sokhom" : (Pirkei Avos) Ethics of Our Fathers ["And you shall build Me (God) a dwelling place, and I shall dwell therein"]...

To complete the report, it is noteworthy to point out the following set activities of the Association of the Wyszkower in Israel:

The non–profit fund: Loans of more than 200–300 Israeli pounds are given out, which in annual sales relates to 22,200 Israeli pounds.

Social aide: Twice a year, for Passover and Sukkos, help is given to needy compatriots. Also over one year, in unusual circumstances, help is provided.

"Beis Wyszkow": Every Tuesday, once a week, there are gatherings and meetings of the administration, committees, and activists in the Association. In the evening, all the compatriots also discuss their issues with the Association. In the "Beis Wyszkow" there are also the annual memorials, meetings, and we are also planning to set up a library.

Memorial evening: Each year, on one of the Ten Days of Repentance [between Rosh Hashanah and Yom Kippur], we hold the annual evening in memory of the destroyed Jewish community of Wyszkow. Through invitations and announcements in the press and on the radio, we let everyone know about the evening's event. After the memorial, there is the annual general meeting of the Association, with reports of the activities and elections to the officials.

The Prayer House: We are planning to set up a House of Prayer in our place, and to bring a Torah scroll from New York, and to build a marble ark for it, and a bookcase for the religious books.

Yizkor Book: As these lines are being written, the Yizkor Book is already at the printer. Truthfully. With the publishing of the Yizkor Book, an obstacle arises. We know, however, that the long wait will be compensated with the content, appearance, and distinction of the book.

Memorial room: Completion of the "Beis Wyszkow" will not be realized, if the memorial room will not be set up as required for the eternal memory of the tortured Wyszkow martyrs. In this room each compatriot will be able to be alone with the holy memory of his dear ones, and also learn a chapter of Mishnayos [Talmud study], read our Yizkor Book ... For this goal, we already received the sum of 1,200 Israeli pounds from the Ladies' Auxiliary in New York.

Women's committee at the Khanukas Habayis celebration ["Dedication to new home"] of "Beis Wyszkow."

Our Officials

The administration of the Association of Wyszkower in Israel consists of the following persons:

Chairman – Sztelung Menakhem. Vice chairman – Kowic Khaim, Mitelsbakh Yakov. Secretary – Wilenski Yerakhmiel. Vice secretary – Kaspi Menakhem. Non–profit fund committee: Sztelung Menakhem, Yekhieli Pinkhas, Bismonowski Rivka, Wilenski Yerakhmiel. Committee of the "Beis Wyszkow" – Sztelung Menakhem, Wilner Avrohom, Yekhieli Pinkhas. Book committee: Sztelung Menakhem, Wilenski Yerakhmiel, Yekhieli Pinkhas, Kaspi Menakhem. Control committee: Yanisz Yosef, Kwaitek Avrohom.

With emotion and satisfaction, we end the fifteen–year active and creative work of the Association of Wyszkower in Israel.

***Please note that the written content appearing on pages 214-220 is virtually the same as that appearing on pages 206-213. To save paper, the text was not duplicated.**

[Page 215]

Dedication of "House of Wyszków" in Tel-Aviv, 1962 The crowd in the hall.

[Page 216]

R. Yaakov Dovid Pshetitsky Z"L

[Page 220]

לזכר עולם

האבן הזאת תהיה לנו לגל-עד

ולמזכרת נצח לזכר הורינו אחינו

אחיותינו נשינו וטפינו הקדושים

בני קהילת **וישקוב**

והסביבה (עיי נהר בוג פולין)

שנהרגו ושנשחטו ונשרפו ונקברו חיים

אחרי עינויים קשים עיי האכזרים הנאצים

הגרמנים וגרודיהם הארורים ימ"ש בשנות

התרצ"ט ה'תש"ה, ארץ אל תכסי דמם

וזכרם הטהור לא ימוש מקרבנו, תנצב"ה

מנציחים יוצאי וישקוב בישראל ובגולה

The memorial plaque on Mount Zion in Jerusalem commemorating the Jewish community in Wyszków, which was annihilated by the Germans

[Page 221]

Vishkov Association of New York
by Yekhiel Burshteyn
Translated by David Goldman

1

Our Vishkov Association in New York is now sixty years old – a rather respectable age. Our members have given their time, health and labor for our organization, and have maintained and cared for their beloved memories. When we get together, we talk about Vishkov of former times and its Jews, community, Jewish institutions, large and small streets, and houses were once our cradles stood. We think of our Vishkov Association as a living monument that we have created on free American soil in honor of our former town that no longer exists. We want to care for this monument and constantly give it new life, similar to the way we constructed a living memorial for Vishkov in the free Jewish State with the aid we provided Israel through the building we established in our names. Now we have created a special unified Vishkov Aid Committee for Israel, about which I will write later in this survey.

2

Over the more than sixty years of the existence and work of our association we have had great and important times. The association's establishment itself was an important event that took place in times totally different from those we are in today when there is highly developed and vibrant Jewish life here in America. In this book, it is worthwhile to reconstruct a picture of life in that former period, when our compatriot [landsmanshaft] association in New York was founded, alongside an array of other ethnic organizations.

The immigrant Jew from the cities and shtetls of Eastern Europe felt lonely on New York's East Side in those days. The leading activists in the Jewish neighborhoods were called Yehudim, and were primarily concerned with philanthropy. They didn't take into consideration the feelings and opinions of the new immigrants about how to build their various institutions. The attitude of the radicals toward the common immigrant in Jewish New York was no better: as far as they were concerned the poor peddler would never turn into a bourgeois who ought to disappear, and the immigrants' religious needs were certainly of no concern whatsoever.

The immigrants started to become organized; their longing for the customs and traditions of the old country, as well as their loneliness, created the need for compatriot organizations. Helping each other in times of trouble and assisting new immigrants to get settled and then bring over their family therefore played a very large role. This was how in a rather short time hundreds of compatriot organizations with hundreds of thousands of members developed at that time. In addition, the more the new immigrant became more Americanized and accustomed to his new environment, the more proud and confident he felt. His low self-esteem and inferiority complex disappeared, and the compatriot organization to which he belonged assisted him immensely.

The significance of the compatriot organizations in Jewish life in America at that time began to grow, and their influence continued to spread. It should be noted that the trade union campaign in America on behalf of the Histadrut in Israel deserves a lot of credit for increasing the importance of our compatriot organizations. The trade union campaign on behalf of the Histadrut was the first event that attracted compatriot organizations to become involved, and to this very day our organizations have a respectable place in Israel. For many years there has existed a special department in the United Jewish Appeal for our organizations. In addition, large Jewish educational institutions, such as Yeshiva University in New York, have appreciated the importance of attracting the compatriot organizations to become involved in financially assisting their institutions.

This was how our Vishkov Association was established in 1896 in New York in the same way as other associations were founded. In the beginning the Vishkov compatriots used to get together over a glass of beer every Sabbath evening to share memories of the old country and to provide the new immigrant with lodging and pay the "Shop" to teach the new immigrant a trade. Hirsh-Meir Kotlowitz, one of our compatriots, was one of the greatest people involved in communal hospitality. Many of us still remember him today. Although he was himself a poor laborer, his modest apartment was always open to newly arrived immigrants; he assisted them with his advice and with his actions.

Due to the constant influx of new immigrants, the compatriot groups multiplied and grew larger. Soon they had to rent special halls for their weekly meetings. Their expenses also grew. Instead of relying constantly on contributions, they established membership dues. Eventually we came to the conclusion that it was appropriate for our association to have a managing committee. In December 1904 we established what was then known as the Independent Vishkov Immigration Support Association.

[Page 222]

The following individuals were chosen for the managing committee: Avraham Mittelsberg, president; Yechezkel Parover, vice president; Shmuel Gemara, financial secretary; Morris Topfel, recording secretary and Shmuel Wideletz, cashier.

The most important goal of the new Vishkov organization was to assist the recent "green" compatriots, both financially and emotionally. Over time, the members became settled in their new country and brought over their families. However, soon new problems arose, such as the need to be able to provide medical assistance, build a cemetery, etc. At that time we had a doctor, the well-known community activist, Dr. Nathan Rotnov, who was hired annually and provided free medical assistance to members. Later on he played an important role at the Hebrew University of Jerusalem. Dr. Rotnov was an active member in the Vishkov Association for a long time.

The old Vishkov Assistance Association, which was founded in 1896, had its own cemetery; its financial situation improved as well. The very first immigrants of our shtetl belonged to the old association. One of those members was the late David Feingold, who some of us remember to this very day. According to our late compatriot, Chaim Aharon Yoskovich, even before the old association, there was a first Vishkov society under the name Ezrat Achim [Fraternal Assistance]. Yoskovich was a vice-president of the society, which only existed for a short time.

The new task was to merge the two organizations: the old 1896 Vishkov association and the new 1904 association; the merger was accomplished in 1906. The total financial assets of the new unified organization amounted to four hundred and eight dollars and 31 cents, and the association had a total membership of 142. The unified organization started providing material for its members; it offered financial assistance in the sum of six dollars a week in the event of illness of any of its members. This was in addition to the assistance provided to the newcomers.

Our Vishkov Association was one of the first compatriot organizations that became concerned with the cultural situation of its members. The association fought against the germanization of Yiddish that at that time was occurring in the Jewish associations, both in the management of the organization and in the spoken language used in the meetings. We were virtually the only ones who were concerned, therefore, that the bylaws of the association were written in good, clean Yiddish. To achieve that purpose, we hired the well-known Yiddish journalist Yaakov Pfeffer, who wrote our bylaws, which are the same as the ones we use today (with some minor changes). This contrasted with the way other associations' bylaws were written in a mixture of Yiddish and German. The leaders of our association also fought against the heretical movements and disgusting practices that could be seen in the Jewish neighborhoods in New York. We didn't allow our members to participate in the open revelry that took place on sad Jewish occasions such as the Ninth of Av [commemorating the destruction of the Temples in Jerusalem], and prohibited the repugnant tradition of holding a communal meal after the death of a member, etc.

3

When World War I broke out, the Vishkov Association became heavily involved in all aspects of the war effort: it invested in Liberty Bonds, in savings plans, and donated significant sums of money to the Red Cross and other aid organizations on behalf of those suffering in Europe because of the war. The association also assisted its members who had gone off to war. Because of the war it was decided to disband the youth organization called The Vishkov Young Men that had been established earlier, and it merged with the Vishkov Association. Aside from the members of the former Vishkov Young Men, the association took in other new members. Our association needed a large hall where it could hold its meetings. At that time, the Vishkov Association also began to become involved in general Jewish community life in the United States. To the extent that we were financially able we supported an array of important institutions and activities. In one case, we also provided assistance to the shirt-workers' union that had gone out on strike.

Apart from the above activities, our association distinguished itself in its work on behalf of those suffering in Vishkov because of the war, and collected thousands of dollars from among our members. Right after the war our compatriot Benny Dovriss traveled as our special emissary to bring aid to the impoverished Jewish population of Vishkov. During the First World War we also participated in establishing the American Jewish Congress, which supported the historical resolution that called for the rebirth of a Jewish state in the Land of Israel [this would have been the Balfour Declaration]. Our delegates to the American Jewish Congress were our compatriots Benny Dovriss and Paul Kramer. Morris Topfel, who became our president in 1914, deserves a lot of credit for the Vishkov Association's expanded activity in those days.

4

One of the things that stimulated the desire to establish compatriots' associations in New York – as mentioned earlier – was the problem of cemeteries. Although in the old country it was possible to have a single cemetery for the entire community, this was not possible in New York because of the diversity of the Jewish population. In the early years, our Vishkov Association owned a small cemetery, part of the Mt. Zion Cemetery near New York. In 1911 the Association purchased a larger property at the Mt. Hebron Cemetery, but due to a shortage of funds, we were unable to construct a fence around the cemetery until 1923. The president at the time, Max Baslav, energetically took on the mission to build one. In 1923 a special fence committee that was set up executed the project. The issue was so important that to this day the Vishkov members are grateful to that committee for their work to set up the fence and at the same time increased the Association's assets by six hundred dollars.

[Page 223]

The success in carrying out the work on the fence led not only to concern on behalf of the dead, but also provided important work for the living. There was an initiative to build our own building, a Vishkov center in New York, where all the compatriots could get together and engage in social activities. This impulse was a common one in Jewish life in those days because of good economic times and growing employment. Our association became very active in order to carry out the plan for the Vishkov center. It was the finest and most interesting period in the lives of Vishkov compatriots.

5

There were, however, internal disputes. Some of the large contributors quietly agitated against the plan. A proposal to dissolve the building fund that we had already put together was accepted in May, 1925, and the money was returned to the contributors. Nevertheless, because of our various undertakings that were part of the building fund several thousand dollars remained in the Association's funds.

At the time of the depression in the United States after 1929 our association did not give up its work in providing assistance for Vishkov compatriots, including for Vishkov itself. The Association provided financial assistance to its members and arranged free Chanukah concerts and other kinds of entertainment for members and their families.

Our association was intensively involved in activities during the Second World War. We bought thirty thousand dollars of government bonds, and hundreds of our young men served in the army. We participated in the United Jewish Appeal and in efforts on behalf of the Histadrut in Palestine, HIAS, yeshivas etc.

We still feel strongly about our responsibilities as a compatriots' organization. The truth is that we share our fate with the other compatriots' organizations in which the older members are the majority and the young people haven't become involved. We made valiant attempts and spent quite a bit of money to get the youth involved, but without success. We can only say that in our Vishkov Association we are emphasizing those things which are strongly rooted in Jewish nationalism and an attachment to Jewish traditions which we brought with us from the old country.

We are as involved as we ever were in campaigns on behalf of the United Jewish Appeal campaigns, the Histadrut, HIAS, yeshivas in New York, etc., and we are proud of the fact that our compatriots' association, to the extent possible, has contributed a brick to the building of the Jewish state. In this way we are striving with all our strength to maintain the beautiful traditions of our Vishkov Association in New York, from its establishment until this very day.

6

We should take this opportunity to make special mention in this survey of the activities of the General United Vishkov Aid Committee which was founded at the end of the First World War in 1918, and was an initiative of our Vishkov Association in New York. As with all of our work, in our United Vishkov Aid Committee we were concerned with all of the beautiful old traditions we were raised with. We did our aid work quietly, without any fanfare, and thereby always remembered what we learned in cheder, that 'man does not live by bread alone.' We provided assistance to the needy residents of our hometown Vishkov, and supported the Beis Yosef yeshiva and other institutions in Vishkov when they still existed.

Vishkov Ladies' Organization in New York]

As soon as our United Aid Committee was founded, we began an energetic and aggressive campaign, and collected thousands of dollars. In 1920, as mentioned earlier, we sent our compatriot Benny Dovris as our special delegate to bring and distribute aid among the needy Jews in Vishkov. We continued with our assistance work until the situation stabilized in Poland and the wounds of the First World War were healed somewhat. The Vishkov Aid Committee's activity subsided, but not for long.

[Page 224]

In 1927-28 we again began to receive appeals for assistance from Vishkov. Our committee received a number of tearful letters for the Vishkov community, from the various institutions as well as from ordinary Jews in town, who complained about their situation. They wrote that poverty had spread again among the Jews in town. The economic and political situation of the Jews in Poland was becoming critical, and there was mass unrest against Jews. The livelihood of the Jews was badly affected.

The leaders and activists of the United Vishkov Aid Committee went to work to respond to the calls for help from our hometown. The heads of the Committee included the following activists: Morris Topfel, chairman; Mrs. Chekhanov, vice-chairman; Shmuel Videletz, cashier; Leo Chernin, finance secretary and Benny Zimmerman, recording secretary. The following served on the executive committee: Jake Zilberstein, Max Holland, William Radziminsky, Isaac Bengal, Rachel Radziminsky, Paul Kramer, Mrs. Molly Paraver, Morris Bernstein, Avraham Goldstein, Moshe Bornstein, Jacob Chelonko, Morris Levy, Avraham Aldak, Chaim-Aharon Jacobovich, Avraham Goldman and Sam Yagoda. They organized a theater event and undertook an energetic campaign. In a short time they collected a larger sum of money with which we assisted the charity fund, yeshiva, Talmud Torah, sick fund and hundreds of families in Vishkov.

7

Our United Vishkov Aid Committee asked the Vishkov community to set up their own committee representing all sections of the Jewish community, so that the collected monies could be distributed for the various needs in a democratic manner. The Vishkov community organized a united committee, and our Vishkov Aid Committee in New York received official notification about this. In Vishkov, the members were: Moshe Ostry, Moshe Pshemyarover, Yaakov Gemara (who is now in New York), Yosef Bindusky, Moshe Stern, Yehuda-Yosef Maltchik, Hershel Borstein, Nissan Bsheshinsky, Yitzchak Ber Rosenberg, Baruch Stollik and Mordechai Mendel Allenberg. They sent us a group photo of the committee which we published in our Association's newsletter.

Among the aid we provided for our hometown, we strongly supported the traditional ma'os chittim campaign (financial assistance for Passover). Our Vishkov compatriots in New York arranged all sorts of events such as Purim meals and Purim concerts, to which the activists William and Rachel Radziminsky devoted themselves and made a great contribution. Those events brought in a large amount of money, and because of it the Aid Committee was able to send contributions for Passover every year for the poor Jews in Vishkov. Of course, we didn't limit ourselves to such activities. We looked for constructive ways to assist the needy in our hometown throughout the entire year.

In 1937-1938, we received a letter from the community in Vishkov that reported that assistance was not only needed for the poor of Vishkov but also for Jews expelled from nearby villages such as Shchanka, who had arrived in Vishkov. We therefore had to expand our work, and the Aid Committee was reorganized for that purpose. Yechiel Borstein was selected as finance secretary and Rachel Radziminsky as vice-chairman. We began a new energetic campaign, and the response of the compatriots was a warm one. This encouraged us to then hold a theater performance in Maurice Schwartz's Art Theater which presented I. J. Singer's Brothers Ashkenazi. The event yielded around three thousand dollars for our aid work.

Over the years, we regularly (three times, often more – four times a year) sent assistance to the above-mentioned institutions in Vishkov. In the winter we sent money for heating for poor Jews. Several hundred families benefited from the Passover Ma'os Chittim campaign. The sum of two hundred dollars was sent to repair the fence at the cemetery in Vishkov. Besides our yearly donations for the charity fund in Vishkov, we gave money to the American

Joint Distribution Committee who also contributed thousands of dollars. Thanks to this effort, the Vishkov Fund received a special sum of two thousand dollars.

The important aid work that the Vishkov charity fund provided with the money we sent in those years has been extensively described in the publication, Folks Hilf [People's Aid] which was published by the leadership of the charity movement in Poland. In the account, special mention was made of the fact that money was being provided to Jews expelled from neighboring villages of Shchanka, Brianchik, Poremba and Divky. This money assisted people with their livelihoods. This was how we helped out the poor Jews in our hometown and in the nearby areas as long as it was possible to send help. With the outbreak of World War Two, the activity of our United Vishkov Aid Committee was suspended temporarily.

8

At the end of 1944 we started to resuscitate the Aid Committee. We understood that we had to be prepared extend assistance to the hapless remnant of the Vishkov community after the war ended. Right after the end of the war, we established contact with some of our compatriots who at that time were located in Silesia and in the refugee internment camps in Germany. Our first act was to provide food packages to some individual compatriots whose addresses we had obtained. At that time we found out that there were survivors also in Sweden and Italy, and we immediately send food packages and other forms of assistance. There was an urgent need for prayer shawls and prayer books when survivors from Vishkov asked us for them. It gave us tremendous satisfaction to meet such requests. Meanwhile, when the survivors of the Vishkov community left Silesia and, together with other Vishkov survivors, started to move to Israel, we quickly sent off needed assistance to them in the Jewish homeland.

[Page 225]

With even greater sums we helped out a number of new Vishkov arrivals in New York, and for some of them we were able to obtain housing and furniture. Our United Aid Committee continues to provide annual contributions to the United Jewish Appeal. During the Arab invasion of Israel in 1948 we made a special contribution of $ 1,500, and between 1919 and 1948 our United Vishkover Aid Committee collected and distributed sixty thousand dollars. In recent years we have been concentrating on providing assistance to the survivors from Vishkov who live in Israel.

9

It is worth mentioning our Vishkov Tehillim [Psalms] Society that is actually quite a bit older than our association. Being traditional Jews, our compatriots continued their traditional life-style and established a Vishkov Tehillim Society in New York, which also owns a synagogue on the Old East Side of New York.

The New York Vishkov Tehillim Society has a beautiful and long-standing history. Documents that have been preserved till today show that the Society was founded in a hundred years ago in 1864. The synagogue, which still stands today on the East Side, was built by the Society sixty years ago, in 1904. It was built by our compatriot, the late Moshe Fleischman, and his son-in-law, Yehudah Ratkovsky. The synagogue's founder, Moshe Fleischman, was president of the Vishkov Tehillim Society for many years. The synagogue also established its own chevra kaddisha [burial society] over ninety years ago, when the Society did not yet have its own building for its synagogue. For many many years one of our members was the Shepser Rabbi, Rabbi Yehoshua, the son of Rabbi Moshe Yosef, and when he passed away, we suffered a great loss; we continue to maintain his memory.

The synagogue of the Vishkov Tehillim Society carried a good reputation on the East Side, and we still have loyal congregants who are businessmen and devoted activists. Our Society has always felt an important responsibility for keeping our compatriots and friends together who celebrate weddings and other events in our synagogue, and who feel as if the synagogue is the same as the one in the old country. Our compatriots also gather together in the synagogue for traditional celebrations at Chanukah, Purim and Simchat Torah. To this day, if someone is looking for one of our compatriots, all they have to do is ask for him in the synagogue and someone will be able to help.

Over the years our Vishkov Tehillim Society always supported various charitable organizations and yeshivas in New York. A large share in this important work was our Vishkov Ladies' Auxiliary, which was always involved in our United Vishkov Aid Committee. The Vishkov Ladies' Auxiliary can take pride in its important work which is imbued with the finest Jewish traditions.

10

I would like to end with a brief look at the new institution we have established – the United Vishkov Aid Committee for Israel – through which we are centralizing our work for our surviving compatriots in the Jewish State. The United Vishkov Aid Committee for Israel was organized in 1957, with Mrs. Rachel Radziminsky as its chairman; Mrs. Radziminsky had been involved with our Aid activities for many years. W. Radziminsky is the cashier and Charles Applebaum is the executive secretary. The following Vishkov organizations are included in this committee:

Vishkov Tehillim Society;

Vishkov Association, with Morris Topfel as its president and G. Zeidenberg as its vice-president.

The Vishkov branch of the Workmen's Circle.

The first Vishkov Ladies' Auxiliary, with Mrs. Molly Parover as its president and Mrs. Enny Fein as its secretary.

The Ladies' Auxiliary of the Vishkov Tehillim Society, with Rachel Radziminsky as chairman.

The Vishkov Building Club, founded four years ago by our compatriots Rabbi Zvi Bronstein, Rabbi Silver, Saul and Mindel Steinmark, Lilly Yoskovitch and Charles Applebaum.

We fervently hope that the United Vishkov Aid Committee for Israel will be able to rise to its calling and carry out great work which is needed to help our compatriots in the Jewish State to get settled and build their homes in their own land. Through this effort, we will eternalize the holy names of our destroyed hometown of Vishkov and build a memorial to it in the reborn Jewish State.

[Page 226]

We also expect that the unified effort on behalf of Israel will be beneficial to our various Vishkov organizations that have been established in New York. The idea that we and Israel will help each other is a general principle applicable to our Vishkov compatriots as well. We know that the work for Israel can keep us together so that our organizations can continue to exist and that we can continued to maintain the traditions and memory of our hometown.

Wyszkower in New York
Translated by Pamela Russ

Reprinted from the "Morgen Zhurnal" ["Morning Journal"], December 28, 1939, New York. Section: Reports, observations, and illuminations of Aharon Benjamin: "What you hear, and what is going on at the Jewish People's Associations – 700 houses are destroyed in their hometown."

A visit to the Wyszkower Benevolent Society: Wyszkow is a town near Warsaw. During the times that the Nazi armies besieged the area and hailed down shrapnel and bombs, the town was completely destroyed.

From reports – indirectly, of course, which the landsmann [compatriots] received, we learned that about 700 homes went up in smoke. The number of victims was great. The number of dead, how great the loss was, and how great the tragedy, we cannot yet describe. But those who followed the growth of the slaughter behind Warsaw, know that the numbers provided are certainly not exaggerated.

The United Relief Committee, which includes the Wyszkower Benevolent Society and its Ladies Auxiliary,

The United Wyszkower Committee in New York

the Workman's Circle branch, the Khevra Tehilim Anshei Wyszkow [Wyszkower] synagogue, and its Ladies Auxiliary, all assumed the task of quickly raising a minimum of $5,000. According to what the Society officials relate, the Wyszkower Benevolent Society is the force behind the relief work and its members – and have the most active workers on the relief committee from the very first day. Morris Tappel, president of the Society, is chairman of the Relief Committee from the very first day, no less than 22 years old. Those very active for their town are: Shmuel Widelec, Yakov Zilberstajn, Max Holand, Mr. and Mrs. Radziminski, and the chairladies of the two auxiliaries – Molly Parower and Rivka Ritchman.

With time, the Wyszkower compatriots sent over approximately $60,000. They send over more than $3,000 annually and support the local yeshiva, Talmud Torah, Bikur Cholim [volunteer organization to help the sick], handworkers' union, fund for the sick, and the non–profit funds. Last year, they sent $1,000 for the non–profit fund, to which Joint [American Jewish Joint Distribution Committee] added another $1,000. Recently, they arranged with Joint for constructive work in Wyszkow, but the war disrupted these plans.

In connection with their new relief activities, the treasurer of their Relief Committee promised that he would give a donation from his own pocket that would amount to exactly the same figure that the activity would bring in.

A large part of the information provided, was given to me by the president Morris Teppel and the secretary Harry Burstajn.

The Society helps the poor and sick members. They gave a member with consumption enough to cure himself, and when he came out healthy they bought him a boarding house in the mountains because the doctor told him that the city would be death for him. With time, he improved and enlarged the place. Another member had a heart problem, so they sent him to the country to cure himself, and they paid the bills at the grocer and butcher for his family. They support the Moishev Zekeinim [Seniors Residence] Bnei Yisroel on Jefferson Street, the United Yeshiva Foundation, the Unions Campaign, Charity Federation, Denver Sanatorium, American Jewish Congress.

[Page 227]

The Los Angeles Wyszkower Society
by Avrohom–Dovid Taff, Los Angeles
Translated by Pamela Russ

The speedy and vital help which we gave to our Wyszkower who saved themselves from Hitler's destruction in Poland and Germany, enabled our compatriots to enter Israel healthier, better dressed, in good spirits, and filled with hope, and knowing that they have a large family of compatriots in lucky America that feel their great pain and are prepared to help them get organized and become part of those who are building and strengthening the State of Israel – and we haven't disappointed them.

We immediately established a loan fund which functions successfully under the directorship of a group of old, established Wyszkower who are devoted to the humanitarian work of helping the newly–arrived compatriots. Through this loan fund, many were assisted in becoming independently productive, so that they would not require further support. We sent over enough funds, and now the fund lends monies to non–Wyszkower needy as well.

But our work is not yet complete. In our efforts to help those who survived, we also remembered our holy martyrs – the thousands of Wyszkower who died by the hands of the Nazis simply because they were Jews and did not have any possibility to save themselves. Therefore, it was our holy mission not to forget them. We set up a committee for this goal, to help realize the project of establishing a center in Israel that would serve as a memorial for our holy martyrs and at the same time provide for the cultural, intellectual, and perhaps also the material interests of our compatriots. Towards this goal, we have already raised a significant amount of money, although not yet an adequate sum. This is a great and holy task and needs to be developed as a serious, holy undertaking for each Wyszkower Jew, wherever he lives, and that he give his support toward realizing this important project.

It is a great honor and pleasure for me to stand at the head of such a group, where each of its members, so willingly, freely, and eagerly, according to his strength and beyond, contributed to the success of our society, not only in the support which we have given, but also with our assistance in helping to evolve our society into one of the most beautiful and cultural in Los Angeles.

In the name of our membership, I would like to send greetings to all the compatriots in Israel, especially to the executives of the loan fund who sincerely devoted their activities to reducing the needs of our Wyszkower. I also wish to greet our compatriots in Detroit, Chicago, Argentina, and Mexico, who contributed to the first aid as well as to the loan fund. I also wish to send a warm greeting to the New York building group, who a little late, but not too late, addressed the needs of our compatriots in Israel in an organized manner. I wish them success and hope that their contribution to the project will be a significant one.

The Committee of the Society of the Wyszkower in Los Angeles

[Page 228]

Wyszkower in Los Angeles
by H. Muszkat, Los Angeles
Translated by Pamela Russ

Who was the first wanderer of the Jewish nation? One opinion is that it was the Patriarch Abraham who was the first. Obeying [God's command to Abraham] to "Go forth from your land and from your birthplace" [Genesis 12:1] – he traveled to other places.

We, having grown and been raised in our beloved city, were forced to leave Wyszkow and travel to the far ends of the world. There were all kinds of reasons for this traveling. Some were searching for more freedom for themselves, more purpose in life, and more material opportunities for working their way up. We traveled so that once and for all, we could put an end to the situation of being refugees.

This happened 70 years ago. A group of young people organized themselves to leave the town. They knocked on the shutters of my father's home. He was supposed to emigrate with them. At the last minute, as we has saying good–bye to his wife and his newborn son, he changed his mind and decided not to leave them. So, in his later years, this son left his parents one dark night, and they waited to hear good things from him.

Our Wyszkower compatriots spread out to all the American cities. These were particularly of the Galveston group. There were no naÃ¯ve Jews at that time, who would allow themselves to be convinced by the philanthropists of the time, who showed a great fear that Jews would not want to settle again in the large cities. So, they wanted to ease the immigration to the agricultural regions of the distant western America. Unfortunately, they did not find what they were looking for in the west. There was no business, not even for the local Americans. And if they did find work, it was slave–like labor, to which the Wyszkower were not accustomed. They left these new regions, therefore, and went even on foot, for hundreds and thousands of miles, and went to a large center where they hoped to find compatriots. But the main thing was – that they searched for a livelihood ... We also went to warmer places. And that's how Wyszkower came to Los Angeles and remained here.

For the Wyszkower residents, there existed an inner longing to live in a homey environment and to create their own landsmanschaft [immigrant benevolent society for hometown compatriots] such as the one in New York. At the first meeting of the Wyszkower in Los Angeles, the excitement was great when they saw the large number of those present.

In August 1946, it was decided to establish a landsmanschaft organization that would distribute aid to all the Wyszkower in the world. The society took on the character of a non–political institution that takes care of all Wyszkower, without exception. An administration was elected, and they designated the honored officials, and the search for Wyszkower who survived the Holocaust, began.

In the Jewish newspaper that was printed in Lodz (Dos Neue Leben, "The New Life"), we placed an announcement saying that we were looking for Wyszkower who needed help. It did not take long and we received a letter from Poland with a list of 210 Wyszkower names. These were the survivors of the Holocaust who had saved themselves in Russia. In the letter, they described how their situation was terrible. They were naked and barefoot. They could not settle in Wyszkow because there was not even one house left intact. Second, they were told to go to Silesia where many houses were left after the Germans were sent out of Poland.

Our society, that comprised more than twenty people, went to work with great energy. We had to raise the necessary monies to buy all kinds of things. The work had many challenges. But we did this work with great commitment and self–sacrifice. We will never forget one specific episode: One of our women, who worked at preparing the packages, was not feeling well. She simply could not bend over. But she did not want to cease her work in these holy tasks, so even though she was ill, she carried out her role. She sat on the floor and moved herself from one box to the next in order to put in the things for those who were in need.

The men packed and tied up the packages, wrote the addresses and a list of the things that were put into each package. They also added a few warm words.

We received a letter from a teacher that they opened a school, but there is not one Jewish book for the children. So we organized a box of Jewish books. We also sent away a box of Tu b'Shevat sweets [for the 15th of the Hebrew month of Shevat, celebrating the onset of spring, or "The New Year of the Trees"] for the children. This gift excited everyone because the children had never in their lives tasted such treats because they were born in the terrible times of the war years.

[Page 229]

After dealing with the main needs, we understood that it was worthwhile to organize constructive aid and to put the people on their feet. There was a great desire – but little finances. At the same time, our compatriot Yisroel Asman, of blessed memory, traveled to Israel where he met with the Wyszkower. He called together a meeting and listened to everyone's complaints, especially from the new Olim [immigrants to Israel] who needed basic assistance to set themselves up in this country. We immediately sent over the first $500, which became the foundation for the newly established Wyszkower loan fund in Israel. We had to go through many great difficulties in order to raise $10,000 for the loan fund.

Our inside efforts were to: set up a memorial for the decimated Jewish community in Wyszkow, a center in the name of the holy martyrs of Wyszkow, that would be in the center of Israel were we would gather to meet. We are joyous that the dream has been realized.

Various Activities
by Beltche Taff (Yelin), Los Angeles
Translated by Pamela Russ

It's already a long time since I left my town of Wyszkow. But to forget the childhood years, which we all experienced in Wyszkow – is impossible. With our own strength, we had to break through to a new road in life, acquire knowledge and wisdom, in order to be part of the struggle for existence. We searched for and we found all the different "isms": in Bundism, folkism, Zionism, and so on. It happened more than once that our physical hunger was stilled with a beautiful presentation, with incessant discussions, in order to find the right way to freedom.

Difficult to forget this town!

Before my eyes stands the bridge across the River Bug, those quiet and calm evenings of our strolls there.

The Friday nights are unforgettable, when everything in town was enveloped in a sort of Sabbath holiness. From a distance, the Shabbath candles sparkled in the smooth river, that divides the town in half; or the Shabbath strolls in the nearby forest that embraced you with secret stillness.

We here, in Los Angeles, with trepidation, have received the horrific news about the Hitlerist murderers. We have begun to take an interest in the compatriots who survived the great catastrophe. Through our notice in the press, many Wyszkower responded, asking for help. As an organized landsmanschaft, we began to send over aid. With our first sum of money, the loan fund in Israel was set up for the Wyszkower needy.

We, in Los Angeles, meet often, and demonstrate activity in many areas: help for Israel (United Appeal), the Jerusalem University, the Histadrut campaign, and so on: and local Jewish problems.

We will not forget the memory of our compatriot Yisroel Asman, of blessed memory.

The Union of **Wyszkow** and Surrounding Areas in Argentina
Aryeh Shtelung, Buenos Aires
Translated by Pamela Russ

The following report includes the organizational and social activities of the Wyszkower landsmanschaft [trans: Immigrant benevolent organizations formed and named after the members' birthplace or East European residence, for mutual aid, hometown aid, and social purposes – Jewish Virtual Library] in Argentina over forty years.

In 1921, in Buenos Aires, a committee of Wyszkower was organized with the goal of helping their compatriots, new immigrants that came to Argentina in large groups. There were Wyszkower in Argentina much earlier, even before the First World War, but in small number. These were – mainly men. Only after the war did families unite, and that's how the number of compatriots grew.

The lively energy behind creating a landsmanschaft organization in Buenos Aires was Yehoshua Dubner, of blessed memory. As treasurer, that was one of the most important positions at the time, he demonstrated great initiative as he founded the Union of the Wyszkower. The first meetings and gatherings of the compatriots were held in his home. Each newly arrived individual was welcomed into his home with fatherly concern and warmth, received a meal, and comfort in his loneliness. His wife Faige, may she rest in peace, helped him greatly in these holy tasks.

[Page 230]

In the year 1928, the immigration to Argentina increased. With the arrival of more compatriots, the committee was reorganized. A non-profit fund was established in order to distribute small loans to the immigrants. This work continued – with small interruptions – until 1939.

With the outbreak of World War Two, the Wyszkower in Argentina, who also felt the cruelty of the war, decided to help their compatriots practically on the other side of the ocean, when, as war victims, they would need the help and support. None of us could foresee the gruesome destruction of the Polish Jewry, and among them – our Jewish Wyszkower. Clearly, during the war years we had no connection with our hometown, and we comforted ourselves with local activity. Also, here there were many unfortunate and sick Wyszkower who needed support. With the assistance of the loan fund, we distributed small interest-free loans.

From the first news that we received from the compatriots around the large world, we learned that our Wyszkow had been almost completely destroyed at the beginning of the war; that our near and dear ones died a horrible death. We did not even have any basic means of helping them.

We heard that many Wyszkower succeeded in saving themselves in Russia, but a large number of them were in exile and in very distant places. As soon as we received news from there, or found out an address of our compatriot – a package was sent to him. Sadly, not every package reached the right address and we were very upset about that.

When the war ended we were of the first landsmanschaft organizations that responded to the needs of those who, as repatriates, returned from Russia, or came from the forests or the "Aryan" side, or saved themselves from the death camps. The tragic reports of the remaining survivors in Poland and Germany, gave us a clear picture of the tremendous tragedy that our Wyszkower experienced in the war years. We immediately mobilized aid on a large scale: packages of clothing to Poland and Germany, and financial support for the sick and for those incapable of work.

A large transport of clothes (195 kilo) was sent over to the Wyszkower in Lower Silesia. Much of the clothing was sewn by individual Wyszkower tailors in Buenos Aires. Later, we heard the news that about half of the transport of clothing, shoes, and linen, did not reach our Wyszkower.

When the State of Israel was established our organization could not remain indifferent to the great national problems of the State and of the Jewish People, and we participated in all the campaigns. In that manner, we gave the representative of the Haganah [Jewish underground paramilitary organization], Ruth Klieger, who visited Buenos Aires in the year 1948, a large donation and also took care that each Wyszkower who came to the Land of Israel, would receive a food package and other forms of help.

Administration of the United Society of Wyszkow and surrounding areas, in Argentina – 1957-59

[Page 231]

All these activities were conducted with the accompaniment of frequent jolts in the administration from anti-national elements, which in the year 1949, led to a split. At that time, we named our landsmanschaft "Union of Wyszkow and Surrounding Areas, in Argentina" and also included ourselves in the Central Union of the Polish Jews and in the National Council.

The circumstances that caused the split are described in the following proclamation, that appeared in the Jewish press in Buenos Aires:

Open Declaration of the Wyszkower Landsleit Union

We, the undersigned members of the Wyszkower Landsleit Union, consider it our obligation to explain to the public about the behavior of the Union's administration. At the last General Assembly, on Saturday, the 30th of the month, we were forced by a majority of voices, to place on the daily agenda the question of the aid campaign for the State of Israel. But with great fuss and pandemonium, almost terrorizing those assembled, a decision was passed with a majority of only two voices not to support the United Campaign committee, but to remain neutral (a total of 25 members agreed with this proposal). Considering this decision as anti-nationalist, which is against the convictions of the majority of the members of the Wyszkower Landsleit Union, who are nationalist Jews and wholeheartedly wish to join all the Jews and the entire organized community in the holy work of helping the State of Israel through the only authorized and united campaign committee, twenty some members, in protest, left the assembly. Disregarding the fact that almost half of those present at the assembly had left, and therefore there was no quorum, the former administration conducted the meeting and also elected a new management. We, the undersigned, who are the majority of the membership, unauthorize the newly elected administration that we decide was not legally elected. We ask the former administration that within fifteen days they should call a new meeting in order to elect an administration. Until a new meeting is called, and a new legal administration is elected, there is no right for the illegally elected administration to take over management and the monies of the loan fund, and also the funds from the assistance fund of the Union.

We reserve the right to take on the necessary social resources in case the former administration does not fulfill our rightful demands.

Yakov Bronstajn	Shia Rotbard
Borukh Ismakh (Yismakh)	Itche Gruszke
Yisroel Czembal	Mottel Gruszke
Yakov Shtelung	Y. Gruszke
Velvel Rotbard	Hershel Shtajman
Velvel Senderowic	Yosef Faktor
Avrohom Zgryzek	Avrohom Bramberg
Sender Holcman	Yakov Altmark
Meyer Ismakh	Yidel Rotbard
Fishel Zgryzek	Shmuel Wjater
Yitzkhok Maimon	Yidel Dzhyk
Yekusiel Altmark	Mendel Wengel
Yisroel Dajk	Moishe Shustak
Aron Czembal	Yakov Monkita
Yosef Papowski	S. Sokol
Simkha Krystal	Shmerl Malczyk
Hershel Ismakh	Moishe Malczyk
Avrohom Bernstajn	B. Goldfoder
Shimon Aronson	Simkha Poskowicz
Avrohom Blaske	Shloime Prager
Leibel Wilenski	Osher Mitlzbakh
Yitzkhok Zlatonwiazda	Mordekhai Tandeter
Yisroel Tenenboim	Aryeh Shtelung
Hershel Rynek	Avrohom Dubner
Yosef Nowominski	Khase Hutenski
Yitzkhok Baharav	Yekhiel Weiss
Mordekhai Ismakh	Eliyahu Shreider
	Nakhum Grinberg

At that time, we also received reports from Israel that the reorganized landsmanschaft (Irgun Yotzei Wyszkow b'Yisroel) set its goal to help the new immigrants. Their first achievement was: to set up a loan fund as practical aid for the new immigrants. At an administration meeting, we decided to collaborate in establishing this important institution, and immediately sent over the necessary funds. To this day, we help individual Wyszkower in Israel and in Poland, while at the same time, managing a loan fund for the needy here in Buenos Aires.

When the question of a Yizkor Book was placed on the agenda, we decided in a most excited manner, and with our whole hearts, to support this project. Also, the idea of building a House of Wyszkow in Tel Aviv, incited us to new activity. We were delighted that for these two important projects of our landsmannschaften in Israel and in the world – the Book of Wyszkow and the House of Wyszkow – Argentina contributed its material and morale help. The $2,000, materials, pictures, and remembrances for the book, were a valuable support for the achievements of the Wyszkower in Israel.

Regretfully, I would like to underwrite that the Wyszkower of the second Union in Buenos Aires declined to participate in all the holy work and went on their own.

[Page 232]

The activities and initiatives of the Wyszkower in Argentina, both in the framework of the landsmanschaft and in the general national organizations and institutions in Argentina, such as: the Sholom Aleichem schools, the Keren Kayemet organizations, the Central Union of Polish Jewish, the National Council, the Jewish Community, the Culture Center and more from Dr. Ringelblum, YIVO, and others.

According to our assessment, there are over 250 Wyszkower families in Argentina, including Rosario and Cordova – two larger provincial cities. Our Society comprises about 200 members. In the first years, the central leadership was managed by our friends Yehoshua Dubner, of blessed memory, and Velvel Rotbard. When our Society was established, at the same time a Women's Committee was set up, which is active to this day.

With our initiative, a Wyszkower landsmanschaft was set up in Rosario as well. In the year 1959, we successfully created a landsmanschaft organization in Montevideo (Uruguay) that comprises about 50 families and is very active.

Several years ago, we held an event for the Forest of the Martyrs and collected a sum of 16,000 Pesos for this objective. We turned to the second Society of the Wyszkower in Buenos Aires that they join us in planting a small forest in the Forest of the Martyrs – they declined. They demonstrated a similar response when we approached them about collaborating on the publication of a Yizkor Book.

Wyszkower Women's Committee in Argentina

From our side, we elected a publishing committee in the persons of Yisroel-Moishe Czembal, Aryeh Shtelung, Borukh Yismakh, Yakov Shtelung, Alter Kapolowyc, and Moishe Kwiatek.

Our Efforts in the Years 1949-59

Administration in the year 1949: Borukh Yismakh – President; Bronstajn – secretary; Yisroel Moishe Czembal – treasurer; Sender Holcman – vice-president; Yakov Shtelung – protocol secretary; Simkha Krystal – acting secretary.

Loan fund: Velvel Rotbard – secretary; Yekusiel Altmark – treasurer; Avrohom Zgryzek, Yitzkhok Baharav, Mordekhai Tandeczazh, Aryeh Shtelung, Yitzkhok Najman, Yakov Monkito, Shimon Aronson – administration members; Moishe Kwiatek, Hersh Rynek, and Shloime Prager – review committee.

Women's Committee in the Society (established in the year 1949): president – Hinde Prager; secretary – Malke Rynek, Laya Shtelung; treasurer – Hendel Rotbard; speakers: Eva Yismakh, Zlatke Bronstajn, Nekhama Berenstajn, Dvoire Wengel, Brokho Rynek, Khana Rajcik, Faige Baharav, Rokhel Czembal.

1950: President – Borukh Yismakh; vice-president – Moishe Kwiatek; secretary – Yakov Bronstajn; protocol secretary – Yakov Shtelung; acting secretary – Simkha Krystal; treasurer – Yisroel Moishe Czembal; pro-treasurer – Aryeh Shtelung.

Loan fund: Velvel Rotbard, Yekusiel Altmark, and Yosef Papowski; speakers: Shlomo Prager, Mordekhai Yismakh, Shmuel Rajczik, Avrohom Zgryzek, Sender Holcman, Simkha Paskowic, Anshel Rubinowyc, Yakov Monkito.

Women's Committee: same as in the year 1949.

1951: President – Yisroel Moishe Czembal; vice-president – Anshel Rubinowyc; secretary – Aryeh Shtelung; protocol secretary – Yosef Papowski (also acting secretary); treasurer – Moishe Kwiatek; protocol treasurer – Mordekhai Yismakh.

Loan fund: Yekusiel Altmark and Velvel Rotbard; speakers – Yakov Shtelung, Borukh Yismakh, Sender Holcman, Elias Schreiber, Yakov Bronstajn, Nokhum Grinberg, Sender Wengel, Shloime Prager, Alter Koplowyc, Yakov Fluda.

Review Committee: Simkha Krystal, Avrohom Zgryzek, Simkha Paskowyc.

Women's Committee: same as in the year 1949.

1953: Chairman – Yisroel Moishe Czembal; vice chairman – Velvel Rotbard; secretary – Aryeh Shtelung; protocol secretary - Alter Koplowitz; treasurer – Moishe Kwiatek; protocol treasurer – Shmuel Rajczik; acting secretary – Yosef Papowski.

Loan fund: Treasurer – Mordekhai Yismakh, Sender Wengel, Yekusiel Altmark. Speakers: Borukh Yismakh, Anshel Rubinwyc, Betzalel Rubinowyc, Yakov Bronstajn, Yitzkhok Gruszke, Leybel Wilenski, Yakov Monkita, Avrohom Rubin, Avrohom Bernstajn.

Review Committee: Yakov Shtelung, Yisroel Sokol, Simkha Paskowyc.

Women's Committee: President – Eva Yismakh; secretary – Laya Shtelung; treasurer – Tama Brenstajn, Dora Wengel, Khana Rajcik, Zlata Bronstajn, Rokhel Czembal, Sarah Altmark, Hendel Rotbard, Felicia Rubinowyc, Rebecca Rubinowyc, Ette Zgryzek.

1956: President – Aryeh Shtelung; vice-president – Shmuel Rajcik; secretary – Alter Koplowyc; official treasurer – Moishe Kwiatek; pro-treasurer – Sender Wengel; acting secretary – Yosef Popowski; speakers – Yisroel Czembal, Borukh Yismakh, Yakov Shtelung, Mordekhai Yismakh, Avrohom Berenstajn, Carlos Rubinowitz, Yekusiel Altmark, Yitzkhok Gruszke, Yoel Gwizdolski.

[Page 233]

Review Committee: Velvel Rotbard, Yakov Paljukh, Yosef Przesczelenjec.

Loan fund: Mordekhai Yismakh, Alter Kaplowyc, Yakov Zgryzek.

Women's Committee: President – Eva Yismakh, Dora Wengel, Khama Berenstajn, Khana Rajcik, Dora Gwizdalski Felicia Rubinowitz, Zlate Bronstajn, Lyuba Koplowitz, Rokhel Czembal, Lieba Dajk, Hendel Rotbard, Leah Shtelung.

1959: President – Borukh Yismakh; vice president – Y.M. Czembal, Moishe Postolski. Secretary – Yosef Papowski, Alter Koplowyc, Hershel Rynek. Treasurers – Aryeh Shtelung, Sender Wengel, Mordekhai Njedwicki. Speakers – Yakov Levin, Avrohom Berenstajn, Yoel Gwizdalski, Shmuel Rajcik, Meyer-Leyb Holcman, Leybel Lisowicki.

Loan Fund: Mordekhai Yismakh, Alter Koplowyc, Yakov Zgryzek, Borukh Yismakh, Meyer-Leyb Holcman, Moishe Kwiatek, Aryeh Shtelung.

Review Committee: Yakov Shtelung, Moishe Kwiatek, Leybel Lisowicki.

Women's Committee: Same as in the year 1956.

Other Activities of the Wyszkower Landsleit – According to the Jewish Press in Argentina

July 28, 1953, with the attendance of a large number of members, the annual General Meeting was held under the chairmanship of President Y.M. Czembal. The pro-secretary, Y. Papowski, read the minutes of the previous meeting that were approved. The secretary, Aryeh Shtelung, gave a detailed report of the activities of the entire period and underlined that for the landsleit in Israel food packages were sent for the sum of 22,000 Pesos, they helped the landsleit with immediate needs with the sum of more than 6,000 Pesos, they supported schools and cultural institutions with more than 2,000 Pesos, for Israel funds – 2,000 Pesos. The balance of the fund was read out by the treasurer M. Kwiatek, and he showed, with numbers, the distinguished work done for that period. A. Rotbard gave a report of the loan fund. Forty-one loans of 500 Pesos were distributed.

Also, a written report was read, sent by the "Organization of Wyszkower in Israel" about their work during the first five months of the year, that was done on a grand scale with the assistance of our Society. Their loan fund distributed loans to 107 people for a hundred pounds, totaling 10,700 pounds, 500 pounds was from the fund for the needy for aid. After the review committee concluded that the books were in order, the suggestion of A.

Zgryzek to greet and express the loyalty of the outgoing management for their past work, was unanimously accepted.

A membership fee was agreed upon at two Pesos per month as minimum. As was customary, the one candidate list presented by the permanent committee was accepted, with the following participants:

Y.M. Czembal, A. Shtelung, M. Kwiatek, A. Rubinowitz, A. Rotbard, B. Yismakh, A. Kopljowitz, Y. Papowski, M. Yismakh, Y. Berenstajn, K. Altmark, S. Wengel, Sh. Rajczik, B. Rubinowitz, Sh. Wolinski, Y. Monkita, Y. Gruzhka, and A. Rubin. Review Committee: Yisroel Sokol, Yakov Shtelung, and Simkha Poskowitz.

Women's Committee: Eva Yismakh, Khana Rajczyk, Nekhama Berenstajn, Dora Wengel, Laya Shtelung, Zlatke Bronstajn, Rukhtzhe Czembal, Ette Zgryzek, Emma Rotbard, Felicia Rubinowitz, Sarah Altmark, and Rebecca Rubinowitz.

Decisions by the Administration

On July 15, the first meeting of the newly-elected administration was held, with the following constituents:

Y.M. Czembal – president. A. Rotbard – vice president. A. Shtelung – secretary. A. Kopljowitz – pro-secretary. M. Kwiatek – treasurer. Sh. Rajczyk – pro-treasurer. Y. Papowski – protocol secretary.

For the loan fund: M. Yismakh – treasurer; S. Wengel and K. Altmark.

Women's Committee: Eva Yismakh – president; Khana Rajczyk – secretary; Nekhama Berenstajn – treasurer. After confirming the incoming registrants as members and taking out loans, the correspondence was read and two delegations were formed: one for the evening honoring the artist Leon Brest for his retirement; and a second for the celebration and evening of departure for the poet A. Sutzkower.

To those addresses sent by the "Organization of Wyszkower in Israel" a transport of thirty food packages of ten kilo was sent.

Our committee members felt their duty towards the United Campaign and summoned all the Wyszkower to fill their obligations as quickly as possible to the State of Israel. In the central office of Puero-Don 667, there were activities for this goal every evening.

The administration was preparing a memorial gathering at the cemetery in Tablada for the Sunday before Yom Kippur, September 13, at the monument of the holy martyrs, to commemorate our parents, sisters and brothers, and friends who were killed by the Nazi murderers in sanctification of God's Name and the Holy Nation.

First Family Gathering

With great success, the first family gathering that took place on August 16, organized by the newly elected Women's Committee with the president at the head being Eva Yismakh. It took place at the house on Terada 4421.

[Page 235]

Despite the fact that it was cold and rainy all day, some 60 members assembled, men and women.

The event was opened by Eta Zgryzek, a member of Women's Committee, and the hostess of the home that provided the tea. This was an opportunity to celebrate the birth of a grandson. At the suggestion of the Keren Kayemet activist A. Shtelung, the grandfathers A. Zgryzek and Y. Monkita paid the sum of 200 Pesos to inscribe the newborn child into the "Sefer Hayeled" [book of birth records], and the father Fishel Zgryzek contributed 100 Pesos to the Society. The assembly was dedicated also to officials that were taking over, and was primarily conducted by president Y.M. Czembal who spoke so beautifully at that event about the deeper meaning of a landsmannschaft organization and about friendly gatherings. Friend Y. Shtelung spoke about future work, and about the State of Israel – M. Yismakh. Member Aharon Czembal delivered the greetings. The president of the Women's Committee, Eva Yismakh, had the final words, as she thanked all those present who came to the first Tea of the Women's Committee.

Song numbers were performed by our beloved friends Sh. Aryeh, Kh. Moishe, and P. Yosel. The assembled left behind a nice amount of money for the Society's fund. In the end, Mrs. Kaplowitz announced that she offers her house to the Women's Committee in honor of the Society's aid work.

Other Activities

At the meeting of April 28, chaired by vice president A. Rubinowitz, a large amount of correspondence was read that was comprised of letters from various local social institutions, such as: DAIA [Delegacion de Asociaciones Israelitas Argentinas; Argentine affiliate of the Latin American Jewish Congress and World Jewish Congress], literary and journal unions, Keren Kayemet l'Yisroel, center of landsmanschaften, and letters from North America and from the State of Israel. All the letters were dealt with satisfactorily. The secretary gave a report of the first four months of the year 1953. He remarked that even though during this period there were months of the so-called "cucumber [pickle] season," still we could note a reasonable time of activity. First, the film project that took place in January was noted, which thanks to the responsibility of the entire administration, was a great success and enabled us to help the needy with thousands of Pesos. The second project was the departure gathering for the administration members Borukh and Eva Yismakh, for their visit to Israel, that took place in the month of February. Regardless of the great heat, a large crowd was present that filled the salon of the confiteria [sweetshop] "Tel Aviv"; among those represented were a great number of institutions. This act was a very great event, because besides the respect and acknowledgement for those who were leaving, the bond between our Society and the Land of Israel was expressed through all the means of work for Israel. The third task was sending out a transport on the first days of March, of thirty food packages at ten kilos for the landsleit in Israel.

During this time, the loan fund gave out a large number of loans of 500 Pesos. They visited members who were sick, and took great interest in their situations. The Society was part of the farewell gathering for the leader of the Keren Kayemet l'Yisroel, friend M. Graiwer and his wife, for their Aliyah [immigration] to Israel with a delegation.

At the invitation of YIVO [Yidisher Vissenshaftlekher Institut; Institute for Jewish Research], we called upon the entire administration and all our members to be present at the celebratory event of the opening of the collective exhibition of pictures and sculptures organized by the division of sculpting art, in memory of our national martyrs, in connection with the tenth memorial day of the uprising of the Warsaw Ghetto. We were represented by a delegation at the social conference about publishing the hundredth book of the series "The Polish Jewry." Our members were at the important event on the 27th of Nissan, to commemorate the heroes of the uprisings in the ghettoes. The event was organized by DAIA and landsmanschaft centers. The Society participated in the celebration of the 30th year jubilee of the literary and journalistic writers' union. H.D. Nomberg was present at the banquet along with a delegation. A delegation comprising Czembal, Shtelung, and Kwiatek visited the office of Keren Kayemet l'Yisroel. They gave a large sum towards putting up a tombstone for the Wyszkow community in the Forest of Martyrs. With the secretarial direction, during that time, the administration members collected a sum of 8.274.50 Pesos at various festive events, for Keren Kayemet l'Yisroel. We delivered to the administration of the journal "Dos Nayeh Vort" ["The New Word"] a list of about one hundred addresses of subscribers. In the meeting of the United Campaign that took place, three administration members were present as delegates.

Greetings from Israel

The welcome that the Society organized for the administration members Eva and Borukh Yismakh for their return from Israel brought together a large crowd of landsleit who gathered around covered tables in the salon of the central, Poeire Dan 667, from one end to the other. Friend Shlinger generously provided tea and baked goods, and the crowd participated with song, led by our friend Kwiatek and Shtelung. The evening was opened by the president Y. Czembal with greetings for the returnees Borukh and Eva Yismakh. He underlined the joy that the trip went by peacefully and expressed his confidence that their trip to Israel would give them more impetus to fortify the important and necessary work, of which they themselves were convinced there [in Israel].

[Page 236]

After landsman Yankel Paliukh read his own piece especially written for this welcome, Eva Yismakh had the first words, bringing greetings from the Women's Committee of the Organization of Wyszkower in Israel, for all the Wyszkower women in Argentina, and asked that they help fulfill the promise that she gave in Israel in the name of the women in Argentina to raise the means for meeting their important aid work.

At that event, there was a meeting held for the newspaper "Dos Nayah Vort" ["The New Word"], and Borukh Yismakh delivered the words as he held the crowd attentively for over an hour with his descriptions of the Wyszkower and the great assistance work for the landsleit that the "Irgun Yotzei Wyszkow" was doing there.

There are five hundred Wyszkower families in Israel, of which 100 are newcomers. Almost all of them needed urgent help: some with urgent needs for daily life, and some for taking out loans from the loan fund to set up a home, to buy work tools, and so on. And above all, the morale help that the newcomer feels that he is not alone, that there is a body that is thinking of him without considering his political leanings. However, the means for helping are small in relation to the actual needs. To this day, help has been coming from Los Angeles, Detroit, and from our Society. The so-called "progressive" Wyszkower Union of Koning 122 did not respond to any of the projects of the "Irgun Yotzei Wyszkow" ["Organization of Wyszkower"]. Even the first list of 22 addresses of the seriously needy refugees, broken, and incapable of work,

having sent food packages to them several years back – they remained
in the files, not attended to. Therefore, the obligation remained on our Society
to increase the work and amass more means for the aid work. Also, the
Wyszkower in Rosaria, Cordoba, Montevideo, and Brazil would not be
permitted to remain idle, but must also increase means for aiding the
landsmanschaft in Israel that takes care of the needy Wyszkower refugees,
and must send aid through our Society, or send directly to the "Irgun Yotzei
Wyszkow b'Yisroel" ["Organization of Wyszkower in Israel"].

Extended Activities

With the attendance of a great many activists, on Wednesday the 27th of the
previous month, a large meeting was held to put together a candidate list for a
new administration and Women's Committee for the General Meeting that
would take place on the 28th of this coming month. The following points were
also addressed:

United Campaign: Until the General Meeting, all the members in the first
list of new candidates, must have filled their obligations for the State of Israel.
They can do that as part of the sub-committee, as well as in the Special
Commission of the Central on Pueira 667. Without the receipt of the United
Campaign, as resolved by DAIA, one cannot sit at any social table.

Keren Kayemet l'Yisroel: We had the meeting for puting up the gravestone
for our town of Wyszkow in the Forest of the Martyrs. After giving over the first
quota, new contributions came in, but only to give a greater sum to the second
quota. Therefore, all the members, and all the landsleit in general, must pay
their dues to the office or directly in the office of the Keren Kayemet l'Yisroel,
for the "Forest of the Martyrs of Wyszkow" account.

Jewish Arts Stage: With great pleasure, we welcome the creation of the
acting stage under the management of the registrant Dovid Likht. On the
acting stage, we see a truly national-progressive company for theater. We are
obligated to support it morally and materially. We ask the landsleit to
participate in all their activities, and particularly in the performances of the
center, with all their national landsmanschaften.

Culture Work: Since we do not have the capacity to run culture activities
on our own, we invite the members to attend the culture evenings that the
central office organizes for all its registered landsmanschaften and in the first
lineup, the lectures of the public universities about Jewish culture and
literature.

Help for Aliyah: At the presentation of a young landsman who experienced a "hakhshara" ["training farm"] and immigrated to Israel as a pioneer, a definitive amount of money was designated towards this journey.

Loan Fund: It was decided to begin an undertaking to increase the founding capital of the loan fund so that very soon they could give out loans of 1,000 Pesos.

At the administrative meeting on the 29th of September, four new members were confirmed, and some contributions towards loans. Some letters arrived from the "Irgun Yotzei Wyszkow b'Yisroel" with a report of this year's activities. They gave out 114 loans at a total of more than 15,000 pounds. From the urgent fund, 500 pounds were distributed to 28 people as a one-time aid. Also, there was a report about the trip of secretary Farbstajn to North America, which assisted in the collection of 5,000 pounds for the loan fund.

On Sunday, September 13, in the cemetery in Tablada near the monument, there was the annual collective Yizkor [memorial] gathering in honor of the martyrs of Wyszkow. There were about 150 landsleit present for their deceased ones. About the destruction of Wyszkow, in the context of a collective memory, Y.M. Czembal spoke of the Forest of Martyrs, as an eternal commemoration of those who perished. A cantor conducted the religious ceremony.

About Two Activists in Wyszkower Society in Argentina
Y.M. Czembal (on his 60th birthday)
by Y. Leiles
Translated by Pamela Russ

The activities of our landsmanschaft in Argentina are closely connected with the name of one of its most devoted friends – Yisroel Moishe Czembal. Born to religious, hard-working parents, after World War One he is flooded with new thoughts that the world could be better and nicer. He helps establish the Poalei Tziyon, where extensive "enlightened" work takes place. Because of the war of Poland with the Bolsheviks, he has to serve in the army. His Party work, therefore, is interrupted. When he returns, he finds his Party split into the right and left wings of the Poalei Tziyon. He joins up with the latter and participates in the founding of the "Society's evening courses for workers" where great cultural work takes place, such as: lectures, library, sports, and so on. He works along with the administration of the large city library, delivers lectures in the youth organization circles. His home becomes the holding place for all the leading friends and representatives that come from Warsaw and Wyszkow.

When a Jewish People's School of the TZISHA [Central Jewish School Organization] was established in town, he is selected as vice-chairman of the school administration.

He participates as a delegate, or later as an invitee in various gatherings and discussions which the Central Committee of Poalei Tziyon invites to Warsaw. He participates as a delegate in the first Pro-Palestine Congress that for the first time in Poland's history, takes place in the meeting room of the Warsaw City Council. He is of the few provincial friends which the World Union put forth on the candidate list of the party of the World Congress for Labor Israel, that took place in Berlin, in the year 1927.

Over eight years (1925-1933), that means for two terms of office, he is the representative for the Jewish workers and general people in the Wyszkower City Council. He never stumbles. He always considers the interests of the workers and general population, and, accords to the lines of his party – the leftist Poalei Tziyon.

Until he leaves Poland, he works as well in the general Jewish institutions, such as: the Jewish People's Bank, member of the Council, and chairman of the non-profit loan fund, that provides for 50% of the entire Jewish population.

His goal is to immigrate to the Land of Israel. As a skilled laborer (baker) he goes to the Palestine office for a work permit and takes the exam. But the certificate is not given to him because he is a leftist Poalei Tziyon member. That's how, years later, he is forced to immigrate to Argentina.

In the year 1936, he leaves Poland and comes to Buenos Aires, leaving behind in his home town, a wife and child. He has to take care of a livelihood and also bring over his family. Nonetheless, he immediately assumes Party work. He steps into the administration of the Sholom Aleichem synagogue, is elected as member in the Central Committee of the Party, is active in the former group "Friends of the Workers of Palestine," and administration member for the league for workers in Israel. Today we meet him as a member of the Central Committee of the Party, executive member of the Center's Sholom Aleichem School, first vice-chairman of the sub-committee of Keren Kayemet l'Yisroel, of the sub-committee of the United Campaign, member of the plenum of the land-secretary of Keren Kayemet l'Yisroel, member of the plenum of Magbit [fundraising foundation for Israel]. He also works actively for the landsmanschaft of his home town Wyszkow, where he takes an active office in the presidium.

Today he is president of the Union of Wyszkow and the surrounding areas. He also helped create the National Council of the Landsmanschaften and was one of their vice-chairmen.

Yakov Shtelung
(50 years of a social activist)
by Y. M. Czembal
Translated by Pamela Russ

Yankel Shtelung was born in Wyszkow to very Khassidic parents. His father, Reb Khaim Henokh, of blessed memory, was a Gerer khassid and worked as a writer in the wood business. He was one of the most honored businessmen in the town. Every year – he was a voluntary reciter of Musaf [late morning prayers] on the Days of Awe in the Gerer shtiebel [informal synagogue].

Yankel was the fourth child (of seven), had a good head for learning in kheder [elementary religious school], and later – in the yeshiva. His parents were certain that he would most definitely grow up and become a real Torah scholar. But at that time, different winds were blowing in Poland, and also blew into Wyszkow. Yankel Shtelung was the first in his home to bring these new winds into these establishments of khassidus.

At the age of just 15, we see him as the founder of the Poalei Zionist Youth Organization in Wyszkow. He immediately becomes the recognized leader, both ideologically and practically. He was delegated to the first country meeting of the youth that was in the year 1919 in Warsaw.

In the year 1920, when the Bolsheviks took over Wyszkow, friend Yankel joined the civilian military, and helped create RevKam (Revolutionary Committee), and was active in installing the new powers. When he left the city because of the Bolsheviks, he was later arrested by the Poles outside of Wyszkow, and he was put before a war trial. He was sentenced to death, but thanks to much intervention and the fact that he was of such a young age, he was permitted to leave the prison walls after six months.

[Page 237]

In the year 1921, after the split of Poalei Tzion, he was of the first and most active in establishing the youth organizations of the left Poalei Tzion. In the year 1921, he stepped into the party and remained the representative and head of the youth.

In the year 1922, he had to interrupt his socio-political activities, because he was called up to military service in the Polish army. His rebellious nature could not withstand the anti-Semitic behaviors in the army. When he went to see the Sejm deputies [Polish Parliament] about anti-Semitism in the military, the first to sign was ... Yakov Shtelung. There, it was said, that letters to soldiers, that were written in Yiddish, were ripped up and not given over to the receiver. For this act, Y. Shtelung was put before the inner court of his division and was given the highest punishment that they could mete out.

When he returned from military duty, he again became active in the movement, and was exceptional in the elections in the Community City Council. He was often a delegate to conferences and meetings in Warsaw. In the second term of office in the Wyszkower city council, he was already of age, and he was presented as a candidate in second place on the Poalei Tziyon list.

His efforts to immigrate to Israel were realized in the year 1925, going there illegally because the leftist Poalei Tziyon members, as was known, were not given travel permits. He reached Israel during a great crisis, but he fought with all his strength to organize himself and bring over his wife and child. As an illegal immigrant, he was unable to bring over his family – and he was forced to leave Israel and go back to Poland.

When he returned to Wyszkow, even before he was working or before he was organized, he threw himself into the Party work as secretary, correspondent of the Party press. He was the Party address in the broadest sense of the term, for the local friends and for those who came from the Central.

He demonstrated great energy as he organized the porter-workers, and technical secretary, servicing them in whatever they needed.

The difficult economic conditions in Wyszkow urged him to emigrate – this time to Argentina. In the year 1934, he came to Buenos Aries with his wife and child. The same thing happened here as did in his home town. Even before he was able to set himself up in the new city, he got in touch with the Party members, and helped build the Sholom Aleichem school in several regions of the town, worked on the school administration, and in the Party. He "visited all the houses," in order to encourage Jewish children to come to the Jewish school. First, though, for a significant amount of time, a prolonged illness interrupted this fruitful community work.

It has already been many years that he has been a member of the Central Committee of the Left Poalei Tziyon, a member of the plenum of the Tzisha [Central Jewish School Organization], member of the culture commission of the Party. He had special merits in our Wyszkower Landsmanschaft Society when help was being organized for those who suffered in the war, refugees, and repatriates in Poland, Germany, and Israel. He was also active in the Central Agency of the Polish Jews in Argentina in the National Council.

The fifty years of the life of Yakov Shtelung (until 120!) means 35 years of rich activity for the good of the community, particularly for our Wyszkower.

Wyszkower in Uruguay
by Sh. Grapa & Kh. Wenger, Montevideo
Translated by Pamela Russ

The Jewish migration from Poland after World War One, reached even Uruguay, one of the southern countries on the American continent and from the year 1933 – from Germany. Clearly, even the Wyszkower Jews found their refuge here, fleeing the anti-Semitic Poland.

Wyszkow in Uruguay

After the end of World War Two, a group of Wyszkower in Uruguay gathered together at the landsman's Binem Bronstajn, where it was decided to establish a Wyszkower landsmanschaft. At this first meeting, H. Borukh Yismakh participated, as a special delegate of the Wyszkower in Argentina. Also, our second meeting took place with a delegate from Argentina – Mr. Aryeh Shtelung. The goals that we set – were very clear and precise: to support the Wyszkower landsleit everywhere they needed help; to perpetuate the memory of the deceased Wyszkower Jews through actively helping by publishing the Yizkor Book. In a General Meeting of the Wyszkower in Montevideo it was decided to establish the landsmanschaft and especially to carry out the tasks for the Yizkor Book.

[Page 238]

Then a committee was selected of eleven people, along with a Women's Committee of seven. It was also decided to organize internal, mutual aid and social activities, such as bikur cholim [attending to the sick], assemblies, and contacts.

The number of Wyszkower in Uruguay was not large (about 40 families). Nonetheless, we frequently organized gatherings at prepared tables, as well as presentations and culture projects. Among them – a performance of "Motel Peysi dem Khazan's" ["Motel Peysi the Cantor's Son," the last novel written by the Yiddish author Sholem Aleichem], in the novel of "Sholom Aleichem Yohr" [Sholom Aleichem Year"]. Every year, in the [Hebrew] month of Elul [generally August/September] we presented the memorial act for our deceased brothers and sisters.

We also helped establish the House of Wyszkow in Tel Aviv.

Wyszkower in Cuba
by Cz. Apelboim
Translated by Pamela Russ

In the 1920s, there was a great emigration flow out of Poland. Because of the limited entry to the United States, the flow turned to South and Central American countries. Many Wyszkower left our town at that time and came to Cuba.

The social life in Cuba was not established overnight. This took years of pioneering and difficult work, in which our landsleit were exceptional in every area. In praise of our city of Wyszkow, it is also worth mentioning the work of our landsleit in building a new settlement.

One of our landsman helped establish the "Agudas Yisroel" [Orthodox community organization] and was the initiator for building a ritual bath and forming a minyan [quorum for prayers] for praying on Shabbath and on the Jewish holidays. We also took part in the directorship of the only respected culture union. We also assisted to bring in the spirit on Spanish Street, by organizing unions, struggling for rights and professional interests.

The founder of the Poalei Tziyon organization in Cuba was actually one of our landsman. He was a member of the Palestine office, he went to a conference as a delegate in the United States, and he organized for the first time in Cuba the ninth yahrzeit [anniversary of the death] of Ber Borokhow. He was also a leader of an independent education circle, was respected in many organizations, participated in many conferences, had his own creations, and so on.

There were about 80-90 Wyszkower in Cuba.

It was difficult to imagine the assimilation that drew in the children who were born in Cuba. Some ran off to larger Jewish settlements, such as Mexico, or to Israel, and the main place – to the United States.

Today, in Cuba, there remains a small community. They have worked themselves up materially, but distanced themselves from one another, torn away from whatever ties they had with Wyszkower.

The Wyszkower in Germany Ask for Help
by Y.M. Kurt Kepel
Translated by Pamela Russ

(Reprinted from "The Forward" January 3, 1946. Article: "The Survivors Are Alone and Need Help" by Y.M. Kurt Kepel : In Wyszkow, out of 5,000 People, 100 Were Saved.)

Mr. Harry Burstajn, the secretary of the Wyszkower Benevolent Society, who lives on 501 West 189th Street in New York, received a tragic letter from several surviving Jews in Wyszkow. They write:

"We Wyszkower that came from Russia, seven people in total, write to you that we found only non-Jews in our home town, and not one Jew. The Germans shot then burned our parents, brothers, and sisters. We are in no position to write it all. Another person would never believe it. We, being in Russia, did not believe this either. Blood is pouring out of our hearts as we are writing this letter to you. From a town such as Wyszkow, where there were 5,000 Jews, only about 100 remain. There are maybe 20 still in Poland, all spread out, and the rest are in Russia. We know about all of them. Whoever wishes, can write to us and we will reply.

"Now we are in Germany, in the area that is occupied by Americans. A Mr. Yoskowitz is here, who is taking an interest in the Wyszkower. We came here from Poland especially because people told us that in the city of Weiden, Yoskowitz is asking about Wyszkower. We ask that you help us with whatever you can. We are roaming around like gypsies. Our home town of Wyszkow no longer exists. We visited Wyszkow. There is not one house there. Even the cemetery is destroyed. Wheat is growing there.

[Page 239]

"There is no place for us in Poland because the German generation is already planted in with the Poles. It happens that the few surviving Polish Jews are attacked and then the rest are killed. We have no home. We are with the Jewish Committee. We are sleeping on benches, as if we would never have had a home. In one word – it can never be any worse in this world as it is for us – broken survivors. We beg you once again, do not forget us.

"We ask you to search for Avrohom Najmark and Moishe Najmark. They live in New York. Shmuel Leyb Brzezhinski writes to them. They are his mother's brothers.

"Poland is no longer a home for the Jews. Now, in Poland, there are Jews who are shot – this is a daily event. The Jews are leaving – or better said, fleeing from Poland. They leave everything behind because they have to sneak across borders. No one is letting us in. It happens, that at the border, they take away our last groshen [pennies]. Not one Jew lives in Wyszkow. A Jewish baker lived in Pultusk. At night, they shot him and his entire family."

These are the signatories of the letter:

Itcze Meyer Wysocki; Moishe Polek's son and his wife Shifra and two sons Velvel and Yisroel; Shmuel Leyb Brzezhinski; Elye Mikholke's and his wife Faige, daughter of Khaim Nisen; Gedalia Dobres, Shloime Gedalia's and Mordekhai Yosel's grandson.

A group of Wyszkower survivors of the Holocaust in Munich, Germany – 1946
First row, from right: **A.P. Shultz, unknown**
Second row: **Wengrow, Wysocki, Markuschamer, Postolski, Krauze**
Third row: **Sredni, Pakht, Szwarcbord, Wysocki**

[Page 243]

Remember

by Dr. M. Dvorszki, S. Shalom

Translated by Chava Eisenstein

Remember the Holocaust of the Jewish Folk
Remember the loss and the defiance
It is a signal for you, a lesson
For all generations to come
May the memory follow you
And be with you forever
When you are out in the open
When you awake or retire to bed
Our wiped-out brothers, their memory
Shall stand before you and be engraved
In your flesh, blood, and bones:
Grate your teeth and remember:
When you eat your bread; Remember
While drinking your water; Remember
When music reaches your ears; Remember
At sunrise, Remember
And when night falls, Remember
At festivities, holidays, - Relive and Remember!

Dr. M. Dvorszki

The Jewish Nation will remember its children –
sons and daughters, soldiers in the Israel
Defense Forces. The brave the loyal, who risked
their lives in the War of Independence, for the
revival of Israel; Remember O Israel, be blessed
with offspring, and mourn the glory of youth,
the lust of heroism, the sanctified desire and the
self-sacrifice from those who were killed in this
arduous battle! May the heroes of the War of
Liberation and Victory be sealed forever in the
hearts of all Israel.

S. Shalom

[Page 244]

Kaddish

by Yerakhmiel Wilenski

Translated by Chava Eisenstein

With profound feelings of sanctity, we step forward to say the "Kaddish" on our parents, brothers, sisters, our dear children, and all our fellow Jews of the sacred community of Wyszkow.

Our dear beloved pleasurable brothers and sisters, righteous, respected families, precious Jews and public activists, who were degraded, tortured, and murdered. They martyred only for being Jews, thereby sanctifying the holiness of G-d, together with all other Jewish congregations over Europe, when the Nazi beast assigned them for slaughter and annihilation. Their remaining ashes are scattered all over the world, and where they rest is unknown.

May the souls of our dear community, which was wiped out by the Nazi murderers – may their name and memory be obliterated - rest in saintly elevated peace.

Wyszkow, our hometown, for hundreds of years had thousands of Jewish families living in her a pure, holy life, in accordance with Jewish tradition, serving as symbol for the best of humanity. Our community and its inhabitants – were burnt to ashes in fire and a big part of its survivors diminished in wandering, or were murdered when discovered in hiding places, they actualized during their many stations of wanderings – who will perish in fire - and who in water, who by hunger and who by thirst, who by a blade and who by plague, and who in the infamous gas chambers...

Where can be found that much tears and eyes, to cry day and night the death of our casualties, who's fate was the same as the fate of the martyrs of all times and ages, since the destruction of The Temple – our national home. The Spanish martyrs, victims of the Crusades, martyrs of Khmelnitsky Riots in 1648, of the wicked pogroms of Petliura, and so many more.

Generations of bereavement, rivers of tears from orphans, from widows, bereft mothers, tortured parents who witnessed their own flesh and blood – their dear children, being murdered by the butchers May their names be blotted out.

- Their memory, and the enormous sorrow of our bereaved nation, the largest in our times, for which condolences has yet to be found, shall last forever and ever.

- All this shall be inscribed in print.

Forever will we remember them – as we remember Jerusalem!

In name of the Yizkor–book team
Yerakhmiel Wilenski

———

[Page 245]

The list of the Jews of Wyszkow who fell, perished and died during World War II and later

[Page 247]

א Alef	
AVRAMCZYK	Avramtshe
AVRAMCZYK	Khaim
AVRAMCZYK	Moshe-Joseph
AVRAMCZYK	Sima
AVRAMCZYK	Feige-Mala
AVRAMCZYK	Shayndl
AVRAMCZYK	Shamai
AUSLANDER	Ita and children
AUSLANDER	Barukh
ASMAN	Mordekhai, wife and children
ASMAN	Fishl wife and children
AISMAN	Benyamin and wife
AICHENBAUM	Bajle
AICHENBAUM	Yaakov and wife
OLAND	Beinish and wife
OLAND	Gite daughter of Tzirl
OLAND	David
OLAND	Khaim-Ber
OLAND	Yitzkhak
OLAND	Yitzkhak, wife and children
OLAND	Yankl son of Tzirl
OLAND	Tema
OLAND	Motl
OLAND	Fishl son of Tzirl

OLAND	Freide daughter of Tzirl
OLAND	Shia
OLAND	Sarag-Rojzw
OLAND	Tzirl
OLAND	Malka
OLDAK	Bunem wife and children
OLDAK	Berish, wife and children
OLDAK	Gershon
OLDAK	David-Leib
OLDAK	Hershl
OLDAK	Khana-Malka
OLDAK	Tovah
OLDAK	Charne
OLDAK	Joseph
OLDAK	Yisroel, wife and children
OLDAK	Mendl, wife and children
OLDAK	Kalman
OLDAK	Sarah
ALTMAN	Aba
ALTMARK	Velvl
ALTMARK	Yaakov, wife and children
ALTMARK	Shimon, wife andchildren
ALTMARK	Avraham Yitzkhak, wife and children
OLENBERG	Aharon
OLENBERG	Gedlia, wife and children
OLENBERG	Khaya
OLENBERG	Yisroel
OLENBERG	Malka
OLENBERG	Mnukha

OLENBERG	Mordekhai-Mendl
OLENBERG	Moshe-Ber and wife
OLENBERG	Miriam
OLENBERG	Naomi
OLENBERG	Nasan, wife and children
OLENBERG	Pese
OLENBERG	Krusha
OLENBERG	Rive
OLSHAKER	Yekhiel, wife and children
OLSHAKER	Yaakov, wife and children
OSWIETSKY	Yehoshua-Yitzkhak
OSWIETSKY	Yitzkhak, wife and children
OSWIETSKY	Leah
OSWIETSKY	Leib, wife and children
OSWIETSKY	Leyzer, wife and children
OSWIETSKY	Pinye and wife
OSTROWIAK	Binyamin
OSTROWIAK	Khaim
OSTROWIAK	Khana
OSTROWIAK	Pueh
OSTROWIAK	Pelte
OSTROWIAK	Pese
OSTROWIAK	Reuven
OSTROWIAK	Shmuel
OSTROWIAK	Rochel
OSTRY	Binyamin-Moshe
OSTRY	David-Hersh and wife
OSTRY	Khaviva
OSTRY	Khaya-Nekhe

OSTRY	Yisroel-Mayer
OSTRY	Liba
OSTRY	Malka
OSTRY	Moshe-Zelig and wife
OSTRY	Moshe-Joseph, wife and children
OSTRY	Feige
ORENSHTEIN	Simkha, wife and children

ב Bet

BOGDAN	Yaakov
BOGDAN	Rivkah
BOGDAN	Raizele
BODER	Motl and wife
BORMAN	Itshe and wife
BORMAN	Zelman
BORNSHTEIN	Avraham
BORNSHTEIN	Berl
BORNSHTEIN	Velvl, wife and children
BORNSHTEIN	Khana-Leah
BORNSHTEIN	Mirtshe
BORNSHTEIN	Malka
BORNSHTEIN	Menakhem
BORNSHTEIN	Feige
BORNSHTEIN	Pese
BORNSHTEIN	Rajzl
BASHITZ	Khenokh
BASHITZ-JAKUBAWITZ	Kehle
BASHITZ	Joseph
BAHARAV	Avraham

BAHARAV	Aharon
BAHARAV	Bronthshe
BAHARAV	Gitl, husband Klieger & their 4 children
BAHARAV	Gitele
BAHARAV	Hershl, wife and children
BAHARAV	Yosele
BAHARAV	Joseph and his wife Nekha
BAHARAV	Yisroel, wife and children
BAHARAV	Manye
BAHARAV	Manyele
BAHARAV	Moshe, wife and children
BAHARAV	Feigele
BAHARAV	Feivl son of Hershl
BAHARAV	Feivl son of Joseph
BAHARAV	Feivl, wife and child
BAHARAV	Perl
BAHARAV	Rivkah
BAHARAV	Rajzele
BAHARAV	Sholom
BAHARAV	Sarah---the mother
BUNDUSKY	Joseph and wife
BURSHTIN	Avraham, wife and children
BURSHTEIN	Itshe
BURSHTEIN	Bunem, wife and children
[Page 248]	
BURSHTEIN	Bunem and wife
BURSHTEIN	Bajle-Rokhel
BURSHTEIN	Ben-Tzion and wife
BURSHTEIN	Khana
BURSHTEIN	Khana

BURSHTIN	Khana-Rokhel
BURSHTIN	Yekhezkel, wife and children
BURSHTIN	Yaakov and wife
BURSHTEIN	Yisroel-Yitzkhak
BURHSTEIN	Mikhal
BURSHTIN	Shlomo
BURSHTEIN	Shmerl
BUREK	Yitzkhak
BUREK	Feivl
BZOZA	Esther
BZOZA	Yaakov
BZEZSHINSKY	Aba
BZEZSHINSKY	Nasan and wife
BIALOSTOTSKY	Yitzkhak-Hersh
BIALOSTOTSKY	Pinkhas and family
BIALOSTOTSKY	Rivkah
BLUM	Aba
BLUM	Hershl
BLUM	Ete
BLUM	Tzvia-Gitl
BLUMENSHTEIN	Yehoshua (Shokhet) and family
BLUMENSHTEIN	Yitzhak and family
BLUMENSHTEIN	Yaakov (Shokhet) and family
BLUMSHTEIN	Leyzer
BENGELSDORF	Urke
BENGELSDORF	Gnendl, husband and child
BENGELSDORF	Khaim, wife and children
BENGELSDORF	Khana-Hinde
BENGELSDORF	Mishke

BENGELSDORF	Moshe, wife and children
BERLINERBLAU	Mordekhai
BERLINERBLAU	David-Hersh
BRODATCH	David
BRODATCH	Lohtshe
BRODER	Esther
BRODER	Hadasah
BRODER	Khaya
BRODER	Ykhezkel and family
BRODE	Motl and wife
BRODER	Rokhel
BRODER	Shlomo
BRODER	Sarah with the children
BRAMA	Breindl daughter of Malkhiel
BRAMA	Kana and her children
BRAMA	Motl
BRAMA	Mikhal
BRAMA	Rivka
BRAMA	Shayne-Sarah
BROMBERG	Aizik
BROMBERG	Shlomo, wife and children
BRONSHTEIN	Bunem, son of r. Itshe Shokhet
BRONSHTEIN	Berl
BRONSHTEIN	Zelde-Malka daughter of Yaakov-David
BRONSHTEIN	Khava
BRONSHTEIN	Yaakov-David and wife Rokhel
BRONSHTEIN	Yitzkhak-Yaakov, son of Bunem
BRONSHTEIN	Fishl
BRONSHTEIN	Shlomo, son of Yaakov-David

BRUKHANKSY	Malkhiel, wife and children
BROK	Nakhum and wife
BROK	Moshe, wife and children
BRESLER	Zelde

ג Gimmel

GOSHELTZANI	Henye
GOSHELTZANI	Ziske
GOSHELTZANI	Yehuda-Leib
GOLDBARSHT	Yehshua-Eliezer
GOLDWASSER	
GOLDMAN	Arye
GOLDMAN	Manye
GOLDMA	Malka
GOLDMAN	Eli-Mayer and wife Elke
GANZGLOZ	father, mother and children
GUTMAN	Eliyahu (Eli) wife and children
GUTSTADT	Dr. and wife
GURMAN	Esther
GURMAN	Bajle
GURMAN	Khayke
GURMAN	Joseph
GURMAN	Mordekhai
GURNEY	David
GURNEY	Joseph
GURNEY	Shoshke
GURNEY	Shifra
GIBUR	Khana
GIBUR	Joseph
GIBUR	Leah

GIBUR	Sarahke
GLOWASH	Shmuel
GLOWATSH	Shmuel
GLOWINSKY	Rokhel and children
GLOWINSKY	Rokhel
GLOWINSKY	Shmiel and wife
GLOWINSKY	Shniel
GLIKSBERG	Yisroel
GLIKSBERG	Yisroel
GERSHONOWITZ	Avramel
GERSHONOWITZ	Joseph
GERSHONOWITZ	Yaakov and wife
GERSHONOWITZ	Yitzkhak
GERSHONOWITZ	Mikhal
GERSHONOWITZ	Rojze
GERSHONOWITZ	Sarah
GERSHONOWITZ	Simkha and wife
GRABINA	Avraham-Hersh
GRABINA	Eliezer
GRABINA	Zeev
GRABINA	Zakharia
GRABINA	Yaakov
GRABINA	Yisroel
GRABINA	Sholom
GROMAN	Breine
GROMAN	Velvl
GROMAN	Mendl
GRANAT	Avraham-David
GRANAT	Reuven and wife

GRANEK	Khava
GRANEK	Yitzkhak
GRANEK	Shepsl
GROSWIRT	
GROSWIRT	Itshe
GROSWIRT	Mayer
GROSWIRT	Kopl
GRUSHKA	Toviah
GRUSHKA	Yehoshua-Berl and wife Khaya
GRIZEK	Avraham
GRIZEK	Avraham, wife and children
GRIZEK	Yitzkhak, wife and children
GRIZEK	Mendl
GRIZEK	Mendl, wife and children
GRIZEK	Mendl, wife and children
GRINBERG	Aba
GRINBERG	Avraham-Mayer
GRINBERG	Barukh
GRINBERG	Golde

[Page 249]

GRINBERG	Dvorah
GRINBERG	Hersh-Pinkhas
GRINBERG	Kheptsah
GRINBERG	Yekhezkel, wife and children
GRINBERG	Yaakov
GRINBERG	Yaakov
GRINBERG	Yidl
GRINBERG	Moshe-Mendl
GRINBERG	Pese
GRINBERG	Tzirl

GRIMBERG	Reuven
GRINBERG	Rokhel
GRINBERG	Sholom
GRINBERG	Shmuel-Yitzkhak
ד **Dalet**	
DOBRES	Barukh-David and children
DOBRES	Khana-Tovah
DOBRES	Yente
DOBRES	Leahtshe
DOBRES	Rivkah
DOBRES	Sarah-Mindl
DOBRES	Shlomo-Yaakov
DOMB	Basha
DOMB	Yekhiel-Mayer, wife and children
DOMB	David-Leib
DON	Irke, wife Esther and children
DON	Itzl
DON	Esther
DON	Golde
DON	David-Leib
DON	Khaim wife and children
DON	Khaim
DON	Yehoshue
DON	Rivkah
DON	Shaul
DZBANEK	Esther, husband and children
DZENGAL	Gitl
DZENGAL	Tovah
DZENGAL	Joseph

DZENGAL	Yidl
DZENGAL	Yitzkhak
DZENGAL	Moshe
DZENGAL	Rivkah
DZENGAL	Rakhel
DZENKEWITZ	Boris
DZENKEWITZ	Khana
DZENKEWITZ	Yospe
DZENKEWITZ	Yisroel
DZENKEWITZ	Moshe
DZENKEWITZ	Faryde
DZENKEWITZ	Rokhel
DEREN	Yisroel and son

ה Hey

HOLLAND	Berl
HOLLAND	Yitzkhak, wife and children
HOLLAND	Beinish and wife
HOLLAND	Yehoshue
HOLLAND	Motl
HOLLAND	Sarah-Rayze
HOLLAND	Fishl
HOLLAND	Royze
HOLTZMAN	Esther
HOLTZMAN	Brakha
HOLTZMAN	Golde
HOLTZMAN	Dobe
HOLTZMAN	Hinde
HOLTZMAN	Hershl
HOLTZMAN	Hersh and family

HOLTZMAN	Zelman
HOLTZMAN	Khaya-Sarah
HOLTZMAN	Khaim and family
HOLTZMAN	Khaim, wife and children
HOL[TZMAN	Yaakov
HOLTZMAN	Yaakov, wife and children
HOLTZMAN	Leah
HOLTZMAN	Libe
HOLTZMAN	Menakhem
HOLTZMAN	Moshe-Yitkhak and 5 children
HOLTZMAN	Feige
HOLTZMAN	Feige-Leah
HOLTZMAN	Shlomo-Yaakov
HOLTZMAN	Simkha-Noakh, wife and children
HOLTZMAN	Sarah
HOLTZKENER	Moshe and children
HOLTZKENER	Frayde, daughter, nee MINTSHE
HILLER	Khaykl
HILLER	Rokhel
HILLER	Reltshe
HILLER	Khana
HIRLIKHT	Shimon

ו **Vav**

WOMENBERG	Asher and wife
WONSOWER	Aizik
WONSOWER	Eltw and children
WONSOWER	Barukh
WONSOWER	Khaim
WONSOWER	Yaakov

WONSOWER	Feige-Leah
WONSOWER	Fishl nd family
WONSOWER	Rivkah-Leah
WONSOWER	Rokhel-Leah
WONSOWER	Sarah
WIATER	Aharon
WIATER	Gitl
WIATER	David, wife and children
WIATER	Khentshe
WIATER	Yaakov
WIATER	Libe
WIATER	Leahtshe
WIATER	Tzipe
WIGODA	Zisl and children
WIGODA	Khaya
WIGODA	Yehuda
WIGODA	Yehoshue
WIGODA	Yisroel
WIGODA	Mnukhak
WIGODA	Mendel
WIGODA	Reuven

[Page 250]

WIGODA	Shmuel
WIGODA	Sarah
WIGODA	Khaya
WIGODA	Yehuda
WIGODA	Yisroel
WIGODA	Reuven
WILENSKI	Itke
WILENSKI	Berish

WILENSKI	Beile
WILENSKI	David
WILENSKI	Pese
WILENSKI	Mendl
WINTER	Mordekhai, wife and children
WAINBERG	Itke
WAINBERG	Esnah
WAINBERG	Zelde
WAINBERG	Khaim-Hersh
WAINBERG	Tscharne-Rayzl
WAINBERG	Moshe, wife and children
WAINBERG	Noakh, wife and children
WAINBERG	Shepsl, wife and children
WAINBERG	Binem and wife
WAINBERG	Khana-Rokhel
WAINBERG	Khava
WAINBERG	Yeshaiahu
WAINBERG	Yaakov
WAISBOIM	Shlomo
WAISBOIM	Sarah-Itah
WAINBRUM	Khana and husband
WAIAIBRUM	Nemi, husband and children
WAINBRUM	Shmuel, wife and children
WAISBOIM	Reuven
WENGASZ	Esther
WENGASZ	Bella, husband and children
WENGASZ	Joseph
WENGASZ	Moshe
WENGASZ	Sarah

WENGROW	Simkha-Yaakov
WENGEL	

ז Zayin

ZATORSKI	Avraham-Joseph
ZATORSKI	Khaim
ZATORSKI	Yaakov-David
ZATORSKI	Yitzkhak
ZALOWITZ	Itzl, wife and children
ZALOWITZ	Berl, wife and children
ZALOWITZ	Eli, wife and children
ZALOWTZ	Yehudah-Leib, wife and children
ZALTZBERG	Avraham
ZALTZBERG	Brakha
ZALTZBERG	Khana
ZALTZBERG	Mekhtshe
ZALTZBERG	Moshe and children
ZALTZBERG	Simkha
ZALTZSHTEIN	Avraham
ZALTZSHTEIN	Hershl
ZALTZSHTEIN	Perl
ZAREMBSKI	Hershl
ZKHISHANSKI	Avraham and children
ZKHISHANSKI	Dinah
ZKHISHANSKI	Sarah
ZKHISHANSKI	Moshe-Barukh, wife and children
ZWEL	Avraham wife and children
ZWEL	Erke, wife and children
ZWEL	Zeev, wife and children
ZWEL	Moshe, wife and children

ZIGELBOIM	Esther-Malka
ZIGELBOIM	Dvorah-Libe
ZIGELBOIM	Hinde
ZIGELBOIM	Khava
ZIGELBOIM	Yente
ZIGELBOIM	Mordekhai
ZIGELBOIM	Rivkah
ZILBERBERG	Itshe
ZILBERBERG	Sarah
ZILBERBERG	Khaim, wife and children
ZILBERMAN	Malka-Perl
ZISMAN	Zelde
ZISMAN	Khava, husband and children
ZISMAN	Yehoshue
ZISMAN	Sholom and wife
ZISKIND	David
ZISKIND	Malka
ZLATMAN	Shlomo
ZLATMAN	Joseph
ZLATMAN	Yitzkhak
ZLATMAN	
ZMIR	Rokhel
ZENDERLAND	Yehudit
ZENDERLAND	Malka
ZENDERLAND	Sholom and wife
ZENDERLAND	Sarah and family

ט Tet

| TAUB | Esther |
| TAUB | Yonah |

TAUB	Leahtshe
TAUB	Shlomo
TEITELBOIM	Boshke, daughter of Benyomin Domb and her husband
TEITEL	Bela
TISHKOWITZ	Asher, wife and children
TISHKOWITZ	Yehoshue, wife and children
TISJKOWITZ	Shmuel, wife and children
TENTSHA	Esther-SarH
TENTSHA	Gedalia
TENTSHA	David
TENTSHA	Dwoshe
TENTSHA	Joseph
TENTSHA	Yitzkhak-Yaakov
TENTSHA	Menakhem
TENTSHA	Rekhel
TENENBOIM	Khuma-Brakha
TENENBOIM	Yoshe
TENENBOIM	Yehuda
TENENBOIM	Rivkah
TENENBOIM	Rojze and children
TREMBLINSKI	Itshe-Mayer and wife
TREMBLINSKI	Yitzkhak, wife and children
TREMBLINSKI	Yisroel and wife
TREMBLINSKI	Simkha and wife
CZEKHANOWIETZKI	Gitl
CZEKHANOWIETZKI	Leah, her husband Avraham and son Yaakov
CZEKHANOWIETZKI	Miriam

CZERWONAGURA	Berish
CZERWONAGURA	David
CZERWONAGURA	Yidel-Nakhum
CZERWONAGURA	Khava-Tovah
CZERWONAGURA	Leah and 3 children

[Page 251]

ך

Yod

YABLONKA	Avraham
YABLONKA	Feige
YABLKA	Dvorah
YABLKA	Khaim
YABLKA	Yekhezkel
YABLKA	Leah
YABLKA	Mayte
YAGODA	Avraham---son of Ephraim
YAGODA	Avraham
YAGODA	Ephraim and wife
YAGODA	Beile
YAGODA	Hinde
YAGODA	Khaim, wife aand children
YAGODA	Yekhezel-Elimelekh and family
YAGODA	Yaakov-Hoshea and his wife Khaitshe
YAGODA	Yitzkhak
YAGODA	Leahtshe
YAGODA	Mindl
YAGODA	Malka daughter of Radziminski
YAGODA	Moshe, son of Shimon
YAGODA	Feigele
YAGODA	Raize

YAGODA	Shimon
YAGODA	Sarah
YAGODA	Sarah-Hinde
YAZSHEMBSKI	Moshe
YAZSHEMBSKI	Feige-Tzirl
YANOSHEWITZ	Libe Plude
YONISZ	Asher and children
YONISZ	Yaakov, wife and children
YONISZ	Moshe and 2 daughters
YONISZ	Rokhel
YOSKOWITZ	Avraham, wife children
YOSKOWITZ	Dobe and 3 children
YOSKOWITZ	Itke and a son
YOSKOWITZ	Libe husband and children
YOSKOWITZ	Rokhel and 4 children
YAKUBOWITZ	Avraham
YAKUBOWITZ	Zisl
YAKUBOWITZ	Yaakov
YAKUBOWITZ	Khele
YAKUBOWITZ	Moshe
YAKUBOWITZ	Feige
JAKUBOWITZ	Rokhel
YAKUBOWITZ	Rokhel, husband and son
JAKUBOWITZ	Shlomo
JAKUBOWITZ	Sarah
YURMAN	
YEDWAB	Avraham
YEDWAB	Khana-Beila and children
YEDWAB	Yaakov

YEDWAB	Sender-Eliezer
YEDWAB	Shmuel
YISMAKH	Joseph

כ Kaf

KHUMNITZKI	David
KHUMNITZKI	Mendl
KHUMNITZKI	Pese
KHJAN	Brayndl
KHJAN	Yitzkhak
KHJAN	Yisroel
KHZAN	Sarah
KHIN	Dinah
KHIN	Dinah
KHIN	Refel and daughter

ל Lamed

LIBERMAN	Grine
LIBERMAN	Rivkah
LITERE	Khenekh
LITERE	Zelig wife and children
LIKHTMAN	Khana
LIKHTMAN	Yosl
LIKHTMAN	Yitzhak
LIKHTMAN	Shlomo
LAYKHER	Dr. and family
LIS	Avraham-Mirdekhi and wife
LIS	Sarah
LEWIN	Esther
LEWIN	Yaakov

LEWIN	Reuven
LEWIN	Sholom
LEWINER	Eliezer
LEMBERGER	Avrahamand wife
LEMBERGER	Yosl
LEMBERGER	Yehudit
LEMBERGER	Shraga
LERMAN	Avraham and children
LERMAN	Itshe, wife and children
LERMAN	Dvorah, husband and children
LERMAN	Khaya-Sarah, wife of Yaakov-David
LERMAN	Yaakov-David, wife and children
LERMAN	Mordekhai
LERMAN	Feige, wife of Yitzkhak
LERMAN	Rokhel, husband and children
LERMAN	Shlomo
LESHCZINSKI	Dr., wife and family

מ Mem

MALINA	Golde
MALINA	Henokh
MALINA	Joel
MALINA	Joseph
MALINA	Yisroel, wife and children
MALINA	Shayndl
MALINA	Sarah-Rivkah
MALOWANCZIK	Esther
MALOWANCZIK	Khaya-Etel
MALOWANCZIK	Zelig'Malownczik, Yehuda
MALOWANCZIK	Khyne

MALOWANCZIK	Khana
MALOWANCZIK	Tuviah (Feldsher)
MALOWANCZIK	Trayne-Ite
MALOWANCZIK	Yaakov-Dov
MALOWANCZIK	Feige
MORGENSTERN	Rabbi Yaakov-Aryeh

[Page 252]

MORGENSTERN	Rabbi David-Shlomo
MORGENSTERN	Binyomin
MORGENSTERN	Yerakhmiel
MORGENSTERN	Rabbi Yisroel-Yitzkhak
MARKUSHAMER	Khava
MARKUSHAMER	Yaakov
MARKUSKHAMER	Yisroel-Mendl
MARKUSKHAMER	Mayte
MITLSBAKH	Avraham-Gershon and family
MAYKHEMER	Binyomintshe (Biyomtshe)
MAYKHEMER	Mindl
MAYKHEMER	Miriam
MAYKHEMER	Mendl
MAYKHEMER	Etel
MINSKY	Hershl
MINSKY	Yaakov
MINSKY	Mordekhai
MINSKY	Miriam
MINKY	Leibl
MLOTEK	Feivl
MLINAJEWITZ	Shmuel
MLINAJEWITZ	Feige
MLINAJEWITZ	Rokhel

MLINAJEWITZ	Leibl
MLINAJEWITZ	Berish
MLINAJEWITZ	Khaya-Golde
MESING	Berish
MESING	Gitl
MESING	Layzer

נ Nun

NAGEL	Khaya
NAGEL	Yokheved
NAGEL	Yaakov
NAGEL	Pese
NAGEL	Sholom
NOWIGRUD	Brayne
NOWIGRUD	Yitzkhak
NADEL	Dvid
NADEL	Leibish
NADEL	Moshe
NADEL	Nekhema
NADEL	Frayde
NADEL	Tzvi
NAIMAN	Hershl
NAIMAN	Miriam and 2 children
NAIMAN	Pavel
NAIMARK	Bella
NAIMARK	Zelman
NAIMARK	Khava
NAIMARK	Tovtshe
NAIMARK	Yaakov
NAIMARK	Motl

NAIMARK	Mikhel
NAIMARK	Feige
NAIMARK	Peshe
NAIMAEK	Tzipe, husband and children
NAIMARK	Tzirl
NAIMARK	Sholom
NAIMARK	Sarah (sister of Shmuel Brama)

ס Samech

SOREK	Reuven
SOREK	Avraham
SOREK	Itshe-Mordekhai
SOREK	Khana-Leah
SOBOTA	Avraham
SOBOT	Rokhel-Leah
SAPERSTEIN	Eliezer
SAPERSTEIN	Barukh
SAPERSTEIN	Khaya
SAPERSTEIN	Toba-Roize, husband and children
SAPERSTEIN	Yaakov
SAPERSTEIN	Malka-Rokhel
SOKOL	Avraham
SOKOL	Avraham, wife and children
SOKOL	Aharon-Yitzkhak
SOKOL	Hirsh-Joseph, wife and children
SOKOL	son of Aharon
SOKOL	Mayer-Aharon, wife and children
SOKOL	Moshe, son of Avraham
SOKOL	Feige-Yente
SUKENNIK	Aharon

SUKENNIK	Yehuda-Arye
SUKENNIK	Yehudith and her child
SUKENNIK	Joseph
SUKENNIK	Leah and her children
SUKENNIK	Tzadok
SUKENNIK	Shayne-Rivkah
SMOLIK	Itshe
SMOLIK	Barukh
SMOLIK	Gutman
SMOLIK	Menakhem
SMOLIK	Perl
SMOLIK	Tzvi-Joseph
SMOLIK	Rokhel
SMOLAJZ	Yehoshue-Khaim
SMOLAJZ	Leibish
SMOLAJZ	Mendl
SMOLAJZ	Moshe
SMOLAJZ	Shayne-Etke
SMOLAJZ	Sarah and children
SMOLARCZIK	Yaakov
SEROK	Beile
SEROK	Yehoshue
SEROK	Leibl
SEROK	Feigele
SREBRNIK	Esther
SREBRNIK	Khava
SREBRNIK	Yekhezel
SREBRNIK	Yosl
SREBRNIK	Shimon

SREBRNIK	Sarah

ע Ayin

ELBOIM	Eliezer
ELBOIM	Zundl, wife and children
ELBOIM	Khavtshe
ELBOIM	Nakhman
ELBOIM	Peshe
ELBOIM	Shmuel
EPSTEIN	Henye
EPSTEIN	Yitzkhak
EPSTEIN	Feige
EPSTEIN	Dobke, husband and children
EPSTEIN	Rokhele
EPSTEIN	Sholom

[Page 253]

פ Peh

PAZUR	Yaakov-Arye
PAZUR	Motl
PAZUR	Shlomo
PAZUR	Shimon
POTASH	Yehoshue
POTASH	Nemi
PAKHT	Tema and children
PAKHT	Neta
PAKHT	Neta and family
PAKHT	Sarah
PALYUKH	Esther
PALYUKH	Khaim, wife and children
PALYUKH	Yisroel, wife and children

PALYUKH	Feivl, wife and children
PALYUKH	Rivkah
PANIARTSHUK	Martshe
PANIARTSHUK	her parents
PASKEWITZ	Mayer
PASKEWITZ	Rivkah-Rokhel
PASKEWITZ	Zelig
PASKEWITZ	Yitzkhak
PASKEWITZ	Malka
PASKEWITZ	Golde
PASKEWITZ	Paye
POPOWSKY	Avraham, wife and children
POPOWSKY	Gitl
POPOWSKY	Gishe
POPOWSKY	Dvorah
POPOWSKY	Henekh
POPOWSKY	Khaya-Sarah
PORTMOWIETSKY	Yaakov, wife and children
POPOWSKY	Yeshe-Leah
PRZESTRZELENIETZ	Esther
PRZESTRZELENIETZ	Khana
PRZESTRZELENIETZ	Leah
PRZESTRZELENIETZ	Mordekhai-Yidl
PRZESTRZELENIETZ	Moshe
PRZESTRZELENIETZ	Nemi
PRZESTRZELENIETZ	Feige, husband and children
PIENIEK	
PIENIEK	Piniye
PIENIEK	Yaakov

PIENIEK	Simkha
PIENIEK	Binem
PIENIEK	Hene
PIENIEK	Zite
PIENIEK	Mendl, wife and children
PIEKASZ	Dvorah
PIEKASZ	Henokh
PIEKASZ	Moshe
PIEKASZ	Nemi
PIEKASZ	Tziporah
PIEKASZ	Rokhel-Leah
PLOTKA	Yehuda-Leib
PLOTKA	Yosl
PLONTSHAK	Yaakov-Joseph and wife
PLONTSHAK	Sarah-Gitl
PLONTSHAK	Nekhama
PLONTSHAK	Moshe
PLONTSHAK	Simkha
PLOTZKER	Avraml
PLOTZKER	Zelde
PLOTZKER	Yosl
PRAGER	Simkha
PSHETITSKY	Khava-Tovah
PSHETITSKY	Tuviah and family
PSHETITSKY	Yidl-Nakhum
PSHETITSKY	Leah
PSHETITSKY	Leibish
PSHETITSKY	Feivl
PSHETITSKY	Sarah

PSHEMIRAROWER	Baile-Feige and family
PSHEMIRAROWER	Khuma
PSHEMIRAROWER	Yaakov
PSHEMIRAROWER	Moshe
FARBSTEIN	Doba
FARBSTEIN	Yaakov
FARBSTEIN	Yisroel
FIALKOW	David
FIALKOW	Malka and children
FEINZILBER	Khaim-Barukh
FEINZILBER	Yosl
FEINZILBER	Joseph
FEINZILBER	Yaakov
FEINZILBER	Nasan
FEINZILBER	Moshe
FILER	Avraham
FILER	Bluma
FILER	Zelman
FILER	Khava
FILER	Moshe-Hirsh
FINKELSTEIN	Nekhama
FINKELSTEIN	Rokhel
FINKELSTEIN	Shmuel-Khaim
FISHMAN	Shlomo
FISHMAN	Manes
FISHBEIN	Simkha
FISHBEIN	Dvorah-Nekhe
FELNER	Zelman
FELNER	Miriam

FELNER	Rokhel
FELNER	Avraham
FELNER	Khana
FELNER	Ite
FELNER	Malka
FELNER	Yisroel-Yitzkhak
FELNER	Shlomo
FRUMOWITZ	Beltshe
FRUMOWITZ	Khaya
FRUMOWITZ	Feige
FRUMOWITZ	Rokhel
FRUMOWITZ	Shlomo
FRIDMAN	Yosl
FRIDMAN	Joseph
FRIDMAN	Yekhezkel
FRIDMAN	Mendl
FRIDMAN	Sarah
FRIDMAN	Sarah
FRIDMAN	Sarah
FRIDER	Avraham-Yitzkhak
FRIDER	Barukh
FRIDER	Brakha
FRIDER	David, wife and children
FRIDER	Yehudith
FRIDER	
FRIDER	Malka
FRIDER	Moshe, wife and children
FRIDER	Pninah
FRIDER	Shlomo

FRIDER	Sarah
FRIDSHTERN	Velvl and children
FRIDSHTERN	Khaya
FRAIMAN	Simkha, wife and children

[Page 254]

צ Tzadik

TZIWIAK	Barukh
TZIWIAK	Joseph, son of Itshe-Mayer Shokhet
TZIWIAK	Nekhama
TZIWIAK	Rivkah and children
TZITAK	Rokhel
TZINAMON	Moshe-Ber
TZINAMON	Roize
TZEMBAL	Aharon
TZEMBAL	Aizik
TZEMBAL	Boez
TZEMBAL	Berl
TZEMBAL	Basha
TZEMBAL	David-Joseph
TZEMBAL	Zlata
TZEMBAL	Khava and children
TZEMBAL	Khana
TZEMBAL	Khana-Feige
TZEMBAL	Joseph
TZEMBAL	Yente
TZEMBAL	Leibl
TZEMBAL	Malka and children
TZEMBAL	Moshe-Barukh and his wife Khava
TZEMBAL	Nakhman-Leizer

TZEMBAL	Sime
TZEMBAL	Feige-Yente
TZEMBAL	Pinkhas
TZEMBAL	Rozah
TZEMBAL	Rivkah
TZEMBAL	Rivkah
TZEMBAL	Shabtai
TZEMBAL	Shlomo

ק **Kof**

KOTLASZ	Khaya-Rokhel
KOTLASZ	Moshe
KOLO	Nokh
KALUSKI	Henekh
KALUSKI	Zishe and wife
KALUSKI	Khanele
KALUSKI	Yosl, wife and children
KALUPKA	Toba and children
KALUPKA	Leibl and family
KOSOWER	Berl, wife and children
KOPLOWITZ	Berish
KOPLOWITZ	Brakha and husband Tzvi
KOPLOWITZ	Hinde, husband Yaakov and son Yisroel
KOPLOWITZ	Khava
KOPLOWITZ	Yaakov
KOPLOWITZ	Yisroel and son
KOPLOWITZ	Tzvi
KOROSH	Avraham
KOROSH	Khaim
KOROSH	Joseph

KOROSH	Leah-Gitl
KOROSH	Shayne
KWIATEK	Ite
KWIATEK	Berl-David
KWIATEK	Khana
KWIATEK	Khanan
KWIATEK	Tobah
KWIATEK	Yente
KWIATEK	Ete
KOLNER	Menakhem, Shokhet
KIRSHENBOIM	Mordekhai
KIRSHENBOIM	Rokhel
KLEINMAN	Yaakov-Shlomo and children
KLEINMAN	Nasan
KLEINMAN	Feige and children
KLEINMAN	Feige
KLEINMAN	Kreindl
KLEINMAN	Rokhel
KNOSTER	Moshe
KERSH	Joseph
KERSH	Avraham
KERSH	Leah-Gitl
KERSH	Shayne
KERSH	Khava
KLEINMAN	Sarah and children
KRAUZE	Yaakov-Arye
KRAUZE	Shoshe
KRUG	Zelde
KRUG	Pesakh

KREMKEWITZ	Brakha
KREMKEWITZ	Shlomo
KREMKEWITZ	Yokheved
KREMKEWITZ	Yehoshue
KRISHTAL	Khaim
KRISHTAL	Teshe
KRISHTAL	Yehudah and 2 children
KRISHTAL	Pinkhas
KRISHTAL	Fraydke and children
KRONENBERG	Velvl
KRONENBERG	Zelig
KRONENBERG	Rivkah

ר **Resh**

ROZEN	Eliahu
ROZEN	David
RABINOWITZ	Estlher
RABINOWITZ	Gnendl, husband and children
RABINOWITZ	Hinde
RABINOWITZ	Yaakov-Arye
RABINOWITZ	Hadassah and husband
RABINOWITZ	Leah, husband and children
ROGOWITZ	Nute, wife and children
ROZENBOIM	Henekh
ROZENBOIM	Khaim
ROZENBOIM	Leubl, wife and children
ROZENBOIM	Mintshe
ROTHOLTZ	Aharon-Leib, wife and children
ROTHOLTZ	David
ROTHOLTZ	Pesakh

ROKHWEITZ	Shmiryahu
ROKHWEITZ	Rivkah
ROZENBERG	Khaya
ROZENBERG	Yekhiel-Mayer
ROZENBERG	Tzcharne
ROZENBERG	Yidl
ROZENBERG	Yaakov and children
ROZENBERG	Yitzkhak-Ber
ROZENBERG	Leah and children
ROZENBERG	Feige
ROZENBERG	Simkha
ROZENBERG	Sarah, children and grandchildren

[Page 255]

RAPOPORT	Shameyah, wife and children
ROKITE	Khana
ROKITE	Liber
RPKITE	David
RUBINOWITZ	Khaya
RUBINOWITZ	Joseph
RUBINOWITZ	Malka
RUBINOWITZ	Reuven
RUBINOWITZ	Sarah
RUBIN	Avraham, wife and children
RUBIN	Yekhiel-Mayer and wife
RUBINSKY	Hershl and wife
RUBINSKY	Tuviah
RUBINSKY	Joseph
RUBINKY	Mayer
RUBINSKY	Moshe and wife
RUBIN	Elke

RUSZE	Alter
RUSZE	Esther
RUSZE	Hershl
RUSZE	Joseph
RING	Avraham
RING	Khaim
RAYKHMAN	Hersh-Leib and wife
RAYKHMAN	Yaakov-Mayer
RAYKHMAN	Mordekhai
RAYKHMAN	Rivkah
RINEK	Avraham
RINEK	Itke
RINEK	Golde
RINEK	Moshe
RINEK	Serke
RINKE	Tzirl, husband and children

ש **Shin**

SHAKHNOWISKY	Avraham –Mendl
SHAKHNOWISKY	Leah
SHAFRAN	Yidl
SHAFRAN	Mindl, nee KATZ
SHAFRAN	Feige
SCHWARTZBORT	Avraham
SCHWARTZBORT	Ite
SCHWARTZBORT	Esther and children
SCHWARTZBORT	Bunem
SCHWARTZBORT	Leyzer
SCHWARTZBORT	Miriam
SCHWARTZBORT	Tzwia

SHULTZ	Avraham-Pinkhas son of Hershl
SHULTZ	Avraham-Pinkhas son of Khaim
SHULTZ	Ite
SHULTZ	Esther
SHULTZ	Blume
SHULTZ	David
SHULTZ	Hershl
SHULTZ	Khaya
SHULTZ	Khaim
SHULTZ	Khana
SHULTZ	Yokheved
SHULTZ	Yekhiel
SHULTZ	Yaakov
SHULTZ	Yisroel
SHULTZ	Mendl
SHULTZ	Mendl son of Hershl and Yokheved
SHULTZ	Perl
SHULTZ	Tzwia
STARKES	Yisroel
STARKES	Hershl
STARKES	Aizik
STAIMAN	Baile, husband and children
STAIMAN	Khava-Zlata
STAIMAN	Khaya-Sarah
STAIMAN	Yenter-Yehudes
STAIMAN	Yaakov-Arye
STAIMAN	Moshe
STEINBERG	Heniye
STEINBERG	Leibtshe

STEINBERG	Sarah and husband
STIKEL	Golde
STIKEL	Khana-Malka
STIKEL	Layzer
STIKEL	Yitzkhak, wife and children
STIKEL	Etke
STIKEL	Feige-Roza
STELUNG	Khaim-Henekh
STELUNG	Esther-Mindl
STELUNG	Avraham-Moshe
STELUNG	Esther---his wife
STELUNG	Brakhatshe, husband children
STELUNG	Khaya, husband and children
STELUNG	Yokheved
STELUNG	Yosl, wife and 2 children
STELUNG	Mendele
STELUNG	Yitzkhakl
SHTESHIGEL	Mayer
SHTESHIGEL	Tuviah
SHTESHIGEL	Mikhal
SHIKE	Yaakov, wife Esther and children
SHAIKE	Itshe
SHAIKE	Hershl
SHAIKE	Mendl
SHAIKE	Elke
SHAIKE	Sarah
SIKORA	Avraham
SIKORA	Golde
SLAFMIN	Gitl and children

SLAFMIN	Moshe and children
SMIETANKE	Dobe and husband
SMIETANKE	Hinde
SNEG	Tscharne
SNEG	Simkha
SEDLEDSKY	Yitzkhak
SEDLEDSKY	Yerakhmiel
SEDLEDSKY	Moshe
SEDLEDSKY	Sarah
SMIETANKE	Hershl
SEMBERG	Avraham
SEMBERG	Avraham-Yitzkhak
SEMBERG	Aharon
SEMBERG	Ephraim
SEMBERG	Bendet
SEMBERG	Golde
SEMBERG	Hillel
SEMBERG	Hersh-Layzer
SEMBERG	Khayatshe
SEMBERG	Khayke
SEMBERG	Khaim-Velvl
SEMBERG	Tuba
SEMBERG	Joseph-Leib
SEMBERG	Malka and daughter Fruma
SEMBERG	Moshe-Aharon
SEMBERG	Moshe
SEMBERG	Pesakh
SEMBERG	Kalman
SEMBERG	Rivkah-Rokhel

SEMBERG	Shlomo
SEMBERG	Shmuel
SEMBERG	Simkha
SEMBERG	Shimon
SEFTEL	Geula
SEFTEL	Feige
SEFTEL	
SHRON	Ite
SHRON	Elimelekh
SHRON	Libe
SHRON	Feivl
SHRON	Ruth

[Page 257]

Rabbis in Wyszkow
by The Rabbis of Wyszkow
Translated by Chava Eisenstein

R. Abba'le Z"L

As a child, I remember hearing about the great and pious Rabbi Abba'le Z"L. He lived in simplicity and poverty his entire life. He would chop and prepare wood for himself outside, in the yard. When people came to seek his judgement, or came to inquire about a kosher–related ruling etc., he would leave the axe and wear his rabbinic hat and capote, enter his rabbinate room, rule the law and go back to his work. He didn't receive payment and his wife, the Rebitzin, sold baking–yeast (heiven). In the rabbinic field he was well known, for he corresponded and wrote "Answers" to many great Torah figures at the time, he also kept up a yeshivah, where boys from the surrounding cities came to learn. He resided in Wyszkow around the years 1830–1865.

Rabbi Israel Ben–Zion Rosenbaum Z"L

"The Old Rabbi" he was called, in my childhood years. There was a great rabbinic look to him; High forehead, a long white beard adorned his face, a pair of brilliant eyes and a constant smile, with which he welcomed warmly each and every one. He ascended from a large ramified rabbinic dynasty. His brother was the Rabbi of Radzymin near Warsaw. Late in the night, we would hear him learning in a most beautiful melody, early morning he was already at the big synagogue where he attended prayers and collected charity for the poor; his salary, too, he distributed to the poor, and he himself chose to live in poverty. His wife, the rebbitzin, would complain and beg to receive part of his pay.

He left after lengthy rabbinical correspondence, which he held with the top rabbis of then, like his father–in–law the great tzadik of Bruk Z"L and Rabbi Joseph of Serock Z"L and the Lomza Rabbi, author of "Divrei Malkhiel" (see: Divrei Malkhiel, part 5 portion: 55, 180, 193, and 273), which discusses children who died upon circumcision, divorce issues etc. in which he refers to him: "To my dear friend and famous Torah giant etc. Rabbi Israel Ben–Zion, Rabbi of Wyszkow, etc."

Rabbi Menahem Mendel'e Bressler ZTZ"L[1]

They called him Rabbi Mendel'e moreh–horaah (rabbinic authority). He was son of the great and pious man of Brok Z"L, and son–in–law of Rabbi Israel Ben–Zion Z"L, mentioned above. A pupil and pal of the Old Rabbi of Ger Z"L, author of the famous "Sfas Emes." He was beloved and revered by all folks of the city with his brilliance and by issuing halakhic resolutions. He acquired many followers, even amongst opponents to Khasidism.

As he first came to Wyszkow, still being supported by his father–in–law, the rabbi, he learned with the best students of the city a daily lesson in Talmud and its interpreters. Being nominated as rabbinical authority of the city was followed by much dispute. The opponent representatives lead by Rav Manish, presented their delegate, a Lithuanian orator who possessed a lovely pleasant voice, but with not an outstanding Torah knowledge. In contrary, all the Khasidic shtiebels in the city backed Reb Mendel'e.

The quarrel rose that much until once, on the day of Hoshanah–Rabba, after the representative of the opponents conducted his speech in the great synagogue, a big commotion arose, which resulted into a violent fight. Four policemen came to set order, but did not manage to control the chaos, they called Russian soldiers (Cossacks) for assistance, they settled at the Senator Solovoy City Square, and then after dispersed the crowd while using force and locked up the synagogue until after the holidays. The aftereffects of these events left their mark for many years later. On the one hand, this caused the making of groups, and on the other hand – it caused all the groups to unite, and the launching of different "Khevrah's" (societies): the Khevrah of "Ein Yaakov" and their "enlightened" Reb Khaim Joshuah, who learned with them every evening tales of our Sages. The Khevrah "Torah" led by R. Mordekhai Kaufman Z"L. "Khok L'Israel" with Rav Zisha Kloski Z"L at the head. "Bikur Kholim" and "Linat Ha'Zedek" headed by Rabbi Moshe Goldsmith Z"L, and more.

After the dispute died down, the entire congregation recognized the greatness of Rabbi Mendel'e. His name became popular amongst the rabbis of that time with his response. In the book that the Lomza Rabbi put out "Divrei Malkiel" he quotes a number of rabbinical responses to him (part 5 portion 203 and 280, discussing witness forgery of debits etc.) where he refers to him with highly respected titles.

His grandchildren – residues of his family, live in Israel.

Rabbi Jacob Aryeh Morgenstern Z"L

After the departure of the Old Rabbi in 1907–1908, Rabbi Jacob Aryeh Morgenstern was appointed Rabbi of the city. This too faced earlier a strong disapproval. This time it was a quiet dispute amongst the khassidic shtiebels in the city. The Ger and Otwock followers wanted Reb Mendel'e, but the Radzymin and Amshinow khassidim backed Rabbi Morgenstern as the right candidate. The masses and the mitnagdim did not introduce an applicant of their own, thereby they were free to support any one of the presented nominees. Rabbi Morgenstern was rooted in a most prominent stately rabbinic family, a fifth generation of the revered Rabbi Mendele of Kotsk, son–in–law of the Old Rabbi of Amshinow, a brother–in–law of the Ostrov Rabbi and cousin of the Rabbi of Sokolov – son of the Lomza Rabbi and son to the sister of the Rabbi of Radzymin. The latter, the Rabbi of Radzymin, to whom also the city's mitnagdim came for counseling and blessings, opted for his brother's son, Rabbi Morgenstern.

Being The Rabbi, he conducted the community with a forceful firm hand. There were cases when he banned figures, thus causing an uproar in the city. When the rabbi opened his yeshiva, 50 students studied under the headship of Reb. Abraham'le Koszk'er, the Rabbi took custody and cared for its subsistence, the yeshiva neighbored him, for it was in the Radzoymin shtiebel.

The rabbi's family grew larger; nine sons and one daughter. His son Reb Israel Isaac was appointed rabbi in Serock. The latest rabbi of Wyszkow, was also his son, Reb David Shlomo Z"L. He was chosen when his father was still living, and after the passing of The Rabbi of Radzymin and was appointed as his replacement. His daughter – the sole survivor of his extensive family is the wife of the Rabbi of Amshinow, she and her husband merited to settle in Jerusalem and establish a yeshiva and a center for Torah scholars.

[Page 258]

The Rabbi of Poremba, and Halakhic Ruler in Wyszkow

At about 1921–1922, after the departure of Rabbi Mendele, Rabbi Karelenstein, the Rav in the nearby town Poremba, was appointed as halakhic ruler in Wyszkow. He was an Alexander khasid and exceptionally well–versed in all Torah sections and commentaries.

Prior to when the khasidim of Alexander and Otwock offered him as candidate, they wished to allocate Rabbi Mendele's son, Reb Shalom, as the rabbinic ruling figure in the city. Nevertheless, in light of the candidature of the Old Rabbi of Poremba, who was known as a giant in Torah, the nomination was cut off.

The Alexander khasidim would gather around him at the third Shabbat meal, they sang together beautiful songs and clamored to hear his Torah discussions, and khasidic phrases. His custom was to invite over yeshiva boys who have studied in famous yeshivas, and request from them to tell him Torah novelties they know. He would always repeat the same Talmud topics with a renewed sharpened wit, which always surprised the people who heard them.

Rabbi Gedaliah Bukhler, Halakhic Instructor in Wyszkow

In 1932, after the passing of the Rabbi of Poremba, Rabbi Gedalia was appointed to serve as halakhic ruler. He was one of the khasidim of the Rabbi of Otwock. Being candidate, he was supported by the Alexander khasidim as by the opposing groups, against the nominee of the Ger khasidim. In his times, the city went through difficult financial times because of the "NARA" (a nationalistic, anti–Semitic organization in Poland).

He was busy day and night giving judgement according to Torah law for many people of the city that came to him with their disagreements. When Rabbi Morgenstern, who was appointed to replace his father (Rabbi of Lomza) left the city for a few months, he placed Rabbi Gedalia to function all by himself. This went on for a couple of years, until Rabbi David Shlomo Morgenstern became rabbi of the city, replacing his father in 1934.

Rabbi David Shlomo Morgenstern – Latest Rabbi of the Wyszkow Community

Rabbi David Shlomo was only 30 when he became rabbi. Many ordinary Jews loved him for his modesty, proficiency in the Talmud and its commentary. He was knowledgeable and involved in the issues of those times. The so–called Enlightened Jews saw him as a symbol of the progress of public life, as opposed to his father, the zealot, who, as a condition for his leaving the rabbinate, had to be replaced by the appointment of his son, Rabbi David Shlomo.

In his days, the great tragedy befell the city, when Wyszkow was destroyed. Together with him, in 1939, was gone forever the beautiful sanctified community, which blossomed for hundreds of years. Her children were led as sheep to slaughter and the city was mowed and burnt down in the Nazi inferno, its few remainders survived miraculously in incomprehensible ways.

May their soul be connected with the spirit of the Nation.

Honorable Men of Wyszkow

Reb Dov Berish, son of Shalom Zvi Ha'Cohen Wilenski Z"L

Mrs. Khaya Bejla, daughter of Jacob Yekhezkel Grapa Z"L

The two symbolized a pure and honest life, imbued with love and faith, and loyal to Jewish Tradition. They fulfilled all Torah commandments, regardless how simple or how difficult.

"No need to announce the righteous," this is said about the righteous, the honest and purified souls, their memory is engraved in the memory of the folks who lived amongst them, and to them they are only missing in the physical sense, their soul stays with the memory of the nation. Not so when concerning the life of the martyrs, who sanctified the name of G–d solely by their death, a sacred death, together with the greater part of their community members. Only few survived to live. For them – we are commanded: "Remember," "Do Not Forget." It is we who are obligated to perpetuate their memory, and shall never ever forget them.

I do not have sufficient words to describe how great is the loss for our nation, the annihilation of the remarkable community Wyszkow. The city that was filled with Torah scholars, sacred, pure wonderful people, who acted on behalf of the public, gave charity and did kind deeds with humanity, those honest, innocent nice people, the thousands of priceless inhabitants and invaluable youth, large families, treasured Jews, mindful, spiritual individuals, precious souls, pure and innocent children that perished never to be again. Our heart aches when we reminisce of them and their death. We cry over them and do not find solace. Amongst them are my dear family members. May my words, which are in the name of my brother and other family members too, serve as a monument for their memory.

Our father Z"L, emulated the ways of Aharon Ha'Cohen, who loved and pursued peace. His face glowed constantly with a beauty of innocence and morality. Under all conditions, he would speak softly, whoever dealt with him trusted him immediately. He knew to stay away from any domineering position, being the son of the head of the community in his native city Stok, he knew all the ins and outs of public issues. Despite being engaged in doing business all day long, plus his involvement in many other troubles, yet, he permanently set time each evening for study, night after night he learned the common Daily Gemara Page, besides, whenever he had a chance he looked into a sefer. In the icy winter nights, he awoke at the last watch, and would lean over the gemara and learn quietly, humming a sweet tune to the shine of a candle, careful not to awake anyone from sleep. On the Shabbat and holidays, he practiced "Half for the Almighty and half for man" assigning considerable time for Torah study. Many families considered it an honor to invite him, being a Cohen, to a pidyon haben ceremony (redeem the first–born son), they gave him the expensive jewelry as a fee for the redemption, but he would always return it shortly, as a gift for the newly born. People loved him very much, being a living model for doing business with truth and loyalty.

Our dear mother Z"L, toiled all her life at home and with the business. All peoples of the city, Jews and Poles alike, preferred purchasing from her, for she had a very good taste and well understood the needs of her clients. People came to seek her advice about family matters, commerce etc. she was appreciated and admired for her open heart to people in need, and faithful counsel. She was a mother devoted and proud of her children who dedicated themselves to study Torah. She constantly strived to immigrate and live with her family in the Land of Israel, and contribute to its construction.

[Page 259]

At the onset of the war, as the Nazis overtook the city, our parents, with our brother Mendl and sister Etke Z"L, fled to the forest together with many other Wyszkow Jews. They wandered from place to place until they came to the city Wengrow. They managed to rejoice, when their only daughter got married to a nice boy from a prominent family, the father, was fluent in Torah and served as the shokhet and poultry kashrut checker in Wengrow. In 1943, came the end to the holy community of Wengrow, where hundreds of our towns Jews found temporary shelter, with our dear parents, brother and sister Z"L amongst them.

O, how our heart aches the loss of them, may their memory be blessed forever!

Rabbi Yekhiel Wilenski
Member of the Rabbinic Court of Tel–Aviv – Jaffa district
Reb Moshe Wiater Z"L

All the houses at the length of Kosciuszko Street, at the right side, coming from Rynek Street – belonged to him. He donated the land for building the big synagogue, and he sponsored the entire construction of the mizrakh wall including the Holy Ark.

A few years later the synagogue was burnt by the "Striege."(?) As a young boy, different tales were still going around about the old synagogue; that demons and ghosts dwelled there, and other various strange fairy tales which tossed horror in our young hearts.

The community leaders began to rebuild the big synagogue around 1870. They erected three very tall walls containing the women's section, a children's kheider and a yeshiva, the Rabbi's home and the committee offices etc. He, reb Moshe Wiater, built on his own expense the Mizrakh wall and the Holy Ark, which was beautifully decorated by wood carvings and artistic pictures of lions and tigers etc. Reb Moshe reached well into old age, he registered one of his houses as a gift to the "Rabbi" of Radzymin. By the age of 80, he remarried a young woman, the daughter of "Gisha'la" and she gave birth, months after his death, to a daughter she named Masha, for her father. Masha conducted trials against the family, who wanted to remove her from the inheritance. They were a large family, and before the destruction, they were huge in the grain trade. Only one family member survived, and succeeded to get to Israel.

Y. Budna Z"L

He was very well off, the wind mills were his, and he made lots of business in the field of grain and produce. One of his sons was son–in–law of reb David Zawiscinski (see below). Another son represented him in Warsaw where he made huge transactions. In Warsaw, it was said about him, that he makes his money quicker than it can be printed. The Russian government appointed him as supplier. In addition, he owned machine–equipped bakeries, etc.

At the time of Poland's Prime Minister Wladyslaw Grabski, he was a victim of a financial war the government conducted against him, and he was requested for much higher taxes than the norm. When he was invited by the Jewish community to Warsaw, and was asked to contribute an attractive amount to the pre–Pesakh charity fund, he responded: "many years I gave fees for charity from my profits; the previous year I gave a handsome sum from my capital; this year I am required to give from money which is not mine. Who knows, perhaps next year I myself will need to turn to you for assistance? ..."

Reb David Zawiszinski Z"L

Served as expeditor and transporter of goods in the whole area, he had an armada of horse carts and was notorious for being a great host who backed Torah scholars. All of his sons–in–law were Torah persons, like Dan Greenzeig, a Torah scholar from the Alecsander Khasidim, sharp and witty, he was supported by his father–in–law a number of years, and went on to become a successful flour merchant, and representative of the main mills in Zegrze. His second son–in–law served as a Jewish adjudicator in the Warsaw rabbinical court. The third, reb Abba, the son of R. Abraham Hirsch, was a learned Torah scholar and a staunch khasid who would often travel to the "Rebbe" of Ger and for a considered amount of time, his son sustained moneywise the entire family.

Reb Joseph Jacobowitz Z"L

An esteemed and well–to–do merchant who was famous in the wood trade, he also owned a sawmill enterprise and a flourmill. R. Jacobowitz gave sizeable sums of money for charity, his heart was open for all needs of whomever turned to him for assistance. However, he mainly supported the Radzymin yeshiva. His daughter and grandchildren are in Israel.

The Brothers: reb Joshua and reb Borukh Sokol Z"L

Of the prominent figures in Wyszkow, aristocratic Khasidim of the Ger dynasty. They were both wood traders and partners in the wood mill. They came from extensive well–based families. Tens of their descendants live in America and in Israel.

Reb Moshe Ahron Olshker Z"L

A wonderful faithful community activist, he acted on behalf of the public for various causes, like managing the Jewish burial society and the mishnayot (Torah commentaries) organization. His dignified appearance was enhanced with an unceasing cheerfulness, thereby fulfilling the phrase in Psalms: "Delight by serving G–d" – as he would say. People loved and honored him. One of his brothers–in–law was reb Berisch Wilenski.

Reb Isaac–Itshe Olshker Z"L

He was a nobleman, a Ger khasid and a partner in the wood mill with his brother–in–law R. Joshua Sokol, R. Hanokh Kaloski and R. Yossel Spiro Z"L. Two of his sons live in South America and one son is in Israel.

Reb Aharon Firestein Z"L

An enormous Torah scholar that weighed every word before it was uttered. Since he was prosperous, he devoted all his time for Torah study. The more talented Torah youths of the town would ask him to test them, with some of them he would have lessons several times a week on various subjects in the Talmud. His son–in–law was –

[Page 260]

Reb Joseph Spiro Z"L

His father–in–law supported him a number of years, and he was free to study. He was an excelling genius with polished manners and was an esteemed khasid of Ger. When his family grew larger, he became partner in the wood mill with reb Isaac Olshker Z"L. His daughters received a traditional plus a universal education. He engaged in exploring Kabbalah issues, reincarnation etc., he went mad.

Reb Leib Walfish's Z"L

One of the community's prominent and well–off members. His son was reb Berisch Serka. In his younger years, he was considered a prodigy, later he went to Warsaw and opened a business of iron and he became very wealthy, he was wealthier of, Privess, the rich merchant, who was until then the wealthiest in Warsaw. He traveled to Egypt on business and settled there. When the Rabbi of Ger was in Egypt in the 1930's, he stayed in his house. The last year prior the war, he returned to Warsaw and was killed in the death camps.

Reb Borukh Zeitog Z"L

A great scholar and a Ger khasid. The best students of the Beit Midrash attended his lectures on gemara and its interpretations. His son R. Aryeh travelled once by train to Warsaw with merchandise, it was past mid–night and "NARA" gangsters tossed him out the window, it happened near Wolomin. In the morning, he was found dead near the railroad tracks. His son–in–law was reb Leibish Holtzkner, whom he supported for a couple of years, until the family grew and moved to Warsaw, there he opened an enterprise of manufacturing which made him very wealthy. He supported many family members, some were employed at his firm, and some received monthly sustenance. He even supported his brother–in–law's children, one of them, reb

Kopel – grandchild of the so–called reb Boruch Kopel's, was an outstanding Torah scholar.

Reb Zakharya Koplowitz Z"L

One of the rich and influential men in the town. He gave away his house on Strajzatzka Street, near the small synagogue, and turned it into a prayer shtiebel for the Ger khasidim. This house became later a thriving Torah center for all scholars and Jewish youths. In its attic was the club of the Agudas Israel Youth and the library they owned, and there they worked on, and issued a periodical etc.

After his death his devoted wife ran the business (she was called "The Zaharya'likha"), and she married off all the children. One of her sons–in–law was reb Benjamin Winter Z"L. he was a well–educated young–man who was active on behalf of the community's affairs, served as overseer of the community's schools, a part of the bank management and other doings. Some of his grandchildren survived, and live in Israel.

Reb Khaim David Goldwasser Z"L

He was a respected representative at the municipality and of the community's board. Served as intendant of the Ger shtiebel and more. Chana–Basha Z"L, his wife, was an esteemed woman who ran the entire business: the restaurant that was always packed with clients, and the transactions in the capital, and more. He was involved with public matters, knowing he has on whom to rely. Two interesting points characterized his personality and the way he conducted himself.

When he was re–elected to city hall, his health was in poor condition, and his wife Khana–Basha tried her best to free him from public duty. She received a statement from Dr. Ribke saying that he is ill, and with the approval of the municipality, she sent a request to the bureau of the district governor in Pultusk, asking to free him of service at the municipality. She also promised to arrange a big party for the Ger khasidim if her request will be fulfilled. When exactly that happened, she prepared a "Kiddush" for the khasidim, where reb Itsche Meir Shokhet spoke and said: "How wonderful are you Khana–Basha, every other woman, and even if he would have a thousand women like King Solomon had, would prepare a "Kiddush" if her husband would be elected for delegating at city hall or any other honorable position. You instead, wave off honor, and make a "Kiddush" when your husband resigns from this prominent position."

In 1919–1920, at the end of the war between Poland and the Soviet Union, upon their return to Wyszkow, the Poles arrested him together with other Jews, falsely accusing them for siding with the Soviets, and they were just about sentencing them to death. When his friend, the mayor of the city Pawlowski, heard about his arrest, he came to the cellar where they were imprisoned and wanted to free him, but reb Khaim David Z"L would not leave by himself, he would go only with all other prisoners. He yelled, "You know very well that we are all innocent." His firm resistance helped to save the other prisoners too. After this ordeal, his heart weakened, and a half year later, he died.

From his family, one son was left, Israel, in New York. He organized drama classes in Wyszkow. His daughter, Pessy Orenstein, is with her family in Israel. They are from the founders of the settlement "Kfar Hassidim." They were amongst the first to immigrate with the "Rabbi of Yablona."

Reb Khaim Chaikel Hiller Z"L

A knowledgeable man, a scholar and a Ger khasid. He would welcome every one warmly, speak softly and cleverly, and was very understanding. Consequently, he was beloved and respected between most folks of the city. He earned his living from selling newspapers and books. In spite of the heavy burden of having to feed his large family, he still managed to have a constant smile on his face. He provided his children with a Jewish traditional and general education. His four daughters reside in Israel.

Reb Itshe Meir the Shokhet and Tester Z"L

The lively figure and one of the pillars of the Khasidic shtiebel of Ger. He had a lovely deep voice, and would sing at the rebbe's tisch (table), thus, imparting pleasure to all attendees. On the high holidays, he led the prayers, serving as cantor at the main synagogue. When he recited the prayer of the cantor "Here I stand, lacking act and achievement" with his powerful Brittany voice, a tremor would pass through everyone's heart, even the walls would reverberate. Many Khasidic comical gimmicks have been told of him. His son, Borukh Ziviak Z"L was head of the "Agudat Israel" and manager of the boys Kheder of the community. Residues of his family, his sons, and grandchildren are in New York, one grandchild is in Warsaw.

[Page 261]

Collected: Yerahmiel Wilenski, Tel–Aviv
Told by: Leibel Rosenberg, Memphis, Bnei–Brak
Reb Mordekhai Kaufman Z"L

An Alexander khasid and a righteous Torah scholar. He would give his entire being for a fellow Jew. In the last years, he had a kheder and in the evenings he was the "Rebbe" in the "Torah Society" which was in the main synagogue.

Of his entire large family, only one daughter was left, she is in Israel.

Reb Jacob Blumstein Z"L

He was called reb Yankl Shokhet. A khasid of Ger. Pleasant, nice and respected by all. He delivered a learning session of the Daily Gemara page every evening, for 40–50 men in the Ger shtiebel.

He perished in the war together with his family. Survivers: One son in Belgium, and a daughter in Paris.

Reb Gedalia Tence Z"L

Served as slaughterer and overseer and a khasid of Otwock. A learned Torah scholar who feared G–d and was beloved by all, he served as cantor at the high holidays prayers. His entire family was wiped out during the war.

Reb Motl Joskowicz Z"L

Everyone knew him by the nickname "Motl Kowal." He was a hard working blacksmith, actualizing the phrase "Fortunate be he, who toils for his bread." He had a large dignified family, and he cared to give his sons a good education and to marry off his daughters to Torah scholars. His son Abraham Yossl Joskowicz studied Torah, and was a building contractor, he built many houses on Kosciuszko Street (The Warsaw Street) in Wyszkow. His oldest daughter married reb Yekhezkel Friedman, an Alexander khasid, well versed in Torah, who owned a store where he sold iron. His second daughter was the wife of reb Zisha Kloski Z"L, an Alexander khasid who was fluent in the Talmud tractate Kodshim (Holy Things). He delivered a daily lecture for the "Khok L'Israel" society. Upon his engagement, his father–in–law bought him a large set of Talmud volumes of the popular Vilna print. He supported him until his family expanded and he became a locksmith. He also worked part–time for the Wyszkow municipality, being in charge of the proper functioning of the water pumps in the city, for which he received monthly pay. He also knew to invent various iron frames and locks, upon demand. His third daughter married reb Leibish Peshtitski Z"L, one of the respectable men, an activist on behalf of the Zionists of the city.

The rabbinical court attendant, reb Isaac Jacob, lived at the home of reb Motl Kowal; he was very far–sighted, and therefore his eyeglasses were very heavy. Every day reb Motl would honor him by drinking with him a whiskey, and as it was told, he would use his finger to measure generously how much to fill the glass.

His grandchildren that came to Israel: Khaim Kovic and his sister. Hanya Peshtitski. Jehiel Kaluski, and their families.

Reb Zalman Grosbard Z"L

A noble Torah scholar. Was a wholesale dealer and an expeditor. At the synagogue, he read aloud the weekly Torah portion for the whole congregation.

Being business–involved with many people and a known figure in the city authorities, he was once elected as a municipality member of the United Zionist party and the crafts workers. This caused a lot of fighting in the Ger Khasidic shtiebel. The zealots, with reb Itshe Meir Shokhet and tester, at the lead, didn't allow R. Zalman to read from the Scroll and he was replaced by reb Abba Blum. In the middle of the prayers on Shabbat, reb Zalman left the shtiebel, accompanied by three young men, and the following week, they opened a "Ger shtiebel no. 2." The founders were: reb Eliezer Lewiner, reb Chaim Kramer, reb Pessah Newmark, reb Zalman Grosbard, reb Lemil Rubin, reb Leibel Rosenberg, reb Itshe Meir Wysocki, reb Moshe Ostry, Jacob–Leib Holland, Zalman Koniasz, they were joined by reb Berisch Sapirstein of Alexander. They hired a shtiebel in the home of Moshe Berel Cynamon (Moshe–Beryl Stelmakh).

Reb Moshe Beryl Cynamon Z"L

He was one of the well–to–do businessmen, but with bizarre customs. He married off his daughters to Torah–knowledgeable men and provided them with dowry. From the 1920's Moshe–Beryl wandered in the world, he went to Israel and two years later, he left to New York and to additional countries in the United States – and then back to Israel. He made a living from trading with scrap, isolated and neglected and far from his family. He merited seeing the establishment of the State of Israel, and that's where he died.

Reb Itzel Radziminski Z"L

My father of blessed memory was honorable amongst his colleagues. A pious man that gave charity and was beloved and popular by many folks and circles. For a living, he owned a butchery on Kosciuszko Street. After the First World War, he left Wyszkow because of an event, which was unknown for years, and I will reveal it now:

It happened in 1910, a battalion of Cossacks led by their commander, passed by on Kosciuszko Street, exactly then, a huge flowerpot came down falling on the officer, wounding him severely. All tenants, including my father Z"L, were arrested. No one was permitted to go near or talk to them, because they were accused of attempting to kill the officer, or against holding an army of Cossacks in Poland. As it turned out to be, it was done accidently by one of the tenants (the Blind Aharon) who was sightless; When he heard the military orchestra playing, he went over to the window and opened it, when the flowerpot fell downstairs. However, the guardians wished to take advantage of the incident and extort money from them all, so they didn't allow the blind man even say a word. A few days passed and the seven prisoners quietly conferred amongst themselves and decided to put the blame on my father and say that he is the one who did it. Since they were all poor, except for my father Z"L, who was considered wealthy, they figured that that's how they will be freed, and my father, will surely be able to afford to release them temporarily. That is what happened; at the investigation they claimed it was my father who flung the pot, they were all released, and my father was taken to the "Castle" in Warsaw. At the early investigation, they concocted heavy charges against him. The prosecutor told the judge, that his crime is one that deserves death, if by chance the officer will recuperate, and there will be extenuated terms, he will be sent to Siberia. The people in the city didn't know where he was taken to, and the police was not permitted to say anything until the process is over. Rumors spread that he will be transferred to Petersburg, where he will be put on trial, or that he isn't living any more... By chance, my father managed to toss a note from "the Pawiak" prison on which he wrote his address, the whole story and his tragic state, plus a promise for reward to whoever will deliver the note to the family. The Jew who brought me the note was paid. Immediately I traveled to Warsaw, after paying a handsome sum, a lawyer managed to get me to meet with my father. After paying a bribe of thousands of Rubles, I succeeded to get to one of the highest–ranking commanders in chief, and it was agreed, that he would arrange the trial to be postponed for another year, and that the lawyer will ask to get him out on bail. On the way back of the court, it was arranged with the policemen that my father will walk out by himself to the foyer and from there he should disappear. The commander in chief made it under the condition, that he never returns to Wyszkow. All preparations were made for the mission. And after a while, when my father came back to Wyszkow, we had to bribe the chief of the police, not to report my father, for being in the city. He received a monthly bribe, promising, that in case of an inspection, he will let us know beforehand, and my father will have to run. No one of our family knew about this entire arrangement, only I was in on it. We lived in constant fear, and then we began to prepare to go to America, which materialized a few years later, when we came to the land of freedom – New York.

[Page 262]

We had a large and extended family, one daughter was married to a Rabbi, they immigrated to the USA in 1928. As an elderly, at the end of 1959, being crippled and paralyzed, the Rabbi immigrated to Israel, he died in Ramat–Gan in 1961. His son, reb Zeev Radziminski is in New York with his wife Rachel nee Prider. They are a big family and are active for years on behalf of communal affairs, they stand at the head of organizations for Wyszkow landsleit. Thanks to them, many annual donations have been sent over the years, to assist charity matters, like a kheder and a yeshiva. In recent years, they also assisted poor people amongst the immigrants by supplying them with Pesakh staples. After his visit to Israel in 1959, he sent thousands of dollars to set up a Loan Fund and a "Wyszkow Home" in Israel.

Zeev Radziminski, New York

Reb Pinkhas Pieniek

My father Z"L made a living from his store where he sold leather and all necessities for shoemaking. He was a khasid of the Otwock Rabbi, a great scholar and a pious Jew, that was careful with each and every commandment, he loved to help a fellow Jew, and if anyone was in need for a loan, he knew the way to my father Z"L – the store near the plump. That's where the house was too. He was known as a clever and friendly man, people came to him with various problems to seek advice, and he was a member of the community board and vice–attendant at the burial society. On the eighth day of Sukkot –

Simkhat Torah, he arranged every year the festive "Kiddush" for the burial society in our home. He offered barrels of beer and schnaps, platters of finest cakes, legumes and fruits. The men drank and sang passionate beautiful khasidic harmonies.

My father cared for the poor people, they should be able to enjoy Shabbat meals, he would also see to the needs of the guest–visitors from other places that came for a day or two. He gave his boys a traditional Torah education, he sent his son reb Simkha Bunim Z"L, to study at the Lomza yeshiva. His wife Chaya Z"L, nee Wigoda, was his faithful right hand, she brought up the children and provided them with a general education too.

They perished when Wyszkow was destroyed, together with two sons and a daughter. From the family were left, two sons in the USA, and two sons in Israel.

Reb Isaac Ber Rosenberg Z"L

A Torah scholar and an exemplary public activist with an unending smile on his happy face, a lengthy white beard made his fatherly figure seemed to display an inner divine presence. He was a member of the community in general on behalf of the Otwock khasidim, and a colleague at the community's board of education. He took great interest in the youth, who he would approach on a personal level, and influenced them positively. When he would pinch a boy lovingly on his check, the boy would feel a special holy tremor pass through his whole being. He was welcomed and greeted by everyone in the street. For a while, he served as attendant at the burial society, and the joke went around, that if he is to remain the attendant, the burial society will have to go bankrupt, why? Because even when rich people died, he didn't demand from their families high fees, for they would complain that they were left with too little money, and are in need of money to provide for wedding expenses, etc. within the family. He believed them, reasoning, that since the family is interested in their own honor, there is no reason to not agree to their claim.

When he reached old age, after marrying off his children, and remaining alone with his wife Sara nee Wigoda, he dedicated all of his time to Torah study; he would awaken at midnight and learn, and go on until early morning, then he would proceed to morning prayers. His wife controlled the manufacture–shop they owned.

Reb Henokh Rozen Z"L – the "Torah–Teacher" of Lodz

Near the Bug River was his kheder with students who just began to study the Gemara. He was well versed in Torah and was also familiar with universal studies. His daughter assisted him by delivering lessons in Hebrew to the students, and by controlling the boys who were very wild and took advantage of his poor eyesight. Many accounts were told about the pranks the boys played over him. There barely was a student in Wyszkow in the 1920–1930's that did not attend his kheder. He was very harsh and lashed out at the kids. If his daughter coincidently wasn't present, he would always incorrectly hit the truly innocent, instead of those boys who truly misbehaved.

[Page 263]

From his family, one daughter lives in Israel.

Henne Gaszelszani Z"L

A widow, she had a small shop for manufacture near the pub of "Kura." She supported her two sons. Jehuda–Leib, who was one of the best youths in town, a khasidic intelligent young fellow, the chief of the Aguda Youth movement. Another son named Sinka, who was known for his wild mischievous conducts. They all perished at the outset of when the Germans shelled the city.

Reb Samuel Wigoda Z"L

A Torah scholar and pious Otwock khasid, whose outlook, feelings and opinions were holy and pure. The tzitzit he would wear were so long, that they protruded below his coat. When he walked, he held on to his tzitzit, as though to drive away evil "spirits" G–d forbid. He never disputed about ordinary matters, all his arguments were merely around Gemara debates. He scraped out a meager living by dealing with fabric, mainly on market days. He didn't ask for much and his wife Menucha Z"L made peace with their poor luck and didn't complain, somehow she managed to feed and clothe her three sons and three daughters. They perished at the onset of the war, only one daughter, Rachel, was spared, she left for Israel in 1935.

Reb Simkha Shnieg Z"L

A true Torah scholar, fluent in the whole Talmud and the analyses. He studied continually, every day he was in the Otwock khasidic shtiebel learning diligently, non–stop. In spite of being a highly regarded knowledgeable

Talmudist, he was very humble and contributed lots of charity. He held a small bar near the bridge, on Rynek Street, which his wife managed, but he assisted her on market days. His eyes reflected the cleverness of a Torah scholar and his sorrow over the absence of the divine presence for Jews in exile. He and his wife were killed right at the first days of the bombardment of Wyszkow.

Youth that learned Torah Z"L

Most youths in our city were immersed most of their life in learning Torah. There was a yeshiva in Wyszkow since 1870. In our time, the yeshiva of the Radzymin Rebbe was famous, it was renewed in 1921 by reb Avrehm'le Kocker, and in 1928, the "Novradhok" yeshiva opened in Wyszkow, headed by the dean reb Simon Hefetz Z"L. the youth of the city formed an important part amongst the students in these yeshivos, who were primarily populated with yeshiva boys from all over Poland.

This youth was not going to make do with the local yeshivos, they aimed much higher, to learn in the famous yeshivos in Poland and in Lithuania. Doing so, they will also fulfill the saying in the Mishna "wander out to learn Torah".

Many boys came from Wyszkow to learn at the famous Lomza yeshiva, some became outstanding students, and many of them immigrated to Israel. We will remember the sacred: reb David Bszoza, Khaim Isaac Krimlowski, Simkha Pieniek, Shlomo Taub, Zvi Oldak, Zvi Brukhanski and more. Some of who were aiming high and some were hoped to fill public positions and become social activists, being from the best and excellent figures with a broad understanding and optimistic belief in the future of the Jewish people. Reb Menashe Kaveh, who was considered a genius, attended the famous yeshiva of Lublin. Other youths traveled to several yeshivos that had spread in Poland, like Novardhok, Ostrow, Bialystok, Warsaw, and so on. My younger brother, Joseph Srebernik Z"L, was a brilliant assiduous student, he studied in Warsaw and was sent later to Riga by the Lubavitcher yeshiva, to start a circle of influential figures with Khabad theories.

The loss of this youth, some of who were alive and thrived at the youth parties in our city, a priceless treasure to the future of our people. We cry over this and wish to perpetuate their dear memory forever.

Menakhem Kaspi

The Wyszkow Bakers
Reb Shoel'ke the Baker

I remember that when he grew old he discontinued baking and his sons Dovid'l and Moshe became bakers. His daughter ("Khana the Baker", or Khana Tyk), who was married to reb Khaim Yankel Tik, a Ger khasid, made him become a baker too. He was her second marriage. It was told, that her first husband, sat all day in the Beit Midrash and learned, and was not aware of any worldly possessions, he didn't even know how money looks like, when he returned home from his daily study, he would ask around "where does Shoel'ke the Baker live?"

Her son–in–law was a great scholar, his name was reb Chaim Meir Lis Z"L, he was a Lubavitch khasid, and circulated Khabad theories amidst the public. Although he was busy making a living, he gave his spare time to form groups that learn Khabad studies. His charming approach was capturing, he was a rare personality for his understanding character, and Torah knowledge. He was highly revered and beloved by everyone.

Dovid Leib the Baker

Was considered one of the 36 pious men for who's merits keep up the universe. All night he baked while humming tunes, at dawn he went to the synagogue, where he would say all 150 psalms, pray the Morning Prayer, thereafter, he would go around collecting money for the poor and distribute it to them. At noon, he finally came home, his wife Tova shouted and screamed at him, but he merely smiled and accepted his lot with calm and peace. However, his wife did all transactions regarding the bakery – buying the flour, making payments, selling to stores.

[Page 264]

Yisroel Mendel the Baker

Reb Yisroel Mendel Markus was an expert in his work. His wife Meitah and their daughters helped him in the business. He would always tell stories of the war between Russia and Turkey, which he had participated. The bakery was in the cellar, at the corner of the streets Rynek and Pultuska. From time to time rain would flood the cellar, nonetheless, he was always happy and jolly.

Residues of the family: Two daughters in Israel, and one in the USA.

Reb Abraham Farbstein

"Avrehmel the carter" they called him. Tall, broad shoulders, well built, his large beard combed neatly, dressed tidily. In spite of his trade, he quite differed from his peers; with his soft speech, his manners, and being an observant Jew who prayed at dawn in the small synagogue of the "Tehillim" club. His only son Jacob studied with topmost teachers and was an intelligent, well–versed scholar, an open minded and good–mannered youth. His marriage took place in Radzymin, and he was supported for a number of years by his father–in–law. When he was on his own, he returned to Wyszkow with his wife Doba, a wonderful woman that in spite of her being busy feeding and educating her many children, she found time to help her husband in his work. In his last years, Avrehmel worked for the family of Khaim Dovid Goldwasser. He was entrusted with the keys of the restaurant and the cooling room of beer and beverages.

From his family, five grandchildren; three boys and two girls of his son Jacob Z"L, immigrated to Israel.

Reb Jacob Markuskhamer

A Torah scholar and a genius as a bachelor, people called him "Yankel Yisroel Gershon's." He was a "Proprietor" of two houses on Rynek Street and owned a bagel bakery, and an oven, where Jews placed their chulent before Shabbat. His wife Khava Z"L took charge of all the matters. They did many kind acts for the community and donated charity. Khava managed the kitchen of the "Beis Joseph" yeshiva and cared for all the students' needs. They themselves had a large family, sons and daughters who were highly esteemed by the community.

Residues of the family are in America, both, their sons and daughters are social figures involved with public affairs. Thus, they continue their parents' tradition, in fit with our era. In their merit that the Wyszkow association operates successfully.

Reb Avrahmke the Teacher

Was one of the latest soldiers of the Czar's army, where he served for thirty years, managing to cross the entire Far East. He was a healthy portly man with a lengthy grey beard and a dignified appearance. His kheder was in the small synagogue of the "Tehillim Society" for boys from very young children, up to when they begin to learn the "Khumash." Being a follower of the Alexander rebbe, he lodged at the khasidic shtiebel on Shabbat, for quite a few years. He would tell wondrous stories of his wanderings in China, Manchuria, Caucasus, Uzbekistan and more. Tales about Jews who made boundless efforts and went from place to place to teach Jewish soldiers the religion of their predecessors, he himself also reached out to save far–off brethren from falling out of our nation.

At the third Shabbat meal, he would always do storytelling, stories that took place in the 1870's.

From his family, his daughter, Shprinza, resides in Israel.

Leibel Rosenberg, Bnei–Brak

Reb Isaac Epstein Z"L

Was at the head of the Wyszkow community for several years, and a ckhasid of Ger. He saw to it that communal life should run smoothly as much as possible. He bore the burden of the society and its needs, and regardless of his public and political position, he was revered and admired by the entire community. He had a glorious appearance and a fatherly approach to his subjects, but at different occasions, when necessary, he knew to be assertive too. He conducted the community with serenity and forethought. He raised a large family. Two of his sons are in New York, and two daughters are in Israel.

Reb Zalman Felner Z"L

A revered Alexander khasid, well–informed and well–versed of Torah. One of the pioneers in the building industry of Wyszkow. He manufactured floor tiles, steps, and construction blocks, being the sole provider in the whole surrounding area. He employed his fellow Jews, giving them good terms, befitted to the perceptions of then... his daughters received a high–leveled education.

One son and one daughter live in Israel.

Reb Berisch Czervonogura Z"L

A Ger khasid and Torah master, who fulfilled every commandment to its most. A modest man in every way that was committed to study Torah, to prayer, and to his children's education. His wife Golda Z"L was a pious woman who managed the store. When the war broke out the family went wandering, until they reached Siberia. Reb Berisch died in Arkhangelsk. Golda, at late age managed to get to Israel, where she lived with her daughter in Tel–Aviv for a couple of years.

Reb Isaac Hirsch Rotbard Z"L

A revered Alexander khasid, served as a cantor by the prayers of the high holidays. He suffered deprivation and poverty all his life. Yet, he accepted his fate and relayed an illuminating face with a warm heart.

From his family, two sons and one daughter live in Israel.

Reb Shmuel Brama Z"L

A wonderful public missioner. He had a workshop and was busy laboring all day long; the evenings he devoted for Torah study, for prayer and for action for the many public affairs. He immigrated to Israel in 1936 with his family, and died in 1957.

Translator's Footnote:

1. Zeykher Tsadik Levrokhe = may the memory of the righteous be blessed

[Page 265]

Founders and the Management
of The Lodovi Bank for Several Years
Translated by Chava Eisenstein

Public activists for improving the economy and commerce in Wyszkow

First Row, from the right: **Avraham Marcuskhamer, Yaakov Pshemiaraver;**

Middle: **Fishl Bronshtein, Shmuel Brama, Moshe-David Yoskowitz, Nakhman Dobres, Eli-Mayer Goldman;**

Top: **E. Boorstin, Kzhan, Modekhai Winter**

May they rest in peace!

Righteous Gentiles during World War II
by Stanislaw Wolski, Mayor
Translated by Chava Eisenstein

In 1930, Mr. Wolski was appointed to stand at the head of the municipality of Wyszkow. Despite that Mr. Wolski was an applicant of "Sanaczia," the ruling party which Marshal Pilsudski initiated, which tended partly to deprive the minor Jews in Poland, he related to them properly and sympathized with their problems; and he bothered the municipality to impart decent life orders, and have proper social relations towards the population, of which the Jews too, enjoyed.

Mr. Wolski demonstrated his great courage and nobility in the horror days of the war. We are familiar with actions to save Jewish lives of Wyszkow. He himself hid two orphaned girls, daughters of Joseph-Yikhya Robinowitz z"l, and doing that, he endangered his and his family's life. At the end, he succeeded to transfer them, by having forged official papers, to work at a plant in Germany. The British freed these two Robinowitz daughters in 1945, and later they came to Israel.

S. Wolski died in 1946, the Jewish refugees of Wyszkow will forever remember the noble figure of one of the great righteous gentiles.

[Page 268]

Obituaries

[Page 269]

The Wyszkower Aid Society in New York that is already
functioning for 70 years, mourns the passing of

Reb Mordekhai Czekhanow, of blessed memory,
(Born 1891, died November 21, 1960)

One of the most prominent members in the last 45 years,
praiseworthy, devoted activist for Wyszkower relief.

In sorrow for the great loss

V. Radziminsky – President
J. Zajdenberg – Vice-president

A Word on His Grave

A righteous man goes before you –
Took his final steps on this earth.
Scores of years with Mordekhai. How fortunate that
It was destined for us to be together.

Mordekhai was our teacher –
We had to understand him,
That it is not more beautiful in human life
Than to love others, not just yourself.

His heart bled for human suffering
His heart trembled for Jewish pain;
Still, his smile never wanted to leave him,
He felt: that the Jewish nation will not die out.

Mordekhai had a heart and a desire
That for another person's pain and need
Not only to help with his feelings
But also to share his piece of bread.

We honor and give respect to his name –
Mordekhai the warm person and fiery Jew
To the wreath of flowers I add
My own flower, my Jewish song ...

Tch. Apelboim

[Page 270]

My deepest sorrow for the great loss of thousands of Wyszkower *landsleit,* holy martyrs, who were murdered by Nazi hands and are no longer here with us.

On their unknown graves – my hot tears.

Honor their memory!

Morris Topel, New York

President of the Wyszkower Society, New York, who has held office for over ten years. Renowned among all the *landsleit,* even outside of New York, as an energetic social activist. For years, chairman of the Relief Committee. After World War One, sent over tens of thousands of dollars to Wyszkow to ease the needs and to support many institutions.

[Page 271]

In Eternal Memory

Our beloved and unforgettable husband and father

Avrohom Mordekhai (Max) Czekhanow, of blessed memory

(born in Wyszkow 1891 – died in New York, November 21, 1960)

Greatly supported community projects; participated for many years in the activities in the Wyszkower Societies in New York; was secretary of the Wyszkower United Relief; raised his family in his spirit, putting forward his traditions and also perpetuating his name through planting trees in the *Keren Kayemet* forests in Israel.

With pain and honor, we will always remember his name.

Also, all those who knew him and worked with him, will not forget his devotion for the nation and for our *landsleit*.

Forever:

His wife: **Molly Czekhanow**, New York
The children: **Benny Czekhanow and Manya Goldman**, New York
Sister-in-law: **Faige Jakubowycz and children**, Israel

[Page 272]

In Eternal Memory

Mr. Yakov Zilberstajn *Hakohen*, **of blessed memory**

One of the most devoted activists in the Wyszkower Society, and in general for Wyszkower *landsleit*. There was no task too difficult for him. Neither rain nor snow stopped him from his mission. He held many positions, was president of the Society, chairman of the Relief Committee, treasurer, and more. He was always encouraging others. He himself had a generous hand and urged others to give.

Twelve years ago, the Zilberstajn family and all other Wyszkower *landsleit* lost their beloved and honored Yakov Zilberstajn. He is greatly missed by the Wyszkower *landsleit* and it is difficult to find someone who can take his position, who, with such energy and success, could conduct his work for the Wyszkower *landsleit*.

Yakov Zilberstajn, may he rest in peace, will not be forgotten.

His work in community projects is chaired by his wife Molly and the children, who are in sadness all these years, for their dear father and beloved husband. They also loyally take part [in addressing] all Wyszkower problems. They also contributed $100 towards the Yizkor Book.

Honor his memory!

The Wyszkower Society, New York;
Wife **Molly Zilberstajn and children**

[Page 273]

United Wyszkower Aid Committee for Israel

We, Wyszkower *landsleit* in New York, gathered together on November 29, 1959, for a memorial gathering, organized by the United Wyszkower Aid Society for Israel – to remember the 20th *yahrtag* [date of death] of the mass murder in our home town of Wyszkow, committed by the Nazi murderers in the Second World War –

Express our pain for the thousands of murdered holy martyrs, our *landsleit*, and our very own dear ones.

We shout out our pain for the millions of holy martyrs of our nation, destroyed by the Nazis only because they were children of the Jewish People.

And we take upon us the obligation to help the surviving *landsleit* in Israel, who need help.

At the same time, we acknowledge our *landsleit* in Israel for their initiative and great efforts in publishing the Yizkor Book, that will be held sacred.

And we will make great attempts to fulfill the slogan: The Wyszkower Yizkor Book in every Wyszkower home.

Chairman of the meeting:
Morris Topel

Secretary of the United Wyszkower Committee:
Charles (Khano) Apelboim

[Page 274]

The holy memory of our husband and father

Charles (Yekhezkel) Parower z"l

He was a distinguished leader of the Landsmannshaft, had great merit for Wyszkower countrymen, and held important office: finance-secretary of Wyszkower Relief. For many years was president and secretary of the Wyszkower Society. Recently --- finance secretary of Relief and protocol secretary of the Society.

We are also here expressing our sorrow on the great loss of the Jewish People and the destruction of thousands of Wyszkower compatriots in World War II

Honor their holy memory

To perpetuate with honor

Molly, Abe and Max Parower and Families

[Page 275]

For Eternal Memory
of our dear Parents

Chaya Tova Parower z"l   **David Parower z"l**
Died January 10, 1959   Died June 17, 1957

Both were active and respected in the Wyszkower Compatriots'
organization in New York.

Glory and honor to their memory!

Their dear children are eternalizing –
Son: **Abraham Parower, wife and children**
Daughters: **Beila Maizer, Rojza Denker,
Yetta Telinger and Families**

For Eternal Memory

For the Millions of Jewish Martyrs who died in World War II
And the holy names of the deceased and perished family [members]

My Husband: **Charles (Bezalel) Frost** – Died March 1, 1952 in New
York
Parents: **R' Nisan and Rojza Lis**, O"H Their graves destroyed in
Wyszkow
Brothers: **Abraham Lis and his wife, Feyga Raizal** – died in Russia
Their young daughter **Chaja Sarah Lis** – died in Warsaw
Aaron Yaakov Lis and wife Pesha with their 4 children – Died in Russia

Honor Their Memory!

For eternity: **Chava Frost**, New York
Active Leaders in the Wyszkower Organizations in New York

[Page 276]

For Eternal Memory

Max Holland z"l

For many years, he was of the most devoted activists for the Society. Thanks to him, the projects of the Society had great success and enabled it to send thousands of dollars of aid for needy Wyszkower countrymen.

His death is a great loss for his family and for all countrymen.

His social work is currently being conducted by his wife—Feyge Holland – may she have many years. She continuously helped her husband in his noble activity. She was his "helpmate."

In perpetuity:
Feyge Holland and Family, New York

[Page 277]

Eternal Honor to my dear Parents

R' Shmuel Mayer and Khaya Brakha Wideletz z''l

Prominent communal leaders, exemplary people.

The light of their traditional spirit and philanthropy will always shine for us.

With great honor for them:
Daughter, Molly Leibowitz and family, New York

For Eternal Memory

My mother: **Itka**
My grandmother: **Rivkah Rokhel**
My sisters: **Paya and Rojne, with their husbands and children**
Who died as a result of the Nazis in 1942

For Eternity:
Yankel Aronek and wife, Bronx, New York

[Page 278]

For Remembrance for our dear mother and wife

Paje Rokhel Toffel

Her Soul is in Eden
Died in New York, 1946

For many years she was connected with Wyszkower Relief work:
Founder and first president of "Wyszkower Ladies Auxiliary" of the
Society of Psalms of the People of Wyszkow, New York. Continued the
presidential office to her last day.

Her death is a loss for Wyszkower countrymen and for her entire family.

We are here expressing our sadness over the death
Of millions of martyrs of the Jewish People, and for the thousands
Of Wyszkower who died.

Honor their memory!

In perpetuity:

Her husband: **Morris Toffel**, New York
Sons:
Samuel and wife Gertrude Toffel
Mayer and wife Charlotte Toffel

Daughters:
Sarah and husband Dr. Joseph Weisbrodt
Basha and husband Louis Gutman
Miriam and husband Ted Robinson

[Page 279]

For Eternal Memory
Our Dear Parents

R' Shmuel-Mayer Wideletz z"l

Khaya-Brakha Wideletz z"l

Of the important workers and leaders of the Wyszkower Organization in New York:
Known for their sincerity and extensive assistance for the many needy:
Beloved and respected in the widest circles.

Their sons:
Yaakov Wideletz and Family, New York
Binyamin Wideletz and Family, New York
Wideletz Family, New York

Glory and honor to their memory!

[Page 280]

For Eternal Memory

Our Dear Parents

Khana Leah Frieder
Died in New York
5 Tevet, 5718 - 1958

Rikl   **and**   **R' Itzl Radziminsky**
Died in New York   Died in Wyszkow
Sivan 5702 - 1943   14 Elul, 5695 - 1935

The unforgettable sister and brother with their families

Zechariah Radziminsky

Malka, Simon Jagoda and their children

Rojza Radziminsky
Wife of Zechariah

The sons of Zechariah Radziminsky

We remember their young cutoff lives with sorrow and pain and in constant mourning for their tragic destruction by the Nazi murderers.

For perpetuity:
Velvel, Rokhel Radziminsky and family,, New York

Honor their Holy Memory!

[Page 281]

For Eternal Memory

We are expressing our deepest sorrow on the great loss of 6
million Jewish martyrs, in the time of World War II
We remember a great pain the loss of our own:

Our dear father: **Leibl Apfelboim z"l**

Our brother-in-law **Abraham Schnitzer z"l**
Died in Plonsker Ghetto

Our dear mother: **Tova Apfelboim**
Died before the war.
Her grave was destroyed by the Nazis.

Our sister **Liptshe Schnitzer**, with her 19-year-old son
Mordekhai z"l
Died in the gas chambers in Auschwitz.

Beltshe Najman. Died in Russia from sorrow
and great pain, her eldest daughter, **Khana**, 13 years
old.
Lost after a bombardment by the Nazis, on the way to
Russia.

Our brother. **Shlomo Apfelboim with his wife and 2
children**,
their fate unknown.

**Perpetuated by their children, sisters, and brother
Miriam, Avraham and Khanna Apfelboim**
United States

[Page 282]

To Remember

With great pain in my heart, we remember here, among the six million holy ones
that have fallen from the Nazi murderous hands, also our own holy ones:

Dear Mother: **Rivkah-Rokhel Raikhman**

Dear Sister: **Itke with her daughters: Paye, Rojze and grandchildren**
Died on Yom Kippur 1942, in Wengrow

The sons of brother **Avraham-Moshe Raikhman:**
Yaakov-Mayer and Mordekhai Raikhman
Died in the mass slaughter in Wyszkow, September 1939
At that time also fell our cousin **Khaim-Shepsl Golansky**.

We remember also our cousins, the brothers:
Their Memory Is Eternal!, who died of hunger in their wanderings; and
nephew **Khatzkel Broder**, who died in the first bombardment in
Wyszkow.

The sister of **Rivka-Rokhel Raikhman:**
Khana-Fayge Tzembal
Died in her own house, after the first bombardment of Wyszkow.

And Dear Mother **Mindl**, also a sister of Rivkah-Rokhel.
Her grave was destroyed. The same thing happened to her dear brother
Aharon Raikhman.

We remember here, in memory, our dear fathers.

Aharon Raikhman and Shimshon Aronek

Their Memory Is Eternal!

**In Constant Mourning for the Raikhman and Aronek Families Yitzkhak and
Itkele Raikhman**
Brooklyn, NY

[Page 283]

The active, respected Landsleit in New York, the brothers:

Benny Tzimmerman and wife, Yankl Tzimmerman and wife, Moshe Tzimmerman and wife

The sisters: **Tillie (Taube) Tshernin, Anna Fine and her husband**

Express their sorrow on the Great Jewish Holocaust in the Second World War and attach great honor, to remember forever, the shining names of:

Their Mother: Their Father:

Etel Tzimmerman,
rest in peace
Died in New York

Always devoted herself to
giving charity to the needy.

**R' Mordekhai-Alter
Tzimmerman,**
rest in peace
Died in New York

First secretary for the
Wyszkower Society in New
York until his death.

Brother: **Yaakov Tzimmerman**

Tillie's husband and brother-in-law:
Louie (Leybel) Tshernin,
rest in peace 1947, held the
office of the vice-president
and other honored positions
of Wyszkower Society.

Son of Tillie and Louie Tshernin

At the age of 23, he fell as a heroic fighter in the American Army, on the slaying fields of Holland in 1945.

Honor Their Memory!

Delivered by:
Benny and Rose Tzimmerman and Family, New York

[Page 284]

For Remembrance

My dear father

R' Simkha Bunem b"r Yisroel Grosbard, z"l

A respected community activist, founder of Gerer Shtiebl (Prayer house) Number 2

Died in Wyszkow on Tisha b'Av 5699 (May 7, 1939)

For my dear husband

R' Moshe Shmuel b"r Dov Beryl Rajmi z"l

Died in Detroit on the 16 November 1957 – 22 Kheshvan 5718

In perpetuity
Roiza Rajmi, Detroit

For Remembrance

Pinye Feinzaig z"l

Helped build the Building Club

Always behaved in a quiet manner, with open hand and a gentle heart.

In Perpetuity:
Khanna Feinzaig, New York

His wife, who represents his good manners and traditions.

For Remembrance

Our Dear Parents

Pinkhas and Gitl Steinberg z"l

In Perpetuity:
Son: **Saul Steinberg and Family**, New York

[Page 285]

For Eternal Memory

Our dear father

Moshe Hutnitski, z"l

In Perpetuity:
Molly Mirsky, Texas
Khava Khefoy,
Rivkah Rubin, Tulsa
Leah Burak,
Rachel Sherman

In great sorrow we remember

Abe Parower, z"l

He died at the age of 61 years,
19th February 1962

In his honor

In Perpetuity:
Molly and Max Parower and
family, New York

In Remembrance for our dear ones

Husband and father, children and brothers

Shmuel Jedwab   **Yaakov Jedwab**   **Avraham Jedwab**

and

Sender-Leyzer

Died in Vilna Ghetto

In perpetuity
Bejla Jedwab, Texas
Khana Levitt, Texas
Feige Temkin, Monterrey, Mexico

[Page 286

To Remember Forever

In memory of our families and friends, who died during the destruction of
Wyszkow,
as well as those whose graves are scattered throughout the world.

We mourn for the great destruction of all the cities and towns – and our
hometown of Wyszkow.

We mourn for all the Jews who died in the last war.

Wyszkower Union in Los Angeles, California

Y. Ayan	**Yitzkhak Markus**
Leah Asman	**Hersh-Ber Muszkat**
Yechiel Brzoza	**A. Mann**
Khaim Biyalis	**Segal**
Itche Brzoza	**Rivkah Palasz**
Broder	**Moshe Pakht**
Helen Braun	**Moshe Farbstein**
Berenstein	**W. Neuberger**
M. Holtzman	**D. Kohen**
Yitzkhak Wisotzky	**Khaya Klugman**
Shlomo Warshawsky	**Kayitz**
B. Wiener	**Perl Kipper**
A. D. Teff	**Avraham Rotblat**
Yitzkhak Teff	**M. Szlenger**
Khana Levkowitz	**Yotan Sarah (Wengrow)**

[Page 287]

To Remember Forever

To all those here who participated in our aide work for our Wyszkower, for Israeli and local institutions, who are no longer here with us.

Yisroel Asman

Hersh Sokol

Mordekhai (Motl) Dan

Yudel Yablanka (Bunem-Leib teacher's son)

Bluma Najmark

Her daughter Esthers Ayin

Shmuel Pesakh and Miriam Gurman

Avraham Fishel and Feige Neuman

Rivkah Teff

Tziviah Biyales

Moshe and wife Friedman and their two daughters

Ende (the butcher) Goldberg

Sifra Wisotzky

Yaakov Shiger

David Polarz

Yechiel Brzoza

Wyszkower Union in Los Angeles

[Page 288]

We, the two remaining children from our
large family, will never forget:

Our father **Mendl Skarlat**
Who died of hunger in the Warsaw Ghetto.

Our dear mother Golde Skarlat

**Our sister Brakha Kaluski with her
family:**

Rokhel Jonisz with her family
Itche Najman with his children
With his family
Rafel with his family
Itche – The intelligent, social doer

They all died sanctifying G-d's Name as a
result of Nazi murderers somewhere in
Poland.

We also remember our sister **Khana**. Who
was taken from us so young.

Honor her memory!

Pese Kayitz (Skarlat) and family
Malkah Marcus (Skarlat) and family
Los Angeles

Sixteen years since the Nazis have cut off
your beautiful, honest life. You taught us,
your children, to love other people, love our
people and actively help build and preserve
our culture. We will never forget you and
never forgive the murderers, who have killed
six million of our people.

Honor your names.

Yaakov ben Shmuel Mordekhai Markuschamer

We want also to remember forever our
mother **Khava bas Yisroel Gershon** with
love and tribute. You also have given your
life and service to our people. You were not
only a good and faithful mother to us, but
also to other children, who came to learn in
our Shtetl. You provided them with food and
board like a mother.

Honor Your Memory!

And we certainly will not forget **Feigele**, our
sweet sister, who devoted her young life to
our people. You helped organize the poor
people in our community. You taught them
how to fight for a better and more beautiful
world. You also, in Mexico, had more energy
to sustain the struggle, and up to the last few
minutes of your life, you held on to your
position. Your name will always be
remembered with love and respect. – **Feigele
Jagoda (Marcuschamer)**, who died on
August 17, 1946.

Children, Brothers and Sister –
**Hersh-Mendl, Avramel,Yitzkhak, Shmuel-
Mordekhai,
Gittl, Moshe, Khaim-Leib and Rivke'le**

[Page 289]

In Remembrance

Rivka Taff

In everlasting memory of our beloved mother

Lynn Blanche Julia
A.D. Taff
Los Angeles

In Remembrance

Moshe and Khaya Peshe Hain [Ayon]

(The teacher)

In memory of our beloved father and mother

Moses and Bessie Hain

May the memories of your life inspire us to carry on
the ideals and principles which you have taught your
children

Joseph, Florence, Carolyn, Michael
Los Angeles – New York – Montrea

[Page 290]

For Remembrance

My father **David Bzoza** – died in
Wyszkow
My mother **Khana** – died in
America
My sister **Bajle Serok** – died
with her husband and child

By the bloody hand of Hitler's
Murderers

A pity for those who are lost and
not here with us.

Yitzkhak Bzoza and family
Los Angeles, California

In Memory

Of our beloved father and mother

Max and Bluma Najmark
And in Memory of our Beloved
Sister
Esther N. Hain

From
Ruth N. Stein and Family
Los Angeles, California

In Remembrance

Of my dear parents

Avraham-Hersh (watchmaker)
znd **Hele-Miriam Broder**
Sister, **Khaya-Tovah**
Brothers **Shmuel-Yitzkhak,
Zekhariah,
Henokh-Mayer**, his wife, two
daughters

Hele, Sarah and son **Avraham-
Hersh**
And brother **Khaim-Yaakov
Margulies**
His wife, children, and
grandchildren
and the entire family

Ephraim Broder and son
Los Angeles, California

In Memory

Our father, mother sister brother and children

Binyamin Khaim Taff, Jospa
Lotshe, Ruchtshe and their children

Avraham Yelin, Malke
Saratshe, David and their children

Itshe and Bajlitshe Taff (Yelin)
And their son
Los Angeles, California

[Page 291]

In Memory

For my dear
parents

**Gedalia and
Libe Rokhman**

Sister **Tobe**,
Her husband
**Avraham-
Yitzkhak
Olenberg**
And their
children

Sister **Khaya-
Sarah**

In memory

Her husband
Goldsmith and
children

In Memory

of our Beloved

Husband and
Father

**Joseph David
Palarz**

Rivkah Palarz and children Los Angeles

In memory .

For my dear parents

Khaim-Mordekhai and Gite-Yokheved Igolowitz

Sister **Rivkah-Rokhel**
her husband **Naphtali Watenberg**
and their chidren
sister **Miriam**,
her husband **Shmuel-Pesakh Gurman**
and sister **Tzviah Bajles**

Ethel Neuberger and family
Los Angeles

In Memory

For my dear parents

Yehuda and Ende (Ende the butcher)

Grandmother **Rajzl Goldberg**

And the entire family

Khana Lefkowitz
Los Angeles

[Page 292]

In Memory

For my dear parents

Yaakov Zelig and Feige Rothblatt
(the answers)

My brother **Mordekhai, Jonathan, Simkha Bunem**
Uncle **Mordekhai-Yudl** (the takazh?), Aunt **Khana**
And the entire family

Avrahm Yitzkhak and family Rothblatt
Los Angeles

In memory

For my dear parents

**Hersh-Leib and Khaya-Rivkah
Holtzman**

Brothers **Eliezer Bunem,
Shmuelke**

Mordekhai Holtzman and family
Los Angeles

For my dear parents

Joseph and Gisha Pakht
Brother **Shlomo and Sarah
Gisha**
Sister **Frumet**
Her husband **Mordekhai-Joseph
Apelboim**
And their son
The entire family and friend

Moshe Pakht and family
Los Angeles

[Page 293]

In Memory

For my dear parents

**Yitzkhak-Hersh and Rotze
Bialostocky**
(**Moshe Leib** cereal maker's son)
Sister **Rivkah** and brother **Pinkhas**

Her husband **Feivl Zilbershtein** and
children
Yokheved, her husband **Eliezer** and
their children
Sister **Khana**, brother **David**
And the whole family

Khaim Bialis, Los Angeles

In Memory

For our dear parents
**Simkha and Sarah
Mushkatenblit**
Our sister
Rojze her husband **Khaninah**
Their daughters Rokhel and
Gitl Goldshtein
Our brother **Aharon-Mayer**
Who did not want to leave the
old parents when their lives
were at the end.
He had to carry them because
they could not go anymore ...
He died in Warsaw Ghetto.

Our brother **Yaakov (Yontshe)**
Who died in the first World
War

My dear children **Moshe** and
Leah
Our entire family, relatives and
friends

Hersh-Ber Mushkat, Los
Angeles
Rivkah Kat, New York

For our dear parents

Henokh and Malkah Bzoza
Our sister **Rochel**, her husband
Zemir,
Their son **Yitzkhak**
Who gave his life for Israel

Yekhiel Bzoza, Los Angeles
Saratshe, Havana

To Remember Forever

Siphra Wisotsky

Died 28 MarKheshvan 5708,
after a serious, short illness

Y. Wisotsky and sons
Los Angeles

In Memory

For **Tzviah Bialis**

Los Angeles

In Memory

For our dear parent
**Yosroel-Yitzkhak and Sarah
Westinyetsky**
Sister **Ziske**, **Esther** and their
families
Brother **Feivl-Aharon** and family

Shlomo and Rivkah Warshawski
Los Angeles

In Memory

For my dear parents **Nakhum
and Bajle**
Sister **Khava** and family
Brother **Khaim-Natan Wengrow**
Brother **Simkha-Yaakov**

Khaitshe Neuman (Wengrow)
Los Angeles

For my dear parents

Moshe and Pearl Holand
Brother **Velvl**, Sister **Khana-Rojze**
Her **Itsche**, Grandmother Khaya-Sara
Aunt Malkah Goldberg
Grandfather Yitzkhak-Aizik,
Grandmother **Esther Rozner**
And the entire family

Khava-Faje Klugmani
Los Angeles

In Memory

For my dear parents
Moshe and Ite Ornshtein
Brother **Simkha** and his family

Pearl Ornshtein
Los Angeles

In Memory

My dear parents **Mendl and Ete Asman**
My Sister **Khava**, her husband
Khaim Kremer and children
And my brother **Yisroel Asman**

Leah Asman
Los Angeles

[Page 294]

Sender Wengel and wife Dora

In memory:
His mother Elke
His brother Avraham wife and
children

Yidl Rajzik

To Perpetuate:
Aunt Esther Brojtman
Aunt Khava Brojtman and
children

Shimon Olemberg

For Remembrance:
His children, D'vorah, Yehudis
His brother Binyamin and family
Sisters, Khaya, Feige, brother-in-
law and children

Velvel Nowogrodski and wife

To Perpetuate:
Yekhiel-Mayer Domb and wife
Golde, son Mendl
Grandmother Bashe Domb
Grandfather Binyamin Domb
Toviah Nowogroski with his wife
Khaya-Peshe

Leib Shtchigel and wife Shtchigel

In memory:
Father Mayer-Yitzkhak Shtchigel
Mother Dobe Shtchigel
Brother Mikhel Shtchigel
Sisters Gitl, Rokhl
Their father Yitzkak-Aryeh Brok
Mother Yospe Brok
Brothers Moshe-Leib Brok

Mordekhai Yismakh and wife Peshe

Forever:
Her father Bunem Borshtein
Mother Malkah-Tova
Sister Bluma-Bajltshe
His father Joseph Yismakh
Sister Leah
Uncle Avraham Popowsky

Yisroel-Moshe Cembal and wife Rokhl

In Memory:
Her father Elter Jelishewski from Radzymin
And his brothers, sisters and family

Shmuel Rajtshik

Forever:
His sister Rivkh and husband Yitkhak Babin
with their son Yaakov

Simkhah Paskowitz and wife

In memory:
The Pshetitsky family –
Moshe, Mayer, Leibish
Yekhezkiel and wife Shayntshe and children
Hendiel Pshetitsky (Rozenberg)
Shayve (Rotenberg)
Shlomo Rotenberg
And children Yisroel, Tzirl, Zisl and Hindl

His Memory:
His father Avraham-Yitzkhak Garfinkel
And wife Miriam-Rivkah, daughter Skarah-Blima
Father Henekh Piekasz and child Moshe'le
Aunt Tziporah and her children Nemeh, Rokhl Leah

Khamah and Avraham Bernshtein

Forever:
Her brother Leibesh Pshetitski
Brother Yekhezkiel, wife and children
Sister Hendl Pshetitski-Rozenberg
Sister Shaive
Brother-in-law Shlomo Rotenberg and their children
Hadas, Tzirl, Yisroel, Zisl, Hendl

He perpetuates his brothers, brothers-in-law and children
All who died as martyrs
Also, Yitzkak Aizik and Moshe Binem Berenshtein
Their wives and children

Moshe Kwiatek

In Memory:
His father Yitzkhak from Kamenczik
And Grandfather Khano from Wyszkow

Yekutiel Altmark and his wife Sarah

For Remembrance:
Her father Yaakov Kershenowitz
Mother Golde-Rivkah with their 3 children

[Page 295]

Borukh Yismakh

To remember the Holy Deceased:
Father Avraham
Mother Gittl
Brothers Shlomo, Velvl, Yossl
Aunts, Nephews, Cousins and
Relatives

Nakhum Greenberg and Family

In Memory:
Father Yekl Greenberg
Brother Borukh
Sisters:
Khaya-Malkah
Sarah
Esther
And their families

Leibl Lipowitzky

In Memory:
Father Joseph, Mother Sarah-
Rivkah
Brothers Berl, Avraham-Tzalke,
Yisroel-Yitzhak
Sisters Enye Gittl, Khaya, Blume,
Feige

Yekutiel Almark

In Memory:
His brother Avraham-Hersh and
family
Sister Rivkah and family

Yitzkhak Zlatagwjazda and wife Nehmi

In Memory:
Her father David Wilenskfi
Her mother Khaya-Bajlw

Zisl K. Burshtein and family

In memory of her husband
Avraham-Leib Burshtein, Rest in
Peace
Died on the 14th Iyar 1944 Buenos
Aires

Yaakov Mesing

In Memory:
Rachel Pelner
Manye Pelner
Zelman Pelner
Died in Wyszkow

Yizkhak Najman and family

In memory:
Mother Khava
Sisters Rojze Garnek
Khaya Najman
Died in Warsaw Ghetto

Yaakov and Shlomo Zilberman
And their families

In Memory:
Mother Malkah-Perl Zilberman
Brother Aizik Zilberman
Sister Khaya-Sarah Zilberman
Sister-in-Law Bajle and her
children

Lean Nowogrodski
And sister Bina Nowogrodski-
Rozner

In Memory:
Mother Nekhamah
Sisters Yehudis
Rajzl
Brother Motl and family

Yisroel Brajtman

In Memory:
Brother David, his wife and child

Avraham Bromberg

In Memory:
Brother-in-Law Joseph Binduski
Sister-in-Law Rachel Binduski

Yisroel Tenenboim and wife
Bajlthse

In Memory:
His mother Ite
Brother Yidl
Her mother Frajde
Sister Yospe

Shmuel Rajczik, wife Khana
and children

In Memory:
Her father Yisroel Prager
Her brothers Simkha Prager and
family
Mendl Prage

[Page 296]

Rivkah and Peshe Kolo
from somewhere near Wyszkow

In Memory:
Mother Dvorah Kolo
Brothers Reuven
Nekhemiah
Shekhna
Sisters Gitl
Aidl and families

Fishl Koplowitz and family

In Memory:
Father Joseph-Aryeh
Mother Khaya Rojze
Brother David and his family
Sisters Esther-Khana
Perl
Feige-Hinde
Died in the war in Poland

Mirl Mondry

In Memory:
Father Yiytzkhak Mondry
Mother Khaya

Khana Goldfaber

In Memory:
Father Avraham-Yitzkhak
Karvat
Brother-In-Law Yisroel Poplowitz
and children

Barukh Autnitzki

In Memory:
Mother Freide
Brothers Shlomo, Mendl, David
Sister Golde
Brother-in-Law
Gershon Zarembski
And children

Sholom Solomon

In Memory:
Mother Khava
Sister Mashe-Rachel
Brother Shlomo
Brother-In-Law Avraham Jagoda
And children

Joseph Popowski and Family

In Memory of their family
Father Mendl
Mother Khava
Sister Feige, her husband and schildren
Brother Moshe-Avraham and his family
Brother Velvl

Leibl Lisowitzki and family

In Memory:
Father Yoseph
Mother Sarah-Rivkah
Brothers Berl, Tzalke and Yisroel-David
Sister Khaya-Blume

Nakhmn Walman

In Memory:
Father Shepsl
Mother-in-Law Rachel
Brother Leibl and family

Yekl Waksman

In Memory:
Sister Feige-Yente

The Brothers Mayer-Leib, Sender and Simkhah Holtzman and families

In Memory:
Father Yaakov Holtzman
Sister Blime, Brother-in-Law Yisroel Shult
Sister Esther Holtzman

Elter Koplowitz and family

In Memory:
Father Berish
Mother Khava
Sister Hinde
Sister Brakha

[Page 297]

Velvl and Hendl Rotbard

In Memory:
Her brothers Hersh-Joseph Sokol
Moshe Sokol
Avraham Sokol
His uncle Khaim Bloom
Aunts Neche
Fraide Nowominski
And their families

Yitzhak and Motl Gruszka and families

In Memory:
Father Yehoshue-Dov
Mother Khaya
Brother Tuviah

Yaakov and Aryeh and Sztelung and families

In Memory:
Father Khaim Henokh
Mother Esther Mindl
Sisters
Khaya Nekhamah Rozenberg
Brakha Dvorah Krimkewitz
Brother Avraham-Moshe
Sztelung
Brother Joseph Sztelung
Brother-in-Law Yekhiel-Mayer
Rozenberg
Brother-in-Law Shlomo
Krimkewitz
Sister-in-Law, Esther
Sister-in-Law, the wife of Joseph
Sztelung
And their children, who died
sanctifying God's Name
And their memory will remain in
our hearts

Yitzkhak Bharav

In Memory
Mother Sarah Bharav
Brothers Joseph, Moshe, Hershl,
and Yisroel
Sisters, Gitl , husband Khaim
Leib (Shokhet and Inspector)
And their families

Mordekhai Njedjewitzki and wife

In Memory:
Brothers-in-Law, Yaakov
Holtzman
Velvl Altmark
Hershl Rujshe
And their families

Yisroel Sokol

In memory:
His brothers Avraham
Hersh-Joseph
Moshe Sokol
And their families

Moshe Postolski and family

In memory of his nephew
Mordekhai-Mendl Postolski

Asher Mitlsbakh and wife Frajde Koplowitz

In Memory:
Their brother-in-law, Barukh
Dobres
Her mother Khava, father Berish
Her sister Hinde-Brakha
And their families

Joseph Nowominski and family

In Memory:
Brother, Yaakov-Aryeh
Sister Nekhe, Brother-in-Law,
Khaim Bloom
Sister Fraide and daughter Yospe
Sister Miriam. Husband and
children

Tzviah Steinman-Ausekhewitz

In Memory:
Father Yaakov-Aryeh Steinman
Mother Khava-Zlate
Sister Bajle and her husband Rav
Avraham
Tzitrin, z"l and children
Brother Moshe, his sister Khaya-
Sarah
His sister, Yente-Khudes
And their families

Motl Wengel and wife, Gitl Postolski-Wengel

In Memory:
His mother Elke Wengel
Brother Avraham and family
Her father
Hersh Postolski
Mother Liptshe-Golde
Sister Leah, Miriam, Yente and
Esther

[Page 298]

**Mordekhai Tandetchazh
and wife Esther-Ite Sokol-
Tandetchazh**

In Memory:
**Her father Avraham Sokol
Brother Mayer-Aharon
Sister-in-law Rokhel
His father Shmuel-Eliezer
Tandetchazh
Mother Mindl**

**Shmuel Pshetitzki and sister
Perl**

In Memory:
**Father Tuviah Pshetitski
Mother Khaitshe
Brothers Yaakov, Feivl, Mendel
Sister Rivkah**

Shia and David Grinberg
in Uruguay

In Memory:
**Mother Mnukah-Dvorah
Father Shmuel-Yitzhak Grinberg
Brothers Hersh-Pinkhas,
Avraham-Mayer,
Yaakov and Aba Grinberg
And their families**

Shaye Gruszka and Family

**Father Mordekhai-Mendl
Mother Khava-Feige
Brothers Avraham, Yekhiel
Sisters Sarah, Etke (died in
Treblinka)**

Yaakov Palukh

In memory:
**Father Yisroel-David
Brother Yidel and family
Sister Zlate and family**

Gitl Kristal

**Father Mordekhai-Mendl
Mother Khava-Feige
Brothers Avraham, Yekhiel
Sisters Sarah, Etke (died in
Treblinke)**

Avraham and Ette Zgrizek

In memory:
**Brother Avraham-Binem
Burshtein and children
Cousin Blime Burshtein and
children**

Etke Rotbard-Schwartzman

In Memory:
Her father Yidel Rotbard
Died in Buenos Aires in the year
1958

Motln Jolkower-Burshtein

In memory:
**Brother-in-law Ephraim Jolowitz
and children**

Aizik Rubin

In Memory:
**His grandmother Libe-Rojze
Rubin**

Avrahm Bluszka

In memory:
Velvl Bluszka
Died in Russia in 1942

Esther-Rokhel Nowigrod-Bszoiniak

In Memory:
**Grandfather Yitzkhak Nowigrod
Grandmother Breine**

Aharon Cembal and children

In memory:
**Father-in-law Shimon Jakobowitz
Sister-in-law Rivkah
Brother-in-law Mendl
Sister-in-law Leah**

Hersh Cymerman and wife

In Memory:
**Malkah Cymerman
Itke Cymerman
Hersh-Leib Cofer
Yidl Cymerman**

[Page 299]

Gedaliah Bengelsdrorf
From Province Cordoba, Argentina

In Memory:
Father Moshe
Died in Wyszkow in the war

Joseph Pjetshelenietz

In Memory:
Father Mordekhai-Yidl
Mother Leah
Sister Esther

Avraham Rubin and family

In Memory:
Mother Liba
Sister Rivkah
Nephew Aizik Rubin

Khaim Zilbershtein and Family

In Memory:
Father Moshe Zilbershtein
Sister Yekl Mentel
Sister-in-law Tova Dan

Nasan Ostry and family

In Memory:
Father David-Tzvi Ostry
Mother Sarah
Brother Moshe-Joseph
Sister Feige
Sister Malka
Sister Khaya-Neche
Sister Libe-Rivke

Hinde Holand-Prager
Shlomo Prager and children

In Memory:
Father Shmuel-Leib Holand
Mother Khava
Sister Dvorah-Rachel
Sisters Rojze, Rachel,
Sarah,Toviah, Khana
Their father Yisroel Pragee
Bother Simkha, wife Rachel
Brother Mendl

Feige Weis-Autnitski

In Memory:
Mother Freide Autnitski
Sister, Golde
Brothers
Mendl
David
Shlomo

Yitzkhak (Itshe) Sokol and wife

In Memory
Her father Reuven Kleinman
Her Mother Malka
Sisters and brothers
Rachel, Yaakov-Shlomo, Kreindl,
Sarahle, Feigele

Yaakov Monkita

In Memory:
Nasan Monkita
Rivkah Popowski

Shmerl Maltshik and wife
Hinde

In Memory:
Father Hershel Holtzman
Mother Khaya-Rivkah
Brothers Moshe
Eliezer
Shaulke
And their families

Hinde Shapira

In Memory:
Father Zelman Holtzman

[Page 300]

In Memory
My Dear Parents

**r' Barukh and Esther Brisk
Husband Binyamin**
Mother-in-law's parents:
**Aizik-Mayer and Yokheved
Krishtal**

Bashke Krishtal

In Memory
My Dear Parents

**r' Wolf-Mayer and Peshe-
Rachel Wenger
Wife Sheine
Sister Beile-Gitl**

Hershl Joseph Wenger

In Memory

**My Dear Mother Dvorah
Grandfather Avraham-Moshe
Brother Motl**

Mnukah Cohen

In Memory

My Dear Parents
**r' Zelik and Libe-Sarah
Zilberman
Sister and son: Esther and
Isaac**

Gedalialh Zilberman

In Memory

**My Dear Step-Father and
Mother
Sholom and Braine Zenderland**
Brothers and sisters:
**Yisroel, Moshe, Khaim, Khava,
Sarah,
Jehuditl and Malka**

Avraham Gliksberg

In Memory

Our Dear Parents
**r' Mordekhai and Khana
Daitcher
Father Mendl Mitzenmakher
Brother Yenkl
Sisters Tzipe and Perl**

**Esther Daitcher
Yitzkhak Mitzenmakher**

In Memory

My Dear Parents
r' Yehuda and Khaya-Sarah
Niestempower
Sisters and brother:
Bashe, Dvorah, Rachel,
Sheindl, and Moshe

Shmuel Niestempower

In Memory

My Dear Parents
r' Avraham and Esther-Hinde
Rybner
Brother Hersh Yenkl

Rachel Rybner-Luzer

In Memory

My Dear Wife
Esther Sarah Lemberg

Shimon Hersh Rostkier

In Memory

My Dear Parents
r' Aba and Esther-Hinde
Altmark
Brothers Shimon and Yenkl
Sister Rojze

Joseph Altmark

In Memory

My Dear Parents
Berish and Golde
Czerwonagora
Avigdor Segal

Our sister, brother, brother-in-law
And their children:
Rajzl, Malka, Khava, Segal
David, Leitshe Czerwonagora
And children Esther, Yisroel
and Mendl

Khoshka and Zindl Segal

In Memory

My Dear Parents
Joseph-Mayer and Malka
Grapa

Our brother and sisters:
Shlomo, Brakha and Kayle

Shalom Grapa

[Page 301]

In Memory

My Dear Parents
**R' Khaim-Shmuel and Tojze
Shiker**

Brother and Sister:
**Yaakov, Motl and
grandchildren
Khaya, Rivkah, Esther and
Rachel**

Moshe Shiker

In Memory

My Dear Parents
**R' Moshe-Hersh and Freida-
Sarah Fieler
R' Hershl and Tzwia-Gitl Blum**

Brothers and Sister:
**Shimon, Mordekhai, Rivkah-
Khaya, Zitl'**

Shlomo Fieler

In Memory

My Dear Parents
**R' Shmuel-Yitzkhak and
Dvorah
Brothers: Aba, Khatzkl,
Avraham-Mayer
Hersh Pinkhas and Yaakov**

Shaul Grinberg

In Memory

My Dear Parents
**R' Khaim-Shepsl and Ita
Galonsky' Brothers and sister:
Berl, Khenokh, Yenkl and
Sarah'**

Shimon Galonsky

In Memory

My Dear Parents
Bunem and Shifra Oldak

Brothers and Sister:
Mendl, Motl, and Tzwia

Yaakov Oldak

In Memory

My Dear Parents
**R' Mordekhai and Khavh
Daitcher**

Sister and Brother-in-law:
**Tzife and Lajzer Friedmakher
Khana and husband**

Hersh Daitcher

In Memory

My Dear Parents
G'dalia and Feige Bronshtein
Sister Mekhshe

Bunem Bronshtein

In Memory

My Dear Parents
R' Abe and Esther-Hinde
Zeltman
Brother Yenkl and sister
Khaya-Feige

Khaya Altmark (Zeltman)

In Memory

My Dear Parents
Yehoshua and Rivka Wenger

Sister and Brothers:
Beltshe, Sarah-Malka, Moshe
and Zecariah

Mordkhai-Joseph Wenger

In Memory

My Dear Parents
R' Yitzkhak –Joseph and
Malka Olsheker
Brother Yaakov and family

Barukh Olsheker

In Memory

My Dear Parents
R' Feivl and Yute Shran

Brother Melekh, his wife and
child

Simkhe-Bunem Shran

In Memory

My Dear Parents
R' Khatzkl and Etel Romianek

Brother, wife and child:
Avraham, Nekhamah and Velvl
Romianek
Sister Zelde, Simkhah
Jakobowitz
And children

Wolf Romianek

[Page 302]

In Memory

My Dear Father
R' Zalmen Radziminsky

Yidl Radziminsky

In Memory

My Dear Wife
Roshke Bronshtein

G'dalia Rombinsky

[Page 303]

To Remember Forever

Founders of the Wyszkow veterans' organizations and members
of its administration who were gathered with their people

Khaim Noson Wengrow, Israel
Rachel Zmir, The Bzoza Home, Israel
Yaakov-David Pshetitsky, Israel
Shaika Pustulsky, Israel
Shmuel Brama, Israel
Berish Safirshtein, Israel
Velvl Rotbard, Argentina

For many years they spent their time working in the desert and helping the
people of our city

May their memory be bound up in the eternal life of our nation

The Wyszkow Foundation in Israel

[Page 304]

For these we cry: And avenge them with disgust, to join the mourners of the world
Yekhezkel [Ezekiel] 28

Our mother
Esther Mindl
rest in peace,
died in Warsaw,
16 Shevat 5694

The gravestone cemetery
Gensha Street
in Warsaw

R' Khaim Henokh Shtelung
z"l
died Warsaw Ghetto
12 Kislev 5701

Our brother
Joseph Shtelung z"l

Our brother **Moshe** his wife **Esther** and children
Mendl and Yitzkhak'el Shtelung

**His wife and two sons
murdered in Jadow Ghetto**

Our sister
Brakh'tza Krimkowitz
died in the First Aktion
in Warsaw

His brother-in-law
Shlomo Krimkowitz
Died in the liquidation
of the Warsaw Ghetto

To Commemorate:
Yaakov Shtelung and Family – Buenos Aires
Aryeh Shtelung and Family – Buenos Aires
Menakhem Shtelung and Family – Tel Aviv

[Page 305

To Remember for Eternity

Our Dear Father

Our Dear Sisters:

Henya and her 2 children
Avraham and Khava

Who died in the Shoah in
France

Dobkeh and husband
Binyamin daughter
Rivkah Rokhel'e Epshtein

His brother-in-law: **Sholom
Epshtein z"l**

May they rest in peace!

The Immortalizers:
Moshe Epshtein, New York
Mendl Epshtein, New York
Beile, Brazil
Malkah Kaluski, Israel
Mitah Daigi, Israel
Esther, Paris

R' Yitzkhak Epshtein z"l
Of the city's dignitaries and
leaders,
community leader until the end
of his days

Gravestone for Jahrzeit, Hoshanna Rabah 1961

To
Remember

Our Dear
Son,
Father,
Husband
and
Brother

**Yehoshua
B'Harab
z"l**

We will always mourn for you, our dearest, who suddenly died in his 39th year of his life, in Buenos Aires.

Your holy memory will always be etched in our broken hearts.

Your good deeds to your parents, wife and family will never be forgotten.

To Immortalize –
Parents: **Yitzkhak and Feige B'Harab** – Israel
Wife: **Rokhel B'Harab** – Buenos Aires
Children: **Shlomo and Mordekhai B'Harab** – Buenos Aires
Sister: **Rivkah Sheinman (B'Harab)** – Buenos Aires

[Page 306]

In eternal memory

My husband and our father

**R' Yaakov Dovid
Pshetitsky z"l**

Died January 15, 1956

A dear person, devoted his heart and soul to his family and the needy in the community. Loved and respected by all.

Founder of the Gemilot Khesed Fund in Wyszkow and in Israel. One of the founders of the Wyszkow Organization and the fund manager until his last day.

May his memory be blessed!

In Commemoration:
His wife: **Sheindl Pshetitsky**
His Daughters: **Dvorah Melowanchik, Hadassa Kaspi, Khava Yekhieli, Khaniah Nagal, Tziporah Holtzman, Rokhel Pshetitsky, Zahava Dudenshtein, Mashe Horowitz**
Sons: **Yisroel and Joseph Pshetitsky**

My Dear Sisters   To Remember Forever

My Dear Parents

Feiga Najmark z"l

R' Pesakh Najmark z"l

Gisha-Rokhel Najmark
née Koplowitz

Esther Najmark z"l

May their memory be bound up in the life of the nation.

To Commemorate:
Khaya Kol (Najmark)
Kibbutz Yifat, Israel

[Page 307]

For Eternal Memory

Our Aunt
Kayle Najmark

Our Dear Parents
R' Yoseph-Mayer and Malka Grapa

Our Dear Sisters:
Brakha and Kayl'tshe

Our Unforgettable Uncle
R' Barukh Sokol z"l

In Memory:
Shmuel Grapa, Mexico
Sholom Grapa, Montevideo
Yehuda Grapa, Mexico
Khana Druynski, Mexico

To Remember for Eternity

Our Dear Father **R' Dov Berish HaKohen Wilenski z"l**

A Torah scholar, modest in his ways, one who loved people,
from the Khasidim of the Rav of Alexander

Our Dear Mother, **Mrs. Bailah Wilenski, nee Grapa**

A righteous woman, engaged in business with people for help and
guidance,
with faith in the community

Our Dear Brother **R' Menakhem Mendl Wilenski z"l**

Our Dear Sister

Itkah Wilenski z"l

Educated in the tradition of our
fathers

Died at the hands of the Nazis in
Wengrow 1943

Their memory be bound up in the bond of the nation's life

To Commemorate:
Avraham Wilner Tel-Aviv
HaRav Yekhiel Wilenski Tel-Aviv
Yerakhmiel Wilenski Tel-Aviv

[Page 308]

To Remember Eternally, Our Dear Parents and Sisters

Ral'tzah Hiller   Rokhel Hiller, rest in peace   R' Khaim Khaikl Hiller z"l

To Commemorate:
Tovah Kryshtal
Malka Wilner
Sarah Kaplan
Leah Rajtzik

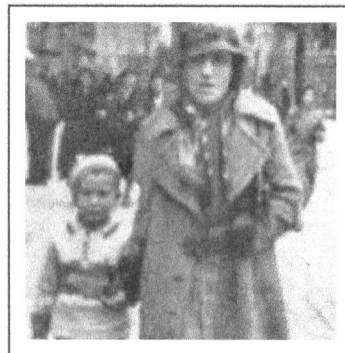

We dedicate this page to
commemorate them with deep
admiration.

We will forever remember our
brave mother, a woman of
valor.

Our father, the most righteous
man of men.

Our blessed and talented sister.

Our sister Khana with her son

To Remember Forever

Our Dear Parents **Zalman and Esther-Brakha Holztman z"l**
(died Sept. 26, 1937 in Wyszkow)

Our Dear Uncle **Tzvi Holtzman**, his wife and 3 sons

Died in the Holocaust years

To Commemorate:
Binah Holtzman-Rukhman, Tel Aviv
Yaakov Holtzman, Canada
Leib Holtzman and Hinda Shapira, Argentina
Tzipora Krauze, Canada

[Page 309]

Eternal memory

| Our dear uncle and his family | Our dear brother and his family | Our dear father | Our dear grandfather |

Reb Yekhiel Olshker, z"l; his wife and six children; died in the Nazi Shoah

Reb Yaakov Olshker z"l, his wife **Liba** and six children, died in the Nazi Shoah

Reb Moshe-Aaron Olshker, z"l, Gabbai [sexton] in the Khevra Kadisha [Burial Society] and in the Khevra Mishnayos [Mishna Study Society]; died on 11 Tishrei, 5681

Reb Yitzkhak-Yosef Olshker, z"l, who died 25 Tammuz 5685

To Commemorate:
Yehudah Ilan (Olshker) and Family, Israel
Shmuel Olshker and Family, Buenos Aires
Borukh Olshker and Family, Montevideo
Fishl Olshker and Family, Brooklyn, New York
Shmuel Burovitz and Family, New York
Betzalel Burovitz and Family, New York

To Remember Forever

Our Dear Uncle   Our Dear Parents

Shmuel-Yaakov Wainberg z"l
Immigrated to Israel 1909
One of the founders of Givat
Shaul, Jerusalem, and create
future generations of builders
of the country.

Shaindel Wainberg z"l
Died 20 Tamuz 5743

Shlomo Wainberg z"l
Immigrated to Israel in 1921
Died 14 Adar 5689 (1929)

Brought to eternal rest on the Mount of Olives, Jerusalem

To Commemorate:
Sorah Segal and Family, Malka Tzekhori and Family,
Khana Shachne and Family, Tovah Rabah and Family,
Laya Lipowsky and Family
Their sons, daughters, nephews and nieces, and grandchildren
Of Reb Shmuel-Yaakov Wainberg z"l

[Page 310]

In Eternal Memory

Our Dear, Unforgettable Parents, Brothers and Sisters – The holy martyrs

His Wife

R' Yitzchak Mondre

Henokh Mondre

Yidl Mondre

To Commemorate:
Avigdor Mondre, Israel
Hershl Mondre, Detroit
Esther Sporta, Israel
Malka Zilberberg, Argentina

[Page 311]

To Remember Forever

My Dear Daughter and Sister

My Husband and Dear Father

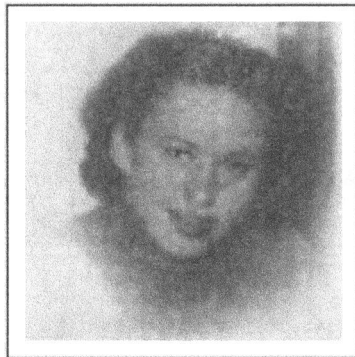

Sorah Jakubowitz z"l
1920-1941
Perished in Ludmir by the hands
of the Nazis, may they be blotted
out. Student at Lvov University,
she promised great things. We
mourn the terrible loss of her life.

**R' Yitzkhak-Mayer Jakubowitz
z"l**
1886-1940

To Commemorate:
His Wife and Mother: **Faige Jakubowitz**, Israel
Daughters & Sisters: **Binah Tabak and family**, Israel
Khana Sokolar and family, Israel
Rokhel Sokolar and family, Israel
Son and Brother: **Pinkhas Jakubowitz and family**, Israel

To Remember Forever

My Sister & husband	My Dear Husband	My Dear Father

Bajla-Faiga & Yaakov Pshemerover z"l
and sons Shaul and Yisroel

R' Khaim-Dovid Goldwasser z"l
Died 21 Adar, 5680 (1920)

R' Shmuel Eliyahu Orenstein z"l
Died 27 Iyar, 1956
K'Far Khasidim
One of the founders of K'Far Khasidim

Our sisters: **Leah Czerwonagura**, husband **David**, & children **Esther, Menakhem and Yisroel**
Malka Shemberg, husband **Yosef-Leib** and daughter **Fruma**
My brother-in-law: **Simkha Orenstein**, his wife and 4 children

To Commemorate:
Pesia Orenstein, Israel
Yisroel Goldwasser, New York

[Page 312]

To Remember Forever

**The Shokhet and Certifier Malkhiel Brukhanski,
and the children of the family**

To Commemorate:
Eliyahu Brukhanski, Israel

To Remember Forever

Our Brother
Yisroel-Mayer Ostry
Memorial Day:
Hoshana Rabah 5718

Our Father
Moshe-Zelig Ostry
Gabbai of the study group
"Path of the Just," Member of
the Board of Gemilas Khesed
["Acts of Loving Kindness"],
walked modestly and Loved all
people.

Our Dear Mother **Khava** z"l – Died Hoshana Rabah 5718

To Commemorate:
Faivel Ostry, Petakh-Tikva
Hintzia, Tel-Aviv
Gitl, Petakh-Tikva

To Remember Our Dear
Parents:
Khaya and Dovid Shredni

To Remember Our Dear
Grandparents:
**Yehuda-Yosef and Mindl
Maltchik**

Yehuda-Joseph Maltchik, z"l

Khaya Shredni,
our uncle
Shmuel Maltchik

Dovid Shredni z"l

To Commemorate:
Eliyahu Shredni
Yaakov Shredni
Hinda Shredni, Israel

[Page 313]

To Remember Forever

Our Dear Brother, his Wife and Children   Our Dear Parents

Dovid and Leah Czerwonagura
Children: **Esther, Mindl and Yisroel**
Died in Warsaw Ghetto

Golde Czerwonagura,
She and her daughter
immigrated to Israel and lived
there for 8 years

Berish Czerwonagura
died in our city Arkhangelsk,
Ger Khasid, a modest man who
had lived all his life in Torah
and prayers, and in teaching his
children. His wife was his
support managed the business
and cared for the family's
livelihood.

May their memories be blessed!

To Commemorate:
Shayndl Rotbard, Israel
Mindl Czerwonagura, Belgium
Yoel Czerwonagura, London
Eli Czerwonagura, Belgium
Khashka Segal, Montevideo

To Remember Forever

Our Dear Parents

R' Yehoshua son of **R' Yitzkhak-Hirsh Wenger** z"l
His wife, the most righteous **Rivkah** z"l
daughter of the Rav of Sterdyn, he was of
Alexander Khasidim.

A scholar and a public servant, Shokhet of
Wyszkow.

Our Dear
Sisters:

**Beltshe,
Sarah-
Malka**

And our
brothers:

**Moshe,
and
Zekhariah**

Beltshe Wenger z"l

Died in Shoah

To Commemorate:
Tziporah and Usher Wenger, Givat Brenner,
Israel
Mordekhai Wenger, Montevideo

To Remember Forever

Our Dear Father and Dear Sisters

R' Yitzkhak Hirsch Rotbard
And children **Itah-Baila, Rivkah and Gitl**

Died in the Shoah in Wyszkow,1939

He was an Alexander Khasid, he led prayers beautifully and devoted
most of his time to Torah and prayer. Despite his suffering in
supporting the family, he did not lose the liveliness of his face.

To Commemorate:
Mordekhai Rotbard and family, Israel
Yisroel Rotbard and family, Israel
Tziporah Stern and family, Israel

[Page 314]

In Eternal Memory

Parents: **Avraham-Joseph and Khaya-Feige**
Sister: **Doba Itke**

Leibish Pshetitsky

Pinye Kryshtal
And son **Avremele**

Tova Kryshtal nee Yoskowitz

To eternalize:

his wife, **Henye
Pshetitsky**

In Memory:
Sons: **Moshe Yoskowitz**
Mendl Yoskowitz
Khaim Yoskowitz
Itche Yoskowitz

Daughters: **Heniye Pshetitsky**
Laytshe Yoskowitz

[Page 315]

To Remember Forever

**Popowsky
Dvorah**

Popowsky Gitl

Kronenberg Zelig
Killed by the
hands
of the Nazis in
Warsaw

To Commemorate:
Kronenberg Nakhum and Yaffa

Popowsky Gishe

To Remember Forever

Yisroel-Yitzkhak Perle
A devoted public
activist, loved all
people. Member of the
City Council.

Fraide Perle
A noble soul, with a
good heart and
sensitivity. She always
yearned for Zion and
helped her
grandchildren
immigrate to Israel

With admiration and respect for their memory

Sarah Ben-Shakhar, Israel
Perle Moshe and his family, Mexico
Brontche Kizl and family, Israel
Etshtein Rivkah and Moshe, Israel

To Remember Forever

Simkha-Bunem Bronshtein

Sarah-Rivkah Bronshtein nee Kronenberg

Yaakov-Yitzkhak Bronshtein

To Commemorate:
Yehoshua Bronshtein, New York
Rakhel Brama, Tel-Aviv

To Remember Forever

R' Avraham-Yitzkhak son of R' Shmuel Frider z"l
His wife **Brokha daughter of R' Velvl**, Rest in Peace

To Commemorate:
Daughter and son-in-law,
Birgenson Mendl and Khava, Haifa

[Page 316]

To Remember Forever

My Dear Parents:
**R' Yekhiel Avraham and
Leah Shultz z"l**
My brothers: **Menakhem,
Dovid and Yaakov**
My sisters: **Tzivia and Perla**
My Uncles: **Khaim Shultz
and his wife Hindl and
children
Hershl and his wife
Yokheved and children**
Grandmother: **Itte Shultz**

**Yokheved Shultz
nee Dzienkewitz**

Khana-'le

**Dzienkewitz Yisroel
His wife Mala
and their daughter
Khana'le**

**Avrohom-Pinkhas
son of Khaim Shultz**

Bertche Dzienkewitz

[Page 317]

To Remember Forever

Our Dear Ones who died and were killed by the hands of the Nazis

Our Father and Our Teacher and Master **Rabbi Khenokh Henekh Kurnet z"l** who died in the prime of his life

Rokhel Srebrnik

Our Sister:
Khana Maizlitz

Our mother, righteous woman
Mrs. Miriam Kurnet, z"l

Our brother:
Yehoshua'le Kurnet z"l

Tziporah (Feiga) z"l

The mourners:
Esther and Moshe Kurnet and their family
Kiryat Borokhov

To Remember Forever

Khaim-Leib Jagoda
Fishl Shemberg

Our Brother and cousin
Avraham Jagode

Our Dear Parents
Moshe-Yaakov and Alte-Khinke Jagode

To Remember:
Jagode Mordekhai, Hadera (Israel)

[Page 318]

Our Dear Sister and Brother   Our Dear Parents

Rakhela and Tzvi (Hershl) Nadel z"l   Khaya-Nekha and R' Yehuda-Aryeh (Leibish) Nadel z"l

Our Sister Sorah z"l   Our Young Brother   Our Dear Sister   Our Dear Brother
                          Moshe'le Nadel   Friedah Nadel   Dovid Nadel z"l

Our hearts are mourning for our dear parents, sisters and brothers; all who were consumed so horribly by the hands of the murderers of the Jewish people.

Our Father – Our teacher and father **R' Yehuda Arye Leibish** son of **R' Khaim Moshe Nadel, z"l** , dear man of many qualities and virtues, exemplary kindness.

Our Mother -- Righteous **Khaya-Nekha** daughter of **R' Yehoshua-Avrohom z"l**. The kindness and dearness were without bounds for the family.

Our Sister – Sarah z"l and her dear family so loving, we will not forget them, especially her closeness and kindness.

Our Brother – **Tsvi (Hershl), z"l**, Dear and delicate oil, devoted to the family.

Our Sister – **Fraide z"l** Dear and lovely.

Our Brother – The young **Moshele z"l**, dear and innocent. We have seen so little of his growth.

Their memory will not be erased from us forever.

May their souls be bound up in the bond of everlasting life.

Those who mourn bitterly:
Yitzkhak Nadel and family
Leah Goldshtein and family
Yaakov Nadel and family

[Page 319]

To Remember Forever

Our Parents: **Elkah Rozah and Moshe Binyamin Ostry**

Our Sister
Ahuva Ostry

To Commemorate:
Their sons: **Shraga, Yitzkhak**
Their daughters: **Rokhel,
Sarah,
Esther, Pninah** –
State of Israel

To Remember Forever

Our Dear Parents:
R' Mordekhai-Mendl and Rivah Olenberg,
Lights of Israel

Our Brothers: **Aharon and Yisroel**
Our Sisters: **Krusah, Naomi, Khaya, Pesia,
Mnukha,
Malka, Miriam and husband Simkha Burshtin**

Their memory be bound forever with the martyrs
of our nation. May G-d Avenge their blood

To Commemorate:
Velvl Olenberg – Haifa
Yitzkhak Olenberg – New York

To Remember Forever Our Dear Ones

Our Father: **Mendl Friedman z"l**
Our Brother **Velvl** his wife **Khaya and
their children**,
may they rest in Eden

To Commemorate:
His wife: **Pesha**
Children: **Yakov Friedman** – Israel
Shlomo, Shayndl and Mikhla – in the Land of
Israel

To Remember Forever

Our Dear Parents: **Yaakov and Dvorah
Farbshtein z"l**
Our Brother **Yisroel**

To Commemorate:
Their sons: **Moshe Farbshtein** – Los Angeles
Simkha and Mordekhai Farbshtein – Haifa
Their daughters:
Tzifah Olenberg, Khaya Ostry – Israel

[Page 320]

To our dear ones and loved ones, we
will never forget
To Remember Forever

Our Brothers: **Yitzkhak Shtikl z"l**
and Eliezer z"l
My Mother: **Feiga-Rozah Shtikl**
z"l
Our Sister: **Khana-Malka, Golda,**
Etka

To Commemorate:
Shtikl Mayer and family, Israel

To our dear ones and loved ones, we
will never forget
To Remember Forever

Feige'le Baharav and her brother
Aharon z"l

To Commemorate:
Their mother: **Dvosha**
Their brother: **Shmuel Baharav and**
family, Israel

Eternal Light
To the pure souls of our dear parents and sisters

Father: **Berish** – He was a modest businessman and lover of all people
Mother: **Khava** – Daughter of the Rav of Wyszkow, of the lineage of rabbis
Sister: **Hinde and husband Yakov and their only son Yisroe**l
Sister: **Brokha and husband Tzvi**
Died in The Shoah

To Commemorate:
Daughter and Sister: **Rokhel Wigoda nee Koplowitz and children** – Tel-Aviv
Son and Brother: **Alter Koplowitz and children**
Daughter and Sister: **Friedah Kronenberg nee Koplowitz and children** – Buenos-Aires

To Remember Forever
Zion, in memory of my dear parents and brothers

Father: **Yisroel** – on a straight road, with clean hands
Mother: **Khaya** – a gentle soul and a dedicated mother
Brother: **Yehuda** – a young man full of ambitions

Yisroel, Khaya and Yehuda Wigoda z"l
Who died in Shoah

Brother Reuven, Taken in Iban
Forever, their memories will be eternalized with honor and love

To Commemorate:
Liber Wigoda and his family, Tel-Aviv

To Remember Forever

Our Dear Parents

Our holy brother and sister
**Shlomo and Zelda-Malkah
Bronshtein**

R' Yaakov-Dovid and Rokhel Bronshtein z"l

To Commemorate:
The sons of **Rabbi Simkha Bunem**, Toronto
Rabbi Tzvi Bronshtein, New York
Gedalia Bronshtein, Argentina
Yisroel-Leyzer Norfilk
Feiga Grosbard, Kfar Saba

Fishl and Khava Bronshtein
Their children **Bunem, Itche and Esther'el**
Died in Jadow, 1943

For Eternal
Memory

Our Dear
Parents

Brother and
Sister

Commemorated
by their
children:
**Yaakov
Bronshtein**,
Argentina
**Breindl
Wilenski**,
Argentina
**Menakhem
Bronshtein**,
New York

[Page 322]

For Eternal Memory

Our Dear Husband and Father

Joseph Rokita z"l

Killed by the Nazis

Honor his memory!

To Commemorate:
His wife: **Khava Rokita**,
Netanya
His son: **Yitzkhak Rokita**,
Netanya

To Remember Forever

Our Dear Father

R' Sholom Yosef Dovid z"l
Son of the Rabbi and Sage R'
Menakhem Zeev Bresler z"l
Righteous teacher in Wyszkow

He died in the first year of his prime,
during his eighteen years of life.

May his memory be blessed!

To Commemorate:
His son: **Arye Bresler**, Kibbutz Einat
His daughter: **Friedah Bresler**, Kibbutz
Einat

For Eternal Memory

Our Dear Brother and Uncle
and his family

Our Dear Father and Husband

**Khaim and Paya Zilberberg
and their children Yisroel
and Khaim**.

R'Shlomo Fishman

Died in Costa Rica 20 Shvat
5718- February 10, 1958

Khaim – Killed in Wyszkow at
the time of the
first bombardment, 5
September 1939; his wife and
children –
in Russia, by the Nazis.

Our Mother, **Khaya-Sorah
Zilberberg**
Died in Bialystok, 1939

Honor their memory!

To Commemorate:
**Nekhama Fishman and Family
Menukhah Najman and Family**

To Commemorate:
His Wife **Nekhama Fishman**
Daughter **Rokhel Lang**
Son **Yisroel Fishman**

[Page 323]

To Remember Forever

**Our Dear Father: Avrohom-
Khaim Rozenboim, z"l**

Our Dear Mother

From a lineage of rabbis and
Torah scholars

His Grandmother: **Mintche
Rozenboim z"l**
His Brother: **Henokh
Rozenboim z"l**
His Aunt: **Friedah Holtzkener
z"l and family**
His Uncle: **Leibl Rozenboim
z"l and family**
Luba and Zelda Bresler z"l

Who Died in the Shoah

May their Memory Be Blessed!

Mrs. Rivkah Rozenboim z"l

She merited arriving in Israel
weak and broken from the
hardships of her wanderings.
Died 3rd day of Tamuz 5720,
June 27, 1960

To Commemorate:
**Khaya Forshtman nee Rozenboim
Sorah Hecht nee Rozenboim**

To Remember Forever

Our Dear Mother

Pesiah Wilenski Wife of **R' Mordekhai Wilenski z"l**

Our Sister **Feiga z"l** Member of the first group of pioneers who came to Israel, 1921 Died in Tel-Yosef, 1929

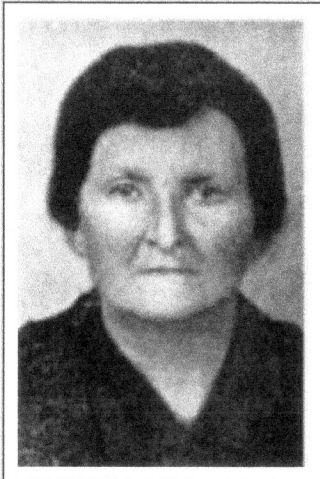

Our Dear Brother **Avrohom Wilenski and family** Died in the Shoah in Warsaw

To Commemorate:
Khaim Shidlu and family, Tel-Aviv
Yehudith Sharfhartz and family, Tel-Aviv
Ezra Wilenski and family, Paris
Dovid Wilenski and family, Paris

To Remember Forever

My Dear Aunt   My Dear Parents

Sorah-Rivkah z"l   **Golda and Yosef Malina**
Wife of R' Hanokh Malina   They died wandering in 1941

To Commemorate:
Khava Malina – Bat-Yam

[Page 324]

To Remember Forever

Kalman Livner
and his wife **Zlata**

Rivkah-Laya Livner
Yekhiel and Khaim Livner

To Commemorate:
Yidl Leib Livner and his Family, Israel

To Remember Forever

Our Dear Parents: **Yehudl-
Nakhum Pshetitsky**
His Wife **Leah**

Who died in the Days of The
Shoah

Our children:
Yidl-Nakhum, born in 1937,
Khava-Tovah, born in 1939

Died While Wandering.

To Commemorate:
Alte and Tzvi Czerwonagura,
Israel
Moshe Pshetitsky, Argentina

To Remember Forever

Aizik Brumberg z"l Our Dear Father

To Commemorate:
Sorah Lojnkoff
Maleh Brumberg

To Remember Forever

Yosef-Mayer and Khaya-Sorah Rubinowitz

Of the Distinguished Alexander Khasidim

To Commemorate:
Grandchildren: **Sharon Zelman**, Israel
Sharon Bunem, Argentina
Miriam, Argentina
Kalman, Soviet Union

[Page 325]

To Remember Forever

Our Dear Sisters:

Gitl and husband **Moshe Shlafmitz z"l**
and their children: **Khaya, Altah, Yeshayahu and Menakhem z"l**
Laya Rozenberg and her children
Laya and Moshe z"l Tova Kwiatek z"l

Aunt: **Elka** and her son **Avrohom Rubin z"l**

My cousin: **Yekhiel Rubin** and his wife, **Khava z"l**

Aunt: **Rokhel Finkelshtein** and husband and daughter **Nekhemah z"l**

To Commemorate:
Tessa Kwiatek, Tel-Aviv

To Remember Forever

Our Dear Parents:

R' Beryl-Dovid and Itah Kwiatek z"l

Our Sisters:
Esther and her husband **Yehudah Kryshtal**
and their children **Khaim and Shoshana z"l**

Pninah z"l

May Their Memory Be Blessed!

To Commemorate:
Rivkah Kwiatek, Tel-Aviv
Matl Kwiatek, Tel-Aviv

To Remember Forever

My Dear Mother: **Miriam Czekhnowitzky z"l**
My Dear Sisters: **Leah** and husband **Avrohom**
and son **Yaakov z"l**
Gitl Czekhnowitzky z"l

To Commemorate:
Alta Kwiatek nee Czekhnowitzky, Tel-Aviv

In Remembrance

Our Dear Sister
Laya Jabloka

With her children:
Yekhezkel, Khaim, Mayte, and Dvorah

To Commemorate:
Zaltzshtein Yokheved, Tel-Aviv
Javner Khava, Tel-Aviv

For Remembering

From wife
Kh. Kiwaikes nee Deutcher

To Commemorate
The Family Wyszkower Association, Montevideo

[Page 326]

For Eternal Remembrance

Our Dear Mother

Khaya Rubinowitz
Our Father:
Yosef-Mayer Rubinowitz

Bother:
Reuven Rubinowitz

Sisters:
Malka and Sorah Rubinowitz

Murdered by the Nazis

To Commemorate:
Wurzehayzer Rokhel, Israel
Glass Brokhe, Israel

To Commemorate:
Khaim Shidlu and family, Tel-Aviv
Yehudith Sharfhartz and family, Tel-Aviv
Ezra Wilenski and family, Paris
Dovid Wilenski and family, Paris

To Remember Forever

My Unforgettable Son   My Dear Husband

Kershenowitz Alter   **Kershenowitz Yitzkhak**

Who were murdered by the hands of the Nazis

Moshe-Dovid Kershenowitz
Yosef and his wife **Frumat** and their children:
Khaya, Itche Kershenowitz
Yaakov, Rojzah, Mikhel, Avrohom and Sorah Kershenowitz

To Commemorate:
Golde and Mayer Kershenowitz, Tel-Aviv

To Remember Forever

Our Dear
Father

**R'Khaim-
Yehoshua
Rozenberg
z"l**

To Commemorate:
Leibl, Khaitche Rozenberg and Family
Memphis – Bnai-Brak

To
Remember
Forever

My Dear
Father
**Hershl
Shtzigl
z"l**

Died 19th
Kislev
5696

Of
Blessed
Memory

To Commemorate
His daughter: **Prager Brayne** – Tel-Aviv

To Remember Forever

My Dear Parents

Leizer and Gitl Messing z"l

My Dear Sisters **Manya and Perl**,
who died in Camp Auschwitz

May Their Memory Be Blessed

To Commemorate:
Joseph Messing and his family,
Netanya

To
Remember
Forever

My Dear
Father
**Yosl
Cembal**

My Dear
Mother
**Zlata
Cembal**

My Dear
Sister
**Reitze
Cembal**

My Dear
Brother
**Shlomo
Cembal**

Died
wandering
by the
hands
Of the
Germans
in the city
of Luban,
District of
Minsk.

To Commemorate:
Cembal Tzvi – Ness-Ziona

[Page 327]

For Eternal Memory

Our Dear Parents and Brother

Tuviah Gruszka
Died in Russia from hunger

Yehoshua-Berl and Khava Gruszka z"l

Our Uncles:
Itche-Mayer Gruszka and family
Yankl Grinberg and family

Died in Jadow together with the parents

We will never forget them!

Itche, Motl, Avrohom-Hersh and families – Argentina
Shlomo Gruszka, Israel
Khana (Gruszka) Rubin, America

To Remember Forever

Our Dear Father: **Borenshtein Berl z"l**
Died in 1941 age 57

Our Dear Brother: **Borenshtein Yaakov z"l**

Member of HaPoal HaMizrakhi and one of the founders
of the Hakhshara group in Lomza and Neustadt

Our Dear Brothers:
Khaim and Yitzkhak z"l
In their lives and in their deaths they did not part

Our Sister Laya z"l
She emigrated to Israel in 1935, died in 1952

May their Memories Be Blessed

To Commemorate:
Stempler Brayne and family, Israel
Halperin Paula and family, Israel

Our Dear Parents

**Shimon-Mayer and Shayndl Nowominsky
z"l**

Our Brothers:
**Yaakov and his wife Miriam and their 3
children
Yosef and his wife Pesia nee Pruk, and their
2 daughters
Shlomo, his wife and 2 children**
Our Sister: **Khaya z"l**

Died at the Hands of the Nazis

May Their Memory Be Blessed!

To Commemorate:
Bella Eizenberg and her family, Ramat-Gan
Moshe Nowominsky and his family, Detroit
Simkha Nowominsky and his family, San Francisco

For Eternal Memory

Our Parents

**R' Yehoshua-Aharon b"r Yakov-
Tzvi Malitzinova
Noami, nee Yoskowitz**
Sister: **Rokhel-Leah Tzukrowitz**

Our father Yehoshua was captured
by the Germans that first Sunday
when he left the Beis Medrash, along
with 42 other people, then taken to a
place [forest] with poplars. They
were stripped naked, then thrown
into a pit and burned. My brother
Dovid, managed to escape from
there, with a child in his hands, and
today lives in America.

To Commemorate:
Son and brother:

Potash Moshe-Hertzke, B'nei Brak
Potash Dovid, New York
Tzukrowitz, Israel

For Eternal Memory

Our Mother and Dear Children

Itke Rubin
Died in Bialystok,
September 14, 1943

Yenkl Rubin
Died in Bialystok,
September 14, 1943

Liba Rubin

Khaya-Sorah
Died in Wyszkow, 1936

Manye Rubin
Died in Bialystok,
October 2, 1943

To Commemorate:
Leml and Esther Rubin, Paris

[Page 329]

To Remember Forever

Our Dear Parents, Brother and Sisters

Family of **R' Zalman Pelner**

To Comemmorate:
Raizel Pelner – Daughter
Aharon Pelner – Son

To Remember Forever

My Brother
**Avraham-Dovid
Granat**

My Parents
Reuven and Sorah-Rivkah

Grandfather and his wife
Moshe-Borukh and Khana Tzembal

To Commemorate:
Yisroel Granat, Bat-Yam

To Remember Forever

R' Shmuel Brama z"l

To Commemorate:
Son **Dovid Brama**

Daughters:
Tzfira
Margalit
Esther

Rivkah Brama,
died in Ghetto

To Remember Forever

Our Dear Parents

R'Yaakov-Yehoshua and Khaya Jagoda z"l

My Brother Shimon Jagoda, his wife Malka and their children

To Commemorate:
Avraham Jagoda and his family, Netanya

[Page 330]

**We Will Remember Forever our Dearest
Who Were Exterminated in the Holocaust**

Their memory will never depart from us

The Lerman Family

Our dear parents: **Abraham Lerman** z"l, a Torah disciple and G-d fearing khasid of Ger, one of the "Beit Joseph" yeshiva initiators who was devoted selflessly for the boys' needs, delighted in their joys and took part in their pain.

Faige Lerman z"l, a precious woman and devoted mother to her children in spite of her suffering pain all her life. Died in 1929, at the age of 53.

Our dear sister: **Rachel Lerman** – perished in the Warsaw ghetto with her husband **David Biderman** and their daughters.

Our brothers: **Jacob David** z"l, a pious Torah scholar, pupil of the "Beit Joseph" yeshiva in Makow: his wife **Chaya Sara** nee **Freemen** of Stok, and their six children who died in the Warsaw ghetto.

Isaac z"l, devoted son to his parents, a noble precious soul who was killed at the The Ninth Fort in Kaunas. His wife **Fannya** and their 11-year-old son **Yisroel**, died in the concentration camp Stuthoff.

Mordekhai z"l, killed at the first German raiding over Wyszkow.

Shlomo z"l, perished in the Wilno ghetto.

Our aunt: **Devora** nee **Lerman**, her husband and their single son.

We shed tears at their untimely awfully sorrow death. May their memory be blessed!

Memorialized by:

**Leibel Lerman – Argentina
Leah Director (Lerman) – Israel**

Translated by Chava Eisenstein

[Page 331]

For Eternal Memory

My Dear Parents, Sister and Family

Parents: **Esther Malka and Leibl Hendl z"l**

Sisters: **Sorah-Brayne and Leibl Dan; Khaya and Avrohom Paskewitz and child**
Wife: **Esther and the children Rokhel and Henye**

To Commemorate:
Hendl (Litman) Eliezer and Family, Tel-Aviv

Our Dear Parents

Leibl and Sarah-Brayne Dan z"l

Died in Russia   Died in Warsaw
Tisha-b'Av 1942 Yom Kippur 1939

Honor Their Memory!

To Commemorate:
Their Children: **Itche, Yekhiel and Ada**, Israel

To Remember Forever
Our Dear Families

**R' Yaakov Levin and daughter and sons:
Esther, Reuven and Sholom z"l
Hershl Mishar and daughters and son:
Sorah, Rivkah, Moshe, Feygele and Aharon.**
Our Neighbors: **Family Kalusky and Skarlat.**

We will never be able to restrain our sorrow,
pain, and wrath.
Such people were murdered by the Nazi savage

To Commemorate:
Khaim Levin, Givat Hashlosha
Batya Friedman, New York
Zelig Levin, New York

To Remember Forever

My Dear Parents: **Holtzman Aharon and
Khana-Alta**
My Sister: **Khaya-Sorah and husband Daniel
Aronyok**
My Relatives: **R' Yisroel-Yitzkhak Friedman.
Moshe Shtayfman, his wife Henye and their
children
Golda Shtayfman, husband and their childre
Shoshka Shtayfman, husband and their
children
Shlomo Shtayfman**

To Commemorate:
The Rebbetzin Ete Adler nee Holtzman, Jerusalem

[Page 332]

For Eternal Remembrance

Zeev Holland hy"d
(May G-d Avenge his blood)
(1928-1948)

Immigrated to Israel in 1945

Commemorated by:
His wife, daughter, and the family

Fell in an operation in Tel-Aviv during the War of Independence
on the third day of Adar 2 5708 (March 14, 1948), at the age of twenty.

Translated by Chava Eisenstein

To Eternal Remembrance

The bereft parents commemorate:
Henna and Meyer Shakhne,
Tel-Aviv, 10 King-David Street

Madhava and Shlomo Shakhne hy"d

Fell in combat at the blockade over Jerusalem on the
28'th of Iyar 5708 (June 6, 1948)

Madhava was a Gadn"a member who worked hard
to achieve security for Jerusalem. She was 17 and
attended the Jerusalem gymnasia "Rehavia."

Shlomo, only 10, was an excellent student in forth
class of the "Tahkimoni" school in Jerusalem.

They were single children to their parents,
grandchildren of **Shlomo and Sheina Wimberg** of
Wyszkow.

The beloved and pleasant souls that were connected
in life and at death.

May their memory be sealed forever in the soul and
in the soul of the nation and of those who battle for
Israel's freedom and independence.

Translated by Chava Eisenstein

[Page 333]

Dear Uncle:

**Avrohom-Gershon Mitlzbakh
His dear sons and grandchildren**

My Dear Aunt:

Frayda-Brokhe Perchik z"l

Died at the hands of the Nazi
thugs in Przasnysz,
together with the martyrs of
Poland, in the Nazi camps and
furnaces.

We mourn their cruel death.

May Their Memory Be Blessed!

To Commemorate:
Yaakov Mitlzbakh, Petakh Tikvah

My Dear Parents

R' Yekhiel-Mikhel Mitlzbakh

and his wife **Iteh (nee Holtzman)**

Emigrated to Israel in 1933
Father died 11 Kislev 5698
His wife died May 6, 1953

To Remember Forever

Our Dear Parents, Brothers and Sisters and Sons
of our Families who died in the Nazi Shoah

Our Parents **R' Pinkhas and Khaya Pieniek z"l**

Our Brothers: **Simkha-Bunem and Yaakov z"l,**
Our Sister **Zisl and husband Yehoshua Wigoda and 2 children**

Sons of Our Family:
**Shmuel Wigoda, Yitzkhak-Ber nd Sorah Rozenberg,
Mendl Wigoda, Yehuda-Leib and Ziska Gozheltzani**

May their memory be bound up with the life of the nation.

To Commemorate:
Menakhem Pieniek and Family, Israel
Yitzkhak Pieniek and Family, Israel

[Page 334]

To Remember Forever

My Dear Father, Brother and Sister, z"l

Yosl Srebrenik z"l

Rabbi Shimon Srebrenik z"l

To Commemorate:
Menakhem Caspi, Kiryat Ono
Zalman Tzadok, New York

To Remember Forever

Our Dear Parents

R' Pinkhas Steinberg z"l
9 Tevet 5689

Gitl Steinberg rest in peace
2 Sivan 5715

To Commemorate:
Avraham Steinberg, Ra'anana
Yehuda Steinberg, Tel Aviv

[Page 335] This page was blank.
[Page 336]

"The First Wyszkower Ladies Auxiliary"

Founded by Molly Parawer in 1922, and received the charter (recognized by law) in 1924, and from then on, runs as the "First," and continues regularly with its work, sent help to Wyszkow, now also does aid work for the *landsleit* and for the community at large.

From right, top row: **Yeta Ritchman, Tillie Chernin**; Bottom right: **Molly Parawer, Khava Frost, Anna Fine**.

The work of the "First" is directed by the chairwoman Molly Parawer and the officials:

Vice chairman – **Khava Frost**
Finance secretary – **Annie Fine**
Protocol secretary – **Tillie Chernin**
Tillie Chernin is now finance and protocol secretary

Treasurer – **Itke Richman**
Trustee (controller) – **Francis Margolis**

United Wyszkower Committee in New York

Top: **Richman (Reichman Yitzchok)**; second row from right: **HaRav Tz. Bronstajn, Velvel Radziminsky, Leibel Bromberg, Itke Reichman, Rivka Rosen**.

First row from right: **Tch. Apelboim, Chava Frost, Max Kavitch, Shaul and Mindel Steinmark, Moishe Freedman, and Molly Leibowitz (Widelec)**.

Translated by Pamela Russ

[Page 339]

Index of Geographic Names
Note that the pages listed are the page numbers in the original Yizkor Book, not this translation.

An index of family names referencing page numbers in this book starts on page 737 below.

א   A (E, I, O or U)

Abu-Agila	137
Odessa	124
Uzbekistan	199
Auschwitz	196, 199
Hungary	195, 196
Usawna (Olszanka?)	12
Ural	178
Uruguay	6, 8, 212, 232, 237, 238
Otwock	22, 53, 98, 99, 141
Italy	64, 225
Aleksander	19, 22, 26, 58, 96, 97, 98, 99, 130, 162
Amerika	38, 44, 45, 46,70, 72, 80, 85, 99, 100, 103, 109, 124,128, 129,139, 140, 191, 193, 199, 207, 208, 209, 210, 215, 217, 221, 222, 223, 228, 234, 235
Amselof	193
Amshinov	22, 58, 98, 120, 121, 128
Inzewycz	177
Ostrow	35, 36, 37, 171, 185, 190, 197
Ostrowieck	61
Ostrow- Mazowieck	41, 64, 178, 194, 213, 219
Ostrolenka	11, 14, 38, 57, 90, 123, 132
Argentina	6, 8, 44, 86, 89, 108, 132, 136, 199, 205, 207, 208, 209, 211, 212, 215, 216, 217, 218, 219, 228, 229, 232, 235, 236, 237
Arkhangelsk	131, 198
Eretz-Yisrael	26, 52, 58, 61, 62, 63, 64, 69, 70, 71, 72, 73, 74, 77, 79, 81, 96, 99, 123, 128, 133, 135, 199, 205, 206, 222, 234, 236, 237
Ozstczecze	12

ב   B (V)

"babske-barg"	47
Bavaria	135
Brzoza	12
Vald	12
Bock	61, 76
Baranov	192
Baranowitz	171
Bar-Sheva	136
Bug	11, 12, 14, 17, 25, 45, 47, 50, 58, 82, 101 131, 143, 146, 164, 167, 168, 195, 200
Buenos-Aires	33, 37, 60, 73, 84, 87, 91, 99, 104, 105, 106, 110, 196,

	209, 215, 229, 230, 231, 232, 237
Bialystok	38, 46, 61, 97, 103, 106, 130, 161, 166, 168, 170, 174, 175, 178, 185, 191, 196, 197, 198, 200
Bydgoszcz	195
Biten	177
Bnai Brak	81
Bergen Belsen	196
Berditchev	123
Belina	11
Berlin	134, 166, 236
Brazil	235
Brańszczyk	11, 12, 61, 71, 128, 196, 224
Bronx	201
Bruk	190
Brisk	51
Bryansk(Bransk)	39

ג G

Goworowa	124
Galveston	228
Galicia	115, 117, 118
Ganges	13
Givat Hashlosha	51, 70
Givat Mikhal	65
Gura	11
Ger	19, 22, 26, 58, 96, 97, 98, 99, 121, 122, 123, 128, 131, 132, 146, 148, 153, 162
Grobnik	176
Grodzisk	12
Grodno	170, 185
Grajewe	177
Grokhow	53, 121
Grembkow/Grebkow	12

ד D

Dodzhilov	146
Dalekes	55, 57
Dombrowe/Dabrow	12
Dvina	198
(Deutschland) Germany	44, 46, 57, 64, 137, 168, 171, 214, 225, 227, 230, 237, 239
Dlugosiodlo	57, 61, 79, 86
Dafna	63, 65
Detroit	213, 219, 228, 235
Denir	168
Dereczin	178, 179, 180, 181, 182, 183, 184, 185
South-America	45, 58, 72, 196

ה H

Efraim (mounts)	65

Wyszkow Memorial Book

ן V (W)

Place	Pages
Woleszczyn	192
Warka	99, 120
Warsaw	11, 12, 14, 26, 29, 33, 34, 38, 42, 44, 45, 46, 48, 51, 52, 53, 56, 58, 60, 61, 64, 70, 71, 75, 76, 77, 78, 80, 82, 85, 96, 97, 104, 106, 115, 116, 117, 118, 119,122, 123, 125, 132, 137, 138, 142, 143, 147, 153, 154, 157, 160, 163, 164, 169, 185, 188, 192, 193, 194, 195, 196, 197, 198, 200, 201, 226, 236, 237
Vigoda	23
Wytanki	12
Vilna	82, 117, 176, 185
Wien/Vien/Vienna	115
Wyelitczke	14
Weiden	238
Wisla	19, 50
White Russia	44, 168, 191
Wloclawek	71, 80
Wengrow	42, 43, 129, 165, 178, 190, 197
Wroclaw	196, 199

ז Z

Place	Pages
Zaleczhe/Zalecze	12
Zombrowa	171, 178, 197
Zakroczym	108, 124
Zareby Koscielne	166
Zhomaki/Ziemaki	12
Zyrardow	101, 132

ח Kh (H)

Place	Pages
Haifa	80, 98, 194, 206, 207,208, 210, 214, 215, 217

ט T (Cz)

Place	Pages
Towarne	192
Toloczyn	168, 169
Targovna/Targowa	11
Tiberias	99
Tuchlin	11
Turina	11
Turkistan	43
Tiktin	197
Tluszcz	186
Tehran	206, 214
Trauenstein	135
Trachenbad	193
Treblinka	174, 199
Czajkiewicz	191
Czyzewo	185
Ciechocinek	99
Tshehanovcy	166
Czekanow	90

Czechoslovakia	199
Chelyabinsk	178
Czerwin	121
Czerwinsk	12
Czestochowa/Częstochowa	14, 71

ל Y (J)

Jablone/Jablon	11
Jadow	38, 39, 42, 43, 46, 76, 86, 165, 168, 170, 185
Januszewycz	178
Jericho	65
Dead Sea/ Yam Hamalakh	65
Jedwabne	176
Joszcolt	196
Jerusalem	52, 65, 101, 211, 220, 222
Israel/Yisrael	4, 6, 8, 38, 52, 82, 89, 96, 97, 99, 124, 126, 127, 128, 129, 130, 132, 133, 136, 137, 200, 201, 202 206, 207, 208, 209, 210, 211, 214, 215, 216, 217, 218, 219, 226, 227, 228, 231, 233, 234, 235, 237, 238

ק Kh/K/Ch

Koziol	164
Kfar-Uno	162
Kfar-Khasidim	69
Chęciny	79
Kherson	124

ל L

L'adi	130
Lodz	53, 64, 120, 146, 185, 228
Latin America	89
Lochow	25, 47, 51, 106, 165
Lachowicze	170, 171
Lomza	108, 124, 176
Lomianki	194, 195, 196
London	199
Los Angeles	6, 8, 50, 55, 57, 124, 127, 157, 205, 208, 209, 210, 211, 212, 214, 215, 216, 217, 218, 221, 225, 227, 228, 229, 235
Lubavitz	96
Lod	177
Lublin	96
Luniniec	169
Legnica	202
Lithuania	12, 44
Leipzig	14
Lemberg (Lvov)	33, 45, 125

מ M

| Masovia | 11 |
| Malkin | 105, 165, 166 |

Montevideo	59, 95, 164, 211, 218, 219, 232, 235, 237, 238
Manischewitz	41
Moscow	183, 184, 192, 199
[Page 340]	
Makow	31, 82, 90, 108, 124
Mizac	213, 219
Miadanek	199
Munich	135
Miedzywodzie	192
Machteshim	65
Mlawa	59, 71, 75
"Maavarot"	65
Maale Akrabim	65
Mexico	104, 213, 219, 228, 238
Massada	65
Mrotszk/Mrozyvc	12
Merchavia	115, 117

ב N

Nadgosze	13
Nowydwor	124, 131
Narew	50
Nasielsk	108, 129,
Negev	134, 137
Nahariah	137
Nakhlat Yitzhak	137
Dan River (Nakhal HaDan)	65
Lower Silesia	199, 230
New York	6, 8, 38,43, 48 43, 83, 85, 89, 99, 101, 102, 124, 125, 127, 131, 169, 200, 201, 207, 208, 209, 210, 211, 212, 213, 214, 215, 216, 217, 218, 219, 221, 222, 223, 224, 225, 226, 228,238, 239
Njeman	183
Nitzana	
Ness Ziona	65
Novorodke	99
Netanya	65, 135, 136, 210, 217

ס S

Sobibor	199
Sodawne	190, 197
Son	?
Sochaczew	130
Samarkand	37, 196, 199
Sokolow	189
Sokoly	64
Sodom	65
Sukhodoly/Suchodoly	12
Stok	168, 190
Stokholm	33
Sterdin	97
Struge	201
Siberia	43, 136, 198

Sinai	135, 136
Slobodke	186
Slonim	171, 172, 174, 177, 178, 179
Smolniki	192
Serock/Srotsk	11, 18, 86, 90, 91, 108, 124, 132, 213, 219
Skrazisk	121
Skuszew	25, 100, 168

ע I/E/A (Ayin)

Evron	137
Ein-Gedi	65
Einat	70
Akko	188
England	191
Atlit	136

פ F and P

Pobrusk	193
Powiszla	115, 118
Palestine	44, 74, 77, 88, 154, 157
Falkow	12
Poplawes	43, 88
Paris	14, 177, 196, 199
Poremba	60, 61, 62, 97, 98, 196, 197, 224
Fareinikte Staten (United States)	77, 82, 85, 238
Pozen	55, 142
Pultusk	11, 13, 14, 28, 29, 30, 43, 57, 59, 60, 75, 76, 78, 90, 91, 98, 107, 132, 167, 177, 189, 194, 196, 213, 219, 239
Poland	5, 6, 7, 8, 11, 12, 44, 48, 59, 61, 70, 71, 84, 86, 91, 101, 115, 118, 120, 123, 11, 132, 140, 162, 164, 166, 171, 177, 185, 188, 189, 196, 199, 200, 201, 202, 205, 210, 211, 218, 224, 227, 228, 230, 236, 237, 238, 239
Piotrkow	13
Piasetchny	193
Pinsk	33, 43, 51, 100, 109
Pyeczkali/Pierzchaly	12
Plock	11, 12, 120
FSS"R (USSR)	166
Peterburg	14
Prague	196, 199
Praga	82
Frankreikh (France)	6, 8
Prasznysz	170
Fruszhew/Proszew	12
Pruczewska–Wiulka/Przetycz Wloscianska	12
Puszkow	190
Preisin	?
Petakh-Tikvah	39, 70, 210, 217

צ Tz

Tzfun America (North America)	58

ק K

Kovne	185, 186, 187
Kotlas	198
Kaluszyn	167
Kalish	120
Komorow	178
Kamion	11
Komisarka	35
Kamientchik/Kamieńczyk	11, 61, 91, 130, 196
Canada	99, 213, 219
Kosow	165, 166, 168
Costa Rica	89
Kopiec	192
Kock/Kotsk	53, 120
Cordoba	235
Kartuze Breze	19
Kielcz	131
Kiev	178
Klosow	71
Krakow	12
Krasnaya Sloboda	191

ר R

Radzymin	22, 47, 51, 53, 58, 63, 64, 91, 95, 98, 101, 106, 120, 121, 134, 148, 162, 185, 197
Radzalow	96
Rovno	193
Rosario	235
Rejowiec	192
Ruda Jaworska	180, 182
Ruda Lipiczanska	180, 182
Rukhama	65
Roszan	76, 88, 106
Russia	31, 43, 97, 99, 136, 166, 168, 178, 179, 198, 228, 230, 238
Rybniki	107
Rybienko	13
Rypin	132, 200
Ramat-Gan	11, 78, 80, 163
Rejowski/Rejowiec	192

ש Sh

Sweden	225
Shchanka	61, 224
Szczyrk	192
Szczecin	134, 185
Chicago	228
Silesia	225, 228
Sieczka	185

ת **T**

Tel-Aviv	4, 6, 8, 14, 26, 33, 40, 52, 69, 70, 102, 108, 120, 121, 129, 136,137, 166, 184, 195, 196, 200, 201, 205, 206, 208, 211, 212, 214, 215, 216, 218, 234, 238
Tel Mond	70, 80

[Page 339]

Index of Geographic Names

Note that the pages listed are the page numbers in the original Yizkor Book, not this translation.

א A (E, I, O or U)

Abu-Agila	137
Odessa	124
Uzbekistan	199
Auschwitz	196, 199
Hungary	195, 196
Usawna (Olszanka?)	12
Ural	178
Uruguay	6, 8, 212, 232, 237, 238
Otwock	22, 53, 98, 99, 141
Italy	64, 225
Aleksander	19, 22, 26, 58, 96, 97, 98, 99, 130, 162
Amerika	38, 44, 45, 46,70, 72, 80, 85, 99, 100, 103, 109, 124,128, 129,139, 140, 191, 193, 199, 207, 208, 209, 210, 215, 217, 221, 222, 223, 228, 234, 235
Amselof	193
Amshinov	22, 58, 98, 120, 121, 128
Inzewycz	177
Ostrow	35, 36, 37, 171, 185, 190, 197
Ostrowieck	61
Ostrow- Mazowieck	41, 64, 178, 194, 213, 219
Ostrolenka	11, 14, 38, 57, 90, 123, 132
Argentina	6, 8, 44, 86, 89, 108, 132, 136, 199, 205, 207, 208, 209, 211, 212, 215, 216, 217, 218, 219, 228, 229, 232, 235, 236, 237
Arkhangelsk	131, 198
Eretz-Yisrael	26, 52, 58, 61, 62, 63, 64, 69, 70, 71, 72, 73, 74, 77, 79, 81, 96, 99, 123, 128, 133, 135, 199, 205, 206, 222, 234, 236, 237
Ozstczecze	12

ב B (V)

"babske-barg"	47
Bavaria	135
Brzoza	12
Vald	12
Bock	61, 76
Baranov	192
Baranowitz	171
Bar-Sheva	136
Bug	11, 12, 14, 17, 25, 45, 47, 50, 58, 82, 101 131, 143, 146, 164, 167, 168, 195, 200
Buenos-Aires	33, 37, 60, 73, 84, 87, 91, 99, 104, 105, 106, 110, 196, 209, 215, 229, 230, 231, 232, 237
Bialystok	38, 46, 61, 97, 103, 106, 130, 161, 166, 168, 170, 174, 175, 178, 185, 191, 196, 197, 198, 200

Bydgoszcz	195
Biten	177
Bnai Brak	81
Bergen Belsen	196
Berditchev	123
Belina	11
Berlin	134, 166, 236
Brazil	235
Brańszczyk	11, 12, 61, 71, 128, 196, 224
Bronx	201
Bruk	190
Brisk	51
Bryansk(Bransk)	39

ג G

Goworowa	124
Galveston	228
Galicia	115, 117, 118
Ganges	13
Givat Hashlosha	51, 70
Givat Mikhal	65
Gura	11
Ger	19, 22, 26, 58, 96, 97, 98, 99, 121, 122, 123, 128, 131, 132, 146, 148, 153, 162
Grobnik	176
Grodzisk	12
Grodno	170, 185
Grajewe	177
Grokhow	53, 121
Grembkow/Grebkow	12

ד D

Dodzhilov	146
Dalekes	55, 57
Dombrowe/Dabrow	12
Dvina	198
(Deutschland) Germany	44, 46, 57, 64, 137, 168, 171, 214, 225, 227, 230, 237, 239
Dlugosiodlo	57, 61, 79, 86
Dafna	63, 65
Detroit	213, 219, 228, 235
Denir	168
Dereczin	178, 179, 180, 181, 182, 183, 184, 185
South-America	45, 58, 72, 196

ה H

Efraim (mounts)	65

ו V (W)

Woleszczyn	192

Warka	99, 120
Warsaw	11, 12, 14, 26, 29, 33, 34, 38, 42, 44, 45, 46, 48, 51, 52, 53, 56, 58, 60, 61, 64, 70, 71, 75, 76, 77, 78, 80, 82, 85, 96, 97, 104, 106, 115, 116, 117, 118, 119, 122, 123, 125, 132, 137, 138, 142, 143, 147, 153, 154, 157, 160, 163, 164, 169, 185, 188, 192, 193, 194, 195, 196, 197, 198, 200, 201, 226, 236, 237
Vigoda	23
Wytanki	12
Vilna	82, 117, 176, 185
Wien/Vien/Vienna	115
Wyelitczke	14
Weiden	238
Wisla	19, 50
White Russia	44, 168, 191
Wloclawek	71, 80
Wengrow	42, 43, 129, 165, 178, 190, 197
Wroclaw	196, 199

ז Z

Zaleczhe/Zalecze	12
Zombrowa	171, 178, 197
Zakroczym	108, 124
Zareby Koscielne	166
Zhomaki/Ziemaki	12
Zyrardow	101, 132

ח Kh (H)

Haifa	80, 98, 194, 206, 207, 208, 210, 214, 215, 217

ט T (Cz)

Towarne	192
Toloczyn	168, 169
Targovna/Targowa	11
Tiberias	99
Tuchlin	11
Turina	11
Turkistan	43
Tiktin	197
Tluszcz	186
Tehran	206, 214
Trauenstein	135
Trachenbad	193
Treblinka	174, 199
Czajkiewicz	191
Czyzewo	185
Ciechocinek	99
Tshehanovcy	166
Czekanow	90
Czechoslovakia	199
Chelyabinsk	178
Czerwin	121

Czerwinsk	12
Czestochowa/Częstochowa	14, 71

ל
Y (J)

Jablone/Jablon	11
Jadow	38, 39, 42, 43, 46, 76, 86, 165, 168, 170, 185
Januszewycz	178
Jericho	65
Dead Sea/ Yam Hamalakh	65
Jedwabne	176
Joszcolt	196
Jerusalem	52, 65, 101, 211, 220, 222
Israel/Yisrael	4, 6, 8, 38, 52, 82, 89, 96, 97, 99, 124, 126, 127, 128, 129, 130, 132, 133, 136, 137, 200, 201, 202 206, 207, 208, 209, 210, 211, 214, 215, 216, 217, 218, 219, 226, 227, 228, 231, 233, 234, 235, 237, 238

ק
Kh/K/Ch

Koziol	164
Kfar-Uno	162
Kfar-Khasidim	69
Chęciny	79
Kherson	124

ל
L

L'adi	130
Lodz	53, 64, 120, 146, 185, 228
Latin America	89
Lochow	25, 47, 51, 106, 165
Lachowicze	170, 171
Lomza	108, 124, 176
Lomianki	194, 195, 196
London	199
Los Angeles	6, 8, 50, 55, 57, 124, 127, 157, 205, 208, 209, 210, 211, 212, 214, 215, 216, 217, 218, 221, 225, 227, 228, 229, 235
Lubavitz	96
Lod	177
Lublin	96
Luniniec	169
Legnica	202
Lithuania	12, 44
Leipzig	14
Lemberg (Lvov)	33, 45, 125

מ
M

Masovia	11
Malkin	105, 165, 166
Montevideo	59, 95, 164, 211, 218, 219, 232, 235, 237, 238
Manischewitz	41
Moscow	183, 184, 192, 199

[Page 340]

Makow	31, 82, 90, 108, 124
Mizac	213, 219
Miadanek	199
Munich	135
Miedzywodzie	192
Machteshim	65
Mlawa	59, 71, 75
"Maavarot"	65
Maale Akrabim	65
Mexico	104, 213, 219, 228, 238
Massada	65
Mrotszk/Mrozyvc	12
Merchavia	115, 117

‫נ‬ N

Nadgosze	13
Nowydwor	124, 131
Narew	50
Nasielsk	108, 129,
Negev	134, 137
Nahariah	137
Nakhlat Yitzhak	137
Dan River (Nakhal HaDan)	65
Lower Silesia	199, 230
New York	6, 8, 38, 43, 48 43, 83, 85, 89, 99, 101, 102, 124, 125, 127, 131, 169, 200, 201, 207, 208, 209, 210, 211, 212, 213, 214, 215, 216, 217, 218, 219, 221, 222, 223, 224, 225, 226, 228, 238, 239
Njeman	183
Nitzana	
Ness Ziona	65
Novorodke	99
Netanya	65, 135, 136, 210, 217

‫ס‬ S

Sobibor	199
Sodawne	190, 197
Son	?
Sochaczew	130
Samarkand	37, 196, 199
Sokolow	189
Sokoly	64
Sodom	65
Sukhodoly/Suchodoly	12
Stok	168, 190
Stokholm	33
Sterdin	97
Struge	201
Siberia	43, 136, 198
Sinai	135, 136
Slobodke	186
Slonim	171, 172, 174, 177, 178, 179

Smolniki	192
Serock/Srotsk	11, 18, 86, 90, 91, 108, 124, 132, 213, 219
Skrazisk	121
Skuszew	25, 100, 168

ע I/E/A (Ayin)

Evron	137
Ein-Gedi	65
Einat	70
Akko	188
England	191
Atlit	136

פ F and P

Pobrusk	193
Powiszla	115, 118
Palestine	44, 74, 77, 88, 154, 157
Falkow	12
Poplawes	43, 88
Paris	14, 177, 196, 199
Poremba	60, 61, 62, 97, 98, 196, 197, 224
Fareinikte Staten (United States)	77, 82, 85, 238
Pozen	55, 142
Pultusk	11, 13, 14, 28, 29, 30, 43, 57, 59, 60, 75, 76, 78, 90, 91, 98, 107, 132, 167, 177, 189, 194, 196, 213, 219, 239
Poland	5, 6, 7, 8, 11, 12, 44, 48, 59, 61, 70, 71, 84, 86, 91, 101, 115, 118, 120, 123, 11, 132, 140, 162, 164, 166, 171, 177, 185, 188, 189, 196, 199, 200, 201, 202, 205, 210, 211, 218, 224, 227, 228, 230, 236, 237, 238, 239
Piotrkow	13
Piasetchny	193
Pinsk	33, 43, 51, 100, 109
Pyeczkali/Pierzchaly	12
Plock	11, 12, 120
FSS"R (USSR)	166
Peterburg	14
Prague	196, 199
Praga	82
Frankreikh (France)	6, 8
Prasznysz	170
Fruszhew/Proszew	12
Pruczewska–Wiulka/Przetycz Wloscianska	12
Puszkow	190
Preisin	?
Petakh-Tikvah	39, 70, 210, 217

צ Tz

Tzfun America (North America)	58

ק K

Kovne	185, 186, 187

Kotlas	198
Kaluszyn	167
Kalish	120
Komorow	178
Kamion	11
Komisarka	35
Kamientchik/Kamieńczyk	11, 61, 91, 130, 196
Canada	99, 213, 219
Kosow	165, 166, 168
Costa Rica	89
Kopiec	192
Kock/Kotsk	53, 120
Cordoba	235
Kartuze Breze	19
Kielcz	131
Kiev	178
Klosow	71
Krakow	12
Krasnaya Sloboda	191

ר **R**

Radzymin	22, 47, 51, 53, 58, 63, 64, 91, 95, 98, 101, 106, 120, 121, 134, 148, 162, 185, 197
Radzalow	96
Rovno	193
Rosario	235
Rejowiec	192
Ruda Jaworska	180, 182
Ruda Lipiczanska	180, 182
Rukhama	65
Roszan	76, 88, 106
Russia	31, 43, 97, 99, 136, 166, 168, 178, 179, 198, 228, 230, 238
Rybniki	107
Rybienko	13
Rypin	132, 200
Ramat-Gan	11, 78, 80, 163
Rejowski/Rejowiec	192

ש **Sh**

Sweden	225
Shchanka	61, 224
Szczyrk	192
Szczecin	134, 185
Chicago	228
Silesia	225, 228
Sieczka	185

ת **T**

Tel-Aviv	4, 6, 8, 14, 26, 33, 40, 52, 69, 70, 102, 108, 120, 121, 129, 136, 137, 166, 184, 195, 196, 200, 201, 205, 206, 208, 211, 212, 214, 215, 216, 218, 234, 238

| Tel Mond | 70, 80 |

INDEX

Abelman, 159

Abraham The Melamed, 202

Abraham-Itzkhak The Tailor, 68

Abramchik, 47

Abramczyk, 204, 210, 217, 275

Adamovitch, 420, 425, 426, 429, 430

Adamovitch Bulak, 425, 426

Adler, 712

Aichenbaum, 542

Aisman, 542

Ajbeszyc, 205

Albek, 291

Aldak, 185, 502

Aldok, 418, 422

Aleichem, 186, 535

Alenberg, 52, 193, 210, 211, 486

Aleykhem, 113

Allenberg, 503

Almark, 644

Alshaker, 209

Alter, 96, 103, 230, 291, 335, 342

Alterman, 453

Altman, 142, 167, 543

Altmark, 78, 518, 520, 521, 523, 543, 643, 648, 655, 657

Altmark (Zeltman), 657

Anders, 463

Anielewicz, 248, 249, 250, 251, 253, 254

Anielewycz, 252

Ansky, 271

Apelboim, 481, 536, 607, 612, 638, 719

Apfelboim, 622

Aplboym, 337

Appelbaum, 141

Applebaum, 506

Appleboim, 282

Arad, 279

Arbuz, 453

Aronek, 617, 623

Aronson, 518, 520

Aronyok, 712

Ash, 186, 367

Asman, 142, 267, 268, 269, 270, 271, 272, 273, 274, 308, 325, 513, 514, 542, 629, 630, 641

Astroviak, 53, 223

Ausekhewitz, 649

Auslander, 542

Autnitski, 653

Autnitzki, 646

Avraham's, 373

Avramchik, 47, 50, 52, 57

Avramczyk, 542

Avrem'l The Janitor, 23

Avrom-Borukh The Cobbler, 92

Ayan, 629

Ayger, 105, 107

Ayin, 630

Aynhorn, 109

Ayon, 43, 46, 47, 197, 633

Ayzenshtat, 95

Ayzikl The Teacher, 339, 340

B'harab, 663

B'herev, 44, 46, 47, 50, 51, 54, 56

Ba'harab, 95, 102, 210

Baal Shem Tov, 285

Baal-Shem-Tov, 96, 103

Babek, 179

Babin, 643

Baharav, 230, 275, 289, 290, 387, 389, 457, 462, 477, 518, 520, 545, 546, 690

Baharov, 289, 290

Bahrav, 194

Bajles, 637

Bamasz, 239

Banakh, 192

Barab, 64, 66, 67, 95, 102, 170, 210, 230, 289, 290, 457

Barak, 61, 67

Baranek, 89

Baranow, 447

Barev, 43

Bartashevitch, 7

Bashitz, 545

Bashitz-Jakubawitz, 545

Baslav, 500

Basok, 453

Baukman, 302

Beck, 278, 279

Becker, 309

Beharav, 241

Beharov, 43

Beilis, 131

Belzer, 265

Bendoov, 59

Bengal, 502

Bengelsdorf, 547, 548

Bengelsdrorf, 652

Ben-Gurion, 303, 307

Beniek, 278

Benjamin, 507

Ben-Ono, 492

Ben-Shakhar, 682

Ben-Zion, 583, 584

Berdiczewski, 268

Berenshtein, 643

Berenstajn, 520, 521, 522, 523

Berenstein, 629

Berish, 587

Berlinerblau, 548

Bernshtein, 643

Bernshteyn, 58

Bernstajn, 518, 521

Bernstein, 502

Beynish The Porter, 93

Bharav, 648

Bialas, 142

Biales, 489

Bialik, 28, 142, 174

Bialis, 639, 640

Bialistok, 56, 61, 68

Bialostocky, 639

Bialostotsky, 547

Bialystocka, 411

Bialystok, 142

Biberman, 302

Biderman, 710

Bilak, 454

Binduski, 120, 645

Bindusky, 503

Birgenson, 683

Bismanowski, 466

Bismonowski, 494

Bitmanowski, 472

Biyales, 630

Biyalis, 629

Black Hershl, 349

Blaske, 518

Bloom, 648, 649

Blum, 243, 547, 595, 656

Blumenshtein, 547

Blumshtayn, 56

Blumshtein, 547

Blumstajn, 193, 194

Blumstein, 594

Bluszka, 652

Boder, 545

Bodnik, 226

Bogdan, 545

Bomza, 109

Bookshtayn, 44

Boorstin, 605

Borenshtein, 705

Borenshteyn, 57

Borenstajn, 469, 471

Borman, 545

Bornshtein, 545

Bornstein, 502

Borochov, 160

Borokhow, 536

Borshtein, 642

Borstein, 503

Bradatch, 44

Brajtman, 645

Brak, 173, 334

Brama, 54, 175, 194, 334, 475, 477, 478, 548, 566, 604, 605, 659, 683, 709

Bramberg, 518

Brame, 241

Bransk, 334

Branstajn, 414

Bratmakher, 159

Braun, 629

Brenstajn, 521

Bresler, 58, 72, 141, 144, 145, 549, 694, 696

Bressler, 68, 584

Brest, 523

Brisk, 654

Brock, 74

Broda, 254

Brodach, 367

Brodacz, 333

Brodakh, 360

Brodatch, 44, 333, 548

Brode, 548

Brodek, 57

Broder, 280, 548, 623, 629, 634

Brojtman, 642

Brok, 192, 549, 642

Bromberg, 548, 645, 719

Brome, 182

Bromo, 179

Bronshtein, 47, 548, 605, 657, 658, 683, 692, 693

Bronshteyn, 54

Bronstajn, 160, 161, 181, 192, 241, 518, 520, 521, 522, 523, 534, 719

Bronstein, 173, 175, 506

Bronstejn, 485

Bronsztejn, 488, 492

Brontche, 682

Bruk, 51, 102, 486

Brukhanksy, 549

Brukhanski, 239, 242, 258, 265, 491, 600, 675

Brumberg, 699

Brun, 465

Brzezhinski, 537, 538

Brzhesinski, 158

Brzhoza, 152, 153, 158

Brzoza, 207, 367, 629, 630

Bsheshinsky, 503

Bszoiniak, 652

Bszoza, 600

Bukhler, 586

Buksboim, 159

Bulak, 419, 420, 425, 426

Bulmstajn, 192

Bundusky, 546

Bunem, 699

Burak, 627

Burek, 547

Burovitz, 670

Burshtein, 546, 547, 644, 652

Burshteyn, 57, 121, 229, 496

Burshtin, 121, 229, 546, 547, 688

Burstajn, 508, 537

Burstyn, 27, 185

Bursztyn, 244, 261

Byalis, 479

Bz'hoza, 69

Bzezshinsky, 547

Bzhaze, 239, 240

Bzhezhinski, 54, 149

Bzhoza, 69, 94, 170, 229, 243, 273, 367, 369

Bzhozeh, 46

Bzhozha, 477, 478, 479

Bzhuzha, 192, 193

Bzoza, 69, 71, 95, 547, 634, 639, 659

Carlyle, 267

Casimir, 13

Casimir I, 5

Caspi, 472, 717

Cazenelson, 453

Cembal, 234, 478, 643, 652, 704

Chafetz, 201

Chait, 156

Chatskel The Teacher, 313

Chechenoviecki, 43

Chekhanov, 35, 43, 502

Chekhnizer, 449

Chelminske, 6

Chelonko, 502

Chernin, 502, 718

Chervonagura, 44

Cherwonagura, 101

Chlebowski, 5

Chorazycki, 279

Chrobry, 10, 13

Chutnitsky, 76

Cielak, 4, 12, 68, 78, 89, 94, 100, 104, 109, 114, 115, 119, 120, 124, 209, 223, 228, 278, 279, 320, 331, 337, 339, 343, 346, 349, 353, 354, 356, 357, 359, 362, 367, 371

Ciwiak, 179, 469

Clare, 43, 53, 58

Cofer, 652

Cohen, 21, 206, 654

Conrad, 5

Cymerman, 652

Cynamon, 95, 595

Cytrin, 224, 226, 227

Cytrinek, 149

Cytryn, 224, 225, 226, 227

Cywiak, 200, 204, 332

Czar Nicholas Ii, 38

Czekhanow, 607, 610

Czekhanowietzki, 559

Czekhnowitzky, 701

Czembal, 155, 156, 158, 159, 160, 161, 162, 177, 180, 182, 184, 185, 518, 520, 521, 522, 523, 524, 525, 526, 528, 529, 531

Czembel, 152

Czerniakow, 467, 468

Czervonogura, 603

Czerwonagora, 655

Czerwonagura, 101, 560, 674, 678, 698

Czuker, 158

Dabkin, 146

Daigi, 662

Daitcher, 654, 656

Dajk, 518, 522

Dan, 94, 114, 630, 652, 711, 712

De Cielak, 4, 68, 78, 89, 94, 100, 104, 109, 115, 120,
124, 209, 223, 228, 320, 331, 337, 339, 343, 346,
349, 353, 354, 356, 357, 359, 362, 367, 371

Deges, 308

Denker, 614

Deren, 553

Dergycz, 152, 155

Deutcher, 170, 701

Deutsher, 163

Director, 710

Director (Lerman), 710

Direktor, 432

Direktor (Lerman), 432

Djuvag, 308

Dmowski, 117, 119

Dobres, 78, 211, 538, 552, 605, 649

Domb, 54, 57, 193, 200, 202, 210, 400, 552, 559, 642

Don, 552

Dorembus, 240

Dostoyevsky, 187

Dovche, 116

Dovid Leib The Baker, 601

Dovris, 502

Dovriss, 499

Drozdowski, 149

Druynski, 666

Dubanik, 46

Dubner, 515, 518, 519

Dudenshtein, 664

Duke Of Masovia, 5

Dvorah The Knitter, 53

Dvorszki, 539

Dzbanek, 308, 309, 310, 311, 552

Dzengal, 552, 553

Dzenkewitz, 553

Dzenkiewicz, 460, 461

Dzhbanek, 157

Dzhbank, 157

Dzhigan, 120, 122

Dzhyk, 518

Dzienkewitz, 684

Dziga, 122

Dzigan, 122

Dżigan, 122

Edelman, 192

Ehrlikh, 46

Eibeschitz, 270

Eikenboim, 54

Einstein, 272

Eisenstat, 158, 159

Eisenstein, 14, 133, 142, 163, 173, 218, 255, 284,
291, 292, 296, 304, 305, 306, 380, 390, 453, 476,
539, 540, 583, 605, 606, 710, 713, 714

Eizenberg, 706

Elbein, 67

Elboim, 47, 50, 180, 184, 185, 192, 194, 210, 229,
230, 418, 422, 442, 444, 459, 568

Elenberg, 452, 461

Eliezer, 711

Eliezer (Litman), 711

Eli-Mayer The Baker, 120

Eli-Meir, 308

Elke-Shoshe The Wagon-Driverin, 120

Elye-Mayer The Baker, 120

Ende The Butcher, 637

Epshtayn, 46

Epshtein, 210, 212, 662

Epshteyn, 50, 52, 57

Epstajn, 145, 183, 185, 458

Epstein, 31, 32, 69, 141, 568, 603

Epsteyn, 69, 95, 210, 212

Epsztein, 101, 210, 212

Epsztejn, 200, 202, 210, 212

Erlich, 453

Erlikht, 192, 193, 194

Ernst, 268

Ernstajn, 160, 161

Ershinke The Water-Carrier, 308

Esterzon, 240

Esthersohn, 142

Etshtein, 682

Eyger, 322, 323

Facht, 75

Faige The Fishmonger, 401

Fajncajn, 459

Faktor, 518

Falker, 111

Farbshtein, 689

Farbshtejn, 478

Farbshteyn, 115

Farbstajn, 528

Farbstein, 60, 175, 571, 602, 629

Farbsteyn, 479

Farbsztejn, 472, 473, 475, 478, 479, 481, 482, 484, 485, 491

Farentyazh, 120

Fayntsayg, 95

Federgreen, 373

Feigenblat, 455, 456

Fein, 506

Feingold, 498

Feinstein, 59

Feintzeig, 44, 49

Feinzaig, 95, 626

Feinzeig, 414

Feinzilber, 571

Feldsher, 564

Felner, 174, 179, 207, 571, 572, 603

Ferdman, 69

Feyge The Blind Yeast Seller, 102

Fialkow, 571

Fieler, 656

Filer, 571

Filidovitch, 425, 430, 431

Filipovski, 45

Filler, 78

Fine, 624, 718

Finkelshtein, 700

Finkelstajn, 159

Finkelstein, 35, 58, 449, 571

Firestein, 591

Fischer, 18

Fishbein, 571

Fishel, 630

Fisher, 94, 109, 120, 294

Fishke The Fireman, 219

Fishkes, 308

Fishman, 571, 695

Fleischman, 505

Fluda, 420, 422, 430, 521

Flude, 418

Forshtman, 696

Fraiman, 573

Frank, 269, 270

Frankel, 471

Frayman, 389

Freedman, 3, 719

Freemen, 710

Freider, 384, 386

Freint, 149, 156

Frider, 77, 572, 573, 683

Fridman, 210, 308, 572

Fridshtern, 573

Frieder, 620

Friedmakher, 656

Friedman, 54, 594, 630, 689, 712

Frishman, 171, 177

Fromowycz, 243

Fronton, 384, 386

Frost, 615, 718, 719

Frumowitz, 572

Frumowycz, 400, 404, 408

Frydman, 207

Fular, 445

Fulje, 414

Funt, 95

Galonsky, 656

Gamre, 179

Ganzgloz, 549

Garfinkel, 643

Garnek, 77, 645

Gaszelszani, 599

Gelernter, 218

Gelman, 227, 449

Gemara, 498, 503

Gemora, 398

Gershkovski, 54

Gershon, 291, 632

Gershon's, 602

Gershonovitch, 77

Gershonowitz, 550

Gibur, 549, 550

Gilbert, 95

Gilczik, 447

Giterman, 180, 184

Glass, 702

Glat, 159

Gliksberg, 550, 654

Glowash, 550

Glowatsh, 550

Glowinsky, 550

Golanski, 400

Golansky, 623

Goldbarsht, 549

Goldbarszt, 481, 486

Goldberg, 181, 630, 637, 641

Goldfaber, 646

Goldfadn, 113

Goldfoder, 518

Goldma, 549

Goldman, 43, 47, 56, 95, 99, 101, 145, 174, 181, 193,
    210, 217, 239, 275, 400, 496, 502, 549, 605, 610

Goldshtein, 639, 687

Goldsmith, 584, 636

Goldstein, 163, 200, 230, 502

Goldsztejn, 479

Goldsztejn (Nudel), 479

Goldvaser, 69

Goldvasser, 46, 433

Goldwasser, 61, 67, 69, 75, 308, 477, 478, 549, 592,
    602, 674

Golomb, 146

Goodman, 94, 109

Gorni, 141

Gosheltzani, 549

Gottlieb, 150

Gozheltzani, 716

Grabina, 211, 550

Grabski, 589

Graetz, 149

Graiwer, 525

Granat, 73, 77, 550, 708

Granek, 551

Grapa, 4, 12, 68, 78, 89, 94, 100, 104, 109, 115, 120,
    124, 209, 223, 228, 230, 278, 279, 320, 331, 337,
    339, 343, 346, 349, 353, 354, 356, 357, 359, 362,
    367, 371, 459, 476, 492, 534, 587, 655, 666, 667

Grapa-Cielak, 12

Gravitzky, 60, 63, 67, 68

Greenbaum, 60

Greenberg, 68, 644

Greenfeder, 373

Greenzeig, 589

Grimberg, 552

Grinberg, 192, 194, 418, 518, 521, 551, 552, 650, 656, 705

Grinboim, 46

Griniski, 287

Grinski, 287

Grizek, 551

Grobams, 453

Grobas, 453, 454

Groman, 550

Grosbard, 95, 144, 145, 192, 207, 241, 595, 626, 692

Grossbart, 141

Groswirt, 551

Grudko, 266

Grushka, 551

Gruszka, 648, 650, 705

Gruszke, 518, 521

Gruzhka, 523

Gunter, 441

Gureni, 240

Gurman, 549, 630, 637

Gurner, 144, 145, 193, 206, 210

Gurney, 46, 51, 549

Gurni, 30, 170, 210, 275, 384

Gurshtein, 77

Gutmacher, 174

Gutman, 249, 549, 618

Gutshtat, 51, 101

Gutstadt, 549

Gutstat, 180, 183, 185

Gwizdalski, 522

Gwizdolski, 521

Gzhende, 395

Habsburżanki, 13

Hain, 633, 634

Haldak, 179

Halenberg, 57

Halperin, 705

Hartglas, 60

Hartman, 78, 89, 120, 320, 331, 337, 339

Hecht, 696

Hefetz, 600

Heifetz, 211, 224, 225, 226

Heler, 378

Hendlis, 256

Hershele The Water Carrier, 320

Hershenkeh, 54, 55

Hershinke The Helper, 115

Hershl Melamed, 349, 352

Hershl The Teacher, 349, 352

Hershl The Water Carrier, 118

Hersh-Leyb The Shingle-Maker, 354, 357

Hertel, 270

Hertz, 439

Hertzl, 277

Herzl, 174, 194, 242, 243

Hesse, 277

Hiler, 192

Hiller, 57, 61, 67, 102, 554, 593, 668

Hinkeleh, 54, 55

Hirlikht, 554

Hirsch, 142, 590

Hirschbein, 186

Hirshfeld, 97

Hock, 312

Holand, 192, 241, 400, 508, 641, 652

Holand-Prager, 652

Holcman, 116, 360, 473, 479, 484, 518, 520, 521, 522

Holcman-Rakhman, 473

Holczman, 170, 197

Holdak, 275, 276

Holdin, 400

Holenberg, 461

Holland, 54, 57, 61, 67, 73, 78, 175, 186, 304, 502, 553, 595, 616, 713

Hollman, 453

Holtsman, 95

Holtzkener, 554, 696

Holtzkner, 591

Holtzman, 47, 54, 95, 116, 553, 554, 629, 638, 647, 653, 664, 669, 712, 715

Holtzman-Rukhman, 669

Holztman, 669

Horowitz, 664

Hutenski, 518

Hutnitski, 627

Igla, 455

Igolowitz, 637

Ihrlikht, 44, 240, 241, 243

Ilan, 133, 670

Ilan (Olshker), 670

Ismaj, 231

Ismakh, 518

Itche-Metch The Musician, 343

Itche-Meyer The Shoykhet, 102

Itche-Meyer The Slaughterer, 332

Jabloka, 701

Jablonski, 455

Jabotinsky, 212

Jacob-Ariye The Butcher, 333

Jacobovich, 502

Jacobowitz, 218, 590

Jaffe, 35, 58, 449

Jagoda, 175, 176, 193, 417, 620, 632, 646, 709

Jagoda (Marcuschamer), 632

Jagode, 686

Jakobowitz, 652, 657

Jakubovich, 310

Jakubovitch, 308

Jakubowitz, 561, 673

Jakubowycz, 169, 170, 180, 183, 192, 194, 240, 242, 261, 610

Jakubowycz-Tabak, 169

Janek, 409

Janis, 177

Januszewycz, 417, 418, 420, 421, 422, 428

Jaskowycz, 145, 177

Javner, 701

Jazhemski, 159, 160, 161

Jedwab, 628

Jelishewski, 643

Jolkower, 652

Jolkower-Burshtein, 652

Jolowitz, 652

Jonasowycz, 180

Jonisz, 631

Joskowicz, 594

Joskowycz, 149, 181

Jungheiser, 453

Jurman, 152, 153, 155

Juskowycz, 148

Kacyzne, 150

Kaftal, 289

Kahan, 466

Kahn, 43, 46, 77

Kalatz, 308

Kalb, 327

Kalisch, 256

Kalish, 211, 257

Kalisher, 174

Kaloski, 590

Kalupka, 574

Kaluski, 43, 44, 56, 57, 102, 141, 144, 145, 152, 153, 157, 202, 206, 207, 210, 211, 243, 277, 414, 461, 475, 478, 479, 481, 484, 486, 574, 595, 631, 662

Kalusky, 50, 51, 52, 308, 712

Kanal, 456

Kaplan, 668

Kaplovitch, 214

Kaplowitz, 524

Kaplowyc, 522

Kapolowyc, 520

Karelenstein, 585

Karl Ferdinand The Plotzker Bishop, 6, 7

Karol, 157

Karpel, 322, 323

Kartufel, 77

Karvat, 646

Karzin, 446

Kasche-Macher's, 142

Kashemakher, 318

Kaspi, 14, 288, 380, 490, 494, 601, 664

Kaspi (Serbernik), 380

Kaspi (Srebrenik), 14

Kat, 639

Katz, 578

Katzav, 414

Katzfke, 312

Kaufman, 205, 421, 584, 594

Kaveh, 600

Kavitch, 719

Kawe, 170

Kayitz, 629, 631

Kayitz (Skarlat), 631

Kazhimiesz I, 5

Kepel, 537

Kerner, 46, 50, 101, 219

Kersh, 575

Kershenowitz, 643, 702

Khafetz, 220

Khaim, 241

Khanhas, 57

Khano, 643

Khashmal, 492

Khatzkls, 57

Khazanovich, 59

Khefoy, 627

Khelenowski, 154

Kheyfetz, 221

Khiles, 158

Khin, 562

Khjan, 562

Khofets, 211

Khofetz, 53

Khumnitzki, 562

Khutnicki, 179

Khzan, 562

Khzhan, 47, 181

King Gustav Adolf Of Sweden, 7

King Jan I Olbracht, 13

King John I Albert, 13

King Sigismund I, 6, 9, 12, 13

King Sigismund Ii Augustus, 13

King Sigismund Iii, 6, 7

King Sigismund Vasa Iii, 13

King Zygmunt August, 9

King Zygmunt August Ii, 13

King Zygmunt The First, 6, 9, 12, 13

King Zygmunt The Third, 6, 7

King Zygmunt Vasa Iii, 13

Kipper, 629

Kiris, 78

Kirshenboim, 575

Kirzhner, 95

Kiszczak, 454

Kiwaikes, 701

Kleinman, 575, 653

Kleinweis, 456

Klepycz, 266

Klieger, 516

Kliger, 290

Kloski, 584, 594

Klosky, 97

Klugman, 629

Klugmani, 641

Knaster, 120, 161

Knoster, 575

Kocker, 600

Kohen, 629

Kohn, 95

Kol, 665

Kol (Najmark), 665

Kolner, 280, 575

Kolo, 574, 646

Komarov, 419, 420, 425, 426

Kon, 279

Koniasz, 595

Kopel, 592

Kopljowitz, 523

Koplowicz, 461

Koplowitz, 173, 175, 176, 521, 522, 574, 592, 646, 647, 649, 665, 691

Koplowyc, 521, 522

Kopolovitch, 56, 327

Kornet, 291

Korosh, 574, 575

Kortzkedi, 297

Koslowska, 71

Kosower, 574

Koszk'er, 585

Kotlasz, 574

Kotlowitz, 497

Kovic, 595

Kovitz, 472

Kowal, 594, 595

Kowic, 494

Kraga, 76

Kramer, 178, 220, 499, 502, 595

Krasucki, 159

Kraushar, 270

Krauze, 4, 12, 68, 78, 89, 94, 100, 104, 108, 109, 115, 120, 124, 209, 223, 228, 279, 320, 331, 337, 339, 343, 346, 349, 353, 354, 356, 357, 359, 362, 367, 371, 538, 575, 669

Krawczik, 394

Kremer, 57, 356, 641

Kremkewitz, 576

Kretsmer, 390

Krimkewitz, 648

Krimkowitz, 661

Krimlowski, 600

Krishtal, 57, 101, 576, 654

Krishtol, 61, 67

Kristal, 101, 650

Kronenberg, 142, 275, 276, 576, 682, 683, 691

Krug, 575

Kruk, 159

Kryshtal, 668, 681, 700

Krystal, 192, 518, 520, 521

Krysztal, 101

Kulaski, 461

Kupchick, 16

Kuper, 96

Kuperstok, 265

Kurlap, 325, 327

Kurnet, 192, 194, 685

Kwaitek, 494

Kwiatek, 102, 207, 478, 480, 489, 520, 521, 522, 523, 525, 526, 575, 643, 700, 701

Kzhan, 605

Lajcher, 101, 278, 279, 371, 372

Lakher, 57

Landau, 43, 46

Landinski, 224

Lang, 695

Laycher, 278, 372

Laykher, 24, 278, 372, 562

Lefkowitz, 637

Lehman, 20

Leibowitz, 617, 719

Leibowitz (Widelec), 719

Leicher, 180, 183, 184, 185, 278, 279

Leichera, 278

Leichert, 278, 279

Leikher, 278

Leikin, 453

Leiles, 529

Lemberg, 50, 655

Lemberger, 563

Lerman, 223, 225, 432, 433, 563, 710

Lerner, 53

Leshchinski, 51

Leshczinski, 563

Leshtshinski, 101

Lesinski, 101

Levin, 43, 46, 50, 51, 57, 95, 97, 102, 141, 144, 152,
    153, 157, 522, 712

Leviner, 102

Levinsky, 224

Levitt, 628

Levkowitz, 629

Levsky, 454

Levy, 502

Lew, 159

Lewenstein, 291

Lewin, 141, 145, 149, 562, 563

Lewiner, 193, 595

Lewinger, 563

Leycher, 278

Leykher, 48, 50, 51, 55, 278, 279

Leyzer The Ropemaker's Son, 309

Liba, 471

Liberman, 270, 562

Lichtenbaum, 253

Lichtman, 101

Lieber, 477

Likht, 527

Likhtenshteyn, 95

Likhtman, 101, 562

Lipkin, 226

Lipowitzky, 644

Lipowsky, 671

Lis, 28, 50, 101, 203, 562, 601, 615

Lisman, 158

Lisowicki, 522

Lisowitzki, 647

Litera, 432

Litere, 562

Litman, 711

Livner, 698

Loifer, 159

Łojek, 127, 128

Lojnkoff, 699

Loketch, 309

Lomzher, 224

Loyek, 127, 128

Lublin, 204

Luzer, 655

Lys, 177

M'lamed, 56

Maczowsher Duke, 5

Mahler, 159

Maimon, 369, 518

Maimonides, 369

Maimonidis, 38

Maizer, 614

Maizlitz, 685

Malavantchik, 308

Malawanczyk, 158

Malchik, 54

Malczik, 179

Malczyk, 149, 182, 185, 241, 518

Malina, 152, 192, 193, 194, 563, 697

Malinowsky, 409, 410

Malitzinova, 706

Malkhiel, 239

Malkhiel The Ritual Slaughterer, 386

Malkhiel The Shoykhet, 101

Malovanchik, 371, 372

Malovantchik, 101, 279, 280, 281

Malovantczyk, 278, 279

Malowanczik, 563, 564

Malowanczyk, 101, 223, 244, 276, 371, 372

Maltchik, 503, 677

Maltshik, 653

Mann, 629

Marcus, 77, 96, 109, 631

Marcus (Skarlat), 631

Marcuschamer, 76, 96, 109, 119, 223

Marcuskamer, 96

Marcuskhamer, 96, 605

Margalit, 492

Margolis, 718

Margulies, 634

Markhavka, 175

Markhevka, 101

Markhevke, 54

Markish, 71, 150

Markus, 245, 601, 629

Markuschamer, 4, 68, 78, 89, 94, 100, 104, 109, 114, 115, 120, 124, 209, 223, 228, 229, 278, 279, 316, 320, 331, 337, 339, 343, 346, 349, 353, 354, 356, 357, 359, 362, 367, 371, 538, 632

Markuschamer De Cielak, 4, 68, 78, 89, 94, 100, 104, 109, 115, 120, 124, 209, 223, 228, 320, 331, 337, 339, 343, 346, 349, 353, 354, 356, 357, 359, 362, 367, 371

Markushamer, 564

Markushjamer, 223

Markuskhamer, 53, 57, 96, 241, 564, 602

Markuskhammer, 479

Marx, 160

Mastboim, 159

Mates, 331

Mates-Faivl The Storekeeper, 353, 356

Mateusz, 131

Maykhemer, 564

Meier-Beinish, 328

Mejer, 203

Melowanchik, 664

Mendelson, 159

Mentel, 652

Mermelstein, 362

Mesing, 23, 193, 565, 645

Messing, 704

Meyer, 230, 234

Meyer Beinish, 328

Meyer-Beinish, 328

Miasnik, 431

Miera, 193

Mikhalkes, 328, 329, 373

Mikholke's, 538

Milewsky, 410, 411, 412

Minkowski, 265

Minky, 564

Minsky, 564

Mirsky, 627

Mishar, 712

Misharik, 69

Mitelsbakh, 144, 145, 149, 152, 153, 472, 473, 475, 479, 484, 486, 490, 494

Mitelzbakh, 466

Mitlesbakh, 157

Mitlsbakh, 68, 343, 346, 349, 353, 354, 356, 357,
     359, 564, 649

Mitlzbakh, 518, 715

Mittelbach, 141

Mittelsbach, 97

Mittelsberg, 498

Mitzenmakher, 654

Mizlutz, 291

Mlinajewitz, 564, 565

Mlotek, 564

Molotek, 53

Mondre, 672

Mondrey, 47, 50

Mondry, 56, 95, 96, 210, 242, 245, 277, 492, 646

Monkita, 518, 521, 523, 524, 653

Monkito, 520, 521

Montefiore, 82

Moov (Shmuleh The Sexton), 54

Morgenshtern, 58

Morgenstern, 34, 217, 219, 231, 244, 245, 290, 564,
     584, 585, 586

Morgensztern, 202

Morgenthau, 82, 89

Morgnshtern, 101

Morgnsztern, 101

Moskowycz, 242

Motl The Kosher Slaughterer, 337

Munchausen, 366

Musberg, 296, 298, 303

Mushkat, 294, 308, 337, 639

Mushkatenblit, 639

Muskat, 479

Muszkat, 511, 629

Nadel, 565, 687

Nagal, 664

Nagel, 173, 176, 565

Naimaek, 566

Naiman, 78, 95, 565

Naimark, 565, 566

Najman, 95, 210, 414, 460, 461, 477, 478, 520, 622,
     631, 645, 695

Najmark, 192, 537, 630, 634, 665, 666

Nakhum The Fisher, 367

Naumberg, 45

Nayman, 210, 389

Neiman, 44, 95, 210

Neuberger, 629, 637

Neuman, 64, 66, 67, 630, 640

Neumark, 170

Newman (Wengrow), 640

Newmark, 141, 595

Niestempower, 655

Niestenpover, 120, 121, 123

Niger, 272

Nisen, 54, 538

Nissenboim, 44

Njedjewitzki, 648

Njedwicki, 522

Nodel, 241

Norfilk, 692

Novgrocki, 175

Novodvorski, 454

Novodworski, 456

Novominski, 44, 95

Nowigrod, 652

Nowigrod-Bszoiniak, 652

Nowigrud, 565

Nowogrodski, 159, 161, 642, 645

Nowogrodski-Rozner, 645

Nowogrudski, 458

Nowominski, 241, 518, 648, 649

Nowominsky, 706

Noyke The Water Carrier, 316

Nudel, 102, 192, 478, 479, 481

Offenbach, 270

Oland, 542, 543

Oldak, 204, 210, 351, 352, 543, 600, 656

Olemberg, 642

Olenberg, 202, 209, 210, 211, 212, 543, 544, 636,
    688, 689

Olleshker, 133

Olshaker, 192, 209, 544

Olsheker, 657

Olshker, 590, 591, 670

Orenshtein, 545

Orenstein, 95, 142, 186, 593, 674

Orensztejn, 95, 477, 478

Orensztejn (Goldwasser), 477

Orensztejn-Goldwasser, 478

Ornshtein, 641

Ortell, 12

Osenholtz, 477

Osichkin, 174

Osman, 320, 324, 474, 478

Oster, 57

Ostri, 180, 182, 466

Ostroviak, 75

Ostrovyak, 98, 223

Ostrowiak, 101, 334, 544

Ostrowik, 175

Ostry, 50, 175, 179, 472, 503, 544, 545, 595, 652,
    676, 688, 689

Oswietsky, 544

Pacht, 348, 350

Pakht, 108, 350, 479, 481, 538, 568, 629, 638

Palarz, 636

Palasz, 629

Paliukh, 526

Paljukh, 522

Paluchi, 313

Palukh, 124, 129, 492, 650

Palukhl, 111

Palyukh, 344, 568, 569

Paniartshuk, 569

Paniatczyk, 192, 194

Papier, 455

Papowski, 518, 521, 522, 523

Paraver, 502

Parawer, 718

Parover, 498, 506

Parower, 508, 613, 614, 627

Paskewitz, 569, 711

Paskornik, 406

Paskowic, 521

Paskowitz, 643

Paskowyc, 521

Pastalski, 177

Paszkornik, 407

Pat, 104, 108

Pavlovski, 63

Pavlowski, 25

Pazor, 173, 174, 175, 176

Pazur, 568

Peczenik, 216

Pelner, 645, 708

Pepke The Cobbler's Son, 121

Perchik, 715

Peretz, 113, 171, 186, 268, 272, 273

Perla, 292

Perle, 141, 682

Pesakh, 630

Peshtitski, 595

Peterzeil, 159

Pfeffer, 498

Piekasz, 570, 643

Pieniek, 569, 570, 597, 600, 716

Pienik, 57, 432

Pietrushka, 270

Pilidovitch, 420

Pilsudski, 24, 175, 606

Pinkhas, 241

Pinsker, 277

Pitchnik, 44

Pitsenik, 95

Piyenik, 47

Pjetshelenietz, 652

Plocker, 185

Ploczker, 183

Plonchik, 57

Plonczak, 204

Plontschak, 50

Plontshak, 570

Plotka, 570

Plotzker, 570

Plukalowski, 158

Polarz, 630

Polek, 538

Polker, 313

Polocker, 180

Polstolski, 75, 76

Polukhlekh, 308

Poniatowski, 6, 12

Poplowitz, 646

Popovsky, 77

Popowski, 158, 159, 161, 244, 371, 393, 521, 647, 653

Popowsky, 569, 642, 682

Portmowietsky, 569

Poskowicz, 518

Poskowitz, 523

Postolski, 50, 179, 180, 182, 184, 185, 210, 477, 479, 485, 522, 538, 649

Postolski-Wengel, 649

Posztolski, 210

Potash, 568, 706

Povlovski, 66

Prage, 645

Pragee, 652

Prager, 148, 193, 270, 461, 518, 520, 521, 570, 645, 652, 703

Prider, 597

Primar, 455

Pruk, 706

Przerębski, 6, 8, 13

Przeszczelenjec, 522

Przestrzeleniec, 101

Przestrzelenietz, 569

Przeticki, 180, 185, 473, 474, 475, 477, 478, 479, 480, 481, 482, 483

Przetycki, 102

Pseticki, 179

Pshemerover, 674

Pshemiaraver, 605

Pshemirarower, 571

Pshemyarover, 503

Pshemyierover, 101

Psheshchelinietz, 57

Psheshtshelyenyietz, 101

Pshetitski, 101, 386, 387, 643

Pshetitski-Rozenberg, 643

Pshetitsky, 44, 495, 570, 643, 659, 664, 681, 698

Pshetitsky (Rozenberg), 643

Pshetitzki, 44, 210, 211, 650

Pshshchelenitz, 46

Pshtitski, 102

Pszeticki, 394, 415

Pszetitski, 281

Pszhetitski, 210, 211

Pustulsky, 659

Putermilkh, 454, 455

Pzhemirover, 47

Pzhetitski, 50

Pzieticki, 466

Rabah, 671

Rabbi Aba'le, 320, 321

Rabbi Abba'le, 583

Rabbi Avrumele From Sochaczew, 286

Rabbi David Shlomo, 256

Rabbi Elimelekh Jehuda, 257

Rabbi Israel Isaac Of Rotzk, 257

Rabbi Jacob Aryeh, 255

Rabbi Joseph Of Amshinov, 257

Rabbi Joseph Of Serock, 583

Rabbi Menakhem Mendel Of Kotzk, 256

Rabbi Mendele Of Kotsk, 585

Rabbi Mordekhai Of Skrazisk, 257

Rabbi Shabtai Tzvi, 269

Rabbi Shimon, 33

Rabbi Yaakov Aryeh, 255, 256

Rabbi Yosef Dela Reina, 268

Rabenu Gershom Of Mainz, 335

Rabin, 78, 339, 362, 366

Rabinovich, 47

Rabinowitz, 576

Radziminski, 211, 488, 508, 560, 596, 597

Radziminsky, 502, 503, 506, 607, 620, 621, 658, 719

Radzyminski, 211

Raikhman, 623

Raisen, 113, 186

Rajcik, 520, 521, 522

Rajcyk, 182

Rajczik, 521, 523, 645

Rajczyk, 523

Rajmi, 626

Rajtshik, 643

Rajtzik, 668

Rajzik, 642

Rakhman, 473, 479, 484, 485

Rambam, 369

Rampa, 201

Rapoport, 43, 44, 56, 577

Rappaport, 177, 269

Rashi, 200, 332, 335, 350, 352

Raspe, 366

Ratkovsky, 505

Raykhman, 578

Reb Avrahmke The Teacher, 602

Reb Benjamin The Stutterer, 205

Reb Butcheh The Baker, 53

Reb Hershl The Historian, 109

Reb Herszynke The Assistant Shamos, 201

Reb Itsche, 26

Reb Itshe Meir The Shokhet, 593, 595

Reb Khaim The Historian, 109

Reb Levi Of Berditchev, 263

Reb Nata, 30

Reb Shimon, 21, 30, 31, 33

Reb Shoel'ke The Baker, 601

Reb Szmul The Shamos, 200, 201

Reb Tuwia The Shamos, 200

Reb Yankel The Shokhet, 29, 30, 31, 32

Reb Yankel The Smith, 32

Reb Yisroel, 30, 32

Reb Zalmele Khosid The Tzadik, 265

Refoelkes, 373, 376

Reichman, 61, 67, 74, 719

Reiness, 174

Reiss, 492

Reyzele Di Zogerin, 346

Reyzl Di Zogerin, 347, 348

Reyzman, 387

Ribka, 63, 66

Ribke, 592

Richman, 718, 719

Rinek, 46, 75, 95, 308, 309, 578

Ring, 461, 578

Ringelblum, 159, 252, 519

Rinke, 578

Ritchman, 508, 718

Ritter, 11

Robinowitz, 606

Robinson, 618

Rogav, 68

Rogowitz, 576

Rokhman, 636

Rokhweitz, 577

Rokita, 694

Rokite, 577

Rombinsky, 658

Romianek, 657

Roosevelt, 89

Rosen, 159, 719

Rosenbaum, 583

Rosenberg, 64, 66, 67, 97, 142, 157, 174, 175, 192, 210, 211, 333, 477, 503, 594, 595, 598, 603

Rosenblatt, 75

Rosenfeld, 456

Rosenzweig, 100

Rosner, 170

Rostkier, 655

Rotbard, 207, 241, 464, 465, 518, 519, 520, 521, 522, 523, 604, 648, 652, 659, 678, 680

Rotbard-Schwartzman, 652

Rotblat, 254, 479, 492, 629

Rotenberg, 193, 255, 643

Rothblatt, 638

Rotholtz, 576

Rothstein, 361

Rotnov, 498

Rozen, 53, 223, 576, 599

Rozenberg, 44, 47, 50, 52, 57, 120, 149, 202, 204, 210, 211, 359, 360, 361, 452, 488, 577, 643, 648, 700, 703, 716

Rozenboim, 58, 576, 696

Rozenstajn, 192, 194

Rozenzweig, 418, 419, 420, 426, 428, 429, 431

Rozhanski, 453

Rozner, 641, 645

Rpkite, 577

Rubenstajn, 439

Rubin, 47, 50, 53, 57, 70, 71, 124, 157, 223, 228, 333, 337, 343, 346, 349, 353, 354, 356, 357, 359, 371, 387, 400, 407, 521, 523, 577, 595, 627, 652, 700, 705, 707

Rubin (Gruszka), 705

Rubinky, 577

Rubinowitz, 521, 522, 523, 524, 577, 699, 702

Rubinowyc, 521

Rubinsky, 577

Rubinwyc, 521

Rujshe, 648

Rukhman, 669

Ruppen, 144

Russ, 1, 4, 71, 129, 144, 152, 169, 177, 178, 180, 192, 197, 214, 216, 220, 221, 231, 234, 239, 244, 249, 258, 265, 267, 268, 273, 275, 277, 316, 320, 325, 359, 373, 377, 378, 393, 397, 398, 400, 415, 432, 439, 445, 451, 452, 457, 467, 469, 472, 507, 509, 511, 514, 515, 529, 531, 534, 536, 537, 719

Rusze, 578

Ruzha, 161

Ruzhe, 158, 160, 161

Rybner, 655

Rybner-Luzer, 655

Rynek, 334, 518, 520, 522

Safirshtein, 659

Salanter, 53, 223

Saperstajn, 251

Saperstein, 114, 566

Sapersztejn, 480

Sapirstein, 76, 595

Sapirsztejn, 207

Sawiski, 455

Scheinfield, 255

Schildt, 4, 12, 68, 115

Schmerling, 253

Schnitzer, 622

Schreiber, 521

Schultz, 252

Schwartz, 371, 503

Schwartzbort, 578

Schwartzman, 652

Sedledsky, 581

Seftel, 582

Segal, 45, 95, 153, 389, 629, 655, 671, 678

Segalowycz, 159

Seligsohn, 280, 281, 282, 289, 290, 294, 308

Semberg, 581, 582

Sender-Leyzer, 628

Senderowic, 518

Serbernik, 284, 380

Serevnik, 34

Serka, 591

Serok, 567, 634

Severin, 8, 10, 13

Shachne, 671

Shafar, 46

Shafran, 578

Shaiga, 76

Shaike, 580

Shakhne, 714

Shakhnowisky, 578

Shalom, 539

Shapira, 44, 46, 51, 653, 669

Shapiro, 69, 216

Sharfhartz, 697, 702

Sharkevich, 63, 66

Shayke, 229

Shazar, 270

Shchigel, 44

Shedlecki, 175

Shedletski, 101

Shedletzki, 173

Shedlezki, 176

Sheinman, 663

Sheinman (B'harab), 663

Shemberg, 674, 686

Shenberg, 211

Sherinski, 456

Sherman, 627

Sherok, 77

Shidletsky, 308

Shidlu, 697, 702

Shiffer, 46

Shifman, 407

Shiger, 630

Shike, 580

Shiker, 656

Shikur, 77

Shimon The Melamed, 116

Shkariat, 67

Shkarlat, 43, 44, 46, 50, 56, 69, 76, 94, 95, 96, 115, 118, 308, 386

Shkarlat (Marcus), 96

Shkarlat (Marcuskhamer), 96

Shlafmitz, 700

Shlinger, 526

Shlit'a, 223

Shlizoner, 120

Shmilkis, 53

Shmuel The Purger, 19

Shmule The Beadle, 244

Shmuleh The Sexton (Moov), 54

Shneider, 74

Shnek, 57

Shnieg, 599

Shoikhet, 290

Shokhet, 67, 573, 592

Sholem–Mehkhel's, 368

Shoshkes, 467

Shpira, 170

Shran, 387, 389, 657

Shredni, 677

Shreider, 518

Shrik, 94

Shron, 57, 582

Shtajman, 518

Shtayfman, 712

Shtaynman, 226

Shtchigel, 102, 642

Shteinberg, 46

Shtellung, 97

Shtelung, 3, 51, 56, 102, 152, 156, 228, 258, 259,
     472, 475, 515, 518, 520, 521, 522, 523, 524, 525,
     526, 531, 532, 533, 534, 660, 661

Shtelung Sokol, 228

Shtern, 50

Shteshigel, 580

Shtikl, 690

Shtokfish, 2, 4

Shtoyb, 120

Shtzigl, 703

Shukrin, 101

Shult, 647

Shults, 389

Shultz, 57, 67, 466, 483, 490, 538, 579, 684

Shumacher, 122

Shumakher, 120

Shustak, 518

Shuster, 74, 393

Shvanek, 74

Siedlecki, 101

Siemowit, 5

Sikora, 580

Silver, 288, 491, 506

Silverberg, 77

Simin, 38

Singer, 503

Sirota, 84, 214

Skarlat, 158, 192, 216, 394, 460, 461, 631, 712

Skarlet, 142

Skladkowski, 117, 119

Skladovski, 49

Slafmin, 580, 581

Smietanka, 215

Smietanke, 581

Smolajz, 567

Smolarczik, 567

Smolik, 567

Sneg, 581

Sobolewski, 245

Sobolewskyi, 246

Sobot, 566

Sobota, 566

Sokal, 464

Sokol, 44, 47, 56, 94, 137, 158, 160, 228, 258, 459,
     518, 521, 523, 566, 590, 630, 648, 649, 650, 653,
     666

Sokolar, 673

Sokolov, 38, 174

Sokol-Tandetchazh, 650

Solomon, 646

Sorek, 566

Spiro, 590, 591

Sporta, 672

Srebernik, 600

Srebnik, 57, 389

Srebnik (Khatzkls), 57

Srebrenik, 14, 717

Srebrnik, 201, 205, 206, 567, 568, 685

Srebro, 415

Sredni, 162, 185, 538

Staiman, 579

Stajnberg, 192, 242

Stanislaver, 38

Stanislaw August, 6

Stanisław August, 12

Starkes, 579

Starowiecki, 161

Stazinski, 66

Stein, 634

Steinberg, 450, 579, 580, 626, 717

Steinman, 226, 449, 649

Steinman-Ausekhewitz, 649

Steinmark, 506, 719

Stelmakh, 595

Stelung, 149, 159, 160, 161, 162, 192, 197, 198, 241,
   414, 466, 580

Stempler, 705

Stern, 185, 217, 503, 680

Stetchiner, 226

Stikel, 580

Stolak, 455

Stolik, 100, 101, 102, 103, 209, 223, 389, 480

Stoller, 74

Stollik, 503

Stolner, 224, 225

Stulik, 101, 102, 103

Sukennik, 566, 567

Surek, 160

Sutzkower, 523

Szaiman, 465

Szapira, 204

Szczanko, 416

Szejnberg, 211

Szembek, 10, 13

Szimanka, 411

Szimanska, 411, 412

Szlanczik, 439

Szlenger, 629

Szlyzaner, 416

Sznek, 204

Szniadower, 400

Szron, 204, 206

Sztelung, 102, 228, 481, 484, 485, 486, 487, 489,
   490, 491, 494, 648

Sztokfish, 483, 484, 490

Szukegnik, 223

Szulc, 207

Szumacher, 122

Szuster, 204

Szwarcbord, 538

Szwarcz, 244, 245, 246

Tabak, 169, 673

Taff, 509, 514, 633, 635

Taff (Yelin), 514

Taharness, 312

Tandeczazh, 520

Tandeczsat, 193

Tandetchazh, 650

Tandeter, 518

Tappel, 508

Taub, 101, 558, 559, 600

Tchekhanogura, 389

Tchekhanov, 282

Tchekhanovietska, 102

Tchervanagura, 77

Tchervonogureh, 56

Tchimbarovitch, 8

Tchishever, 95

Teff, 96, 479, 629, 630

Teitel, 559

Teitelboim, 559

Telinger, 614

Temkin, 628

Tence, 594

Tenenbaum, 192, 305

Tenenboim, 193, 194, 246, 518, 559, 645

Tentsha, 559

Tentshe, 57

Teppel, 508

Tik, 95, 152, 153, 211, 601

Tishkowitz, 559

Tisjkowitz, 559

Toebbens, 252

Toffel, 618

Toib, 241

Tolstoy, 187

Topel, 609, 612

Topfel, 498, 499, 502, 506

Traidenis, 12

Traine's, 335

Trane's, 331, 332

Trebernik, 54

Treger, 148

Trembelinski, 74

Tremblinski, 559

Treydom, 5, 12

Trojden, 5, 12

Troonk, 38

Tschechonowietski, 141

Tsembal, 74, 75

Tshernin, 624, 625

Tsimet, 78

Tsinamon, 95

Tsitrin, 224, 225, 226, 227, 449

Tsytrin, 450

Tszekhanovietska, 102

Tunkel, 150

Turkov, 251

Turtletaub, 100, 104

Tyk, 601

Tzadok, 717

Tzarkin, 287

Tzekhori, 671

Tzembal, 50, 51, 234, 235, 573, 574, 623, 708

Tzimerman, 488

Tzimmerman, 624, 625

Tzinamon, 573

Tzitak, 573

Tzitrin, 53, 649

Tziviak, 56

Tziwiak, 573

Tzluyak, 50

Tzukrowitz, 706

Umyal, 218

Urke The Driver, 309

Ussishkin, 144

Val, 159

Valerek, 121

Valman, 77

Vangazh, 57

Vasa, 7, 8, 13

Vayslits, 229

Vaza, 13

Vengazh, 47

Venger, 331, 332, 333, 338, 386

Vengersh, 212

Vengozh, 47, 50

Vengrov, 43, 44, 46, 50, 70, 74, 101, 116, 210

Vernik, 50

Videletz, 502

Vigoda, 37, 71

Vilenski, 101

Vinter, 50

Visotski, 57, 333

Visotzky, 50

Vistenetski, 75

Vistinetski, 94

Vitkind, 226

Volinski, 57

Volman, 51

Volvishes, 313

Von Eibeschitz, 270

Von Munchausen, 364

Von Münchhausen, 366

Waiaibrum, 556

Wainberg, 556, 671

Wainbrum, 556

Waisboim, 556

Wajngrow, 177

Wajnmakher's, 276

Wajntraub, 432

Waksman, 647

Walfish, 591

Walman, 647

Warsawski, 492

Warshawski, 640

Warshawsky, 629

Wasa, 7, 13

Wasertreger, 105

Watenberg, 637

Waza, 13

Weikhart, 237

Weinreich, 159

Weis, 653

Weis-Autnitski, 653

Weisbrodt, 618

Weisman, 292

Weisman (Perla), 292

Weiss, 518

Wejngrow, 480

Wendilowska, 412, 413, 414

Wengasz, 556

Wengel, 416, 420, 421, 425, 429, 518, 520, 521, 522, 523, 557, 642, 649

Wenger, 200, 205, 271, 331, 335, 337, 338, 534, 654, 657, 680

Wengrov, 182

Wengrow, 473, 477, 478, 538, 557, 629, 640, 659

Wenkhleska, 455

Westinyetsky, 640

Wiater, 555, 588, 589

Widelec, 508, 719

Wideletz, 498, 617, 619

Wiener, 629

Wiernicki, 194

Wiernik, 184, 204, 278, 279

Wigoda, 477, 555, 598, 599, 691, 716

Wilenskfi, 644

Wilenski, 2, 101, 206, 284, 472, 476, 479, 481, 484, 485, 486, 487, 488, 489, 490, 491, 494, 518, 521, 540, 541, 555, 556, 587, 588, 590, 594, 667, 693, 697, 702

Wilenski-Grapa, 476

Wilensky, 466

Wilner, 254, 466, 481, 482, 483, 484, 485, 489, 490, 494, 667

Wimberg, 714

Winemakher, 142

Winter, 556, 592, 605

Winzber, 421

Wisotsky, 640

Wisotzky, 629, 630

Wistinjeczka, 158

Wistinyeczka, 158

Wistnizkis, 174

Wjater, 518

Wolerek, 120, 121

Wolinski, 523

Wolman, 160, 185

Wolski, 606

Womenberg, 554

Wonsewer, 422

Wonsower, 554, 555

Wonswer, 173, 174, 175

Wurzehayzer, 702

Wysocki, 333, 538, 595

Wystiniecki, 239

Yaakov The Shokhet, 23

Yablanka, 630

Yablka, 560

Yablonka, 560

Yacobovitch, 50

Yagoda, 44, 46, 502, 560, 561

Yakov Yosef The Scribe's Son, 242

Yakov-Yisroel The Teacher, 316, 359

Yakubovicz, 94, 210

Yakubovitch, 210

Yakubowitz, 561

Yakubowycz, 185

Yanisz, 480, 494

Yankef-Aryeh The Butcher, 333

Yankl The Shoykhet, 102

Yanoshewitz, 561

Yanosowycz, 185

Yanovich, 78

Yaushzon, 38

Yazshembski, 561

Yechieli, 466

Yedvab, 77

Yedvob, 46

Yedwab, 561, 562

Yekhieili, 487

Yekhieli, 472, 483, 484, 486, 488, 490, 494, 664

Yekhieli (Shultz), 483, 490

Yelin, 514, 635

Yismach, 161, 186

Yismakh, 231, 492, 518, 520, 521, 522, 523, 524, 525, 526, 534, 562, 642, 644

Yisroel The Tailor, 70

Yitzchaki, 335, 352

Yitzkhok-Ber The Khossid, 317

Yitzkhok-Yakov The Sexton, 328, 375

Yonasowycz, 182

Yonish, 50

Yonisz, 484, 561

Yoskovich, 498

Yoskovitch, 46, 47, 506

Yoskowitz, 537, 561, 605, 681, 706

Youngsteyn, 387

Yungshtayn, 46

Yungshteyn, 95, 113

Yungshteyn (Goldman), 95

Yurman, 69, 308, 561

Z'lenow, 142

Zajdenberg, 607

Zajdenstat, 267

Zalman, 285

Zalowitz, 557

Zalowtz, 557

Zaltzberg, 557

Zaltzshtein, 557, 701

Zaluski, 10

Zamir, 306, 307, 477, 478

Zamir (Bzhozha), 477, 478

Zar, 158

Zarembski, 557, 646

Zatorski, 219, 557

Zawiscinski, 589

Zawiszanski, 414

Zawiszinski, 589

Zeidenberg, 506

Zeitlin, 38, 84, 89, 90, 94, 95, 104, 105, 107, 108, 267

Zeitog, 56, 591

Zelik, 120, 123, 359

Zelman, 699

Zeltman, 77, 193, 657

Zenderland, 558, 654

Zerubabel, 159

Zgrizek, 652

Zgryzek, 518, 520, 521, 522, 523, 524

Zhelenitz, 70

Zhemovit, 5

Zhepka, 185, 240

Zhitlowski, 268

Zigelboim, 558

Zilberberg, 558, 672, 695

Zilberman, 121, 123, 558, 645, 654

Zilberman-Niestenpover, 121, 123

Zilbershtein, 639, 652

Zilberstajn, 508, 611

Zilberstein, 502

Zimmerman, 502

Zimmermann, 209

Zisha The Pot Merchant, 310

Ziskind, 558

Zisman, 558

Zissman, 47, 57

Ziviak, 593

Zkhishanski, 557

Zlatagwjazda, 644

Zlatman, 249, 558

Zlatonwiazda, 518

Zmir, 558

Zor, 158

Zotorski, 173, 175, 176

Zrenchi, 61

Zrumber, 18

Zuchter, 333

Zuckerman, 252

Zukerman, 252, 453

Zundel, 30

Zuzel, 30, 31, 77, 78, 101, 192, 194, 333

Zwel, 557

Zysman, 204